CENTRE FOR EDUCATIONAL RESEARCH
AND INNOVATION

INDICATORS OF EDUCATION SYSTEMS

EDUCATION AT A GLANCE
OECD indicators

ORGANISATION FOR ECONOMIC CO-OPERATION AND DEVELOPMENT

ORGANISATION FOR ECONOMIC CO-OPERATION AND DEVELOPMENT

Pursuant to Article 1 of the Convention signed in Paris on 14th December 1960, and which came into force on 30th September 1961, the Organisation for Economic Co-operation and Development (OECD) shall promote policies designed:

— to achieve the highest sustainable economic growth and employment and a rising standard of living in Member countries, while maintaining financial stability, and thus to contribute to the development of the world economy;

— to contribute to sound economic expansion in Member as well as non-member countries in the process of economic development; and

— to contribute to the expansion of world trade on a multilateral, non-discriminatory basis in accordance with international obligations.

The original Member countries of the OECD are Austria, Belgium, Canada, Denmark, France, Germany, Greece, Iceland, Ireland, Italy, Luxembourg, the Netherlands, Norway, Portugal, Spain, Sweden, Switzerland, Turkey, the United Kingdom and the United States. The following countries became Members subsequently through accession at the dates indicated hereafter: Japan (28th April 1964), Finland (28th January 1969), Australia (7th June 1971), New Zealand (29th May 1973) and Mexico (18th May 1994). The Commission of the European Communities takes part in the work of the OECD (Article 13 of the OECD Convention).

Publié en français sous le titre :
REGARDS SUR L'ÉDUCATION
LES INDICATEURS DE L'OCDE

© OECD 1995
Applications for permission to reproduce or translate all or part
of this publication should be made to:
Head of Publications Service, OECD
2, rue André-Pascal, 75775 PARIS CEDEX 16, France

Foreword

This third edition of *Education at a Glance* presents a set of 49 international education indicators covering the 1991/92 school year. The set has been put together under the INES Project on international education indicators developed by the Centre for Educational Research and Innovation (CERI) in co-operation with the new OECD Unit for Education Statistics and Indicators.

The publication of this set of indicators marks the completion of efforts begun in 1992 to develop a system for collecting, screening and processing education statistics that would bring together statistical information of a very diverse nature from several sources.

The indicators as defined at the General Assembly of the INES Project held in Lugano, Switzerland in September 1991 provide regularly updated information on the organisation and operation of education systems. They provide information on the way the systems react to the changes in policy priorities and contemporary developments in society. The third version, more diversified and comprehensive than the previous two (1992 and 1993), facilitates the comparison of education systems and the study of possible extensions.

Education at a Glance is the fruit of considerable collective efforts on the part of researchers, statisticians, data producers, policy officials and civil servants. As with the previous editions, its preparation would not have been possible without the financial, material and technical support of the four countries responsible for the INES Project Networks – the Netherlands, Sweden, the United Kingdom (Scotland) and the United States. In addition, its publication has been greatly facilitated by the allocation to the INES Project of a special grant from the National Center for Education Statistics (NCES) of the United States. It is published on the responsibility of the Secretary-General of the OECD.

ALSO AVAILABLE

OECD Education Statistics, 1985-1992/Statistiques de l'enseignement de l'OCDE, 1985-1992 (bilingual)

Measuring the Quality of Schools/Mesurer la qualité des établissements scolaires (bilingual)
FF 120 FFE 155 £20 US$ 29 DM 47

Measuring What Students Learn/Mesurer les résultats scolaires (bilingual)
FF 110 FFE 140 £17 US$ 27 DM 40

Education and Employment/Formation et emploi (bilingual)
FF 90 FFE 115 £14 US$ 22 DM 34

Expectations of the Final Stage of Compulsory Education/Le dernier cycle de l'enseignement obligatoire : quelle attente ? (bilingual)
FF 120 FFE 155 £20 US$ 29 DM 47

Decision-Making Processes in the Education Systems of 14 OECD Countries (forthcoming)

Prices charged at the OECD Bookshop.
The OECD CATALOGUE OF PUBLICATIONS and supplements will be sent free of charge
on request addressed either to OECD Publications Service,
or to the OECD Distributor in your country.

Table of contents

INTRODUCTION 7

READERS' GUIDE 15

I. CONTEXTS OF EDUCATION

Demographic Context

C01:	Educational attainment of the population	19
C02:	Gender differences in education	24
C03:	Youth and population	30

Social and Economic Context

C11:	Labour force participation and education	32
C12:	Unemployment among youth and adults	39
C13:	National income per capita	44

Opinions and Expectations

C21:	Importance of school subjects	47
C22:	Importance of qualities/aptitudes	50
C23:	Public confidence in the schools	53
C24:	Educational responsibilities of schools	56
C25:	Respect for teachers	59
C26:	Priorities in school practice	62
C27:	Decision-making at school level	65

II. COSTS, RESOURCES AND SCHOOL PROCESSES

Financial Resources

Expenditure on education

F01:	Educational expenditure relative to GDP	71
F02:	Expenditure of public and private educational institutions	78
F03:	Expenditure for educational services per student	86
F04:	Allocation of funds by level of education	95
F05:	Current and capital expenditure	102

Sources of educational funds

F11:	Funds from public and private sources	108
F12:	Public funds by level of government	115
F13:	Share of education in public spending	121

Participation in Education

P01:	Participation in formal education	124
P02:	Early childhood education	129
P03:	Participation in secondary education	134
P04:	Transition characteristics from secondary to tertiary education	141
P05:	Entry to tertiary education	149
P06:	Participation in tertiary education	152
P08:	Continuing education and training for adults	157

Processes and Staff

Instructional time

P11:	Teaching time per subject	164
P12:	Hours of instruction	167

School processes

P21:	Grouping within classes	171

Human resources

P31:	Staff employed in education	174
P32:	Ratio of students to teaching staff	178
P33:	Teaching time	181
P34:	Teacher education	184
P35:	Teacher compensation	187
P36:	Teacher characteristics	192

Educational R&D

P41:	Educational R&D personnel	197
P42:	Educational R&D expenditure	201

III. RESULTS OF EDUCATION

Student Outcomes

R04:	Progress in reading achievement	207
R05:	Amount of reading	210

Table of contents

System Outcomes

R11:	Upper secondary graduation	213
R12:	University graduation	217
R14:	University degrees	220
R15:	Science and engineering personnel	224

Labour Market Outcomes

R21:	Unemployment and education	227
R22:	Education and earnings	232
R23:	Educational attainment of workers	239
R24:	Labour force status for leavers from education	247

IV. ANNOTATED ORGANISATION CHARTS OF EDUCATION SYSTEMS

Australia	253
Austria	255
Belgium (Flemish and French communities)	259
Canada	263
Czech Republic	265
Denmark	267
Finland	271
France	273
Germany	276
Greece	279
Hungary	281
Ireland	283
Italy	287
Japan	289
Netherlands	293
New Zealand	295
Norway	297
Portugal	301
Spain	303
Sweden	305
Switzerland	309
Turkey	311
United Kingdom (England and Wales)	313
United States	315
Russia	317

V. ANNEXES

Annex 1: Notes	320
Annex 2: Data sources	338
Annex 3: Technical notes	349
Annex 4: Glossary	366
Annex 5: Participants in the INES Project	370

Introduction

The third edition of *Education at a Glance* presents a larger and more detailed set of indicators than its predecessors, with the aim of providing the basis for a better understanding of the variety of factors and relationships that determine educational performance.

At a time when education is receiving increased priority but, like other areas of public spending, is facing the prospect of limited public funds, understanding better the internal processes that determine the relationship between educational expenditures and educational outcomes is particularly important. Furthermore, in a period of near-record unemployment, with heavy emphasis on policies that will improve the performance of labour markets, Member countries are seeking to enhance their understanding of connections between education and employment. Education and training figured centrally in the policy recommendations of *The OECD Jobs Study,* and the supporting analytic report *Evidence and Explanations*, published in 1994. And as global influences have greater impact on societies and on economic activity, educational performance has to be considered at a level beyond the traditional national context.

A volume of statistical indicators cannot on its own produce an accurate understanding of any of these relationships. Indicators nevertheless are an important source of information for policy-makers, providing insights into the functioning of their own, as well as other education systems. In this edition of *Education at a Glance*, each indicator is presented squarely in the context of the policy issues it raises.

The present set of indicators provides educational policy-makers with a richer array of international data than has ever been available before. There is more detailed information about educational processes, the context in which education systems are set, and relationships between educational and non-educational variables. The growing scope of coverage is important in itself but, at the same time, governments are looking for a set that is relevant to their policy-making needs. Such a focus would help reduce the considerable resources needed to develop and produce indicators. A major challenge for the OECD is to achieve a balanced transition from its pioneering development of new sets of education indicators to regular collection and publication on a long-term basis.

In addition to continuing the series of existing indicators, this volume introduces a number of new indicators:

- *The close relationship between education and the labour market* is explored from several angles. Indicators R21 and R22 confirm the link between educational attainment and both job prospects and expected earnings, as similar indicators have done in the past. Indicator R24, however, looks at the employment of those leaving education in a more dynamic context, by examining their labour market status one year and five yers later.

Indicator R23 examines in detail another aspect of the different experiences of groups educated to different levels: the occupations and industrial sectors in which they find themselves. What is interesting here is not simply that some sectors employ better-qualified personnel than others, but that the differences between sectors and occupations in any one country are more important than the differences for any one sector across countries. In other words, the relationships between employment and education are to a large extent global. A parallel result is provided in indicator P08 on adult participation in job-related education and training. This indicator shows that in predicting individuals' participation, their previous level of educational attainment proves more of a factor than whether they live in a country with high or low levels of training overall. This reinforces the message to policy-makers that targeted measures to encourage greater participation by less-qualified groups are more important than attempts merely to raise the overall level of training activity. More generally, since patterns of inequality of prospects for the less-qualified are similar across countries, raising qualification levels can have impact on labour markets. The fact that those with a

Introduction

particular level of qualification experience similar labour market benefits everywhere – whatever the proportion of the population receiving that qualification – suggests that qualifications are more than a mere screening mechanism whose advantages disappear when the number of people obtaining them increases.

• *Structural variations in education systems and educational expenditure* illustrate potential alternatives for policy-makers seeking better value for money. Analysis of expenditure from public and private sources (F02 and F11) gives a more detailed picture than hitherto available of various ways of supporting educational institutions: public and private funding and control, and public subsidy to private organisations. These data show that private provision is not always merely an "add-on" to a predominantly public system, and that governments seeking to redefine the balance of responsibilities can consider an entire range of existing models. Within public education, the varying patterns of spending on different items suggest further policy options – for example with regard to the proportion of current expenditure devoted to teachers' pay. Indicator F05 shows that in primary and secondary education, this proportion varies from around half of current expenditure in some countries to over 80 per cent in others. Also in the first systematic international comparison of teachers' pay, indicator P35 shows that structure is at least as important to the picture as the overall level: the most striking differences between countries have to do with ratios of maximum to minimum pay (from 1.2 in Norway to 2.6 in Portugal) and the time needed to reach the maximum (from 9 years in the United Kingdom to 45 years in Spain).

Structural differences in modes of participation also represent various options at each educational level. Indicator P02, on early childhood education, compares for the first time not just the rate of participation at various ages, but the characteristics of transition from early childhood to primary education; indicator P04 does the same for the secondary-to-tertiary transition. These analyses illustrate that the options for increasing educational participation at various ages are not confined to a single type of education. Indicator P03, on secondary education, shows another possibility: part-time enrolment. Although this is not at present a significant option at the upper secondary level in many countries, it is likely to be considered increasingly so in all post-compulsory sectors in the coming years.

• *The demands made on education by society* are examined in new survey evidence presented in this edition. While any survey of public opinion needs to be interpreted with caution, these results raise important questions for educational policy-makers. It is no longer possible to regard education as a "closed" system, and future policy development is bound to be influenced by the interaction between professional and public opinion. Indicators C21 to C23 present interesting information on the public's view of what schools should be teaching and how well subjects are taught. Two results are especially striking. First, there is overall a high level of agreement on several basic "qualities" (e.g. self-confidence, job-relevant skills) that should be taught and a high level of support for the core subjects, but much less importance is attached to certain other subjects, such as social studies. Secondly, there is consistently higher confidence in the teaching of important subjects than in the teaching of important qualities. This message is again closely related to the labour market link: skills and knowledge that will help get a job are among the public's highest priorities for schools in almost all countries.

There is less public consensus about the way schools should be run. Opinion is particularly divided as to whether various decisions should be taken at the school level, with average levels of support for school-based decision-making ranging from 17 per cent in Spain to 60 per cent in the United States. It is interesting to note that an indicator (on the loci of decision-making) included in the 1993 edition of *Education at a Glance* showed that in practice, fewer decisions are delegated to school level in the United States than in any other country. Clearly, by providing more detailed data both on educational processes and on the demands made on education, indicators can point to ways in which expectations might come closer to being fulfilled.

Developments and new features

This edition of *Education at a Glance* includes 49 indicators (see Chart 1) that have been prepared and discussed by the Technical Group of data producers, within

Introduction

the OECD Unit for Education Statistics and Indicators, and by four Networks of countries which co-operate in developing indicators of common interest in accordance with the policy priorities of the Member countries and the conceptual framework proposed by the OECD.

This set of indicators almost fully realises the set of indicators which was set forth in 1991 – the beginning of the production phase of OECD work in this area. Four additional categories of indicators appear for the first time, representing a substantial increase in information. With the inclusion of a new section on the opinions and expectations of users of the education system (indicators C21 to C27) the contexts of education can now be considered more complete. These new indicators were developed by Network D, and involved data collected by means of a questionnaire distributed to a sample of around 1 000 adults in each of 12 Member countries in Autumn 1993 and at the very beginning of 1994. The survey referred specifically to the final years of compulsory education. The same questions were asked in all countries about the importance of school subjects; the level of confidence in the way subjects are taught; schools responsibility for the personal and social development of students; respect for teachers; and the public's views on school practices (such as assigning regular homework, the way discipline is maintained and keeping parents well informed) and on the autonomy of schools.

The inclusion of figures measuring public perception of several common educational issues is an important innovation. The data allow the reader to contrast the opinion of the public with the empirical results provided by other indicators. For example, it is now possible to compare the level of respect for secondary teachers with the level of their remuneration; views about the autonomy of schools with their effective decision-making responsibility; or the importance that the public attributes to school subjects with the nature and goals of school curricula. This innovation opens analytical perspectives that merit further examination and suggest a need to reconsider the functions of such surveys in the development of education policies.

Reorganisation of the section on expenditure

The section dealing with expenditure on education and sources of educational funds (indicators F01 to F05 and F11 to F13) has been substantially reorganised.

In the Autumn of 1993, the OECD began an extensive remodelling of its statistics and indicators of education expenditures, with three goals in mind: to produce an improved, expanded and more valid set of finance indicators; to establish a more comprehensive and coherent international database in the area of education finance, and to develop a single, unified instrument for collecting finance data, one that could replace the previous OECD/INES data forms and the UNESCO-OECD-EUROSTAT joint questionnaires. A more specific objective was to tackle some of the comparability problems that had been revealed by the International Expenditure Comparability Study, an in-depth inquiry into the validity of expenditure comparisons, sponsored by the U.S. National Center for Education Statistics in collaboration with the OECD.

The resulting new finance data collection questionnaires, with their accompanying definitions and instructions, were used on a trial basis to collect expenditure statistics for this edition of *Education at a Glance*. The experiment was successful, and a decision has been taken by the international agencies concerned to use the new instrument, after some further additions and refinements, as the basis for the joint collection of international finance statistics. Naturally, the OECD finance indicators have been revised to correspond with, and benefit from, the restructured and expanded statistics. What follows are brief summaries of, first, the main changes in expenditure statistics, and second, the principal differences between the finance indicators in this volume and those in the previous editions.

Changes in the expenditure statistics

Revision of the data collection instrument entailed *a)* development of a restructured, expanded set of expenditure categories and *b)* preparation of new, more detailed definitions and instructions for data providers. The most important features of the revised expenditure categories are as follows:

i) there is a clear distinction in the restructured statistics (and hence in the revised expenditure indicators) between information on education expenditures or costs and information on sources of education funds;

ii) the new instruments include explicit categories of transfer payments and subsidies. This makes it pos-

Introduction

sible to trace flows of education funds from initial sources to ultimate users and to calculate both initial (before transfer) and final (after transfer) distributions of education funding by source;

iii) the revised structure allows separate reporting for public and private educational institutions, and makes a further distinction between government-dependent and private educational institutions. Thus it is now possible to compare the expenditure shares of the different types of institutions among countries, and match expenditure and enrolment figures correctly for the purpose of calculating expenditure per student;

iv) the instrument separates expenditures by or for educational institutions from subsidies to students; the distinction becomes especially relevant at the level of tertiary education;

v) there is greater specificity in the breakdown of expenditures by use or resource category, including further differentiation of personnel compensation by type of personnel and a distinction between basic educational services and ancillary services. However, these features are not yet reflected in the data submissions of most countries.

The most important change in the definitions and instructions is a general one. The new finance data collection questionnaires are accompanied by much more specific, operationally detailed guidelines for data providers than were previously available. This additional detail eliminates some of the earlier ambiguity regarding categories and classifications, and thus helps lessen some of the former comparability problems.

In addition, some important substantive changes in definitions affect the education finance statistics for this year's *Education at a Glance*. Most notably, the definition of early childhood education has been broadened to cover at least all centre-based programmes serving children aged 3 to 5; countries have been asked to include expenditures for adult education programmes "comparable or equivalent to" programmes of regular schools; private firms' expenditures towards training apprentices have been recognised as part of education spending; a particular method of quantifying the cost of retirement (pensions) has been employed. Several of these definitional changes may have caused discrepancies between the indicators in this volume and similarly labelled indicators in earlier editions.

The finance indicators

In line with the changes in education expenditure statistics outlined above, this edition of *Education at a Glance* presents a restructured set of finance indicators. The following comments explain, indicator by indicator, the principal changes.

Indicator F01, "Educational expenditure relative to GDP", is similar to the identically labelled indicator in the 1993 edition of *Education at a Glance*, but new features now make it possible *a)* to determine the shares of GDP accounted for by public and private institutions, and *b)* to compare educational shares of GDP with or without public subsidies for student living expenses. In addition, the broadened statistical coverage of education spending has in some cases resulted in higher shares of GDP than would have been calculated using the definitions from earlier editions.

Indicator F02, "Expenditure of public and private educational institutions", is a new indicator, based on data distinguishing expenditures for public, government-dependent private and independent private institutions.

Indicator F03, "Expenditure for educational services per student", integrates two closely related sets of figures that were presented separately in previous versions of *Education at a Glance* – expenditures per student in equivalent U.S. dollars, and expenditures per student relative to per capita GDP. As an aid to interpretation, the indicator also includes an *index* of expenditure per student, expressed relative to expenditure per student of the OECD area as a whole. The expenditure per student figures now reflect costs of educational institutions only, not subsidies for student living. As a result, the comparisons of expenditure per tertiary student can differ sharply from those presented in the previous versions of *Education at a Glance*.

In response to the hotly debated issue of whether expenditures for research should be included in comparisons of tertiary spending per student, this edition offers a supplemental analysis showing how the expenditure per student figures, for selected countries, would be affected by deletion of the research component. This analysis appears in Annex 3.

Indicator F04, "Allocation of funds by level of education", also brings together two related sets of statis-

Introduction

tics that were presented separately in the previous edition – figures on expenditure shares by education level (expressed relative to the corresponding enrolment shares) and figures on relative expenditure per student by level. The indicator differs from its predecessors, however, in that – as with F03 – only the expenditures of educational institutions, not subsidies for student living expenses, are taken into account.

With regard to "Current and capital expenditure" (F05), the statistical separation of subsidies from purchases of educational resources, together with certain changes in the definitions of personnel and other resource categories, may lessen some of the serious comparability problems associated with earlier versions of this indicator.

Indicator F11, "Funds from public and private sources", makes use of the restructured data on sources and flows of educational funds. Having previously covered only initial sources of funds, this redesigned indicator now also covers final sources, taking public-to-private transfers into account. In particular, there is some (although not yet complete) coverage of tuition fees and other household payments to institutions, and the offsetting subsidies (scholarships, etc.) from public sources.

Indicator F12, "Public funds by level of government", also uses upgraded data to compare countries with respect to the shares of public funds originating from and finally expended by the central, regional and local levels of government. Its earlier version covered initial sources of funds only, without accounting for transfers among levels of government.

Finally, Indicator F13, "Share of education in public spending" now presents the education shares of public spending both with and without pubic subsidies for student living expenses.

Comparability: improvements and lingering problems

As a result of improvements in the collection instrument and instructions and the continuing dialogue between the OECD Secretariat and national data providers, the data are to some extent more comparable. For example, through clearer definitions, there is now more uniform coverage of expenditures for early childhood education, and far less confusion over definitions of initial and final expenditures. Moreover, some countries have produced fuller coverage of their expenditure statistics, either by assembling data from previously unused sources or by estimating previously unreported components of spending, making their data more comparable to those of other countries. Nevertheless, significant comparability problems remain, viz:

Many countries still omit some or all education expenditures of households and other private entities. These countries thus understate expenditures (e.g. in calculating spending relative to GDP), and must be excluded from comparisons of public and private shares of education spending.

Most countries with major apprenticeship systems (other than Germany) have not reported the costs incurred by private firms with regard to training in the workplace. As a result, their expenditures are seriously understated in comparison with those of countries that rely on school-based modes of training.

Consistency has not been achieved in the coverage of expenditures for ancillary services, such as student lodging, meals and transportation. There are also problems in comparing subsidies for student living expenses across countries.

Problems connected with research funding still hamper expenditure comparisons at the tertiary level. On the one hand, countries differ in the extent to which they include research outlays in their expenditure figures; on the other, no satisfactory method has yet been devised for excluding the research component of spending.

Comparisons of expenditure per tertiary student are also impaired by problems in quantifying full-time-equivalent (FTE) tertiary enrolment – especially in cases where countries do not recognise the concept of part-time university education.

A problem affecting comparisons at all levels is incomplete or inconsistent measurement of expenditures for retirement (pensions) of education personnel. The magnitude of potential errors makes this a high-priority area for improvement of national statistics.

Finally, differences in the definitions of levels of education – early childhood, primary, secondary and ter-

Introduction

tiary – still reduce the validity of many expenditure comparisons. This problem highlights the importance of reforming the ISCED taxonomy of educational programmes – an effort in which the OECD is now involved, along with other international agencies.

Regarding the other sections...

Another new and important feature is the presentation of indicators about teaching time, teachers' initial training and their characteristics (indicators P33 to P36). These data, the result of a special survey organised by Network C, make it possible to compare some components of policies dealing with teachers in OECD countries. The indicators do not cover teaching staff in tertiary education. Further refinements will be required for a broader and more comparable set of data on educational staff, and ongoing conceptual and analytical work will be needed to determine which human resource indicators are essential for a basic overview of the quality of the education system. The attempt to use IEA data from the background questionnaires of the Reading Literacy Study for calculating indicators on school practices was not very successful. The data had been collected to serve as an aid in interpreting student reading scores; they were not appropriate for constructing general indicators on school practices.

Yet another first is the inclusion of information on a key factor in education systems: efforts in the area of educational research. This is a relatively low-funded, low-staffed sector that has not really been explored at the international level in any sort of comparative perspective. The two indicators P41 and P42 provide data on personnel resources and expenditure allocated to educational R&D, which is a highly labour-intensive process. The question that arises from the data now available is whether OECD countries have the resources to develop the level of research activity demanded by education systems.

The section on participation in education is already on firm conceptual ground, but numerous unresolved definition problems continue to influence the comparability of results. The future technical manual for education statistics and indicators will improve the situation. The noteworthy addition this year is the indicator on continuing education and training for adults (P08), developed and prepared by Network B. The data cover participation in job-related continuing education and training in 12 countries and offer analysis of that participation by both age group and educational background.

There is less innovation featured in the section dealing with results of education, where the OECD continues to encounter data problems in the three areas of student, system, and labour market outcomes.

In the area of student outcomes, the main issue is the lack of sources providing internationally comparable data on student achievement. This year, only two indicators have been calculated using 1991 data from the latest Reading Literacy Study. In the area of system outcomes, the problems mostly have to do with definitions. Developments in upper secondary and tertiary education are not adequately covered by the existing classification schemes. Moreover, many concepts – such as that of new entrants into tertiary education or part-time education – are not very well defined in operational terms. In several cases, providing truly comparative information is simply not possible. For this reason it has been necessary once again to drop the indicator on the university survival rate. In the area of labour market outcomes, two new indicators appear: the educational attainment of workers (R23) and the labour force status for leavers from education (R24). Both of these indicators reveal aspects of the incidence of education at labour market level which are important for explaining the employment problems encountered by many workers.

The publication's geographical coverage has been expanded significantly: Poland and Russia have been added to the Central and Eastern Europe group of countries.

Also for this edition, in response to a general request from the OECD countries, a new section containing annotated organisation charts of the countries' education systems is included at the end of the volume. These charts, along with the accompanying comments provided by each country, allow a fuller understanding of indicator data and help avoid misleading comparisons.

Finally, it is important to note that *Education at a Glance* is published jointly with a companion volume, *OECD Education Statistics, 1985-1992*, that includes all the raw data used to calculate the indicators and the historical series dating from 1985.

Introduction

Readers who are interested in having a fuller understanding of the set, or of knowing the factors and problems that influenced the choice and calculation of the indicators, can refer to the four reports prepared by the Networks of the INES Project. These reports, soon to be published by the OECD, provide a unique inside view of the theoretical, conceptual and technical problems encountered in preparing the indicators as well as current development trends in the area of the international education indicators.

Future directions

Major efforts will now be made to reduce the number of indicators. This will imply a revision of the criteria used for selecting indicators and the implementation of a procedure for preparing explicit policy-oriented indicators each year. In this perspective, it is important to relate the results to national educational goals and standards.

Increased knowledge of national goals provides a broad context in which to examine the entire indicator set, and a sense of the direction for developing new policy-relevant indicators.

In two pilot studies, the INES Network A tested the possibility of eliciting information on education goals that could be used to develop indicators for *Education at a Glance*. The pilot studies demonstrated the feasibility of undertaking a low-cost, but nevertheless systematic survey of national goals for education. The initial indicators on GOALS, slated for publication in the next version of *Education at a Glance*, will assess the degree of incorporation of four national goals that were common across many of the OECD countries (To Achieve Basic Levels of Literacy, To Achieve Excellence in Education for All Students, To Achieve Equal Access to Educational Opportunity, and To Achieve Lifelong Learning).

Another development envisaged for the next version of *Education at a Glance* will be the preparation of indicators showing disparities within and across countries. The current country averages allow comparison only of overall levels of investment or participation in education. Those results are important and useful, but they provide less than a full picture. The INES Project will develop and publish indicators of expenditure and staff disparities to reflect intra-country variation in resources. Finally, this version will make it possible to calculate indicators showing trends over a period of five years, between 1988, the reference year for the first version of the publication, and 1993, the reference year of this publication.

Costs, Resources and School Processes

Financial resources

Expenditure on education
- F01: Educational expenditure relative to GDP
- F02: Expenditure of public and private educational institutions
- F03: Expenditure for educational services per student
- F04: Allocation of funds by level of education
- F05: Current and capital expenditure

Sources of educational funds
- F11: Funds from public and private sources
- F12: Public funds by level of government
- F13: Share of education in public spending

Participation in education
- P01: Participation in formal education
- P02: Early childhood education
- P03: Participation in secondary education
- P04: Transition characteristics from secondary to tertiary education
- P05: Entry to tertiary education
- P06: Participation in tertiary education
- P08: Continuing education and training for adults

Processes and staff

Instructional time
- P11: Teaching time per subject
- P12: Hours of instruction

School processes
- P21: Grouping within classes

Human resources
- P31: Staff employed in education
- P32: Ratio of students to teaching staff
- P33: Teaching time
- P34: Teacher education
- P35: Teacher compensation
- P36: Teacher characteristics

Educational R&D
- P41: Educational R&D personnel
- P42: Educational R&D expenditure

Contexts of Education

Demographic context
- C01: Educational attainment of the population
- C02: Gender differences in education
- C03: Youth and population

Social and economic context
- C11: Labour force participation and education
- C12: Unemployment among youth and adults
- C13: National income per capita

Opinions and expectations
- C21: Importance of school subjects
- C22: Importance of qualities/aptitudes
- C23: Public confidence in the schools
- C24: Educational responsibilities of schools
- C25: Respect for teachers
- C26: Priorities in school practice
- C27: Decision-making at school level

Results of Education

Student outcomes
- R04: Progress in reading achievement
- R05: Amount of reading

System outcomes
- R11: Upper secondary graduation
- R12: University graduation
- R14: University degrees
- R15: Science and engineering personnel

Labour market outcomes
- R21: Unemployment and education
- R22: Education and earnings
- R23: Educational attainment of workers
- R24: Labour force status for leavers from education

Readers' guide

Country abbreviations

Australia	AUS	Japan	JPN
Austria	OST	Luxembourg	LUX
Belgium	BEL	Netherlands	NET
Canada	CAN	New Zealand	NZL
Czech Republic	CZC	Norway	NOR
Denmark	DEN	Poland	POL
Finland	FIN	Portugal	POR
France	FRA	Russia	RUS
Germany	GER	Spain	SPA
Greece	GRE	Sweden	SWE
Hungary	HUN	Switzerland	SWI
Iceland	ICE	Turkey	TUR
Ireland	IRE	United Kingdom	UKM
Italy	ITA	United States	USA

Country coverage

No information was provided by Luxembourg. A number of countries did not provide data for subsets of indicators, in which case the corresponding row in the tables is left blank.

"Germany (FTFR)" refers to the former territory of the Federal Republic of Germany, "Germany (TFGDR)" to the former German Democratic Republic, and simply "Germany" to the territory of the Federal Republic of Germany after unification on 3 October 1990.

Austria, Finland and Sweden were not members of the European Community in the data reference year, and are therefore grouped under "Other Europe" in the tables.

The samples of schools and students drawn from the IEA reading literacy study (see indicators R04 and R05) were restricted to British Columbia for Canada and the French community for Belgium.

Data sources

Sources of indicator data are presented in detail in Annex 2. The main sources are as follows:
- The data for indicators C01 and C02, C11 and C12, P08, and R21 to R24 are derived from household and labour force surveys conducted by the countries.
- The data for indicator C03 are derived from the demographic database of the OECD, and EUROSTAT.
- The figures for indicator C13, the indices of purchasing power parity (PPP) and the data on total public expenditure are derived from the National Accounts database of the OECD.
- The data for indicators F01 to F05, F11 to F13, P01 to P06, P31 and P32, P41 and P42, and R11 to R15 were provided by the national authorities.
- Indicators C21 to C27, P11, P33 to P36 are based on data derived from special INES surveys.
- Indicators P12 and P21 are based on special surveys conducted by the International Association for the Evaluation of Educational Achievement (IEA).

ISCED levels

ISCED refers to the International Standard Classification of Education. It is used as a means of compiling internationally comparable statistics on education. The classification distinguishes among seven levels of education (see Glossary for details). Synoptic updated graphs showing the structure of the education system, corresponding theoretical durations and the typical starting and ending ages of the main educational programmes by ISCED level, are presented in Annex 3.

Readers' guide

Mean scores

The *OECD total* is the value of the indicator for the entire OECD area, treated as one country. See Annex 3 for a description of the procedures used for the calculations.

The *country mean* is the simple average of the indicator values of all countries. It is sometimes referred to as the value for the "typical" country. A description of calculations is provided in Annex 3.

Reference periods

The indicators included in this report cover the school year 1991/92. By convention, they are referred to as 1992 education indicators. The fiscal years considered for calculating finance indicators are as follows: 1992 for Austria, Belgium, the Czech Republic, Denmark, Finland, France, Germany, Greece, Hungary, Ireland, Italy, Luxembourg, the Netherlands, Norway, Poland, Portugal, Russia, Spain, Switzerland and Turkey; April 1991 to March 1992 for Canada, Japan and the United Kingdom; and July 1991 to June 1992 for Australia, New Zealand, Sweden and the United States.

Rounding of data

Data may not always add to the totals indicated because of rounding.

Symbols

Four symbols are employed in the tables and graphs:

- Magnitude is either negligible or zero.
- X Data included in another category of the question, or in another question.
  Data not applicable because the question does not apply.
- ... Data not available, either because they were not collected in the country, or due to non-response.

I

CONTEXTS OF EDUCATION

C01: Educational attainment of the population

C01(A): PERCENTAGE OF THE POPULATION THAT HAS ATTAINED A SPECIFIC HIGHEST LEVEL OF EDUCATION

C01(B): PERCENTAGE OF THE POPULATION THAT HAS ATTAINED AT LEAST UPPER SECONDARY EDUCATION

POLICY ISSUES

There are marked inequalities in levels of educational attainment between Southern Europe and the rest of the OECD countries. Assuming that educational attainment is closely related to the skills and competencies of the labour force, these findings have serious implications for job creation and economic development in Southern European countries. Across Member countries generally, more thought should be given to further education (and upskilling) for the 35-64 age groups.

KEY RESULTS

Levels of educational attainment vary greatly across OECD Member countries. In some, around four-fifths of the population aged 25 to 64 have attained upper secondary or tertiary education. Thus, only one-fifth of the population in these countries has attained levels lower than upper secondary education. In some countries in Southern Europe, the educational structure of the adult population shows a different profile, with one-fifth or even less having attained upper secondary or tertiary education, and around four-fifths having attained levels lower than upper secondary.

All countries show large variations in educational attainment from one age group to another, with younger groups attaining higher levels.

DESCRIPTION AND INTERPRETATION

In most OECD countries, more than half of the population aged between 25 and 64 have completed at least upper secondary education. In four countries – Germany, Norway, Switzerland and the United States – around 80 per cent have attained this level. In Portugal and Turkey, on the other hand, the proportion is around 15 per cent. Low percentages are also found in Greece (one-third), Italy and Spain (one-fourth in both).

Thus, the countries in Southern Europe have the lowest proportions of persons having attained upper secondary or tertiary education among OECD countries. However, the educational structure is changing rather rapidly in Southern Europe, with younger generations obtaining more education than their elders. In Greece, Italy, Portugal, Spain and Turkey, the proportion of persons attaining upper secondary education is three to six times higher among those aged 25 to 34 than among 55 to 64 year-olds. As regards tertiary education, the proportion for the younger age group is two to four times larger than the older age group in these countries.

In fact, younger age groups have higher levels of educational attainment generally. This is a result of the expansion of education in all countries through the past decades. On average, as much as 65 per cent of persons aged 25 to 34 have attained at least upper secondary education in OECD countries. Among those aged 55 to 64, less than 40 per cent have attained this level. The difference between these generations ranges from as much as 51 percentage points in Finland to only 11 percentage points in New Zealand.

The proportion of the population that has received tertiary education also varies greatly across countries. More than 40 per cent of the population in Canada and around 30 per cent in the United States have attained this level. In Austria, Italy, Portugal and Turkey, less than 10 per cent have attained tertiary level.

DEFINITIONS

Educational attainment is expressed as the percentage of the adult population (25 to 64 year-olds) that has completed a certain highest level of education defined according to the ISCED system. The education system of many countries has changed considerably since the ISCED classification was adopted. Many educational programmes and study courses now in existence therefore cannot be easily classified. The countries do not always classify diplomas and qualifications at the same ISCED levels, even if they are received at roughly the same age or after a similar number of years of schooling.

C01: Educational attainment of the population

C01 : Niveau général de formation

Table C01(A):
Percentage of the population 25 to 64 years of age that has attained a specific highest level of education (1992)

Tableau C01(A) :
Pourcentage de la population âgée de 25 à 64 ans ayant atteint son niveau de formation le plus élevé (1992)

	Early childhood, primary and lower secondary education / *Education préscolaire, enseignement primaire et secondaire*	Upper secondary education / *Enseignement secondaire 2ᵉ cycle*	Non-university tertiary education / *Enseignement non universitaire*	University education / *Enseignement universitaire*	Total / *Total*	
North America						***Amérique du Nord***
Canada	29	30	26	15	100	*Canada*
United States	16	53	7	24	100	*Etats-Unis*
Pacific Area						***Pays du Pacifique***
Australia *	47	30	11	12	100	** Australie*
Japan	...	...	...	...	...	*Japon*
New Zealand	43	33	13	11	100	*Nouvelle-Zélande*
European Community						***Communauté européenne***
Belgium	55	25	11	9	100	*Belgique*
Denmark	41	40	6	13	100	*Danemark*
France	48	36	6	10	100	*France*
Germany	18	60	10	12	100	*Allemagne*
Greece **	66	21	3	10	100	*** Grèce*
Ireland	58	25	9	8	100	*Irlande*
Italy	72	22	x	6	100	*Italie*
Luxembourg	...	...	...	...	...	*Luxembourg*
Netherlands	42	37	x	21	100	*Pays-Bas*
Portugal **	86	7	2	5	100	*** Portugal*
Spain	77	10	3	10	100	*Espagne*
United Kingdom	32	49	8	11	100	*Royaume-Uni*
Other Europe - OECD						***Autres pays d'Europe - OCDE***
Austria	32	61	x	7	100	*Autriche*
Finland	39	43	8	10	100	*Finlande*
Iceland	...	...	...	...	...	*Islande*
Norway	21	54	13	12	100	*Norvège*
Sweden	30	46	12	12	100	*Suède*
Switzerland	19	60	13	8	100	*Suisse*
Turkey	86	9	x	5	100	*Turquie*
Country mean	**45**	**36**	**8**	**11**	**100**	***Moyenne des pays***

* 1993 data
** 1991 data
See Annex 1 for notes

* données 1993
** données 1991
Voir notes en annexe 1

C01: Educational attainment of the population

C01 : Niveau général de formation

Chart C01(A):
Percentage of the population 25 to 64 years of age that has attained a specific highest level of education (1992)

Graphique C01(A) :
Pourcentage de la population âgée de 25 à 64 ans ayant atteint son niveau de formation le plus élevé (1992)

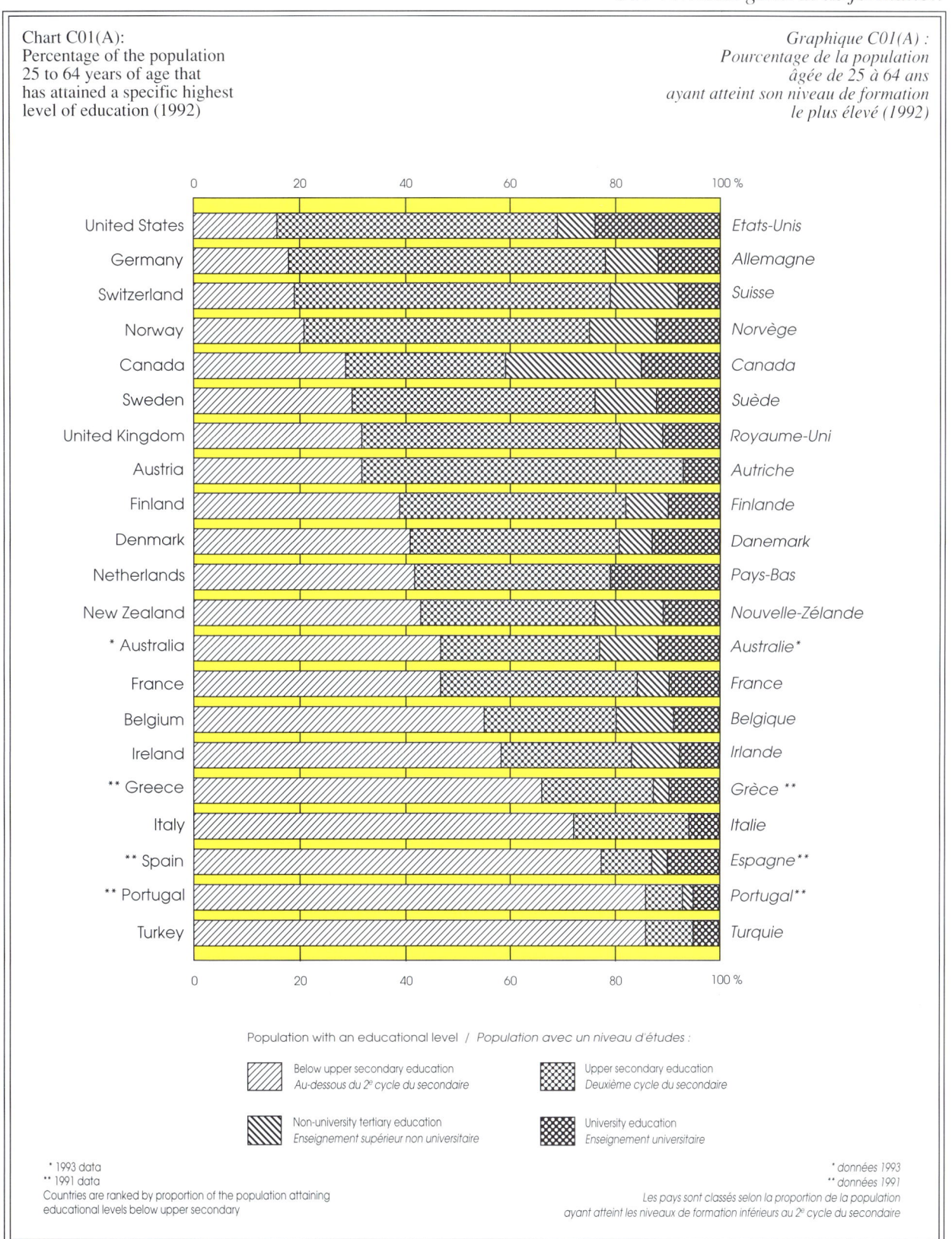

United States		Etats-Unis
Germany		Allemagne
Switzerland		Suisse
Norway		Norvège
Canada		Canada
Sweden		Suède
United Kingdom		Royaume-Uni
Austria		Autriche
Finland		Finlande
Denmark		Danemark
Netherlands		Pays-Bas
New Zealand		Nouvelle-Zélande
* Australia		Australie*
France		France
Belgium		Belgique
Ireland		Irlande
** Greece		Grèce **
Italy		Italie
** Spain		Espagne**
** Portugal		Portugal**
Turkey		Turquie

Population with an educational level / *Population avec un niveau d'études :*

- Below upper secondary education / *Au-dessous du 2e cycle du secondaire*
- Upper secondary education / *Deuxième cycle du secondaire*
- Non-university tertiary education / *Enseignement supérieur non universitaire*
- University education / *Enseignement universitaire*

* 1993 data
** 1991 data
Countries are ranked by proportion of the population attaining educational levels below upper secondary

* données 1993
** données 1991
Les pays sont classés selon la proportion de la population ayant atteint les niveaux de formation inférieurs au 2e cycle du secondaire

C01: Educational attainment of the population

C01: Niveau général de formation

Table C01(B):
Persons having attained at least upper secondary education, by age group (in %) (1992)

Tableau C01(B) :
Personnes ayant terminé au moins le deuxième cycle de l'enseignement secondaire, par groupe d'âge (en %) (1992)

	Age groups / Groupes d'âge				Difference in attainment between age groups / Différence des niveaux de formation entre groupes d'âge			
	25 - 34 (a)	35 - 44 (b)	45 - 54 (c)	55 - 64 (d)	(a) – (b)	(b) – (c)	(c) – (d)	
North America								*Amérique du Nord*
Canada	81	78	66	49	3	12	17	Canada
United States	87	88	83	73	-2	6	10	Etats-Unis
Pacific Area								*Pays du Pacifique*
Australia *	57	56	51	42	0	6	8	* Australie
Japan	...	...	...	...	...	...	...	Japon
New Zealand	60	58	55	49	1	4	6	Nouvelle-Zélande
European Community								*Communauté européenne*
Belgium	60	52	38	24	8	13	15	Belgique
Denmark	67	61	58	45	6	3	14	Danemark
France	67	57	47	29	10	10	18	France
Germany	89	87	81	69	2	6	12	Allemagne
Greece **	52	39	26	17	14	13	8	** Grèce
Ireland	56	44	35	25	12	9	10	Irlande
Italy	42	35	21	12	8	14	9	Italie
Luxembourg	...	...	...	...	...	...	...	Luxembourg
Netherlands	68	61	52	42	7	9	11	Pays-Bas
Portugal **	21	17	10	7	4	6	4	** Portugal
Spain	41	24	14	8	17	11	5	Espagne
United Kingdom	81	71	62	51	10	9	11	Royaume-Uni
Other Europe - OECD								*Autres pays d'Europe - OCDE*
Austria	79	71	65	50	8	6	16	Autriche
Finland	82	69	52	31	13	17	21	Finlande
Iceland	...	...	...	...	...	...	...	Islande
Norway	88	83	75	61	5	8	15	Norvège
Sweden	83	76	65	48	7	11	17	Suède
Switzerland	87	84	78	70	3	7	7	Suisse
Turkey	21	14	9	5	7	5	4	Turquie
Country mean	**65**	**58**	**50**	**38**	**7**	**9**	**11**	*Moyenne des pays*

* 1993 data
** 1991 data
See Annex 1 for notes

* données 1993
** données 1991
Voir notes en annexe 1

C01: Educational attainment of the population

C01: Niveau général de formation

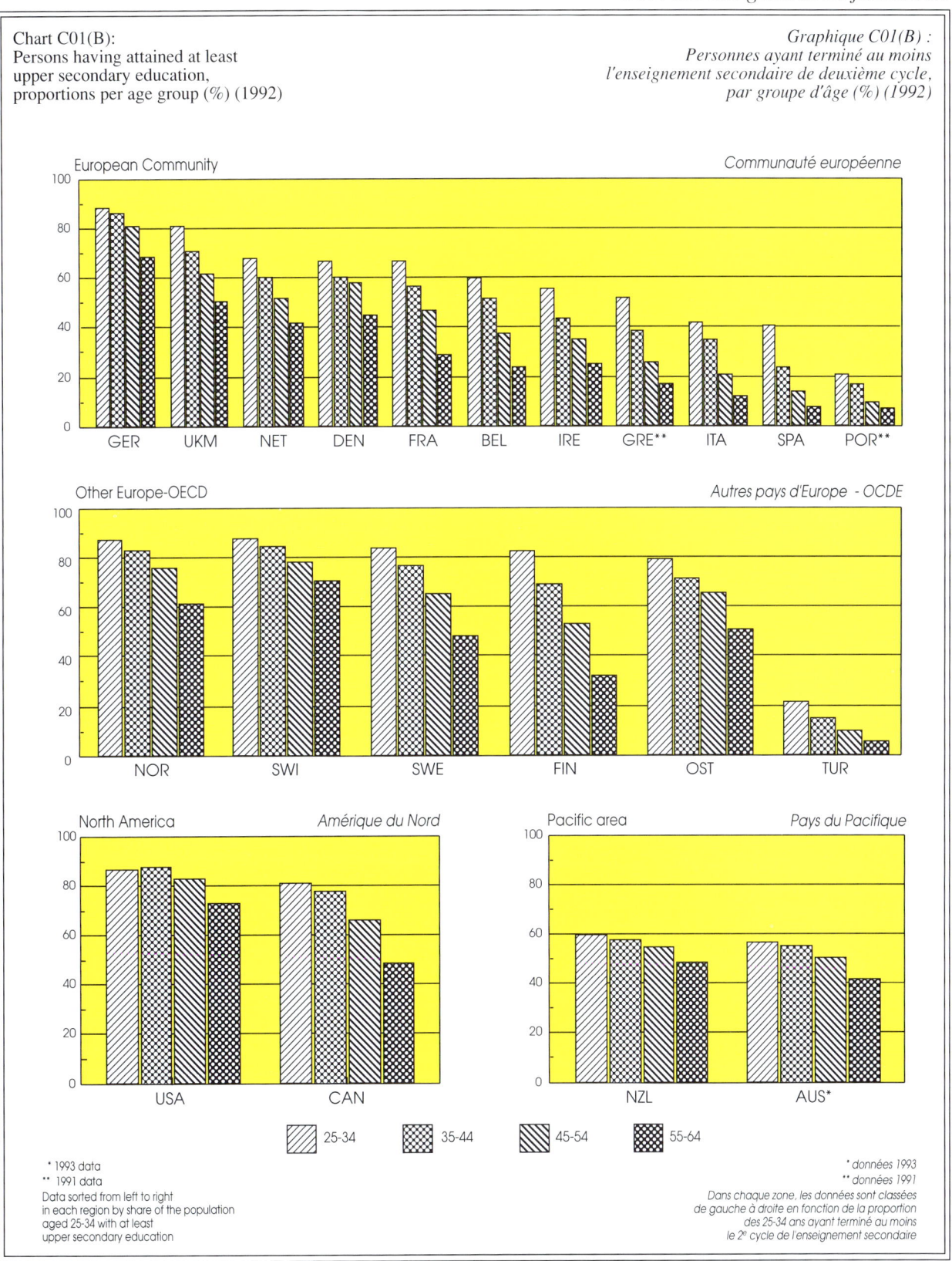

Chart C01(B):
Persons having attained at least upper secondary education, proportions per age group (%) (1992)

Graphique C01(B):
Personnes ayant terminé au moins l'enseignement secondaire de deuxième cycle, par groupe d'âge (%) (1992)

European Community — *Communauté européenne*
GER, UKM, NET, DEN, FRA, BEL, IRE, GRE**, ITA, SPA, POR**

Other Europe-OECD — *Autres pays d'Europe - OCDE*
NOR, SWI, SWE, FIN, OST, TUR

North America — *Amérique du Nord*
USA, CAN

Pacific area — *Pays du Pacifique*
NZL, AUS*

Age groups: 25-34, 35-44, 45-54, 55-64

* 1993 data
** 1991 data
Data sorted from left to right in each region by share of the population aged 25-34 with at least upper secondary education

* données 1993
** données 1991
Dans chaque zone, les données sont classées de gauche à droite en fonction de la proportion des 25-34 ans ayant terminé au moins le 2e cycle de l'enseignement secondaire

C02: Gender differences in education

C02(A): PROPORTION OF WOMEN AMONG THOSE ATTAINING SPECIFIC LEVELS OF EDUCATION

POLICY ISSUES

There is insufficient opportunity and/or incentive for women to reach the same levels of educational attainment as men in OECD countries.

KEY RESULTS

In most OECD countries, women form the majority of those who have attained only primary and lower secondary education. The same holds true for the group attaining only non-university tertiary education. Men are in a clear majority among those who have attained university education. In no OECD country do as many women aged 25 to 64 hold university qualifications as men in the same age group. In five countries, Belgium, Germany, Switzerland, Turkey and the United Kingdom, the proportion of women among university graduates in this age group is below 40 per cent.

Frequently, within the group attaining upper secondary education as the highest level, men outnumber women. That is not the case, however, in Canada, Finland, Greece, Ireland, Switzerland or the United States, where the female proportion is just above 50 per cent.

DESCRIPTION AND INTERPRETATION

Women are generally over-represented among those ending their education at a level below upper secondary. In Austria, Germany and Switzerland, around two-thirds of those educated at these levels are women. In Australia, New Zealand and the United Kingdom, their share is about 60 per cent.

In more than half the countries, women are over-represented in non-university tertiary education. Programmes at that level are often of short duration, and lead to particular occupations with many more women than men. This over-representation is particularly pronounced in Belgium, New Zealand and the United Kingdom. The share is even higher in Portugal, but the total number of persons receiving non-university tertiary education is very small in that country.

In all countries, there is a striking male over-representation with regard to university education.

These tendencies are much stronger among older age groups. Thus, the average female over-representation at primary and lower secondary levels is more pronounced among 45 to 54 and 55 to 64 year-olds than among 25 to 34 and 35 to 44 year-olds. Male over-representation at upper secondary level is higher among the older age groups. For those with non-university tertiary education there is a split picture. More women than men hold this qualification among those aged 25 to 34 and 35 to 44, whereas the opposite situation applies for the older age groups. Among university graduates the average proportion of women is only around 35 per cent in the age groups 45 to 54 and 55 to 64. This proportion is approximately 10 percentage points higher for those aged 25 to 34 and 35 to 44. Some countries have as many female as male university graduates, but this applies only to the age group 25 to 34. At this level and at this age, Portugal and Spain have a female proportion of around 55 per cent. However, it must be noted that neither country reports any non-university tertiary education (see *OECD Education Statistics, 1985-1992*).

In addition to these differences, men and women often choose different fields of study — a tendency that ultimately leads them to different parts of the labour market, even if they have received the same level of education.

DEFINITIONS

This indicator is defined as the proportion of women among all persons in a specific age group having attained a certain level of education. As with the preceding indicator, caution must be exercised with regard to the classification of the education levels.

C02: Gender differences in education

C02 : Niveau de formation par sexe

Table C02(A):
Proportion of women in the total population 25 to 64 years of age having attained a specific level of education (1992)

Tableau C02(A) :
Proportion de femmes dans la population âgée de 25 à 64 ans ayant un niveau spécifique de formation (1992)

	Early childhood, primary and lower secondary education / *Education préscolaire, enseignement primaire et secondaire*	Upper secondary education / *Enseignement secondaire 2e cycle*	Non-university tertiary education / *Enseignement non universitaire*	University education / *Enseignement universitaire*	Total / *Total*	
North America						*Amérique du Nord*
Canada	50	55	50	45	51	*Canada*
United States	50	53	56	46	51	*Etats-Unis*
Pacific Area						*Pays du Pacifique*
Australia *	61	35	50	45	50	** Australie*
Japan	...	...	...	...	...	*Japon*
New Zealand	57	39	68	40	51	*Nouvelle-Zélande*
European Community						*Communauté européenne*
Belgium	51	47	60	34	50	*Belgique*
Denmark	55	43	57	47	49	*Danemark*
France	55	46	56	46	51	*France*
Germany	68	49	35	35	49	*Allemagne*
Greece **	52	53	40	40	51	*** Grèce*
Ireland	47	58	54	41	50	*Irlande*
Italy	52	48	x	43	51	*Italie*
Luxembourg	...	...	...	...	...	*Luxembourg*
Netherlands	56	45	x	42	49	*Pays-Bas*
Portugal **	52	46	74	48	52	*** Portugal*
Spain	53	46	34	48	51	*Espagne*
United Kingdom	59	46	60	36	50	*Royaume-Uni*
Other Europe - OECD						*Autres pays d'Europe - OCDE*
Austria	65	43	x	43	50	*Autriche*
Finland	49	52	52	42	50	*Finlande*
Iceland	...	...	...	...	...	*Islande*
Norway	51	50	51	40	49	*Norvège*
Sweden	47	50	54	46	49	*Suède*
Switzerland	66	52	25	32	50	*Suisse*
Turkey	52	34	x	30	50	*Turquie*
Country mean	**55**	**47**	**51**	**41**	**50**	*Moyenne des pays*

* 1993 data
** 1991 data
See Annex 1 for notes

* données 1993
** données 1991
Voir notes en annexe 1

C02: Gender differences in education

C02 : Niveau de formation par sexe

Chart C02(A):
Proportion of women in the total population 25 to 64 years of age having attained a specific level of education (1992)

Graphique C02(A) :
Pourcentage de femmes dans la population âgée de 25 à 64 ans ayant atteint un niveau spécifique de formation (1992)

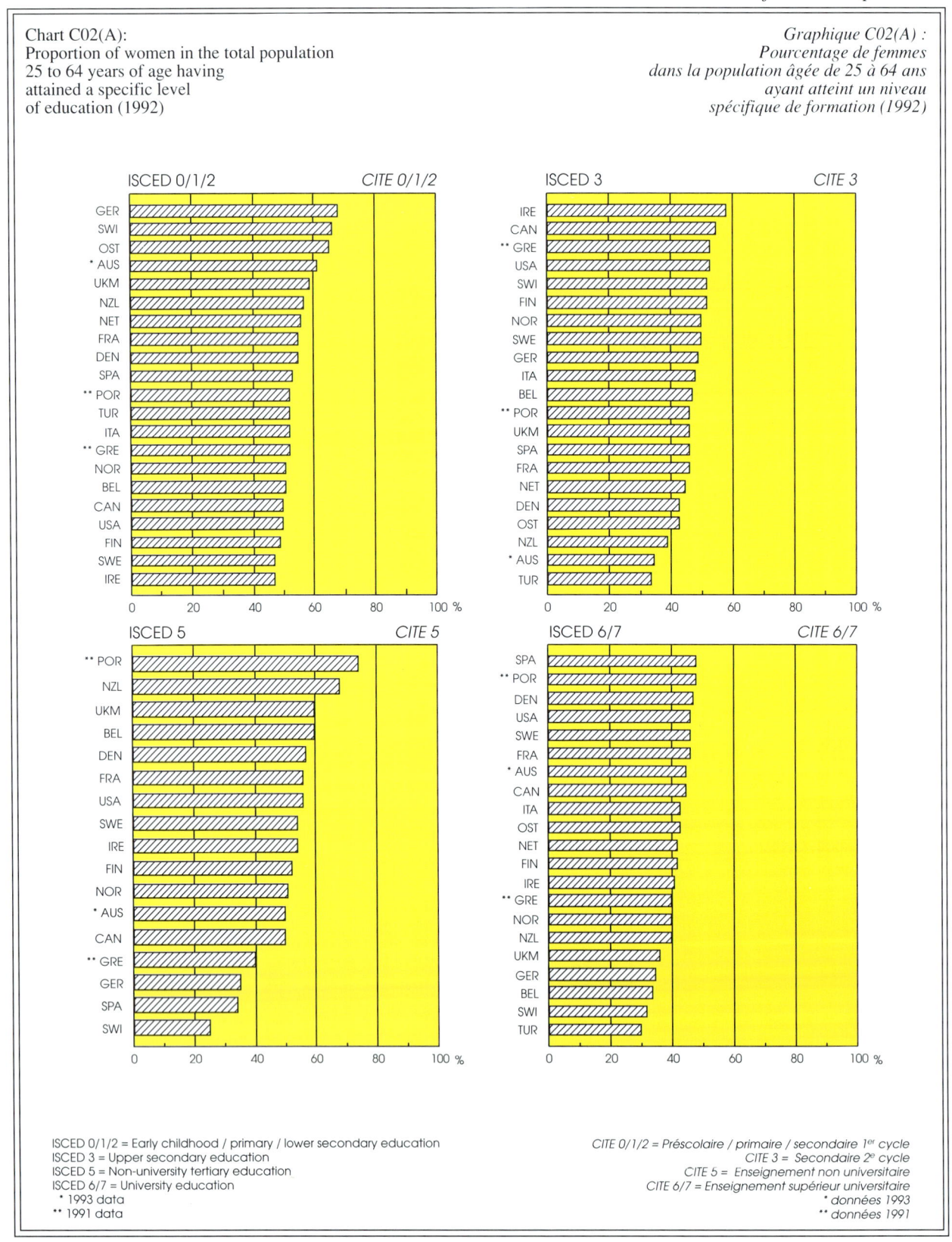

ISCED 0/1/2 = Early childhood / primary / lower secondary education
ISCED 3 = Upper secondary education
ISCED 5 = Non-university tertiary education
ISCED 6/7 = University education
 * 1993 data
 ** 1991 data

CITE 0/1/2 = Préscolaire / primaire / secondaire 1er cycle
CITE 3 = Secondaire 2e cycle
CITE 5 = Enseignement non universitaire
CITE 6/7 = Enseignement supérieur universitaire
 * données 1993
 ** données 1991

C02: Gender differences in education

C02(B): INDEX OF GENDER DIFFERENCES IN EDUCATION

POLICY ISSUES

There is insufficient opportunity and/or incentive for women to reach the same levels of educational attainment as men in OECD countries.

KEY RESULTS

In most countries, differences in the educational attainment of men and women have been reduced since the 1960s. In all but one country, the evolution is in a direction that favours women.

In half of the countries, women aged 25 to 34 are advantaged in educational attainment: more women than men have completed upper secondary education, and have reached a tertiary qualification.

DESCRIPTION AND INTERPRETATION

Positive index scores indicate that men are advantaged; negative index scores indicate that women are advantaged.

In most Western European countries, men still hold the advantage when it comes to educational attainment. In Austria and Switzerland, this advantage is considerable. On the other hand, in the Nordic and North American countries and (especially) in Ireland, women are advantaged. In Southern European countries the differences tend to be smaller, and generally in favour of women.

Turkey is the only country where the gender gap has widened, and in favour of men.

Men are most advantaged in Australia and Switzerland. In Denmark, Germany and the Netherlands women have vastly improved their educational attainment. In half the countries, the advantage crossed over from men to women.

In most countries, the gender differences are most pronounced in the lower educational categories. Differences in tertiary education are most significant in only four countries: Denmark, the Netherlands, Spain and Switzerland. As noted above, Australia and Switzerland both show wide differences favouring men. In Switzerland the high index score is caused mainly by the relatively low number of women (in comparison with men) with university education. In Australia the index score reflects the high proportion of males with trade qualifications, classified as upper secondary, as well as higher education retention rates for males until recent years. Female participation levels in Australia now exceed those for males as post-compulsory school and higher education levels.

The index is a composite of (dis)advantage scores in the lower and higher educational categories. In some countries advantages for men or women work in opposite directions, a phenomenon that can produce an overall evenness of the index. The score for Italy, zero, does not mean that there are no gender differences, but that the advantages and disadvantages of men and women are balanced.

The index conceals gender differences by not taking into account the different fields of study in secondary and tertiary education.

DEFINITIONS

The indicator is based on the assumption that possessing a diploma or degree of tertiary education is an advantage, and that not having completed upper secondary education is a disadvantage. If the percentage of *men* who have not completed upper secondary education is higher than the percentage of *women*, then men are disadvantaged. If the percentage of women who have completed tertiary education is higher than the percentage of men having such an education, then women are in a position of advantage.

The index of gender differences in education is calculated in accordance with the procedures described in the relevant technical note in Annex 3.

C02: Gender differences in education

C02 : Niveau de formation par sexe

Table C02(B) :
Index of gender differences in education
by age group (in %) (1992)

Tableau C02(B) :
Indice de disparité des niveaux de formation
par sexe et groupe d'âge (en %) (1992)

	Ages 25-34 25-34 ans	Ages 55-64 55-64 ans	
North America			**Amérique du Nord**
Canada	-1.2	4.2	Canada
United States	-0.8	3.4	Etats-Unis
Pacific Area			**Pays du Pacifique**
Australia *	8.3	12.2	* Australie
Japan	...	...	Japon
New Zealand	2.4	6.7	Nouvelle-Zélande
European Community			**Communauté européenne**
Belgium	-0.9	7.0	Belgique
Denmark	-0.2	10.3	Danemark
France	0.9	6.5	France
Germany	3.4	18.4	Allemagne
Greece	...	...	Grèce
Ireland	-2.8	-1.0	Irlande
Italy	0.0	5.1	Italie
Luxembourg	...	...	Luxembourg
Netherlands	2.1	11.7	Pays-Bas
Portugal **	-1.8	2.6	** Portugal
Spain	-1.2	4.5	Espagne
United Kingdom	2.8	10.7	Royaume-Uni
Other Europe - OECD			**Autres pays d'Europe - OCDE**
Austria	5.8	15.4	Autriche
Finland	-1.6	2.2	Finlande
Iceland	...	...	Islande
Norway	-1.4	5.3	Norvège
Sweden	-1.6	1.3	Suède
Switzerland	7.8	16.8	Suisse
Turkey	7.2	3.0	Turquie

* 1993 data
** 1991 data
See Annex 1 for notes

* données 1993
** données 1991
Voir notes en annexe 1

C02: Gender differences in education

C02 : Niveau de formation par sexe

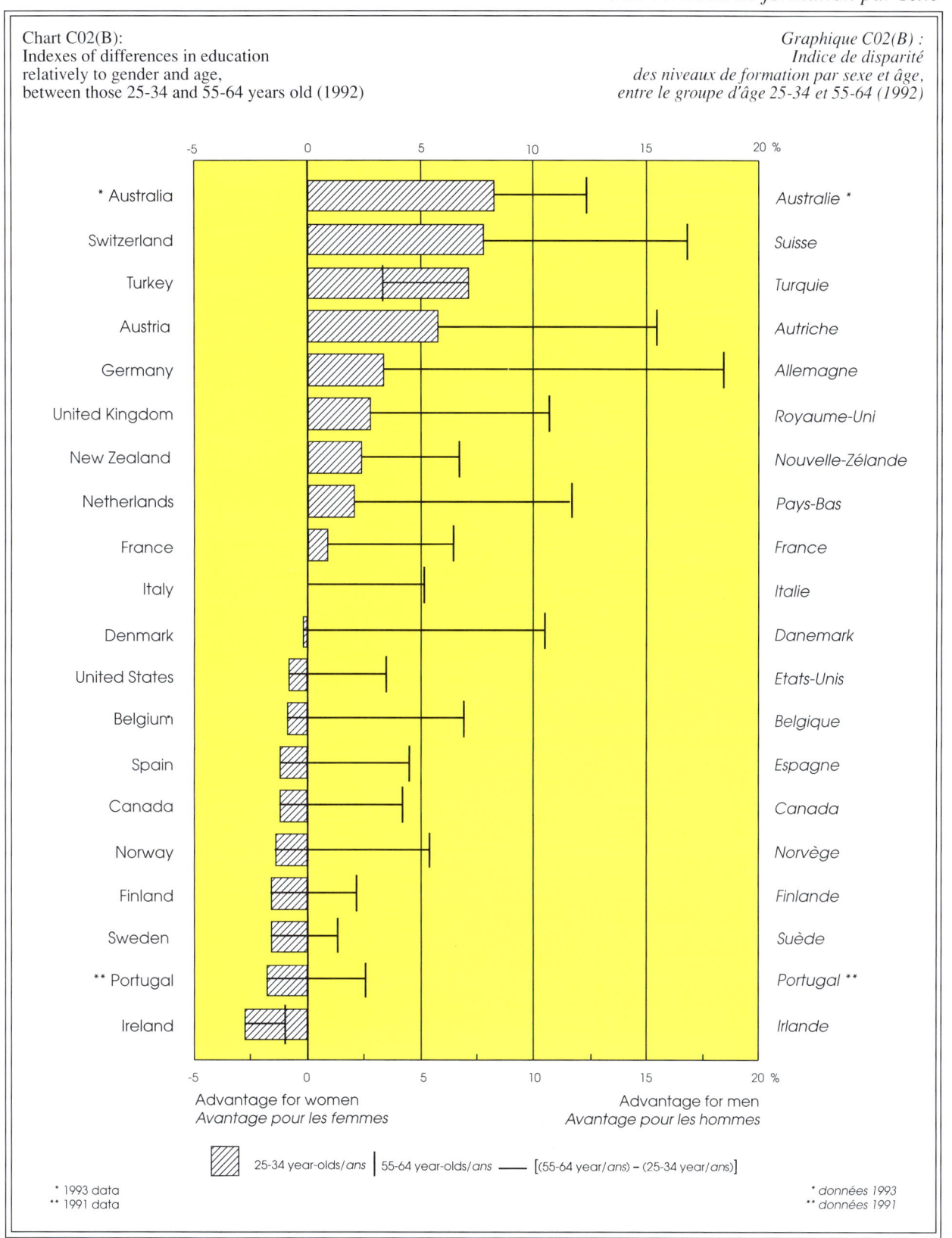

Chart C02(B):
Indexes of differences in education
relatively to gender and age,
between those 25-34 and 55-64 years old (1992)

*Graphique C02(B) :
Indice de disparité
des niveaux de formation par sexe et âge,
entre le groupe d'âge 25-34 et 55-64 (1992)*

* Australia		Australie *
Switzerland		Suisse
Turkey		Turquie
Austria		Autriche
Germany		Allemagne
United Kingdom		Royaume-Uni
New Zealand		Nouvelle-Zélande
Netherlands		Pays-Bas
France		France
Italy		Italie
Denmark		Danemark
United States		Etats-Unis
Belgium		Belgique
Spain		Espagne
Canada		Canada
Norway		Norvège
Finland		Finlande
Sweden		Suède
** Portugal		Portugal **
Ireland		Irlande

Advantage for women — Advantage for men
Avantage pour les femmes — Avantage pour les hommes

25-34 year-olds/*ans* | 55-64 year-olds/*ans* — [(55-64 year/*ans*) − (25-34 year/*ans*)]

* 1993 data
** 1991 data

* données 1993
** données 1991

C03: Youth and population

THE RELATIVE SIZE OF THE YOUNG POPULATION

POLICY ISSUES

The number of young people in a population influences the amount of funding and organisational efforts a country must put towards its education system. Larger proportions of young people suggest both more people to be educated and fewer people in the workforce. Therefore, countries with larger young populations must allocate a greater proportion of their national income to education in order to devote the same proportion of domestic product to each student.

KEY RESULTS

Turkey has the largest proportion of population aged between 5 and 14, namely nearly 22 per cent. It is closely followed by other, generally less prosperous countries: Ireland, Poland, Portugal and Russia. In these countries, 5 to 14 year-olds outnumber 15 to 24 year-olds. At the other end of the spectrum, Germany has the smallest proportion of 5 to 14 year-olds, followed closely by Denmark and Switzerland.

DESCRIPTION AND INTERPRETATION

The proportion of population aged 5 to 14 ranges from 10 per cent in Germany (FTFR) to over 21 per cent in Turkey. In most countries, the proportion of population aged 5 to 14 ranges between 11 and 14 per cent. The proportion of population falling into the 15 to 24 age group is slightly larger.

The least prosperous countries must devote a greater share of weak GDP to education to achieve the same absolute level of spending of the most prosperous countries, and then distribute this spending over more students.

DEFINITIONS

The relative size of the young population is the number of people aged 5 to 29 per 100 people in the total population. The total population includes all persons settled in the country, regardless of citizenship, educational or labour market status.

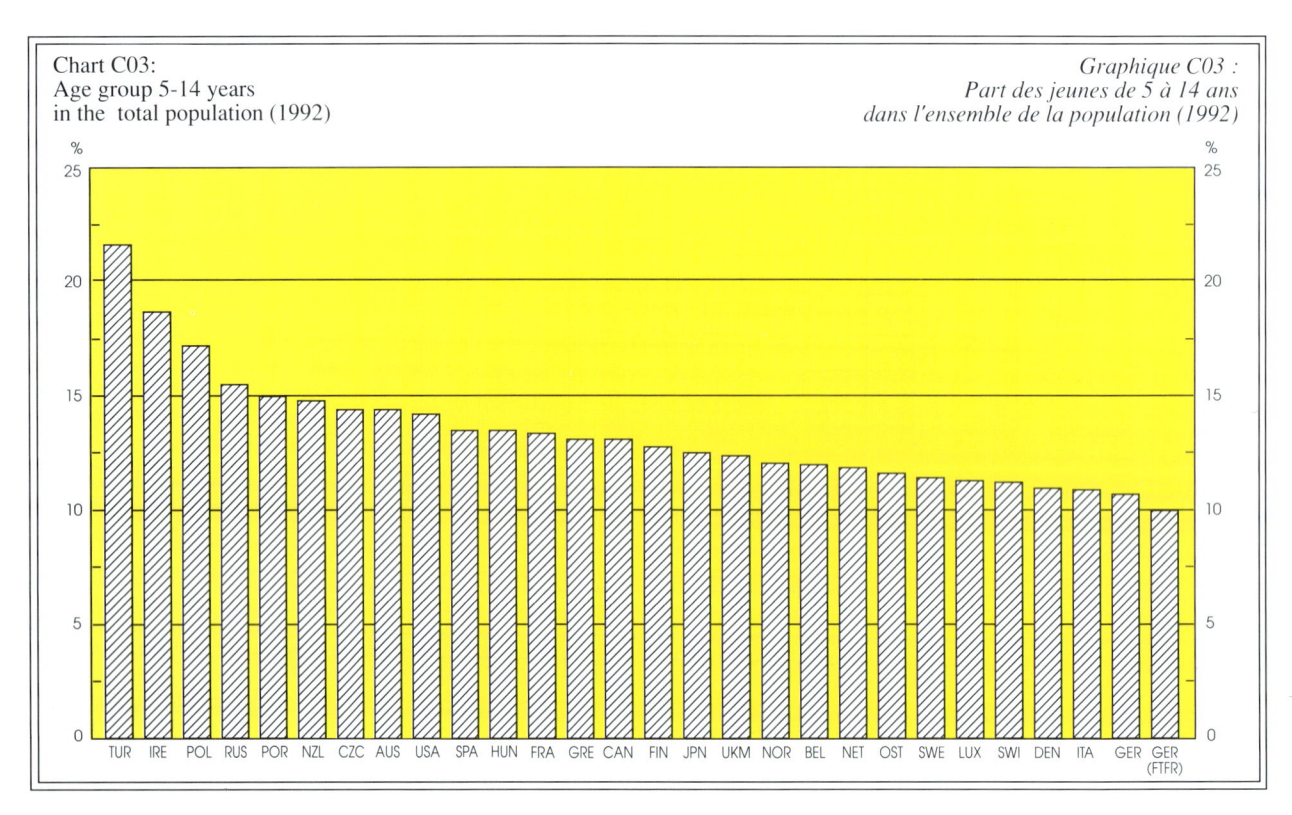

Chart C03:
Age group 5-14 years
in the total population (1992)

*Graphique C03 :
Part des jeunes de 5 à 14 ans
dans l'ensemble de la population (1992)*

C03: Youth and population

C03 : Jeunes et ensemble de la population

Table C03:
Share of persons in age groups
varying from 5 to 29 years
in the total population (in %) (1992)

*Tableau C03 :
Population âgée de 5 à 29 ans
dans l'ensemble de la population
(en %) (1992)*

	5-29	5-14	15-24	25-29	
North America					*Amérique du Nord*
Canada	34.7	13.1	13.4	8.2	*Canada*
United States	36.3	14.2	14.2	8.0	*Etats-Unis*
Pacific Area					*Pays du Pacifique*
Australia	38.2	14.4	15.8	8.0	*Australie*
Japan	34.5	12.5	15.5	6.4	*Japon*
New Zealand	39.0	14.8	16.2	8.0	*Nouvelle-Zélande*
European Community					*Communauté européenne*
Belgium	33.4	12.0	13.4	8.0	*Belgique*
Denmark	33.4	11.0	14.3	8.1	*Danemark*
France	35.5	13.4	14.6	7.6	*France*
Germany (FTFR)	31.9	10.0	13.0	9.0	*Allemagne (ex-terr. de la RFA)*
Germany	32.4	10.7	12.8	8.8	*Allemagne*
Greece	35.2	13.1	14.5	7.6	*Grèce*
Ireland	42.8	18.7	17.1	7.0	*Irlande*
Italy	34.7	10.9	15.4	8.4	*Italie*
Luxembourg	32.6	11.3	12.7	8.6	*Luxembourg*
Netherlands	35.4	11.9	14.9	8.6	*Pays-Bas*
Portugal	42.3	15.0	17.6	9.8	*Portugal*
Spain	38.6	13.5	16.8	8.4	*Espagne*
United Kingdom	34.7	12.4	14.1	8.2	*Royaume-Uni*
Other Europe - OECD					*Autres pays d'Europe - OCDE*
Austria	34.9	11.6	14.5	8.8	*Autriche*
Finland	33.1	12.8	12.7	7.5	*Finlande*
Iceland	...	...	...	...	*Islande*
Norway	34.7	12.1	14.9	7.7	*Norvège*
Sweden	31.9	11.4	13.2	7.3	*Suède*
Switzerland	32.9	11.2	13.2	8.5	*Suisse*
Turkey	49.7	21.6	19.9	8.2	*Turquie*
Country mean	**35.9**	**13.1**	**14.8**	**8.1**	*Moyenne des pays*
Central and Eastern Europe					*Europe centrale et orientale*
Czech Republic	36.5	14.4	15.4	6.7	*République tchèque*
Hungary	34.5	13.5	15.1	5.9	*Hongrie*
Poland	38.3	17.2	14.4	6.7	*Pologne*
Russia	36.1	15.5	13.4	7.2	*Russie*

See Annex 1 for notes

Voir notes en annexe 1

C11: Labour force participation and education

LABOUR FORCE PARTICIPATION RATE BY LEVEL OF EDUCATIONAL ATTAINMENT

POLICY ISSUES

The level of educational attainment is a factor influencing participation rates in the labour force and the quality of economic activity.

KEY RESULTS

The higher the level of education, the higher labour force participation is. Differences in participation rates between the educational levels are much larger among women than among men.

Men have higher participation rates than women at all levels. This difference between the genders is on average around 10 percentage points among those with university education, but more than 30 percentage points at levels below upper secondary.

DESCRIPTION AND INTERPRETATION

Overall labour force participation rates, while uniformly high, vary substantially across countries, ranging from around 60-65 per cent of the population of 25 to 64 year-olds in Ireland and some of the Southern European countries to around 80-90 per cent of the population in the Nordic countries, Switzerland and the United States [Table C11(3)].

These large variations are to a large extent due to differences in participation rates for women. Sweden has the highest and Turkey the lowest, and the range between them is more than 50 percentage points. With regard to men, Switzerland has the highest and Austria and Belgium the lowest participation rate, but only 14 percentage points separate the extremes.

The same type of pattern can be seen at each educational level. The variation in labour force participation rates between the countries is much larger for women than for men, as is the variation between educational levels in each country. These variations are influenced by social, cultural and economic factors in the different countries.

Differences between countries with regard to women's labour market behaviour seem, however, to be decreasing. Among younger women aged 25 to 34, the range in labour force participation rates between countries is much smaller than among older women.

DEFINITIONS

The labour force participation rate is calculated as the percentage of the population that belongs to the labour force. The labour force is defined in accordance with *OECD Labour Force Statistics*.

C11: Labour force participation and education

C11 : Taux d'activité et niveau de formation

Table C11(1):
Labour force participation rate by level of educational attainment for men 25 to 64 years of age (1992)

Tableau C11(1) :
Taux d'activité par niveau de formation pour la population masculine âgée de 25 à 64 ans (1992)

	Early childhood, primary and lower secondary education / Education préscolaire, enseignement primaire et secondaire	Upper secondary education / Enseignement secondaire 2e cycle	Non-university tertiary education / Enseignement non universitaire	University education / Enseignement universitaire	Total / Total	
North America						*Amérique du Nord*
Canada	76.2	89.4	91.4	93.8	86.8	*Canada*
United States	75.2	89.8	94.1	93.8	88.7	*Etats-Unis*
Pacific Area						*Pays du Pacifique*
Australia	82.9	89.8	90.7	94.8	88.0	*Australie*
Japan	...	...	...	...	...	*Japon*
New Zealand	82.2	87.5	90.9	95.0	86.8	*Nouvelle-Zélande*
European Community						*Communauté européenne*
Belgium	73.4	88.9	92.5	91.8	81.3	*Belgique*
Denmark	78.8	90.8	94.1	94.9	87.1	*Danemark*
France	77.4	90.6	95.4	91.2	85.1	*France*
Germany	80.2	85.6	89.4	93.8	86.7	*Allemagne*
Greece	...	...	...	...	...	*Grèce*
Ireland	82.4	93.4	94.3	93.6	86.5	*Irlande*
Italy	81.8	89.6	x	93.9	84.5	*Italie*
Luxembourg	...	...	...	...	...	*Luxembourg*
Netherlands	77.1	88.5	x	91.3	85.0	*Pays-Bas*
Portugal	83.3	91.1	91.1	96.0	84.7	*Portugal*
Spain	82.9	92.2	95.3	90.5	85.2	*Espagne*
United Kingdom	79.4	91.1	93.2	94.2	88.6	*Royaume-Uni*
Other Europe - OECD						*Autres pays d'Europe - OCDE*
Austria	71.6	83.6	x	93.1	81.7	*Autriche*
Finland	73.1	89.5	89.2	93.4	83.6	*Finlande*
Iceland	...	...	...	...	...	*Islande*
Norway	75.3	89.8	91.0	95.9	87.9	*Norvège*
Sweden	90.8	94.8	94.7	96.1	93.7	*Suède*
Switzerland	91.8	95.5	96.3	97.6	95.4	*Suisse*
Turkey	87.6	92.1	x	93.6	88.5	*Turquie*
Country mean	**80.2**	**90.2**	**92.7**	**93.9**	**86.8**	*Moyenne des pays*

See Annex 1 for notes

Voir notes en annexe 1

C11: Labour force participation and education

C11 : Taux d'activité et niveau de formation

Chart C11(1):
Range in labour force participation rates for men in the population aged 25 to 64 by level of educational attainment (1992)

Graphique C11(1) :
Taux d'activité des hommes dans la population de 25 à 64 ans selon le niveau de formation (1992)

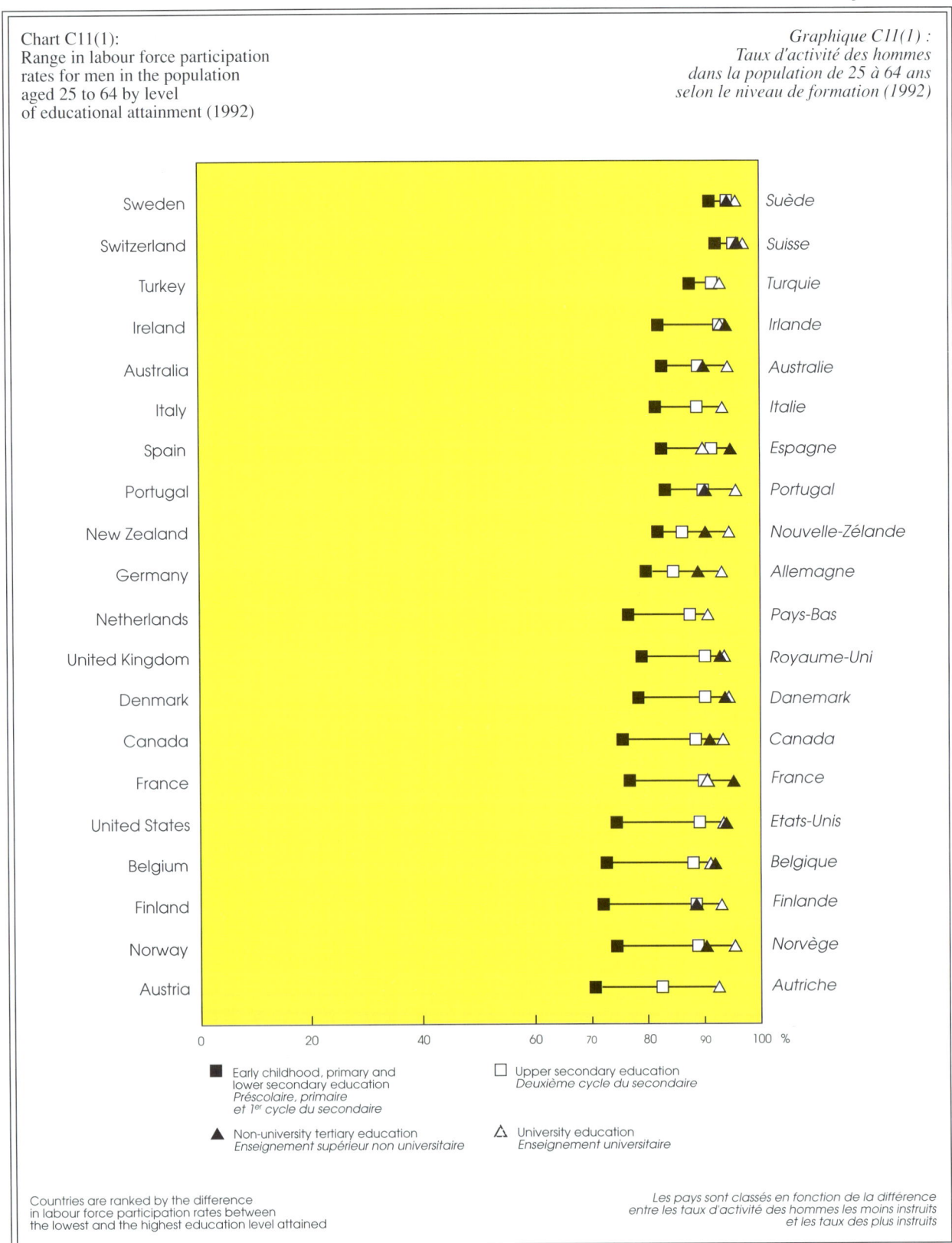

Sweden		Suède
Switzerland		Suisse
Turkey		Turquie
Ireland		Irlande
Australia		Australie
Italy		Italie
Spain		Espagne
Portugal		Portugal
New Zealand		Nouvelle-Zélande
Germany		Allemagne
Netherlands		Pays-Bas
United Kingdom		Royaume-Uni
Denmark		Danemark
Canada		Canada
France		France
United States		Etats-Unis
Belgium		Belgique
Finland		Finlande
Norway		Norvège
Austria		Autriche

■ Early childhood, primary and lower secondary education
Préscolaire, primaire et 1er cycle du secondaire

□ Upper secondary education
Deuxième cycle du secondaire

▲ Non-university tertiary education
Enseignement supérieur non universitaire

△ University education
Enseignement universitaire

Countries are ranked by the difference in labour force participation rates between the lowest and the highest education level attained

Les pays sont classés en fonction de la différence entre les taux d'activité des hommes les moins instruits et les taux des plus instruits

C11: Labour force participation and education

C11: Taux d'activité et niveau de formation

Table C11(2):
Labour force participation rate by level of educational attainment for women 25 to 64 years of age (1992)

*Tableau C11(2) :
Taux d'activité par niveau de formation pour la population féminine âgée de 25 à 64 ans (1992)*

	Early childhood, primary and lower secondary education / *Éducation préscolaire, enseignement primaire et secondaire*	Upper secondary education / *Enseignement secondaire 2e cycle*	Non-university tertiary education / *Enseignement non universitaire*	University education / *Enseignement universitaire*	Total / *Total*	
North America						*Amérique du Nord*
Canada	48.5	72.0	79.6	84.3	68.9	*Canada*
United States	45.6	70.7	81.0	82.2	70.0	*États-Unis*
Pacific Area						*Pays du Pacifique*
Australia	53.4	62.2	75.7	82.3	60.8	*Australie*
Japan	...	...	...	...	...	*Japon*
New Zealand	55.5	65.8	75.9	81.0	63.8	*Nouvelle-Zélande*
European Community						*Communauté européenne*
Belgium	39.7	67.5	80.4	83.4	54.6	*Belgique*
Denmark	68.3	86.6	92.8	92.3	79.4	*Danemark*
France	54.6	74.9	84.7	81.9	65.7	*France*
Germany	46.1	67.3	80.9	82.4	64.2	*Allemagne*
Greece	...	...	...	...	...	*Grèce*
Ireland	29.2	54.3	71.4	79.8	43.9	*Irlande*
Italy	36.6	69.3	x	86.4	46.2	*Italie*
Luxembourg	...	...	...	...	...	*Luxembourg*
Netherlands	38.4	63.2	x	77.4	53.8	*Pays-Bas*
Portugal	48.4	85.2	91.0	94.4	54.0	*Portugal*
Spain	34.8	65.9	76.7	81.9	42.9	*Espagne*
United Kingdom	54.2	71.4	77.7	83.6	66.4	*Royaume-Uni*
Other Europe - OECD						*Autres pays d'Europe - OCDE*
Austria	42.8	61.1	x	82.0	54.7	*Autriche*
Finland	66.4	80.1	82.4	89.4	75.9	*Finlande*
Iceland	...	...	...	...	...	*Islande*
Norway	55.1	76.7	86.6	89.2	74.6	*Norvège*
Sweden	81.0	91.2	93.9	94.1	89.1	*Suède*
Switzerland	61.3	70.2	78.8	82.1	69.1	*Suisse*
Turkey	31.4	41.3	x	82.2	33.4	*Turquie*
Country mean	**49.6**	**69.8**	**81.8**	**84.6**	**61.6**	*Moyenne des pays*

See Annex 1 for notes

Voir notes en annexe 1

C11: Labour force participation and education

C11: Taux d'activité et niveau de formation

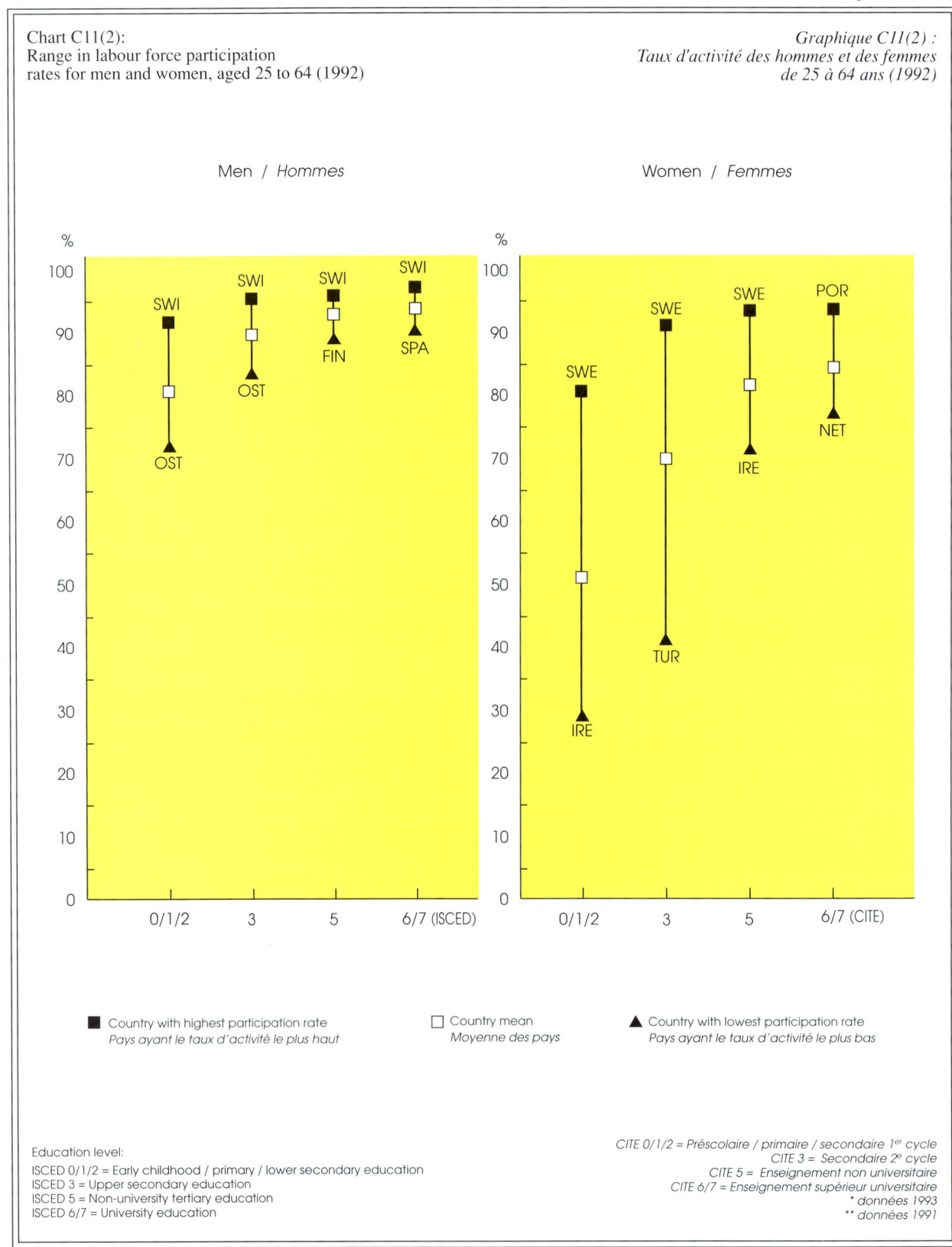

Chart C11(2):
Range in labour force participation rates for men and women, aged 25 to 64 (1992)

Graphique C11(2):
Taux d'activité des hommes et des femmes de 25 à 64 ans (1992)

Men / Hommes

ISCED	Highest	Mean	Lowest
0/1/2	SWI (~92)	(~81)	OST (~71)
3	SWI (~95)	(~90)	OST (~83)
5	SWI (~96)	(~93)	FIN (~88)
6/7	SWI (~97)	(~94)	SPA (~90)

Women / Femmes

ISCED	Highest	Mean	Lowest
0/1/2	SWE (~81)	(~52)	IRE (~29)
3	SWE (~92)	(~70)	TUR (~41)
5	SWE (~94)	(~82)	IRE (~70)
6/7	POR (~94)	(~85)	NET (~77)

■ Country with highest participation rate / *Pays ayant le taux d'activité le plus haut*
□ Country mean / *Moyenne des pays*
▲ Country with lowest participation rate / *Pays ayant le taux d'activité le plus bas*

Education level:
ISCED 0/1/2 = Early childhood / primary / lower secondary education
ISCED 3 = Upper secondary education
ISCED 5 = Non-university tertiary education
ISCED 6/7 = University education

CITE 0/1/2 = Préscolaire / primaire / secondaire 1er cycle
CITE 3 = Secondaire 2e cycle
CITE 5 = Enseignement non universitaire
CITE 6/7 = Enseignement supérieur universitaire
* *données 1993*
** *données 1991*

C11: Labour force participation and education

C11: Taux d'activité et niveau de formation

Table C11(3):
Labour force participation rate by level of educational attainment for men and women 25 to 64 years of age (1992)

Tableau C11(3):
Taux d'activité par niveau de formation pour 100 personnes de la population âgée de 25 à 64 ans (1992)

	Early childhood, primary and lower secondary education / *Éducation préscolaire, enseignement primaire et secondaire*	Upper secondary education / *Enseignement secondaire 2e cycle*	Non-university tertiary education / *Enseignement non universitaire*	University education / *Enseignement universitaire*	Total / *Total*	
North America						*Amérique du Nord*
Canada	62.4	79.9	85.5	89.6	77.8	*Canada*
United States	60.3	79.7	86.7	88.4	79.2	*États-Unis*
Pacific Area						*Pays du Pacifique*
Australia	65.1	80.2	83.2	89.2	74.4	*Australie*
Japan	...	...	...	...	...	*Japon*
New Zealand	67.0	79.1	80.9	89.5	75.2	*Nouvelle-Zélande*
European Community						*Communauté européenne*
Belgium	56.1	78.8	85.3	88.9	68.0	*Belgique*
Denmark	73.0	88.9	93.4	93.7	83.3	*Danemark*
France	64.9	83.5	89.4	86.9	75.3	*France*
Germany	57.0	76.7	86.5	89.8	75.6	*Allemagne*
Greece	...	...	...	...	...	*Grèce*
Ireland	57.3	70.7	81.9	87.9	65.2	*Irlande*
Italy	58.2	79.8	x	90.7	65.1	*Italie*
Luxembourg	...	...	...	...	...	*Luxembourg*
Netherlands	55.4	77.0	x	85.5	69.7	*Pays-Bas*
Portugal	65.1	88.4	91.0	95.2	68.8	*Portugal*
Spain	57.6	80.2	89.0	86.4	63.7	*Espagne*
United Kingdom	64.5	82.1	84.0	90.3	77.5	*Royaume-Uni*
Other Europe - OECD						*Autres pays d'Europe - OCDE*
Austria	52.8	73.9	x	88.4	68.1	*Autriche*
Finland	69.8	84.7	85.7	91.8	79.8	*Finlande*
Iceland	...	...	...	...	...	*Islande*
Norway	65.0	83.2	88.8	93.3	81.4	*Norvège*
Sweden	86.2	93.0	94.3	95.2	91.4	*Suède*
Switzerland	71.7	82.2	91.9	92.7	82.3	*Suisse*
Turkey	58.3	74.7	x	90.2	61.3	*Turquie*
Country mean	**63.4**	**80.8**	**87.3**	**90.2**	**74.2**	*Moyenne des pays*

See Annex 1 for notes

Voir notes en annexe 1

C11: Labour force participation and education

C11: Taux d'activité et niveau de formation

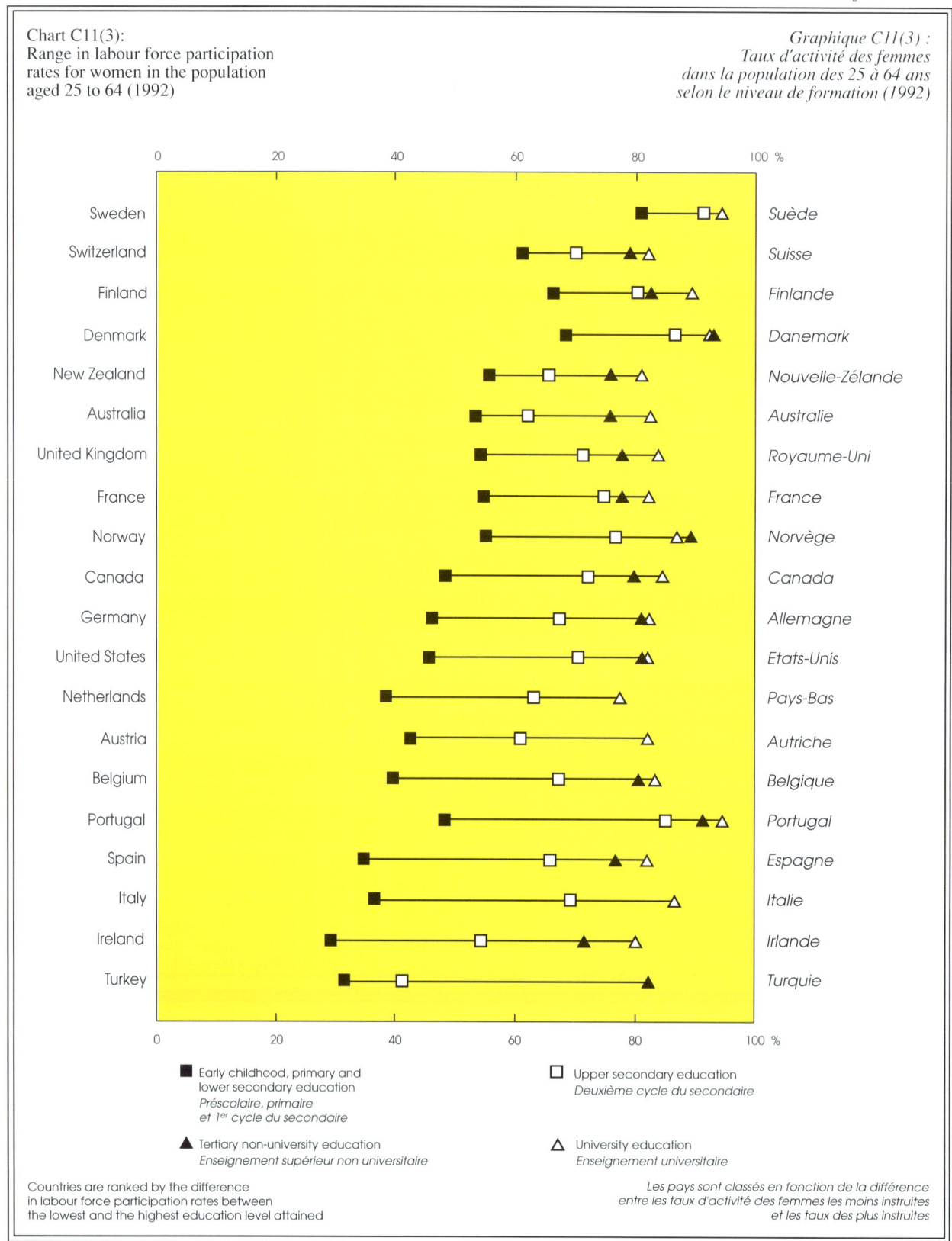

Chart C11(3):
Range in labour force participation rates for women in the population aged 25 to 64 (1992)

Graphique C11(3):
Taux d'activité des femmes dans la population des 25 à 64 ans selon le niveau de formation (1992)

Sweden		Suède
Switzerland		Suisse
Finland		Finlande
Denmark		Danemark
New Zealand		Nouvelle-Zélande
Australia		Australie
United Kingdom		Royaume-Uni
France		France
Norway		Norvège
Canada		Canada
Germany		Allemagne
United States		Etats-Unis
Netherlands		Pays-Bas
Austria		Autriche
Belgium		Belgique
Portugal		Portugal
Spain		Espagne
Italy		Italie
Ireland		Irlande
Turkey		Turquie

■ Early childhood, primary and lower secondary education
Préscolaire, primaire et 1er cycle du secondaire

□ Upper secondary education
Deuxième cycle du secondaire

▲ Tertiary non-university education
Enseignement supérieur non universitaire

△ University education
Enseignement universitaire

Countries are ranked by the difference in labour force participation rates between the lowest and the highest education level attained

Les pays sont classés en fonction de la différence entre les taux d'activité des femmes les moins instruites et les taux des plus instruites

C12: Unemployment among youth and adults

C12(A): UNEMPLOYMENT RATES BY GENDER AND AGE GROUP

C12(B): YOUTH LABOUR FORCE PARTICIPATION AND UNEMPLOYMENT

POLICY ISSUES

Youth labour force participaton and the deeply troubling phenomenon of youth unemployment are both linked to factors influencing the decision whether to stay in school or enter the workforce. Students need to feel (justifiably) confident that education will effectively prepare them for the working world. In this respect, the success stories of Japan and Germany merit special attention.

KEY RESULTS

In every country except Germany (FTFR), youth are more likely to find themselves unemployed than any other portion of the labour force. When measured as a percentage of the population aged 15-24, the percentage of unemployed youths ranges from 2 per cent in Japan to 16.6 per cent in Spain [see Table C12(B)].

Labour force participation among youths also varies across countries [see Table C12(B)]. Over 65 per cent of youths aged 15 to 24 participate in the labour force in four countries: Australia, Canada, Denmark and the United Kingdom. Five countries – Belgium, France, Hungary, Italy and Poland – have youth labour force participation rates below 45 per cent. The percentage of unemployed youths appears unrelated to the percentage of youths participating in the labour force.

DESCRIPTION AND INTERPRETATION

Labour force participation and unemployment among youths reflect factors influencing their decision whether to stay in school or enter the workforce. High rates of labour force participation may reflect societal expectations that youths leave school and enter the labour force at an earlier age. High unemployment, particularly among youths, often provides an incentive for students to stay longer in school. In the short term, the prospect of an extended job search serves as a disincentive to enter the labour force. More generally, employment prospects tend to be brighter for people with more skills, education, and training.

Germany (FTFR) excepted, unemployment rates are higher among youths than among other labour force participants. In Germany, low unemployment rates among young women lead to lower overall unemployment rates among youths. The youth unemployment rate is also low (4.4 per cent) in Japan, which has a low total unemployment rate (2.2 per cent). The apparent success of those two countries in keeping youth unemployment relatively low raises interesting questions about what makes the school-to-work transition so effective.

DEFINITIONS

The unemployment rate is the percentage of people in the labour force (the currently active population) without work (i.e. not in paid employment or self-employment). Labour force participation is defined as the proportion of the population that *a)* is working for pay, *b)* is self-employed, or *c)* meets the following two conditions: seeking work (i.e. taking specific steps in a specified recent period to seek paid employment or self-employment); and currently available for work.

Tables C12(A) and C12(B) present two different measures of the youth unemployment rate. Table C12(A) presents the proportion of all people who are in the labour force and not full-time students who are not employed. Table C12(B) presents the proportion of the total population aged 15 to 24 who are in the labour force and not currently working for pay or self-employed.

C12: Unemployment among youth and adults

C12: Chômage des jeunes et des adultes

Table C12(A):
Unemployment rates for men and women
by age group (1992)

*Tableau C12(A):
Taux de chômage par sexe
et groupe d'âge (1992)*

	\multicolumn{3}{c}{Total unemployment rate (age 15-64) *Taux de chômage global (15-64 ans)*}	
	M + W / H + F	Men / *Hommes*	Women / *Femmes*	
North America				*Amérique du Nord*
Canada	11.4	12.1	10.4	*Canada*
United States	7.8	8.9	6.6	*Etats-Unis*
Pacific Area				*Pays du Pacifique*
Australia *	10.9	11.8	9.6	* *Australie*
Japan	2.2	2.1	2.2	*Japon*
New Zealand	10.2	11.1	9.0	*Nouvelle-Zélande*
European Community				*Communauté européenne*
Belgium	9.6	6.8	13.6	*Belgique*
Denmark	10.7	9.7	11.7	*Danemark*
France	10.1	8.0	12.8	*France*
Germany (FTFR)	5.8	5.4	6.4	*Allemagne (ex-terr. de la RFA)*
Germany	6.1	4.7	8.0	*Allemagne*
Greece	9.0	5.7	14.5	*Grèce*
Ireland	15.6	15.6	15.6	*Irlande*
Italy	11.7	8.2	17.5	*Italie*
Luxembourg	16.0	...	...	*Luxembourg*
Netherlands	6.6	5.0	8.3	*Pays-Bas*
Portugal **	6.1	4.1	8.8	** *Portugal*
Spain	18.5	14.4	25.8	*Espagne*
United Kingdom	9.7	11.6	7.2	*Royaume-Uni*
Other Europe - OECD				*Autres pays d'Europe - OCDE*
Austria	3.7	3.6	3.9	*Autriche*
Finland	12.9	15.0	10.6	*Finlande*
Iceland	...	...	...	*Islande*
Norway	6.0	6.7	5.2	*Norvège*
Sweden	4.8	5.7	3.8	*Suède*
Switzerland	3.1	2.5	3.8	*Suisse*
Turkey	8.1	8.3	7.5	*Turquie*
Central and Eastern Europe				*Europe centrale et orientale*
Czech Republic	3.1	2.3	4.2	*République tchèque*
Hungary	9.9	11.0	8.7	*Hongrie*
Poland	13.5	12.3	14.9	*Pologne*
Russia	...	...	...	*Russie*

* 1993 data
** 1991 data
See Annex 1 for notes

*données 1993
**données 1991
Voir notes en annexe 1

C12: Unemployment among youth and adults

C12: Chômage des jeunes et des adultes

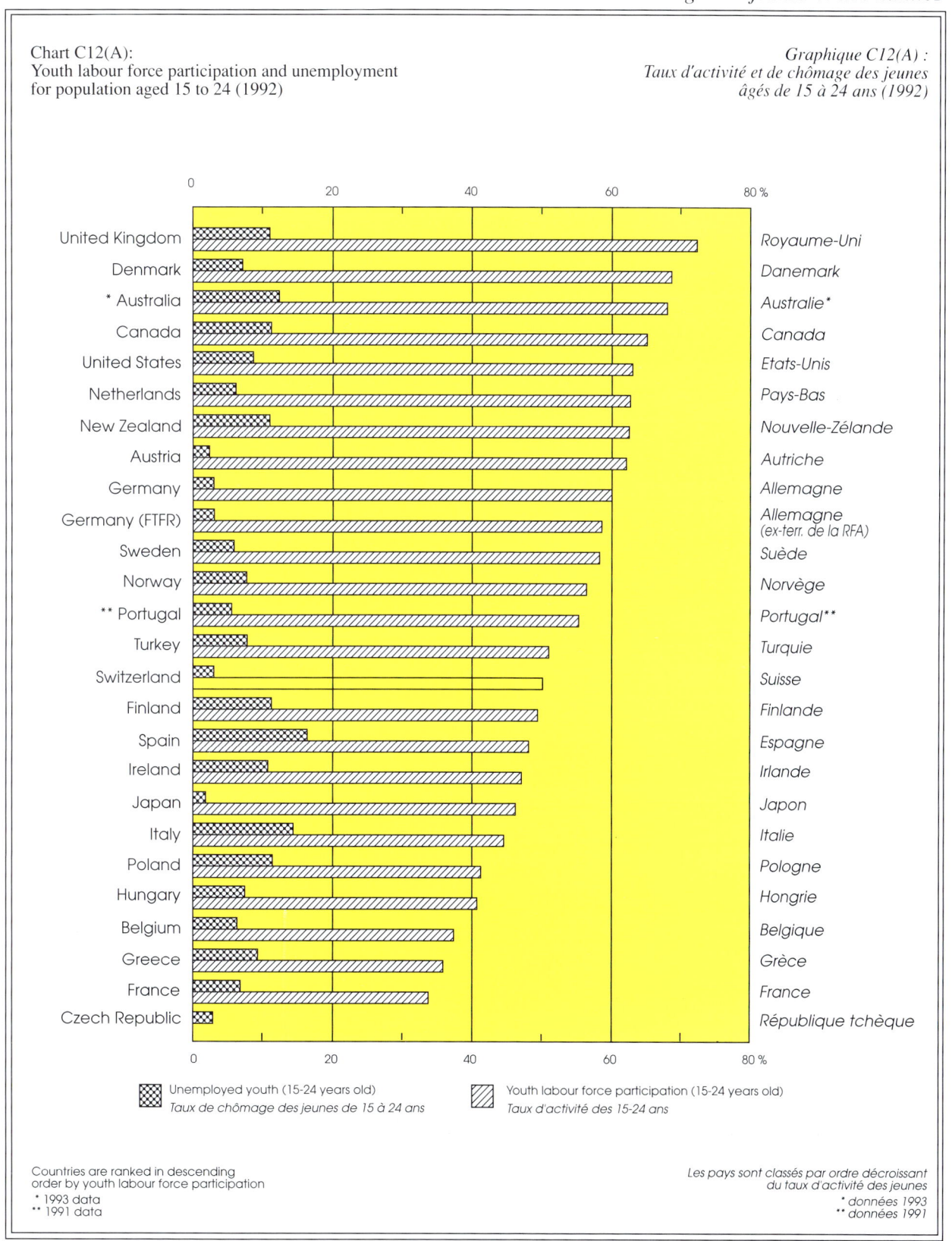

Chart C12(A):
Youth labour force participation and unemployment for population aged 15 to 24 (1992)

Graphique C12(A) :
Taux d'activité et de chômage des jeunes âgés de 15 à 24 ans (1992)

Countries (top to bottom): United Kingdom, Denmark, *Australia, Canada, United States, Netherlands, New Zealand, Austria, Germany, Germany (FTFR), Sweden, Norway, **Portugal, Turkey, Switzerland, Finland, Spain, Ireland, Japan, Italy, Poland, Hungary, Belgium, Greece, France, Czech Republic

Royaume-Uni, Danemark, Australie, Canada, Etats-Unis, Pays-Bas, Nouvelle-Zélande, Autriche, Allemagne, Allemagne (ex-terr. de la RFA), Suède, Norvège, Portugal**, Turquie, Suisse, Finlande, Espagne, Irlande, Japon, Italie, Pologne, Hongrie, Belgique, Grèce, France, République tchèque*

Legend:
- Unemployed youth (15-24 years old) / Taux de chômage des jeunes de 15 à 24 ans
- Youth labour force participation (15-24 years old) / Taux d'activité des 15-24 ans

Countries are ranked in descending order by youth labour force participation
* 1993 data
** 1991 data

Les pays sont classés par ordre décroissant du taux d'activité des jeunes
* données 1993
** données 1991

C12: Unemployment among youth and adults

C12: Chômage des jeunes et des adultes

Table C12(B):
Youth labour force participation and unemployment as a percentage of the population 15 to 24 years of age, men and women (1992)

Tableau C12(B):
Taux d'activité et de chômage des jeunes en pourcentage de la population âgée de 15 à 24 ans, hommes et femmes (1992)

	Unemployed youth as a percentage of all persons in the population 15-24 years of age / *Jeunes au chômage par rapport au total de la population âgée de 15 à 24 ans*	Youth in the labour force as a percentage of all persons in the population 15-24 years of age / *Jeunes actifs par rapport au total de la population âgée de 15 à 24 ans*	
North America			*Amérique du Nord*
Canada	11.6	65.1	*Canada*
United States	8.9	63.0	*Etats-Unis*
Pacific Area			*Pays du Pacifique*
Australia *	12.5	68.2	* *Australie*
Japan	2.0	46.4	*Japon*
New Zealand	11.2	62.6	*Nouvelle-Zélande*
European Community			*Communauté européenne*
Belgium	6.6	37.4	*Belgique*
Denmark	7.5	68.8	*Danemark*
France	7.1	34.0	*France*
Germany (FTFR)	3.3	60.1	*Allemagne (ex-terr. de la RFA)*
Germany	3.2	58.6	*Allemagne*
Greece	9.7	36.0	*Grèce*
Ireland	11.0	47.2	*Irlande*
Italy	14.6	44.7	*Italie*
Luxembourg	...	...	*Luxembourg*
Netherlands	6.5	62.8	*Pays-Bas*
Portugal **	5.7	55.4	** *Portugal*
Spain	16.6	48.2	*Espagne*
United Kingdom	11.2	72.5	*Royaume-Uni*
Other Europe - OECD			*Autres pays d'Europe - OCDE*
Austria	2.7	62.2	*Autriche*
Finland	11.6	49.5	*Finlande*
Iceland	...	...	*Islande*
Norway	7.8	56.6	*Norvège*
Sweden	6.3	58.5	*Suède*
Switzerland	3.2	50.4	*Suisse*
Turkey	8.2	51.3	*Turquie*
Central and Eastern Europe			*Europe centrale et orientale*
Czech Republic	3.0	...	*République tchèque*
Hungary	7.7	40.9	*Hongrie*
Poland	11.7	41.5	*Pologne*
Russia	...	...	*Russie*

* 1993 data
** 1991 data
See Annex 1 for notes

* données 1993
** données 1991
Voir notes en annexe 1

C12: Unemployment among youth and adults

C12: Chômage des jeunes et des adultes

Chart C12(B):
Youth labour force participation and unemployment for population aged 15 to 24 (1992)

Graphique C12(B):
Taux d'activité et de chômage des jeunes âgés de 15 à 24 ans (1992)

Spain	Espagne
Italy	Italie
* Australia	Australie*
Poland	Pologne
Finland	Finlande
Canada	Canada
New Zealand	Nouvelle-Zélande
United Kingdom	Royaume-Uni
Ireland	Irlande
Greece	Grèce
United States	Etats-Unis
Turkey	Turquie
Norway	Norvège
Hungary	Hongrie
Denmark	Danemark
France	France
Belgium	Belgique
Netherlands	Pays-Bas
Sweden	Suède
** Portugal	Portugal**
Germany	Allemagne
Germany (FTFR)	Allemagne (ex.-terr. de la RFA)
Switzerland	Suisse
Czech Republic	République tchèque
Austria	Autriche
Japan	Japon

Unemployed youth (15-24 years old)
Taux de chômage des jeunes de 15 à 24 ans

Youth labour force participation (15-24 years old)
Taux d'activité des 15-24 ans

Countries are ranked in descending order by youth unemployment
* 1993 data
** 1991 data

Les pays sont classés par ordre décroissant du taux de chômage des jeunes
* *données 1993*
** *données 1991*

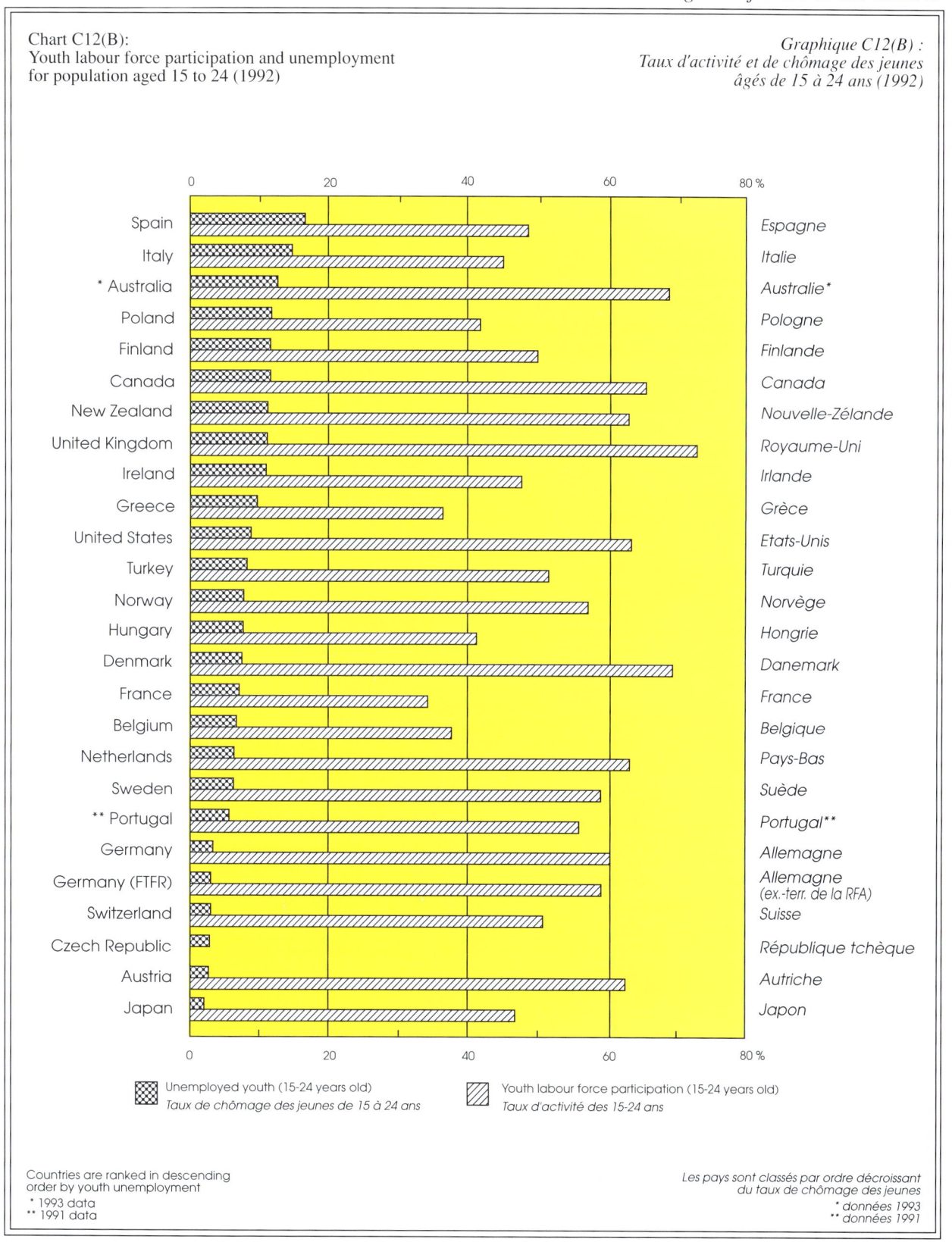

C13: National income per capita

GDP PER CAPITA, 1982-1992

POLICY ISSUES

Gross domestic product (GDP) per capita provides a measure of a country's prosperity and ability to finance educational programmes among other things. More prosperous countries can invest a higher absolute level of resources in education for the same percentage of GDP. At the other end of the spectrum, less affluent countries must spend a greater percentage of their per capita GDP to achieve the same level of spending on education. They must also spend a greater percentage on other basics, and so education must compete for a share of even more limited resources.

KEY RESULTS

The range of per capita GDP among OECD countries is very wide. The most prosperous country, the United States, has a per capita GDP that is more than twice the GDP of the three poorest countries: Greece, Portugal and Turkey.

DESCRIPTION AND INTERPRETATION

Average per capita GDP (reported in constant dollars) has increased steadily over the decade. In 1982, the average was US$ 10 703. By 1992, this average had reached US$ 13 020.

As noted above, vast disparities exist in the GDP per capita, though differences between the richest and poorest countries have diminished somewhat. In 1982, five countries had a GDP per capita less than one-half that of the most prosperous country. By 1992, only four countries were in this position. In general, countries' growth rates were unrelated to their 1982 rankings.

Turkey has remained the least prosperous nation over the period covered, and the United States and Switzerland have maintained their respective positions as the most and second most prosperous nations. However, rankings of countries in the middle have shifted. For example, in 1982, Norway ranked ninth from the bottom; by 1992, it had overtaken five other countries.

Growth disparities in countries' per capita GDP have also been dramatic. GDP per capita in Iceland and New Zealand grew less than 10 per cent over the period covered, while in Ireland it grew by over 40 per cent. The least prosperous countries tended to have less growth, although there were exceptions to this as well. Ireland, for example, experienced a very high growth rate.

Comparing this indicator with C03, the relative size of the young population, it appears that the least prosperous countries must educate the largest number of students. In these nations, already thin resources must be spread that much farther.

DEFINITIONS

GDP per capita is measured in accordance with definitions used by the OECD for calculating national accounts statistics; thus it is expressed in national currency units per US dollar. It is measured at 1985 price levels, and adjusted for differences in the purchasing power parity index (PPP) of 1985. The total population, by which the GDP is divided, includes all persons settled in the country, regardless of citizenship, educational, or labour market status.

The chart represents the proportional growth in per capita GDP between 1982 and 1992. The figures presented there are derived by dividing the 1992 per capita GDP by that of 1982 and multiplying the result by 100.

C13: National income per capita

C13 : Revenu national par habitant

Table C13:
GDP per capita in 1982, 1985, 1990 and 1992 at 1985 price levels and converted using PPPs (US dollars)

*Tableau C13 :
PIB par habitant en 1982, 1985, 1990 et 1992 aux niveaux de prix de 1985 convertis en PPA (dollars E-U)*

	GDP per capita (1992) / PIB par habitant (1992)	1992	1990	1985	1982	Annual change (in %) / Variation annuelle (en %)	
Turkey	3 960	121	119	100	91	2.6	Turquie
Greece	6 350	109	107	100	95	1.2	Grèce
Portugal	7 210	126	123	100	102	2.0	Portugal
Ireland	9 940	135	127	100	95	3.3	Irlande
Spain	10 110	126	123	100	95	2.6	Espagne
New Zealand	11 270	99	100	100	94	0.4	Nouvelle-Zélande
Finland	12 000	103	116	100	93	0.9	Finlande
United Kingdom	12 820	112	116	100	91	1.8	Royaume-Uni
Iceland	13 450	105	110	100	97	0.7	Islande
Italy	13 620	117	115	100	95	1.9	Italie
Netherlands	13 630	115	113	100	94	1.8	Pays-Bas
Sweden	13 650	105	109	100	93	1.1	Suède
Australia	13 900	108	107	100	90	1.7	Australie
Norway	13 920	110	106	100	87	2.2	Norvège
Belgium	14 000	118	115	100	97	1.8	Belgique
Denmark	14 100	108	107	100	89	1.8	Danemark
Austria	14 240	116	113	100	94	1.9	Autriche
France	14 670	114	113	100	97	1.4	France
Canada	15 440	105	109	100	89	1.5	Canada
Japan	15 450	128	122	100	91	3.2	Japon
Germany (FTFR)	15 940	118	114	100	93	2.2	Allemagne (ex-terr. de la RFA)
Luxembourg	17 080	124	121	100	89	3.0	Luxembourg
Switzerland	17 400	109	112	100	95	1.3	Suisse
United States	18 360	109	110	100	90	1.8	Etats-Unis
Country mean	**13 020**	**113**	**113**	**100**	**93**	**1.8**	**Moyenne des pays**

C13: National income per capita

C13 : Revenu national par habitant

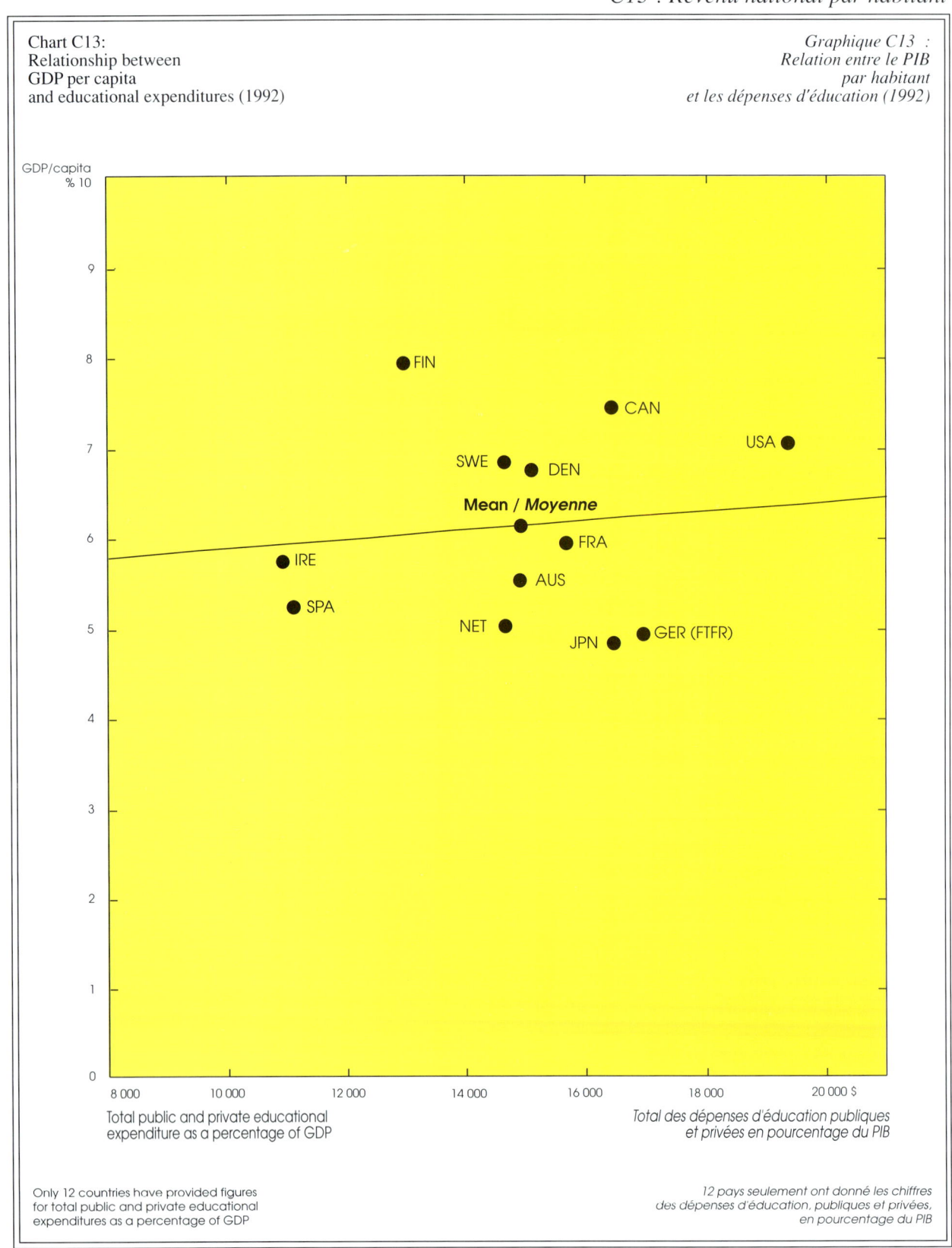

Chart C13:
Relationship between
GDP per capita
and educational expenditures (1992)

Graphique C13 :
Relation entre le PIB
par habitant
et les dépenses d'éducation (1992)

Total public and private educational expenditure as a percentage of GDP

Total des dépenses d'éducation publiques et privées en pourcentage du PIB

Only 12 countries have provided figures for total public and private educational expenditures as a percentage of GDP

12 pays seulement ont donné les chiffres des dépenses d'éducation, publiques et privées, en pourcentage du PIB

C21: Importance of school subjects

C21: IMPORTANCE OF SECONDARY SCHOOL SUBJECTS

POLICY ISSUES

When public perception of what should be taught in school does not match the current policy agenda – or developments such as rapid technological advance – governments must take such (possibly unexpected) input into account.

KEY RESULTS

There is a high level of agreement across countries regarding the importance of two subjects: native (school) language and mathematics; the latter subject is viewed as one of the top two priorities in all countries except the Netherlands. Some subjects – such as social studies – receive very different rankings.

Foreign languages receive an equally high ranking in all but two countries (the United Kingdom and the United States).

The arts have the lowest priority in all countries except Switzerland and the United States, where technology/technical studies rank lowest.

Technology/technical studies are generally ranked near the bottom. The countries in which technology/technical studies receive their highest ranking are Austria, Portugal, Spain and the United Kingdom.

DESCRIPTION AND INTERPRETATION

Both the table and the chart provide a country-by-country comparison of the importance given by the general public in twelve OECD countries to subjects in secondary school curriculum. Figures refer to the percentage of respondents who said that a subject was "essential" or "very important". The table lists all ten subjects used in the survey, while the chart highlights only four: three top-priority subjects, and one showing wide variation among countries: social subjects.

The table also provides a "subject average", an overall measure of the importance accorded to the ten subjects by individual countries. At the bottom of the table are the "country averages" for each subject.

On each chart, the cross-country average for the subject is represented by a horizontal line. The size of the column above or below the horizontal line shows how far any individual country differs from the cross-country average.

Country averages are useful because:

• They offer a view of the international ranking of subjects.

• In conjunction with the subject average, they show the extent to which a subject's ranking within any individual country is similar or dissimilar to its international ranking.

• Represented as lines on the charts, they allow visual identification of countries that fall above or below country averages.

Subject averages are useful because:

• They give a reading of how the public in any individual country responded overall. This may say something about the strength with which people in various countries express their views, or it may show absolute differences among countries.

• The importance of any individual subject within a country can be gauged in comparison with the subject average for that country – that is, the hanging bars chart may be drawn for any individual country using the subject average as a base line.

In conclusion, the most value to be derived from the indicator may lie in examination of relative relationships within and across countries rather than simply by making a comparison of raw percentages.

DEFINITIONS

The indicator refers to the percentage of the general public who responded "essential" or "very important" to this question: "The following are ten examples of things that young people study or could study in secondary school. In your view how important are each of these?" (It should be noted that one or two optional items were added in some countries.)

Other response categories were "fairly important", "not very important", "not at all important", "not sure either way" or, in some countries, "don't know".

C21: Importance of school subjects

C21 : Importance des matières d'enseignement

Table C21:
Percentage of respondents who thought the subjects were "essential" or "very important" (1993/94)

Tableau C21 :
Pourcentage des répondants qui estimaient que les matières étaient "essentielles" ou "très importantes" (1993/94)

	Physical education / Sciences physiques	The arts / Education et pratiques artistiques	The sciences / Sciences expérimentales	Foreign languages / Langues étrangères	Native (school) language / Langue maternelle	Social subjects (e.g. History, Geography) / Histoire, géographie	Mathematics / Mathématiques	Education for citizenship / Education civique	Technology technical studies / Technologie	Information technology (e.g. Computing) / Informatique	Subject average within each country / Moyenne des matières par pays	
Austria	73	43	67	91	92	72	92	64	60	79	**73.2**	Autriche
Belgium (Flemish community)	63	29	57	88	86	44	80	66	53	77	**64.3**	Belgique (Communauté flamande)
Denmark	38	36	46	79	85	41	81	46	...	55	**56.3**	Danemark
Finland	61	31	53	87	77	49	84	35	39	71	**58.9**	Finlande
France	50	31	63	87	97	69	88	67	47	69	**66.8**	France
Netherlands	41	31	64	85	90	47	69	41	42	75	**58.6**	Pays-Bas
Portugal	71	55	76	85	91	75	86	73	66	76	**75.5**	Portugal
Spain	52	44	65	72	67	66	73	66	63	66	**63.4**	Espagne
Sweden	54	31	65	87	94	58	91	70	38	63	**65.0**	Suède
Switzerland	67	58	63	77	84	62	82	65	52	71	**68.1**	Suisse
United Kingdom	41	26	66	56	88	50	93	36	57	72	**58.4**	Royaume-Uni
United States	62	47	85	53	92	80	96	77	36	86	**71.3**	Etats-Unis
Country average for each subject	**56.0**	**38.4**	**64.1**	**79.0**	**86.9**	**59.5**	**84.6**	**59.0**	**50.3**	**71.5**		**Moyenne des pays pour chaque matière**

See Annex 1 for notes

Voir notes en annexe 1

C21: Importance of school subjects

C21 : Importance des matières d'enseignement

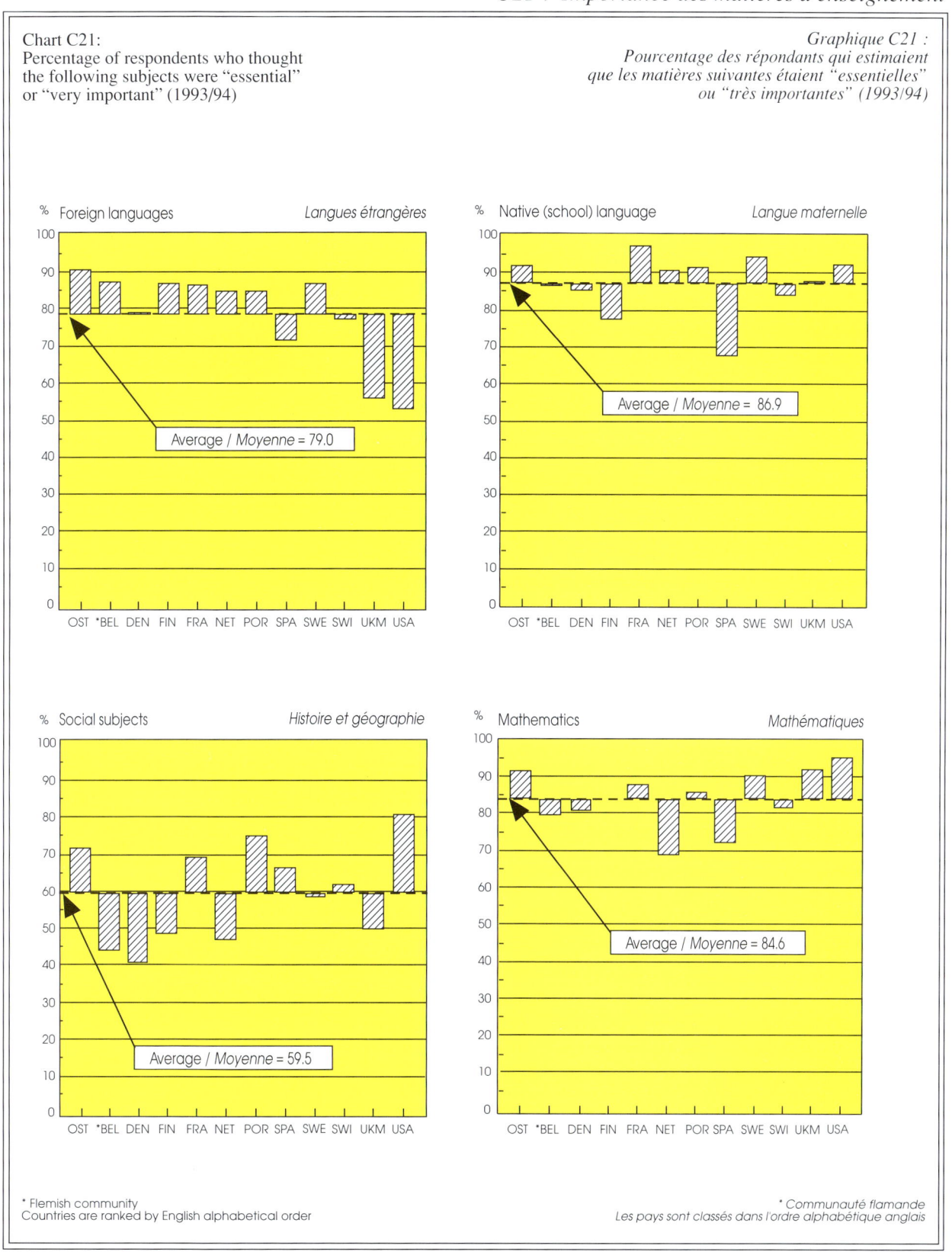

Chart C21:
Percentage of respondents who thought the following subjects were "essential" or "very important" (1993/94)

Graphique C21 :
Pourcentage des répondants qui estimaient que les matières suivantes étaient "essentielles" ou "très importantes" (1993/94)

Foreign languages / Langues étrangères
Average / Moyenne = 79.0

Native (school) language / Langue maternelle
Average / Moyenne = 86.9

Social subjects / Histoire et géographie
Average / Moyenne = 59.5

Mathematics / Mathématiques
Average / Moyenne = 84.6

Countries: OST, *BEL, DEN, FIN, FRA, NET, POR, SPA, SWE, SWI, UKM, USA

* Flemish community
Countries are ranked by English alphabetical order

* Communauté flamande
Les pays sont classés dans l'ordre alphabétique anglais

C22: Importance of qualities/aptitudes

C22: IMPORTANCE OF QUALITIES/APTITUDES

POLICY ISSUES

What can be done to enhance secondary school's ability to develop aptitudes and qualities such as self-confidence? The public place a high priority on such qualities, although they are difficult to quantify.

KEY RESULTS

On the whole, countries rate personal, social and vocational qualities and/or aptitudes higher than curriculum subjects. The country averages range from 88.4 to 64.2 per cent for qualities, as compared with 86.9 to 38.4 per cent for subjects (Table C21).

"Self-confidence" and "skills and knowledge to get a job" are consistently rated as high priorities in all countries.

"Understanding of other countries of the world" has a significantly lower country average than the seven others, and is rated as a bottom priority (or bottom equal) in ten of the twelve countries. Austria and Switzerland are exceptions with "understanding other countries" higher than "being a good citizen".

The latter quality shows the least consistency in its ranking across countries — high in Portugal, middle in Belgium (Flemish community) and Finland, and low in Austria and Switzerland.

DESCRIPTION AND INTERPRETATION

Both the table and the chart provide a country-by-country comparison of the importance that the general public in twelve OECD countries attach to qualities. Figures refer to the percentage of respondents who said that a quality was "essential" or "very important". The table lists all eight qualities, while the chart highlights four of qualities rated as most important.

The table provides a "qualities average", an overall measure of the importance accorded to the eight qualities by individual countries. The country averages for each quality are at the bottom of the table.

The chart presents country averages as a horizontal line. This allows an "at a glance" reading of the level of priority given to that quality across countries.

The size of the column above or below the horizontal line shows how much any individual country differs from the country average.

In interpreting the information, it is helpful to set these data alongside those on the importance of subjects (Indicator C21). Useful comparisons can be made in two areas in particular: *i)* qualities averages in relation to subject averages; and *ii)* country averages for subjects and for qualities.

Within this indicator it is also useful to examine country averages, because:

• They give a view of international consensus on the ranking of qualities.

• They show the extent to which a qualities ranking within any individual country is similar or dissimilar to its international ranking.

• They allow visual identification of countries that fall above or below the line.

Qualities averages give a reading of how the public in any country responded overall. In addition, the importance of any individual quality within a country can be gauged in comparison with the qualities average for that country.

DEFINITIONS

This indicator refers to the percentage of the general public who responded "essential" or "very important" to this question: "The following are qualities that young people may have developed by the end of their compulsory schooling. In your view, how important is it that schools aim to develop such qualities?".

Other response categories were: "fairly important", "not very important", "not at all important" and "not sure either way" or, in some countries, "don't know".

C22: Importance of qualities/aptitudes

C22 : Importance de certaines qualités

Table C22:
Percentage of respondents who thought the following qualities were "essential" or "very important" (1993/94)

Tableau C22 :
Pourcentage des répondants qui estimaient que les qualités suivantes étaient "essentielles" ou "très importantes" (1993/94)

	Self-confidence / La confiance en soi	How to live among people from different backgrounds / La capacité de vivre avec des personnes de différents milieux	A desire to continue studies or training / La motivation à poursuivre des études ou à compléter sa formation	An understanding of other countries of the world / La compréhension des autres pays du monde	Skills and knowledge which will help to get a job / Les compétences et les connaissances utiles pour trouver un emploi	Skills and knowledge which will help to continue studies or training / Les compétences et les connaissances permettant des études ou une formation ultérieures	A lifestyle which promotes good health / Un mode de vie équilibré et sain	Being a good citizen / Un esprit et un comportement civiques	**Qualities average within each country / Moyenne des qualités par pays**	
Austria	93	83	79	71	92	88	83	68	**82.3**	Autriche
Belgium (Flemish community)	90	81	75	61	85	78	78	80	**78.5**	Belgique (Communauté flamande)
Denmark	87	84	65	61	75	70	61	63	**70.6**	Danemark
Finland	89	87	68	62	82	76	77	76	**77.1**	Finlande
France	93	83	87	64	91	84	85	82	**83.5**	France
Netherlands	90	85	73	63	80	83	61	65	**74.8**	Pays-Bas
Portugal	82	82	81	71	85	85	86	87	**82.6**	Portugal
Spain	75	73	70	65	77	73	72	75	**72.5**	Espagne
Sweden	90	75	68	61	85	80	72	76	**75.9**	Suède
Switzerland	93	88	76	74	89	86	79	58	**80.4**	Suisse
United Kingdom	89	73	69	49	91	...	72	82	**75.1**	Royaume-Uni
United States	89	82	88	67	94	90	83	86	**84.8**	Etats-Unis
Country average for each quality	**88.4**	**81.3**	**74.8**	**64.2**	**85.5**	**81.2**	**75.7**	**74.9**		**Moyenne des pays pour chaque qualité**

See Annex 1 for notes

Voir notes en annexe 1

C22: Importance of qualities/aptitudes

C22 : Importance de certaines qualités

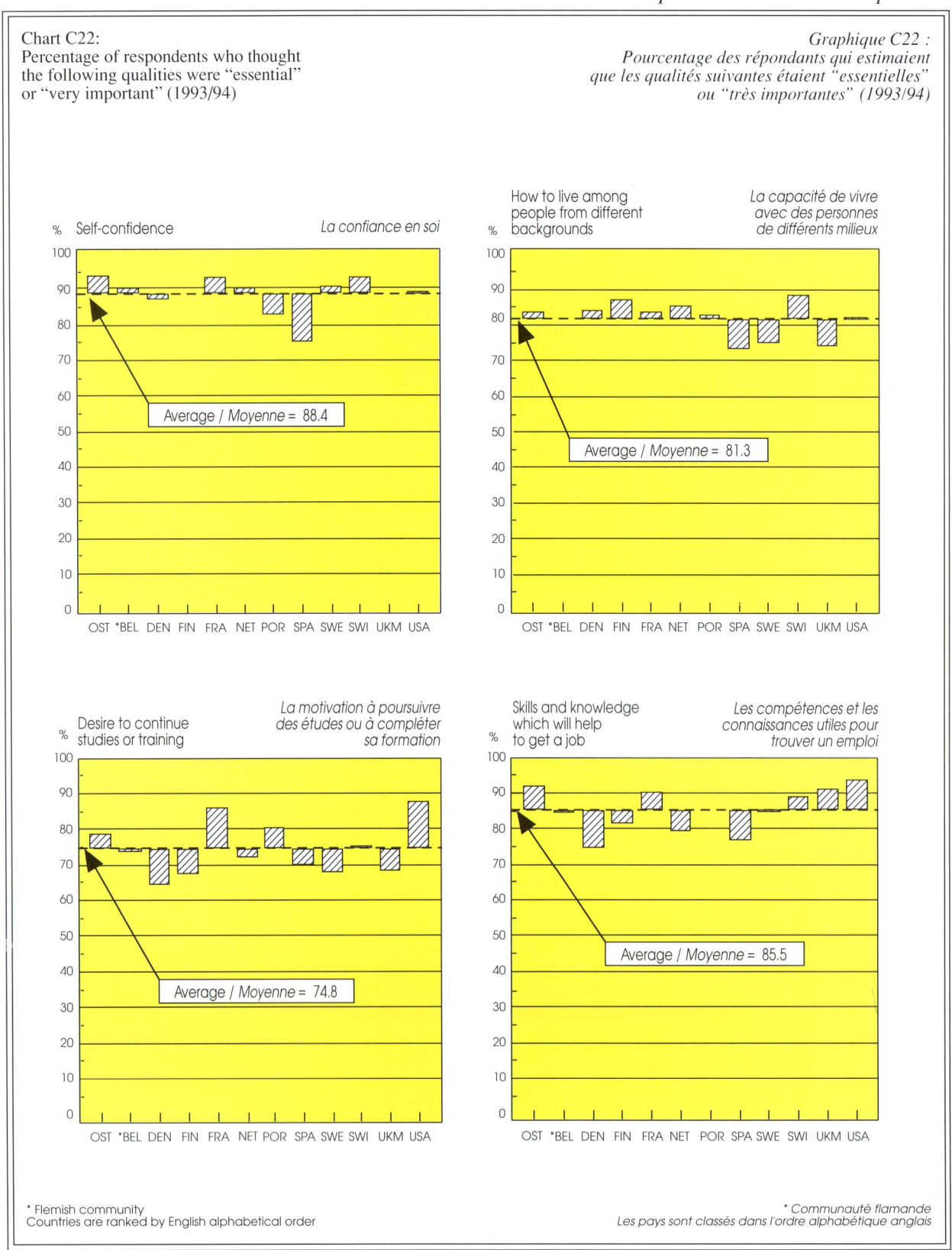

Chart C22:
Percentage of respondents who thought the following qualities were "essential" or "very important" (1993/94)

Graphique C22 :
Pourcentage des répondants qui estimaient que les qualités suivantes étaient "essentielles" ou "très importantes" (1993/94)

Self-confidence / La confiance en soi
Average / Moyenne = 88.4

How to live among people from different backgrounds / La capacité de vivre avec des personnes de différents milieux
Average / Moyenne = 81.3

Desire to continue studies or training / La motivation à poursuivre des études ou à compléter sa formation
Average / Moyenne = 74.8

Skills and knowledge which will help to get a job / Les compétences et les connaissances utiles pour trouver un emploi
Average / Moyenne = 85.5

Countries: OST, *BEL, DEN, FIN, FRA, NET, POR, SPA, SWE, SWI, UKM, USA

* Flemish community
Countries are ranked by English alphabetical order

* Communauté flamande
Les pays sont classés dans l'ordre alphabétique anglais

C23: Public confidence in the schools

C23: CONFIDENCE IN THE TEACHING OF SUBJECTS AND DEVELOPMENT OF QUALITIES

POLICY ISSUES

The gap between confidence in the achievement of objectives and the perceived importance of those objectives may, in terms of policy, be taken as one index of satisfaction or dissatisfaction with schools. Where precisely is improvement needed? What can be done in practical terms?

KEY RESULTS

The general public's confidence in the teaching of important subjects is consistently higher than its confidence in the development of important qualities – except in Portugal, where they are equal.

The difference between the two levels is marginally higher in two or three countries (e.g. in Denmark, Spain and the United States – 4 to 9 percentage points) and very much higher in three others (Finland, France and Sweden – 22 percentage points).

Confidence in the teaching of important subjects in France is high in absolute terms (84 per cent) and relatively high in comparison with other countries.

In Sweden, the confidence expressed in the development of qualities is low in absolute terms (18 per cent), and in relative terms conspicuously lower than in all other countries.

DESCRIPTION AND INTERPRETATION

The chart shows, for each country, and in two vertical columns, the public's level of confidence in the teaching of subjects and in the development of qualities rated "essential" or "very important".

The columns show the average percentage of important subjects or qualities that respondents believe – i.e., are "very confident" or "fairly confident" – to be well taught. These are subjects or qualities that each respondent deems "essential" or "very important", and the indicator equals the average of percentages across respondents.

The percentage figure is the average confidence figure across all ten subjects. For example, Belgium's (Flemish community) 72 per cent confidence in teaching of subjects is the average confidence figure across all 10 subjects. The 58 per cent figure for Belgium (Flemish community) is the average confidence figure across all eight qualities. Both are calculated by taking only those responses where people say that a subject or quality is "essential"/"very important" and then ascertaining whether or not they say they are "very confident"/"fairly confident" that subject is taught well.

The "country average" is calculated by averaging the confidence figure for each of the twelve countries. This is done twice, once for subjects, once for qualities. The two are represented in the chart by two horizontal lines, one solid (subjects) and one dotted line (qualities).

The table simply provides the figures on which the chart is based. A number of different measures might be used in interpreting the results:
• The satisfaction rating may be taken as the height of the column.
• The relative degree of satisfaction with subjects as compared with qualities may be read as the difference in height between the two relevant columns.
• Individual countries may be compared with the average across countries by examining the difference between the column height and the horizontal (country average) line.

DEFINITION

A subject or quality is regarded as important by a respondent if he or she said it was "essential" or "very important". The respondent is confident about the teaching of the subject if he or she also indicated that he or she was "very" or "fairly" confident it was taught (or developed) well.

The indicator is calculated using a four-step procedure finding:
• The number of times a respondent rated a subject or quality "essential" or "very important" (*a*).
• The number of times a respondent also said he or she was "very" or "fairly" confident about the teaching of the subject or quality (*b*).
• The average *b/a* for each respondent.
• The average for all respondents in each country, which forms the percentage score for the country.

C23: Public confidence in the schools

C23 : Confiance du public envers l'école

Table C23:
Percentage of respondents who viewed subjects as important and who thought they were taught well, and percentage of respondents who thought qualities were important and that they were developed well
(1993/94)

Tableau C23 :
Pourcentage des répondants qui estimaient que les matières étaient importantes et qu'elles étaient bien enseignées, et pourcentage des répondants qui estimaient que les qualités étaient importantes et que leur acquisition était favorisée
(1993/94)

	Average confidence in important subjects *Appréciation moyenne de l'importance des matières*	Average confidence in important qualities *Appréciation moyenne de l'importance des qualités*	
Austria	78	63	*Autriche*
Belgium (Flemish community)	72	58	*Belgique (Communauté flamande)*
Denmark	75	69	*Danemark*
Finland	77	55	*Finlande*
France	84	62	*France*
Netherlands	64	51	*Pays-Bas*
Portugal	58	58	*Portugal*
Spain	46	37	*Espagne*
Sweden	40	18	*Suède*
Switzerland	76	63	*Suisse*
United Kingdom	63	47	*Royaume-Uni*
United States	63	59	*Etats-Unis*
Country average	**66.2**	**53.4**	***Moyenne des pays***

See Annex 1 for notes

Voir notes en annexe 1

C23: Public confidence in the schools

C23 : Confiance du public envers l'école

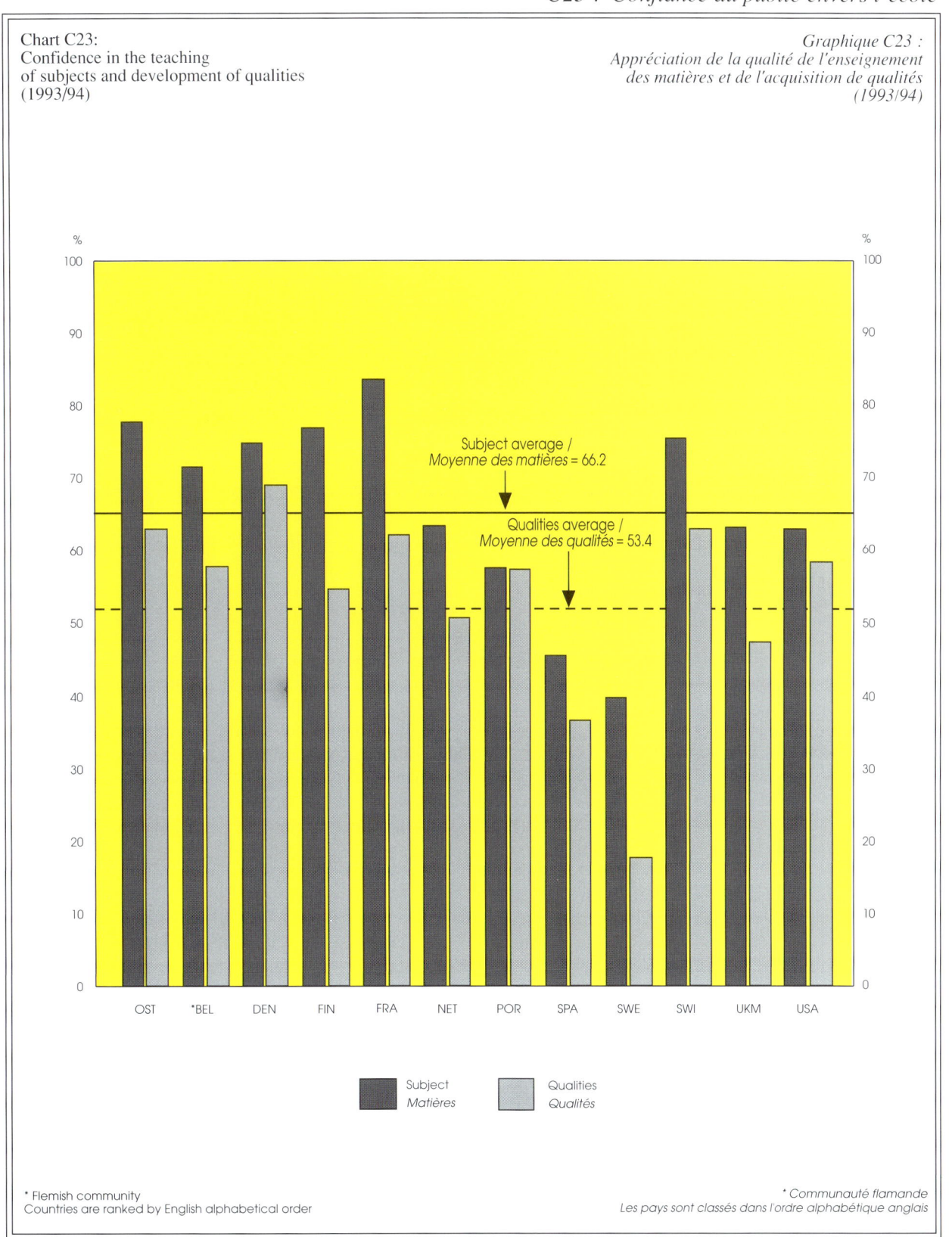

Chart C23:
Confidence in the teaching of subjects and development of qualities (1993/94)

Graphique C23 :
Appréciation de la qualité de l'enseignement des matières et de l'acquisition de qualités (1993/94)

Subject average / Moyenne des matières = 66.2

Qualities average / Moyenne des qualités = 53.4

Countries (left to right): OST, *BEL, DEN, FIN, FRA, NET, POR, SPA, SWE, SWI, UKM, USA

Legend: Subject / Matières — Qualities / Qualités

* Flemish community
Countries are ranked by English alphabetical order

* *Communauté flamande*
Les pays sont classés dans l'ordre alphabétique anglais

C24: Educational responsibilities of schools

C24: HOME SCHOOL BALANCE FOR THE PERSONAL AND SOCIAL DEVELOPMENT OF YOUNG PEOPLE

POLICY ISSUES

Outside the schoolroom, what can be done to enhance home/community efforts towards nurturing the personal and social development of young people?

KEY RESULTS

In all countries, there is strong feeling that responsibilities for personal and social education should be shared between home and school. Denmark and Finland are the only exceptions, with more than half the population ascribing major responsibility to the home.

There are wide variations among countries in the percentage of the public assigning a major responsibility for personal and social development to the home.

In four countries (France, Portugal, Spain and the United Kingdom), less than 20 per cent of the public see the home as having more responsibility than the school.

There is a strong consensus across all countries that schools should not have the main responsibility for personal and social development. Portugal is the only country where more than 10 per cent of the public indicate the home should have less responsibility than the school.

DESCRIPTION AND INTERPRETATION

With the exception of Portugal, all of the variations among countries in the percentage of people assigning most responsibility to the school fall within the survey's margin of error. Therefore, these figures should be regarded as approximately equal. The remaining interest, then, lies with the balance of shared responsibility and home responsibility, and the country breakdown as shown on the chart is most revealing.

Only in the Nordic countries – Denmark and Finland – did more than half of the sample (55 per cent) find that the home should bear more responsibility than the school. In the nine other countries, the majority of persons believed the responsibility should be shared, with percentages in six of the nine ranging from 53 to 67 per cent. France, Spain and the United Kingdom had the lowest share (14-15 per cent) of persons placing primary responsibility with the home.

It would be interesting to explore further the countries that fall well above and well below the country average for home responsibility. Policy context as well as current practice will be important in any attempt to explain the meaning or implications of those findings.

DEFINITIONS

The indicator refers to percentages of the general public who responded "main"/"shared equally"/"less" to the following question: "How much responsibility do you think the school should have (compared with the home) for the personal and social development of young people?".

C24: Educational responsibilities of schools

C24 : Responsabilités éducatives de l'école

Table C24:
Percentage of people who answered how much responsibility they thought the home should have compared to school for the personal and social development of young people (1993/94)

Tableau C24 :
Pourcentage de la population qui a répondu à la question sur la responsabilité que la famille devrait avoir par rapport à l'établissement scolaire en ce qui concerne l'épanouissement personnel et social des jeunes (1993/94)

	Home should have more responsibility than the school / *La famille devrait avoir plus de responsabilité que l'établissement scolaire*	Home should share responsibility equally with the school / *La famille devrait avoir autant de responsabilité que l'établissement scolaire*	Home should have less responsibility than the school / *La famille devrait avoir moins de responsabilité que l'établissement scolaire*	
Denmark	55	43	2	*Danemark*
Finland	55	44	1	*Finlande*
Netherlands	44	53	3	*Pays-Bas*
Austria	42	55	3	*Autriche*
Sweden	38	60	2	*Suède*
United States	34	63	3	*Etats-Unis*
Belgium (Flemish community)	28	65	7	*Belgique (Communauté flamande)*
Portugal	18	67	14	*Portugal*
Spain	15	80	5	*Espagne*
United Kingdom	14	81	5	*Royaume-Uni*
France	14	79	7	*France*
Country average	**32.5**	**62.8**	**4.7**	***Moyenne des pays***

See Annex 1 for notes

Voir notes en annexe 1

C24: Educational responsibilities of schools

C24 : Responsabilités éducatives de l'école

Chart C24:
Percentage of people who answered how much responsibility they thought the home should have compared to school for the personal and social development of young people (1993/94)

Graphique C24 :
Pourcentage de la population qui a répondu à la question sur la responsabilité que la famille devrait avoir par rapport à l'établissement scolaire en ce qui concerne l'épanouissement personnel et social des jeunes (1993/94)

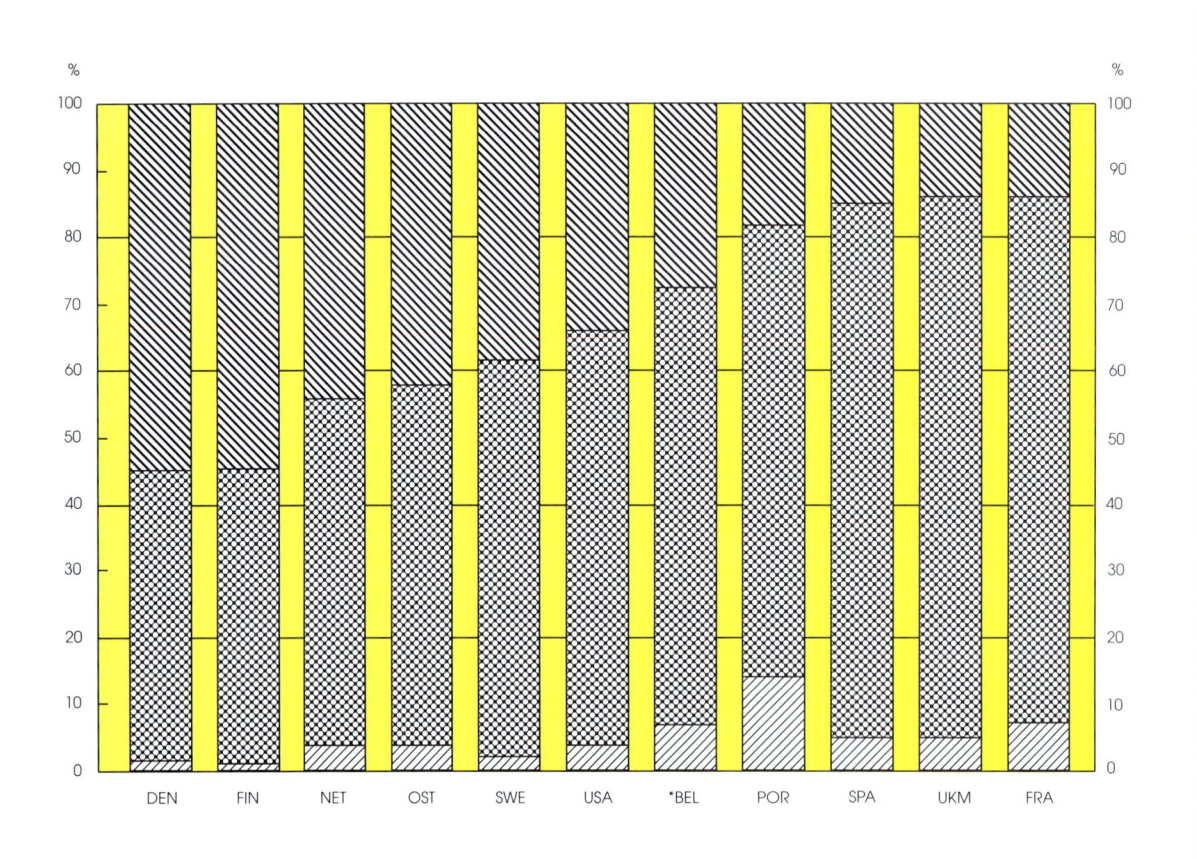

- Less responsibility than the school / *Moins de responsabilité que l'établissement*
- More responsibility than the school / *Plus de responsabilité que l'établissement*
- Responsibility shared equally with the home / *Autant de responsabilité*

* Flemish community
Countries are ordered as the percentage who felt the home should have more responsibility than the school for the personal and social development of young people

* *Communauté flamande*
Les pays sont classés par ordre décroissant selon que la population attribuait plus de responsabilité à la famille

C25: Respect for teachers

C25: RESPECT FOR SECONDARY TEACHERS

POLICY ISSUES

In providing information on the general public's level of respect for secondary teachers, this indicator translates into support or lack of support for the teaching profession. How people perceive the profession is likely to affect recruitment and the quality of new entrants. The information is likely to be of most use when taken together with that of other indicators on teachers, such as salary levels and working conditions.

KEY RESULTS

There is wide variation from country to country in the percentages of persons who said that teachers are "very" or "fairly respected", with figures ranging from 32 per cent in Spain to 74 per cent in Austria.

In all but three countries, less than 10 per cent think teachers are "very respected". Austria and the United States stand out from the overall pattern trend with around one person in five saying that teachers are "very respected".

Taking the eleven countries together, one in three of the general public considers that teachers are "not very respected".

In no country do more than 10 per cent of the public say that teachers are "not at all respected".

The percentage saying that they are "not sure" or "don't know" ranges in ten countries from 2 to 10 per cent. A notable exception is Portugal, where one in four said that they are "not sure" or "don't know".

DESCRIPTION AND INTERPRETATION

In the chart, countries are presented in alphabetical order from left to right. The column represents the percentage of the public who said that teachers were "very" or "fairly" respected. The average across countries for these two response categories is 57.6 per cent, and is represented by the horizontal line. Each individual country may then be seen as exceeding or falling short of that average rating.

DEFINITIONS

This indicator refers to the percentage of the general public who responded "very respected" or "fairly respected" to the question: "In your opinion how respected are secondary teachers as a profession?".

Other response categories were: "not very respected", "not at all respected" and "not sure either way".

C25: Respect for teachers

C25 : Considération accordée aux enseignants

Table C25:
Different levels of respect
for secondary teachers
as professionals (percentage, 1993/94)

*Tableau C25 :
Différents niveaux de considération
pour les enseignants du secondaire en tant
que professionnels (pourcentage, 1993/94)*

	Very respected / *Très bien considérés*	Fairly respected / *Assez bien considérés*	Very and fairly respected / *Très et assez bien considérés*	Not very respected / *Pas très bien considérés*	Not at all respected / *Mal considérés*	Not sure / *Sans opinion*	
Austria	18	57	74	18	3	4	*Autriche*
Belgium (Flemish community)	8	56	64	29	6	2	*Belgique (Communauté flamande)*
Denmark	7	52	59	35	2	3	*Danemark*
Finland	7	51	58	40	2	...	*Finlande*
France	8	47	55	35	9	2	*France*
Netherlands	5	55	61	33	2	4	*Pays-Bas*
Portugal	12	47	59	13	3	25	*Portugal*
Spain	3	29	32	49	9	10	*Espagne*
Sweden	7	40	48	37	6	9	*Suède*
United Kingdom	7	49	56	32	6	7	*Royaume-Uni*
United States	20	48	68	24	5	3	*Etats-Unis*
Country average	**9.3**	**48.3**	**57.6**	**31.3**	**4.8**	**6.9**	***Moyenne des pays***

See Annex 1 for notes

Voir notes en annexe 1

C25: Respect for teachers

C25 : Considération accordée aux enseignants

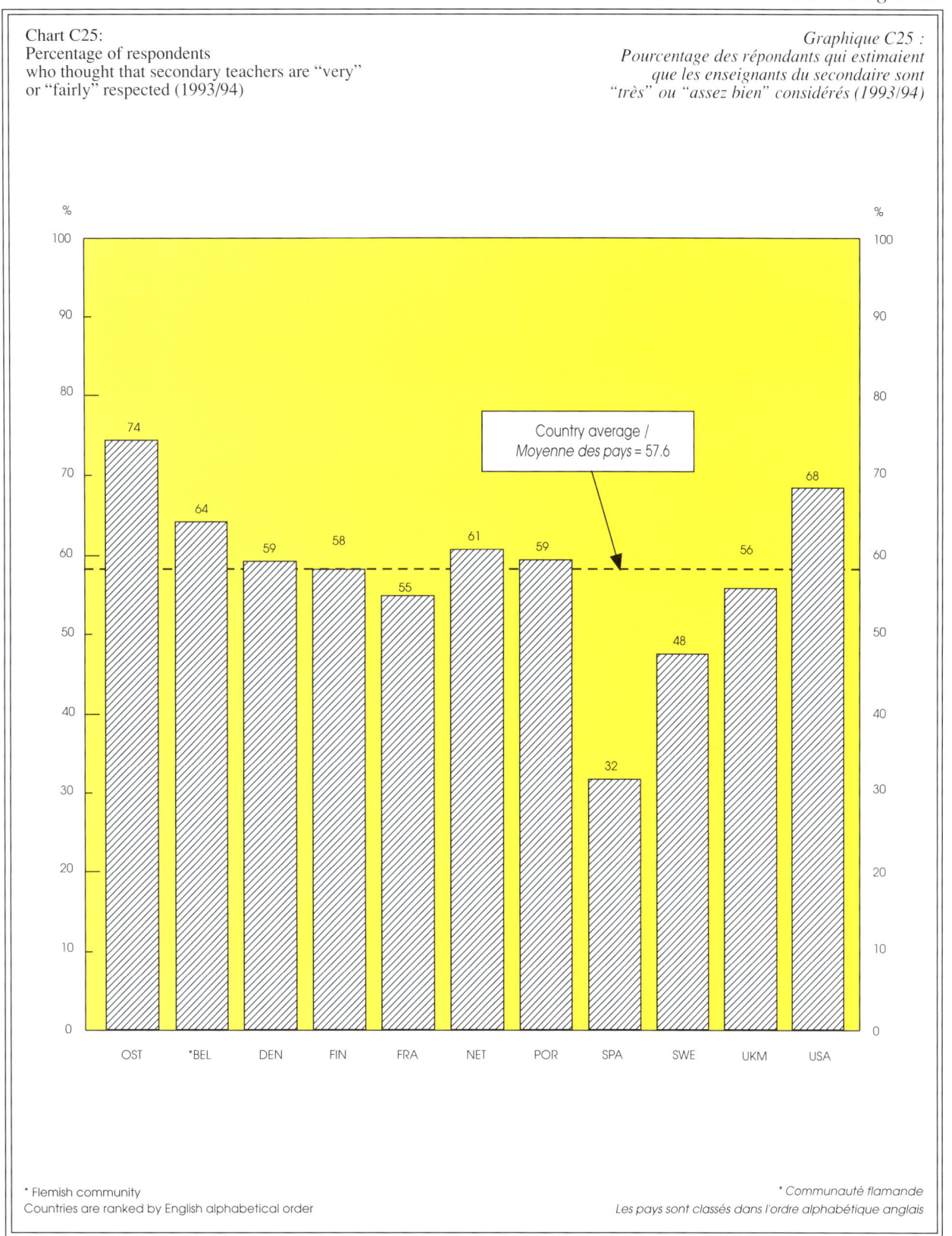

Chart C25:
Percentage of respondents who thought that secondary teachers are "very" or "fairly" respected (1993/94)

Graphique C25 :
Pourcentage des répondants qui estimaient que les enseignants du secondaire sont "très" ou "assez bien" considérés (1993/94)

Country	%
OST	74
*BEL	64
DEN	59
FIN	58
FRA	55
NET	61
POR	59
SPA	32
SWE	48
UKM	56
USA	68

Country average / *Moyenne des pays* = 57.6

* Flemish community
Countries are ranked by English alphabetical order

* *Communauté flamande*
Les pays sont classés dans l'ordre alphabétique anglais

C26: Priorities in school practice

C26: PRIORITIES IN SCHOOL PRACTICE

POLICY ISSUES

This indicator provides information about the public's perception of effective school practices on which the public would like to see greatest investment of energy and resources.

KEY RESULTS

There is strong support among the general public in all countries for "helping with difficulties in learning", which is ranked as a top priority in each.

"Keeping parents well informed" is rated highly overall (country average: 82.3 per cent), and is also rated highly within eleven of the twelve countries. France, though, gives it relatively less weight than most other priorities.

"Careers advice and guidance" is rated highly overall (country average: 80.2 per cent), and rated highly within each of the twelve countries.

"Maintaining discipline" is seen in four countries (Finland, France, the United Kingdom and the United States) as a top priority, and in Finland and France it is ranked significantly higher than "keeping parents well informed".

"Regular homework" has the lowest country average overall (57.5 per cent), and is also low on the list in every country.

"A wide range of subjects taught" shows the greatest variation among countries; it is rated very low in Finland and relatively high in Belgium, Switzerland and the United States.

DESCRIPTION AND INTERPRETATION

The general public were asked to respond to seven aspects of school practice, each of which is shown in graphic and tabular form for the twelve countries. Each of the seven charts illustrates one aspect of school practice, with countries shown alphabetically from left to right. The average for all countries taken together ("country average") is represented by a horizontal line. The distance of any country above or below the horizontal line shows the distance from the country average.

The table gives the same information in percentages, and also provides a "school practices" average which shows, for an individual country, the average response rate for all seven aspects of practice.

The "school practices" average is particularly useful in interpreting the figures, because it gives an immediate reading of the relative priority rating of any school practice for one country. For example, while "keeping parents well informed" is rated as "essential"/"very important" by 76 per cent of the public in France, this is not a high priority when it is noted that their school practices average 80.3 per cent.

The school practices average also makes it possible to take into account differences in response between Denmark and Spain, where it is generally quite low (59 per cent) as against the United States, for example, where it is generally high (87 per cent).

DEFINITIONS

This indicator refers to percentages of the general public who responded "essential" or "very important" to the following question: "In your view, how important are each of the following for schools to emphasize in order to achieve their goals?".

Other response categories were: "fairly important", "not very important", "not at all important" and "not sure either way" or, in some countries, "don't know".

C26: Priorities in school practice

C26 : Aspects prioritaires de l'action des écoles

Table C26:
Percentage of respondents who thought it is "essential" or "very important" for schools to emphasize the following practices in order to achieve their goals (1993/94)

*Tableau C26 :
Pourcentage des répondants qui estimaient qu'il est "essentiel" ou "très important" que l'école prête une attention particulière aux aspects suivants pour s'acquitter de sa mission (1993/94)*

	Careers advice and guidance / L'aide à l'orientation des élèves et les informations sur les métiers	Helping with difficulties in learning / L'aide aux élèves en difficulté	Strong leadership from the headteacher / Une direction ferme assurée par le chef d'établissement	Maintaining discipline / Le maintien de la discipline dans l'établissement	Regular homework / Des devoirs donnés à la maison régulièrement	A wide range of different subjects taught / Un large éventail de disciplines enseignées	Keeping parents well informed and involved / L'information et la participation des parents d'élèves	**School practices average within each country / Moyenne générale par pays**	
Austria	93	92	47	73	57	70	86	**73.9**	Autriche
Belgium (Flemish community)	76	92	73	81	58	74	85	**76.9**	Belgique (Communauté flamande)
Denmark	66	81	46	56	39	51	74	**59.1**	Danemark
Finland	74	89	42	91	71	29	72	**66.8**	Finlande
France	93	94	82	89	57	70	76	**80.3**	France
Netherlands	81	92	61	69	60	67	83	**73.4**	Pays-Bas
Portugal	81	87	69	79	67	38	87	**72.6**	Portugal
Spain	71	76	38	60	39	55	74	**58.9**	Espagne
Sweden	77	88	62	79	49	48	80	**69.1**	Suède
Switzerland	82	92	56	67	52	71	88	**72.5**	Suisse
United Kingdom	85	94	75	90	63	70	87	**80.5**	Royaume-Uni
United States	84	92	85	93	78	79	95	**86.6**	Etats-Unis
Country average for earch school practice	**80.2**	**89.1**	**61.4**	**77.1**	**57.5**	**60.2**	**82.3**		*Moyenne des pays pour chaque aspect*

See Annex 1 for notes

Voir notes en annexe 1

C26: Priorities in school practice

C26 : Aspects prioritaires de l'action des écoles

Chart C26:
Percentage of respondents who thought it is "essential" and "very important" for schools to emphasize the following practices in order to achieve their goals (1993/94)

Graphique C26 :
Pourcentage des répondants qui estimaient qu'il est "essentiel" ou "très important" que l'école prête une attention particulière aux aspects suivants pour s'acquitter de sa mission (1993/94)

Careers advice and guidance — *L'aide à l'orientation des élèves et les informations sur les métiers* — 80.2

Helping with difficulties in learning — *L'aide aux élèves en difficulté* — 89.1

Strong leadership from the headteacher — *Une direction ferme assurée par le chef d'établissement* — 61.4

Maintaining discipline — *Le maintien de la discipline dans l'établissement* — 77.1

Regular homework — *Des devoirs donnés à la maison régulièrement* — 57.5

A wide range of subjects taught — *Un large éventail de disciplines enseignées* — 60.2

Keeping parents well informed and involved — *L'information et la participation des parents d'élèves* — 82.3

* Flemish community
Countries are ranked by English alphabetical order

* Communauté flamande
Les pays sont classés dans l'ordre alphabétique anglais

C27: Decision-making at school level

C27: IMPORTANCE OF DECISION-MAKING AT SCHOOL LEVEL

POLICY ISSUES

This indicator shows aspects of school management for which people favour more local control. Devolution of responsibility to schools is a common policy issue among OECD countries, and one in which public views may confirm or question policy and practice.

KEY RESULTS

There is wide variation among countries with regard to support for school-level decision-making. There is also wide variation in the types of decision-making that are seen as most appropriate for schools.

In one country (the United States), a majority are in favour of schools exercising autonomy in all areas.

The areas for which school-level decision-making receives the strongest support are teacher selection and promotion, how the school budget is spent, and how subjects are taught. The areas in which it is least supported are what subjects are taught and teachers' salaries and working conditions.

In some countries (e.g. the United States), views are fairly consistent across all six areas of decision-making. In other countries, the public differentiate sharply between one area and another. For example, in Sweden, 51 per cent favour local control of school budgets, but only 17 per cent favour letting schools set teacher salaries. In the Netherlands, 47 per cent favour school control of teacher selection and promotion, but only 15 per cent want local control over the subjects taught.

The area in which there is widest divergence from country to country is teacher selection and promotion.

DESCRIPTION AND INTERPRETATION

The percentage of respondents who viewed it as "very important" that schools have control over each of six areas of decision-making is shown in the chart and the table. The chart provides for each country a six-strand "web", and each of the six sectors between strands corresponds to an aspect of school-level decision-making. The distance the shaded area reaches from the centre of the web indicates the percentage of people favouring local control of the function indicated.

As well as giving an at-a-glance view of overall support among countries, the charts show how support leans towards certain kinds of decision-making. In Sweden, for example, the web extends more to the left (teacher selection and control over school budgets).

The table adds two other pieces of information. The country average at the bottom shows those areas of school-level decision-making that receive most and least support across all countries. The "items average" allows each area of school-level decision-making to be viewed at relative to the average for any individual country.

The context of national policy and practice is an important one in examining the meaning and implications of the data. For example, in France there is relative strong support for selecting and promotion of teachers at school level although this is not national practice of policy. A similar level of support is expressed in the United Kingdom where it is policy. This underlines the value of setting the indicator alongside others, such as levels of decision-making and resourcing and, of considering the findings in a wider national context, for example, awareness of how decisions are taken is likely to differ both between and within countries.

DEFINITIONS

The indicator refers to the percentage of a sample of the general public who responded "very important" to each of ten items following the question: "In your opinion, how important is it that the following decisions are made by the individual school itself?".

Other response categories were: "fairly important", "not very important", "not at all important" and "not sure either way".

C27: Decision-making at school level

C27 : Prise de décision au niveau de l'établissement

Table C27:
Percentage of respondents who thought it was "very important" for decisions to be made by schools themselves (1993/94)

*Tableau C27 :
Pourcentage des répondants qui estimaient qu'il est "très important" que les décisions soient prises par les établissements scolaires eux-mêmes (1993/94)*

	What subjects are taught / *Le choix des disciplines enseignées*	How subjects are taught / *La manière d'enseigner ces disciplines*	Amount of time spent teaching each subject / *Temps consacré à l'enseignement de chaque discipline*	How the school budget is spent / *L'utilisation des crédits de l'établissement*	Teacher selection and promotion / *Le recrutement et la promotion des enseignants*	Teachers' salaries and working conditions / *Le salaire et les conditions de travail des enseignants*	**Items average within each country** / *Moyenne des rubriques par pays*	
Austria	31	36	28	33	31	18	**29.6**	*Autriche*
Belgium (Flemish community)	22	41	27	36	39	26	**31.9**	*Belgique (Communauté flamande)*
Denmark	20	32	16	34	31	12	**24.0**	*Danemark*
Finland	18	35	26	40	34	22	**28.9**	*Finlande*
France	34	56	51	50	59	43	**48.7**	*France*
Netherlands	15	35	22	31	47	24	**28.9**	*Pays-Bas*
Portugal	44	55	50	56	51	37	**48.8**	*Portugal*
Spain	13	19	17	19	20	13	**16.9**	*Espagne*
Sweden	23	38	24	51	44	17	**32.8**	*Suède*
Switzerland	18	32	21	22	26	14	**22.0**	*Suisse*
United Kingdom	39	50	44	57	50	32	**45.3**	*Royaume-Uni*
United States	53	60	57	64	67	57	**59.8**	*Etats-Unis*
Country average for each item	**27.7**	**40.6**	**31.8**	**41.0**	**41.6**	**26.2**		*Moyenne des pays pour chaque rubrique*

See Annex 1 for notes

Voir notes en annexe 1

C27: Decision-making at school level

C27 : Prise de décision au niveau de l'établissement

Chart C27:
Importance of decisions at school level

Graphique C27 :
Importance des décisions
au niveau de l'établissement scolaire

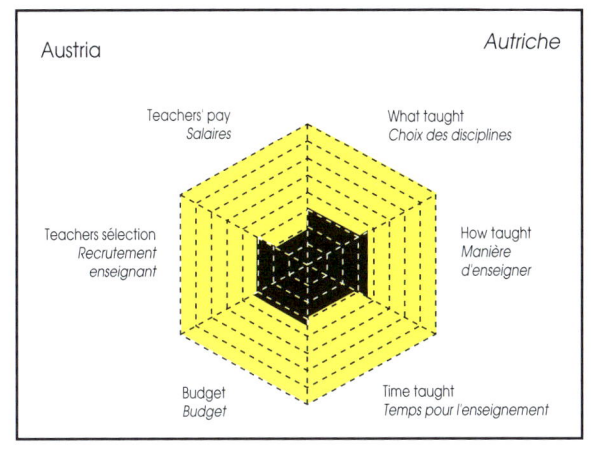

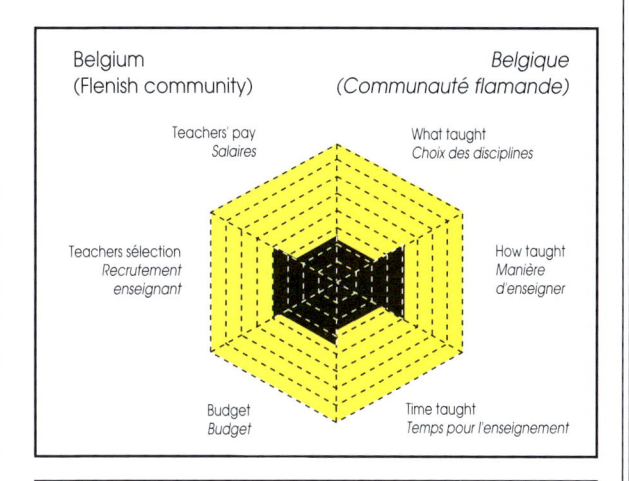

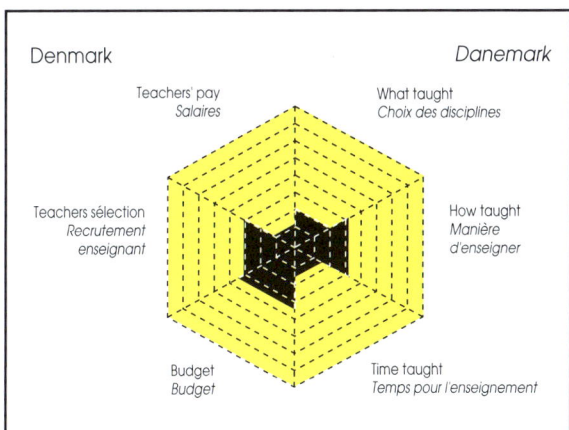

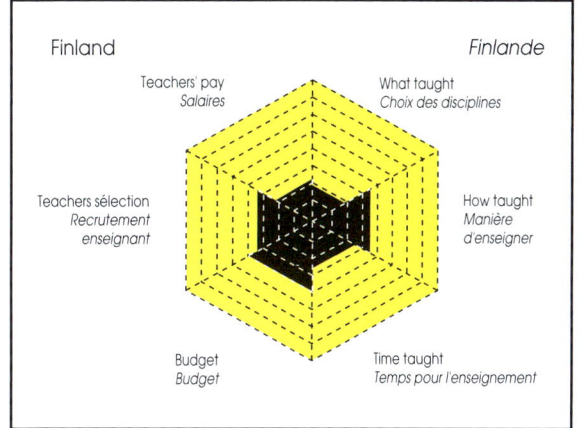

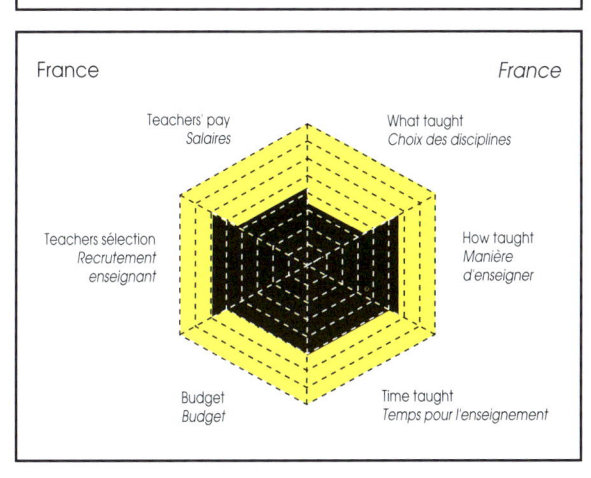

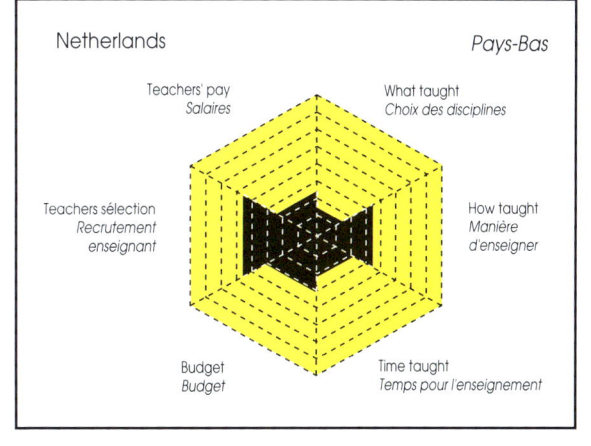

Countries are ranked by English alphabetical order.
The scale is in units of 10%.
The distance from the centre along a strand of the web shows the percentages which are given in the table.
The greater the distance the greater the percentage who thought it was very important for decisions to be made by the schools themselves.

Les pays sont classés dans l'ordre alphabétique anglais.
Echelle en unités de 10 %.
La distance du maillage à partir du centre correspond aux pourcentages indiqués dans le tableau.
Plus la distance est grande, plus est élevé le pourcentage de ceux qui pensent qu'il est important que les écoles prennent des décisions.

67

C27: Decision-making at school level

C27 : Prise de décision au niveau de l'établissement

Chart C27: Importance of decisions at school level

Graphique C27 : Importance des décisions au niveau de l'établissement scolaire

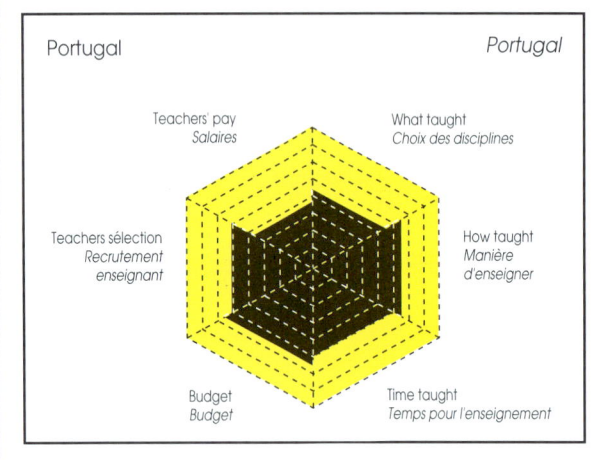

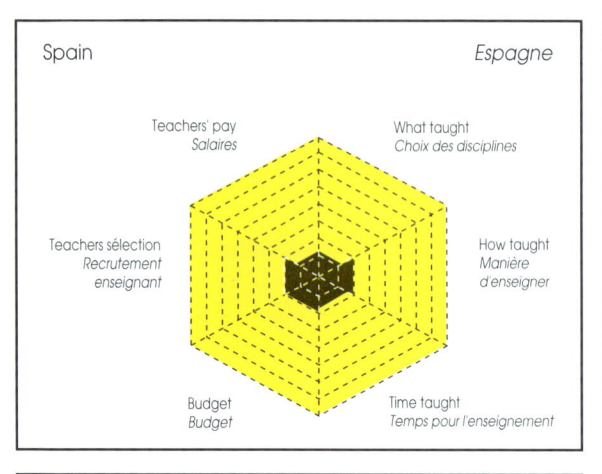

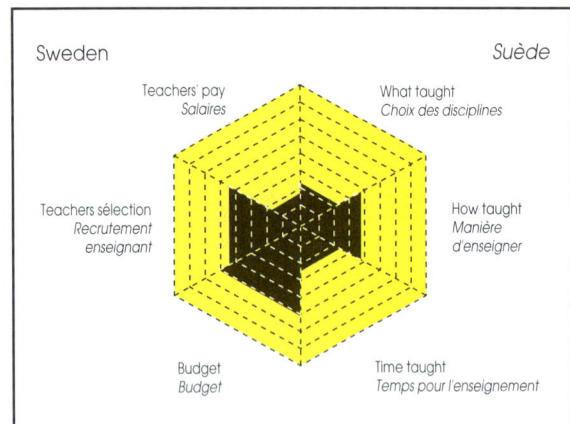

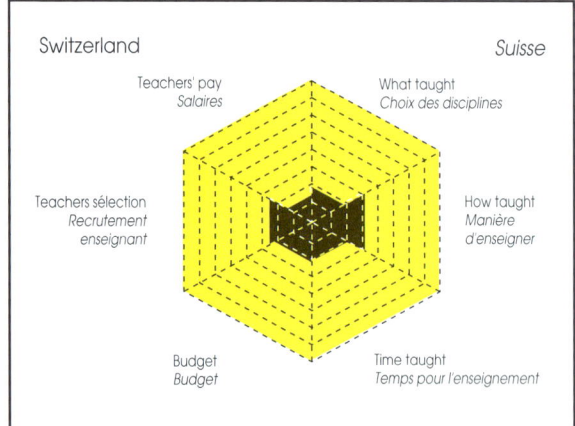

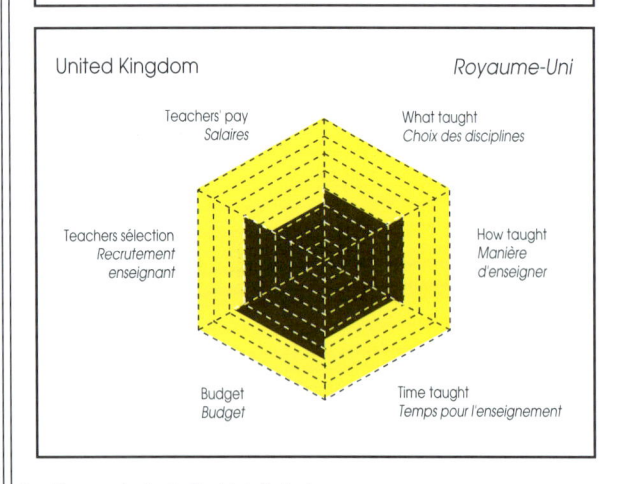

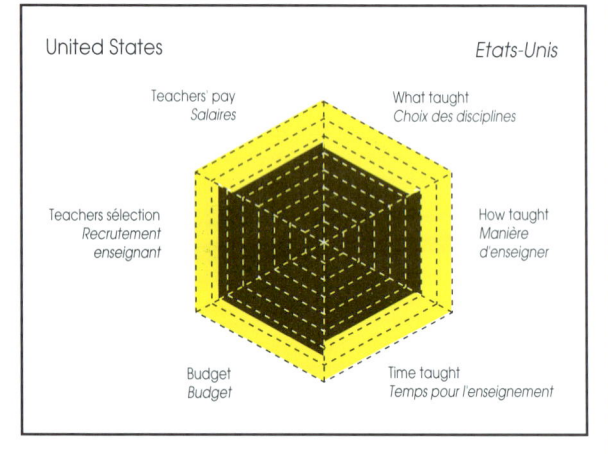

Portugal / Portugal

- Teachers' pay / Salaires
- What taught / Choix des disciplines
- Teachers sélection / Recrutement enseignant
- How taught / Manière d'enseigner
- Budget / Budget
- Time taught / Temps pour l'enseignement

Spain / Espagne

- Teachers' pay / Salaires
- What taught / Choix des disciplines
- Teachers sélection / Recrutement enseignant
- How taught / Manière d'enseigner
- Budget / Budget
- Time taught / Temps pour l'enseignement

Sweden / Suède

- Teachers' pay / Salaires
- What taught / Choix des disciplines
- Teachers sélection / Recrutement enseignant
- How taught / Manière d'enseigner
- Budget / Budget
- Time taught / Temps pour l'enseignement

Switzerland / Suisse

- Teachers' pay / Salaires
- What taught / Choix des disciplines
- Teachers sélection / Recrutement enseignant
- How taught / Manière d'enseigner
- Budget / Budget
- Time taught / Temps pour l'enseignement

United Kingdom / Royaume-Uni

- Teachers' pay / Salaires
- What taught / Choix des disciplines
- Teachers sélection / Recrutement enseignant
- How taught / Manière d'enseigner
- Budget / Budget
- Time taught / Temps pour l'enseignement

United States / Etats-Unis

- Teachers' pay / Salaires
- What taught / Choix des disciplines
- Teachers sélection / Recrutement enseignant
- How taught / Manière d'enseigner
- Budget / Budget
- Time taught / Temps pour l'enseignement

Countries are ranked by English alphabetical order.
The scale is in units of 10%.
The distance from the centre along a strand of the web shows the percentages which are given in the table.
The greater the distance the greater the percentage who thought it was very important for decisions to be made by the schools themselves.

Les pays sont classés dans l'ordre alphabétique anglais.
Echelle en unités de 10 %.
La distance du maillage à partir du centre correspond aux pourcentages indiqués dans le tableau.
Plus la distance est grande, plus est élevé le pourcentage de ceux qui pensent qu'il est important que les écoles prennent des décisions.

II

COSTS, RESOURCES, AND SCHOOL PROCESSES

F01: Educational expenditure relative to GDP

EXPENDITURES FOR EDUCATION RELATIVE TO GROSS DOMESTIC PRODUCT (GDP)

POLICY ISSUES

The broadest policy decision that each country must make (explicitly or implicitly) in the realm of education finance concerns the share of total national resources to devote to educational activities. A closely related task is to divide educational resources among the various levels of education. Another choice concerns the share to be channelled to education through the public sector.

KEY RESULTS

The OECD countries as a whole spend 6.1 per cent of their collective GDP to support their educational institutions (all levels combined); most of that, 4.9 per cent, goes to support public institutions. The education share of GDP rises to 6.5 per cent when the indicator is broadened to include subsidies for students as well as funds for institutions.

The percentage of GDP spent for educational institutions varies from 4.8 to 7.9 among the individual countries. The share of GDP that goes to public institutions generally ranges from 3.6 to 7.3 per cent; an exception is the Netherlands, where the percentage is much lower because of the high degree of reliance on private institutions.

Public spending for primary and secondary education (including subsidies to the private sector) amounts to 3.5 per cent of GDP for OECD as a whole, varying from 2.6 to 5.1 per cent among the individual countries. Public spending for tertiary education averages 1.1 per cent of GDP; it generally ranges from 0.8 to 2.4 per cent among the individual countries, but accounts for only 0.3 per cent of GDP in Japan.

DESCRIPTION AND INTERPRETATION

Ideally, this indicator would compare countries with respect to shares of GDP devoted to education without differentiating either between public and private institutions, or between funds from public and private sources. However, because many countries are still unable to report private funding, it is necessary to emphasize comparisons of expenditures from public sources and expenditures of public institutions, even though these yield a less-than-complete picture of national efforts to support education. (In this indicator, the category "private institutions" includes both government-dependent and independent institutions.)

Table F01(A) shows large disparities in the share of GDP put towards public educational institutions. Canada, Finland and Hungary each spend 7.2 or 7.3 per cent of GDP for such institutions, while Australia, Japan, Germany (FTFR), the Netherlands, Spain and the United Kingdom spend 4.5 per cent or less. However, the disparities are smaller when the expenditures of private institutions are taken into account, with most countries spending between 5 and 7 per cent of GDP on public and private institutions combined.

As can be seen from Tables F01(B), it is possible to compare many countries with respect to the share of GDP devoted to *public* expenditure on education, but only a handful can be compared with respect to spending from both public and private sources.

The percentages of GDP devoted to public expenditures for primary and secondary education are highest (between 4.1 and 5.0 per cent) for the Nordic countries (Denmark, Finland, Norway, Sweden), Switzerland and Hungary; they are lowest (3.2 per cent or less) for countries in the Pacific area (Australia, New Zealand and Japan), Germany (FTFR) and the Czech Republic. The remaining European countries and the United States fall into the mid range, with public expenditures between 3.3 and 3.8 per cent of GDP. Inclusion of funds from private sources raises the GDP shares of France, Japan and the United States by around one-tenth, and the share of Spain by about one-sixth.

The typical OECD country devotes 1.4 per cent of its GDP to public funding of tertiary education (including subsidies for student living expenses); only a small – often negligible – additional percentage comes from private sources. Countries spending significantly larger fractions of GDP on tertiary education (2 per cent or more) include the English-speaking countries of Australia, Canada and New Zealand, plus Denmark and Finland. Most Western European countries outside the Nordic area – Belgium, France, Germany (FTFR), Italy, Spain, the United Kingdom, Austria and Switzerland – appear from these

F01: Educational expenditure relative to GDP

figures to allocate relatively low fractions of GDP (1.2 per cent or less) to tertiary education. However, the inclusion of now-omitted private funds and expenditures for research would raise these percentages significantly for some countries. Japan spends a smaller percentage of its GDP on tertiary education than the other OECD countries – only 0.8 per cent, including both public and private funds.

The percentage of GDP spent by public authorities for all levels of education combined varies by more than a factor of two among the OECD countries. At the high end, with public expenditures exceeding 7 per cent of GDP, are the Nordic countries and Canada; at the low end are Japan and Germany (FTFR), with public outlays of 3.6 and 4.1 per cent of GDP respectively. It should be noted that the inclusion of private expenditures has an important effect on the relative positions of such countries as France, Japan, Spain and the United States.

The results mentioned here and presented in the tables are affected by various data gaps and comparability problems. Among the major problems (apart from omitted private expenditures) are uneven coverage of spending for pre-primary education, the omission of private costs of apprenticeship programmes, inconsistent measurement of pension costs, and uneven coverage of expenditures of tertiary institutions for research and ancillary services.

DEFINITIONS

In this indicator, multiple measures of educational expenditure and its components are expressed as percentages of GDP.

The figures on expenditures for educational institutions in Table F01(A) exclude two forms of spending outside the institutions: direct household purchases of educational goods and services; and subsidies for student living expenses, see F11 and Chart F11. Expenditures relative to GDP, for public institutions and public and private institutions combined, are calculated for primary and secondary education; tertiary education; the sub-total of primary, secondary, and tertiary education; and all levels of education combined. (The last includes expenditures for early childhood education and expenditures not allocated by level.)

Tables F01(B) distinguish between education funds originating in the public and private sectors. This distinction is based on the *initial* source of funds and does not reflect subsequent public-to-private or private-to-public transfers. A major reason for the differentiation is to allow comparisons to include the many countries that are able to report only expenditures from public sources.

The first of the two columns under the heading "Funds originating in the public sector" includes only public expenditures for educational institutions; the second includes expenditures for institutions plus public subsidies to the private sector. The latter consist mostly of scholarships and other forms of financial aid to students. The amounts shown under "Funds originating in the private sector" consist mainly of tuition and other fees (net of offsetting public subsidies) paid to educational institutions by students or households. The final column of Tables F01(B) is total expenditure from both public and private sources. Public subsidies have been netted out where necessary to avoid double counting.

F01: Educational expenditure relative to GDP

F01 : Dépenses d'éducation en pourcentage du PIB

Table F01(A):
Educational expenditure as a percentage of GDP by type of institution (1992)

Tableau F01(A) : Dépenses d'éducation en pourcentage du PIB par type d'établissement (1992)

	Public institutions only / Etablissements publics seuls				Public and private institutions combined / Etablissements publics et privés				
	Primary and secondary education	Tertiary education	Primary, secondary and tertiary education	All levels of education combined *	Primary and secondary education	Tertiary education	Primary, secondary and tertiary education	All levels of education combined *	
North America									*Amérique du Nord*
Canada	...	2.4	...	7.2	...	2.4	...	7.4	*Canada*
United States	3.9	1.6	5.6	5.7	4.3	2.5	6.7	7.0	*Etats-Unis*
Pacific Area									*Pays du Pacifique*
Australia	...	1.8	...	4.5	...	1.9	...	5.5	*Australie*
Japan	2.8	0.3	3.1	3.6	3.1	0.8	3.9	4.8	*Japon*
New Zealand	...	...	...	...	...	...	...	...	*Nouvelle-Zélande*
European Community									*Communauté européenne*
Belgium	...	...	...	...	...	...	...	...	*Belgique*
Denmark	3.9	1.3	5.2	6.2	4.1	1.3	5.4	6.7	*Danemark*
France	3.4	0.9	4.3	5.1	4.0	1.0	5.0	5.9	*France*
Germany (FTFR)	2.4	1.0	3.4	3.7	3.4	1.0	4.4	4.9	*Allemagne (ex-terr. de la RFA)*
Germany	...	...	...	...	...	...	...	...	*Allemagne*
Greece	...	...	...	...	...	...	...	...	*Grèce*
Ireland	3.7	1.4	5.1	5.7	3.7	1.4	5.1	5.7	*Irlande*
Italy	...	...	...	...	...	...	...	...	*Italie*
Luxembourg	...	...	...	...	...	...	...	...	*Luxembourg*
Netherlands	0.8	0.8	1.6	1.7	3.0	1.4	4.5	5.0	*Pays-Bas*
Portugal	4.0	0.9	4.9	5.2	...	...	...	...	*Portugal*
Spain	2.9	0.9	3.8	4.2	3.7	0.9	4.7	5.2	*Espagne*
United Kingdom	4.0	0.1	4.1	4.1	...	0.8	...	...	*Royaume-Uni*
Other Europe - OECD									*Autres pays d'Europe - OCDE*
Austria	...	...	...	...	...	...	...	...	*Autriche*
Finland	4.6	1.8	6.4	7.3	4.9	1.9	6.8	7.9	*Finlande*
Iceland	...	...	...	...	...	...	...	...	*Islande*
Norway	...	...	...	...	...	...	...	...	*Norvège*
Sweden	4.6	1.0	5.6	6.7	4.6	1.0	5.6	6.8	*Suède*
Switzerland	...	...	...	...	...	...	...	...	*Suisse*
Turkey	...	...	...	...	...	...	...	...	*Turquie*
Country mean	3.4	1.2	4.6	5.1	3.9	1.4	5.3	6.1	*Moyenne des pays*
OECD total	3.4	1.2	4.7	4.9	3.9	1.7	5.5	6.1	*Total OCDE*
Central and Eastern Europe									*Europe centrale et orientale*
Czech Republic	...	...	...	...	...	...	...	...	*République tchèque*
Hungary	4.7	1.6	6.3	7.3	4.8	1.6	6.3	7.3	*Hongrie*
Poland	...	...	...	...	...	...	...	...	*Pologne*
Russia	...	...	...	...	...	...	...	...	*Russie*

See Annex 1 for notes
* Including early childhood education and undistributed

Voir notes en annexe 1
* Education préscolaire et dépenses non affectées incluses

F01: Educational expenditure relative to GDP

F01 : Dépenses d'éducation en pourcentage du PIB

Table F01(B1):
Educational expenditure as a percentage of GDP
for primary and secondary education
by origin of funds (1992)

*Tableau F01(B1) :
Dépenses d'éducation en pourcentage du PIB
par source de financement, enseignement primaire
et secondaire (1992)*

	Funds originating in the public sector — Direct public expenditure for educational institutions / *Dépenses directes des administrations publiques pour les établissements*	Funds originating in the public sector — Total public expenditure, including subsidies to the private sector / *Ensemble des dépenses des administrations publiques, incluant les subventions au secteur privé*	Funds originating in the private sector — Private payments to educational institutions (net of public subsidies) / *Paiements privés aux établissements (net des subventions publiques)*	Total expenditure from both public and private sources / *Ensemble des dépenses provenant des secteurs public et privé*	
North America					*Amérique du Nord*
Canada	...	...	...	...	*Canada*
United States	3.9	3.9	0.4	4.3	*Etats-Unis*
Pacific Area					*Pays du Pacifique*
Australia	2.9	3.0	...	...	*Australie*
Japan	2.8	2.8	0.3	3.1	*Japon*
New Zealand	3.2	3.2	...	...	*Nouvelle-Zélande*
European Community					*Communauté européenne*
Belgium	3.2	3.4	...	...	*Belgique*
Denmark	4.0	4.5	-	4.5	*Danemark*
France	3.7	3.8	0.3	4.2	*France*
Germany (FTFR)	2.5	2.6	...	...	*Allemagne (ex-terr. de la RFA)*
Germany	...	...	...	...	*Allemagne*
Greece	...	...	...	...	*Grèce*
Ireland	3.6	3.7	...	...	*Irlande*
Italy	3.4	3.4	...	...	*Italie*
Luxembourg	...	...	...	...	*Luxembourg*
Netherlands	2.9	3.3	-	3.4	*Pays-Bas*
Portugal	...	...	...	...	*Portugal*
Spain	3.3	3.3	0.5	4.1	*Espagne*
United Kingdom	4.0	4.1	...	...	*Royaume-Uni*
Other Europe - OECD					*Autres pays d'Europe - OCDE*
Austria	3.7	3.7	...	...	*Autriche*
Finland	4.8	5.0	...	...	*Finlande*
Iceland	...	...	...	...	*Islande*
Norway	5.0	...	...	...	*Norvège*
Sweden	4.6	5.1	-	5.1	*Suède*
Switzerland	3.8	4.1	...	...	*Suisse*
Turkey	...	...	...	...	*Turquie*
Country mean	**3.6**	**3.7**	...	**4.1**	***Moyenne des pays***
OECD total	**3.5**	**3.5**	...	**4.0**	***Total OCDE***
Central and Eastern Europe					*Europe centrale et orientale*
Czech Republic	3.0	3.0	...	...	*République tchèque*
Hungary	4.3	4.4	...	...	*Hongrie*
Poland	...	...	...	...	*Pologne*
Russia	...	...	...	...	*Russie*

See Annex 1 for notes

Voir notes en annexe 1

F01: Educational expenditure relative to GDP

F01 : Dépenses d'éducation en pourcentage du PIB

Table F01(B2):
Educational expenditure as a percentage of GDP
for tertiary education by origin of funds (1992)

*Tableau F01(B2) :
Dépenses d'éducation en pourcentage du PIB
par source de financement, enseignement supérieur (1992)*

	Funds originating in the public sector — Direct public expenditure for educational institutions / *Dépenses directes des administrations publiques pour les établissements*	Funds originating in the public sector — Total public expenditure, including subsidies to the private sector / *Ensemble des dépenses des administrations publiques, incluant les subventions au secteur privé*	Funds originating in the private sector — Private payments to educational institutions (net of public subsidies) / *Paiements privés aux établissements (net des subventions publiques)*	Total expenditure from both public and private sources / *Ensemble des dépenses provenant des secteurs public et privé*	
North America					*Amérique du Nord*
Canada	2.1	2.4	0.1	2.6	*Canada*
United States	1.2	1.3	1.1	2.6	*Etats-Unis*
Pacific Area					*Pays du Pacifique*
Australia	1.5	1.9	0.4	2.3	*Australie*
Japan	0.3	0.3	0.5	0.8	*Japon*
New Zealand	1.4	2.0	...	...	*Nouvelle-Zélande*
European Community					*Communauté européenne*
Belgium	0.6	0.9	...	...	*Belgique*
Denmark	1.3	2.0	-	2.0	*Danemark*
France	0.8	0.9	0.1	1.1	*France*
Germany (FTFR)	0.9	1.0	...	...	*Allemagne (ex-terr. de la RFA)*
Germany	...	...	...	...	*Allemagne*
Greece	...	...	...	...	*Grèce*
Ireland	1.0	1.3	0.3	1.6	*Irlande*
Italy	0.8	0.8	...	...	*Italie*
Luxembourg	...	...	...	...	*Luxembourg*
Netherlands	1.2	1.8	-	1.8	*Pays-Bas*
Portugal	...	...	...	...	*Portugal*
Spain	0.8	0.8	0.2	1.1	*Espagne*
United Kingdom	0.8	1.1	-	1.1	*Royaume-Uni*
Other Europe - OECD					*Autres pays d'Europe - OCDE*
Austria	1.1	1.2	...	...	*Autriche*
Finland	1.9	2.2	...	...	*Finlande*
Iceland	...	...	...	...	*Islande*
Norway	1.4	...	...	...	*Norvège*
Sweden	1.0	1.6	-	1.6	*Suède*
Switzerland	1.1	1.2	...	...	*Suisse*
Turkey	...	...	...	...	*Turquie*
Country mean	**1.1**	**1.4**	...	**1.7**	***Moyenne des pays***
OECD total	**1.0**	**1.1**	...	**1.9**	***Total OCDE***
Central and Eastern Europe					*Europe centrale et orientale*
Czech Republic	0.6	0.7	...	...	*République tchèque*
Hungary	1.1	1.3	...	...	*Hongrie*
Poland	...	...	...	...	*Pologne*
Russia	...	...	...	...	*Russie*

See Annex 1 for notes

Voir notes en annexe 1

F01: Educational expenditure relative to GDP

F01 : Dépenses d'éducation en pourcentage du PIB

Table F01(B3):
Educational expenditure as a percentage of GDP for all levels of education combined by origin of funds (1992)

Tableau F01(B3) :
Dépenses d'éducation en pourcentage du PIB par source de financement, tous niveaux scolaires confondus (1992)

	Funds originating in the public sector — Direct public expenditure for educational institutions / *Dépenses directes des administrations publiques pour les établissements*	Funds originating in the public sector — Total public expenditure, including subsidies to the private sector / *Ensemble des dépenses des administrations publiques, incluant les subventions au secteur privé*	Funds originating in the private sector — Private payments to educational institutions (net of public subsidies) / *Paiements privés aux établissements (net des subventions publiques)*	Total expenditure from both public and private sources / *Ensemble des dépenses provenant des secteurs public et privé*	
North America					**Amérique du Nord**
Canada	6.9	7.2	0.2	7.6	Canada
United States	5.3	5.4	1.6	7.2	Etats-Unis
Pacific Area					**Pays du Pacifique**
Australia	4.8	5.5	0.7	6.2	Australie
Japan	3.6	3.6	1.1	4.8	Japon
New Zealand	5.9	6.5	...	...	Nouvelle-Zélande
European Community					**Communauté européenne**
Belgium	5.5	6.0	...	...	Belgique
Denmark	6.1	7.6	0.2	7.8	Danemark
France	5.4	5.5	0.4	6.2	France
Germany (FTFR)	3.9	4.1	...	...	Allemagne (ex-terr. de la RFA)
Germany	...	...	...	...	Allemagne
Greece	...	...	...	...	Grèce
Ireland	5.2	5.6	0.4	6.0	Irlande
Italy	5.0	5.1	...	...	Italie
Luxembourg	...	...	...	...	Luxembourg
Netherlands	4.6	5.6	–	5.8	Pays-Bas
Portugal	...	...	...	...	Portugal
Spain	4.5	4.6	0.7	5.8	Espagne
United Kingdom	4.9	5.2	...	...	Royaume-Uni
Other Europe - OECD					**Autres pays d'Europe - OCDE**
Austria	5.7	5.8	...	...	Autriche
Finland	7.7	8.3	...	...	Finlande
Iceland	...	...	...	...	Islande
Norway	7.6	...	...	...	Norvège
Sweden	6.7	7.7	0.1	7.8	Suède
Switzerland	5.3	5.7	...	...	Suisse
Turkey	...	...	...	...	Turquie
Country mean	**5.5**	**5.8**	...	**6.5**	**Moyenne des pays**
OECD total	**4.9**	**5.1**	...	**6.5**	**Total OCDE**
Central and Eastern Europe					**Europe centrale et orientale**
Czech Republic	4.8	4.8	...	...	République tchèque
Hungary	6.4	6.6	...	...	Hongrie
Poland	...	...	...	...	Pologne
Russia	...	...	...	...	Russie

See Annex 1 for notes

Voir notes en annexe 1

F01: Educational expenditure relative to GDP

F01 : Dépenses d'éducation en pourcentage du PIB

Chart F01:
Expenditure for educational institutions as a percentage of GDP by type of institution (1992)

*Graphique F01 :
Dépenses d'éducation en pourcentage du PIB par type d'établissement (1992)*

Primary and secondary — *Primaire et secondaire*

Tertiary — *Supérieur*

All levels combined — *Tous niveaux confondus*

Legend:
- Public institutions only / *Etablissements publics seuls*
- Private institutions / *Etablissements privés*

Countries are ranked in order of decreasing expenditures from public educational institutions as a percentage of GDP

Les pays sont classés en ordre décroissant des dépenses d'éducation des établissements publics en pourcentage du PIB

* Expenditure from private institutions have not been reported

* Les dépenses des établissements privés n'ont pas été communiquées

F02: Expenditure of public and private educational institutions

EXPENDITURE OF PUBLIC AND PRIVATE EDUCATIONAL INSTITUTIONS

POLICY ISSUES

Debates over privatisation, institutional diversity, the involvement of religious organisations in education, and the desirability of public subsidies for privately controlled schools have led some OECD countries to reassess the roles of public and private educational institutions. This indicator compares countries with respect to the shares of educational expenditure accounted for by public institutions, private institutions that are substantially publicly funded ("government-dependent" institutions), and private institutions that receive little or no public money ("independent" private institutions).

The indicator should be considered together with indicator P01, which shows the enrolment shares of the same three types of institutions.

KEY RESULTS

Public institutions account for the main share of expenditure for primary and secondary education in most countries, but government-funded private schools account for the largest share of expenditure in the Netherlands and significant, albeit lesser, shares in France and Spain. The large fraction of German secondary expenditure going to independent private institutions refers to costs incurred by private firms under the "dual system" of training apprentices.

Private pre-primary schools account for the dominant share of expenditures at that level in Japan and the Netherlands and major shares in Germany (FTFR), Spain and the United States, but they play minor or negligible roles in most of the other countries for which data are available.

Public institutions spend between 90 and 99 per cent of the total funds for tertiary education in most countries, but private institutions account for about 35 per cent of total tertiary spending in the United States, 44 per cent in the Netherlands, 62 per cent in Belgium and 60 per cent in Japan. Moreover, according to the definition used here, which is based on institutional governance rather than sources of funding, 78 per cent of spending for tertiary education in the United Kingdom qualifies as expenditure of government-dependent private institutions.

DESCRIPTION AND INTERPRETATION

Of the 14 countries that have reported expenditures by type of institution for all levels of education combined, eight report that public institutions account for at least 92 per cent of the total spending of public and private institutions. The countries reporting smaller shares of public institutions are the United States (82 per cent), Japan and Germany (FTFR) (75 per cent), France (86 per cent), Spain (80 per cent) and the Netherlands (only 35 per cent). The Netherlands figure reflects that country's high levels of enrolment in government-funded private institutions.

The expenditure shares of private institutions are understated in some cases. For example, some countries lack data on the expenditures of private occupational or trade schools, and some have omitted the expenditures of certain pre-primary institutions. Perhaps more importantly, an estimate of private expenditures for training apprentices has been provided only by Germany (FTFR).

The classification of institutions as public or private is generally clear-cut, but there are a few ambiguities. The case of United Kingdom tertiary institutions has been mentioned above. Ireland's primary and secondary schools have been described elsewhere as government-dependent private (i.e. church-operated) schools, but have been classified as public schools in the data submitted to the OECD. The distinction between government-dependent and independent private schools is clear in most instances, with ambiguity in only a few cases.

DEFINITIONS

The tables present the shares of total national expenditures for educational institutions accounted for by public institutions, government-dependent private institutions, and independent private institutions.

Public institutions are those owned and controlled by central, regional or local governments. Private institutions are owned and controlled by private (non-governmental) organisations, including business firms, religious organisations, and other non-profit entities.

The distinction between government-dependent and independent private institutions is based on the extent of government funding: the former receive substantial portions of their funding (at least 50 per cent, but usually much more) from public authorities; the latter receive little or no government money.

F02: Expenditure of public and private educational institutions

F02 : Dépenses des établissements d'enseignement publics et privés

Table F02(1):
Expenditure shares of public and private educational institutions for early childhood education (1992)

Tableau F02(1) :
Répartition en pourcentage des dépenses publiques et privées par type d'établissement, éducation préscolaire (1992)

	Public institutions / *Établissements publics*	Government-dependent private institutions / *Établissements privés subventionnés*	Independent private institutions / *Établissements privés non subventionnés*	All private institutions / *Ensemble des établissements privés*	All institutions / *Ensemble des établissements*	
North America						*Amérique du Nord*
Canada	...	.	...	...	...	*Canada*
United States	64.7	13.1	22.2	35.3	100.0	*Etats-Unis*
Pacific Area						*Pays du Pacifique*
Australia	...	...	...	...	...	*Australie*
Japan	30.2	.	69.8	69.8	100.0	*Japon*
New Zealand	...	...	...	...	...	*Nouvelle-Zélande*
European Community						*Communauté européenne*
Belgium	...	...	...	...	...	*Belgique*
Denmark	98.7	1.3	x	1.3	100.0	*Danemark*
France	89.1	10.7	0.2	10.9	100.0	*France*
Germany (FTFR)	62.2	37.8	.	37.8	100.0	*Allemagne (ex-terr. de la RFA)*
Germany	...	...	...	...	...	*Allemagne*
Greece	...	...	...	...	...	*Grèce*
Ireland	98.3	.	1.7	1.7	100.0	*Irlande*
Italy	...	.	...	...	...	*Italie*
Luxembourg	...	...	...	...	...	*Luxembourg*
Netherlands	32.9	67.1	x	67.1	100.0	*Pays-Bas*
Portugal	...	...	...	...	...	*Portugal*
Spain	64.2	5.2	30.6	35.8	100.0	*Espagne*
United Kingdom	100.0	.	.	x	100.0	*Royaume-Uni*
Other Europe - OECD						*Autres pays d'Europe - OCDE*
Austria	94.0	6.0	x	6.0	100.0	*Autriche*
Finland	100.0	x	.	x	100.0	*Finlande*
Iceland	...	...	...	...	...	*Islande*
Norway	100.0	x	-	x	100.0	*Norvège*
Sweden	100.0	-	.	-	100.0	*Suède*
Switzerland	...	...	...	...	...	*Suisse*
Turkey	...	.	...	...	...	*Turquie*
Country mean	**79.6**	...	...	**20.4**	**100.0**	***Moyenne des pays***
Central and Eastern Europe						*Europe centrale et orientale*
Czech Republic	...	...	...	...	...	*République tchèque*
Hungary	99.8	0.2	.	0.2	100.0	*Hongrie*
Poland	...	...	...	...	...	*Pologne*
Russia	...	...	...	...	...	*Russie*

See Annex 1 for notes

Voir notes en annexe 1

F02: Expenditure of public and private educational institutions

F02 : Dépenses des établissements d'enseignement publics et privés

Table F02(2):
Expenditure shares of public and private educational institutions for primary education (1992)

*Tableau F02(2) :
Répartition en pourcentage des dépenses publiques et privées par type d'établissement, enseignement primaire (1992)*

	Public institutions / Établissements publics	Government-dependent private institutions / Établissements privés subventionnés	Independent private institutions / Établissements privés non subventionnés	All private institutions / Ensemble des établissements privés	All institutions / Ensemble des établissements	
North America						*Amérique du Nord*
Canada	...		...	...	...	*Canada*
United States	93.6	.	6.4	6.4	100.0	*Etats-Unis*
Pacific Area						*Pays du Pacifique*
Australia	...	...	...	...	...	*Australie*
Japan	99.2	.	0.8	0.8	100.0	*Japon*
New Zealand	...	...	...	...	...	*Nouvelle-Zélande*
European Community						*Communauté européenne*
Belgium	...	...	...	...	...	*Belgique*
Denmark	94.6	5.4	x	5.4	100.0	*Danemark*
France	88.1	11.7	0.2	11.9	100.0	*France*
Germany (FTFR)	99.4	0.6	.	0.6	100.0	*Allemagne (ex-terr. de la RFA)*
Germany	...	...	...	...	...	*Allemagne*
Greece	...	...	...	...	...	*Grèce*
Ireland	98.5	.	1.5	1.5	100.0	*Irlande*
Italy	...	.	...	...	...	*Italie*
Luxembourg	...	...	...	...	...	*Luxembourg*
Netherlands	32.4	67.6	x	67.6	100.0	*Pays-Bas*
Portugal	...	...	...	...	...	*Portugal*
Spain	71.3	24.5	4.2	28.7	100.0	*Espagne*
United Kingdom	...	.	...	...	...	*Royaume-Uni*
Other Europe - OECD						*Autres pays d'Europe - OCDE*
Austria	99.6	0.4	x	0.4	100.0	*Autriche*
Finland	98.7	1.3	.	1.3	100.0	*Finlande*
Iceland	...	...	...	...	...	*Islande*
Norway	98.7	1.2	-	1.3	100.0	*Norvège*
Sweden	99.3	0.7	.	0.7	100.0	*Suède*
Switzerland	...	...	...	...	...	*Suisse*
Turkey	...	.	...	...	...	*Turquie*
Country mean	**89.4**	...	...	**10.6**	**100.0**	*Moyenne des pays*
Central and Eastern Europe						*Europe centrale et orientale*
Czech Republic	...	...	...	...	...	*République tchèque*
Hungary	99.3	0.7	.	0.7	100.0	*Hongrie*
Poland	...	...	...	...	...	*Pologne*
Russia	...	...	...	...	...	*Russie*

See Annex 1 for notes

Voir notes en annexe 1

F02: Expenditure of public and private educational institutions
F02 : Dépenses des établissements d'enseignement publics et privés

Table F02(3):
Expenditure shares of public and private educational institutions for secondary education (1992)

Tableau F02(3) :
Répartition en pourcentage des dépenses publiques et privées par type d'établissement, enseignement secondaire (1992)

	Public institutions / Établissements publics	Government-dependent private institutions / Établissements privés subventionnés	Independent private institutions / Établissements privés non subventionnés	All private institutions / Ensemble des établissements privés	All institutions / Ensemble des établissements	
North America						*Amérique du Nord*
Canada	...	.	...	...	...	Canada
United States	92.2	.	7.8	7.8	100.0	États-Unis
Pacific Area						*Pays du Pacifique*
Australia	...	...	...	...	...	Australie
Japan	84.4	.	15.6	15,6	100.0	Japon
New Zealand	...	...	...	...	...	Nouvelle-Zélande
European Community						*Communauté européenne*
Belgium	...	...	...	...	...	Belgique
Denmark	94.7	5.3	x	5.3	100.0	Danemark
France	82.0	17.3	0.7	18.0	100.0	France
Germany (FTFR)	64.0	4.8	31.2	36,0	100.0	Allemagne (ex-terr. de la RFA)
Germany	...	...	...	...	...	Allemagne
Greece	...	...	...	...	...	Grèce
Ireland	99.7	.	0.3	0.3	100.0	Irlande
Italy	...	.	...	...	...	Italie
Luxembourg	...	...	..	...	...	Luxembourg
Netherlands	20.6	79.4	x	79.4	100.0	Pays-Bas
Portugal	...	...	...	...	...	Portugal
Spain	80.0	11.5	8.5	20.0	100.0	Espagne
United Kingdom	...	...	...	...	...	Royaume-Uni
Other Europe - OECD						*Autres pays d'Europe - OCDE*
Austria	99.3	0.7	x	0.7	100.0	Autriche
Finland	91.8	8.2	.	8.2	100.0	Finlande
Iceland	...	...	...	...	...	Islande
Norway	93.7	6.3	-	6.3	100.0	Norvège
Sweden	98.9	1.1	.	1.1	100.0	Suède
Switzerland	...	...	...	...	...	Suisse
Turkey	...	...	...	...	...	Turquie
Country mean	**83.5**	...	...	**16.5**	**100.0**	**Moyenne des pays**
Central and Eastern Europe						*Europe centrale et orientale*
Czech Republic	...	...	...	...	...	République tchèque
Hungary	98.8	1.2	.	1.2	100.0	Hongrie
Poland	...	...	...	...	...	Pologne
Russia	...	...	...	...	...	Russie

See Annex 1 for notes — Voir notes en annexe 1

F02: Expenditure of public and private educational institutions

F02 : Dépenses des établissements d'enseignement publics et privés

Table F02(4): Expenditure shares of public and private educational institutions for tertiary education (1992)

Tableau F02(4) : Répartition en pourcentage des dépenses publiques et privées par type d'établissement, enseignement supérieur (1992)

	Public institutions / Établissements publics	Government-dependent private institutions / Établissements privés subventionnés	Independent private institutions / Établissements privés non subventionnés	All private institutions / Ensemble des établissements privés	All institutions / Ensemble des établissements	
North America						*Amérique du Nord*
Canada	99.5	.	0.5	0.5	100.0	*Canada*
United States	65.1	.	34.9	34.9	100.0	*Etats-Unis*
Pacific Area						*Pays du Pacifique*
Australia	...	...	...	...	...	*Australie*
Japan	40.4	.	59.6	59.6	100.0	*Japon*
New Zealand	...	...	...	...	...	*Nouvelle-Zélande*
European Community						*Communauté européenne*
Belgium	38.2	61.8		61.8	...	*Belgique*
Denmark	100.0		.		100.0	*Danemark*
France	90.5	6.7	2.7	9.5	100.0	*France*
Germany (FTFR)	98.7	1.3	.	1.3	100.0	*Allemagne (ex-terr. de la RFA)*
Germany	...	...	...	...	...	*Allemagne*
Greece	...	...	...	...	...	*Grèce*
Ireland	99.0	.	1.0	1.0	100.0	*Irlande*
Italy	...	.	...	...	...	*Italie*
Luxembourg	...	...	...	...	...	*Luxembourg*
Netherlands	56.2	43.8	x	43.8	100.0	*Pays-Bas*
Portugal	...	...	...	...	...	*Portugal*
Spain	92.2	.	7.8	7.8	100.0	*Espagne*
United Kingdom	22.2	77.8	-	77.8	100.0	*Royaume-Uni*
Other Europe - OECD						*Autres pays d'Europe - OCDE*
Austria	91.9	8.1	x	8.1	100.0	*Autriche*
Finland	95.6	4.4	.	4.4	100.0	*Finlande*
Iceland	...	...	...	...	...	*Islande*
Norway	94.6	5.4	-	5.4	100.0	*Norvège*
Sweden	98.9	-	1.1	1.1	100.0	*Suède*
Switzerland	...	...	...	...	...	*Suisse*
Turkey	...	...	...	...	...	*Turquie*
Country mean	**78.9**	...	...	**21.1**	**100.0**	***Moyenne des pays***
Central and Eastern Europe						*Europe centrale et orientale*
Czech Republic	...	...	...	...	...	*République tchèque*
Hungary	99.5	0.5	.	0.5	100.0	*Hongrie*
Poland	...	...	...	...	...	*Pologne*
Russia	...	...	...	...	...	*Russie*

See Annex 1 for notes

Voir notes en annexe 1

F02: Expenditure of public and private educational institutions
F02 : Dépenses des établissements d'enseignement publics et privés

Table F02(5):
Expenditure shares of public and private educational institutions for primary and secondary education (1992)

*Tableau F02(5) :
Répartition en pourcentage des dépenses publiques et privées par type d'établissement, enseignement primaire et secondaire (1992)*

	Public institutions / Établissements publics	Government-dependent private institutions / Établissements privés subventionnés	Independent private institutions / Établissements privés non subventionnés	All private institutions / Ensemble des établissements privés	All institutions / Ensemble des établissements	
North America						*Amérique du Nord*
Canada	95.6	.	4.4	4.4	100.0	*Canada*
United States	92.9	.	7.1	7.1	100.0	*Etats-Unis*
Pacific Area						*Pays du Pacifique*
Australia	...	...	...	...	...	*Australie*
Japan	90.9	.	9.1	9.1	100.0	*Japon*
New Zealand	...	...	...	...	...	*Nouvelle-Zélande*
European Community						*Communauté européenne*
Belgium	...	...	...	...	...	*Belgique*
Denmark	94.7	5.3	x	5.3	100.0	*Danemark*
France	83.6	15.8	0.6	16.4	100.0	*France*
Germany (FTFR)	70.0	4.1	25.9	30.0	100.0	*Allemagne (ex-terr. de la RFA)*
Germany	...	...	...	...	...	*Allemagne*
Greece	...	...	...	...	...	*Grèce*
Ireland	99.2	.	0.8	0.8	100.0	*Irlande*
Italy	...	.	...	...	...	*Italie*
Luxembourg	...	...	...	...	...	*Luxembourg*
Netherlands	25.0	75.0	x	75.0	100.0	*Pays-Bas*
Portugal	...	...	...	...	...	*Portugal*
Spain	77.4	15.4	7.2	22.6	100.0	*Espagne*
United Kingdom	...	...	...	...	...	*Royaume-Uni*
Other Europe - OECD						*Autres pays d'Europe - OCDE*
Austria	99.4	0.6	x	0.6	100.0	*Autriche*
Finland	94.7	5.3	.	5.3	100.0	*Finlande*
Iceland	...	...	...	...	...	*Islande*
Norway	95.5	4.5	-	4.5	100.0	*Norvège*
Sweden	99.1	0.9	.	0.9	100.0	*Suède*
Switzerland	...	...	...	...	...	*Suisse*
Turkey	...	.	...	...	...	*Turquie*
Country mean	**86.0**	...	...	**14.0**	**100.0**	***Moyenne des pays***
Central and Eastern Europe						*Europe centrale et orientale*
Czech Republic	...	...	...	...	...	*République tchèque*
Hungary	99.0	1.0	.	1.0	100.0	*Hongrie*
Poland	...	...	...	...	...	*Pologne*
Russia	...	...	...	...	...	*Russie*

See Annex 1 for notes

Voir notes en annexe 1

F02: Expenditure of public and private educational institutions

F02 : Dépenses des établissements d'enseignement publics et privés

Table F02(6):
Expenditure shares of public and private educational institutions for all levels of education combined (1992)

Tableau F02(6) :
Répartition en pourcentage des dépenses publiques et privées par type d'établissement, tous niveaux scolaires confondus (1992)

	Public institutions / Établissements publics	Government-dependent private institutions / Établissements privés subventionnés	Independent private institutions / Établissements privés non subventionnés	All private institutions / Ensemble des établissements privés	All institutions / Ensemble des établissements	
North America						*Amérique du Nord*
Canada	97.0	.	3.0	3.0	100.0	*Canada*
United States	82.0	0.5	17.5	18.0	100.0	*Etats-Unis*
Pacific Area						*Pays du Pacifique*
Australia	...	...	...	...	...	*Australie*
Japan	75.0	.	25.0	25.0	100.0	*Japon*
New Zealand	...	...	...	...	...	*Nouvelle-Zélande*
European Community						*Communauté européenne*
Belgium	...	...	...	...	...	*Belgique*
Denmark	93.5	3.4	3.0	6.5	100.0	*Danemark*
France	85.9	13.2	0.9	14.1	100.0	*France*
Germany (FTFR)	75.2	6.2	18.6	24.8	100.0	*Allemagne (ex-terr. de la RFA)*
Germany	...	...	...	...	...	*Allemagne*
Greece	...	...	...	...	...	*Grèce*
Ireland	99.1	.	0.9	0.9	100.0	*Irlande*
Italy	...	.	...	...	...	*Italie*
Luxembourg	...	...	...	...	...	*Luxembourg*
Netherlands	34.6	65.4	x	65.4	100.0	*Pays-Bas*
Portugal	...	...	...	...	...	*Portugal*
Spain	79.6	11.3	9.0	20.4	100.0	*Espagne*
United Kingdom	...	...	...	...	...	*Royaume-Uni*
Other Europe - OECD						*Autres pays d'Europe - OCDE*
Austria	96.9	3.1	x	3.1	100.0	*Autriche*
Finland	93.4	6.6	.	6.6	100.0	*Finlande*
Iceland	...	...	...	...	...	*Islande*
Norway	93.8	6.2	-	6.2	100.0	*Norvège*
Sweden	99.2	0.6	0.2	0.8	100.0	*Suède*
Switzerland	...	...	...	...	...	*Suisse*
Turkey	...	...	...	...	...	*Turquie*
Country mean	**85.0**	...	...	**15.0**	**100.0**	*Moyenne des pays*
Central and Eastern Europe						*Europe centrale et orientale*
Czech Republic	...	...	...	...	...	*République tchèque*
Hungary	99.2	0.8	.	0.8	100.0	*Hongrie*
Poland	...	...	...	...	...	*Pologne*
Russia	...	...	...	...	...	*Russie*

See Annex 1 for notes

Voir notes en annexe 1

F02: Expenditure of public and private educational institutions

F02 : Dépenses des établissements d'enseignement publics et privés

Chart F02:
Expenditure shares of public and private educational institutions for primary and secondary, tertiary and all (1992)

*Graphique F02 :
Répartition en pourcentage des dépenses publiques et privées, enseignement primaire et secondaire, supérieur, et tous niveaux confondus*

Primary and secondary — *Primaire et secondaire*
(OST, IRE, SWE, HUN, CAN, NOR, FIN, DEN, USA, JPN, **MEAN**, FRA, SPA, GER (FTFR), NET)

Tertiary — *Supérieur*
(DEN, CAN, HUN, IRE, SWE, GER (FTFR), FIN, NOR, SPA, OST, FRA, **MEAN**, USA, NET, JPN, BEL, UKM)

All levels combined — *Tous niveaux confondus*
(HUN, SWE, IRE, CAN, OST, NOR, DEN, FIN, FRA, **MEAN**, USA, SPA, GER (FTFR), JPN, NET)

Public institutions only / *Etablissements publics seuls*
Private institutions / *Etablissements privés*

Countries are ranked in order of decreasing expenditure share of public educational institutions

Les pays sont classés par ordre décroissant des dépenses d'éducation des établissements publics

F03: Expenditure for educational services per student

F03: EXPENDITURE PER STUDENT

POLICY ISSUES

A perennial issue facing education policy-makers around the world is whether the amount spent on each student's education is too low, too high, or "just right", given the conflicting demands for improved and more accessible education on the one hand, and for avoiding undue burden for taxpayers on the other. A major consideration is how a country's investment in education (human capital formation) compares with the investments of other countries. This indicator provides figures on expenditure per student in absolute terms (in US dollars) relative to the average expenditure per student for the OECD area as a whole, and relative to each country's per capita GDP.

KEY RESULTS

The OECD countries as a whole spend about $4 170 per student in primary education, $5 170 per student in secondary education, and $4 700 per student in primary and secondary education combined. However, these OECD-wide averages, especially for primary education, are strongly influenced by the high expenditure level in the largest country, the United States. The levels of spending per student in the "typical" OECD country, as represented by the country mean, are: primary, $3 410; secondary, $4 760; and primary and secondary combined, $4 180.

For OECD as a whole, expenditure per student averages 20.8 per cent of per capita GDP at the primary level and 26.7 per cent at the secondary level.

Even excluding the highest-spending and lowest-spending countries, the range in expenditure per student is wide: from about $2 000 to over $4 500 at the primary level and from less than $3 000 to over $6 000 at the secondary level.

The range in reported spending per pre-primary student is even greater – from under $2 000 to more than $7 000, but this reflects wide variations in the types of early childhood services whose costs have been included in the expenditure figures – see below.

The OECD countries as a whole spend an average of $10 030 per tertiary student, or about 49 per cent of per capita GDP. The country mean, which may be more representative of the "typical" OECD country, is much lower – $7 940 per student or, on average, 45 per cent of the country's per capita GDP. Some countries spend less than $6 000 per tertiary student, while others spend $12 000 or more.

DESCRIPTION AND INTERPRETATION

The data used in calculating expenditure per student include only the expenditures of educational institutions. Public subsidies for student living expenses are excluded. This represents a procedural departure from *Education at a Glance* in previous years. Therefore, the expenditure-per-student figures for some countries, especially relative to tertiary education, are not comparable with those in the earlier editions.

The figures presented for most countries are expenditures per student in public educational institutions. Many countries have only small numbers of private institutions, or have no data on private school expenditures. However, for a few countries where government-dependent private schools play major roles in primary and secondary education – Belgium, France, the Netherlands and Spain – it was decided to present figures both for public schools and for public and government-dependent private schools combined. Similarly, the table for tertiary education includes, for a few countries, expenditures of private institutions and public and private institutions combined.

Of the 18 countries for which data are available on expenditure per primary student, five spend $2 500 per student or less; seven spend between $2 500 and $4 000 per student; and six spend over $4 000 per student. The countries that spend the most (over $4 200 per student) are Denmark, Norway, Sweden and the United States; those that spend the least (less than $2 300) are Hungary, Ireland, New Zealand and Spain.

At the secondary level, five countries spend $6 000 or more per student; five spend $3 500 per student or less; seven spend between $3 500 and $6 000. The highest-spending countries are Austria, Belgium, Germany (FTFR), Norway, Sweden and the United States. (The Austrian and German figures take into account, in different ways, the systems of apprenticeship training of these countries; see Annex 3.)

To interpret the figures on pre-primary spending per student, one must consider the differences between the Nordic countries and all the others. Pre-primary insti-

F03: Expenditure for educational services per student

tutions in the Nordic countries often provide extended day and evening care for young children, the costs of which are included in reported spending per student. Thus, Denmark, Finland, Norway and Sweden report expenditures of $6 000 per student or more, while all the other OECD countries report spending per student in the range of $1 000 to $3 300. Moreover, the spending levels of some of the latter countries may be understated, because the distinction between full-day and part-day programmes has not been taken into account in calculating spending per full-time-equivalent student.

Expenditure per tertiary student varies by more than a factor of three. Of the 21 countries for which data are available, five – Canada, Japan, Switzerland, the United Kingdom and the United States – report expenditures of more than $10 000 per student (the figure for United States private institutions is over $20 000). Twelve countries report expenditures of between $6 000 and $10 000 per student. The remaining four countries – Austria, the Czech Republic, Italy and Spain – report expenditures of less than $6 000 per student, with the Czech Republic and Spain reporting only about $3 600 and $3 800, respectively.

As one would expect, higher income countries tend to spend more per student at all levels of education, but the correlation is far from perfect. As can be seen from Charts F03, the relationship between expenditure per student and per capita GDP is generally positive, but considerable variation in spending exists among both the richer and the poorer countries.

The following points should be considered in interpreting differences in expenditures per student:

• These do not always reflect variations in the real resources provided to students (e.g. variations in teacher/student ratios). In some cases, they reflect variations in relative prices. For example, a country may appear to spend an above-average amount because the salaries of its teachers are high relative to the country's general price level.

• The figures on spending per student are affected by certain problems in comparing expenditures among countries. For example, countries differ in whether, or to what extent, they have reported funds from private sources; whether they have included amounts spent by business firms to train apprentices; and how they measure the cost of pensions for education personnel. The results are sometimes strongly affected – especially at the tertiary level – by differences in how countries define full-time, part-time and full-time-equivalent enrolment.

• An important comparability problem at the tertiary level is that the expenditures of some countries include essentially all spending for research in institutions of higher education, whereas the data from other countries exclude separately funded or separately budgeted research. This problem is addressed in a special supplement to this indicator in Annex 3.

DEFINITIONS

Expenditure per student in national currency is calculated by dividing the total expenditures of or for educational institutions of a particular type (public, government-dependent private, independent private), and at a particular level of education, by the corresponding full-time-equivalent (FTE) enrolment. The result is then translated into US dollars by dividing it by the purchasing power parity (PPP) exchange rate between that country's currency and the US dollar.

The index of relative expenditure per student (OECD = 100) is calculated by dividing each country's expenditure per student by expenditure per student in the OECD area as a whole (both figures expressed in US dollars). The expenditure-per-student figure for the OECD area as a whole is a weighted average of the individual country figures, in which the weights are the countries' FTE enrolments.

Expenditure per student relative to per capita GDP is calculated by expressing expenditure per student in units of national currency as a percentage of per capita GDP, also in national currency. In cases where the educational expenditure and GDP data pertain to different annual periods, an inflation factor is used to adjust for the discrepancy (see Annex 3).

The specific PPP rate used to convert other national currencies into US dollars is that pertaining to gross domestic product, as published in OECD's National Accounts Database. It is essential to use PPP rates rather than market exchange rates to convert other national currencies into US dollars, because market exchange rates are affected by many factors (interest rates, trade policies, expectations for economic growth, etc.) that have little to do with the current, relative domestic purchasing powers of different countries. The PPP rates are presented in *OECD Education Statistics, 1985-1992*.

F03: Expenditure for educational services per student

F03 : Dépenses d'éducation par élève

Table F03(1):
Expenditure per student for early childhood education (1992)

Tableau F03(1) :
Dépenses unitaires pour l'éducation préscolaire (1992)

	Type of institution	Expenditure per student (US dollars converted using PPPs) / Dépenses unitaires (en équivalent dollars E-U convertis en PPA)	Index: Expenditure per student as a percentage of OECD total / Indice : Dépenses unitaires en pourcentage du total OCDE	Expenditure per student relative to per capita GDP / Dépenses unitaires en proportion du PIB par habitant	Type d'établissement	
North America						*Amérique du Nord*
Canada		...	...	...		*Canada*
United States	Public	3 210	107	14.1	Public	*Etats-Unis*
Pacific Area						*Pays du Pacifique*
Australia		...	...	...		*Australie*
Japan	Public	3 020	101	15.7	Public	*Japon*
New Zealand	Public	1 900	63	13.4	Public	*Nouvelle-Zélande*
European Community						*Communauté européenne*
Belgium	Public	2 350	78	13.0	Public	*Belgique*
	Public and gvt-dep *	1 860	62	10.3	Public et privé sub *	
Denmark	Public	6 300	210	35.8	Public	*Danemark*
France	Public	2 630	88	14.2	Public	*France*
	Public and gvt-dep *	2 580	86	14.0	Public et privé sub *	
Germany (FTFR)	Public	3 350	112	16.5	Public	*Allemagne (ex-terr. de la RFA)*
Germany	Public	...	...	...	Public	*Allemagne*
Greece		...	...	...		*Grèce*
Ireland	Public	1 750	58	13.7	Public	*Irlande*
Italy	Public	3 280	109	18.9	Public	*Italie*
Luxembourg		...	...	...		*Luxembourg*
Netherlands	Public and gvt-dep *	2 230	74	13.2	Public et privé sub *	*Pays-Bas*
Portugal		...	...	...		*Portugal*
Spain	Public	2 100	70	16.4	Public	*Espagne*
	Public and gvt-dep *	2 090	70	16.3	Public et privé sub *	
United Kingdom	Public	1 860	62	11.8	Public	*Royaume-Uni*
Other Europe - OECD						*Autres pays d'Europe - OCDE*
Austria	Public	3280	110	18.2	Public	*Autriche*
Finland	Public	6280	210	43.4	Public	*Finlande*
Iceland		...	...	...		*Islande*
Norway	Public	7 350	245	41.6	Public	*Norvège*
Sweden	Public	6 070	202	36.5	Public	*Suède*
Switzerland	Public	1 890	63	8.5	Public	*Suisse*
Turkey		...	...	...		*Turquie*
Country mean		**3 430**	**114**	**20.1**		*Moyenne des pays*
OECD total		**3 000**	**100**	**16.0**		*Total OCDE*
Central and Eastern Europe						*Europe centrale et orientale*
Czech Republic	Public	1 240	41	17.3	Public	*République tchèque*
Hungary	Public	1 640	55	23.9	Public	*Hongrie*
Poland		...	...	...		*Pologne*
Russia		...	...	...		*Russie*

See Annex 1 for notes
* Public and government-dependent private

Voir notes en annexe 1
* Public et privé subventionné

F03: Expenditure for educational services per student

F03 : Dépenses d'éducation par élève

Table F03(2):
Expenditure per student for primary education (1992)

Tableau F03(2) :
Dépenses unitaires pour l'enseignement primaire (1992)

	Type of institution	Expenditure per student (US dollars converted using PPPs) / *Dépenses unitaires (en équivalent dollars E-U convertis en PPA)*	Index: Expenditure per student as a percentage of OECD total / *Indice : Dépenses unitaires en pourcentage du total OCDE*	Expenditure per student relative to per capita GDP / *Dépenses unitaires en proportion du PIB par habitant*	Type d'établissement	
North America						*Amérique du Nord*
Canada		...	...	...		*Canada*
United States	Public	5 600	135	24.5	Public	*Etats-Unis*
Pacific Area						*Pays du Pacifique*
Australia						*Australie*
Japan	Public	3 530	85	18.3	Public	*Japon*
New Zealand	Public	2 030	49	14.4	Public	*Nouvelle-Zélande*
European Community						*Communauté européenne*
Belgium	Public	2 910	70	16.1	Public	*Belgique*
	Public and gvt-dep *	2 390	57	13.2	Public et privé sub *	
Denmark	Public	4 220	101	24.0	Public	*Danemark*
France	Public	3 000	72	16.2	Public	*France*
	Public and gvt-dep *	2 900	70	15.6	Public et privé sub *	
Germany (FTFR)	Public	2 980	72	14.7	Public	*Allemagne (ex- terr. de la RFA)*
Germany	Public	...	...	...	Public	*Allemagne*
Greece		...	...	...		*Grèce*
Ireland	Public	1 770	43	13.9	Public	*Irlande*
Italy	Public	4 050	97	23.3	Public	*Italie*
Luxembourg		...	...	...		*Luxembourg*
Netherlands	Public and gvt-dep *	2 560	62	15.1	Public et privé sub *	*Pays-Bas*
Portugal		...	...	...		*Portugal*
Spain	Public	2 270	54	17.7	Public	*Espagne*
	Public and gvt-dep *	2 030	49	15.9	Public et privé sub *	
United Kingdom	Public	3 120	75	19.7	Public	*Royaume-Uni*
Other Europe - OECD						*Autres pays d'Europe - OCDE*
Austria	Public	4 010	96	22.2	Public	*Autriche*
Finland	Public	3 850	93	26.6	Public	*Finlande*
Iceland		...	...	...		*Islande*
Norway	Public	4 480	108	25.3	Public	*Norvège*
Sweden	Public	4 840	116	29.1	Public	*Suède*
Switzerland	Public	3 560	85	16.0	Public	*Suisse*
Turkey		...	...	...		*Turquie*
Country mean		**3 410**	**82**	**19.5**		*Moyenne des pays*
OECD total		**4 170**	**100**	**20.8**		*Total OCDE*
Central and Eastern Europe						*Europe centrale et orientale*
Czech Republic		...	...	...		*République tchèque*
Hungary	Public	1 840	44	26.6	Public	*Hongrie*
Poland		...	...	...		*Pologne*
Russia		...	...	...		*Russie*

See Annex 1 for notes
* Public and government-dependent private

Voir notes en annexe 1
* Public et privé subventionné

F03: Expenditure for educational services per student

F03 : Dépenses d'éducation par élève

Table F03(3):
Expenditure per student for secondary education (1992)

Tableau F03(3) :
Dépenses unitaires pour l'enseignement secondaire (1992)

	Type of institution	Expenditure per student (US dollars converted using PPPs) / Dépenses unitaires (en équivalent dollars E-U convertis en PPA)	Index: Expenditure per student as a percentage of OECD total / Indice : Dépenses unitaires en pourcentage du total OCDE	Expenditure per student relative to per capita GDP / Dépenses unitaires en proportion du PIB par habitant	Type d'établissement	
North America						**Amérique du Nord**
Canada		...	...	...		Canada
United States	Public	6 470	125	28.3	Public	Etats-Unis
Pacific Area						**Pays du Pacifique**
Australia		...	...	...		Australie
Japan	Public	3 900	75	20.2	Public	Japon
New Zealand	Public	2 620	51	18.5	Public	Nouvelle-Zélande
European Community						**Communauté européenne**
Belgium	Public	6 470	130	37.3	Public	Belgique
	Public and gvt-dep *	5 150	100	28.5	Public et privé sub *	
Denmark	Public	4 940	96	28.0	Public	Danemark
France	Public	5 870	114	31.7	Public	France
	Public and gvt-dep *	5 430	105	29.3	Public et privé sub *	
Germany (FTFR)	Public	4 260	82	20.9	Public	Allemagne (ex-terr. de la RFA)
	Public and private	6 210	120	30.5	Public et privé	
Germany	Public	...	...	...	Public	Allemagne
Greece		...	...	...		Grèce
Ireland	Public	2 770	54	21.7	Public	Irlande
Italy	Public	4 700	91	27.1	Public	Italie
Luxembourg		...	...	...		Luxembourg
Netherlands	Public and gvt-dep *	3 310	64	19.5	Public et privé sub *	Pays-Bas
Portugal		...	...	...		Portugal
Spain	Public	3 140	61	24.6	Public	Espagne
	Public and gvt-dep *	2 790	54	21.8	Public et privé sub *	
United Kingdom	Public	4 390	85	27.8	Public	Royaume-Uni
Other Europe - OECD						**Autres pays d'Europe - OCDE**
Austria	Public	6 420	124	35.6	Public	Autriche
Finland	Public	4 820	93	33.3	Public	Finlande
Iceland		...	...	...		Islande
Norway	Public	6 200	120	35.1	Public	Norvège
Sweden	Public	6 050	117	36.4	Public	Suède
Switzerland		...	...	...		Suisse
Turkey		...	...	...		Turquie
Country mean		**4 760**	**92**	**27.6**		**Moyenne des pays**
OECD total		**5 170**	**100**	**26.7**		**Total OCDE**
Central and Eastern Europe						**Europe centrale et orientale**
Czech Republic		...	...	...		République tchèque
Hungary	Public	2 000	39	29.1	Public	Hongrie
Poland		...	...	...		Pologne
Russia		...	...	...		Russie

See Annex 1 for notes
* Public and government-dependent private

Voir notes en annexe 1
* Public et privé subventionné

F03: Expenditure for educational services per student

F03 : Dépenses d'éducation par élève

Table F03(4):
Expenditure per student for primary and secondary education (1992)

Tableau F03(4) :
Dépenses unitaires pour l'enseignement primaire et secondaire (1992)

Country	Type of institution	Expenditure per student (US dollars converted using PPPs) / Dépenses unitaires (en équivalent dollars E-U convertis en PPA)	Index: Expenditure per student as a percentage of OECD total / Indice : Dépenses unitaires en pourcentage du total OCDE	Expenditure per student relative to per capita GDP / Dépenses unitaires en proportion du PIB par habitant	Type d'établissement	
North America						**Amérique du Nord**
Canada		...	...	...		Canada
United States	Public	6 010	128	26.3	Public	Etats-Unis
Pacific Area						**Pays du Pacifique**
Australia		...	...	...		Australie
Japan	Public	3 710	79	19.3	Public	Japon
New Zealand	Public	2 340	50	16.6	Public	Nouvelle-Zélande
European Community						**Communauté européenne**
Belgium	Public	4 660	99	25.8	Public	Belgique
	Public and gvt-dep *	3 840	82	21.2	Public et privé sub *	
Denmark	Public	4 660	99	26.4	Public	Danemark
France	Public	4 600	98	24.9	Public	France
	Public and gvt-dep *	4 380	93	23.7	Public et privé sub *	
Germany (FTFR)	Public	3 860	82	19.0	Public	Allemagne (ex-terr. de la RFA)
	Public and private	5 230	111	25.7	Public et privé	
Germany	Public	...	...	...	Public	Allemagne
Greece		...	...	...		Grèce
Ireland	Public	2 240	48	17.6	Public	Irlande
Italy	Public	4 470	95	25.7	Public	Italie
Luxembourg		...	...	...		Luxembourg
Netherlands	Public and gvt-dep *	2 990	64	17.6	Public et privé sub *	Pays-Bas
Portugal		...	...	...		Portugal
Spain	Public	2 840	60	22.2	Public	Espagne
	Public and gvt-dep *	2 500	53	19.5	Public et privé sub *	
United Kingdom	Public	3 780	80	23.9	Public	Royaume-Uni
Other Europe - OECD						**Autres pays d'Europe - OCDE**
Austria	Public	5 490	117	30.5	Public	Autriche
Finland	Public	4 350	93	30.1	Public	Finlande
Iceland		...	...	...		Islande
Norway	Public	5 420	115	30.7	Public	Norvège
Sweden	Public	5 450	116	32.8	Public	Suède
Switzerland		...	...	...		Suisse
Turkey		...	...	...		Turquie
Country mean		**4 180**	**89**	**24.2**		**Moyenne des pays**
OECD total		**4 700**	**100**	**23.9**		**Total OCDE**
Central and Eastern Europe						**Europe centrale et orientale**
Czech Republic	Public	1 280	27	17.8	Public	République tchèque
Hungary	Public	1 950	41	28.4	Public	Hongrie
Poland		...	...	...		Pologne
Russia		...	...	...		Russie

See Annex 1 for notes
* Public and government-dependent private

Voir notes en annexe 1
* Public et privé subventionné

F03: Expenditure for educational services per student

F03 : Dépenses d'éducation par élève

Table F03(5):
Expenditure per student for tertiary education (1992)

Tableau F03(5) :
Dépenses unitaires pour l'enseignement supérieur (1992)

	Type of institution	Expenditure per student (US dollars converted using PPPs) / Dépenses unitaires (en équivalent dollars E-U convertis en PPA)	Index: Expenditure per student as a percentage of OECD total / Indice : Dépenses unitaires en pourcentage du total OCDE	Expenditure per student relative to per capita GDP / Dépenses unitaires en proportion du PIB par habitant	Type d'établissement	
North America						*Amérique du Nord*
Canada	Public	12 350	123	63.3	Public	*Canada*
United States	Public	11 880	118	52.0	Public	*Etats-Unis*
	Independent private	20 300	202	88.9	Privé non subventionné	
	Public and private	13 890	138	60.8	Public et privé	
Pacific Area						*Pays du Pacifique*
Australia	Public	6 600	66	39.0	Public	*Australie*
Japan	Public	11 850	118	61.5	Public	*Japon*
	Independent private	5 630	56	29.2	Privé non subventionné	
	Public and private	7 140	71	37.1	Public et privé	
New Zealand	Public	6 080	61	43.0	Public	*Nouvelle-Zélande*
European Community						*Communauté européenne*
Belgium	Public	6 850	68	37.9	Public	*Belgique*
	Public and gvt-dep *	6 590	66	36.4	Public et privé sub *	
Denmark	Public	6 710	67	38.1	Public	*Danemark*
France	Public	6 020	60	32.5	Public	*France*
	Private	4 090	41	22.1	Privé	
	Public and private	5 760	57	31.1	Public et privé	
Germany (FTFR)	Public	6 550	65	32.2	Public	*Allemagne (ex-terr. de la RFA)*
Germany	Public	...	...	...	Public	*Allemagne*
Greece		...	...	...		*Grèce*
Ireland	Public	7 270	72	56.9	Public	*Irlande*
Italy	Public	5 850	58	33.7	Public	*Italie*
Luxembourg		...	...	...		*Luxembourg*
Netherlands	Public and gvt-dep *	8 720	87	51.5	Public et privé sub *	*Pays-Bas*
Portugal		...	...	...		*Portugal*
Spain	Public	3 770	38	29.4	Public	*Espagne*
United Kingdom	Public	15 060	150	95.2	Public	*Royaume-Uni*
	Gvt-dep **	9 400	94	59.4	Privé subventionné **	
	Public and gvt-dep *	10 370	103	65.6	Public et privé sub *	
Other Europe - OECD						*Autres pays d'Europe - OCDE*
Austria	Public	5 820	58	32.3	Public	*Autriche*
Finland	Public	8 650	86	59.7	Public	*Finlande*
Iceland		...	...	...		*Islande*
Norway	Public	8 720	87	49.4	Public	*Norvège*
Sweden	Public	7 120	71	42.9	Public	*Suède*
Switzerland	Public	12 900	129	58.0	Public	*Suisse*
Turkey		...	...	...		*Turquie*
Country mean		**7 940**	**79**	**45.3**		***Moyenne des pays***
OECD total		**10 030**	**100**	**49.0**		***Total OCDE***
Central and Eastern Europe						*Europe centrale et orientale*
Czech Republic	Public	3 590	36	50.2	Public	*République tchèque*
Hungary	Public	9 690	97	140.8	Public	*Hongrie*
Poland		...	...	...		*Pologne*
Russia		...	...	...		*Russie*

See Annex 1 for notes
* Public and government-dependent private
** Government-dependent private only

Voir notes en annexe 1
* Public et privé subventionné
** Privé subventionné seulement

F03: Expenditure for educational services per student

F03 : Dépenses d'éducation par élève

Chart F03:
Public expenditure per student
in relation to GDP per capita (1992)

Graphique F03 :
Dépenses publiques unitaires
en proportion du PIB par habitant (1992)

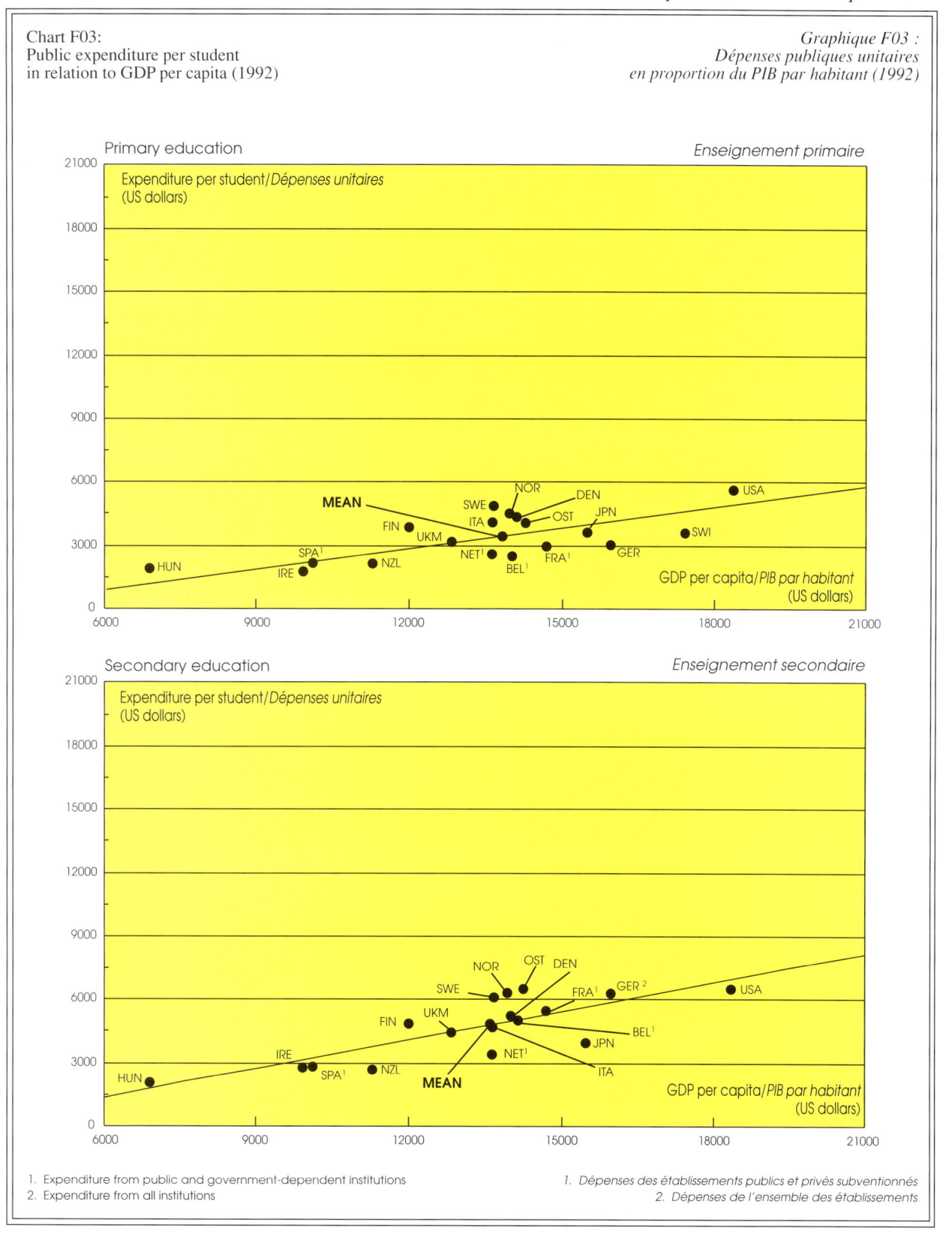

Primary education — *Enseignement primaire*

Expenditure per student/*Dépenses unitaires* (US dollars)

Countries plotted: HUN, IRE, SPA¹, NZL, FIN, UKM, NET¹, BEL¹, SWE, ITA, NOR, FRA¹, OST, DEN, JPN, GER, SWI, USA; MEAN shown.

GDP per capita/*PIB par habitant* (US dollars)

Secondary education — *Enseignement secondaire*

Expenditure per student/*Dépenses unitaires* (US dollars)

Countries plotted: HUN, IRE, SPA¹, NZL, FIN, UKM, SWE, NOR, OST, DEN, NET¹, FRA¹, ITA, GER², BEL¹, JPN, USA; MEAN shown.

GDP per capita/*PIB par habitant* (US dollars)

1. Expenditure from public and government-dependent institutions
2. Expenditure from all institutions

1. *Dépenses des établissements publics et privés subventionnés*
2. *Dépenses de l'ensemble des établissements*

F03: Expenditure for educational services per student

F03 : Dépenses d'éducation par élève

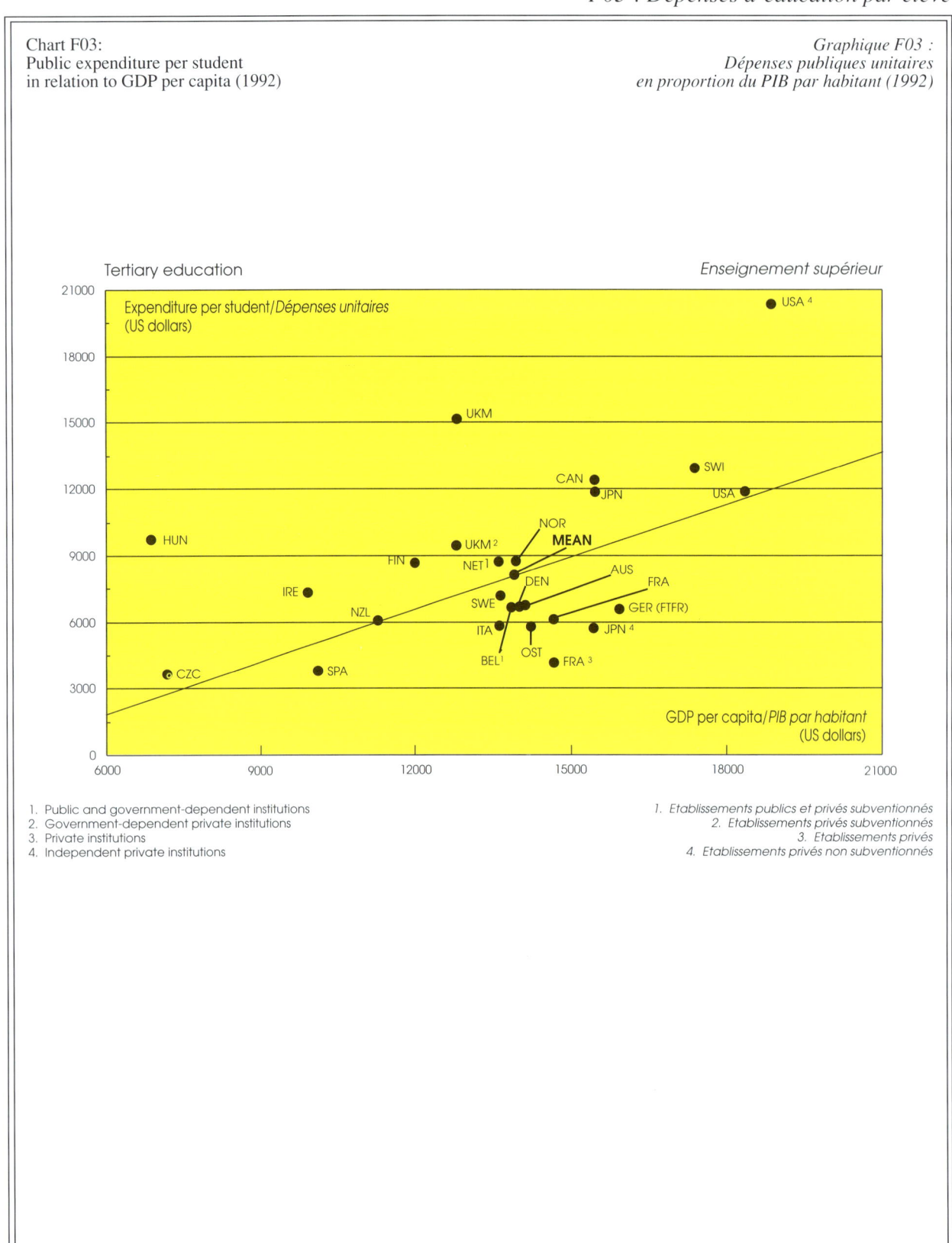

Chart F03:
Public expenditure per student
in relation to GDP per capita (1992)

*Graphique F03 :
Dépenses publiques unitaires
en proportion du PIB par habitant (1992)*

Tertiary education — *Enseignement supérieur*

Expenditure per student/*Dépenses unitaires* (US dollars)

GDP per capita/*PIB par habitant* (US dollars)

1. Public and government-dependent institutions
2. Government-dependent private institutions
3. Private institutions
4. Independent private institutions

1. *Etablissements publics et privés subventionnés*
2. *Etablissements privés subventionnés*
3. *Etablissements privés*
4. *Etablissements privés non subventionnés*

F04: Allocation of funds by level of education

EXPENDITURE AND ENROLMENT SHARES BY LEVEL OF EDUCATION

POLICY ISSUES

In elaborating its strategy for developing human resources, how should a country distribute resources across the various stages of education? Some countries emphasize broad access to higher education, for example, while others invest in near-universal education for children as young as two or three. It is difficult to compare the distribution of resources by level directly, but this indicator seeks to accomplish the task indirectly by: *a)* comparing each country's distribution of expenditures by level to the corresponding distribution of enrolments; and *b)* comparing relative expenditures per student at different levels.

KEY RESULTS

For the typical OECD country, the percentage distribution of education expenditures by level is as follows: pre-primary, 7 per cent; primary, 26 per cent; secondary, 45 per cent; and tertiary, 22 per cent. These percentages differ greatly among countries, reflecting differences in (among other things) the duration of each stage of education and rates of participation in pre-primary, upper secondary, and tertiary education.

The percentages of national education expenditures devoted to pre-primary and primary education are generally smaller than the corresponding percentages of enrolment – on average, 30 and 26 per cent smaller, respectively, reflecting the relatively low amounts spent per student at these levels. The percentage devoted to secondary education is slightly greater (by about 4 per cent on average) than the corresponding percentage of enrolment.

Because countries spend much more per student at the tertiary education level than at others, the percentage of total expenditures devoted to tertiary education is sharply higher – 1.8 times larger on average – than the corresponding percentage of enrolment.

For the OECD area as a whole, expenditure per student in pre-primary education averages about 14 per cent less than expenditure per student in primary education, while expenditures per student at the secondary and tertiary levels are, respectively, 28 and 127 per cent higher on average than expenditure per primary student [Table F04(B)].

DESCRIPTION AND INTERPRETATION

Because of differences among countries in the starting age and durations of pre-primary, primary and secondary education, it is not possible to compare expenditure shares by level directly. For example, in a comparison between a country with four years of primary schooling and one with six years, it is not unreasonable to expect the primary share of expenditures in the latter country to be about 50 per cent larger because of the difference in duration alone. To make meaningful comparisons, it is necessary to consider the expenditure share of each level relative to the corresponding share of enrolment. The results are best shown by plotting expenditure shares against enrolment shares, as in Charts F04.

The pre-primary share of expenditures is only 0.5 to 0.8 times as large as the enrolment share in most countries; in the Nordic countries, however, the expenditure share is about 10 per cent greater than the enrolment share. This exceptional feature of the Nordic countries (illustrated in Chart F04) is explained by the fact that these countries almost alone spend substantially more per pre-primary student than per primary student.

The primary share of expenditures is 0.7 to 0.9 times as great as the enrolment share in most cases, signifying that primary students receive a share of funding less than proportional to their numbers. This ratio is lowest in Belgium, France and Switzerland (0.6) and highest in Italy, Japan and Sweden (0.9).

Expenditure per secondary student is about 40 per cent greater on average than expenditure per primary student, but some countries spend only about 10 per cent more (Hungary, Japan and Sweden) while others spend around 100 per cent more per secondary student (Belgium, France and Switzerland). For most countries, the secondary share of expenditures is between 0.9 and 1.2 times as large as the secondary share of enrolment.

The relative amount spent per tertiary student varies widely among countries, ranging from only 145 to 160 per cent of expenditure per primary student in Austria, Italy and Sweden to more than 300 per cent in

F04: Allocation of funds by level of education

Hungary, Ireland, Japan, the Netherlands, Switzerland and the United Kingdom. Correspondingly wide variations in the relationship between the tertiary expenditure share and the tertiary enrolment share can be seen in Chart F04. The expenditure share is only 1.3 to 1.5 times as great as the enrolment share in some cases, but more than 2.5 times as great in others.

DEFINITIONS

The expenditure share for each level of education is expressed as a percentage of the total expenditure for all levels of education combined. Expenditures for both public and government-dependent private schools are taken into account where data are available; otherwise, only the expenditures of public institutions are included. Expenditures for educational institutions alone are considered; subsidies for student living expenses are not counted. Expenditures classified as "not allocated by level" are excluded from these calculations.

The enrolment share for each level is calculated similarly: full-time-equivalent (FTE) enrolment at the level in question, expressed as a percentage of FTE enrolment at all levels of education combined.

As an aid to interpreting the results, the ratio of expenditure share to enrolment share is shown in the tables for each level of education. A ratio below 1.0 indicates that the level receives a share of funds less than proportional to its enrolment; a ratio greater than 1.0 indicates a share more than proportional to its enrolment.

The relative expenditure per student for each level of education is calculated by expressing expenditure per student for the level in question as a percentage of expenditure per student for primary education in the same country. (Because expenditure per student at the primary level has been taken as the standard of comparison, relative expenditure per student in primary education is always 100, by definition.)

F04: Allocation of funds by level of education

F04 : Répartition des crédits par niveau d'enseignement

Table F04(A1):
Shares of expenditure and of enrolment
for early childhood and primary education in public
and government-dependent private institutions (1992)

Tableau F04(A1) :
Répartition en pourcentage des dépenses et des effectifs
pour l'éducation préscolaire et l'enseignement primaire
dans les établissements publics et privés subventionnés (1992)

	Early childhood education / Education préscolaire			Primary education / Enseignement primaire			
	As a percentage of expenditure at all levels combined	As a percentage of enrolment at all levels combined	Ratio of expenditure to enrolment	As a percentage of expenditure at all levels combined	As a percentage of enrolment at all levels combined	Ratio of expenditure to enrolment	
North America							*Amérique du Nord*
Canada	...	3.7	...	...	38.7	...	Canada
United States	3.5	6.1	0.6	34.2	41.6	0.8	Etats-Unis
Pacific Area							*Pays du Pacifique*
Australia	...	...	...	...	...	...	Australie
Japan	1.6	2.2	0.8	42.0	47.5	0.9	Japon
New Zealand (PUB)	4.0	6.0	0.7	26.9	37.5	0.7	(PUB) Nouvelle-Zélande
European Community							*Communauté européenne*
Belgium	8.9	18.1	0.5	21.2	33.6	0.6	Belgique
Denmark	14.6	13.1	1.1	23.1	30.0	0.8	Danemark
France (PUB)	11.5	22.1	0.5	20.1	34.9	0.6	(PUB) France
Germany (FTFR)	7.0	...	...	15.6	...	...	Allemagne (ex-terr. de la RFA)
Germany	...	...	...	...	...	...	Allemagne
Greece	...	7.0	...	...	40.1	...	Grèce
Ireland	8.3	12.7	0.7	27.8	41.4	0.7	Irlande
Italy	7.8	10.9	0.7	24.0	26.9	0.9	Italie
Luxembourg	...	...	...	...	...	...	Luxembourg
Netherlands	6.7	10.9	0.6	23.2	32.8	0.7	Pays-Bas
Portugal	2.4	...	...	38.1	...	...	Portugal
Spain	6.3	8.0	0.8	22.9	29.8	0.8	Espagne
United Kingdom	1.6	3.7	0.4	30.9	42.0	0.7	Royaume-Uni
Other Europe - OECD							*Autres pays d'Europe - OCDE*
Austria	7.0	13.3	0.5	19.9	25.5	0.8	Autriche
Finland	8.8	8.0	1.1	26.5	35.7	0.7	Finlande
Iceland	...	...	...	...	...	...	Islande
Norway (PUB)	11.4	9.4	1.2	25.9	35.0	0.7	(PUB) Norvège
Sweden	16.8	15.4	1.1	29.2	34.2	0.9	Suède
Switzerland	3.7	11.2	0.3	21.7	35.1	0.6	Suisse
Turkey	...	1.1	...	...	58.7	...	Turquie
Country mean	**7.3**	**9.6**	**0.7**	**26.3**	**36.9**	**0.7**	**Moyenne des pays**
OECD total	**7.0**	**11.0**	**0.7**	**32.3**	**40.5**	**0.8**	**Total OCDE**
Central and Eastern Europe							*Europe centrale et orientale*
Czech Republic (PUB)	12.7	14.4	0.9	...	24.6	...	(PUB) République tchèque
Hungary	12.4	17.6	0.7	18.3	22.9	0.8	Hongrie
Poland	...	...	...	...	...	...	Pologne
Russia	...	24.6	...	...	37.3	...	Russie

See Annex 1 for notes
(PUB) means that percentages refer to shares
of public expenditure and enrolment only

Voir notes en annexe 1
(PUB) signifie que les pourcentages concernent uniquement
les répartitions des dépenses et des effectifs des établissements publics

F04: Allocation of funds by level of education

F04 : Répartition des crédits par niveau d'enseignement

Table F04(A2):
Shares of expenditure and of enrolment for secondary and tertiary education in public and government-dependent private institutions (1992)

Tableau F04(A2) :
Répartition en pourcentage des dépenses et des effectifs pour l'enseignement secondaire et supérieur dans les établissements publics et privés subventionnés (1992)

	Secondary education / *Enseignement secondaire*			Tertiary education / *Enseignement supérieur*			
	As a percentage of expenditure at all levels combined	As a percentage of enrolment at all levels combined	Ratio of expenditure to enrolment	As a percentage of expenditure at all levels combined	As a percentage of enrolment at all levels combined	Ratio of expenditure to enrolment	
North America							*Amérique du Nord*
Canada	...	37.2	...	37.1	20.4	1.8	*Canada*
United States	34.5	36.3	1.0	27.9	16.0	1.7	*Etats-Unis*
Pacific Area							*Pays du Pacifique*
Australia	...	...	...	...	...	...	*Australie*
Japan	45.7	46.8	1.0	10.7	3.6	3.0	*Japon*
New Zealand (PUB)	39.5	42.7	0.9	29.6	13.8	2.2	*(PUB) Nouvelle-Zélande*
European Community							*Communauté européenne*
Belgium	50.2	36.9	1.4	19.8	11.4	1.7	*Belgique*
Denmark	41.8	42.1	1.0	20.6	14.8	1.4	*Danemark*
France (PUB)	49.8	49.4	1.0	18.7	13.8	1.4	*(PUB) France*
Germany (FTFR)	52.6	...	...	24.8	...	...	*Allemagne (ex-terr. de la RFA)*
Germany	...	...	...	...	...	...	*Allemagne*
Greece	...	43.3	...	...	9.7	...	*Grèce*
Ireland	39.0	37.1	1.1	24.3	8.8	2.8	*Irlande*
Italy	50.0	48.2	1.0	18.2	14.1	1.3	*Italie*
Luxembourg	...	...	...	...	...	...	*Luxembourg*
Netherlands	39.9	43.7	0.9	30.2	12.6	2.4	*Pays-Bas*
Portugal	40.0	...	...	19.5	...	...	*Portugal*
Spain	51.3	48.6	1.1	19.5	13.7	1.4	*Espagne*
United Kingdom	46.8	45.1	1.0	20.7	9.2	2.3	*Royaume-Uni*
Other Europe - OECD							*Autres pays d'Europe - OCDE*
Austria	51.5	44.0	1.2	21.6	17.2	1.3	*Autriche*
Finland	38.3	40.5	0.9	26.4	15.8	1.7	*Finlande*
Iceland	...	...	...	...	...	...	*Islande*
Norway (PUB)	43.1	42.1	1.0	19.5	13.5	1.4	*(PUB) Norvège*
Sweden	36.4	38.7	0.9	15.0	11.7	1.3	*Suède*
Switzerland	52.6	43.8	1.2	22.1	10.0	2.2	*Suisse*
Turkey	...	33.3	...	...	7.0	...	*Turquie*
Country mean	**44.6**	**42.1**	**1.0**	**22.4**	**12.5**	**1.8**	***Moyenne des pays***
OECD total	**42.6**	**41.9**	**1.0**	**25.7**	**14.8**	**1.8**	***Total OCDE***
Central and Eastern Europe							*Europe centrale et orientale*
Czech Republic (PUB)	...	55.1	...	15.0	5.9	2.6	*(PUB) République tchèque*
Hungary	47.6	54.3	0.9	21.7	5.2	4.2	*Hongrie*
Poland	...	...	...	...	...	...	*Pologne*
Russia	...	26.1	...	...	12.1	...	*Russie*

See Annex 1 for notes
(PUB) means that percentages refer to shares of public expenditure and enrolment only

Voir notes en annexe 1
(PUB) signifie que les pourcentages concernent uniquement les répartitions des dépenses et des effectifs des établissements publics

F04: Allocation of funds by level of education

F04 : Répartition des crédits par niveau d'enseignement

Table F04(B):
Relative expenditure per student by level of education (primary=100) in public and government-dependent private institutions (1992)

*Tableau F04(B) :
Dépenses unitaires relatives, par niveau scolaire (primaire=100), établissements publics et privés subventionnés (1992)*

	Early childhood education / *Education préscolaire*	Primary education / *Enseignement primaire*	Secondary education / *Enseignement secondaire*	Tertiary education / *Enseignement supérieur*	
North America					*Amérique du Nord*
Canada	...	...	...	...	*Canada*
United States	69	100	115	212	*Etats-Unis*
Pacific Area					*Pays du Pacifique*
Australia	...	...	...	...	*Australie*
Japan	85	100	110	336	*Japon*
New Zealand (PUB)	94	100	129	299	*(PUB) Nouvelle-Zélande*
European Community					*Communauté européenne*
Belgium	78	100	215	275	*Belgique*
Denmark	145	100	129	181	*Danemark*
France (PUB)	90	100	175	236	*(PUB) France*
Germany (FTFR)	...	...	...	...	*Allemagne (ex-terr. de la RFA)*
Germany	...	...	...	...	*Allemagne*
Greece	...	...	...	...	*Grèce*
Ireland	97	100	156	410	*Irlande*
Italy	81	100	116	145	*Italie*
Luxembourg	...	...	...	...	*Luxembourg*
Netherlands	87	100	129	340	*Pays-Bas*
Portugal	...	...	...	...	*Portugal*
Spain	103	100	137	185	*Espagne*
United Kingdom	59	100	141	305	*Royaume-Uni*
Other Europe - OECD					*Autres pays d'Europe - OCDE*
Austria	67	100	150	160	*Autriche*
Finland	148	100	127	226	*Finlande*
Iceland	...	...	...	...	*Islande*
Norway (PUB)	164	100	139	195	*(PUB) Norvège*
Sweden	128	100	110	149	*Suède*
Switzerland	53	100	195	359	*Suisse*
Turkey	...	...	...	...	*Turquie*
Country mean	**97**	**100**	**142**	**251**	***Moyenne des pays***
OECD total	**86**	**100**	**128**	**227**	***Total OCDE***
Central and Eastern Europe					*Europe centrale et orientale*
Czech Republic (PUB)	...	...	...	...	*(PUB) République tchèque*
Hungary	88	100	110	523	*Hongrie*
Poland	...	...	...	...	*Pologne*
Russia	...	...	...	...	*Russie*

See Annex 1 for notes

(PUB) means that percentages refer to shares of public expenditure and enrolment only

Voir notes en annexe 1

(PUB) signifie que les pourcentages concernent uniquement les répartitions des dépenses et des effectifs des établissements publics

F04: Allocation of funds by level of education

F04 : Répartition des crédits par niveau d'enseignement

Chart F04:
Shares of educational expenditure and shares of enrolment (1992)

Graphique F04 :
Pourcentage des dépenses d'éducation et pourcentage des effectifs (1992)

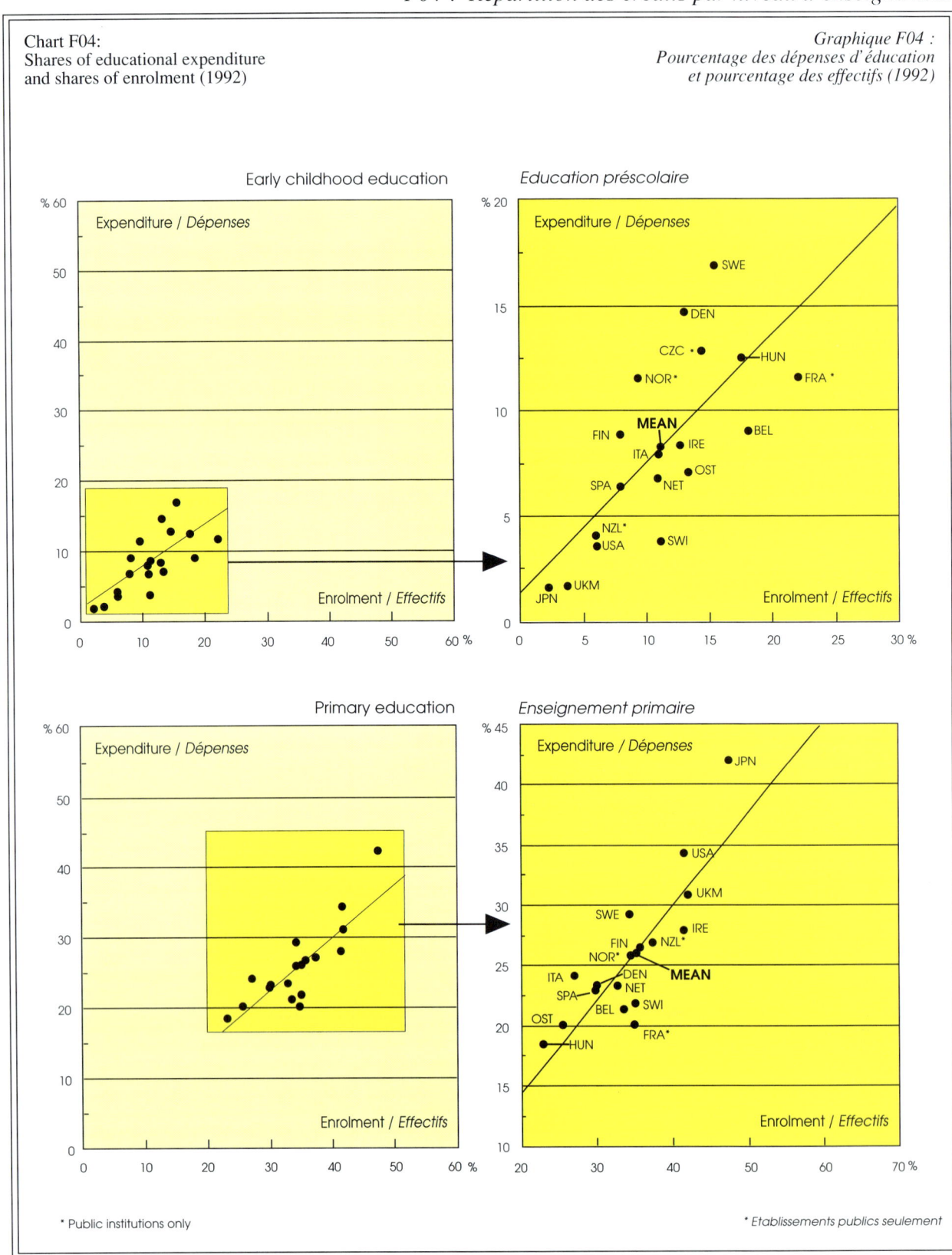

Early childhood education — *Education préscolaire*

Primary education — *Enseignement primaire*

* Public institutions only

* *Etablissements publics seulement*

F04: Allocation of funds by level of education

F04 : Répartition des crédits par niveau d'enseignement

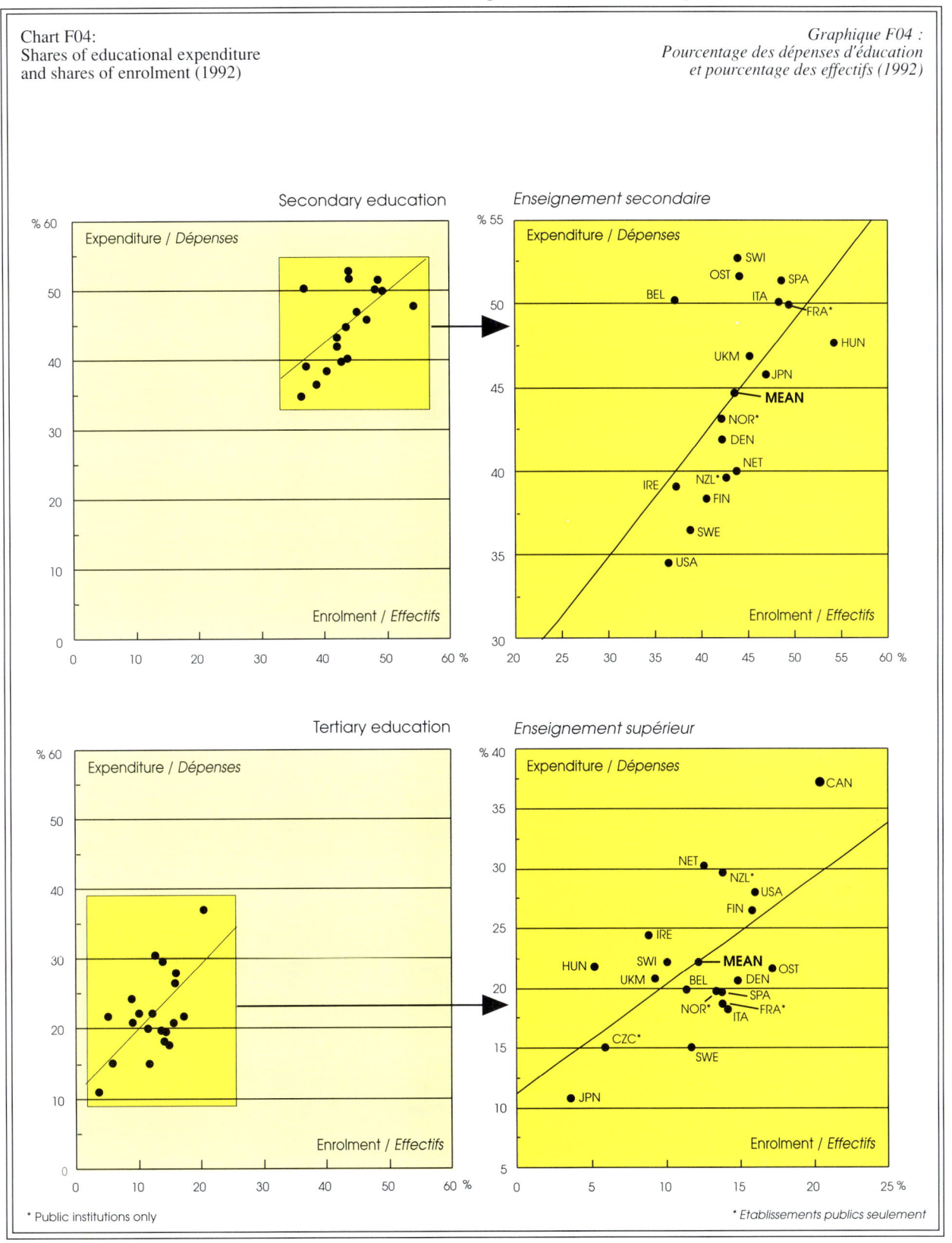

Chart F04:
Shares of educational expenditure and shares of enrolment (1992)

Graphique F04 :
Pourcentage des dépenses d'éducation et pourcentage des effectifs (1992)

Secondary education — *Enseignement secondaire*

Tertiary education — *Enseignement supérieur*

* Public institutions only

* *Etablissements publics seulement*

F05: Current and capital expenditure

EDUCATIONAL EXPENDITURE BY RESOURCE CATEGORY

POLICY ISSUES

Given the total funds available for education, each country's policy-makers must decide how to spend the funds most effectively. In particular, they must select appropriate mixes of personnel and other resources for their educational institutions.

KEY RESULTS

Countries have been compared with respect to, first, the division of spending between current and capital outlay and, second, the distribution of current expenditures among compensation of teaching personnel, compensation of non-teaching personnel, and spending for non-personnel resources. For the OECD area as a whole, about 91 per cent of spending for all levels of education combined is current expenditure and about 9 per cent is capital expenditure. The capital share is larger at the tertiary level than at the primary-secondary level for most countries.

Expenditures for staff compensation (including both salary and non-salary compensation) account for over 80 per cent of total current spending for primary-secondary education in most countries (the figure for the OECD area as a whole is 84 per cent). The reported staff compensation share of total current spending is substantially lower at the tertiary level – 72 per cent for the OECD area as a whole – but still exceeds 65 per cent in most countries.

The fraction of total current expenditure spent on teaching staff is, for the OECD area as a whole, 62 per cent at the primary-secondary level and 47 per cent at the tertiary level.

DESCRIPTION AND INTERPRETATION

There is a wide variation among countries with regard to percentages of capital spending. At the primary-secondary level, the reported capital share ranges from below 3.5 per cent (Belgium, Ireland, Italy and Portugal) to over 11 per cent in Austria and Hungary and more than 16 per cent in Japan. At the tertiary level, some countries report capital shares of just over 5 per cent (Canada, Finland and the United Kingdom), whereas others report 18 per cent or more (Austria, Italy, Spain and Switzerland). These variations may be due partly to definitional differences among the countries.

Most countries report that staff compensation accounts for between 80 and 95 per cent of current spending for primary and secondary institutions, and between 65 and 75 per cent of current spending for tertiary institutions. Substantially lower staff compensation percentages are reported by Denmark, Japan and the United Kingdom at the primary-secondary level and by Austria, Belgium Denmark, Japan and Norway at the tertiary level.

The division of staff compensation expenditures between teaching and non-teaching staff is not clear-cut. Some countries define "teachers" narrowly, limiting the term to persons who teach students in the classroom; others use a broader definition that includes heads of schools and other professional personnel. Because of these (and other) definitional differences, the wide variations in reported percentages of expenditures for non-teaching staff should be viewed with caution. In the case of primary and secondary education, these percentages range from less than 2 per cent in Belgium and less than 4 per cent in Ireland to about 25 per cent in Denmark and the United States.

DEFINITIONS

The current and capital shares of expenditures are the percentages of total expenditures for the level of education in question, reported as current expenditures and capital expenditures, respectively. Only expenditures for educational institutions are considered in these calculations; subsidies for student living expenses are excluded.

Calculations cover the expenditures of public institutions or, where available, those of public institutions and government-dependent private institutions combined.

The shares of current expenditure allocated to compensation of teachers, compensation of other staff, total staff compensation, and other (non-personnel) current outlays are calculated by expressing the respective amounts as percentages of total current expenditures. In some cases, compensation of teaching staff means compensation of classroom teachers only, but in others it includes that of heads of schools and other professional educators.

F05: Current and capital expenditure

F05 : Dépenses de fonctionnement et dépenses en capital

Table F05(1):
Expenditure by resource category for primary and secondary education in public and government-dependent private institutions (1992)

Tableau F05(1) :
Dépenses d'éducation par nature pour l'enseignement primaire et secondaire, établissements publics et privés subventionnés (1992)

	Percentage of total expenditure / *Répartition des dépenses totales*			Percentage of current expenditure / *Répartition des dépenses de fonctionnement*			
	Current / *Fonctionnement*	Capital / *Capital*	Compensation of teachers / *Rémunération des enseignants*	Compensation of other staff / *Rémunération des autres personnels*	Compensation of all staff / *Rémunération de l'ensemble du personnel*	Other current expenditure / *Autres dépenses de fonctionnement*	
North America							*Amérique du Nord*
Canada	...	...	...	...	...	...	*Canada*
United States	91.2	8.8	61.4	25.1	86.5	13.5	*États-Unis*
Pacific Area							*Pays du Pacifique*
Australia	...	...	...	...	...	...	*Australie*
Japan (PUB)	83.7	16.3	56.6	11.3	67.9	32.1	*(PUB) Japon*
New Zealand	...	...	...	...	...	...	*Nouvelle-Zélande*
European Community							*Communauté européenne*
Belgium	99.6	0.4	82.2	1.2	83.4	16.6	*Belgique*
Denmark (PUB)	94.0	6.0	49.2	25.6	74.8	25.2	*(PUB) Danemark*
France	90.5	9.5	...	...	86.1	13.9	*France*
Germany (FTFR) (PUB)	93.0	7.0	...	...	87.8	12.2	*(PUB) Allemagne (ex-terr. de la RFA)*
Germany	...	...	...	...	...	...	*Allemagne*
Greece	...	...	...	...	...	...	*Grèce*
Ireland (PUB)	96.9	3.1	86.5	3.9	90.3	9.7	*(PUB) Irlande*
Italy (PUB)	96.7	3.3	78.9	15.7	94.6	5.4	*(PUB) Italie*
Luxembourg	...	...	...	...	...	...	*Luxembourg*
Netherlands	95.1	4.9	...	...	81.2	18.8	*Pays-Bas*
Portugal (PUB)	96.5	3.5	...	...	97.9	2.1	*(PUB) Portugal*
Spain	91.8	8.2	...	...	87.2	12.8	*Espagne*
United Kingdom	94.9	5.1	59.7	15.8	75.5	24.5	*Royaume-Uni*
Other Europe - OECD							*Autres pays d'Europe - OCDE*
Austria	88.9	11.1	70.9	11.2	82.1	17.9	*Autriche*
Finland	95.7	4.3	66.5	16.4	82.9	17.1	*Finlande*
Iceland	...	...	...	...	...	...	*Islande*
Norway (PUB)	96.0	4.0	...	...	78.3	21.7	*(PUB) Norvège*
Sweden	...	...	...	...	...	...	*Suède*
Switzerland (PUB)	93.2	6.8	82.8	7.7	90.5	9.5	*(PUB) Suisse*
Turkey	...	...	...	...	...	...	*Turquie*
Country mean	**93.6**	**6.4**	**69.5**	**13.4**	**84.2**	**15.8**	*Moyenne des pays*
OECD total	**91.1**	**8.9**	**62.5**	**20.3**	**83.6**	**16.4**	*Total OCDE*
Central and Eastern Europe							*Europe centrale et orientale*
Czech Republic (PUB)	89.5	10.5	...	...	44.3	55.7	*(PUB) République tchèque*
Hungary	88.3	11.7	...	...	...	...	*Hongrie*
Poland	...	...	...	...	...	...	*Pologne*
Russia	...	...	...	...	...	...	*Russie*

See Annex 1 for notes
(PUB) means that percentages refer to shares of public expenditure and enrolment only

Voir notes en annexe 1
(PUB) signifie que les pourcentages concernent uniquement les répartitions des dépenses et des effectifs des établissements publics

F05: Current and capital expenditure
F05 : Dépenses de fonctionnement et dépenses en capital

Table F05(2):
Expenditure by resource category for tertiary education in public and government-dependent private institutions (1992)

Tableau F05(2) :
Dépenses d'éducation par nature pour l'enseignement supérieur, établissements publics et privés subventionnés (1992)

	Percentage of total expenditure / Répartition des dépenses totales			Percentage of current expenditure / Répartition des dépenses de fonctionnement			
	Current / Fonctionnement	Capital / Capital	Compensation of teachers / Rémunération des enseignants	Compensation of other staff / Rémunération des autres personnels	Compensation of all staff / Rémunération de l'ensemble du personnel	Other current expenditure / Autres dépenses de fonctionnement	
North America							*Amérique du Nord*
Canada	94.7	5.3	40.3	25.8	66.1	33.9	*Canada*
United States	92.4	7.6	50.4	23.2	73.6	26.4	*Etats-Unis*
Pacific Area							*Pays du Pacifique*
Australia	...	...	...	...	...	...	*Australie*
Japan (PUB)	86.5	13.5	41.6	17.6	59.2	40.8	*(PUB) Japon*
New Zealand	...	...	...	...	...	...	*Nouvelle-Zélande*
European Community							*Communauté européenne*
Belgium	99.0	1.0	57.6	0.3	58.0	42.0	*Belgique*
Denmark (PUB)	85.5	14.5	42.1	17.9	60.0	40.0	*(PUB) Danemark*
France	91.0	9.0	...	...	72.6	27.4	*France*
Germany (FTFR) (PUB)	87.6	12.4	...	...	75.9	24.1	*(PUB) Allemagne (ex-terr. de la RFA)*
Germany	...	...	...	...	...	...	*Allemagne*
Greece	...	...	...	...	...	...	*Grèce*
Ireland (PUB)	89.3	10.7	53.3	21.7	75.0	25.0	*(PUB) Irlande*
Italy (PUB)	70.7	29.3	32.2	35.7	67.8	32.2	*(PUB) Italie*
Luxembourg	...	...	...	...	...	...	*Luxembourg*
Netherlands	93.1	6.9	...	...	71.2	28.8	*Pays-Bas*
Portugal (PUB)	82.5	17.5	...	...	72.1	27.9	*(PUB) Portugal*
Spain	80.0	20.0	...	...	80.6	19.4	*Espagne*
United Kingdom	94.6	5.4	45.7	29.3	75.1	24.9	*Royaume-Uni*
Other Europe - OECD							*Autres pays d'Europe - OCDE*
Austria	80.8	19.2	32.3	23.5	55.9	44.1	*Autriche*
Finland	94.8	5.2	46.0	19.4	65.4	34.6	*Finlande*
Iceland	...	...	...	...	...	...	*Islande*
Norway (PUB)	84.1	15.9	...	...	64.7	35.3	*(PUB) Norvège*
Sweden	...	...	...	...	...	...	*Suède*
Switzerland (PUB)	80.2	19.8	58.2	25.0	83.2	16.8	*(PUB) Suisse*
Turkey	...	...	...	...	...	...	*Turquie*
Country mean	**87.5**	**12.5**	**45.4**	**21.8**	**69.2**	**30.8**	***Moyenne des pays***
OECD total	**90.2**	**9.8**	**47.3**	**23.8**	**71.8**	**28.2**	***Total OCDE***
Central and Eastern Europe							*Europe centrale et orientale*
Czech Republic (PUB)	88.6	11.4	...	...	47.9	52.1	*(PUB) République tchèque*
Hungary	90.7	9.3	...	...	...	...	*Hongrie*
Poland	...	...	...	...	...	...	*Pologne*
Russia	...	...	...	...	...	...	*Russie*

See Annex 1 for notes
(PUB) means that percentages refer to shares of public expenditure and enrolment only

Voir notes en annexe 1
(PUB) signifie que les pourcentages concernent uniquement les répartitions des dépenses et des effectifs des établissements publics

F05: Current and capital expenditure
F05 : Dépenses de fonctionnement et dépenses en capital

Table F05(3):
Expenditure by resource category for all levels of education combined in public and government-dependent private institutions (1992)

Tableau F05(3) :
Dépenses d'éducation par nature pour tous les niveaux scolaires confondus, établissements publics et privés subventionnés (1992)

	Current / Fonctionnement	Capital / Capital	Compensation of teachers / Rémunération des enseignants	Compensation of other staff / Rémunération des autres personnels	Compensation of all staff / Rémunération de l'ensemble du personnel	Other current expenditure / Autres dépenses de fonctionnement	
Percentage of total expenditure							
Percentage of current expenditure							
North America							*Amérique du Nord*
Canada	93.1	6.9	54.1	20.2	74.3	25.7	*Canada*
United States	91.6	8.4	58.4	24.6	83.0	17.0	*Etats-Unis*
Pacific Area							*Pays du Pacifique*
Australia	...	...	...	...	...	...	*Australie*
Japan (PUB)	84.9	15.1	50.9	15.0	65.9	34.1	*(PUB) Japon*
New Zealand	...	...	...	...	...	...	*Nouvelle-Zélande*
European Community							*Communauté européenne*
Belgium	98.9	1.1	75.7	2.6	78.4	21.6	*Belgique*
Denmark (PUB)	92.9	7.1	47.8	23.9	71.7	28.3	*(PUB) Danemark*
France	91.6	8.4	...	...	83.5	16.5	*France*
Germany (FTFR) (PUB)	90.9	9.1	...	...	83.4	16.6	*(PUB) Allemagne (ex-terr. de la RFA)*
Germany	...	...	...	...	...	...	*Allemagne*
Greece	...	...	...	...	...	...	*Grèce*
Ireland (PUB)	95.1	4.9	77.8	8.5	86.3	13.7	*(PUB) Irlande*
Italy (PUB)	91.8	8.2	64.7	16.7	81.4	18.6	*(PUB) Italie*
Luxembourg	...	...	...	...	...	...	*Luxembourg*
Netherlands	94.6	5.4	...	...	76.5	23.5	*Pays-Bas*
Portugal (PUB)	93.4	6.6	...	...	92.1	7.9	*(PUB) Portugal*
Spain	89.7	10.3	...	...	86.0	14.0	*Espagne*
United Kingdom	94.9	5.1	57.7	17.7	75.4	24.6	*Royaume-Uni*
Other Europe - OECD							*Autres pays d'Europe - OCDE*
Austria	88.0	12.0	53.3	16.2	69.5	30.5	*Autriche*
Finland	96.0	4.0	58.9	18.0	76.9	23.1	*Finlande*
Iceland	...	...	...	...	...	...	*Islande*
Norway (PUB)	93.3	6.7	...	...	76.3	23.7	*(PUB) Norvège*
Sweden	...	...	...	...	...	...	*Suède*
Switzerland (PUB)	84.3	15.7	71.5	14.4	85.9	14.1	*(PUB) Suisse*
Turkey	...	...	...	...	...	...	*Turquie*
Country mean	**92.1**	**7.9**	**61.0**	**16.2**	**79.2**	**20.8**	***Moyenne des pays***
OECD total	**91.0**	**9.0**	**57.7**	**21.1**	**79.8**	**20.2**	***Total OCDE***
Central and Eastern Europe							*Europe centrale et orientale*
Czech Republic (PUB)	90.0	10.0	...	...	46.4	53.6	*(PUB) République tchèque*
Hungary	89.6	10.4	...	...	...	...	*Hongrie*
Poland	...	...	...	...	...	...	*Pologne*
Russia	...	...	...	...	...	...	*Russie*

See Annex 1 for notes
(PUB) means that percentages refer to shares of public expenditure and enrolment only

Voir notes en annexe 1
(PUB) signifie que les pourcentages concernent uniquement les répartitions des dépenses et des effectifs des établissements publics

F05: Current and capital expenditure

F05 : Dépenses de fonctionnement et dépenses en capital

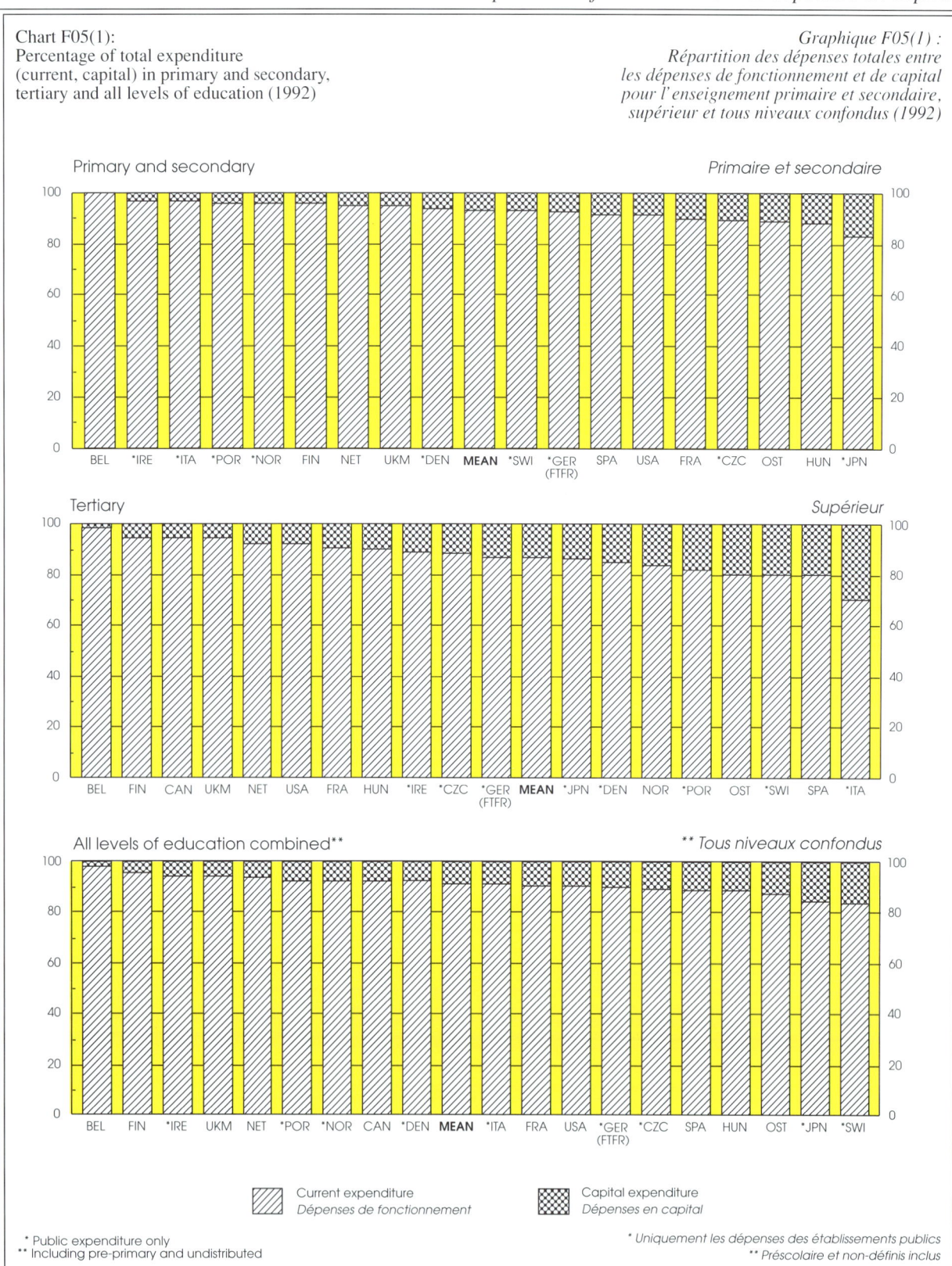

Chart F05(1):
Percentage of total expenditure (current, capital) in primary and secondary, tertiary and all levels of education (1992)

Graphique F05(1) :
Répartition des dépenses totales entre les dépenses de fonctionnement et de capital pour l'enseignement primaire et secondaire, supérieur et tous niveaux confondus (1992)

Primary and secondary — *Primaire et secondaire*

Countries (left to right): BEL, *IRE, *ITA, *POR, *NOR, FIN, NET, UKM, *DEN, **MEAN**, *SWI, *GER (FTFR), SPA, USA, FRA, *CZC, OST, HUN, *JPN

Tertiary — *Supérieur*

Countries (left to right): BEL, FIN, CAN, UKM, NET, USA, FRA, HUN, *IRE, *CZC, *GER (FTFR), **MEAN**, *JPN, *DEN, NOR, *POR, OST, *SWI, SPA, *ITA

All levels of education combined** — *** Tous niveaux confondus*

Countries (left to right): BEL, FIN, *IRE, UKM, NET, *POR, *NOR, CAN, *DEN, **MEAN**, *ITA, FRA, USA, *GER (FTFR), *CZC, SPA, HUN, OST, *JPN, *SWI

Legend:
- ▨ Current expenditure / *Dépenses de fonctionnement*
- ▦ Capital expenditure / *Dépenses en capital*

* Public expenditure only
** Including pre-primary and undistributed

* Uniquement les dépenses des établissements publics
** Préscolaire et non-définis inclus

F05: Current and capital expenditure

F05 : Dépenses de fonctionnement et dépenses en capital

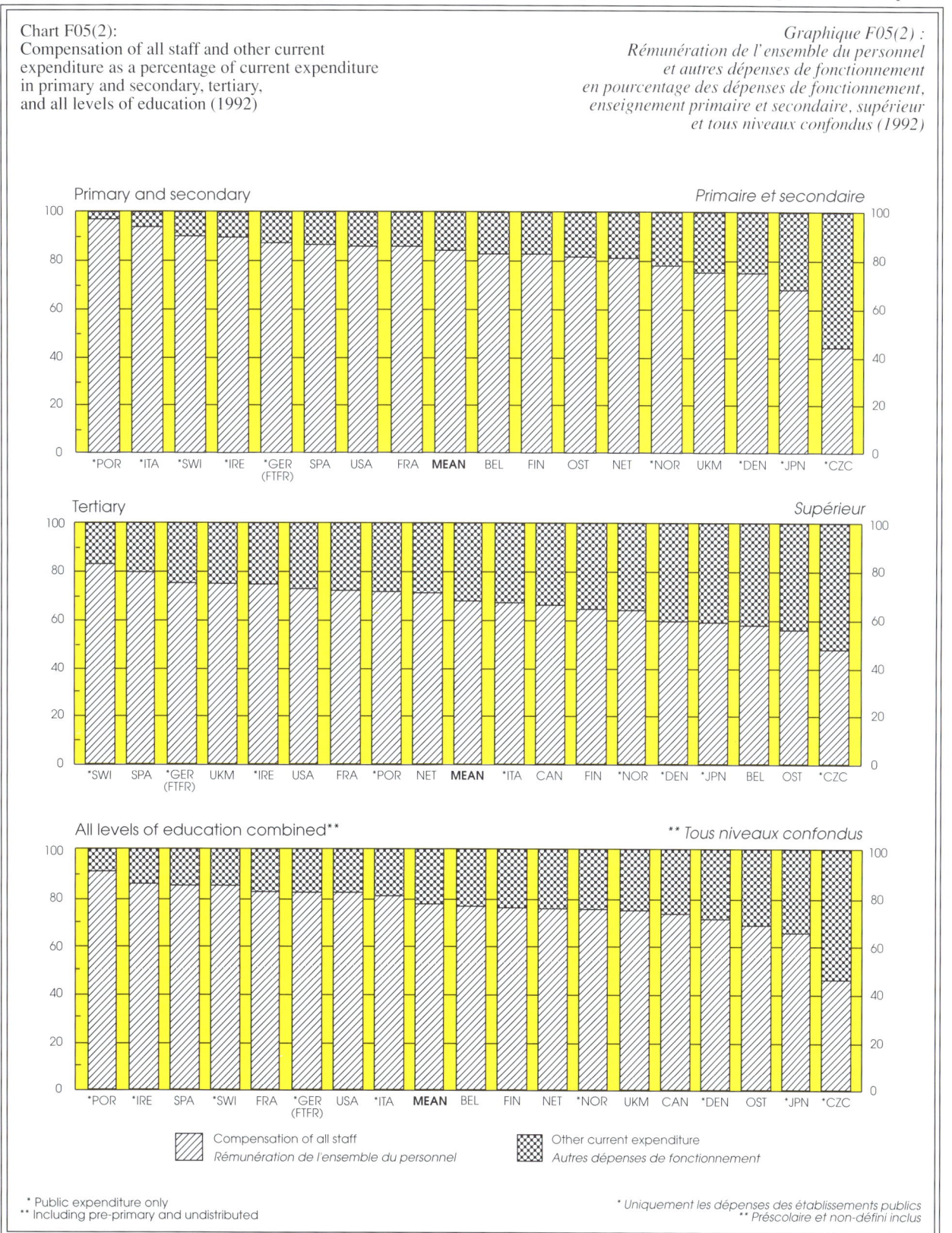

Chart F05(2):
Compensation of all staff and other current expenditure as a percentage of current expenditure in primary and secondary, tertiary, and all levels of education (1992)

Graphique F05(2) :
Rémunération de l'ensemble du personnel et autres dépenses de fonctionnement en pourcentage des dépenses de fonctionnement, enseignement primaire et secondaire, supérieur et tous niveaux confondus (1992)

Primary and secondary — Primaire et secondaire
*POR, *ITA, *SWI, *IRE, *GER (FTFR), SPA, USA, FRA, MEAN, BEL, FIN, OST, NET, *NOR, UKM, *DEN, *JPN, *CZC

Tertiary — Supérieur
*SWI, SPA, *GER (FTFR), UKM, *IRE, USA, FRA, *POR, NET, MEAN, *ITA, CAN, FIN, *NOR, *DEN, *JPN, BEL, OST, *CZC

All levels of education combined** — ** Tous niveaux confondus
*POR, *IRE, SPA, *SWI, FRA, *GER (FTFR), USA, *ITA, MEAN, BEL, FIN, NET, *NOR, UKM, CAN, *DEN, OST, *JPN, *CZC

Compensation of all staff / Rémunération de l'ensemble du personnel
Other current expenditure / Autres dépenses de fonctionnement

* Public expenditure only
** Including pre-primary and undistributed

* Uniquement les dépenses des établissements publics
** Préscolaire et non-défini inclus

107

F11: Funds from public and private sources

FUNDS FROM PUBLIC AND PRIVATE SOURCES

POLICY ISSUES

A vigorously debated issue in some countries is whether or to what degree the costs of education should be borne by the individuals who benefit rather than by society as a whole. This question is especially relevant at the beginning and end stages of education – early childhood education on one hand, and tertiary education on the other – where the practice of full or near-full public funding is less dominant than at the primary and secondary levels.

KEY RESULTS

The following results pertain only to the relatively few countries – eight in the case of primary and secondary education, eleven in the case of tertiary – that have provided reasonably complete data on education expenditures from private sources.

The average share of education funds generated in the private sector (all levels of education combined) is 8 per cent, and the average private share of final expenditures (counting funds transferred from the public sector) is 16.0 per cent.

Private funding plays a much more important role in tertiary education than at any other level. On average, 13.9 per cent of all tertiary spending originates in the private sector. The private share of final expenditures for tertiary education (counting scholarships and other subsidies to students) averages 31.5 per cent.

DESCRIPTION AND INTERPRETATION

Because many countries have been unable to provide complete (or, in some cases, any) data on education funds from private sources, this indicator has been calculated for only a minority of the OECD countries. It is expected that more countries will be able to provide data on private expenditures in the future.

Among the countries represented, the shares of education funds originating in the private sector (all levels of education combined) range from 1.6 per cent in Sweden and 2.9 per cent in Denmark to 22.6 per cent in the United States and 24.0 per cent in Japan.

The private shares of final education expenditures are higher than the initial shares because the former reflect funds that are transferred to as well as generated in the private sector; the former are found mainly in the form of scholarships and other subsidies for students. The private shares of expenditures (for all levels of education combined) after transfers range from 7.0 per cent in Canada and 8.8 per cent in France to over 24 per cent in both the United States and Japan. The Nordic countries, the Netherlands and Australia have very small initial private shares, but substantial private shares after transfers.

Countries differ greatly in the degree of private funding of tertiary education. Only very small shares originate in the private sector in Australia, Canada, Denmark and Sweden. In contrast, over 45 per cent of all tertiary spending in the United States and over 60 per cent of all tertiary spending in Japan derives from private sources.

The final private shares of tertiary spending are sharply higher than the initial private shares in most cases. For example, the initial and final private shares in Denmark are 1.2 per cent and 37.9 per cent, respectively. The differences are accounted for by public subsidies to students or households, most of which are subsidies for student living expenses. Note that the figures on private spending do not include student living expenses (for housing, meals, etc.) *except* to the extent that they are publicly subsidised. If all living expenses were included, the private shares of both initial and final tertiary spending would be much higher. If student living expenses were excluded entirely from the calculations (regardless of whether they were subsidised), the initial and final private shares of spending would differ only slightly.

The main indicator tables do not take into account direct household purchases of educational goods and services – e.g. purchases of books, paper, calculators, school uniforms and other personal items used at school. Most countries have no data on the costs of these items, but a few have developed estimates from household surveys. Table F11(B) shows the effects of including the direct purchases for four countries with such surveys. The result is to raise the private shares of initial spending (all levels of education combined) of Canada, France and the United States by 2 to 3 percentage points, and the private share of Spain by more than 7 percentage points. Some of the effects on private shares of tertiary spending are considerably greater. It is reasonable to conclude that the omis-

F11: Funds from public and private sources

sion of direct purchases results in substantial understatement of the private sector's contribution to education spending.

DEFINITIONS

The initial public and private shares of education funds are the percentages of total education spending originating in, or generated by, the public and private sectors. Total education spending is here defined as total expenditures for educational institutions plus the publicly subsidised portion of student living expenses. Initial public spending includes both direct public expenditures for educational institutions and transfers to the private sector. Initial private spending includes tuition fees and other student or household payments to educational institutions, *less* the portion of such payments offset by public subsidies.

The final public and private shares are the percentages of education funds expended directly by public and private purchasers of educational services. Final public spending includes direct public purchases of educational resources and payments to educational institutions, but excludes transfers to households and other private entities. Final private spending includes tuition fees and other private payments to educational institutions (whether or not offset by public subsidies), plus the publicly subsidised portion of student living expenses.

Direct household purchases of educational goods and services are excluded from the main calculations of initial and final shares, but are reflected in Table F11(B) covering the four countries for which data on direct purchases are available.

F11: Funds from public and private sources

F11 : Fonds publics et fonds privés

Table F11(A1):
Shares of funds from public and private sources
for primary and secondary education (1992)

Tableau F11(A1) :
Répartition par source des financements publics et privés
de l'enseignement primaire et secondaire (1992)

in %	Initial funds (before transfers between levels of government and from public-to-private) *Sources initiales (avant transferts entre échelons administratifs et du public au privé)* Public sources *Financement public*	Private sources *Financement privé*	Final funds (after transfers between levels of government and from public-to-private) *Sources finales (après transferts entre échelons administratifs et du public au privé)* Public sources *Financement public*	Private sources *Financement privé*	en %
North America					*Amérique du Nord*
Canada	95.5	4.5	95.5	4.5	*Canada*
United State	90.9	9.1	90.9	9.1	*Etats-Unis*
Pacific Area					*Pays du Pacifique*
Australia	...	...	...	...	*Australie*
Japan	91.1	8.9	91.1	8.9	*Japon*
New Zealand	...	...	...	...	*Nouvelle-Zélande*
European Community					*Communauté européenne*
Belgium	...	...	...	...	*Belgique*
Denmark	100.0		88.4	11.6	*Danemark*
France	93.4	6.6	92.1	7.9	*France*
Germany (FTFR)	...	...	...	...	*Allemagne (ex-terr. de la RFA)*
Germany	...	...	...	...	*Allemagne*
Greece	...	...	...	...	*Grèce*
Ireland	...	...	...	...	*Irlande*
Italy	...	...	...	...	*Italie*
Luxembourg	...	...	...	...	*Luxembourg*
Netherlands	100.0	-	88.1	11.9	*Pays-Bas*
Portugal	...	...	...	...	*Portugal*
Spain	87.8	12.2	86.4	13.6	*Espagne*
United Kingdom	...	...	...	...	*Royaume-Uni*
Other Europe - OECD					*Autres pays d'Europe - OCDE*
Austria	...	...	...	...	*Autriche*
Finland	...	...	...	...	*Finlande*
Iceland	...	...	...	...	*Islande*
Norway	...	...	...	...	*Norvège*
Sweden	100.0	-	91.3	8.7	*Suède*
Switzerland	...	...	...	...	*Suisse*
Turkey	...	...	...	...	*Turquie*
Country mean	**94.8**	**5.2**	**90.5**	**9.5**	***Moyenne des pays***
Central and Eastern Europe					*Europe centrale et orientale*
Czech Republic	...	...	...	...	*République tchèque*
Hungary	...	...	...	...	*Hongrie*
Poland	...	...	...	...	*Pologne*
Russia	...	...	...	...	*Russie*

See Annex 1 for notes

Voir notes en annexe 1

F11: Funds from public and private sources

F11 : Fonds publics et fonds privés

Table F11(A2):
Shares of funds from public and private sources
for tertiary education (1992)

*Tableau F11(A2) :
Répartition par source des financements publics et privés
de l'enseignement supérieur (1992)*

in %	Initial funds (before transfers between levels of government and from public-to-private) *Sources initiales (avant transferts entre échelons administratifs et du public au privé)*		Final funds (after transfers between levels of government and from public-to-private) *Sources finales (après transferts entre échelons administratifs et du public au privé)*		en %
	Public sources *Financement public*	Private sources *Financement privé*	Public sources *Financement public*	Private sources *Financement privé*	
North America					*Amérique du Nord*
Canada	97.4	2.6	84.7	15.3	*Canada*
United States	54.5	45.5	49.6	50.4	*Etats-Unis*
Pacific Area					*Pays du Pacifique*
Australia	100.0	-	78.1	21.9	*Australie*
Japan	39.7	60.3	39.7	60.3	*Japon*
New Zealand	...	...	...	...	*Nouvelle-Zélande*
European Community					*Communauté européenne*
Belgium	...	...	...	...	*Belgique*
Denmark	98.8	1.2	62.1	37.9	*Danemark*
France	91.1	8.9	83.7	16.3	*France*
Germany (FTFR)	...	...	...	...	*Allemagne (ex-terr. de la RFA)*
Germany	...	...	...	...	*Allemagne*
Greece	...	...	...	...	*Grèce*
Ireland	83.3	16.7	66.8	33.2	*Irlande*
Italy	...	...	...	...	*Italie*
Luxembourg	...	...	...	...	*Luxembourg*
Netherlands	100.0	-	70.5	29.5	*Pays-Bas*
Portugal	...	...	...	...	*Portugal*
Spain	83.4	16.6	77.2	22.8	*Espagne*
United Kingdom	100.0	-	77.7	22.3	*Royaume-Uni*
Other Europe - OECD					*Autres pays d'Europe - OCDE*
Austria	...	...	...	...	*Autriche*
Finland	...	...	...	...	*Finlande*
Iceland	...	...	...	...	*Islande*
Norway	...	...	...	...	*Norvège*
Sweden	99.3	0.7	62.9	37.1	*Suède*
Switzerland	...	...	...	...	*Suisse*
Turkey	...	...	...	...	*Turquie*
Country mean	**86.1**	**13.9**	**68.5**	**31.5**	*Moyenne des pays*
Central and Eastern Europe					*Europe centrale et orientale*
Czech Republic	...	...	...	...	*République tchèque*
Hungary	...	...	...	...	*Hongrie*
Poland	...	...	...	...	*Pologne*
Russia	...	...	...	...	*Russie*

See Annex 1 for notes

Voir notes en annexe 1

F11: Funds from public and private sources

F11 : Fonds publics et fonds privés

Table F11(A3):
Shares of funds from public and private sources
for all levels of education combined (1992)

Tableau F11(A3) :
Répartition par source des financements publics et privés
de l'enseignement, tous niveaux scolaires confondus (1992)

in %	Initial funds (before transfers between levels of government and from public-to-private) / Sources initiales (avant transferts entre échelons administratifs et du public au privé) Public sources / Financement public	Private sources / Financement privé	Final funds (after transfers between levels of government and from public-to-private) / Sources finales (après transferts entre échelons administratifs et du public au privé) Public sources / Financement public	Private sources / Financement privé	en %
North America					**Amérique du Nord**
Canada	97.3	2.7	93.0	7.0	Canada
United States	77.4	22.6	75.6	24.4	Etats-Unis
Pacific Area					**Pays du Pacifique**
Australia	100.0	-	86.5	13.5	Australie
Japan	76.0	24.0	75.7	24.3	Japon
New Zealand	...	...	...	...	Nouvelle-Zélande
European Community					**Communauté européenne**
Belgium	...	...	...	...	Belgique
Denmark	97.1	2.9	78.6	21.4	Danemark
France	93.3	6.7	91.2	8.8	France
Germany (FTFR)	...	...	...	...	Allemagne (ex-terr. de la RFA)
Germany	...	...	...	...	Allemagne
Greece	...	...	...	...	Grèce
Ireland	93.1	6.9	86.5	13.5	Irlande
Italy	...	...	...	...	Italie
Luxembourg	...	...	...	...	Luxembourg
Netherlands	100.0	-	83.5	16.5	Pays-Bas
Portugal	...	...	...	...	Portugal
Spain	86.3	13.7	84.1	15.9	Espagne
United Kingdom	...	...	...	...	Royaume-Uni
Other Europe - OECD					**Autres pays d'Europe - OCDE**
Austria	...	...	...	...	Autriche
Finland	...	...	...	...	Finlande
Iceland	...	...	...	...	Islande
Norway	...	...	...	...	Norvège
Sweden	98.4	1.6	85.3	14.7	Suède
Switzerland	...	...	...	...	Suisse
Turkey	...	...	...	...	Turquie
Country mean	**91.9**	**8.1**	**84.0**	**16.0**	**Moyenne des pays**
Central and Eastern Europe					**Europe centrale et orientale**
Czech Republic	...	...	...	...	République tchèque
Hungary	...	...	...	...	Hongrie
Poland	...	...	...	...	Pologne
Russia	...	...	...	...	Russie

See Annex 1 for notes

Voir notes en annexe 1

F11: Funds from public and private sources
F11 : Fonds publics et fonds privés

Table F11(B):
Private shares of funds by level of education excluding or including direct household purchases (1992)

Tableau F11(B) :
Répartition des financements privés de l'enseignement avec ou sans les données sur les achats directs par les ménages (1992)

	Initial funds (before transfers between levels of government and from public-to-private) / *Sources initiales (avant transferts entre échelons administratifs et du public au privé)*			Final funds (after transfers between levels of government and from public-to-private) / *Sources finales (après transferts entre échelons administratifs et du public au privé)*			
	Primary and secondary education / *Enseignement primaire et secondaire*	Tertiary education / *Enseignement supérieur*	All levels of education / *Tous niveaux confondus*	Primary and secondary education / *Enseignement primaire et secondaire*	Tertiary education / *Enseignement supérieur*	All levels of education / *Tous niveaux confondus*	
Canada							*Canada*
excluding DHP	4.5	2.6	2.7	4.5	15.3	7.0	*avec ADM*
including DHP	5.8	8.1	5.5	5.8	20.1	9.7	*sans ADM*
France							*France*
excluding DHP	6.6	8.9	6.7	7.9	16.3	8.8	*avec ADM*
including DHP	9.6	15.2	10.1	10.9	22.0	12.2	*sans ADM*
Spain							*Espagne*
excluding DHP	12.2	16.6	13.7	13.6	22.8	15.9	*avec ADM*
including DHP	18.3	23.8	21.2	19.6	29.4	23.3	*sans ADM*
United States							*Etats-Unis*
excluding DHP	9.1	45.5	22.6	9.1	50.4	24.4	*avec ADM*
including DHP	9.6	48.2	24.4	9.6	52.9	26.1	*sansADM*

See Annex 1 for notes
DHP: Direct household purchases

Voir notes en annexe 1
ADM : Achats directs par les ménages

F11: Funds from public and private sources

F11 : Fonds publics et fonds privés

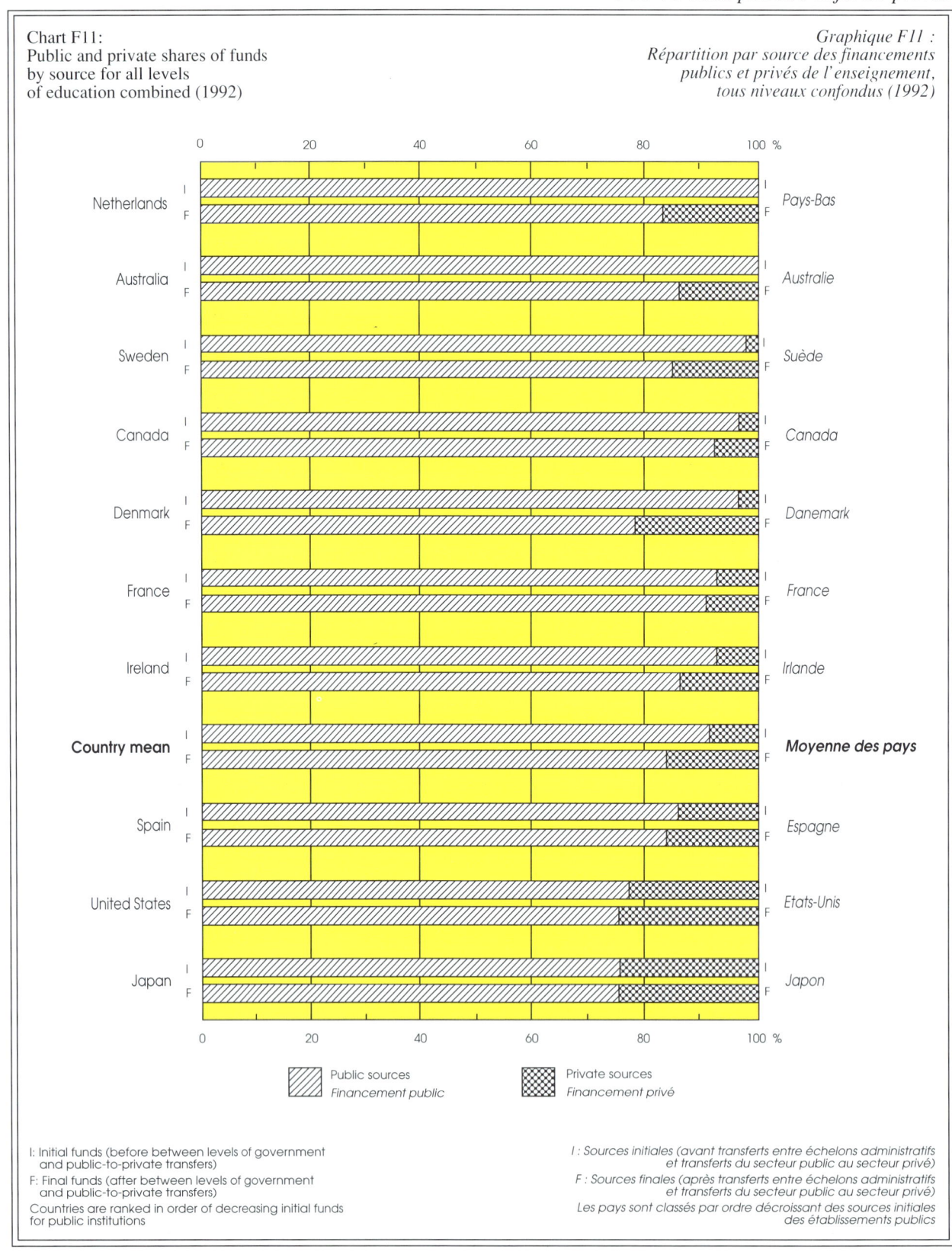

Chart F11:
Public and private shares of funds by source for all levels of education combined (1992)

Graphique F11 :
Répartition par source des financements publics et privés de l'enseignement, tous niveaux confondus (1992)

Netherlands	I / F		Pays-Bas
Australia	I / F		Australie
Sweden	I / F		Suède
Canada	I / F		Canada
Denmark	I / F		Danemark
France	I / F		France
Ireland	I / F		Irlande
Country mean	I / F		**Moyenne des pays**
Spain	I / F		Espagne
United States	I / F		Etats-Unis
Japan	I / F		Japon

Public sources / *Financement public*
Private sources / *Financement privé*

I: Initial funds (before between levels of government and public-to-private transfers)
F: Final funds (after between levels of government and public-to-private transfers)
Countries are ranked in order of decreasing initial funds for public institutions

I : Sources initiales (avant transferts entre échelons administratifs et transferts du secteur public au secteur privé)
F : Sources finales (après transferts entre échelons administratifs et transferts du secteur public au secteur privé)
Les pays sont classés par ordre décroissant des sources initiales des établissements publics

F12: Public funds by level of government

EDUCATIONAL EXPENDITURE BY INITIAL SOURCE OF FUNDS

POLICY ISSUES

Several OECD countries have acted recently to decentralise educational decision-making within the public sector, and others are considering decentralisation measures. An important element of this process is the division of responsibility for, and control over, the funding of education among national, regional and local authorities.

KEY RESULTS

Countries vary widely in how they divide the public sector's responsibility for financing education. In many cases, this division also differs sharply between the primary-secondary and tertiary education sectors of the same country.

Among the diverse patterns observed at the primary-secondary level are the following:
• the central government is both the main initial source and the main final spender of education funds;
• central government is the main initial source but regional or local authorities the main direct purchasers of educational resources;
• regional authorities are both the main initial sources and the main final purchasers;
• funding responsibilities are shared between regional and local authorities.

Usually – but with some notable exceptions – responsibility for financing education is more centralised at the tertiary level than at the primary or secondary levels. In most of the countries for which data are available, the central government has the dominant role as both initial source and final spender of tertiary funds. In a few countries, regional governments play the dominant role; in a third category, responsibilities are shared in various proportions between central government and regional or local authorities.

DESCRIPTION AND INTERPRETATION

Based on the percentages of public funds for primary and secondary education generated and spent by central, regional and local governments, countries can be grouped into the following categories:

1. Central government is both the main initial source and the main final spender of primary-secondary funds: France, Ireland, Italy, the Netherlands and New Zealand.
2. Central government is the main initial source of funds, but regional or local authorities are the main final purchasers of educational services: Austria, Finland, Hungary and the United Kingdom (a special case discussed below).
3. Regional governments are both the main initial sources and the main final spenders of primary-secondary funds: Australia, Belgium, Germany (FTFR) and Japan.
4. Most funding responsibilities are divided between regional and local authorities, with central government playing a minor role: Canada, Switzerland and the United States.
5. Central government shares with regional or local authorities the responsibility for both generating education funds and purchasing educational services: the Czech Republic, Denmark and Spain.

In the following countries, central government plays the dominant role in financing tertiary education, meaning that it is both the initial source and final spender of at least 60 per cent (but often close to 100 per cent) of all funds for tertiary education: Austria, the Czech Republic, Denmark, Finland, France, Hungary, Ireland, Italy, Japan, the Netherlands, New Zealand and the United Kingdom. In Australia, the central government generates most funds but regional governments are the main final spenders.

In Belgium, Canada and Germany (FTFR), regional authorities play the same dominant role as that played by central governments in the countries listed above.

In Spain, Switzerland and the United States, responsibilities for both generating funds and purchasing tertiary education services are shared between the central and regional governments.

Note, however, that these classifications do not take into account flows of general-purpose funds – that is, funds not specifically earmarked for education – from central to regional or local governments, or in some cases from regional governments to localities. If proportionate shares of these general-purpose transfers were attributed to education, the central government's role as initial pro-

F12: Public funds by level of government

vider of funds would appear substantially larger in such countries as Australia, Austria, Canada, Germany (FTFR) and Spain.

Two special cases deserve mention. First, the local authorities responsible for operating schools in the United Kingdom are financed mainly with central government funds. Although these funds consist principally of general-purpose grants and shared revenues, it seems appropriate in this comparison to count the United Kingdom as one of the countries in which the central government is the main source of education funds. Second, the main responsibility for financing education in Belgium is borne by the three language-based communities. Because the Belgian authorities classify the communities as regional governments, Belgium has been included among the countries that assign primary responsibility to regional units.

DEFINITIONS

The initial education expenditure of each level of government – also referred to as the expenditure originating at that level – is the total educational expenditure of all public authorities at the level in question (direct expenditures plus transfers between levels of government and transfers to the private sector), less the transfers received from governments at other levels. Shares of initial expenditure are calculated in relation to the total, consolidated expenditure of all three levels of government. Funds received from international sources have been counted as transfers received by the central government.

As already mentioned, only expenditures specifically designated for education are taken into account in determining initial shares. General-purpose transfers between levels of government, which provide much of the revenue of regional and local governments in some countries, have been excluded from the calculations.

The final expenditure of each level of government is the amount spent directly on educational services by all public authorities at that level. It does not include transfers to other levels of government or to households or other private entities. Shares of final expenditure are calculated in relation to the total direct expenditure for educational services of all levels of government combined.

For the public sector as a whole, final expenditure is less than initial expenditure because some funds generated there are transferred to, and ultimately used by, households and other private parties.

F12: Public funds by level of government

F12 : Financement public par niveau administratif

Table F12(1):
Sources of public funds by level of government
for primary and secondary education (1992)

Tableau F12(1) :
Financement public de l'enseignement par niveau administratif,
enseignement primaire et secondaire (1992)

in %	Sources of initial funds (before transfers between levels of government) *Sources initiales de financement (avant transferts entre échelons administratifs)*				Sources of final funds (after transfers between levels of government) *Sources finales de financement (après transferts entre échelons administratifs)*				en %
	Central	Regional	Local	Total	Central	Regional	Local	Total	
North America									*Amérique du Nord*
Canada	2.4	63.8	33.8	100.0	1.8	8.0	90.3	100.0	*Canada*
United States	7.6	47.9	44.5	100.0	0.8	0.4	98.8	100.0	*Etats-Unis*
Pacific Area									*Pays du Pacifique*
Australia	28.9	71.0	0.1	100.0	0.2	99.8	0.1	100.0	*Australie*
Japan	24.5	75.5	x	100.0	0.3	99.7	x	100.0	*Japon*
New Zealand	100.0	.	.	100.0	100.0	.	.	100.0	*Nouvelle-Zélande*
European Community									*Communauté européenne*
Belgium	x	95.7	4.3	100.0	x	93.5	6.5	100.0	*Belgique*
Denmark	28.4	11.4	60.2	100.0	25.9	13.2	60.8	100.0	*Danemark*
France	74.8	11.7	13.5	100.0	72.9	13.3	13.7	100.0	*France*
Germany (FTFR)	0.6	80.2	19.1	100.0	-	78.1	21.9	100.0	*Allemagne (ex-terr. de la RFA)*
Germany	...	...	...	...	...	...	...	...	*Allemagne*
Greece	...	...	...	...	...	...	...	...	*Grèce*
Ireland	95.7	.	0.1	100.0	84.4	.	15.6	100.0	*Irlande*
Italy	79.0	4.8	16.1	100.0	79.0	4.8	16.1	100.0	*Italie*
Luxembourg	...	...	...	...	...	...	...	...	*Luxembourg*
Netherlands	96.4	-	3.6	100.0	74.7	-	25.3	100.0	*Pays-Bas*
Portugal	...	...	...	...	...	...	...	...	*Portugal*
Spain	48.3	44.6	6.3	100.0	41.9	51.7	6.4	100.0	*Espagne*
United Kingdom	6.5	.	93.5	100.0	3.6	.	96.4	100.0	*Royaume-Uni*
Other Europe - OECD									*Autres pays d'Europe - OCDE*
Austria	69.4	10.4	20.2	100.0	31.8	42.8	25.4	100.0	*Autriche*
Finland	70.6	.	29.4	100.0	14.7	.	85.3	100.0	*Finlande*
Iceland	...	...	...	...	...	...	...	...	*Islande*
Norway	...	...	...	...	...	...	...	...	*Norvège*
Sweden	...	...	...	...	...	...	...	...	*Suède*
Switzerland	3.4	52.2	44.4	100.0	0.5	45.8	53.8	100.0	*Suisse*
Turkey	...	...	...	...	...	...	...	...	*Turquie*
Country mean	**43.4**	**33.5**	**22.9**	**100.0**	**31.3**	**32.4**	**36.2**	**100.0**	***Moyenne des pays***
Central and Eastern Europe									*Europe centrale et orientale*
Czech Republic	68.4	.	31.6	100.0	68.4	.	31.6	100.0	*République tchèque*
Hungary	71.8	x	28.2	100.0	4.1	x	95.9	100.0	*Hongrie*
Poland	...	...	...	...	...	...	...	...	*Pologne*
Russia	...	...	...	...	...	...	...	...	*Russie*

See Annex 1 for notes

Voir notes en annexe 1

F12: Public funds by level of government

F12 : Financement public par niveau administratif

Table F12(2):
Sources of public funds by level of government
for tertiary education (1992)

*Tableau F12(2) :
Financement public de l'enseignement par niveau
administratif, enseignement supérieur (1992)*

in %	Sources of initial funds (before transfers between levels of government) *Sources initiales de financement (avant transferts entre échelons administratifs)*				Sources of final funds (after transfers between levels of government) *Sources finales de financement (après transferts entre échelons administratifs)*				en %
	Central	Regional	Local	Total	Central	Regional	Local	Total	
North America									*Amérique du Nord*
Canada	29.4	70.6	.	100.0	24.5	75.5	.	100.0	*Canada*
United States	36.2	57.9	5.9	100.0	30.7	62.8	6.4	100.0	*Etats-Unis*
Pacific Area									*Pays du Pacifique*
Australia	73.5	26.4	.	100.0	5.4	94.6	.	100.0	*Australie*
Japan	86.0	14.0	x	100.0	85.7	14.3	x	100.0	*Japon*
New Zealand	100.0	.	.	100.0	100.0	.	.	100.0	*Nouvelle-Zélande*
European Community									*Communauté européenne*
Belgium	x	99.6	0.4	100.0	x	98.3	1.7	100.0	*Belgique*
Denmark	87.8	1.3	10.1	100.0	90.2	2.0	7.8	100.0	*Danemark*
France	91.6	4.8	3.6	100.0	90.9	5.2	3.9	100.0	*France*
Germany (FTFR)	16.0	83.1	0.8	100.0	1.4	97.7	1.0	100.0	*Allemagne (ex-terr. de la RFA)*
Germany	...	...	...	...	...	...	...	...	*Allemagne*
Greece	...	...	...	...	...	...	...	...	*Grèce*
Ireland	77.4	.	.	100.0	71.1	.	28.9	100.0	*Irlande*
Italy	99.6	-	0.6	100.0	100.0	.	.	100.0	*Italie*
Luxembourg	...	...	...	...	...	...	...	...	*Luxembourg*
Netherlands	100.1	-	-	100.0	98.2	-	1.8	100.0	*Pays-Bas*
Portugal	...	...	...	...	...	...	...	...	*Portugal*
Spain	49.0	50.0	0.9	100.0	45.6	53.4	1.0	100.0	*Espagne*
United Kingdom	93.6	.	6.4	100.0	63.9	.	36.1	100.0	*Royaume-Uni*
Other Europe - OECD									*Autres pays d'Europe - OCDE*
Austria	98.8	0.3	0.9	100.0	98.8	0.3	0.9	100.0	*Autriche*
Finland	91.7	.	8.3	100.0	84.5	.	15.5	100.0	*Finlande*
Iceland	...	...	...	...	...	...	...	...	*Islande*
Norway	...	...	...	...	...	...	...	...	*Norvège*
Sweden	...	...	...	...	...	...	...	...	*Suède*
Switzerland	44.5	54.7	0.7	100.0	35.1	63.6	1.2	100.0	*Suisse*
Turkey	...	...	...	...	...	...	...	...	*Turquie*
Country mean	**69.1**	**27.2**	**2.3**	**100.0**	**60.3**	**33.4**	**6.3**	**100.0**	*Moyenne des pays*
Central and Eastern Europe									*Europe centrale et orientale*
Czech Republic	100.0	.	x	100.0	100.0	.	-	100.0	*République tchèque*
Hungary	100.0	x	.	100.0	100.0	x	-	100.0	*Hongrie*
Poland	...	...	...	...	...	...	...	...	*Pologne*
Russia	...	...	...	...	...	...	...	...	*Russie*

See Annex 1 for notes

Voir notes en annexe 1

F12: Public funds by level of government

F12 : Financement public par niveau administratif

Table F12(3):
Sources of public funds by level of government
for all levels of education combined (1992)

Tableau F12(3) :
Financement public de l'enseignement par niveau
administratif, tous niveaux scolaires confondus (1992)

in %	\multicolumn{4}{c	}{Sources of initial funds (before transfers between levels of government) / *Sources initiales de financement (avant transferts entre échelons administratifs)*}	\multicolumn{4}{c	}{Sources of final funds (after transfers between levels of government) / *Sources finales de financement (après transferts entre échelons administratifs)*}	en %
	Central	Regional	Local	Total	Central	Regional	Local	Total	
North America									*Amérique du Nord*
Canada	11.5	66.1	22.8	100.4	8.8	28.7	62.5	100.0	*Canada*
United States	15.3	50.1	34.6	100.0	8.4	14.9	76.8	100.0	*Etats-Unis*
Pacific Area									*Pays du Pacifique*
Australia	43.5	56.9	0.1	100.5	3.4	96.4	0.2	100.0	*Australie*
Japan	30.0	70.0	x	100.0	9.9	90.1	x	100.0	*Japon*
New Zealand	100.0	.	.	100.0	100.0	.	.	100.0	*Nouvelle-Zélande*
European Community									*Communauté européenne*
Belgium	14.0	82.7	3.3	100.0	15.4	79.4	5.2	100.0	*Belgique*
Denmark	42.4	7.6	49.8	100.0	37.2	9.4	53.5	100.0	*Danemark*
France	75.5	9.2	15.3	100.0	73.9	10.4	15.7	100.0	*France*
Germany (FTFR)	5.4	76.7	17.9	100.0	1.2	77.7	21.1	100.0	*Allemagne (ex-terr. de la RFA)*
Germany	...	...	...	...	...	...	...	...	*Allemagne*
Greece	...	...	...	...	...	...	...	...	*Grèce*
Ireland	91.8	.	0.1	100.0	83.5	.	16.5	100.0	*Irlande*
Italy	76.5	5.6	17.9	100.0	77.3	3.4	19.3	100.0	*Italie*
Luxembourg	...	...	...	...	...	...	...	...	*Luxembourg*
Netherlands	96.2	0.1	3.8	100.0	79.8	0.1	20.1	100.0	*Pays-Bas*
Portugal	...	...	...	...	...	...	...	...	*Portugal*
Spain	47.1	46.8	5.5	100.0	41.7	52.7	5.6	100.0	*Espagne*
United Kingdom	24.2	.	75.8	100.0	13.7	.	86.3	100.0	*Royaume-Uni*
Other Europe - OECD									*Autres pays d'Europe - OCDE*
Austria	69.7	10.3	20.0	100.0	44.8	31.5	23.7	100.0	*Autriche*
Finland	73.8	.	26.2	100.0	31.4	.	68.6	100.0	*Finlande*
Iceland	...	...	...	...	...	...	...	...	*Islande*
Norway	...	...	...	...	...	...	...	...	*Norvège*
Sweden	...	...	...	...	...	...	...	...	*Suède*
Switzerland	11.9	53.0	35.2	100.0	7.7	49.1	43.2	100.0	*Suisse*
Turkey	...	...	...	...	...	...	...	...	*Turquie*
Country mean	**48.8**	**31.5**	**19.3**	**100.1**	**37.5**	**32.0**	**30.5**	**100.0**	***Moyenne des pays***
Central and Eastern Europe									*Europe centrale et orientale*
Czech Republic	74.2	.	25.8	100.0	74.1	.	25.9	100.0	*République tchèque*
Hungary	72.6	x	27.4	100.0	21.8	x	78.2	100.0	*Hongrie*
Poland	...	...	...	...	...	...	...	...	*Pologne*
Russia	...	...	...	...	...	...	...	...	*Russie*

See Annex 1 for notes

Voir notes en annexe 1

F12: Public funds by level of government

F12 : Financement public par niveau administratif

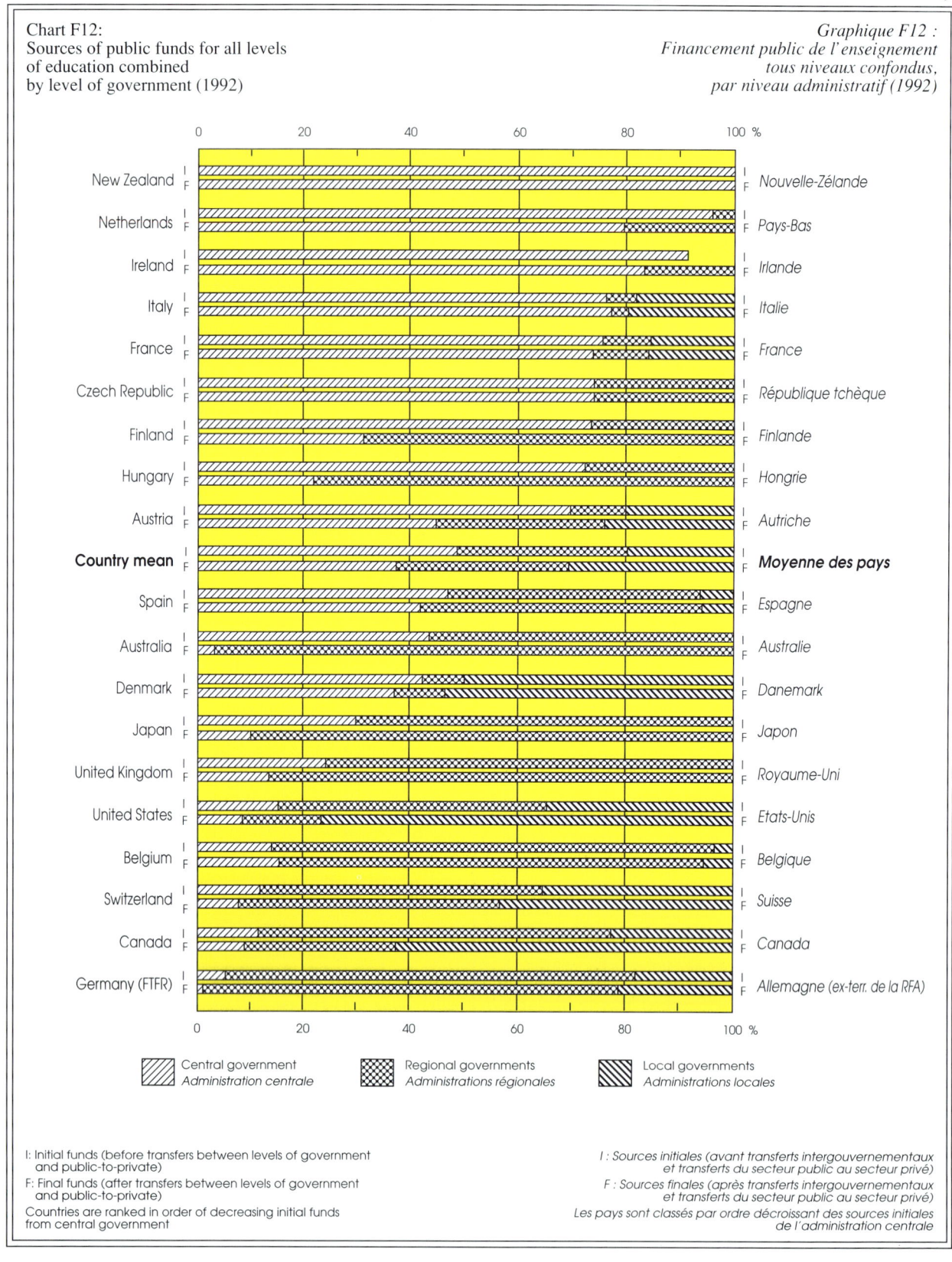

Chart F12:
Sources of public funds for all levels of education combined by level of government (1992)

Graphique F12 :
Financement public de l'enseignement tous niveaux confondus, par niveau administratif (1992)

New Zealand		Nouvelle-Zélande
Netherlands		Pays-Bas
Ireland		Irlande
Italy		Italie
France		France
Czech Republic		République tchèque
Finland		Finlande
Hungary		Hongrie
Austria		Autriche
Country mean		**Moyenne des pays**
Spain		Espagne
Australia		Australie
Denmark		Danemark
Japan		Japon
United Kingdom		Royaume-Uni
United States		Etats-Unis
Belgium		Belgique
Switzerland		Suisse
Canada		Canada
Germany (FTFR)		Allemagne (ex-terr. de la RFA)

Central government / *Administration centrale*
Regional governments / *Administrations régionales*
Local governments / *Administrations locales*

I: Initial funds (before transfers between levels of government and public-to-private)
F: Final funds (after transfers between levels of government and public-to-private)
Countries are ranked in order of decreasing initial funds from central government

I : Sources initiales (avant transferts intergouvernementaux et transferts du secteur public au secteur privé)
F : Sources finales (après transferts intergouvernementaux et transferts du secteur public au secteur privé)
Les pays sont classés par ordre décroissant des sources initiales de l'administration centrale

F13: Share of education in public spending

PUBLIC EXPENDITURE FOR EDUCATION RELATIVE TO TOTAL PUBLIC EXPENDITURE

POLICY ISSUES

Education must compete for public financial support against all the other areas for which government is responsible. Whether education should receive a larger or smaller share of the total public budget is an issue frequently debated everywhere.

KEY RESULTS

About 12 per cent of all public expenditure in a "typical" OECD country is devoted to education: 11 per cent is spent to support educational institutions, and 1 per cent consists of subsidies to the "private sector". On average, 7.9 per cent of total public spending is allocated to primary and secondary education and 2.8 per cent to tertiary education.

Most countries devote between 9 and 14 per cent of total government outlays to education. Primary-secondary education accounts for between 5.4 and 9.6 per cent of total public spending in most cases. The tertiary share is more variable, ranging between 1.5 and 4.9 per cent.

DESCRIPTION AND INTERPRETATION

The education share of the total public sector budget is lowest (below 10 per cent) in Germany (FTFR), Italy and the Netherlands. Those same countries also devote the smallest shares of the public budget to primary and secondary education. The percentage of total public spending allocated to education is highest (more than 14 per cent) in Australia, Canada, the Czech Republic, Hungary, Norway, Switzerland and the United States.

Canada and Australia also devote the largest fractions of public spending to tertiary education (4.7 and 4.9 per cent, respectively). The fact that only 1 per cent of Japan's public budget is allocated to tertiary education is explained in part by Japan's heavy reliance on private financing of tertiary studies. Other countries that spend relatively small shares of public funds on tertiary education (between 1.5 and 1.7 per cent) are Belgium, France and Italy. (Sweden would be included in the group if subsidies to the private sector were not counted.)

Variations in the education share of total public spending reflect differences among countries in the division of responsibility for financing education between the public and private sectors. For instance, countries that require students to pay tuition fees and/or finance most or all of their own living expenses are likely to devote smaller percentages of public funds to tertiary education, other things being equal, than countries that provide "free" tertiary education and/or generous public subsidies to tertiary students.

Moreover, variations in the percentage of the public budget devoted to education also reflect differences in the breadth of the public sector's responsibilities outside education. For example, countries that spend relatively large amounts on their social security and national health care systems [e.g. Austria, France, Germany (FTFR), Sweden] will appear to be spending relatively smaller percentages on education. Moreover, the results of the comparison are sensitive to how total public expenditure is defined. The results would be quite different if, for example, the denominator excluded the expenditures of social security funds, or if it were limited to social programme expenditures only.

DEFINITIONS

In this indicator, each of the following three expenditure variables is expressed as a percentage of the country's total public sector expenditures: *a)* direct public expenditures for educational services; *b)* public subsidies for education to the private sector; and *c)* total educational expenditures (i.e. the sum of direct expenditures and public subsidies). These percentages are calculated for primary and secondary education, tertiary education, and all levels of education combined.

Direct public expenditures for educational services include both the amounts spent directly by governments to hire educational personnel and procure other resources and the amounts provided by governments to institutions (public or private) for use by the institutions themselves to acquire educational resources. Public subsidies include scholarships and other financial aid to students plus certain subsidies to other private entities but exclude the aforesaid payments to institutions.

The data on total public expenditures for all purposes (the denominator in all percentage calculations) have been taken from the OECD National Accounts Database.

F13: Share of education in public spending

F13 : Part de l'éducation dans les dépenses publiques

Table F13:
Public educational expenditure as a percentage of total public expenditure (1992)

*Tableau F13 :
Dépenses publiques d'éducation en pourcentage du total des dépenses publiques (1992)*

	Direct public expenditure for educational services / *Dépenses publiques directes pour les services d'enseignement*			Public subsidies for the private sector / *Subventions publiques au secteur privé*			Total: direct expenditure plus public subsidies to the private sector / *Total : dépenses directes plus subventions publiques au secteur privé*			
	Primary and secondary education	Tertiary education	All levels of education combined	Primary and secondary education	Tertiary education	All levels of education combined	Primary and secondary education	Tertiary education	All levels of education combined	
North America										*Amérique du Nord*
Canada	...	4.1	13.4	...	0.6	0.6	...	4.7	14.0	*Canada*
United States	10.1	3.2	13.8	.	0.3	0.3	10.1	3.5	14.2	*Etats-Unis*
Pacific Area										*Pays du Pacifique*
Australia	7.3	3.9	12.1	0.5	1.1	1.9	7.7	4.9	14.0	*Australie*
Japan	8.7	1.0	11.3	x	x	0.1	8.7	1.0	11.3	*Japon*
New Zealand	...	...	...	...	...	...	...	...	...	*Nouvelle-Zélande*
European Community										*Communauté européenne*
Belgium	5.6	1.1	9.5	0.4	0.4	1.0	6.0	1.5	10.5	*Belgique*
Denmark	6.6	2.1	10.1	0.9	1.2	2.4	7.5	3.3	12.5	*Danemark*
France	7.2	1.6	10.4	0.1	0.1	0.2	7.3	1.7	10.6	*France*
Germany (FTFR)	5.2	1.9	8.0	0.2	0.3	0.5	5.4	2.2	8.5	*Allemagne (ex-terr. de la RFA)*
Germany	...	...	...	...	...	...	...	...	...	*Allemagne*
Greece	...	...	...	...	...	...	...	...	...	*Grèce*
Ireland	8.8	2.5	12.7	0.3	0.6	1.0	9.1	3.2	13.7	*Irlande*
Italy	6.4	1.5	9.2	-	0.1	0.3	6.4	1.6	9.5	*Italie*
Luxembourg	...	...	...	...	...	...	...	...	...	*Luxembourg*
Netherlands	4.9	2.1	8.0	0.7	0.9	1.6	5.6	3.0	9.5	*Pays-Bas*
Portugal	...	...	...	...	...	...	...	...	...	*Portugal*
Spain	7.4	1.8	10.1	0.1	0.1	0.3	7.5	1.9	10.4	*Espagne*
United Kingdom	9.2	1.9	11.3	0.1	0.5	0.6	9.3	2.4	11.9	*Royaume-Uni*
Other Europe - OECD										*Autres pays d'Europe - OCDE*
Austria	7.2	2.2	11.0	-	0.1	0.2	7.2	2.3	11.3	*Autriche*
Finland	8.1	3.1	12.9	0.4	0.6	1.0	8.4	3.7	13.9	*Finlande*
Iceland	...	...	...	...	...	...	...	...	...	*Islande*
Norway	9.2	2.6	14.0	...	...	...	...	...	...	*Norvège*
Sweden	7.0	1.5	10.1	0.7	0.9	1.6	7.7	2.4	11.7	*Suède*
Switzerland	11.1	3.2	15.3	0.8	0.2	1.2	11.9	3.4	16.5	*Suisse*
Turkey	...	...	...	...	...	...	...	...	...	*Turquie*
Country mean	**7.7**	**2.3**	**11.3**	**0.3**	**0.5**	**0.9**	**7.9**	**2.8**	**12.0**	***Moyenne des pays***
Central and Eastern Europe										*Europe centrale et orientale*
Czech Republic	9.6	2.0	15.3	-	0.1	0.1	9.6	2.1	15.3	*République tchèque*
Hungary	12.3	3.2	18.1	-	0.5	0.5	12.4	3.7	18.7	*Hongrie*
Poland	...	...	...	...	...	...	...	...	...	*Pologne*
Russia	...	...	...	...	...	...	...	...	...	*Russie*

See Annex 1 for notes

Voir notes en annexe 1

F13: Share of education in public spending

F13 : Part de l'éducation dans les dépenses publiques

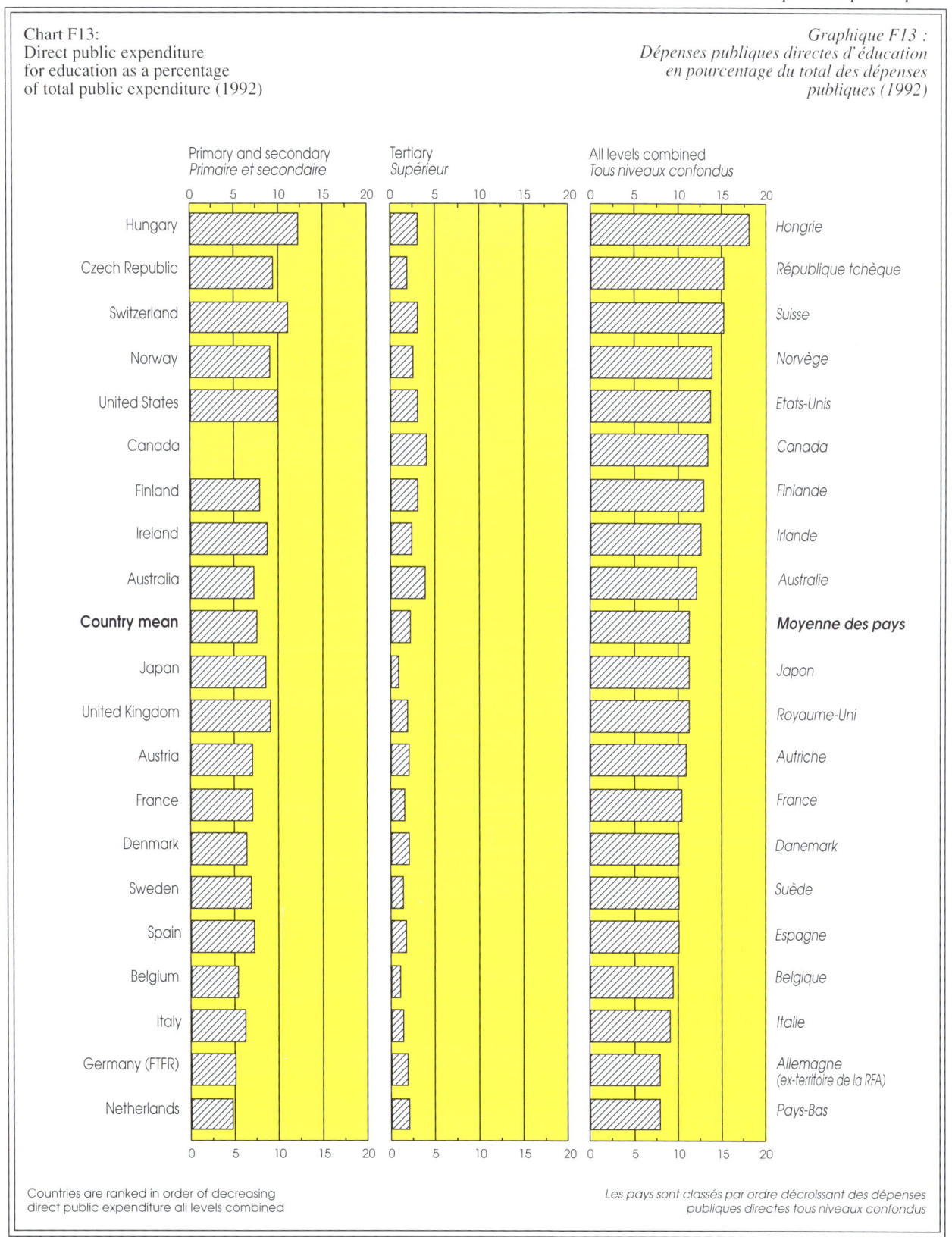

Chart F13:
Direct public expenditure for education as a percentage of total public expenditure (1992)

Graphique F13 :
Dépenses publiques directes d'éducation en pourcentage du total des dépenses publiques (1992)

Primary and secondary / Primaire et secondaire	Tertiary / Supérieur	All levels combined / Tous niveaux confondus

Countries (ranked in order of decreasing direct public expenditure all levels combined):

- Hungary / Hongrie
- Czech Republic / République tchèque
- Switzerland / Suisse
- Norway / Norvège
- United States / Etats-Unis
- Canada / Canada
- Finland / Finlande
- Ireland / Irlande
- Australia / Australie
- **Country mean / Moyenne des pays**
- Japan / Japon
- United Kingdom / Royaume-Uni
- Austria / Autriche
- France / France
- Denmark / Danemark
- Sweden / Suède
- Spain / Espagne
- Belgium / Belgique
- Italy / Italie
- Germany (FTFR) / Allemagne (ex-territoire de la RFA)
- Netherlands / Pays-Bas

Countries are ranked in order of decreasing direct public expenditure all levels combined

Les pays sont classés par ordre décroissant des dépenses publiques directes tous niveaux confondus

P01: Participation in formal education

PARTICIPATION IN FORMAL EDUCATION RELATIVE TO THE POPULATION AGED 5 TO 29

POLICY ISSUES

On the basis of participation and schooling expectancy figures, what modifications should governments pursue with regard to development of their education systems? Do results call for a shift in sectoral priorities?

KEY RESULTS

There are on average more than 50 students enrolled full-time in primary, secondary or tertiary education per 100 persons in the population 5 to 29 years of age. About 20 enrolments separate the two extremes: Turkey (40) and Finland (61).

Part-time schooling, markedly uneven in its development from country to country, concerns, on average, relatively few students; the vast majority attend public institutions.

There is considerable variation in the number of students enrolled in tertiary education relative to the 5 to 29 year-old population, with the figures sometimes doubling between countries.

Differences among countries are put into sharper focus by examining the projected number of years during which a 5 year-old can expect to be enrolled in school, which vary from less than 10 years to 16 years.

DESCRIPTION AND INTERPRETATION

With the exception of Turkey (40) and Russia (45), the indicator for participation in full-time schooling of those 5 to 29 years of age ranges from 49 to 61. For the majority of countries, the number of students is about half the size of the population in that age group. The number is highest (58 or above) in Canada, France and Finland.

These disparities are explained in part by the rather uneven development of tertiary education – from two students per 100 persons 5 to 29 years old in Hungary to 10 in Canada and Finland.

However, participation rates also vary in primary and lower secondary education. Because there is virtually universal enrolment at this level, this variation reflects a purely demographic factor: the relative size of the younger age cohorts within the 5 to 29 year-old population which is highest in Australia and Ireland, and lowest in Austria, Germany (FTFR) and Italy. These differences also contribute to the variation found in the figures for all levels combined.

Whether full-time or part-time, enrolment in public establishments predominates most often. Belgium and the Netherlands, however, provide an exception, with a majority of students in the private government-funded sector. Spain also has a sizeable number of students in this sector. The purely private sector, generally very small, is largest in Japan (12) and the United States (7).

Average schooling expectancy is lowest – 13 years or less – in the Czech Republic, Hungary, Poland, Turkey and Russia. It is highest, 15.5 years or more, in Belgium, Denmark, France, Germany (FTFR) and the Netherlands. In all the other countries the average expectancy is about 14 or 15 years. Taking into account part-time schooling affects the results of the calculations slightly; the gain attains or exceeds half-a-year for Hungary, New Zealand, Norway, Russia, the United Kingdom and the United States.

DEFINITIONS

This indicator shows the number of students enrolled in education per 100 individuals 5 to 29 years of age. Students enrolled in primary, secondary or tertiary education are counted regardless of their age. Also, students enrolled in pre-primary education, even if they are 5 years or older, are excluded.

The expectation of participation relative to the 1991/92 school year is obtained by adding the net enrolment rates for each year of age from 5 (independently if 5, 6 or 7 year-olds attend a pre-primary or primary school) to 29, and dividing by 100. This indicator represents, therefore, the (hypothetical) duration of schooling for a 5 year-old child under current conditions. Should there be a tendency to lengthen (or shorten) studies during the ensuing years, the actual average duration of schooling for the cohort will be higher (or lower). The calculation does not include expected enrolment beyond the age of 29. Full-time equivalents have been calculated using the coefficients supplied by the countries.

P01: Participation in formal education

P01 : Scolarisation dans l'enseignement formel

Table P01(A1):
Number of full-time students per 100 persons
in the population aged 5 to 29 (1992)

*Tableau P01(A1) :
Effectifs scolarisés à plein temps pour 100 personnes
de la population de 5 à 29 ans (1992)*

	Enrolments in public and private education / *Effectifs scolarisés dans l'enseignement public et privé*					Enrolments by type of institution / *Effectifs scolarisés par type d'établissement*			
	Primary and lower secondary / *Primaire et secondaire 1er cycle*	Upper secondary / *Secondaire 2e cycle*	Tertiary / *Enseignement supérieur*	Undefined / *Non défini*	All levels except early childhood education / *Tous niveaux confondus sauf préscolaire*	Public / *Public*	Government-dependent private / *Privé subventionné*	Independent private / *Privé non subventionné*	
North America									*Amérique du Nord*
Canada	36.4	11.6	10.1	.	58.0	55.7	.	2.3	*Canada*
United States	35.9	9.5	8.7	.	54.2	47.6	.	6.5	*Etats-Unis*
Pacific Area									*Pays du Pacifique*
Australia	40.2	6.2	6.9	...	...	...	...	...	*Australie*
Japan	33.6	13.2	7.8	1.1	55.7	43.8	.	11.9	*Japon*
New Zealand	39.2	10.4	5.9	.	55.6	53.8	.	1.8	*Nouvelle-Zélande*
European Community									*Communauté européenne*
Belgium	30.8	15.4	7.5	0.1	53.9	20.7	33.2	.	*Belgique*
Denmark	32.6	13.0	9.4	.	54.9	51.4	3.5	.	*Danemark*
France	35.8	12.3	9.0	1.3	58.4	47.1	...	...	*France*
Germany (FTFR)	29.5	12.0	8.9	.	50.3	...	...	...	*Allemagne (ex-terr. de la RFA)*
Germany	31.1	11.0	7.7	.	49.8	...	...	...	*Allemagne*
Greece	33.9	11.2	4.9	.	50.0	47.0	.	3.0	*Grèce*
Ireland	40.6	10.5	5.1	0.3	56.4	55.8	.	0.7	*Irlande*
Italy	26.1	16.0	7.8	-	50.0	46.7	.	3.3	*Italie*
Luxembourg	...	...	...	...	...	...	...	...	*Luxembourg*
Netherlands	34.3	12.7	7.4	.	54.4	14.0	40.4	-	*Pays-Bas*
Portugal	...	...	...	...	...	...	...	...	*Portugal*
Spain	30.8	17.2	8.6	0.3	56.9	40.4	12.1	4.4	*Espagne*
United Kingdom	35.0	12.7	4.2	.	51.9	44.3	3.7	3.9	*Royaume-Uni*
Other Europe - OECD									*Autres pays d'Europe - OCDE*
Austria	26.7	14.5	9.3	.	50.5	47.2	3.3	-	*Autriche*
Finland	36.0	14.4	10.4	-	60.8	58.5	2.2	-	*Finlande*
Iceland	...	...	...	...	...	...	...	...	*Islande*
Norway	31.3	15.1	8.2	.	54.6	52.1	...	...	*Norvège*
Sweden	32.0	10.7	7.5	.	50.2	49.5	0.7	0.1	*Suède*
Switzerland	32.0	11.7	5.0	0.3	49.1	45.9	1.3	2.0	*Suisse*
Turkey	31.5	5.4	2.8	.	39.7	39.1	.	0.5	*Turquie*
Central and Eastern Europe									*Europe centrale et orientale*
Czech Republic	32.7	15.3	3.3	.	51.2	51.0	0.2	.	*République tchèque*
Hungary	31.4	15.0	2.3	.	48.7	48.2	0.4	.	*Hongrie*
Poland	35.5	13.4	3.7	.	52.6	...	...	...	*Pologne*
Russia	32.3	6.8	6.0	.	45.0	45.0	.	.	*Russie*

See Annex 1 for notes

Voir notes en annexe 1

P01: Participation in formal education

P01 : Scolarisation dans l'enseignement formel

Table P01(A2):
Number of part-time students per 100 persons
in the population aged 5 to 29 (1992)

Tableau P01(A2) :
Effectifs scolarisés à temps partiel pour 100 personnes
de la population de 5 à 29 ans (1992)

	Primary and lower secondary / Primaire et secondaire 1er cycle	Upper secondary / Secondaire 2e cycle	Tertiary / Enseignement supérieur	Undefined / Non défini	All levels except early childhood education / Tous niveaux confondus sauf préscolaire	Public / Public	Government-dependent private / Privé subventionné	Independent private / Privé non subventionné	
North America									*Amérique du Nord*
Canada	.	.	9.6	.	9.6	6.7	.	2.9	*Canada*
United States	-	x	6.7	.	6.7	5.7	.	1.0	*Etats-Unis*
Pacific Area									*Pays du Pacifique*
Australia	.	1.8	17.0	...	...	...	...	...	*Australie*
Japan	.	0.4	0.6	.	0.9	0.4	.	0.6	*Japon*
New Zealand	0.4	2.3	5.1	.	7.8	7.8	-	-	*Nouvelle-Zélande*
European Community									*Communauté européenne*
Belgium	.	0.2	.	7.2	7.4	4.3	3.1	.	*Belgique*
Denmark	.	.	.	.	.	.	.	.	*Danemark*
France	.	.	.	.	.	.	.	.	*France*
Germany (FTFR)	.	0.1	0.2	.	0.3	0.2	...	...	*Allemagne (ex-terr. de la RFA)*
Germany	.	0.1	0.2	.	0.2	.	...	...	*Allemagne*
Greece	.	.	.	.	.	.	.	.	*Grèce*
Ireland	.	0.3	1.6	.	2.0	2.0	.	-	*Irlande*
Italy	-	-	x	-	x	x	x	x	*Italie*
Luxembourg	...	...	...	...	...	...	...	...	*Luxembourg*
Netherlands	1.1	1.7	1.2	.	3.9	1.0	3.0	-	*Pays-Bas*
Portugal	...	...	...	...	...	...	...	...	*Portugal*
Spain	.	1.3	.	.	1.3	1.3	.	.	*Espagne*
United Kingdom	0.2	9.1	2.7	.	12.1	10.2	1.6	0.3	*Royaume-Uni*
Other Europe - OECD									*Autres pays d'Europe - OCDE*
Austria	.	.	.	.	.	.	.	.	*Autriche*
Finland	.	-	-	-	-	-	-	.	*Finlande*
Iceland	...	...	...	...	...	...	...	...	*Islande*
Norway	.	0.2	2.2	.	2.4	1.6	...	...	*Norvège*
Sweden	2.1	4.9	x	.	7.0	7.0	.	.	*Suède*
Switzerland	.	0.2	1.3	.	1.5	0.4	0.6	0.4	*Suisse*
Turkey	.	.	.	.	.	.	.	.	*Turquie*
Central and Eastern Europe									*Europe centrale et orientale*
Czech Republic	.	.	0.3	.	0.3	0.3	.	.	*République tchèque*
Hungary	0.3	1.9	0.9	.	3.1	3.1	-	.	*Hongrie*
Poland	.	.	.	.	.	.	.	.	*Pologne*
Russia	0.2	1.1	3.4	.	4.7	4.7	.	.	*Russie*

See Annex 1 for notes

Voir notes en annexe 1

P01: Participation in formal education

P01 : Scolarisation dans l'enseignement formel

Table P01(B):
Schooling expectancy
for a 5 year-old child (1992)

Tableau P01(B) :
Espérance de scolarisation
pour un enfant de 5 ans (1992)

	Full-time *Plein temps*	Full-time equivalents *Equivalents plein temps*	
North America			*Amérique du Nord*
Canada	14.7	...	*Canada*
United States	14.2	14.8	*Etats-Unis*
Pacific Area			*Pays du Pacifique*
Australia	...	...	*Australie*
Japan	...	...	*Japon*
New Zealand	14.1	14.6	*Nouvelle-Zélande*
European Community			*Communauté européenne*
Belgium	15.5	15.8	*Belgique*
Denmark	15.6	15.6	*Danemark*
France	15.9	15.9	*France*
Germany (FTFR)	15.9	15.9	*Allemagne (ex-terr. de la RFA)*
Germany	...	...	*Allemagne*
Greece	13.7	13.7	*Grèce*
Ireland	14.4	14.6	*Irlande*
Italy	...	...	*Italie*
Luxembourg	...	...	*Luxembourg*
Netherlands	15.8	16.0	*Pays-Bas*
Portugal	...	...	*Portugal*
Spain	15.4	...	*Espagne*
United Kingdom	13.4	14.0	*Royaume-Uni*
Other Europe - OECD			*Autres pays d'Europe - OCDE*
Austria	...	...	*Autriche*
Finland	15.4	15.4	*Finlande*
Iceland	...	...	*Islande*
Norway	14.7	15.6	*Norvège*
Sweden	14.3	14.7	*Suède*
Switzerland	15.0	15.2	*Suisse*
Turkey	9.4	9.4	*Turquie*
Central and Eastern Europe			*Europe centrale et orientale*
Czech Republic	13.1	...	*République tchèque*
Hungary	12.6	13.2	*Hongrie*
Poland	13.0	13.0	*Pologne*
Russia	12.0	12.5	*Russie*

See Annex 1 for notes

Voir notes en annexe 1

P01: Participation in formal education

P01 : Scolarisation dans l'enseignement formel

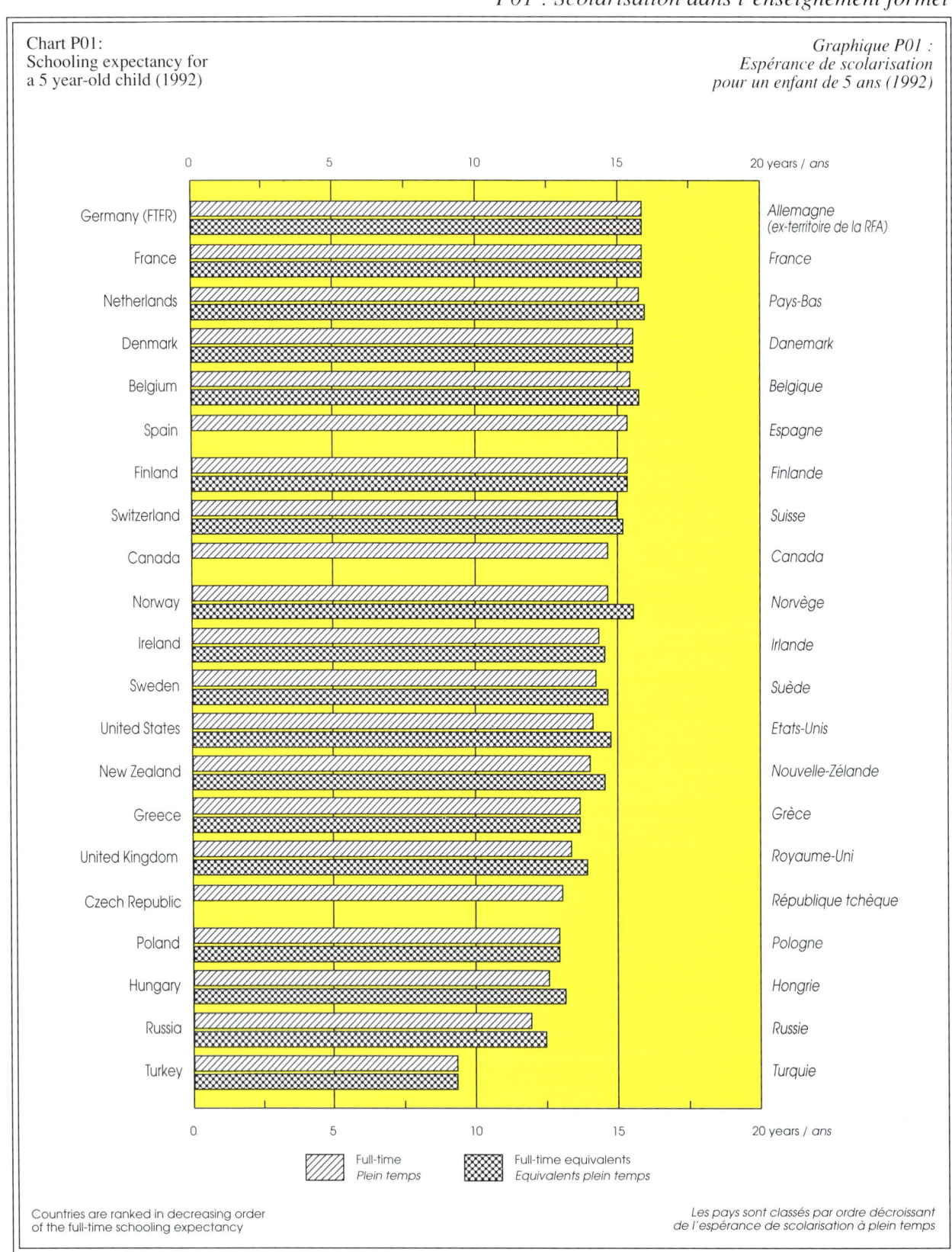

Chart P01:
Schooling expectancy for a 5 year-old child (1992)

Graphique P01 :
Espérance de scolarisation
pour un enfant de 5 ans (1992)

Germany (FTFR)		Allemagne (ex-territoire de la RFA)
France		France
Netherlands		Pays-Bas
Denmark		Danemark
Belgium		Belgique
Spain		Espagne
Finland		Finlande
Switzerland		Suisse
Canada		Canada
Norway		Norvège
Ireland		Irlande
Sweden		Suède
United States		Etats-Unis
New Zealand		Nouvelle-Zélande
Greece		Grèce
United Kingdom		Royaume-Uni
Czech Republic		République tchèque
Poland		Pologne
Hungary		Hongrie
Russia		Russie
Turkey		Turquie

Legend: Full-time / *Plein temps* — Full-time equivalents / *Equivalents plein temps*

Countries are ranked in decreasing order of the full-time schooling expectancy

Les pays sont classés par ordre décroissant de l'espérance de scolarisation à plein temps

P02: Early childhood education

NET RATES OF PARTICIPATION IN EARLY CHILDHOOD AND PRIMARY EDUCATION

POLICY ISSUES

Are the early childhood educational structures currently in place the most effective means of preparing children for later schooling? How long should early childhood education be?

KEY RESULTS

Thirteen out of 20 countries report enrolment rates of at least 30 per cent in early childhood education at age 3; by age 4, about three-fourths of the countries (16 out of 22) report enrolment rates of at least 50 per cent. At age 6, over 90 per cent of children in most countries are enrolled in either early childhood or primary education, and at age 7 participation rates are over 90 per cent in all countries.

The transition from early childhood education to primary education takes place at age 5 in a few countries, but occurs in most countries at age 6. By age 7, the vast majority of children in all countries (except Russia) are enrolled in primary schools.

DESCRIPTION AND INTERPRETATION

This indicator shows rates of participation in early childhood and primary education at each age from 3 through 7. Overall, rates of participation increase for each succeeding year of age. At age 3, about one-third of the countries (seven out of 20) report enrolment rates of over 50 per cent. Rates vary widely among countries, however, ranging from under 20 per cent in Greece, Ireland and Switzerland to over 90 per cent in Belgium, France and Hungary.

At age 4, enrolment rates rise sharply in several countries. Still, there is significant variation between figures which range from less than 30 per cent in Finland, Switzerland, Turkey and the United Kingdom to over 90 per cent in Belgium, France, Hungary, the Netherlands, New Zealand and Spain.

Enrolments at age 5 continue to increase, and begin to divide into early childhood and primary education. The vast majority of children in most countries still attend early childhood education institutions, but in three countries (Australia, New Zealand and the United Kingdom), the majority of 5 year-olds are enrolled in primary schools and the corresponding percentages for Canada and Greece are sizeable [Table P02(B)].

At age 6, participation in education (early childhood and primary) is nearly universal (over 90 per cent) in all but three countries (Finland, Norway and Turkey). Also at this stage, the balance in enrolments shifts even further to primary schools, with majority enrolments in over half the countries. However, in Germany, Ireland, Switzerland and the Nordic countries, a large proportion of children are still enrolled in early childhood education.

Enrolment rates for children aged 7 are nearly universal in all countries, and nearly all enrolments relate to primary school. Only Russia reports that more than 50 per cent of this age group are still enrolled in early childhood education.

While countries differ in their enrolment rates for young children, it must be recognised that those rates are affected significantly by differences in reporting practices. Seven countries (Denmark, Finland, Germany, New Zealand, Norway, Poland and Sweden) report most or all enrolments in "kindergartens" or other "child care" programmes as part of early childhood education (as directed in the reporting instructions). However, at least 13 other countries – Austria, Belgium, Canada, the Czech Republic, France, Hungary, Ireland, Japan, the Netherlands, Spain, Switzerland, the United Kingdom and the United States – report only enrolments in "schools" or "educational institutions". Enrolment rates in this second group of countries are therefore understated, since a large sector of early childhood education has been excluded.

Nine countries report enrolments of children aged 2 in early childhood education [Table P02(A2)]. However, it is difficult to compare enrolment rates of 2 year-olds across countries because of differences in the reporting systems. The instructions permit countries to include 2 year-olds enrolled in centre-based programmes if these centres also serve children aged 3 to 5. Countries such as Belgium, France and Spain therefore include children enrolled in pre-primary schools or *écoles maternelles*. However, most other countries exclude these children, either because 3 is the starting age established by the

P02: Early childhood education

OECD for reporting data on early childhood education, or because countries do not have data on the number of 2 year-olds enrolled in child-care centres.

DEFINITIONS

This indicator is defined as the net enrolment rate for children at each age from 2 to 7 in early childhood education, primary education, and both levels of education combined. Net rates for each year of age are calculated by dividing full-time plus part-time enrolments at that age by the total population of that age.

Most European countries do not distinguish full-time from part-time enrolments in early childhood education; all children are considered as "full-time" in enrolment counts. A few countries, most notably Canada and the United States, do make this distinction and count part-time enrolments. For this indicator, all part-time enrolments are counted as full-time to reflect the number of children participating in early childhood education, regardless of the intensity of participation.

The average duration of early childhood education is calculated by adding the net enrolment rates for each single age and dividing the total by 100.

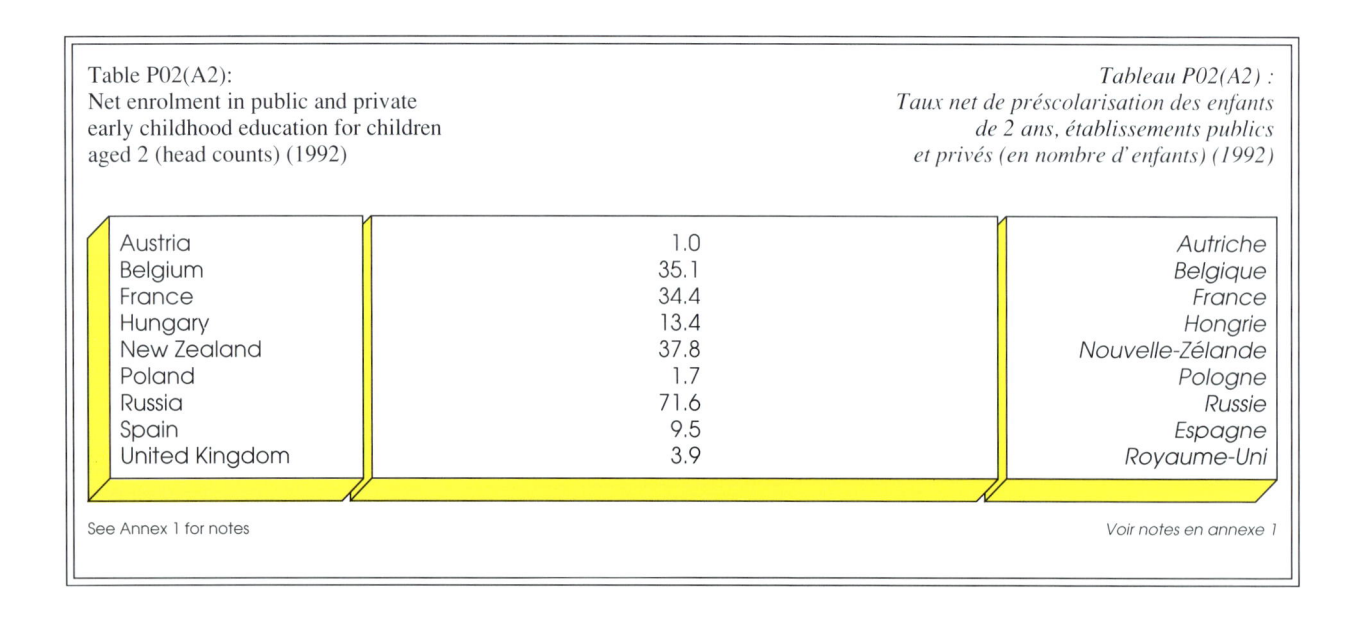

Table P02(A2):
Net enrolment in public and private early childhood education for children aged 2 (head counts) (1992)

*Tableau P02(A2) :
Taux net de préscolarisation des enfants de 2 ans, établissements publics et privés (en nombre d'enfants) (1992)*

Austria	1.0	Autriche
Belgium	35.1	Belgique
France	34.4	France
Hungary	13.4	Hongrie
New Zealand	37.8	Nouvelle-Zélande
Poland	1.7	Pologne
Russia	71.6	Russie
Spain	9.5	Espagne
United Kingdom	3.9	Royaume-Uni

See Annex 1 for notes

Voir notes en annexe 1

P02: Early childhood education

P02 : Education préscolaire

Table P02(A1):
Net enrolment in public and private
early childhood education (head counts) (1992)

Tableau P02(A1) :
Taux net de préscolarisation (en nombre d'enfants),
établissements publics et privés (1992)

	\multicolumn{5}{c	}{Net enrolment rates by single year of age (in %) / Taux net par âge simple (en %)}	Average duration of early childhood education (in years) / Durée moyenne de la préscolarisation (en années)	
	3	4	5	6	7		
North America							*Amérique du Nord*
Canada	.	45.9	69.3	8.3	.	1.24	*Canada*
United States	28.5	53.0	82.8	15.7	1.1	1.81	*Etats-Unis*
Pacific Area							*Pays du Pacifique*
Australia	...	...	...	...	...	...	*Australie*
Japan	23.1	57.6	65.7	.	.	1.46	*Japon*
New Zealand	73.7	92.6	5.4	-	-	2.10	*Nouvelle-Zélande*
European Community							*Communauté européenne*
Belgium	97.7	99.3	97.8	3.8	0.1	3.34	*Belgique*
Denmark	37.9	53.6	61.1	92.6	8.4	2.54	*Danemark*
France	98.8	101.4	99.8	1.0	-	3.35	*France*
Germany (FTFR)	30.8	68.5	78.5	71.0	1.4	2.61	*Allemagne (ex-terr. de la RFA)*
Germany	...	...	...	...	...	...	*Allemagne*
Greece	11.2	48.9	61.5	0.8	.	1.22	*Grèce*
Ireland	1.2	55.7	99.8	54.7	2.5	2.14	*Irlande*
Italy	...	...	...	...	...	...	*Italie*
Luxembourg	...	...	...	...	...	...	*Luxembourg*
Netherlands	-	97.6	98.2	0.5	0.8	1.97	*Pays-Bas*
Portugal	...	...	...	...	...	...	*Portugal*
Spain	37.2	95.8	100.4	.	.	2.43	*Espagne*
United Kingdom	37.0	12.6	0.1	.	.	0.54	*Royaume-Uni*
Other Europe - OECD							*Autres pays d'Europe - OCDE*
Austria	29.0	66.3	86.2	36.3	0.3	2.19	*Autriche*
Finland	24.3	28.1	32.0	57.2	0.6	1.42	*Finlande*
Iceland	...	...	...	...	...	...	*Islande*
Norway	44.0	56.5	65.1	78.2	1.2	2.45	*Norvège*
Sweden	45.2	50.8	60.6	98.3	.	2.55	*Suède*
Switzerland	7.4	26.2	77.1	70.2	2.7	1.84	*Suisse*
Turkey	.	0.3	1.5	8.8	.	0.11	*Turquie*
Country mean	**33.0**	**58.5**	**65.4**	**31.4**	**1.0**	**1.96**	*Moyenne des pays*
Central and Eastern Europe							*Europe centrale et orientale*
Czech Republic	65.7	84.1	99.8	1.9	.	2.52	*République tchèque*
Hungary	99.0	100.5	100.3	6.0	1.2	3.20	*Hongrie*
Poland	78.3	x	x	93.9	2.3	1.76	*Pologne*
Russia	53.9	52.0	51.6	72.4	56.6	3.58	*Russie*

See Annex 1 for notes

Voir notes en annexe 1

P02: Early childhood education

P02 : Education préscolaire

Table P02(B):
Net enrolment rates by single year of age (4 to 7)
in public and private early childhood
and primary education
(head counts) (1992)

Tableau P02(B) :
Taux net de scolarisation par âge simple (de 4 à 7 ans)
dans l'enseignement préscolaire et primaire
(en nombre d'enfants),
établissements publics et privés (1992)

	Age 4 Early childhood education / Préscolaire	Age 4 Primary / Primaire	Age 4 Early childhood and primary education / Préscolaire et primaire	Age 5 Early childhood education / Préscolaire	Age 5 Primary / Primaire	Age 5 Early childhood and primary education / Préscolaire et primaire	Age 6 Early childhood education / Préscolaire	Age 6 Primary / Primaire	Age 6 Early childhood and primary education / Préscolaire et primaire	Age 7 Early childhood education / Préscolaire	Age 7 Primary / Primaire	Age 7 Early childhood and primary education / Préscolaire et primaire	
North America													*Amérique du Nord*
Canada	45.9	.	45.9	69.3	29.9	99.2	8.3	95.4	103.7	.	102.9	102.9	*Canada*
United States	53.0	-	53.0	82.8	5.8	88.6	15.7	86.6	102.3	1.1	102.2	103.3	*Etats-Unis*
Pacific Area													*Pays du Pacifique*
Australia	...	x	...	...	74.2	...	...	98.1	...	...	99.8	...	*Australie*
Japan	57.6	.	57.6	65.7	.	65.7	.	101.9	101.9	.	101.0	101.0	*Japon*
New Zealand	92.6	-	92.6	5.4	99.7	105.1	-	100.8	100.8	-	100.9	100.9	*Nouvelle-Zélande*
European Community													*Communauté européenne*
Belgium	99.3	.	99.3	97.8	1.9	99.7	3.8	96.0	99.8	0.1	99.0	99.1	*Belgique*
Denmark	53.6	-	53.6	61.1	-	61.1	92.6	3.8	96.4	8.4	91.4	99.7	*Danemark*
France	101.4	-	101.4	99.8	1.8	101.5	1.0	99.6	100.6	-	100.2	100.2	*France*
Germany (FTFR)	68.5	-	68.5	78.5	-	78.5	71.0	44.1	115.1	1.4	96.0	97.5	*Allemagne (ex-terr. de la RFA)*
Germany	...	...	...	...	...	...	...	...	...	...	...	...	*Allemagne*
Greece	48.9	.	48.9	61.5	23.7	85.2	0.8	101.7	102.5	.	95.6	95.6	*Grèce*
Ireland	55.7	-	55.7	99.8	0.1	100.0	54.7	44.4	99.1	2.5	98.1	100.5	*Irlande*
Italy	...	...	...	...	...	...	...	...	...	...	...	...	*Italie*
Luxembourg	...	...	...	...	...	...	...	...	...	...	...	...	*Luxembourg*
Netherlands	97.6	0.4	98.0	98.2	0.6	98.8	0.5	97.2	97.7	0.8	99.2	100.0	*Pays-Bas*
Portugal	...	...	...	...	...	...	...	...	...	...	...	...	*Portugal*
Spain	95.8	.	95.8	100.4	.	100.4	.	103.2	103.2	.	103.8	103.8	*Espagne*
United Kingdom	12.6	77.5	90.1	0.1	98.8	98.9	.	98.5	98.5	.	98.9	98.9	*Royaume-Uni*
Other Europe - OECD													*Autres pays d'Europe - OCDE*
Austria	66.3	.	66.3	86.2	.	86.2	36.3	62.2	98.4	0.3	99.7	100.0	*Autriche*
Finland	28.1	-	28.1	32.0	-	32.0	57.2	0.4	57.6	0.6	98.9	99.5	*Finlande*
Iceland	...	...	...	...	...	...	...	...	...	...	...	...	*Islande*
Norway	56.5	.	56.5	65.1	.	65.1	78.2	1.1	79.3	1.2	98.1	99.3	*Norvège*
Sweden	50.8	.	50.8	60.6	.	60.6	98.3	1.6	99.9	.	97.5	97.5	*Suède*
Switzerland	26.2	-	26.2	77.1	0.2	77.3	70.2	28.8	99.0	2.7	97.5	100.1	*Suisse*
Turkey	0.3	.	0.3	1.5	.	1.5	8.8	5.4	14.2	.	93.3	93.3	*Turquie*
Country mean	**58.5**	**31.9**	**62.6**	**65.4**	**16.8**	**79.2**	**31.4**	**63.5**	**93.2**	**1.0**	**98.7**	**99.6**	***Moyenne des pays***
Central and Eastern Europe													*Europe centrale et orientale*
Czech Republic	84.1	.	84.1	99.8	.	99.8	1.9	104.8	106.7	.	102.8	102.8	*République tchèque*
Hungary	100.5	.	100.5	100.3	0.9	101.2	6.0	94.6	100.6	1.2	99.9	101.1	*Hongrie*
Poland	x	.	x	x	.	x	93.9	1.1	95.0	2.3	96.2	98.5	*Pologne*
Russia	52.0	.	52.0	51.6	.	51.6	72.4	26.9	99.3	56.6	43.4	100.0	*Russie*

See Annex 1 for notes

Voir notes en annexe 1

P02: Early childhood education

P02 : Education préscolaire

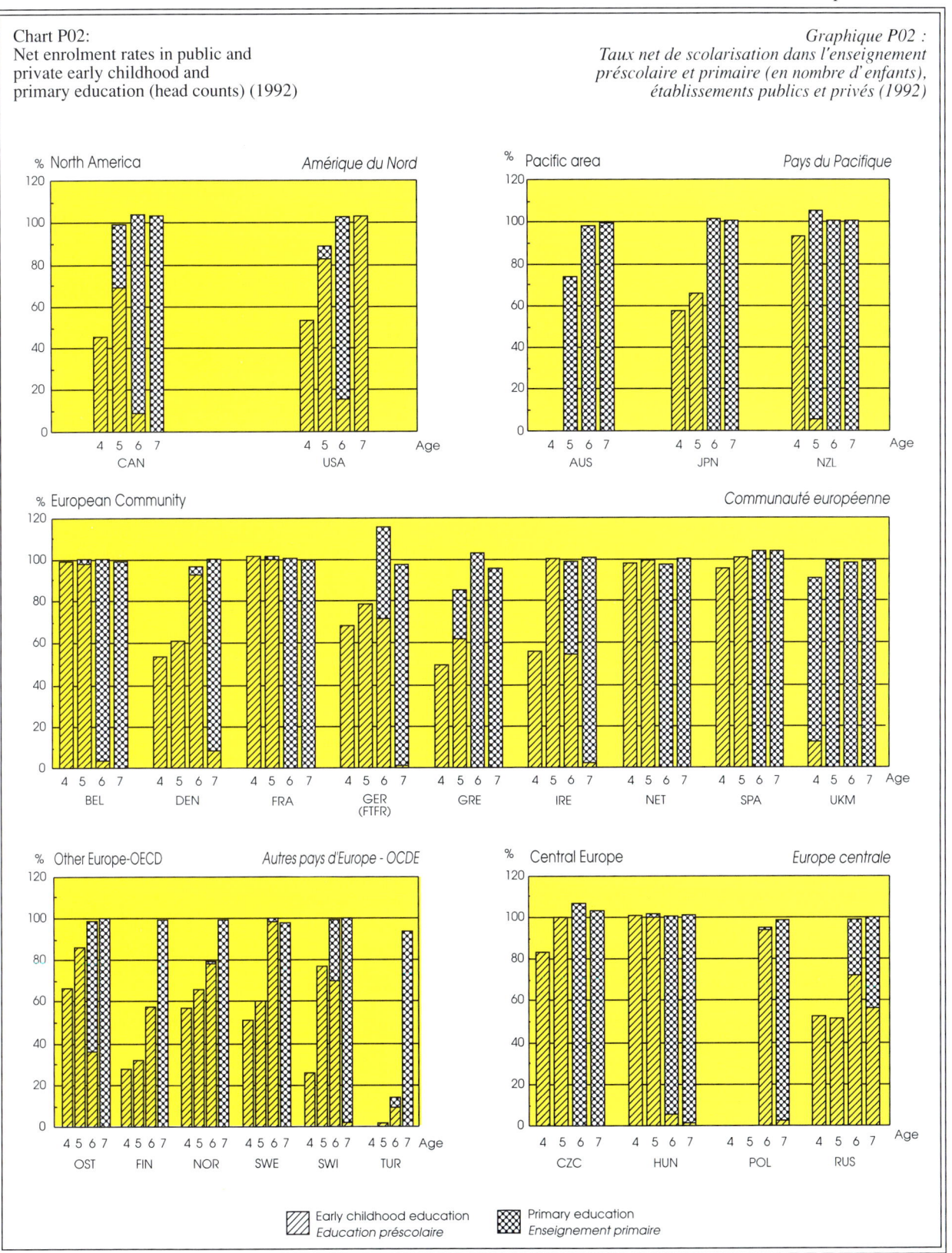

Chart P02:
Net enrolment rates in public and private early childhood and primary education (head counts) (1992)

*Graphique P02 :
Taux net de scolarisation dans l'enseignement préscolaire et primaire (en nombre d'enfants), établissements publics et privés (1992)*

- Early childhood education / *Education préscolaire*
- Primary education / *Enseignement primaire*

133

P03: Participation in secondary education

NET RATES OF PARTICIPATION IN ALL SECONDARY EDUCATION PROGRAMMES

POLICY ISSUES

Some countries offer students who have completed upper secondary education the chance to re-enrol and pursue additional qualifications – and the percentage of 20 year-olds who prefer this option over entry into tertiary education is striking. By the same token, countries with high enrolment rates in vocational institutions or apprenticeship programmes show higher participation rates for upper secondary education. What are the dynamics behind these clear-cut preferences? Are there lessons here for policy-makers in the other countries?

KEY RESULTS

In all but two of the 19 OECD countries for which data are available, at least 90 per cent of 15 year-olds participate in secondary education on a full-time basis. By age 17, however, full-time participation rates drop to less than 80 per cent of the population in almost half the OECD countries. In general, countries where the majority of participants in upper secondary education attend vocational institutions or apprenticeship programmes show higher rates of full-time secondary participation at ages 18 and beyond. Five OECD countries show enrolments in upper secondary education of persons who have completed one programme in upper secondary education and have enrolled in another.

DESCRIPTION AND INTERPRETATION

In most of the OECD and Eastern European countries, the final full year of full-time secondary education occurs at age 17 or 18. Of the 23 countries for which data are available, 17 show rates of full-time secondary participation of 80 per cent or more at age 16, and eleven show comparable participation rates at 17. In six countries (Australia, Hungary, Russia, Spain, Turkey and the United Kingdom) full-time secondary participation drops below 80 per cent at age 16, although at least some of these countries have substantial numbers of students continuing upper secondary education on a part-time basis. Only one country, Germany (FTFR), shows a full-time participation rate greater than 80 per cent at age 18, and only nine countries rates above 50 per cent.

While full-time secondary participation ends for most persons before age 19, ten countries show participation by 10 per cent or more of the population continuing after that age. These countries are Belgium, Canada, Denmark, Finland, France, Germany (FTFR), the Netherlands, Norway, Spain and Switzerland. For at least Denmark, Germany (FTFR) and the Netherlands, these rates include students who have completed one secondary programme (qualification) and are participating in a second programme.

In more than half of the OECD countries, the majority of upper secondary students attend vocational institutions or participate in apprenticeship. In twelve of the 17 countries supplying data, more than half of all upper secondary students (full- and part-time) are enrolled in vocational institutions or apprenticeship, and in six of those countries more than two-thirds. Among European countries, only Spain and Turkey show vocational/apprenticeship participation rates below 50 per cent of upper secondary students.

In some countries, primarily the English-speaking countries and Japan, there are almost no upper secondary institutions differentiated by curriculum – general or vocational – although students pursue different curricula in undifferentiated (or comprehensive) secondary schools. These countries generally show low rates of participation in vocational institutions or have not submitted data on this topic.

In five OECD countries and one Eastern European country, students may complete upper secondary education and then enrol a second or subsequent time. In three countries, Germany, Denmark, and Spain there are 10 or more students enrolled in second or subsequent upper secondary programmes per 100 individuals in the population in the age group most commonly attending this level of education. Most of the students who re-enrol in upper secondary education pursue vocational or apprenticeship education.

DEFINITIONS

Full-time equivalents have been computed using coefficients (numbers of part-time enrolments comprising a full-time enrolment) provided by the countries. Vocational education includes vocational, technical and apprenticeship programmes. Typical age ranges were provided by the countries. Both the part-time coefficients and the age ranges can be found in Annex 3.

P03: Participation in secondary education

P03 : Scolarisation dans le secondaire

Table P03(A1):
Net enrolment in all public and private secondary education
(full-time enrolments) (1992)

Tableau P03(A1) :
Taux net de scolarisation dans l'enseignement secondaire public et privé
(effectifs à plein temps) (1992)

Net enrolment rates by single year of age (in %)
Taux net par âge simple (en %)

	14	15	16	17	18	19	20	21	
North America									*Amérique du Nord*
Canada	99.8	98.7	96.3	72.0	36.9	11.1	14.0	.	*Canada*
United States	98.7	95.7	91.4	72.0	20.6	5.8	1.7	0.6	*Etats-Unis*
Pacific Area									*Pays du Pacifique*
Australia	97.5	92.0	78.7	58.8	14.2	2.8	3.3	x	*Australie*
Japan	101.6	96.8	95.1	90.3	1.8	x	x	x	*Japon*
New Zealand	98.9	96.7	87.8	65.7	20.8	5.9	2.4	1.7	*Nouvelle-Zélande*
European Community									*Communauté européenne*
Belgium	98.9	98.7	97.2	93.6	49.8	25.1	10.6	4.4	*Belgique*
Denmark	93.4	97.8	92.4	80.1	68.9	48.4	28.3	16.3	*Danemark*
France	94.3	94.1	92.1	87.2	58.6	34.0	12.0	3.1	*France*
Germany (FTFR)	93.9	93.1	95.3	92.8	82.3	55.0	29.3	16.0	*Allemagne (ex-terr. de la RFA)*
Germany	...	...	...	...	...	...	...	...	*Allemagne*
Greece	94.2	86.1	88.4	62.1	19.4	10.5	4.7	3.1	*Grèce*
Ireland	97.6	94.3	87.5	70.2	33.1	11.5	7.0	3.6	*Irlande*
Italy	...	...	...	...	...	...	...	...	*Italie*
Luxembourg	...	...	...	...	...	...	...	...	*Luxembourg*
Netherlands	98.7	99.0	97.3	90.8	67.9	42.3	25.4	14.7	*Pays-Bas*
Portugal	...	...	...	...	...	...	...	...	*Portugal*
Spain	100.4	91.0	75.6	66.9	35.5	20.7	17.2	10.6	*Espagne*
United Kingdom	99.6	98.9	75.3	55.3	18.7	4.3	1.9	1.2	*Royaume-Uni*
Other Europe - OECD									*Autres pays d'Europe - OCDE*
Austria	...	...	...	...	...	...	...	...	*Autriche*
Finland	99.8	99.8	94.5	85.8	79.7	26.8	16.5	15.3	*Finlande*
Iceland	...	...	...	...	...	...	...	...	*Islande*
Norway	99.4	99.3	92.8	86.6	77.2	34.6	17.6	11.9	*Norvège*
Sweden	99.7	95.6	89.2	87.0	59.6	11.5	2.7	1.7	*Suède*
Switzerland	98.3	95.8	85.2	82.0	74.2	48.9	20.6	8.2	*Suisse*
Turkey	47.5	45.9	39.3	33.9	19.8	9.7	6.0	.	*Turquie*
Country mean	**95.4**	**93.1**	**86.9**	**75.4**	**44.2**	**21.5**	**11.6**	**5.9**	***Moyenne des pays***
Central and Eastern Europe									*Europe centrale et orientale*
Czech Republic	106.4	90.2	86.9	39.4	.	.	.	.	*République tchèque*
Hungary	88.7	84.4	75.2	45.4	12.2	3.9	1.4	.	*Hongrie*
Poland	1.4	81.6	85.1	81.6	49.8	17.3	5.8	x	*Pologne*
Russia	95.1	59.6	47.7	8.4	0.1	.	.	.	*Russie*

See Annex 1 for notes

Voir notes en annexe 1

P03: Participation in secondary education

P03 : Scolarisation dans le secondaire

Table P03(A2):
Net enrolment in all public and private secondary education (part-time enrolments) (1992)

*Tableau P03(A2) :
Taux net de scolarisation dans l'enseignement secondaire public et privé (effectifs à temps partiel) (1992)*

	14	15	16	17	18	19	20	21	
North America									*Amérique du Nord*
Canada	.	.	.	.	.	.	.	.	*Canada*
United States	-	-	-	-	-	-	-	-	*Etats-Unis*
Pacific Area									*Pays du Pacifique*
Australia	...	...	...	...	...	...	...	...	*Australie*
Japan	.	1.4	1.4	1.4	0.8	0.4	1.1	x	*Japon*
New Zealand	-	-	0.8	2.3	3.7	3.8	3.0	2.4	*Nouvelle-Zélande*
European Community									*Communauté européenne*
Belgium	.	0.6	1.6	2.3	0.7	0.3	0.1	0.1	*Belgique*
Denmark	.	.	.	.	.	.	.	.	*Danemark*
France	.	.	.	.	.	.	.	.	*France*
Germany (FTFR)	-	-	0.2	0.4	0.4	0.4	0.4	0.3	*Allemagne (ex-terr. de la RFA)*
Germany	...	...	...	...	...	...	...	...	*Allemagne*
Greece	.	.	.	.	.	.	.	.	*Grèce*
Ireland	-	-	1.0	0.4	0.7	0.9	0.6	0.5	*Irlande*
Italy	-	-	-	-	-	-	-	-	*Italie*
Luxembourg	...	...	...	...	...	...	...	...	*Luxembourg*
Netherlands	-	0.2	0.5	1.2	2.6	3.6	3.8	3.2	*Pays-Bas*
Portugal	...	...	...	...	...	...	...	...	*Portugal*
Spain	...	...	...	...	...	...	...	...	*Espagne*
United Kingdom	x	1.2	15.4	19.7	15.9	10.1	7.3	6.1	*Royaume-Uni*
Other Europe - OECD									*Autres pays d'Europe - OCDE*
Austria	.	.	.	.	.	.	.	.	*Autriche*
Finland	-	-	-	-	-	-	-	-	*Finlande*
Iceland	...	...	...	...	...	...	...	...	*Islande*
Norway	-	-	0.1	0.4	0.3	0.4	0.4	0.4	*Norvège*
Sweden	-	-	0.4	1.0	3.7	6.0	7.1	7.3	*Suède*
Switzerland	-	-	-	-	0.1	0.2	0.3	0.3	*Suisse*
Turkey	.	.	.	.	.	.	.	.	*Turquie*
Country mean	...	0.2	1.1	1.5	1.5	1.4	1.3	1.1	***Moyenne des pays***
Central and Eastern Europe									*Europe centrale et orientale*
Czech Republic	.	.	.	.	...	...	...	...	*République tchèque*
Hungary	1.3	3.9	3.5	5.7	6.5	5.7	4.5	3.6	*Hongrie*
Poland	.	.	.	.	.	.	.	.	*Pologne*
Russia	.	5.0	x	11.0	.	.	.	.	*Russie*

See Annex 1 for notes

Voir notes en annexe 1

P03: Participation in secondary education

P03 : Scolarisation dans le secondaire

Chart P03(A):
Net enrolment of 16, 17 and 18 year-olds in public and private secondary education (1992)

Graphique P03(A) :
Taux net de scolarisation des jeunes de 16, 17 et 18 ans dans l'enseignement secondaire public et privé (1992)

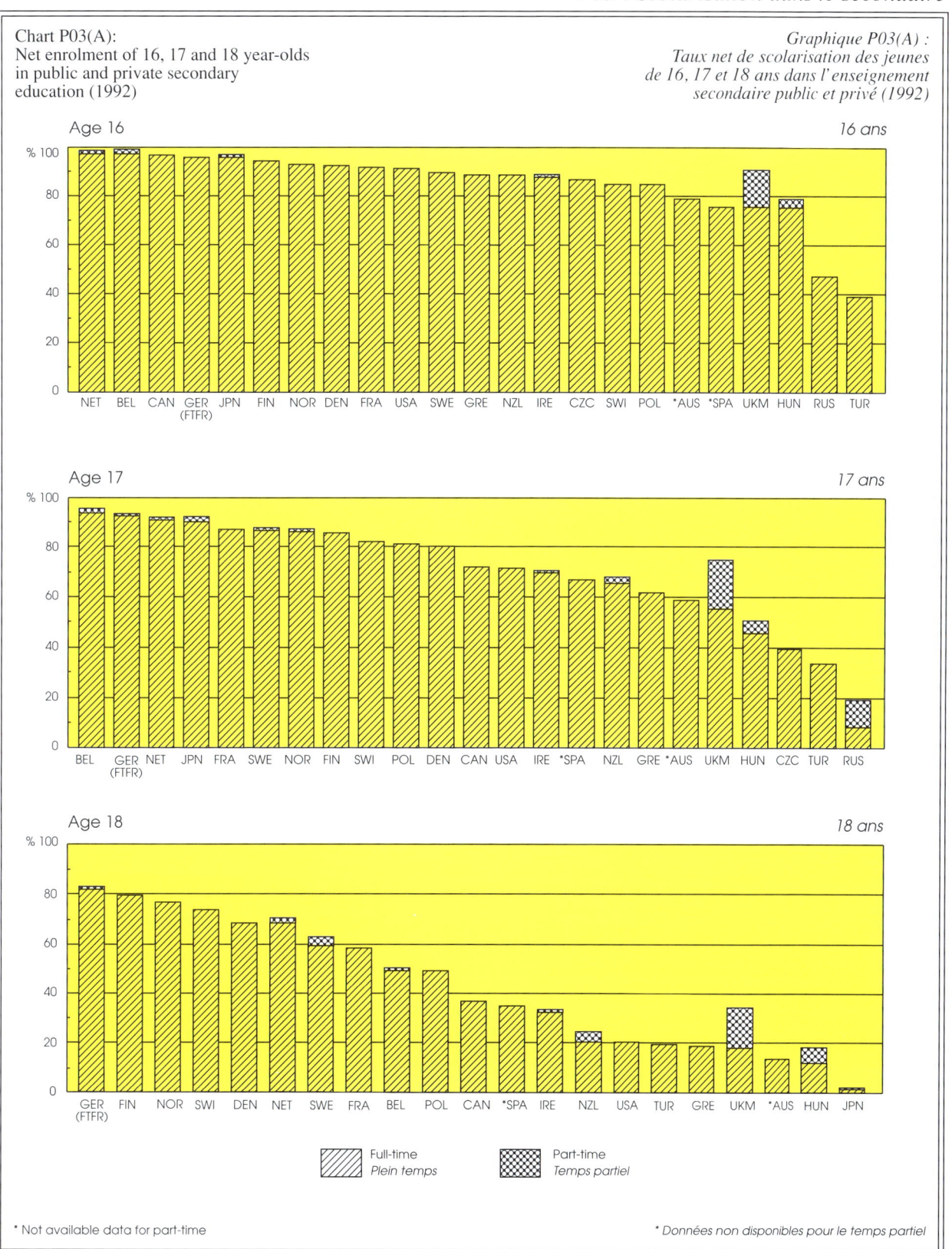

Age 16 / 16 ans

Age 17 / 17 ans

Age 18 / 18 ans

Full-time / Plein temps
Part-time / Temps partiel

* Not available data for part-time
* Données non disponibles pour le temps partiel

P03: Participation in secondary education

P03 : Scolarisation dans le secondaire

Table P03(B):
Percentage of upper secondary students enrolled in public and private general and vocational education (head counts) (1992)

Tableau P03(B) :
Pourcentage des élèves de l'enseignement secondaire du deuxième cycle général et professionnel, établissements publics et privés (en nombre d'individus) (1992)

	General education *Enseignement général*	Vocational education and apprenticeship *Enseignement professionnel et apprentissage*	Total	
North America				*Amérique du Nord*
Canada	...	...	...	*Canada*
United States	...	...	...	*Etats-Unis*
Pacific Area				*Pays du Pacifique*
Australia	75.5	24.5	100.0	*Australie*
Japan	72.5	27.5	100.0	*Japon*
New Zealand	81.2	18.8	100.0	*Nouvelle-Zélande*
European Community				*Communauté européenne*
Belgium	40.8	59.2	100.0	*Belgique*
Denmark	43.8	56.2	100.0	*Danemark*
France	45.9	54.1	100.0	*France*
Germany (FTFR)	20.4	79.6	100.0	*Allemagne (ex-terr. de la RFA)*
Germany	20.2	79.8	100.0	*Allemagne*
Greece	...	...	...	*Grèce*
Ireland	...	...	...	*Irlande*
Italy	32.6	67.4	100.0	*Italie*
Luxembourg	...	...	...	*Luxembourg*
Netherlands	29.9	70.1	100.0	*Pays-Bas*
Portugal	...	...	...	*Portugal*
Spain	58.6	41.4	100.0	*Espagne*
United Kingdom	42.4	57.6	100.0	*Royaume-Uni*
Other Europe - OECD				*Autres pays d'Europe - OCDE*
Austria	24.0	76.0	100.0	*Autriche*
Finland	45.6	54.4	100.0	*Finlande*
Iceland	...	...	...	*Islande*
Norway	40.2	59.8	100.0	*Norvège*
Sweden	...	...	...	*Suède*
Switzerland	26.8	73.2	100.0	*Suisse*
Turkey	56.5	43.5	100.0	*Turquie*
Central and Eastern Europe				*Europe centrale et orientale*
Czech Republic	46.3	53.7	100.0	*République tchèque*
Hungary	25.0	75.0	100.0	*Hongrie*
Poland	25.4	74.6	100.0	*Pologne*
Russia	56.4	43.6	100.0	*Russie*

See Annex 1 for notes

Voir notes en annexe 1

P03: Participation in secondary education

P03 : Scolarisation dans le secondaire

Chart P03(B):
Percentage of upper secondary students enrolled in public and private general and vocational education (head counts) (1992)

Graphique P03(B) :
Pourcentage des élèves de l'enseignement secondaire du deuxième cycle général et professionnel, établissements publics et privés (en nombre d'individus) (1992)

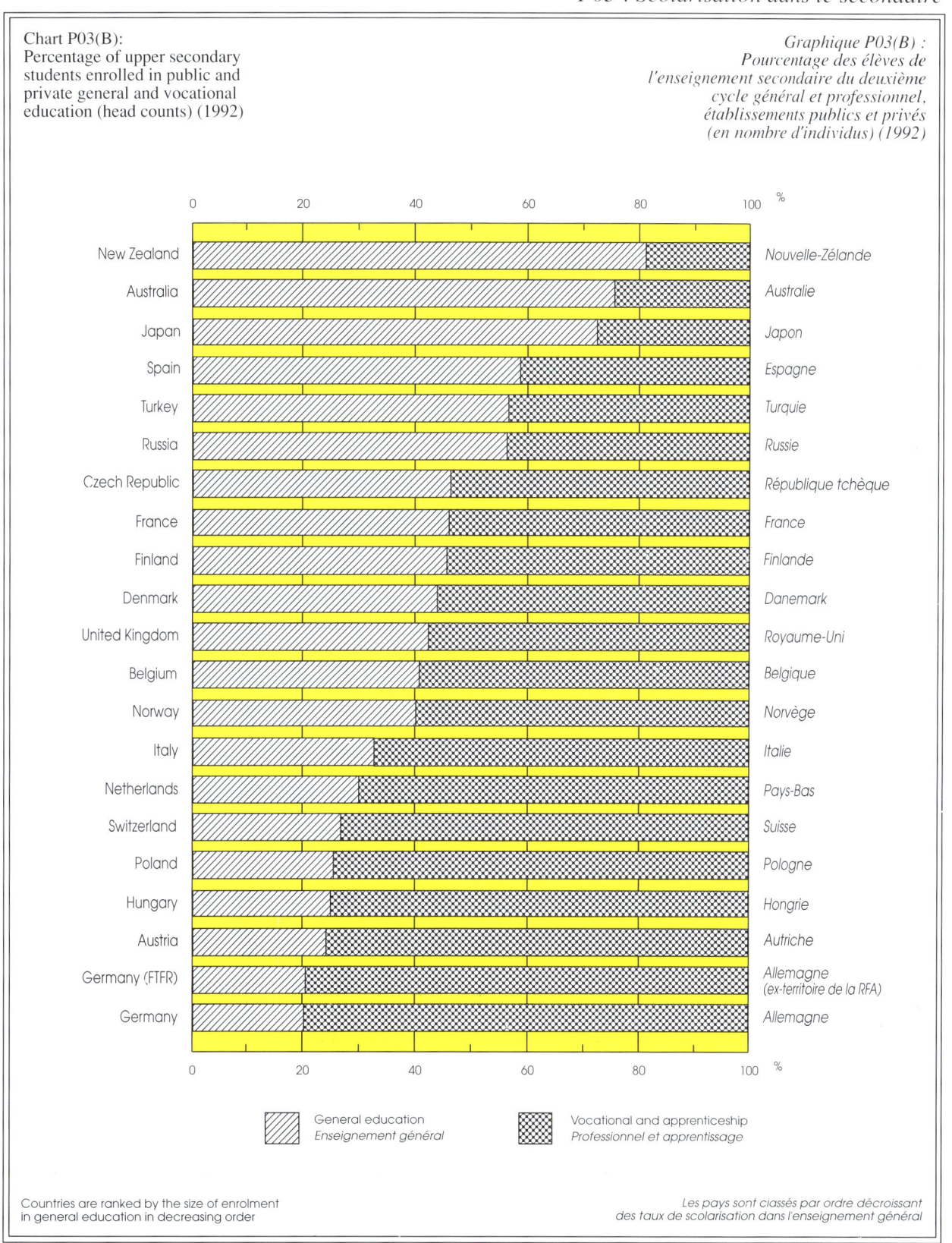

New Zealand	Nouvelle-Zélande
Australia	Australie
Japan	Japon
Spain	Espagne
Turkey	Turquie
Russia	Russie
Czech Republic	République tchèque
France	France
Finland	Finlande
Denmark	Danemark
United Kingdom	Royaume-Uni
Belgium	Belgique
Norway	Norvège
Italy	Italie
Netherlands	Pays-Bas
Switzerland	Suisse
Poland	Pologne
Hungary	Hongrie
Austria	Autriche
Germany (FTFR)	Allemagne (ex-territoire de la RFA)
Germany	Allemagne

Legend:
- General education / Enseignement général
- Vocational and apprenticeship / Professionnel et apprentissage

Countries are ranked by the size of enrolment in general education in decreasing order

Les pays sont classés par ordre décroissant des taux de scolarisation dans l'enseignement général

P03: Participation in secondary education

P03 : Scolarisation dans le secondaire

Table P03(C):
Ratio of enrolled students (full-time equivalents) in public and private upper secondary education, by type of educational programme, to population in the typical age group (1992)

Tableau P03(C) :
Taux de scolarisation (en équivalent plein temps) dans l'enseignement secondaire du deuxième cycle par cursus de formation par rapport à la classe d'âge correspondante, établissements publics et privés (1992)

	First educational programmes / Premier cursus de formation			Second educational programmes / Second cursus de formation			
	Upper secondary education / Enseignement secondaire 2ᵉ cycle	General education / Enseignement général	Vocational education and apprenticeship / Enseignement professionnel et Apprentissage	Upper secondary education / Enseignement secondaire 2ᵉ cycle	General education / Enseignement général	Vocational education and apprenticeship / Enseignement professionnel et apprentissage	
North America							*Amérique du Nord*
Canada	103.5	...	...	.	.	.	*Canada*
United States	87.8	...	...	.	.	.	*Etats-Unis*
Pacific Area							*Pays du Pacifique*
Australia	...	...	...	...	...	...	*Australie*
Japan	100.0	72.5	27.5	-	-	-	*Japon*
New Zealand	99.4	79.7	19.7	3.8	3.8	.	*Nouvelle-Zélande*
European Community							*Communauté européenne*
Belgium	101.6	44.2	57.4	.	.	.	*Belgique*
Denmark	77.8	36.2	41.5	10.0	2.2	7.8	*Danemark*
France	108.7	49.9	58.8	.	.	.	*France*
Germany (FTFR)	100.4	26.2	74.2	21.3	.	1.3	*Allemagne (ex-terr. de la RFA)*
Germany	...	...	...	...	...	...	*Allemagne*
Greece	93.9	...	...	.	.	.	*Grèce*
Ireland	...	...	...	...	...	...	*Irlande*
Italy	78.6	25.6	53.0	-	-	-	*Italie*
Luxembourg	...	...	...	...	...	...	*Luxembourg*
Netherlands	120.4	42.7	77.7	7.5	3.5	4.0	*Pays-Bas*
Portugal	...	...	...	...	...	...	*Portugal*
Spain	113.3	62.8	50.5	20.4	.	20.4	*Espagne*
United Kingdom	125.7	67.4	58.3	x	x	x	*Royaume-Uni*
Other Europe - OECD							*Autres pays d'Europe - OCDE*
Austria	...	...	...	...	...	...	*Autriche*
Finland	...	...	...	...	...	...	*Finlande*
Iceland	...	...	...	...	...	...	*Islande*
Norway	126.6	50.9	75.8	.	.	.	*Norvège*
Sweden	...	...	...	...	...	...	*Suède*
Switzerland	...	...	...	...	...	...	*Suisse*
Turkey	35.6	22.5	13.1	.	.	.	*Turquie*
Country mean	**98.2**	**48.4**	**50.6**	**3.9**	**0.6**	**3.3**	***Moyenne des pays***
Central and Eastern Europe							*Europe centrale et orientale*
Czech Republic	70.1	32.4	37.6	.	.	.	*République tchèque*
Hungary	86.4	19.9	66.5	7.5	-	6.5	*Hongrie*
Poland	...	...	...	...	...	...	*Pologne*
Russia	...	...	...	...	...	...	*Russie*

See Annex 1 for notes

Voir notes en annexe 1

P04: Transition characteristics from secondary to tertiary education

NET RATES OF PARTICIPATION SHOWING PASSAGE FROM SECONDARY TO TERTIARY EDUCATION

POLICY ISSUES

Recent years have seen the dissolving of age boundaries in the transition from secondary to tertiary education. Graph lines have flattened as the process has "widened" to include students ranging from 17 to 24 years old. Does this represent an opportunity for countries to explore new organisational frameworks for learning that are more gradual and take place outside as well as inside the classroom? Or is it in fact a constraint that hampers formulation of coherent education policy?

KEY RESULTS

For 17 year-olds, all countries show much higher rates of full-time enrolment in upper secondary than in tertiary education, and only seven out of 23 countries show total rates of full-time education participation (upper secondary and tertiary combined) of less than 70 per cent. By age 19, however, upper secondary participation rates decline and students are shifting to tertiary education. Three-quarters of the countries show total full-time participation rates (all levels combined) of less than 50 per cent of the age group and the majority of countries have higher full-time enrolments in tertiary than upper secondary education. By age 24, the vast majority of young adults in most countries are no longer in school full-time, almost all remaining full-time participants are in universities, and total full-time participation rates are greater than 15 per cent of the age group in only five countries.

DESCRIPTION AND INTERPRETATION

This indicator shows net rates of full-time participation in upper secondary, non-university tertiary and university education at each year of age from 17 to 24. Overall, rates slope downward for each succeeding year of age. For age 17, only four out of 23 countries (the Czech Republic, Hungary, Russia and Turkey) report overall full-time participation rates of less than 50 per cent of the age group. As full-time upper secondary education ends, the number of countries with overall full-time participation rates below 50 per cent increases, so that by age 19, 15 out of 20 countries reporting complete data have full-time education participation rates (upper secondary and tertiary combined) below 50 per cent of the age group.

After age 19, the decrease in full-time education participation by year of age is gradual but steady. For 20 year-olds, 16 out of 21 countries with complete data report overall full-time participation rates of 20 per cent or greater, with the majority of those participants in tertiary education in all but four countries. Those four – Denmark, Germany (FTFR), the Netherlands and Switzerland – allow students who have completed upper secondary education to pursue additional upper secondary qualifications, which may help account for their relatively high continuing upper secondary participation rates. For those aged 22, nine out of 21 countries report full-time participation rates above 20 per cent of the age group, and all countries except Germany (FTFR) report a majority of their full-time participants in tertiary education. For the 24 age group, only three countries (Denmark, Finland and Norway) report full-time educational participation at more than 20 per cent.

A few countries show full-time participation rates that do not decline steadily over time. Finland shows higher full-time rates for 21 and 22 year-olds than for 19 year-olds, a result of increasing full-time tertiary participation and only a small decline in full-time secondary participation. Sweden shows a substantial increase in full-time participation at age 22 (followed by a substantial decrease the following year), due primarily to a major increase in full-time upper secondary participation.

Some countries count all tertiary participants as enrolled full-time, particularly students in universities, while others do not. If part-time tertiary enrolments had been included, it is likely that overall tertiary participation rates in some countries would be considerably higher.

DEFINITIONS

Net enrolment rates for each year of age are calculated by dividing full-time school enrollees at that age by the total population at that age.

All enrolment rates shown are for full-time students only. Some countries consider all tertiary (or all university) participants to be full-time students, while other countries identify or define some participants as enrolled on a part-time basis. Thus, *this indicator does not show overall rates of education participation*, especially for countries that distinguish part-time enrolments. It should not be used to compare overall tertiary participation rates across OECD countries.

P04: Transition characteristics from secondary to tertiary education

P04 : Spécificités du passage de l'enseignement secondaire à l'enseignement supérieur

Table P04(1):
Transition characteristics at each year of age from 17 through 24: net full-time enrolment rates by level of education in public and private institutions (1992)

Tableau P04(1) :
Spécificités du passage du secondaire au supérieur par année d'âge de 17 à 24 ans : taux de fréquentation à plein temps par niveau scolaire, établissements publics et privés (1992)

	Age 17 / 17 ans				Age 18 / 18 ans				
	Upper secondary education / Enseignement secondaire du 2ᵉ cycle	Non-university tertiary education / Enseignement supérieur non universitaire	University education / Enseignement supérieur universitaire	Total	Upper secondary education / Enseignement secondaire du 2ᵉ cycle	Non-university tertiary education / Enseignement supérieur non universitaire	University education / Enseignement supérieur universitaire	Total	
North America									*Amérique du Nord*
Canada	70.8	2.4	7.0	80.2	36.9	6.3	17.6	60.8	Canada
United States	70.8	1.1	2.2	74.0	20.3	11.9	21.9	54.0	Etats-Unis
Pacific Area									*Pays du Pacifique*
Australia	56.8	4.2	11.0	72.0	13.4	9.5	19.6	42.5	Australie
Japan	90.3	.	.	90.3	1.8	...	...	...	Japon
New Zealand	63.6	1.0	0.5	65.2	19.1	4.4	15.3	38.8	Nouvelle-Zélande
European Community									*Communauté européenne*
Belgium	89.9	0.1	0.6	90.6	47.4	10.6	17.2	75.2	Belgique
Denmark	73.8	-	-	73.8	68.0	0.1	0.4	68.5	Danemark
France	82.9	0.2	1.7	84.9	57.8	4.1	16.0	77.9	France
Germany (FTFR)	81.1	0.6	-	81.7	81.1	1.4	0.3	82.8	Allemagne (ex-terr. de la RFA)
Germany	...	...	...	...	...	...	...	...	Allemagne
Greece	61.4	.	.	61.4	19.1	7.5	18.1	44.7	Grèce
Ireland	69.6	3.2	3.6	76.5	33.0	10.7	13.8	57.5	Irlande
Italy	...	...	...	...	...	...	...	...	Italie
Luxembourg	...	...	...	...	...	...	...	...	Luxembourg
Netherlands	73.1	.	1.6	74.7	62.5	.	10.9	73.4	Pays-Bas
Portugal	...	...	...	...	...	...	...	...	Portugal
Spain	66.9	.	0.3	67.3	35.5	0.2	18.1	53.8	Espagne
United Kingdom	55.3	0.3	1.1	56.7	18.7	2.1	12.8	33.6	Royaume-Uni
Other Europe - OECD									*Autres pays d'Europe - OCDE*
Austria	...	.	-	...	...	...	5.8	...	Autriche
Finland	84.7	0.5	-	85.2	79.5	1.8	0.4	81.7	Finlande
Iceland	...	...	...	...	...	...	...	...	Islande
Norway	86.6	-	-	86.7	77.2	0.3	0.2	77.7	Norvège
Sweden	86.9	.	-	86.9	59.6	0.9	0.2	60.8	Suède
Switzerland	77.5	0.2	-	77.8	73.6	0.5	0.5	74.7	Suisse
Turkey	29.4	0.6	2.2	32.2	19.8	1.2	5.2	26.1	Turquie
Country mean	**72.2**	**0.7**	**1.6**	**74.6**	**43.4**	**4.1**	**10.2**	**60.3**	**Moyenne des pays**
Central and Eastern Europe									*Europe centrale et orientale*
Czech Republic	39.4	.	.	39.4	.	2.6	14.4	17.0	République tchèque
Hungary	45.4	.	.	45.4	12.2	2.6	3.4	18.2	Hongrie
Poland	81.6	.	.	81.6	49.8	0.2	0.5	50.5	Pologne
Russia	8.0	18.7	...	...	0.1	17.8	...	...	Russie

See Annex 1 for notes

Voir notes en annexe 1

P04: Transition characteristics from secondary to tertiary education

P04 : Spécificités du passage de l'enseignement secondaire à l'enseignement supérieur

Table P04(2):
Transition characteristics at each year of age
from 17 through 24: net full-time enrolment rates
by level of education in public and private institutions (1992)

*Tableau P04(2) :
Spécificités du passage du secondaire au supérieur par année d'âge
de 17 à 24 ans : taux de fréquentation à plein temps
par niveau scolaire, établissements publics et privés (1992)*

	Age 19 / *19 ans*				Age 20 / *20 ans*				
	Upper secondary education	Non-university tertiary education	University education	Total	Upper secondary education	Non-university tertiary education	University education	Total	
North America									*Amérique du Nord*
Canada	11.1	10.5	25.4	47.0	14.0	9.6	24.0	47.6	*Canada*
United States	5.6	11.5	25.2	42.4	1.6	7.2	24.1	32.9	*Etats-Unis*
Pacific Area									*Pays du Pacifique*
Australia	2.5	7.7	19.7	29.9	2.6	4.9	15.5	23.0	*Australie*
Japan	x	...	...	...	x	...	...	...	*Japon*
New Zealand	4.8	5.5	19.4	29.6	1.9	4.4	18.5	24.8	*Nouvelle-Zélande*
European Community									*Communauté européenne*
Belgium	23.6	17.2	18.8	59.6	9.5	17.6	16.8	43.9	*Belgique*
Denmark	48.2	0.7	4.3	53.1	28.2	1.9	11.1	41.2	*Danemark*
France	33.8	9.6	21.2	64.6	12.0	11.9	22.7	46.6	*France*
Germany (FTFR)	55.0	2.1	4.0	61.1	29.3	2.3	9.7	41.2	*Allemagne (ex-terr. de la RFA)*
Germany	...	...	...	...	...	...	...	...	*Allemagne*
Greece	10.4	10.6	23.6	44.6	4.6	9.1	11.8	25.6	*Grèce*
Ireland	11.5	11.0	16.6	39.1	6.9	7.9	14.7	29.6	*Irlande*
Italy	...	...	...	...	...	...	...	...	*Italie*
Luxembourg	...	...	...	...	...	...	...	...	*Luxembourg*
Netherlands	41.6	.	19.9	61.5	25.0	.	23.6	48.5	*Pays-Bas*
Portugal	...	...	...	...	...	...	...	...	*Portugal*
Spain	20.7	0.2	23.8	44.8	17.2	0.7	24.8	42.7	*Espagne*
United Kingdom	4.3	2.9	16.7	23.9	1.9	2.2	15.4	19.5	*Royaume-Uni*
Other Europe - OECD									*Autres pays d'Europe - OCDE*
Austria	...	...	12.8	...	...	...	16.1	...	*Autriche*
Finland	26.7	4.0	8.8	39.5	16.4	6.1	13.8	36.3	*Finlande*
Iceland	...	...	...	...	...	...	...	...	*Islande*
Norway	34.6	7.8	6.2	48.6	17.6	9.2	10.1	36.9	*Norvège*
Sweden	11.5	9.1	3.7	24.3	2.7	7.9	6.0	16.5	*Suède*
Switzerland	48.7	1.2	2.7	52.6	20.5	2.6	6.4	29.5	*Suisse*
Turkey	9.7	1.3	7.2	18.2	6.0	1.1	8.0	15.1	*Turquie*
Country mean	**21.3**	**6.3**	**14.7**	**43.6**	**11.5**	**5.9**	**15.4**	**33.4**	*Moyenne des pays*
Central and Eastern Europe									*Europe centrale et orientale*
Czech Republic	.	1.6	12.8	14.4	.	x	12.4	12.4	*République tchèque*
Hungary	3.9	4.2	6.1	14.2	1.4	4.6	6.9	12.9	*Hongrie*
Poland	17.3	5.1	8.5	30.9	5.8	5.8	11.8	23.3	*Pologne*
Russia	.	7.7	...	...	.	2.8	...	...	*Russie*

See Annex 1 for notes

Voir notes en annexe 1

P04: Transition characteristics from secondary to tertiary education

P04 : Spécificités du passage de l'enseignement secondaire à l'enseignement supérieur

Table P04(3):
Transition characteristics at each year of age from 17 through 24: net full-time enrolment rates by level of education in public and private institutions (1992)

Tableau P04(3) :
Spécificités du passage du secondaire au supérieur par année d'âge de 17 à 24 ans : taux de fréquentation à plein temps par niveau scolaire, établissements publics et privés (1992)

	\multicolumn{4}{c	}{Age 21 / 21 ans}	\multicolumn{4}{c	}{Age 22 / 22 ans}	
	Upper secondary education / Enseignement secondaire du 2e cycle	Non-university tertiary education / Enseignement supérieur non universitaire	University education / Enseignement supérieur universitaire	Total	Upper secondary education / Enseignement secondaire du 2e cycle	Non-university tertiary education / Enseignement supérieur non universitaire	University education / Enseignement supérieur universitaire	Total	
North America									*Amérique du Nord*
Canada	.	6.5	21.9	28.4	.	4.2	17.2	21.4	*Canada*
United States	0.5	4.1	23.7	28.3	0.4	2.9	16.3	19.6	*Etats-Unis*
Pacific Area									*Pays du Pacifique*
Australia	x	3.1	10.5	13.6	x	2.2	6.8	9.0	*Australie*
Japan	x	...	...	...	x	...	...	...	*Japon*
New Zealand	1.4	3.2	14.7	19.3	0.9	1.9	9.3	12.1	*Nouvelle-Zélande*
European Community									*Communauté européenne*
Belgium	3.9	12.1	15.1	31.1	1.5	6.2	12.3	20.0	*Belgique*
Denmark	16.3	2.8	15.7	34.7	9.7	3.2	18.2	31.2	*Danemark*
France	3.1	9.4	21.0	33.5	1.0	5.2	17.6	23.8	*France*
Germany (FTFR)	16.0	2.0	13.1	31.1	20.4	1.6	14.9	36.8	*Allemagne (ex-terr. de la RFA)*
Germany	...	...	...	...	...	...	...	...	*Allemagne*
Greece	2.4	5.9	9.9	18.1	x	4.7	3.4	8.1	*Grèce*
Ireland	3.6	3.9	11.9	19.4	1.4	2.2	7.5	11.1	*Irlande*
Italy	...	...	...	...	...	...	...	...	*Italie*
Luxembourg	...	...	...	...	...	...	...	...	*Luxembourg*
Netherlands	14.7	.	24.0	38.7	6.6	.	21.4	28.0	*Pays-Bas*
Portugal	...	...	...	...	...	...	...	...	*Portugal*
Spain	10.6	-	23.4	34.0	6.5	-	21.3	27.9	*Espagne*
United Kingdom	1.2	1.4	11.1	13.7	1.0	0.9	6.3	8.1	*Royaume-Uni*
Other Europe - OECD									*Autres pays d'Europe - OCDE*
Austria	...	...	16.7	...	...	...	16.3	...	*Autriche*
Finland	15.2	8.1	17.0	40.3	12.9	8.1	19.2	40.1	*Finlande*
Iceland	...	...	...	...	...	...	...	...	*Islande*
Norway	11.9	6.9	14.5	33.4	8.4	5.3	16.6	30.3	*Norvège*
Sweden	1.7	7.0	7.4	16.1	13.4	5.8	8.7	27.9	*Suède*
Switzerland	8.2	3.6	8.8	20.5	4.2	3.9	8.9	17.0	*Suisse*
Turkey	.	0.8	7.9	8.8	.	0.5	6.7	7.2	*Turquie*
Country mean	**5.8**	**4.5**	**15.2**	**25.7**	**4.6**	**3.3**	**13.1**	**21.1**	***Moyenne des pays***
Central and Eastern Europe									*Europe centrale et orientale*
Czech Republic	.	x	12.4	12.4	.	x	9.6	9.6	*République tchèque*
Hungary	.	3.1	6.9	10.0	.	1.5	6.3	7.8	*Hongrie*
Poland	x	2.9	12.2	15.1	x	1.3	11.9	13.2	*Pologne*
Russia	.	1.5	...	...	.	0.9	...	...	*Russie*

See Annex 1 for notes — *Voir notes en annexe 1*

P04: Transition characteristics from secondary to tertiary education

P04 : Spécificités du passage de l'enseignement secondaire à l'enseignement supérieur

Table P04(4):
Transition characteristics at each year of age from 17 through 24: net full-time enrolment rates by level of education in public and private institutions (1992)

Tableau P04(4) :
Spécificités du passage du secondaire au supérieur par année d'âge de 17 à 24 ans : taux de fréquentation à plein temps par niveau scolaire, établissements publics et privés (1992)

	Age 23 / 23 ans				Age 24 / 24 ans				
	Upper secondary education	Non-university tertiary education	University education	Total	Upper secondary education	Non-university tertiary education	University education	Total	
North America									*Amérique du Nord*
Canada	.	3.0	11.3	14.3	.	2.1	7.5	9.6	Canada
United States	0.6	2.5	9.5	12.6	0.4	1.4	6.6	8.4	États-Unis
Pacific Area									*Pays du Pacifique*
Australia	x	1.7	4.6	6.3	x	1.4	3.2	4.6	Australie
Japan	x	...	...	...	x	...	...	...	Japon
New Zealand	0.7	1.3	5.4	7.5	0.7	1.1	3.4	5.2	Nouvelle-Zélande
European Community									*Communauté européenne*
Belgium	0.6	2.7	8.2	11.5	0.4	1.0	5.1	6.6	Belgique
Denmark	4.7	3.0	18.7	26.3	3.9	2.6	17.7	24.2	Danemark
France	0.1	2.5	13.2	15.8	0.1	1.1	9.0	10.1	France
Germany (FTFR)	1.6	1.5	15.7	18.7	1.1	1.6	15.7	18.4	Allemagne (ex-terr. de la RFA)
Germany	...	...	...	...	...	...	...	...	Allemagne
Greece	x	4.1	1.9	6.0	x	2.8	0.9	3.7	Grèce
Ireland	0.4	1.0	4.6	6.1	0.4	0.8	2.8	4.0	Irlande
Italy	...	...	...	...	...	...	...	...	Italie
Luxembourg	...	...	...	...	...	...	...	...	Luxembourg
Netherlands	3.9	.	17.6	21.6	3.6	.	12.6	16.2	Pays-Bas
Portugal	...	...	...	...	...	...	...	...	Portugal
Spain	2.8	-	16.5	19.3	1.4	-	12.6	14.0	Espagne
United Kingdom	0.8	0.6	3.8	5.2	0.7	0.5	2.6	3.7	Royaume-Uni
Other Europe - OECD									*Autres pays d'Europe - OCDE*
Austria	...	...	16.2	...	...	...	15.3	...	Autriche
Finland	8.4	7.0	17.8	33.2	5.5	5.2	16.3	27.0	Finlande
Iceland	...	...	...	...	...	...	...	...	Islande
Norway	6.2	4.0	15.9	26.0	4.8	3.1	13.1	21.1	Norvège
Sweden	x	4.9	8.8	13.7	x	4.2	8.2	12.5	Suède
Switzerland	2.6	3.6	8.4	14.6	1.8	3.0	7.6	12.4	Suisse
Turkey	.	0.3	5.3	5.6	.	0.2	4.0	4.1	Turquie
Country mean	**1.8**	**2.4**	**10.7**	**14.7**	**1.3**	**1.8**	**8.6**	**11.4**	**Moyenne des pays**
Central and Eastern Europe									*Europe centrale et orientale*
Czech Republic	.	x	1.4	1.4	.	x	x	1.4	République tchèque
Hungary	.	0.7	4.7	5.4	.	0.3	2.8	3.2	Hongrie
Poland	x	0.8	10.6	11.3	.	0.5	7.8	8.3	Pologne
Russia	.	0.5	...	...	.	0.3	...	...	Russie

See Annex 1 for notes — *Voir notes en annexe 1*

P04: Transition characteristics from secondary to tertiary education

P04 : Spécificités du passage de l'enseignement secondaire à l'enseignement supérieur

Chart P04:
Transition characteristics:
full-time student enrolment
by single year of age
and level of education (1992)

*Graphique P04 :
Spécificités du passage du secondaire
au supérieur : effectifs scolarisés
à plein temps par année d'âge
et par niveau scolaire (1992)*

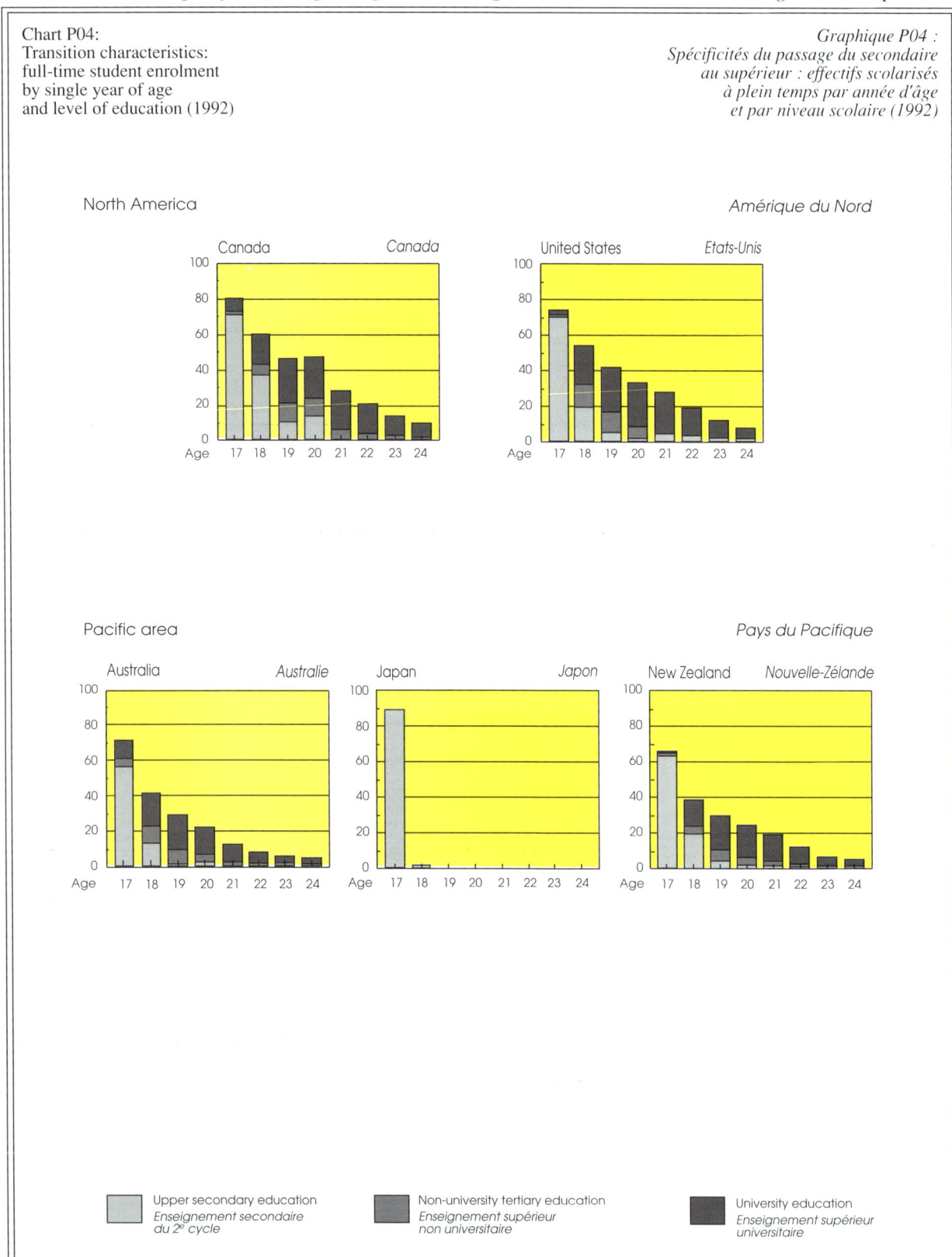

North America / *Amérique du Nord*

Canada / *Canada*

United States / *Etats-Unis*

Pacific area / *Pays du Pacifique*

Australia / *Australie*

Japan / *Japon*

New Zealand / *Nouvelle-Zélande*

- Upper secondary education / *Enseignement secondaire du 2ᵉ cycle*
- Non-university tertiary education / *Enseignement supérieur non universitaire*
- University education / *Enseignement supérieur universitaire*

146

P04: Transition characteristics from secondary to tertiary education

P04 : Spécificités du passage de l'enseignement secondaire à l'enseignement supérieur

Chart P04:
Transition characteristics:
full-time student enrolment
by single year of age
and level of education (1992)

*Graphique P04 :
Spécificités du passage du secondaire
au supérieur : effectifs scolarisés
à plein temps par année d'âge
et par niveau scolaire (1992)*

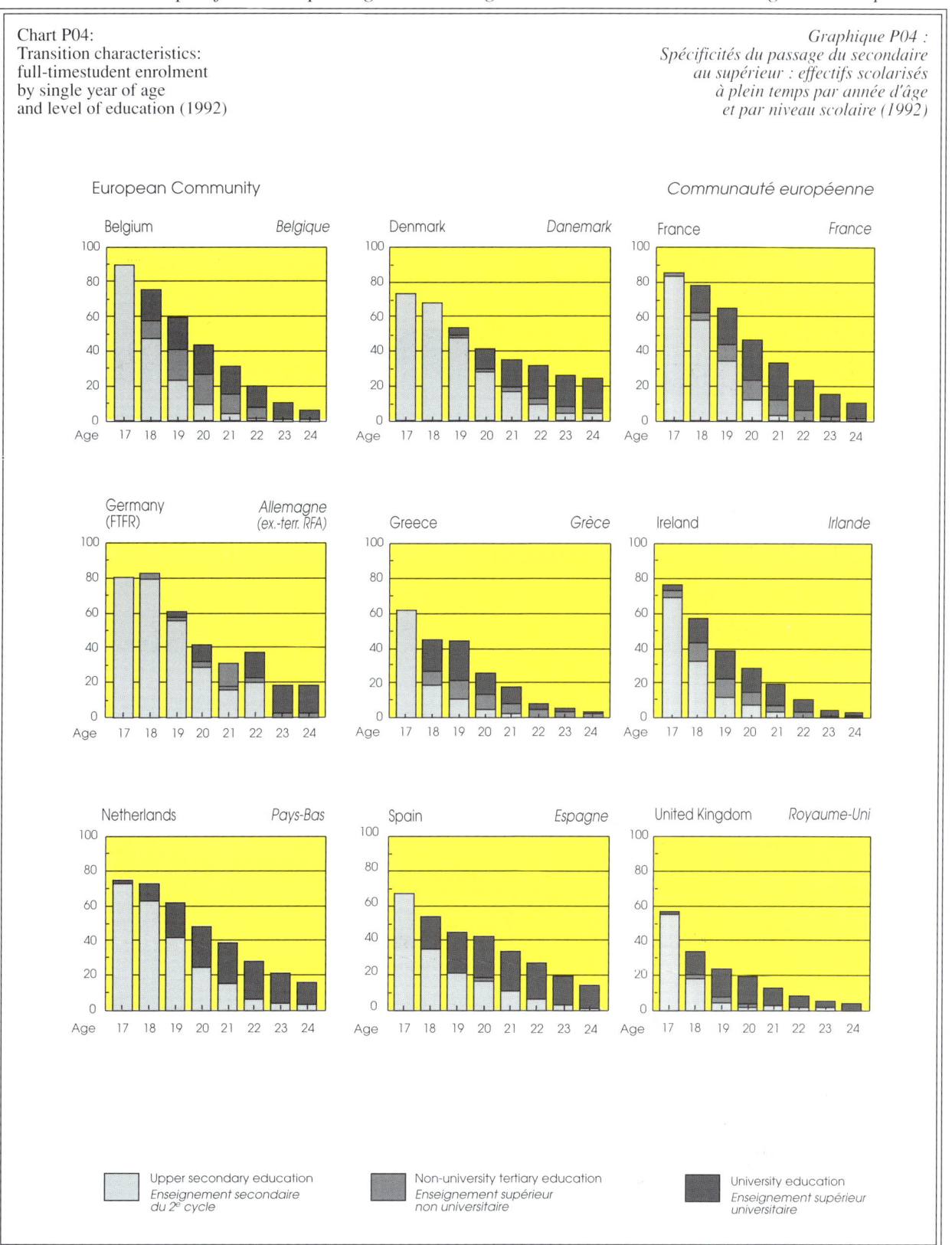

European Community — *Communauté européenne*

Belgium — *Belgique*
Denmark — *Danemark*
France — *France*
Germany (FTFR) — *Allemagne (ex.-terr. RFA)*
Greece — *Grèce*
Ireland — *Irlande*
Netherlands — *Pays-Bas*
Spain — *Espagne*
United Kingdom — *Royaume-Uni*

Upper secondary education / *Enseignement secondaire du 2e cycle*

Non-university tertiary education / *Enseignement supérieur non universitaire*

University education / *Enseignement supérieur universitaire*

P04: Transition characteristics from secondary to tertiary education

P04 : Spécificités du passage de l'enseignement secondaire à l'enseignement supérieur

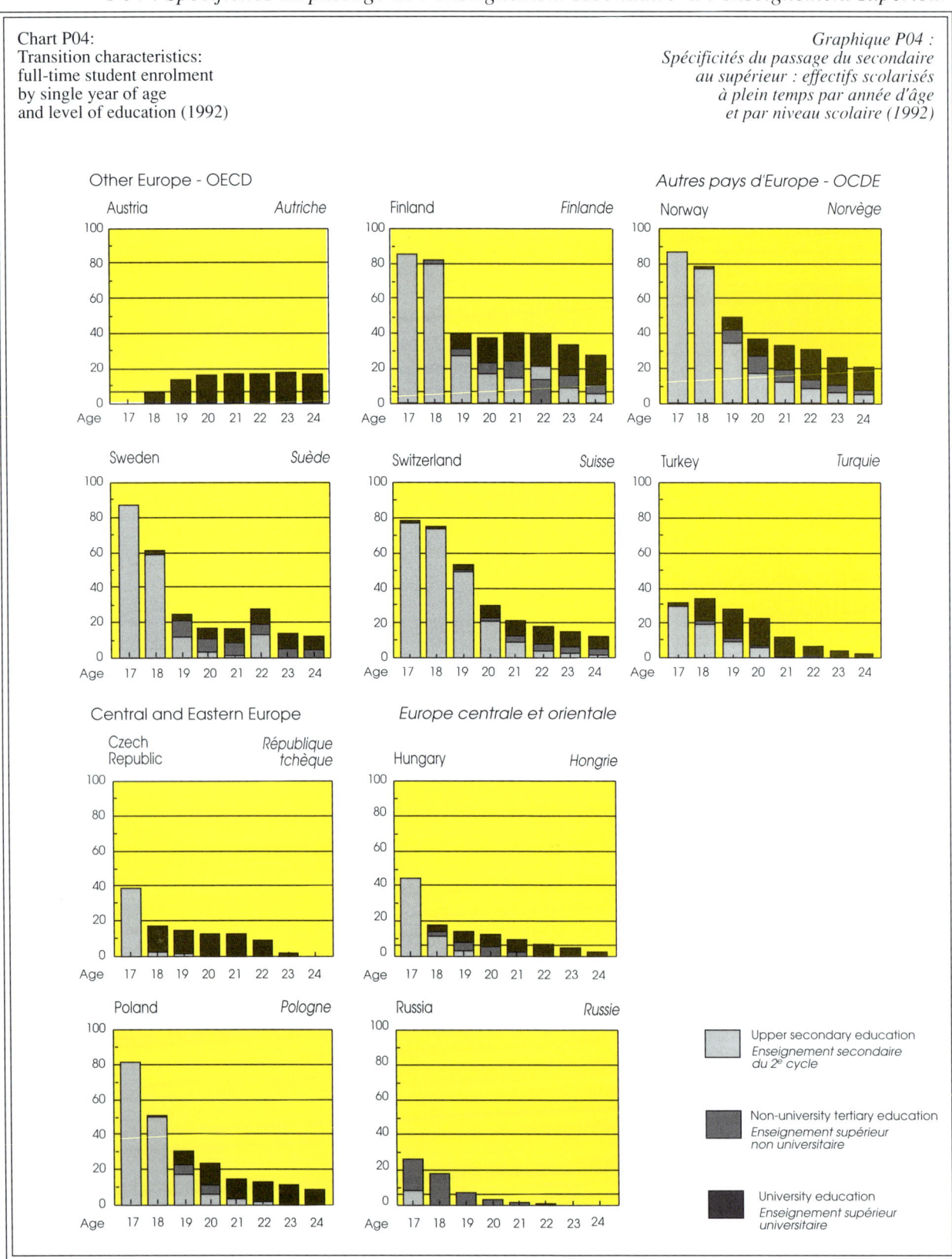

Chart P04:
Transition characteristics:
full-time student enrolment
by single year of age
and level of education (1992)

Graphique P04 :
Spécificités du passage du secondaire
au supérieur : effectifs scolarisés
à plein temps par année d'âge
et par niveau scolaire (1992)

Other Europe - OECD / *Autres pays d'Europe - OCDE*

Austria / *Autriche* — Finland / *Finlande* — Norway / *Norvège*

Sweden / *Suède* — Switzerland / *Suisse* — Turkey / *Turquie*

Central and Eastern Europe / *Europe centrale et orientale*

Czech Republic / *République tchèque* — Hungary / *Hongrie*

Poland / *Pologne* — Russia / *Russie*

Legend:
- Upper secondary education / *Enseignement secondaire du 2ᵉ cycle*
- Non-university tertiary education / *Enseignement supérieur non universitaire*
- University education / *Enseignement supérieur universitaire*

P05: Entry to tertiary education

RATIO OF NEW ENTRANTS INTO FULL-TIME PROGRAMMES LEADING TO A TERTIARY-LEVEL QUALIFICATION

POLICY ISSUES

In most countries, higher numbers of students enter university than non-university tertiary education. Are universities able to accommodate mass higher education? What are the implications with regard to expanding, maintaining or reducing levels of access?

KEY RESULTS

Across the OECD and Eastern European countries, there is a wide variation in the tertiary new entry index, i.e. the number of new full-time entrants per 100 individuals in the population at the most common age for starting tertiary education. The non-university new entry index is higher for women than for men in most countries; the university new entry index is higher for men in about half of the countries.

DESCRIPTION AND INTERPRETATION

It is essential to note two characteristics of the index. First, whereas it is calculated according to the number of people at the age when entrance to tertiary programmes most commonly occurs, the new entrants themselves may be of any age. Secondly, as a result of difficulties in distinguishing between new (first-time) entrants and other entrants, the number of new entrants may be overestimated in some countries. Thus, the index should not be interpreted as the percentage of those at the most common starting age for full-time tertiary education.

In most countries, there are more full-time new entrants to university than to non-university tertiary education relative to the population at the age at which new entrance most commonly occurs. The university new entry index ranges from 8.7 in Hungary to 43.3 in Spain; it is above 20 in 14 out of 19 OECD countries. In contrast, the non-university new entry index is below 20 in most OECD countries – 13 out of 16. Across all countries, it ranges from 0.4 in Italy to 37.3 in Sweden. Sweden and Japan are the only countries where the new entry index is higher for non-university tertiary education than for university education.

DEFINITIONS

New (i.e. first-time) entrants are persons enrolling in any tertiary university and non-university programme for the first time. Students who complete tertiary-level non-degree programmes and transfer to degree programmes are not regarded as new entrants; nor are persons returning to tertiary education after an absence. Foreign students who enrol in a country's education system for the first time in a post-graduate programme are considered new entrants. Each country has identified a theoretical starting year for new entrants to tertiary education, i.e. the age (or average of ages) in which tertiary education typically begins. These ages are shown in Annex 3.

This indicator is also affected by the kinds of data that countries can supply. Some countries are unable to distinguish between first-time and other entrants to full-time tertiary education (or between full- and part-time first-time entrants). In addition, some countries can identify first-time entrants in university but not in non-university tertiary education. The definition of new entrants may also differ across countries.

All of the information shown relates to full-time students only. Some countries consider all tertiary (or all university) participants to be full-time students, while other countries identify or define some participants as enrolled on a part-time basis. Thus, *this indicator does not show the total number of new entrants*, especially for countries that recognise part-time enrolment. It should not be used to compare overall tertiary access rates across OECD countries.

P05: Entry to tertiary education

P05 : Accès à l'enseignement supérieur

Table P05:
Number of new entrants to full-time public and private tertiary education per 100 persons in the theoretical starting âge, men and women (1992)

Tableau P05 :
Taux de nouveaux inscrits dans l'enseignement supérieur à plein temps pour 100 personnes de la population d'âge théorique, établissements publics et privés (1992)

	Non-university tertiary education / Enseignement supérieur non universitaire			University education / Enseignement supérieur universitaire			Total / Total			
	M+W / H+F	Men / Hommes	Women / Femmes	M+W / H+F	Men / Hommes	Women / Femmes	M+W / H+F	Men / Hommes	Women / Femmes	
North America										**Amérique du Nord**
Canada	...	...	...	...	...	...	...	...	...	Canada
United States	...	...	...	...	...	...	...	...	...	Etats-Unis
Pacific Area										**Pays du Pacifique**
Australia	...	...	...	38.3	33.7	43.0	...	...	...	Australie
Japan	29.7	19.3	40.7	25.2	34.1	15.9	55.0	53.4	56.6	Japon
New Zealand	11.8	10.0	13.5	24.9	23.9	26.0	36.7	34.0	39.5	Nouvelle-Zélande
European Community										**Communauté européenne**
Belgium	25.3	19.1	31.8	27.3	29.4	25.1	52.6	48.5	56.9	Belgique
Denmark	11.2	12.8	9.6	41.5	36.4	47.0	52.8	49.2	56.6	Danemark
France	17.3	16.0	18.7	30.6	26.6	34.8	48.0	42.6	53.5	France
Germany (FTFR)	12.5	11.4	13.7	35.3	45.4	24.8	47.8	56.8	38.5	Allemagne (ex-terr. de la RFA)
Germany	16.0	12.6	19.6	33.0	41.4	24.1	49.0	54.0	43.7	Allemagne
Greece	13.4	...	...	15.9	...	...	29.3	...	...	Grèce
Ireland	17.8	17.7	18.0	22.1	21.9	22.3	39.9	39.5	40.4	Irlande
Italy	0.4	0.3	0.6	41.3	41.4	41.2	41.7	41.6	41.8	Italie
Luxembourg	...	...	...	...	...	...	...	...	...	Luxembourg
Netherlands	.	.	.	40.1	40.7	39.4	40.1	40.7	39.4	Pays-Bas
Portugal	...	...	...	...	...	...	...	...	...	Portugal
Spain	-	-	-	43.3	40.8	45.9	43.3	40.8	45.9	Espagne
United Kingdom	10.3	9.9	10.7	26.6	27.5	25.6	36.9	37.4	36.3	Royaume-Uni
Other Europe - OECD										**Autres pays d'Europe - OCDE**
Austria	6.2	4.2	8.4	27.9	27.9	27.9	34.1	32.0	36.3	Autriche
Finland	...	...	...	...	...	...	...	...	...	Finlande
Iceland	...	...	...	...	...	...	...	...	...	Islande
Norway	18.2	15.8	20.8	19.8	15.9	23.9	38.0	31.7	44.6	Norvège
Sweden	37.3	33.6	41.3	14.7	14.1	15.3	52.0	47.7	56.5	Suède
Switzerland	13.0	15.3	10.7	15.2	16.9	13.4	28.2	32.1	24.2	Suisse
Turkey	2.3	3.0	1.6	12.0	14.7	9.0	14.3	17.7	10.7	Turquie
Country mean	**13.5**	**11.8**	**15.3**	**28.2**	**29.6**	**28.0**	**41.1**	**41.2**	**42.4**	**Moyenne des pays**
Central and Eastern Europe										**Europe centrale et orientale**
Czech Republic	4.0	3.2	4.9	13.9	15.9	11.8	17.9	19.1	16.7	République tchèque
Hungary	6.3	...	...	8.7	...	...	15.0	...	...	Hongrie
Poland	9.2	4.3	14.3	19.7	19.6	19.7	28.8	23.9	34.1	Pologne
Russia	...	...	...	...	...	...	...	...	...	Russie

See Annex 1 for notes

Voir notes en annexe 1

P05: Entry to tertiary education

P05 : Accès à l'enseignement supérieur

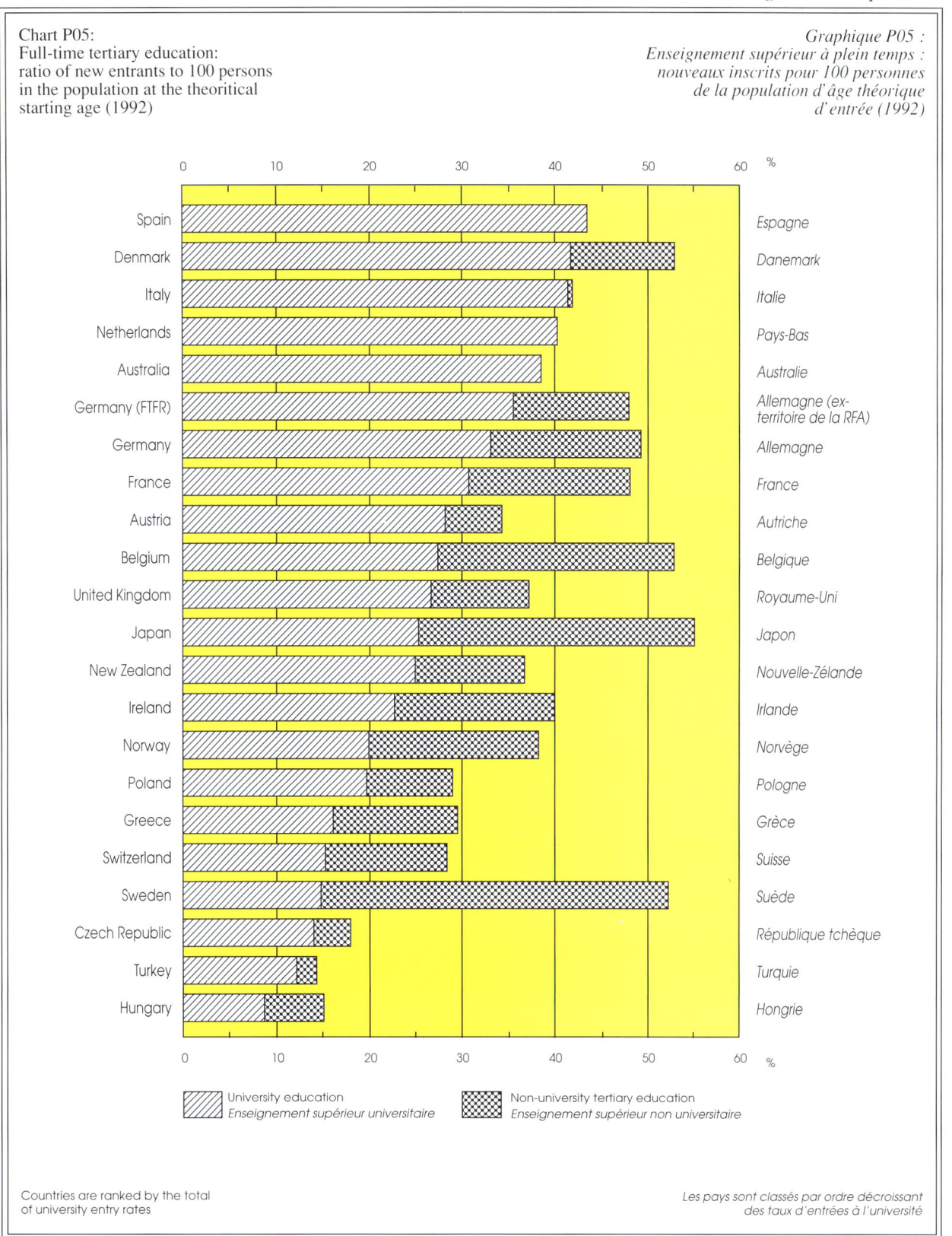

Chart P05:
Full-time tertiary education:
ratio of new entrants to 100 persons
in the population at the theoritical
starting age (1992)

Graphique P05 :
Enseignement supérieur à plein temps :
nouveaux inscrits pour 100 personnes
de la population d'âge théorique
d'entrée (1992)

Spain	Espagne
Denmark	Danemark
Italy	Italie
Netherlands	Pays-Bas
Australia	Australie
Germany (FTFR)	Allemagne (ex-territoire de la RFA)
Germany	Allemagne
France	France
Austria	Autriche
Belgium	Belgique
United Kingdom	Royaume-Uni
Japan	Japon
New Zealand	Nouvelle-Zélande
Ireland	Irlande
Norway	Norvège
Poland	Pologne
Greece	Grèce
Switzerland	Suisse
Sweden	Suède
Czech Republic	République tchèque
Turkey	Turquie
Hungary	Hongrie

University education / *Enseignement supérieur universitaire*
Non-university tertiary education / *Enseignement supérieur non universitaire*

Countries are ranked by the total of university entry rates

Les pays sont classés par ordre décroissant des taux d'entrées à l'université

151

P06: Participation in tertiary education

NET RATES OF PARTICIPATION IN UNIVERSITY AND NON-UNIVERSITY TERTIARY EDUCATION

POLICY ISSUES

Are university enrolment rates disconcertingly low? If so, would this appear to be more related to choice or to access? Is the alternative of non-university tertiary education a viable means of improving links between education and the labour market?

KEY RESULTS

Enrolment rates of 18 to 21 year-olds in university education range from 20 per cent or more in five countries (Canada, France, the Netherlands, Spain and the United States) to below 5 per cent in two (Sweden and Switzerland). With the exception of Australia and Sweden, non-university enrolments are lower than university enrolments.

Total enrolment rates in tertiary education for students 22 to 25 years old are lower thank for 18 to 21 year-olds, with the exception of seven: Denmark, Germany (FTFR), Finland, Norway, Poland, Sweden and Switzerland.

In all countries except Australia, the tertiary education enrolment rate continues to decline as the age group advances. In Australia, the enrolment rate among those 26 to 29 years old is slightly higher than the rate for those aged 22 to 25.

DESCRIPTION AND INTERPRETATION

This indicator shows the proportion of people aged 18 to 29 participating in higher education in 1992; and whether at university or non-university level. The table gives results for three age bands, and shows the extent to which older age groups participate in higher education.

Participation rates for non-university tertiary education varied widely across countries with figures, for 18 to 21 year-olds, ranging from near-zero to around 15 per cent. The Australian figure of 23 per cent reflects the inclusion of Technical and Further Education (TAFE), some of which may be better classified as upper secondary.

In most countries, 18 to 21 year-olds have the highest participation rate in non-university tertiary education. The main exceptions are Denmark and Finland, where the rate was higher for 22 to 25 year-olds.

Among 18 to 21 year-olds, women were more likely than men to participate in the non-university sector, although in general the differences were not large. For 22 to 25 year-olds, men were more likely to participate, with the exception of four countries: Finland, France, Poland and Sweden.

At university level, the countries fell into two groups: the peak age of participation for the majority was 18 to 21, but for some it was 22 to 25.

Women's enrolment rates tended to be higher than men's among 18 to 21 year-olds, but for 22 to 25 year-olds, men tend to have the higher rates.

DEFINITIONS

This indicator is based on calculations of the net enrolment rates for students in three age groups: 18-21, 22-25 and 26-29. Net enrolment rates for each group are obtained by dividing the number of tertiary education students in the age group by the total population in that age group.

These figures are based on head counts, i.e. they make no attempt to distinguish full- and part-time study. In fact, producing standard distinction is extremely difficult. Some countries do not even recognise the concept of part-time study, although in practice part of their provision would be classified as such by other countries.

P06: Participation in tertiary education

P06 : Fréquentation de l'enseignement supérieur

Table P06:
Net enrolment in public and private tertiary education by age group and by type of programme (head counts) (1992)

Tableau P06 :
Taux de fréquentation de l'enseignement supérieur public et privé par groupe d'âge et par type de programme (en nombre d'individus) (1992)

		Ages 18-21 / *18-21 ans*								
		Non-university tertiary education *Enseignement supérieur non universitaire*			University education *Enseignement supérieur universitaire*			Total *Total*		
		M+W H+F	Men *Hommes*	Women *Femmes*	M+W H+F	Men *Hommes*	Women *Femmes*	M+W H+F	Men *Hommes*	Women *Femmes*
North America										
Canada		...	...	...	23.9	20.8	27.2	...	...	...
United States		13.8	12.9	14.7	25.0	22.4	27.7	38.8	35.3	42.4
Pacific Area										
Australia		22.9	26.6	19.2	18.8	17.2	20.4	41.7	43.7	39.6
Japan		...	...	...	...	...	...	...	...	...
New Zealand		7.1	6.2	8.0	18.8	17.4	20.1	25.8	23.6	28.2
European Community										
Belgium		14.5	10.6	18.5	16.9	17.9	15.9	31.4	28.5	34.4
Denmark		1.3	1.2	1.5	7.8	7.3	8.4	9.2	8.5	9.8
France		8.8	8.2	9.4	20.2	17.2	23.4	29.0	25.3	32.8
Germany (FTFR)		2.3	0.8	4.0	7.4	6.8	7.9	9.7	7.6	11.9
Germany		...	...	...	...	...	...	...	...	...
Greece		8.2	7.6	8.9	15.6	13.8	17.5	23.8	21.4	26.4
Ireland		...	...	...	...	...	...	...	...	...
Italy		...	...	...	...	...	...	...	...	...
Luxembourg		...	...	...	...	...	...	...	...	...
Netherlands		.	.	.	20.1	19.8	20.4	20.1	19.8	20.4
Portugal		...	...	...	...	...	...	...	...	...
Spain		0.3	0.3	0.3	22.5	19.7	25.5	22.8	19.9	25.8
United Kingdom		3.9	4.6	3.0	14.2	14.2	14.2	18.0	18.8	17.2
Other Europe - OECD										
Austria		...	...	...	13.1	12.9	13.3	...	...	...
Finland		5.1	3.2	7.1	10.3	10.2	10.4	15.4	13.3	17.5
Iceland		...	...	...	...	...	...	...	...	...
Norway		7.0	6.1	8.0	8.4	7.1	9.8	15.4	13.1	17.7
Sweden		6.3	5.9	6.6	4.3	3.8	4.9	10.6	9.7	11.5
Switzerland		2.4	2.6	2.2	4.8	5.1	4.4	7.2	7.7	6.6
Turkey		1.1	1.5	0.7	7.0	8.3	5.7	8.2	9.8	6.4
Country mean		**6.6**	**6.1**	**7.0**	**14.4**	**13.4**	**15.4**	**20.4**	**19.1**	**21.8**
Central and Eastern Europe										
Czech Republic		1.1	0.7	1.6	...	...	...	...	...	...
Hungary		4.1	3.5	4.6	6.0	5.4	6.6	10.0	8.9	11.2
Poland		3.5	1.5	5.5	8.1	7.3	8.9	11.6	8.9	14.4
Russia		9.5	...	...	...	...	...	...	...	...

See Annex 1 for notes

Voir notes en annexe 1

P06: Participation in tertiary education

P06 : Fréquentation de l'enseignement supérieur

Table P06:
Net enrolment in public and private tertiary education by age group and by type of programme (head counts) (1992)

Tableau P06 :
Taux de fréquentation de l'enseignement supérieur public et privé par groupe d'âge et par type de programme (en nombre d'individus) (1992)

Ages 22-25 / 22-25 ans

	Non-university tertiary education / Enseignement supérieur non universitaire			University education / Enseignement supérieur universitaire			Total / Total			
	M+W / H+F	Men / Hommes	Women / Femmes	M+W / H+F	Men / Hommes	Women / Femmes	M+W / H+F	Men / Hommes	Women / Femmes	
North America										*Amérique du Nord*
Canada	...	...	...	13.9	13.7	14.2	...	...	...	*Canada*
United States	6.5	6.3	6.7	12.1	13.2	11.0	18.6	19.5	17.7	*Etats-Unis*
Pacific Area										*Pays du Pacifique*
Australia	9.2	10.2	8.1	6.2	6.5	5.9	15.4	16.7	14.1	*Australie*
Japan	...	...	...	...	...	...	...	...	...	*Japon*
New Zealand	4.2	4.2	4.1	7.8	8.5	7.0	11.9	12.8	11.1	*Nouvelle-Zélande*
European Community										*Communauté européenne*
Belgium	2.5	2.6	2.4	7.1	8.3	5.9	9.7	10.9	8.3	*Belgique*
Denmark	2.7	3.1	2.3	17.2	15.4	19.1	19.9	18.5	21.4	*Danemark*
France	2.3	2.2	2.5	11.6	10.9	12.4	14.0	13.1	14.9	*France*
Germany (FTFR)	1.7	1.9	1.5	15.2	18.4	11.8	16.9	20.3	13.3	*Allemagne (ex-terr. de la RFA)*
Germany	...	...	...	...	...	...	...	...	...	*Allemagne*
Greece	3.3	3.2	3.4	1.6	2.0	1.2	5.0	5.2	4.7	*Grèce*
Ireland	...	...	...	...	...	...	...	...	...	*Irlande*
Italy	...	...	...	...	...	...	...	...	...	*Italie*
Luxembourg	...	...	...	...	...	...	...	...	...	*Luxembourg*
Netherlands	.	.	.	15.9	18.1	13.6	15.9	18.1	13.6	*Pays-Bas*
Portugal	...	...	...	...	...	...	...	...	...	*Portugal*
Spain	-	-	-	14.9	14.7	15.2	14.9	14.7	15.2	*Espagne*
United Kingdom	2.0	2.2	1.7	4.7	5.3	4.0	6.6	7.5	5.7	*Royaume-Uni*
Other Europe - OECD										*Autres pays d'Europe - OCDE*
Austria	...	...	...	15.4	16.9	13.8	...	...	...	*Autriche*
Finland	5.9	4.5	7.3	16.6	17.1	16.0	22.5	21.7	23.4	*Finlande*
Iceland	...	...	...	...	...	...	...	...	...	*Islande*
Norway	5.1	5.1	5.1	15.3	14.6	16.0	20.4	19.7	21.1	*Norvège*
Sweden	4.6	3.6	5.7	8.1	8.7	7.4	12.7	12.3	13.1	*Suède*
Switzerland	5.4	7.9	2.9	7.8	9.8	5.8	13.2	17.7	8.7	*Suisse*
Turkey	0.3	0.4	0.1	4.9	6.8	3.0	5.2	7.2	3.2	*Turquie*
Country mean	**3.5**	**3.6**	**3.4**	**10.9**	**11.6**	**10.2**	**13.9**	**14.7**	**13.1**	*Moyenne des pays*
Central and Eastern Europe										*Europe centrale et orientale*
Czech Republic	x	x	x	...	...	...	...	...	...	*République tchèque*
Hungary	1.4	1.4	1.5	5.0	5.3	4.7	6.4	6.6	6.2	*Hongrie*
Poland	1.2	0.4	2.1	12.1	11.8	12.5	13.4	12.2	14.6	*Pologne*
Russia	4.6	...	...	...	...	...	...	...	...	*Russie*

See Annex 1 for notes / *Voir notes en annexe 1*

P06: Participation in tertiary education

P06 : Fréquentation de l'enseignement supérieur

Table P06:
Net enrolment in public and private tertiary education by age group and type of programme (head counts) (1992)

Tableau P06 :
Taux de fréquentation de l'enseignement supérieur public et privé par groupe d'âge et par type de programme (en nombre d'individus) (1992)

	\multicolumn{9}{c|}{Ages 26-29 / 26-29 ans}	
	\multicolumn{3}{c|}{Non-university tertiary education / Enseignement supérieur non universitaire}	\multicolumn{3}{c|}{University education / Enseignement supérieur universitaire}	\multicolumn{3}{c|}{Total / Total}	
	M+W / H+F	Men / Hommes	Women / Femmes	M+W / H+F	Men / Hommes	Women / Femmes	M+W / H+F	Men / Hommes	Women / Femmes	
North America										*Amérique du Nord*
Canada	...	...	...	5.6	5.6	5.6	...	...	...	*Canada*
United States	4.1	3.9	4.4	5.4	5.7	5.2	9.5	9.5	9.6	*Etats-Unis*
Pacific Area										*Pays du Pacifique*
Australia	11.4	12.8	10.0	5.4	5.5	5.3	16.8	18.3	15.3	*Australie*
Japan	...	...	...	...	...	...	...	...	...	*Japon*
New Zealand	3.0	3.1	2.9	3.6	3.6	3.6	6.6	6.7	6.5	*Nouvelle-Zélande*
European Community										*Communauté européenne*
Belgium	0.1	0.1	0.1	1.5	2.0	1.0	1.7	2.2	1.2	*Belgique*
Denmark	1.4	1.7	1.1	8.7	8.7	8.8	10.1	10.3	9.8	*Danemark*
France	0.3	0.2	0.4	3.8	3.9	3.6	4.1	4.2	4.0	*France*
Germany (FTFR)	1.4	1.8	0.9	9.6	12.1	6.8	10.9	13.9	7.7	*Allemagne (ex-terr. de la RFA)*
Germany	...	...	...	...	...	...	...	...	...	*Allemagne*
Greece	0.5	0.3	0.6	0.3	0.4	0.2	0.8	0.7	0.9	*Grèce*
Ireland	...	...	...	...	...	...	...	...	...	*Irlande*
Italy	...	...	...	...	...	...	...	...	...	*Italie*
Luxembourg	...	...	...	...	...	...	...	...	...	*Luxembourg*
Netherlands	.	.	.	4.8	5.6	3.9	4.8	5.6	3.9	*Pays-Bas*
Portugal	...	...	...	...	...	...	...	...	...	*Portugal*
Spain	-	-	-	5.4	5.9	5.0	5.4	5.9	5.0	*Espagne*
United Kingdom	1.1	1.2	1.0	1.8	2.1	1.6	2.9	3.3	2.5	*Royaume-Uni*
Other Europe - OECD										*Autres pays d'Europe - OCDE*
Austria	...	...	...	9.0	10.9	7.1	...	...	...	*Autriche*
Finland	2.0	1.3	2.7	8.7	9.1	8.3	10.7	10.4	11.0	*Finlande*
Iceland	...	...	...	...	...	...	...	...	...	*Islande*
Norway	2.5	2.7	2.4	6.5	6.7	6.4	9.0	9.3	8.7	*Norvège*
Sweden	2.7	2.3	3.2	3.8	4.6	3.0	6.5	6.9	6.2	*Suède*
Switzerland	3.0	4.6	1.4	4.0	5.2	2.8	7.1	9.8	4.3	*Suisse*
Turkey	0.1	0.1	-	2.3	3.2	1.3	2.3	3.3	1.3	*Turquie*
Country mean	**2.1**	**2.3**	**1.9**	**5.0**	**5.6**	**4.4**	**6.8**	**7.5**	**6.1**	***Moyenne des pays***
Central and Eastern Europe										*Europe centrale et orientale*
Czech Republic	x	x	x	...	...	...	...	...	...	*République tchèque*
Hungary	0.5	0.6	0.4	1.6	1.8	1.5	2.1	2.3	1.9	*Hongrie*
Poland	x	x	x	x	x	x	x	x	x	*Pologne*
Russia	x	...	...	...	...	...	...	...	...	*Russie*

See Annex 1 for notes

Voir notes en annexe 1

P06: Participation in tertiary education

P06 : Fréquentation de l'enseignement supérieur

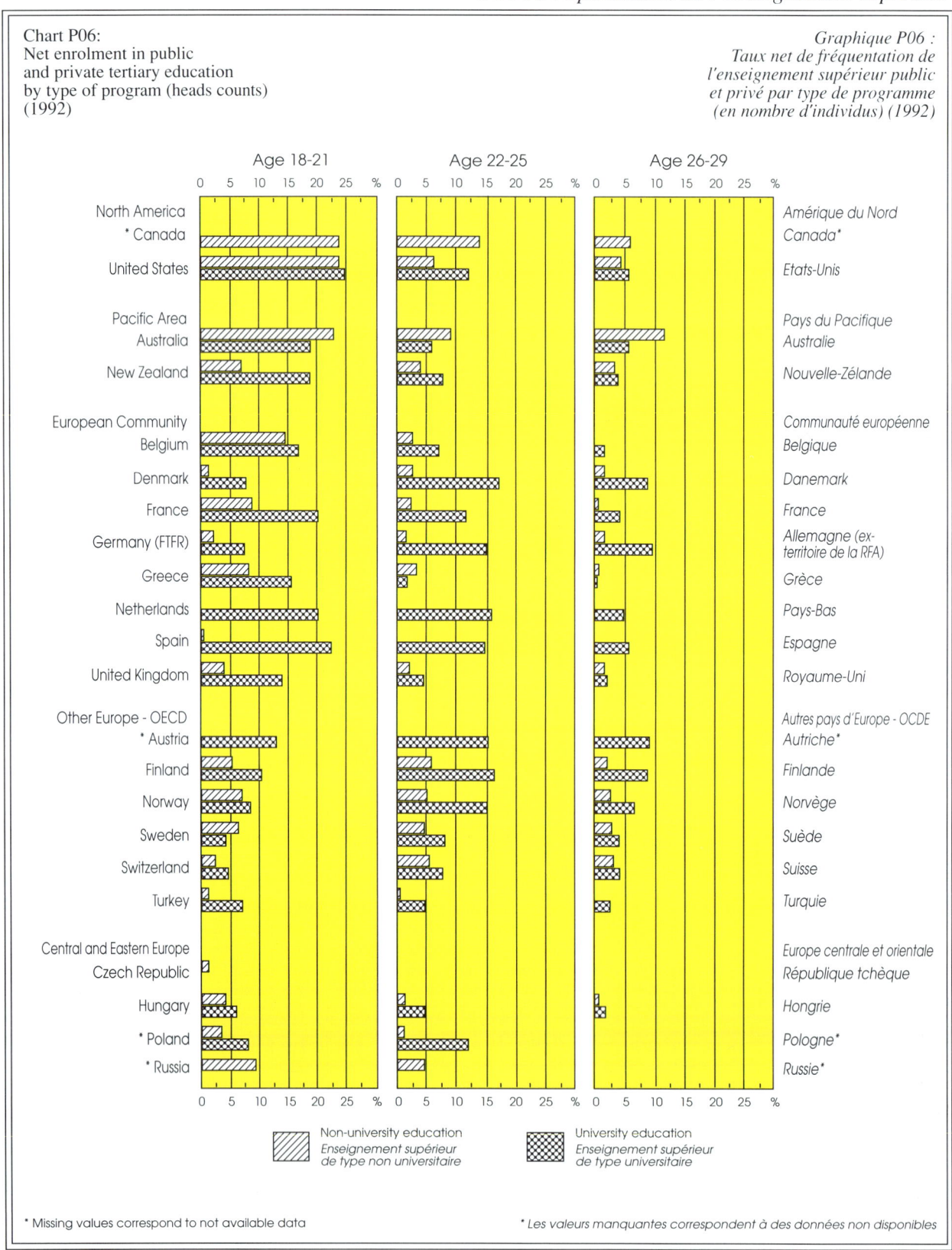

Chart P06:
Net enrolment in public
and private tertiary education
by type of program (heads counts)
(1992)

Graphique P06 :
Taux net de fréquentation de
l'enseignement supérieur public
et privé par type de programme
(en nombre d'individus) (1992)

Region / Country		
North America		Amérique du Nord
* Canada		Canada*
United States		Etats-Unis
Pacific Area		Pays du Pacifique
Australia		Australie
New Zealand		Nouvelle-Zélande
European Community		Communauté européenne
Belgium		Belgique
Denmark		Danemark
France		France
Germany (FTFR)		Allemagne (ex-territoire de la RFA)
Greece		Grèce
Netherlands		Pays-Bas
Spain		Espagne
United Kingdom		Royaume-Uni
Other Europe - OECD		Autres pays d'Europe - OCDE
* Austria		Autriche*
Finland		Finlande
Norway		Norvège
Sweden		Suède
Switzerland		Suisse
Turkey		Turquie
Central and Eastern Europe		Europe centrale et orientale
Czech Republic		République tchèque
Hungary		Hongrie
* Poland		Pologne*
* Russia		Russie*

Non-university education / *Enseignement supérieur de type non universitaire*

University education / *Enseignement supérieur de type universitaire*

* Missing values correspond to not available data

* *Les valeurs manquantes correspondent à des données non disponibles*

P08: Continuing education and training for adults

PARTICIPATION IN JOB-RELATED CONTINUING EDUCATION AND TRAINING

POLICY ISSUES

Is there a way of increasing the participation in job-related continuing education and training of those with low levels of education?

KEY RESULTS

Participation in job-related continuing education and training (CET) is closely linked to the previously attained level of education: in all countries, those with the lowest levels of education also have the lowest levels of participation in CET, while those with a tertiary education attain the highest levels. With the exception of Sweden, participation in CET declines for the oldest age group (45 to 64 year-olds), sometimes sharply.

DESCRIPTION AND INTERPRETATION

Participation of the employed in job-related CET can play a role in remedying the labour market mismatch between knowledge and skills acquired in the formal education system and the knowledge and skills demanded in an ever-changing labour market.

This indicator measures the amount of participation in job-related CET over a period of either twelve months or four weeks preceding the interview survey. Eight of the reporting countries use the longer reference period, and four use the shorter one.

The same participation pattern is observed in almost all reporting OECD countries: younger age groups participate in higher proportions than older age groups. Differences in participation rates between 25 to 34 year-olds and 35 to 44 year-olds are generally small, whereas those between 35 to 44 year-olds and 45 to 64 year-olds are generally quite considerable. The widest variations in the latter case can be found in Canada, France, Norway and the United States. Among the countries with a four-week reference period, Denmark shows the greatest difference in participation between the two oldest age groups.

The participation in job-related CET among the employed can also be seen as reflecting the dynamics of the labour market in a country.

The data point to the conclusion that job-related CET seems to allow those who already have a good stock of skills to continue to develop their competencies, thereby maintaining or furthering their advantage in the labour market. In most reporting countries, the proportion of participants in CET is three-and-a-half to four times as large among those with a tertiary education as among those without upper secondary education. In relative terms, this difference is considerably smaller in Finland and Sweden, and much larger in Canada, Spain, the United Kingdom and the United States.

In the reporting countries 80 to 97 per cent of all participants aged 25 to 64 in job-related CET have already attained at least upper secondary education [Table P08(C)]. This percentage is much higher than the proportion of those who have attained that level in the population of the same age. Significant differences in these proportions can be seen in countries such as Ireland and Spain. In Ireland, those with at least upper secondary education make up 42 per cent of the population 25 to 64 years of age, but account for 80 per cent of CET participation in 1992. In Spain these proportions were 23 and 84 per cent respectively.

The fact that a large majority of participants in job-related CET in all OECD countries have completed at least an upper secondary education may be an indication that CET offerings tend to be geared to their needs, rather than to the needs of those with less education.

DEFINITIONS

Continuing education and training (CET) for adults refers to all kinds of job-related education and training organised, financed or sponsored by authorities; provided by employers; or self-financed.

Job-related CET covers all organised, systematic education and training activities in which people take part in order to: obtain knowledge and/or new skills for a current or future job; increase earnings; improve job and/or career opportunities in a current or other field; and generally improve their opportunities for advancement and promotion.

Continuing education and training for adults does not include military training or full-time studies at ISCED levels 5, 6 and 7.

P08: Continuing education and training for adults

P08 : Education et formation continues des adultes

Table P08(A): Participation in job-related continuing education and training as a percentage of the employed population aged 25 to 64, totals and by educational groups, various years

Tableau P08(A) : Participation à l'éducation et à la formation professionnelles continues en pourcentage de la population active occupée âgée de 25 à 64 ans, ventilée suivant le niveau d'instruction, diverses années

	Year / Année	Early childhood, primary and lower secondary education / Education préscolaire, enseignement primaire et secondaire 1er cycle	Upper secondary education / Enseignement secondaire du 2e cycle	Tertiary education / Enseignement supérieur	Total / Total	
During the 12-month period preceding the survey						*Pendant la période de 12 mois précédant l'enquête*
Canada	1991	13	25	40	30	Canada
Finland	1990	28	47	74	46	Finlande
France	1992	13	31	46	27	France
Germany	1991	11	23	41	27	Allemagne
Norway	1991	17	33	57	37	Norvège
Sweden	1993	21	34	53	36	Suède
Switzerland	1993	16	39	52	38	Suisse
United States	1991	10	30	54	38	Etats-Unis
During the 4-weed period preceding the survey						*Pendant la période de 4 semaines précédant l'enquête*
Denmark	1991	6	14	25	15	Danemark
Ireland	1992	2	4	8	4	Irlande
Spain	1992	1	6	7	3	Espagne
United Kingdom	1992	4	10	19	11	Royaume-Uni

See Annex 1 for notes   *Voir notes en annexe 1*

P08: Continuing education and training for adults

P08 : Education et formation continues des adultes

Chart P08(A):
Participation in job-related continuing education and training as a percentage of the employed, by educational groups

Graphique P08(A) :
Participation à l'éducation et à la formation professionnelles continues en pourcentage des actifs occupés, par niveau d'instruction

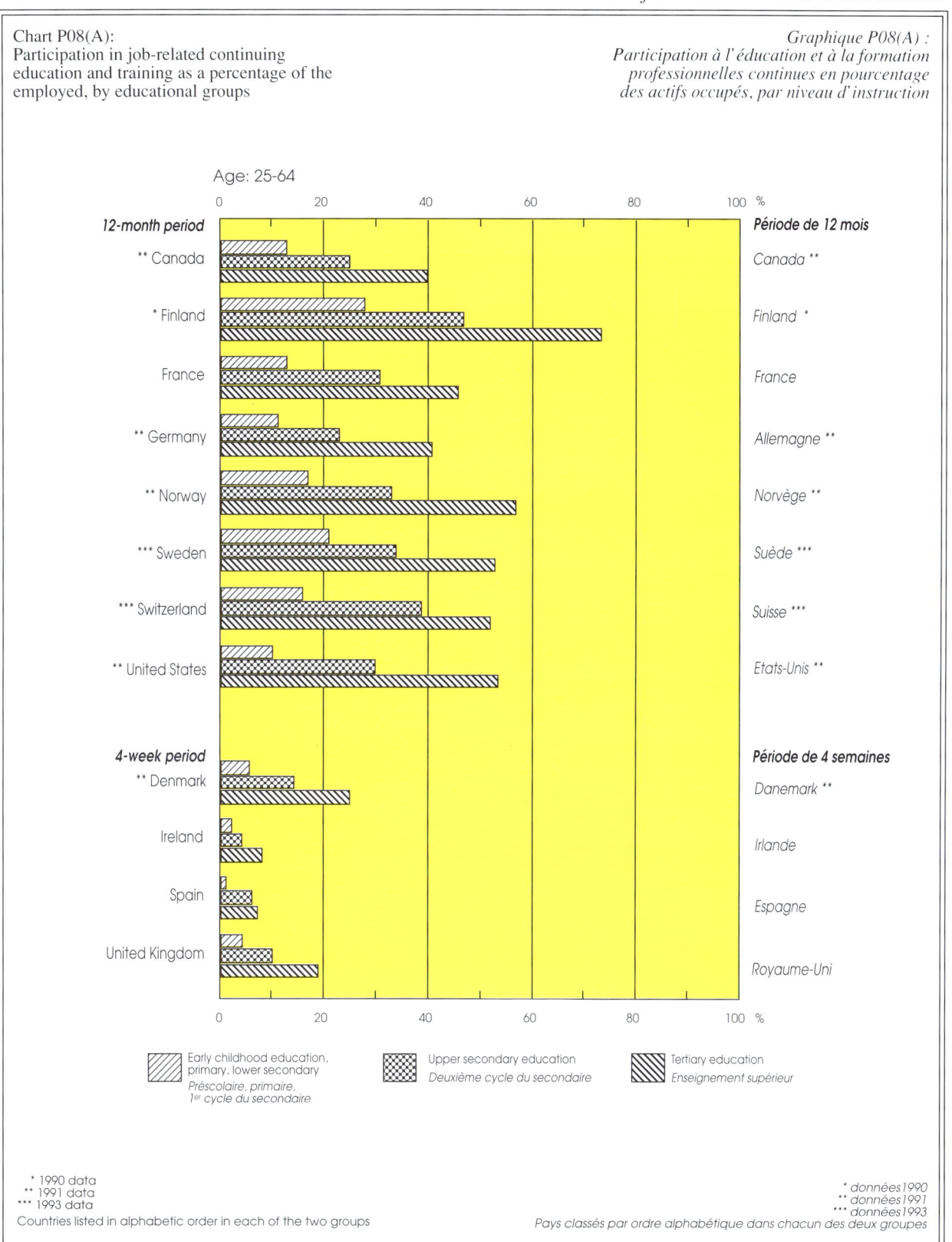

Age: 25-64

12-month period — *Période de 12 mois*

- ** Canada / Canada **
- * Finland / Finlande *
- France / France
- ** Germany / Allemagne **
- ** Norway / Norvège **
- *** Sweden / Suède ***
- *** Switzerland / Suisse ***
- ** United States / Etats-Unis **

4-week period — *Période de 4 semaines*

- ** Denmark / Danemark **
- Ireland / Irlande
- Spain / Espagne
- United Kingdom / Royaume-Uni

Legend:
- Early childhood education, primary, lower secondary / Préscolaire, primaire, 1er cycle du secondaire
- Upper secondary education / Deuxième cycle du secondaire
- Tertiary education / Enseignement supérieur

* 1990 data / données 1990
** 1991 data / données 1991
*** 1993 data / données 1993

Countries listed in alphabetic order in each of the two groups
Pays classés par ordre alphabétique dans chacun des deux groupes

P08: Continuing education and training for adults / P08 : Education et formation continues des adultes

Table P08(B): Participation in job-related continuing and training as a percentage of the employed population aged 25 to 64, totals and by age groups, various years

Tableau P08(B) : Participation à l'éducation et à la formation professionnelles continues en pourcentage de la population active occupée âgée de 25 à 64 ans, totaux et ventilation par tranche d'âge, diverses années

	Year / Année	Age 25-34 / 25-34 ans	Age 35-44 / 35-44 ans	Age 45-64 / 45-64 ans	Total	
During the 12-month period preceding the survey						*Pendant la période de 12 mois précédant l'enquête*
Canada	1991	32	35	23	30	Canada
Finland	1990	51	49	40	46	Finlande
France	1992	43	27	11	27	France
Germany	1991	33	29	21	27	Allemagne
Norway	1991	40	42	30	37	Norvège
Sweden	1993	36	33	41	36	Suède
Switzerland	1993	42	41	34	38	Suisse
United States	1991	37	43	33	38	Etats-Unis
During the 4-week period preceding the survey						*Pendant la période de 4 semaines précédant l'enquête*
Denmark	1991	17	17	11	15	Danemark
Ireland	1992	5	4	2	4	Irlande
Spain	1992	6	2	1	3	Espagne
United Kingdom	1992	12	12	8	11	Royaume-Uni

See Annex 1 for notes

Voir notes en annexe 1

P08: Continuing education and training for adults

P08 : Education et formation continues des adultes

Chart P08(B):
Participation in job-related continuing education and training as a percentage of the employed for different age groups

Graphique P08(B) :
Participation à l'éducation et à la formation professionnelles continues en pourcentage des actifs occupés par groupe d'âge

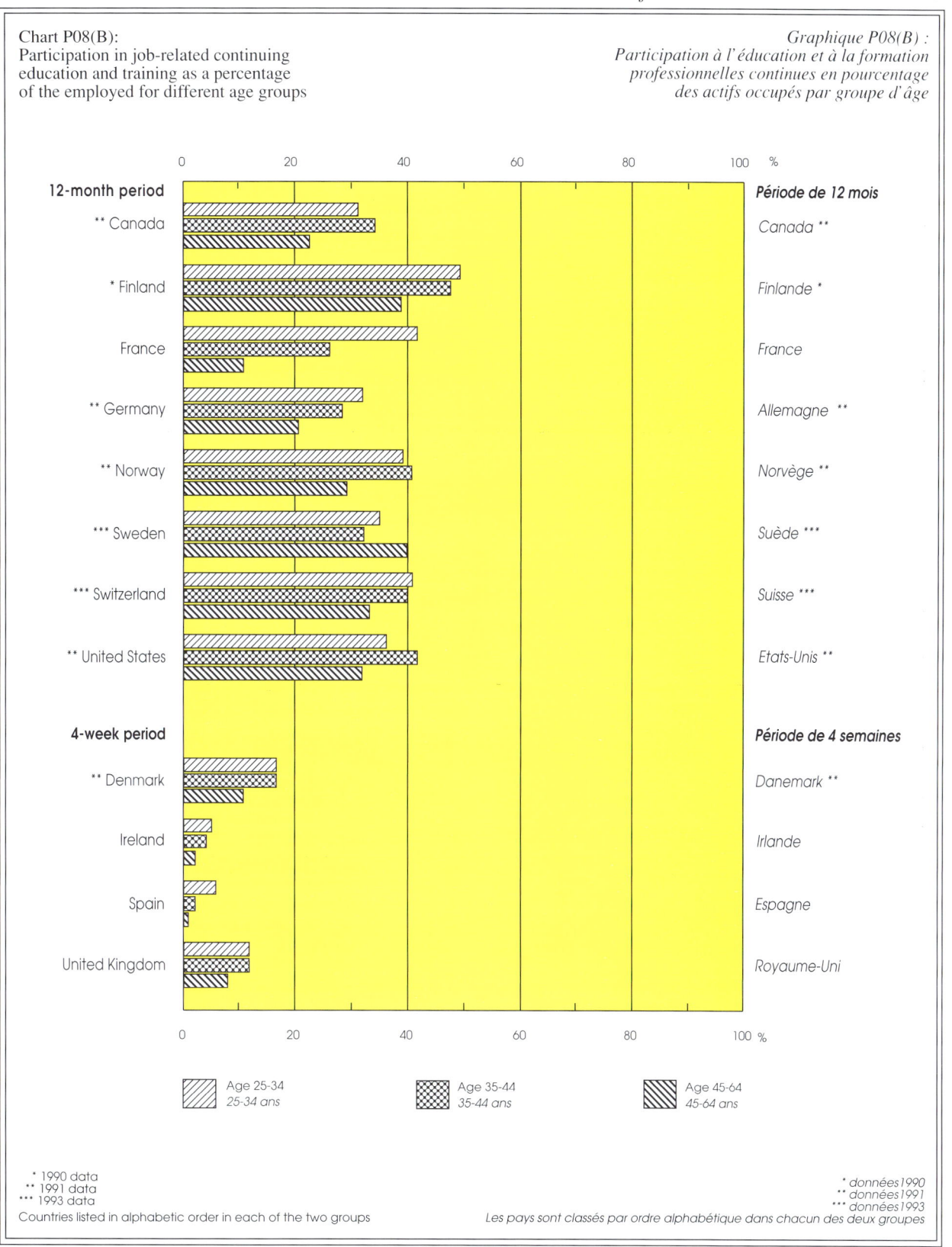

12-month period / *Période de 12 mois*
- ** Canada / Canada **
- * Finland / Finlande *
- France / France
- ** Germany / Allemagne **
- ** Norway / Norvège **
- *** Sweden / Suède ***
- *** Switzerland / Suisse ***
- ** United States / Etats-Unis **

4-week period / *Période de 4 semaines*
- ** Denmark / Danemark **
- Ireland / Irlande
- Spain / Espagne
- United Kingdom / Royaume-Uni

Age 25-34 / 25-34 ans
Age 35-44 / 35-44 ans
Age 45-64 / 45-64 ans

* 1990 data
** 1991 data
*** 1993 data
Countries listed in alphabetic order in each of the two groups

* données 1990
** données 1991
*** données 1993
Les pays sont classés par ordre alphabétique dans chacun des deux groupes

P08: Continuing education and training for adults

P08 : Education et formation continues des adultes

Table P08(C):
Distribution of participants in job-related continuing education and training of the employed population aged 25 to 64, totals and by educational background, various years

Tableau P08(C) :
Répartition des participants à l'éducation et à la formation professionnelles continues dans la population active occupée âgée de 25 à 64 ans, totaux et ventilation par niveau d'instruction, diverses années

	Year / Année	Early childhood, primary and lower secondary education / Education préscolaire, enseignement primaire et secondaire 1er cycle	Upper secondary education / Enseignement secondaire du 2e cycle	Tertiary education / Enseignement supérieur	Total / Total	
During the 12-month period preceding the survey						*Pendant la période de 12 mois précédant l'enquête*
Canada	1991	8	30	62	100	*Canada*
Finland	1990	20	45	35	100	*Finlande*
France	1992	20	47	33	100	*France*
Germany	1991	4	49	47	100	*Allemagne*
Norway	1991	7	55	38	100	*Norvège*
Sweden	1993	14	45	41	100	*Suède*
Switzerland	1993	7	59	34	100	*Suisse*
United States	1991	3	43	54	100	*Etats-Unis*
During the 4-week period preceding the survey						*Pendant la période de 4 semaines précédant l'enquête*
Denmark	1991	12	46	42	100	*Danemark*
Ireland	1992	20	29	51	100	*Irlande*
Spain	1992	16	30	54	100	*Espagne*
United Kingdom	1992	8	51	41	100	*Royaume-Uni*

See Annex 1 for notes

Voir notes en annexe 1

P08: Continuing education and training for adults

P08 : Education et formation continues des adultes

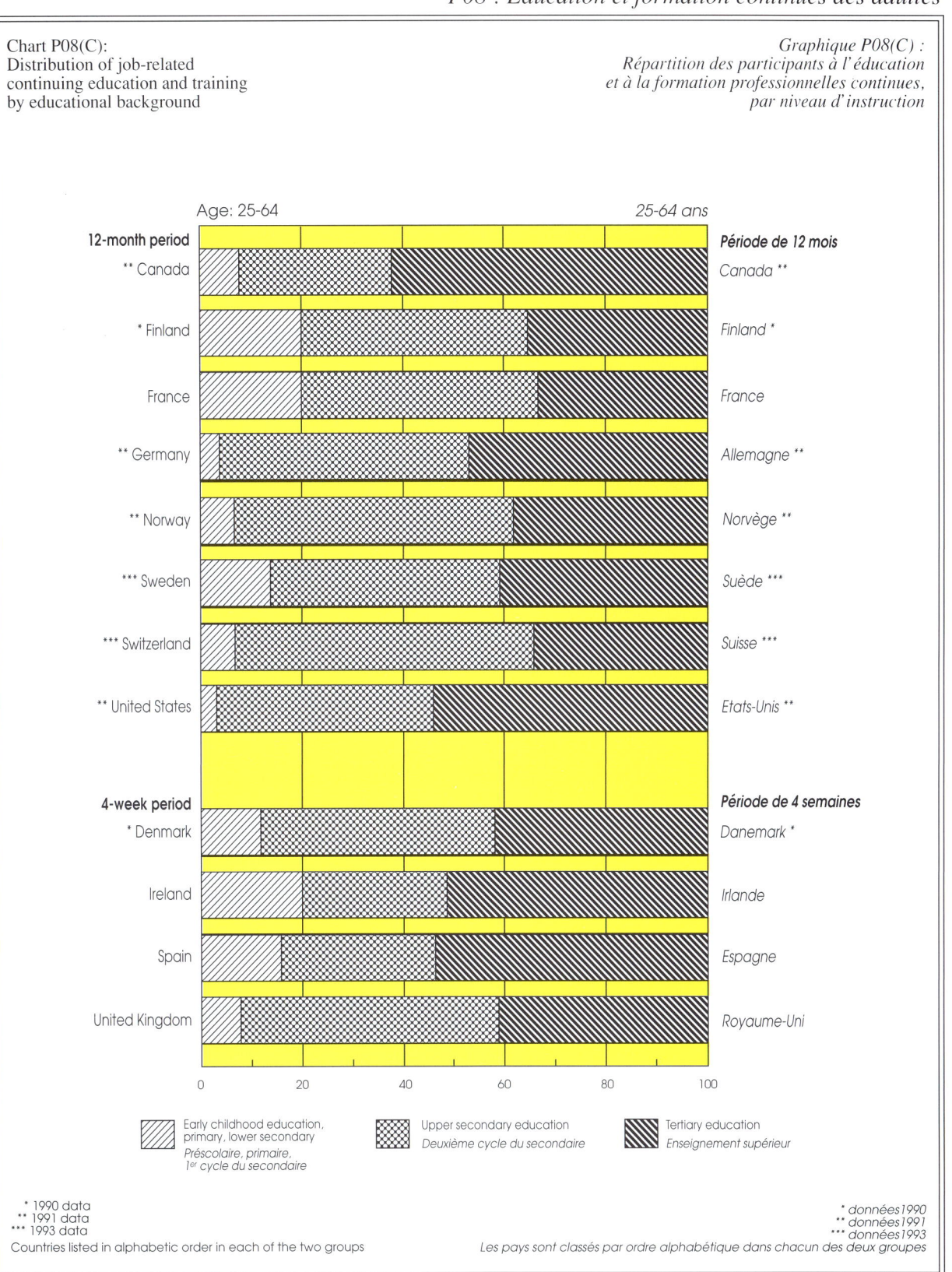

Chart P08(C):
Distribution of job-related continuing education and training by educational background

Graphique P08(C) :
Répartition des participants à l'éducation et à la formation professionnelles continues, par niveau d'instruction

Age: 25-64 / 25-64 ans

12-month period / *Période de 12 mois*
- ** Canada / Canada **
- * Finland / Finland *
- France / France
- ** Germany / Allemagne **
- ** Norway / Norvège **
- *** Sweden / Suède ***
- *** Switzerland / Suisse ***
- ** United States / Etats-Unis **

4-week period / *Période de 4 semaines*
- * Denmark / Danemark *
- Ireland / Irlande
- Spain / Espagne
- United Kingdom / Royaume-Uni

Legend:
- Early childhood education, primary, lower secondary / *Préscolaire, primaire, 1er cycle du secondaire*
- Upper secondary education / *Deuxième cycle du secondaire*
- Tertiary education / *Enseignement supérieur*

* 1990 data
** 1991 data
*** 1993 data

Countries listed in alphabetic order in each of the two groups

* données 1990
** données 1991
*** données 1993

Les pays sont classés par ordre alphabétique dans chacun des deux groupes

163

P11: Teaching time per subject

TEACHING TIME PER SUBJECT AS A PERCENTAGE OF ALL TEACHING TIME

POLICY ISSUES

Assuming that the percentage of teaching time devoted to a given subject provides an indication of the relative importance accorded to that subject, would any shifts in priority seem to be called for?

KEY RESULTS

The largest block of teaching time in public lower secondary education is devoted to languages: 29 per cent as a country mean. In some countries, this time is distributed almost equally between the mother tongue and foreign languages. Mathematics and science together form the next largest block of time, a mean of 23 per cent. Only 8 per cent of teaching time is devoted to vocational skills and technology.

Countries differ considerably in their distribution of teaching time among subjects. In all countries, however, about 40 per cent of teaching time at lower secondary education is devoted to reading, writing, mathematics and science.

DESCRIPTION AND INTERPRETATION

This indicator shows percentages of total teaching time devoted to the major subjects in the curriculum, and thus indicates the relative emphasis given to those subjects. It does not provide information on the total teaching time available for all subjects (in minutes or hours per year), nor on the absolute time devoted to a subject.

In some countries (e.g. the Netherlands and Spain), a portion of teaching time is not included in the prescribed curriculum. That additional time may be devoted to prescribed subjects or to others. If it is devoted to subjects in the prescribed curriculum, there will be an underestimation of the percentage of time for prescribed subjects. In other countries (Belgium and Sweden), there is a distinction between compulsory and optional subjects. In most cases, time devoted to optional subjects has been included in the figures (sometimes in the category "Other"). This can lead to an overestimation of the time devoted to those subjects, if they are not actually taught, and an underestimation of time allotted to compulsory subjects. Time devoted to optional subjects is not included in the Finnish data.

Although the impact of unprescribed time and optional subjects on the distributions is not a major one, these percentages should be interpreted cautiously.

The table and pie chart illustrate that the greatest percentages of teaching time are devoted to language-based subjects – reading and writing in the mother tongue (16 per cent), foreign languages (13 per cent) and social studies (13 per cent) – while the least time is devoted to vocational skills (2 per cent) and religion (5 per cent). Mathematics and science receive 12 and 11 per cent of teaching time, respectively. Arts and physical education both receive 9 per cent, while technology and other subjects take 6 and 10 per cent, respectively.

The percentage of time devoted to reading and writing in the mother tongue varies from a minimum of 10 per cent in Sweden to a maximum of 22 per cent in Italy (more than twice as large). It should be noted that in Ireland and Spain a second "mother tongue" is taught, not classified as a foreign language. Ireland includes both languages in reading and writing (in the mother tongue).

Foreign languages receive 9 or 10 per cent of the time in Finland, Italy, Norway, Sweden and Turkey, but 26 per cent in the Netherlands. It should be noted that the figures for foreign languages in Finland, Norway and Sweden may reflect an underestimation, as there are also elective foreign languages in these countries which are reported under the category "Other". In New Zealand, only 7 per cent of teaching time is devoted to foreign languages. This low figure could partly be explained by the fact that calculations for that country are based solely on grades 1, 2 and 3 of lower secondary education. New Zealand's integrated primary school curriculum does not prescribe foreign languages (and few schools offer them) in grades 1 or above; more time is devoted to them in grades 4 and 5.

There is somewhat less variation among countries for both mathematics and sciences. The share of time devoted to mathematics ranges from 8 per cent in the Netherlands to 16 per cent in New Zealand. Sciences receive the smallest percentage of time from Belgium (6 per cent) and the highest percentage from Portugal (14 per cent).

P11: Teaching time per subject

DEFINITIONS

Teaching time per subject refers to the percentage of the total available teaching time per subject category according to the intended curriculum (school year of reference: 1991/92). "Teaching time" is expressed as a number of lessons (each lesson is assumed to have the same time length). Data cover lower secondary, grades 1 to 5: grade 1 refers to the first year, grade 2 to the second year, etc.

With regard to subject categories, reading and writing refer to the mother tongue; sciences cover physics, chemistry, biology and earth science; social studies refer to geography and history; technology includes information technology; and religion includes history, culture and ethical thinking.

If no specific information on the intended curriculum was available, countries were allowed to report survey data on the implemented curriculum.

Some information on the intended curriculum for primary and upper secondary education is also available, and is reported in *OECD Education Statistics, 1985-1992*.

Table P11:
Teaching time per subject according to the intended curriculum as a percentage of all teaching time (public lower secondary education) (1992)

*Tableau P11 :
Temps d'enseignement par matière selon le programme prévu en pourcentage du temps total d'enseignement (enseignement secondaire du premier cycle, établissements publics) (1992)*

in %	Reading and writing	Mathematics	Sciences	Social studies	Foreign languages	Technology	Arts	Physical education	Religion	Vocational skills	Other	en %
Austria	14	12	13	11	11	6[1]	11	11	6	2[2]	3[3]	Autriche
Belgium	15	13	6	11	13	2[4]	5	8	6	-	23[5]	Belgique
Finland	12	12	12[6]	12[7]	9	-[8]	6	9	4	-	24[9]	Finlande
France	18	14	10	13	17	8	7	11	...	...	1[10]	France
Germany (FTFR)	13	12	11	11	18	-	9	9	6	3[11]	9	Allemagne (ex- terr. de la RFA)
Ireland	19[12]	10	8	16	12	6[13]	12	4	5	-	10	Irlande
Italy	22	10	10	14	10	10	13	7	3	-	-	Italie
Netherlands	16	8	9	14	26	...	10	11	2	2	1	Pays-Bas
New Zealand	20[14]	16[15]	9[16]	9[17]	7[18]	11[19]	7[20]	12[21]	...[22]	6[23]	3[24]	Nouvelle-Zélande
Norway	16	12	9	10	10	...	9	9	7	...	19[25]	Norvège
Portugal	11	13	14	16	17	14[26]	6	6	3[27]	...	...	Portugal
Spain	20	13	10	10	13	6	12	10	6	...	...	Espagne
Sweden	10	12	13	17	9	2	7	9	...	...	21	Suède
Turkey	20	13	13	11	10	...	9	7	7	7	3	Turquie
Country mean	**16**	**12**	**11**	**13**	**13**	**6**	**9**	**9**	**5**	**2**	**10**	**Moyenne des pays**

See Annex 1 for notes

Voir notes en annexe 1

P11: Teaching time per subject

P11 : Temps d'enseignement par matière

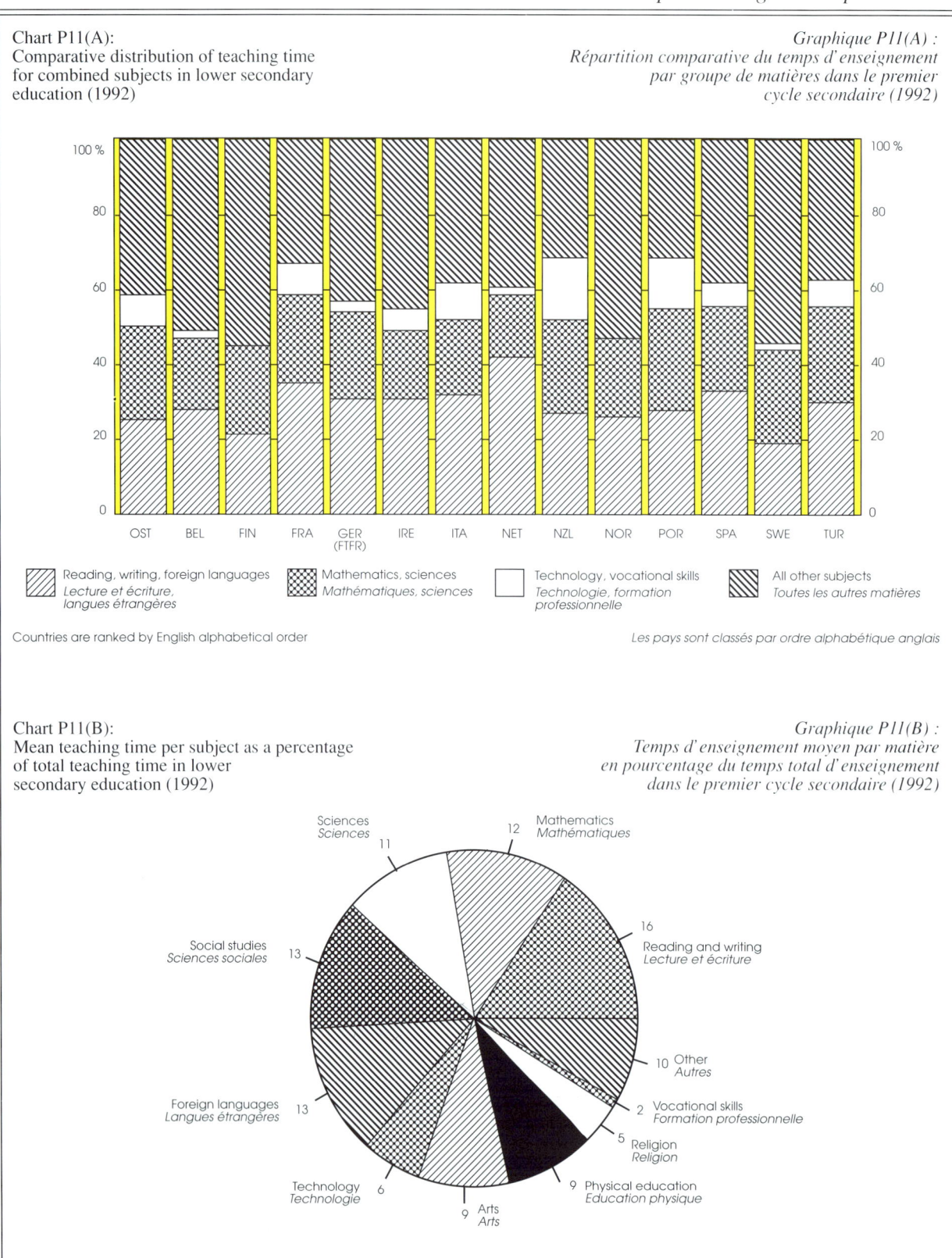

Chart P11(A):
Comparative distribution of teaching time for combined subjects in lower secondary education (1992)

Graphique P11(A) :
Répartition comparative du temps d'enseignement par groupe de matières dans le premier cycle secondaire (1992)

Legend:
- Reading, writing, foreign languages / *Lecture et écriture, langues étrangères*
- Mathematics, sciences / *Mathématiques, sciences*
- Technology, vocational skills / *Technologie, formation professionnelle*
- All other subjects / *Toutes les autres matières*

Countries are ranked by English alphabetical order

Les pays sont classés par ordre alphabétique anglais

Chart P11(B):
Mean teaching time per subject as a percentage of total teaching time in lower secondary education (1992)

Graphique P11(B) :
Temps d'enseignement moyen par matière en pourcentage du temps total d'enseignement dans le premier cycle secondaire (1992)

- Sciences / *Sciences*: 11
- Mathematics / *Mathématiques*: 12
- Reading and writing / *Lecture et écriture*: 16
- Other / *Autres*: 10
- Vocational skills / *Formation professionnelle*: 2
- Religion / *Religion*: 5
- Physical education / *Education physique*: 9
- Arts / *Arts*: 9
- Technology / *Technologie*: 6
- Foreign languages / *Langues étrangères*: 13
- Social studies / *Sciences sociales*: 13

P12: Hours of instruction

HOURS OF INSTRUCTION FOR 9 AND 14 YEAR-OLD PUPILS

POLICY ISSUES

Should countries lengthen the school year or the school week as a means of raising student achievement?

KEY RESULTS

On average, 9 year-old pupils in primary education in the reporting OECD countries receive 825 hours of instruction per year, and 14 year-old pupils receive 959 hours. The mean number of hours varies considerably among countries. In the Netherlands and the United States, pupils in both groups receive over 1 000 hours per year, whereas 9 year-old pupils in Denmark, Germany (FTFR), Germany (TFGDR), Greece and Iceland receive less than 700 hours, and 14 year-olds in Greece and Iceland less than 800.

Some countries show relatively wide variation across schools as well.

DESCRIPTION AND INTERPRETATION

This indicator reports the mean number of hours of instruction offered to 9 and 14 year-old pupils in the school year 1990/91. The number is calculated by multiplying the number of hours per week by the number of weeks per year the school is open. No adjustments have been made for holidays and festivities occurring during those weeks; the indicator is thus an approximation. Within each country, the hours of instruction for 50 per cent of students fall between the upper and lower bounds shown in Chart P12(B).

Table P12 shows that 9 year-old pupils receive the highest number of hours of instruction in the Netherlands (1 019), the United States (1 001) and New Zealand (963). Whereas the difference in hours in both groups between the Netherlands and the United States is not significant, those between the two countries and New Zealand are significant.

The lowest average numbers of hours provided to 9 year-old pupils are found in Iceland (585), Germany (FTFR) (661) and Denmark (662), a significant difference.

With regard to 14 year-old pupils, Table P12 shows that the mean number of hours of instruction is highest in the Netherlands (1 198), Switzerland (1 108) and Belgium (French community) (1 090).

The lowest number of hours is offered to the average 14 year-old pupil in Greece (743) and Iceland (794). In comparing the figures for the two groups, it is interesting to note that the Netherlands offers the highest number of hours of instruction – and Iceland the lowest – to both 9 and 14 year-old pupils.

A higher number of hours of instruction is offered to 14 year-olds than it is to 9 year-olds in almost all countries.

Table P12 and Chart P12(B) also provide information about the amount of dispersion in the hours of instruction within each country. The figures in the column "25th percentile" indicate that 25 per cent of the 9 or 14 year-old pupils receive the given number of hours of instruction or less [e.g. Belgium (French community), 25 per cent of the 9 year-old pupils receive 863 hours of instruction or less]. The figures in the column "75th percentile" indicate that 25 per cent of the 9 or 14 year-old pupils receive the given number of hours of instruction or more [e.g. Belgium (French community), 25 per cent of the 9 year-old pupils receive 926 hours of instruction or more].

The largest dispersion in received hours of instruction among 9 year-old pupils is found in Switzerland; 25 per cent of Swiss 9 year-old pupils are offered 767 hours of instruction or less, and 25 per cent are offered 987 hours or more, a difference of more than 200 hours. In Finland and the Netherlands the dispersion is low. The difference between the 25th and 75th percentile in these countries is only 29 and 16 hours of instruction, respectively.

It should be noted that, first, the hours of instruction as measured in this indicator represent the time pupils spend in the classroom excluding breaks, which can be considered as an upper limit of time on task. Second, hours of instruction that pupils receive should not be confused with "teaching time" as measured in indicator P33; the latter relates to the working conditions of teachers, and the number of hours that they are assigned direct teaching responsibilities.

DEFINITIONS

This indicator is based upon data from the Reading Literacy Study, which was conducted by the International Association for the Evaluation of Educational Achievement. The indicator refers to the number of hours of instruction received by the "average" 9 and 14 year-old pupil per year; the year of reference is 1990/91. See Annex 3 for additional information about the Reading Literacy Study.

P12: Hours of instruction

P12 : Heures de cours

Table P12:
Mean number of hours of instruction per year
and dispersion in hours received by pupils
(standard errors in parentheses) (1991)

*Tableau P12 :
Nombre annuel moyen d'heures de cours
et disparité des heures suivies par les élèves
(erreurs types entre parenthèses) (1991)*

	Mean number of hours of instruction per year / *Nombre moyen d'heures de cours par an*	Number of hours of instruction for the bottom quarter (25th percentile) / *Nombre d'heures de cours pour l'intervalle inférieur (25e centile)*	Number of hours of instruction for the top quarter (75th percentile) / *Nombre d'heures de cours pour l'intervalle supérieur (75e centile)*	
Pupils 9 years of age				*Elèves âgés de 9 ans*
Belgium (French community)	900 (5.4)	863	926	*Belgique (Communauté française)*
British Columbia (Canada)	927 (7.5)	903	975	*Colombie-Britannique (Canada)*
Denmark	662 (2.9)	630	690	*Danemark*
Finland	705 (2.8)	684	713	*Finlande*
France	878 (4.2)	855	914	*France*
Germany (TFGDR)	679 (5.0)	656	713	*Allemagne (ex-RDA)*
Germany (FTFR)	661 (6.1)	610	705	*Allemagne (ex- terr. de la RFA)*
Greece	692 (5.8)	638	722	*Grèce*
Iceland	585 (7.8)	560	624	*Islande*
Ireland	920 (0.0)	920	920	*Irlande*
Netherlands	1 019 (2.5)	1 014	1 030	*Pays-Bas*
New Zealand	963 (2.8)	933	998	*Nouvelle-Zélande*
Spain	909 (5.5)	833	975	*Espagne*
Switzerland	874 (6.6)	767	987	*Suisse*
United States	1 001 (7.3)	927	1 080	*Etats-Unis*
Pupils 14 years of age				*Elèves âgés de 14 ans*
Belgium (French community)	1 090 (8.2)	1 013	1 133	*Belgique (Communauté française)*
British Columbia (Canada)	999 (8.0)	975	1 025	*Colombie-Britannique (Canada)*
Denmark	903 (5.0)	870	958	*Danemark*
Finland	857 (1.3)	855	855	*Finlande*
France	1 047 (7.7)	990	1 102	*France*
Germany (TFGDR)	878 (4.9)	840	912	*Allemagne (ex-RDA)*
Germany (FTFR)	870 (4.6)	833	913	*Allemagne (ex- terr. de la RFA)*
Greece	743 (5.5)	695	788	*Grèce*
Iceland	794 (7.1)	744	840	*Islande*
Netherlands	1 198 (9.4)	1 178	1 280	*Pays-Bas*
New Zealand	982 (5.0)	950	1 000	*Nouvelle-Zélande*
Spain	925 (6.0)	840	1 000	*Espagne*
Switzerland	1 108 (7.0)	1 020	1 216	*Suisse*
United States	1 032 (9.2)	958	1 107	*Etats-Unis*

See Annex 1 for notes

Voir notes en annexe 1

P12: Hours of instruction

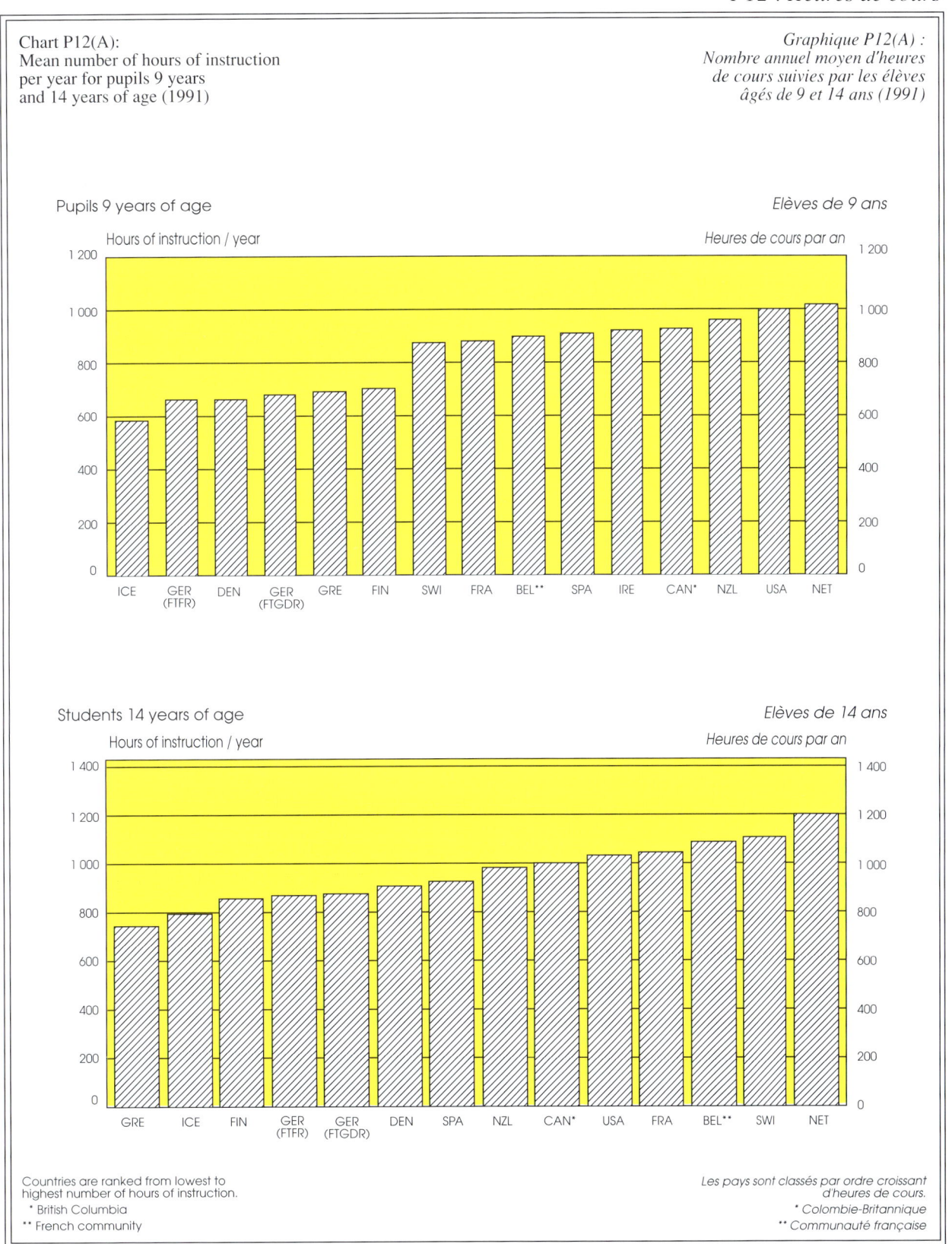

P12 : Heures de cours

Chart P12(A):
Mean number of hours of instruction per year for pupils 9 years and 14 years of age (1991)

Graphique P12(A) :
Nombre annuel moyen d'heures de cours suivies par les élèves âgés de 9 et 14 ans (1991)

Pupils 9 years of age — *Elèves de 9 ans*
Hours of instruction / year — *Heures de cours par an*

Countries (in order): ICE, GER (FTFR), DEN, GER (FTGDR), GRE, FIN, SWI, FRA, BEL**, SPA, IRE, CAN*, NZL, USA, NET

Students 14 years of age — *Elèves de 14 ans*
Hours of instruction / year — *Heures de cours par an*

Countries (in order): GRE, ICE, FIN, GER (FTFR), GER (FTGDR), DEN, SPA, NZL, CAN*, USA, FRA, BEL**, SWI, NET

Countries are ranked from lowest to highest number of hours of instruction.
* British Columbia
** French community

Les pays sont classés par ordre croissant d'heures de cours.
* Colombie-Britannique
** Communauté française

P12: Hours of instruction

P12 : Heures de cours

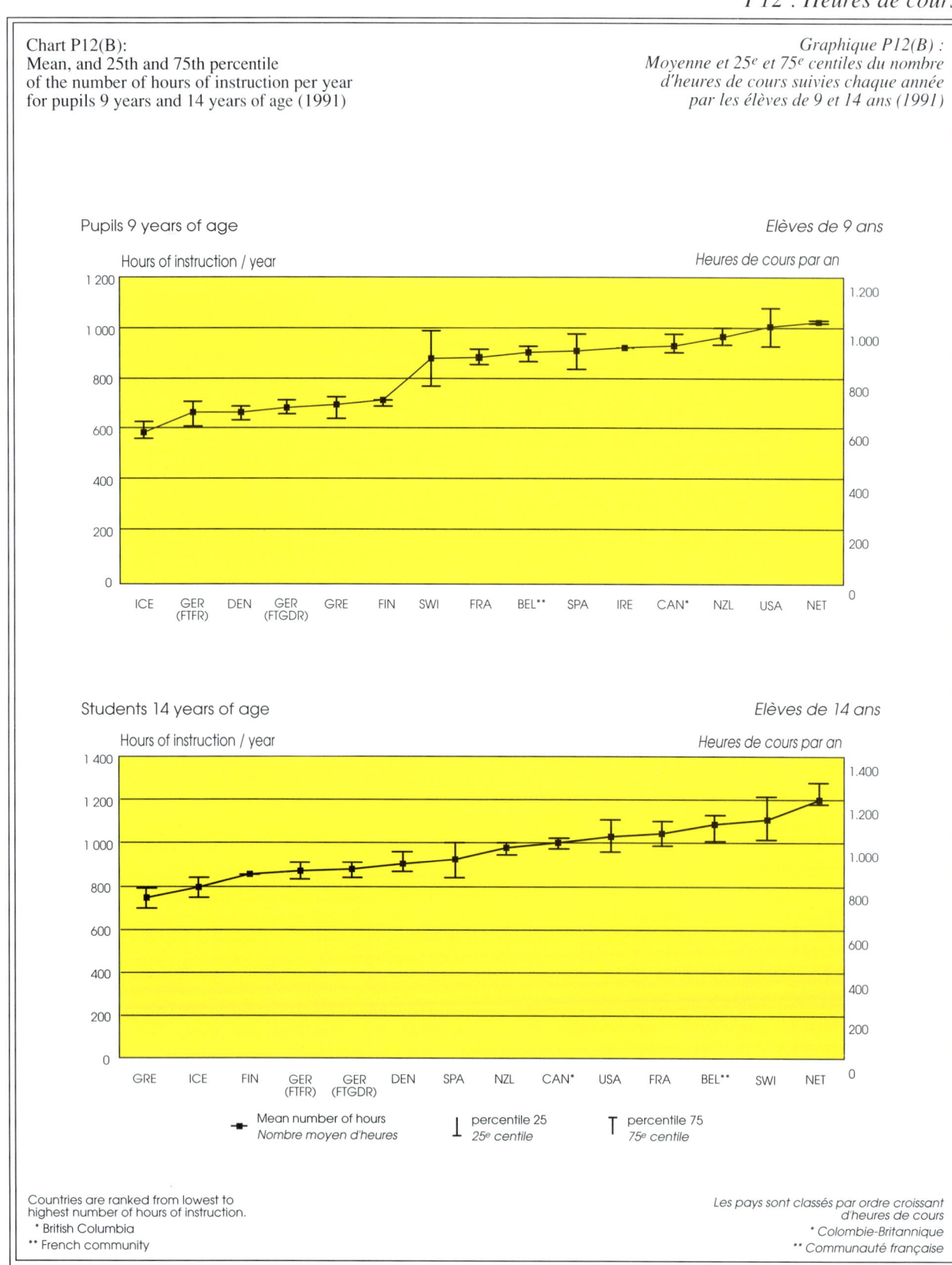

Chart P12(B):
Mean, and 25th and 75th percentile
of the number of hours of instruction per year
for pupils 9 years and 14 years of age (1991)

*Graphique P12(B) :
Moyenne et 25ᵉ et 75ᵉ centiles du nombre
d'heures de cours suivies chaque année
par les élèves de 9 et 14 ans (1991)*

Pupils 9 years of age — *Elèves de 9 ans*

Hours of instruction / year — *Heures de cours par an*

Countries (ranked): ICE, GER (FTFR), DEN, GER (FTGDR), GRE, FIN, SWI, FRA, BEL**, SPA, IRE, CAN*, NZL, USA, NET

Students 14 years of age — *Elèves de 14 ans*

Hours of instruction / year — *Heures de cours par an*

Countries (ranked): GRE, ICE, FIN, GER (FTFR), GER (FTGDR), DEN, SPA, NZL, CAN*, USA, FRA, BEL**, SWI, NET

- Mean number of hours / *Nombre moyen d'heures*
- percentile 25 / *25ᵉ centile*
- percentile 75 / *75ᵉ centile*

Countries are ranked from lowest to highest number of hours of instruction.
* British Columbia
** French community

*Les pays sont classés par ordre croissant d'heures de cours
* Colombie-Britannique
** Communauté française*

P21: Grouping within classes

GROUPING OF 9 YEAR-OLDS WITHIN CLASSES FOR READING AND LANGUAGE LESSONS

POLICY ISSUES

Is the grouping of pupils within classes an effective strategy for adapting instruction to individual needs?

KEY RESULTS

OECD countries vary considerably in the extent to which they group 9 year-old pupils within classes for reading and language instruction. All countries group at least 11 per cent of the pupils by one criterion or another. In almost every country this criterion is ability; pupils within classes are almost never grouped according to age.

DESCRIPTION AND INTERPRETATION

Grouping is a means of adapting instruction to the characteristics of pupils. This indicator shows the extent to which teachers group 9 year-old pupils during reading and language lessons, and the criterion for differentiation. The data are no less relevant for being subject-specific; a considerable part of the school day for 9 year-olds in many countries is in fact devoted to reading and language.

For almost all countries, the most common way of grouping pupils is by ability. None of the considerable research on this practice has produced solid evidence of a link between ability grouping and higher levels of achievement. Some researchers have argued that it is not the way groups are formed, but the teacher's success in coping with ability differences, that determines the achievement of pupils.

It should be noted that the information used for this indicator has to do with grouping within the classroom, not with assigning pupils to classes. Furthermore, grouping does not necessarily imply different ways of providing instruction.

The first column of Table P21 shows the percentage of 9 year-old pupils who are not grouped by their teachers during reading instruction; the other four show the percentage whose teachers most frequently use the grouping criterion listed. Figures in each row add up to 100 per cent. Standard errors are shown in Annex 3. The table shows that pupils in the Netherlands (9 per cent) and New Zealand (6 per cent) are the most likely to be grouped during reading and language lessons, while pupils in Spain (89 per cent) and Greece (84 per cent) are the least likely.

While ability grouping predominates in most countries, interest grouping is also relatively important in Denmark (17 per cent), Finland (14 per cent), Portugal (13 per cent) and Switzerland (12 per cent). As noted above, age is seldom the criterion; only in the United States does grouping by age (12 per cent) occur more frequently than by "interest" (4 per cent) or "other" grouping (7 per cent). Some teachers in the United States may have misinterpreted the study as asking how pupils are assigned to classes, particularly those who typically instruct whole classes. In Switzerland (20 per cent) and Denmark (19 per cent), "other" types of grouping are also relatively important.

DEFINITIONS

Data are from the Reading Literacy Study, which was conducted by the International Association for the Evaluation of Educational Achievement. The year of reference was 1990/91.

The teachers' responses are weighted to represent the school experiences of pupils.

See Annex 3 for additional information about the Reading Literacy Study.

P21: Grouping within classes

P21 : Répartition des élèves en groupes dans les classes

Table P21:
Distribution in percentage of 9 year-old pupils
in various types of grouping for reading
instruction as reported by
their teachers (1991)

*Tableau P21 :
Pourcentage des élèves de 9 ans
répartis en groupes pendant
les cours de lecture,
au dire de leurs enseignants (1991)*

	No grouping / *Aucun groupe*	Ability groups / *Groupes d'aptitudes*	Interest groups / *Groupes d'intérêt*	Age groups / *Groupes d'âge*	Other / *Autres*	
Belgium (French community)	71	16	9	1	3	*Belgique (Communauté française)*
British Columbia (Canada)	57	19	7	2	15	*Colombie-Britannique (Canada)*
Denmark	26	38	17	0	19	*Danemark*
Finland	66	13	14	1	6	*Finlande*
Germany (TFGDR)	24	55	9	0	12	*Allemagne (ex-RDA)*
Germany (FTFR)	63	32	3	0	2	*Allemagne (ex-terr. de la RFA))*
Greece	84	9	4	1	2	*Grèce*
Iceland	41	48	3	1	7	*Islande*
Ireland	49	49	1	1	0	*Irlande*
Netherlands	9	87	0	2	2	*Pays-Bas*
New Zealand	6	83	4	0	7	*Nouvelle-Zélande*
Portugal	69	14	13	0	4	*Portugal*
Spain	89	8	1	1	1	*Espagne*
Switzerland	52	16	12	1	20	*Suisse*
United States	31	45	4	12	7	*Etats-Unis*

See Annex 1 for notes

Voir notes en annexe 1

P21: Grouping within classes

P21 : Répartition des élèves en groupes dans les classes

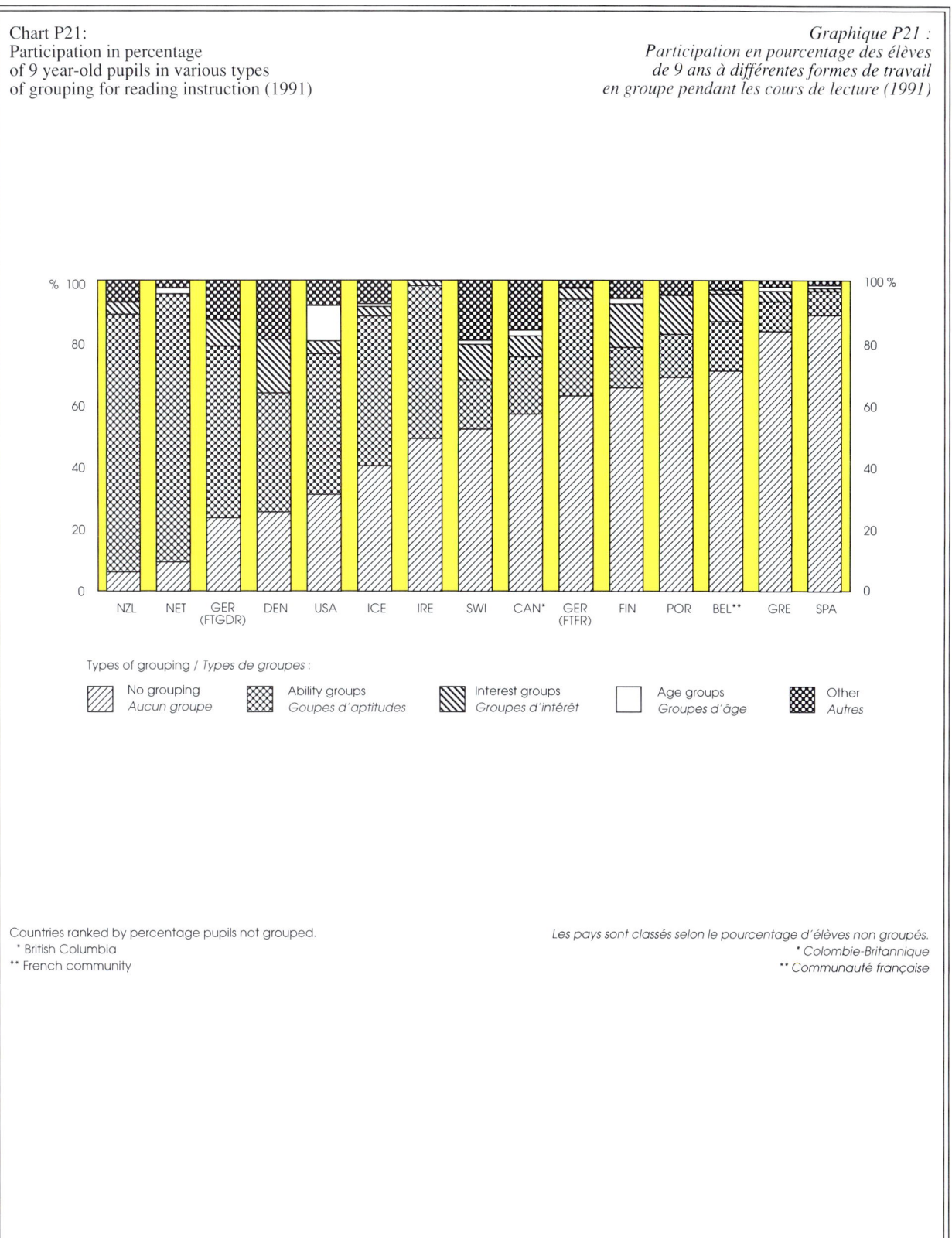

Chart P21:
Participation in percentage
of 9 year-old pupils in various types
of grouping for reading instruction (1991)

Graphique P21 :
Participation en pourcentage des élèves
de 9 ans à différentes formes de travail
en groupe pendant les cours de lecture (1991)

Types of grouping / *Types de groupes* :

- No grouping / *Aucun groupe*
- Ability groups / *Goupes d'aptitudes*
- Interest groups / *Groupes d'intérêt*
- Age groups / *Groupes d'âge*
- Other / *Autres*

Countries ranked by percentage pupils not grouped.
* British Columbia
** French community

Les pays sont classés selon le pourcentage d'élèves non groupés.
* Colombie-Britannique
** Communauté française

P31: Staff employed in education

TEACHING AND NON-TEACHING STAFF AS A PERCENTAGE OF THE TOTAL LABOUR FORCE

POLICY ISSUES

Is education currently understaffed? Overstaffed? Is education in competition with other sectors for available qualified personnel? Is there a proper balance within education between teaching and non-teaching staff? Between public and private financing of their employment?

KEY RESULTS

Teaching staff at all levels represent between 2 and 5 per cent of the total labour force in 16 OECD countries.

Between 8 and 25 per cent of the total teaching staff are in tertiary education. In about half of the countries reporting, tertiary staff comprise between 7 and 12 per cent of all teachers; in the remaining countries, they comprise 17 to 25 per cent.

In ten countries with relevant data, pedagogical and support staff comprise between 17 and 58 per cent of the whole education staff. The country mean is 36 per cent.

DESCRIPTION AND INTERPRETATION

In nearly half of the countries reporting [Australia, Germany (FTFR), Japan, the Netherlands, Turkey, the United Kingdom and the United States], teaching staff comprise between 2 and 3 per cent of the labour force. In all of these countries except Turkey and the United Kingdom, tertiary staff comprise between 17 and 25 per cent of all teaching staff.

In a slightly larger group of countries (Austria, the Czech Republic, Denmark, Finland, France, Ireland, New Zealand and Spain), teaching staff comprise between 3 and 4 per cent of the labour force. In two of these, Austria and New Zealand, 17 and 25 per cent of all teaching staff are at the tertiary level.

Lastly, in three countries (Belgium, Hungary and Italy), teaching staff comprise between 4 and 5 per cent of the labour force. Neither of these countries has a sizeable tertiary level teaching staff.

In most countries, student enrolments represent between 40 and 60 per cent of the labour force. In Ireland and Spain, the ratio of students to labour force participants was larger; in Denmark, Germany, Spain and Switzerland, it was lower.

In three of the countries reporting pedagogical and support staff data, that group combined represents a relatively small share of the overall education staff (between 17 and 25 per cent) in Belgium, the Czech Republic and Italy. In five countries: Finland, France, Germany (FTFR), Hungary and Japan, there are between 36 and 42 pedagogical and support staff for every 100 members of the education labour force. The United States has the largest ratio: 58.

DEFINITIONS

This indicator expresses numbers of full-time-equivalent (FTE) teaching staff, non-teaching staff, and all education staff as percentages of the total labour force in each country in 1991. The figures include staff employed in primary, secondary and tertiary education in both public and private schools.

Teachers are defined as persons whose professional activity involves the transmitting of knowledge, attitudes and skills that are stipulated in a formal curriculum programme to students enrolled in a formal educational institution. Non-teaching staff includes two categories: other pedagogical staff, including principals, headmasters, supervisors, counsellors, psychologists, librarians, etc.; and support staff including clerical personnel, building operations and maintenance personnel, food service workers, etc.

The figures on the size of the total labour force against which the numbers of education staff are compared have been obtained from OECD's *Labour Force Statistics*.

P31: Staff employed in education

P31 : Personnel de l'enseignement

Table P31(A):
Teaching staff as a percentage
of the labour force total
(full-time equivalents) (1992)

Tableau P31(A) :
Personnel enseignant en pourcentage
de la population active totale
(en équivalents plein temps) (1992)

	Public and private education / *Enseignement public et privé*			Students enrolment as a percentage of labour force / *Effectifs scolarisés en pourcentage de la population active*	
	Primary and secondary / *Primaire et secondaire*	Tertiary / *Supérieur*	All levels (including early childhood education) / *Tous niveaux (préscolaire inclus)*		
North America					*Amérique du Nord*
Canada	...	...	...	51.5	*Canada*
United States	2.1	0.5	2.7	49.3	*Etats-Unis*
Pacific Area					*Pays du Pacifique*
Australia	2.3	0.6	2.9	...	*Australie*
Japan	1.7	0.4	2.4	39.9	*Japon*
New Zealand	2.3	0.5	3.3	58.8	*Nouvelle-Zélande*
European Community					*Communauté européenne*
Belgium	3.8	0.3	4.8	58.1	*Belgique*
Denmark	2.7	0.2	3.3	37.4	*Danemark*
France	2.4	0.4	3.3	57.6	*France*
Germany (FTFR)	1.6	0.6	2.4	39.6	*Allemagne (ex-terr. de la RFA)*
Germany	...	...	...	...	*Allemagne*
Greece	...	...	...	48.2	*Grèce*
Ireland	2.8	0.4	3.6	74.8	*Irlande*
Italy	3.5	0.1	4.2	46.5	*Italie*
Luxembourg	...	...	...	...	*Luxembourg*
Netherlands	1.8	0.4	2.4	49.1	*Pays-Bas*
Portugal	...	...	...	...	*Portugal*
Spain	2.6	0.4	3.3	63.5	*Espagne*
United Kingdom	2.2	0.3	2.5	47.2	*Royaume-Uni*
Other Europe - OECD					*Autres pays d'Europe-OCDE*
Austria	3.0	0.5	3.8	43.2	*Autriche*
Finland	...	...	3.1	43.6	*Finlande*
Iceland	...	...	...	...	*Islande*
Norway	...	...	...	46.1	*Norvège*
Sweden	2.3	...	...	41.9	*Suède*
Switzerland	...	...	...	36.0	*Suisse*
Turkey	2.0	0.2	2.2	57.1	*Turquie*
Country mean	**2.4**	**0.4**	**3.1**	**49.5**	***Moyenne des pays***
Central and Eastern Europe					*Europe centrale et orientale*
Czech Republic	2.4	0.3	3.5	46.3	*République tchèque*
Hungary	3.0	0.4	4.2	50.1	*Hongrie*
Poland	...	...	...	50.3	*Pologne*
Russia	...	...	...	...	*Russie*

See Annex 1 for notes

Voir notes en annexe 1

P31: Staff employed in education

P31 : Personnel de l'enseignement

Table P31(B):
Staff employed in education as a percentage of the labour force total (full-time equivalents) (1992)

Tableau P31(B) :
Personnel de l'enseignement en pourcentage de la population active totale (en équivalents plein temps) (1992)

	Teachers / Enseignants	Pedagogical staff / Personnel pédagogique	Support staff / Personnel de soutien	Teachers and pedagogical staff / Enseignants et personnel pédagogique	Pedagogical and support staff / Personnel pédagogique et de soutien	All staff / Ensemble du personnel	
North America							**Amérique du Nord**
Canada	...	...	...	...	...	...	Canada
United States	2.7	1.5	2.1	4.1	3.6	6.2	Etats-Unis
Pacific Area							**Pays du Pacifique**
Australia	2.9	0.3	1.2	3.0	1.5	4.2	Australie
Japan	2.4	x	0.7	x	x	3.1	Japon
New Zealand	3.3	...	...	...	...	...	Nouvelle-Zélande
European Community							**Communauté européenne**
Belgium	4.8	0.6	0.6	5.5	1.2	6.0	Belgique
Denmark	3.3	1.6	0.9	4.9	2.4	5.7	Danemark
France	3.3	...	...	...	2.2	5.5	France
Germany (FTFR)	2.4	...	...	...	...	...	Allemagne (ex- terr. de la RFA)
Germany	...	...	...	...	...	...	Allemagne
Greece	...	...	...	...	...	...	Grèce
Ireland	3.6	...	...	...	...	...	Irlande
Italy	4.2	0.4	0.8	4.2	1.3	5.5	Italie
Luxembourg	...	...	...	...	...	...	Luxembourg
Netherlands	2.4	...	...	...	...	...	Pays-Bas
Portugal	...	...	...	...	...	...	Portugal
Spain	3.3	...	...	...	...	...	Espagne
United Kingdom	2.5	...	...	...	...	...	Royaume-Uni
Other Europe - OECD							**Autres pays d'Europe-OCDE**
Austria	3.8	...	...	...	...	...	Autriche
Finland	3.1	...	...	...	2.0	5.1	Finlande
Iceland	...	...	...	...	...	...	Islande
Norway	...	...	...	...	...	...	Norvège
Sweden	...	...	...	...	...	...	Suède
Switzerland	...	...	...	...	...	...	Suisse
Turkey	2.2	...	...	...	...	...	Turquie
Country mean	**3.1**	...	...	...	**1.8**	**5.2**	**Moyenne des pays**
Central and Eastern Europe							**Europe centrale et orientale**
Czech Republic	3.5	0.7	.	4.2	0.7	4.2	République tchèque
Hungary	4.2	x	2.2	4.2	2.2	6.4	Hongrie
Poland	...	...	...	...	...	...	Pologne
Russia	...	...	...	...	...	...	Russie

See Annex 1 for notes

Voir notes en annexe 1

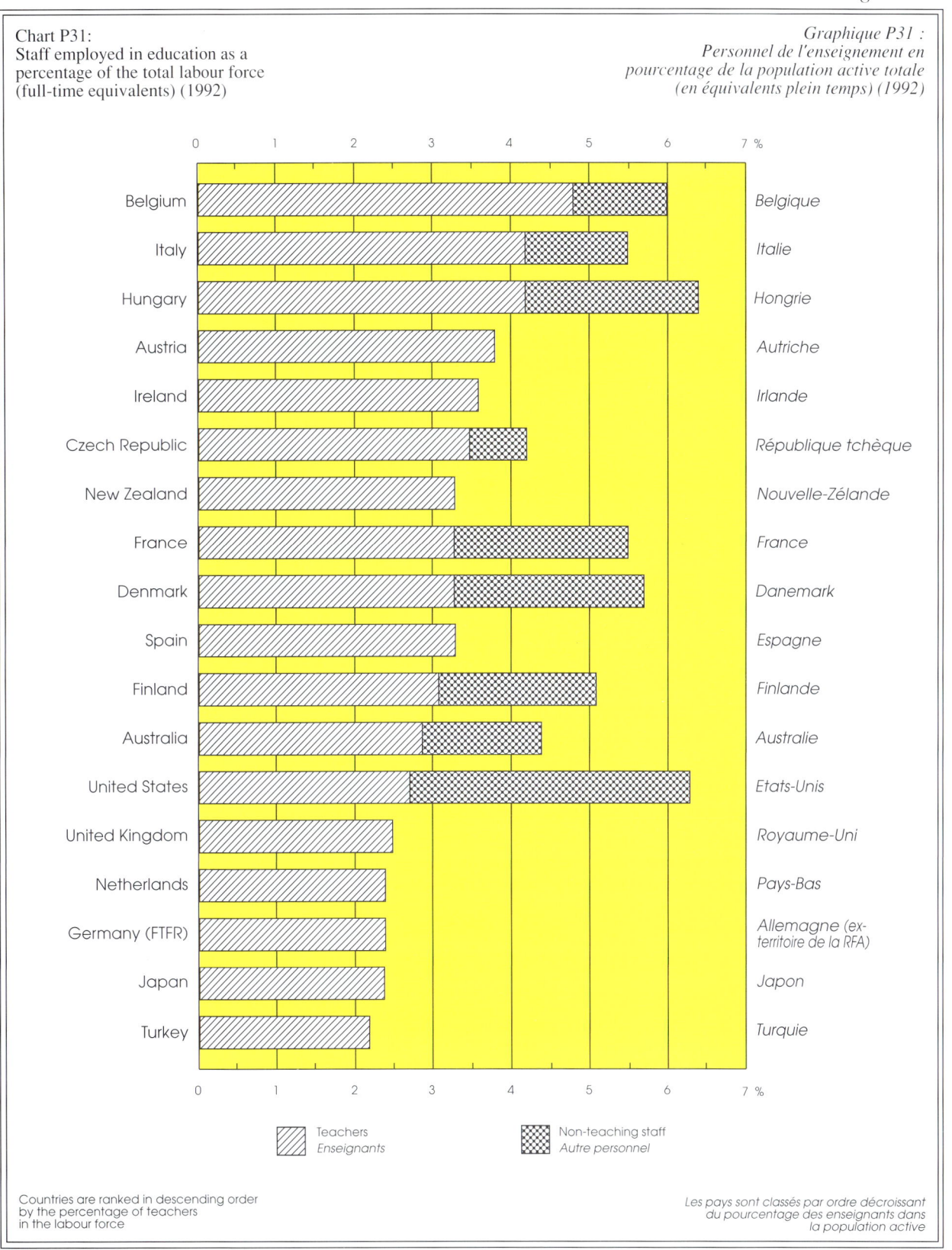

P31: Staff employed in education

P31 : *Personnel de l'enseignement*

Chart P31:
Staff employed in education as a percentage of the total labour force (full-time equivalents) (1992)

*Graphique P31 :
Personnel de l'enseignement en pourcentage de la population active totale (en équivalents plein temps) (1992)*

Belgium		Belgique
Italy		Italie
Hungary		Hongrie
Austria		Autriche
Ireland		Irlande
Czech Republic		République tchèque
New Zealand		Nouvelle-Zélande
France		France
Denmark		Danemark
Spain		Espagne
Finland		Finlande
Australia		Australie
United States		Etats-Unis
United Kingdom		Royaume-Uni
Netherlands		Pays-Bas
Germany (FTFR)		Allemagne (ex-territoire de la RFA)
Japan		Japon
Turkey		Turquie

Teachers / *Enseignants*
Non-teaching staff / *Autre personnel*

Countries are ranked in descending order by the percentage of teachers in the labour force

Les pays sont classés par ordre décroissant du pourcentage des enseignants dans la population active

P32: Ratio of students to teaching staff

RATIO OF STUDENTS TO TEACHING STAFF, BY LEVEL OF EDUCATION

POLICY ISSUES

Should improved student access to teaching resources be considered a priority at lower education levels, rather than as a "bonus" that comes with age?

KEY RESULTS

In most countries, the general pattern is for the ratio of students to teachers to decline as the students progress to higher education levels. For public and private institutions, the country mean for early childhood education (20.1:1) is higher than the mean for primary education (18.5:1) and higher than the mean for secondary education (14.6:1).

DESCRIPTION AND INTERPRETATION

Because older students have more access to teaching resources than younger students, the pattern of a progressively declining ratio of students to teachers can be thought of as producing a "bonus for age". While the pattern is long-established in some countries, in others it may be due to more recent professional or parental influence on policy.

However, it is important to note that all children in early childhood education are counted as full-time even though they attend school only a half-day, and thus utilise less teaching time than those who are present a full day. When a country's early childhood ratio reflects primarily half-day attendance, that ratio needs to be weighted differently from those of other levels.

These figures do not show how teaching time is allocated. For example, they do not show whether resources are used to create a larger number of small classes for general teaching, additional specialist teaching, additional professional activities (preparation, evaluation), or additional administrative work. A relatively small ratio does not necessarily signify that most students are in small classes; classes could be large if teachers have a lot of non-teaching time, or if it is common for classes to have more than one teacher.

Of the 16 countries reporting on early childhood public and private education, seven have ratios between 11:1 and 19:1, three are under 11, and six have ratios above 20:1.

Of the 18 countries reporting on primary education, twelve have ratios between 18:1 and 24:1; four have ratios between 11:1 and 14:1; two countries have relatively high ratios of nearly 26:1 and 29.3:1.

Of the 18 countries reporting all secondary education, one country has a ratio of 23.4:1; four have ratios between 7:1 and 10:1; and 13 have ratios between 12:1 and 19:1.

For most countries reporting lower and upper secondary education separately, the ratios between the two levels are relatively similar. Exceptions are Austria, Germany (FTFR) and Sweden, where ratios are lower in lower secondary education, and the Czech Republic and Turkey where ratios are higher at the lower secondary level. In Turkey, there are more than three times as many students per teacher in lower secondary than in upper secondary schools.

The ratio is not an indicator of class size. The fact that one country has a lower ratio of students to teachers than another does not necessarily mean that classes are smaller in the first country or that pupils in the first country receive larger amounts of instruction. The relationship between the student/teacher ratio and either average class size or the amount of instruction per pupil is complicated by variations among countries in the length of the school year, the number of hours that a student attends class each day, the length of a teacher's working day, the number of classes or students for which a teacher is responsible, and the division of the teacher's time between teaching and other duties.

DEFINITIONS

The ratio of students to teaching staff is obtained by dividing the number of full-time-equivalent (FTE) students at a given level of education by the number of full-time-equivalent teachers at the same level. Students and teachers in both public and private schools have been included in the calculations.

P32: Ratio of students to teaching staff

P32 : Nombre d'élèves par enseignant

Table P32:
Ratio of students to teaching staff,
by level of education (1992)

*Tableau P32 :
Ratio élèves / enseignant,
par niveau d'enseignement (1992)*

	Public education / Enseignement public					Public and private education / Enseignement public et privé					
	Early childhood education / Préscolaire	Primary education / Primaire	Lower secondary education / Secondaire 1er cycle	Upper secondary education / Secondaire 2e cycle	All secondary education / Ensemble du secondaire	Early childhood education / Préscolaire	Primary education / Primaire	Lower secondary education / Secondaire 1er cycle	Upper secondary education / Secondaire 2e cycle	All secondary education / Ensemble du secondaire	
North America											*Amérique du Nord*
Canada	...	...	...	...	...	...	...	...	...	...	*Canada*
United States	...	...	17.7	15.6	16.7	...	...	16.8	15.0	15.9	*Etats-Unis*
Pacific Area											*Pays du Pacifique*
Australia	...	18.0	...	...	12.8	...	18.4	...	...	12.9	*Australie*
Japan	14.5	19.8	17.0	15.5	16.3	18.5	19.8	16.8	16.4	16.6	*Japon*
New Zealand	17.0	18.5	...	...	18.0	8.8	18.5	...	...	17.7	*Nouvelle-Zélande*
European Community											*Communauté européenne*
Belgium	17.5	13.0	...	...	6.7	18.4	13.7	...	...	7.8	*Belgique*
Denmark	10.8	11.1	9.0	10.4	9.6	10.7	10.9	9.1	10.4	9.7	*Danemark*
France	25.8	20.2	...	...	14.0	26.0	20.4	...	...	14.3	*France*
Germany (FTFR)	24.4	19.6	14.6	19.8	16.4	23.9	19.6	14.6	19.0	16.2	*Allemagne (ex- terr. de la RFA)*
Germany	...	...	...	...	...	...	...	...	...	...	*Allemagne*
Greece	...	...	...	...	...	...	...	...	...	...	*Grèce*
Ireland	27.5	25.8	...	...	17.1	27.2	25.6	...	...	17.1	*Irlande*
Italy	11.8	10.5	8.9	9.1	9.0	13.3	10.9	9.0	8.8	8.9	*Italie*
Luxembourg	...	...	...	...	...	...	...	...	...	...	*Luxembourg*
Netherlands	...	...	...	...	...	25.9	23.6	...	...	18.8	*Pays-Bas*
Portugal	...	...	...	...	...	...	...	...	...	...	*Portugal*
Spain	21.5	18.8	16.6	14.5	15.3	23.4	21.2	17.6	15.9	16.6	*Espagne*
United Kingdom	38.1	21.2	16.5	14.9	15.5	38.1	20.8	15.9	14.8	15.2	*Royaume-Uni*
Other Europe - OECD											*Autres pays d'Europe-OCDE*
Austria	17.3	12.2	7.9	11.4	9.4	18.3	12.2	7.7	11.6	9.4	*Autriche*
Finland	...	...	...	...	...	12.5	19.0	...	...	...	*Finlande*
Iceland	...	...	...	...	...	...	...	...	...	...	*Islande*
Norway	...	10.6	8.5	8.2	8.3	...	...	...	...	...	*Norvège*
Sweden	...	11.9	10.4	16.0	12.8	...	11.9	10.6	16.0	13.0	*Suède*
Switzerland	...	...	...	...	...	...	...	...	...	...	*Suisse*
Turkey	16.7	29.4	46.3	13.6	23.7	16.6	29.3	47.5	13.2	23.4	*Turquie*
Country mean	**20.2**	**17.4**	**15.8**	**13.5**	**13.8**	**20.1**	**18.5**	**16.6**	**14.1**	**14.6**	*Moyenne des pays*
Central and Eastern Europe											*Europe centrale et orientale*
Czech Republic	10.9	22.9	17.0	10.6	13.3	10.9	22.9	17.0	10.5	13.2	*République tchèque*
Hungary	11.3	12.6	11.5	14.1	12.7	11.5	12.7	11.6	14.1	12.7	*Hongrie*
Poland	...	...	...	...	...	...	...	...	...	...	*Pologne*
Russia	...	...	...	...	...	...	...	...	...	...	*Russie*

See Annex 1 for notes

Voir notes en annexe 1

P32: Ratio of students to teaching staff

P32 : Nombre d'élèves par enseignant

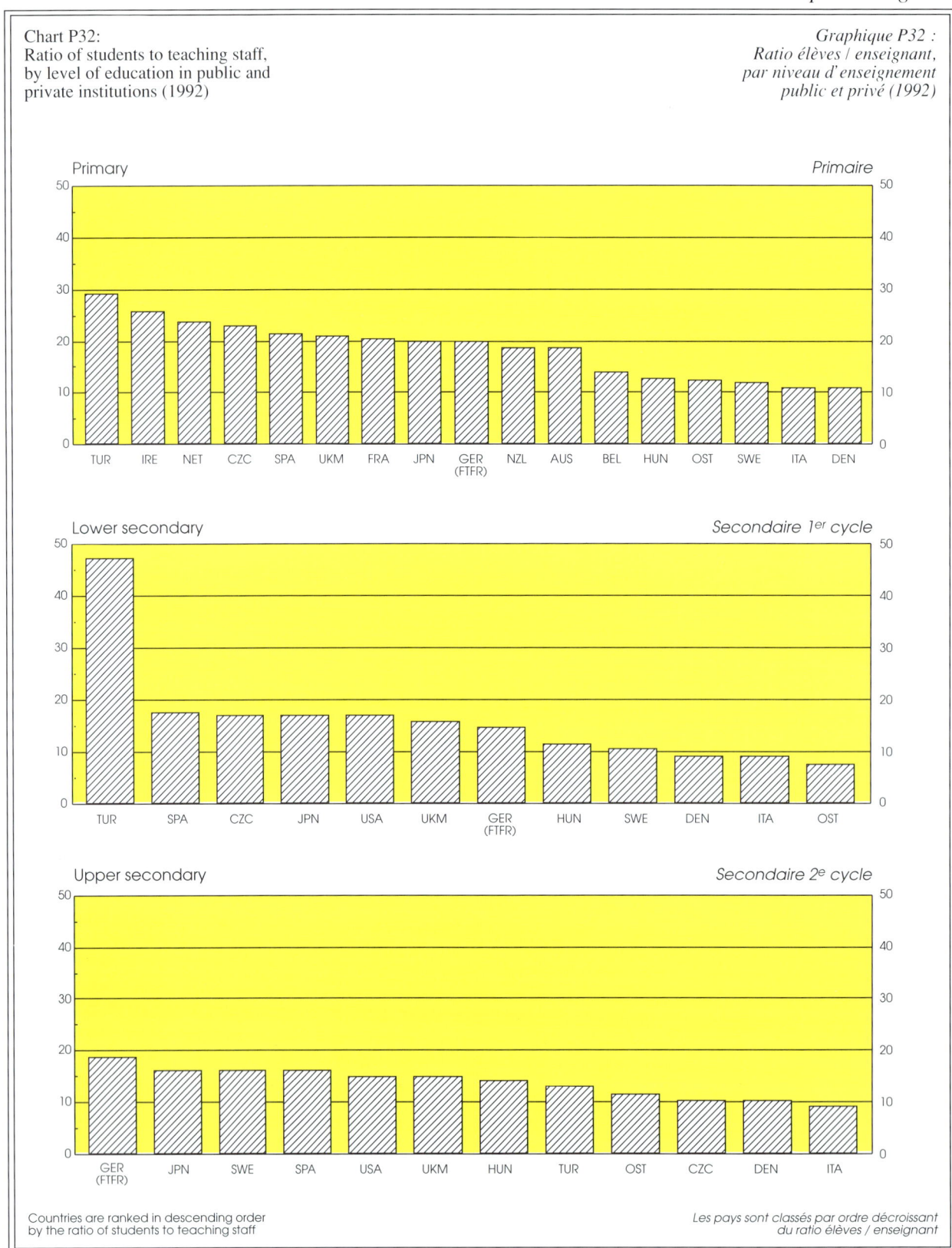

Chart P32:
Ratio of students to teaching staff, by level of education in public and private institutions (1992)

*Graphique P32 :
Ratio élèves / enseignant, par niveau d'enseignement public et privé (1992)*

Primary / *Primaire*

Country	Ratio
TUR	29
IRE	26
NET	24
CZC	23
SPA	21
UKM	21
FRA	20
JPN	20
GER (FTFR)	20
NZL	19
AUS	19
BEL	14
HUN	13
OST	12
SWE	12
ITA	11
DEN	11

Lower secondary / *Secondaire 1er cycle*

TUR	47
SPA	17
CZC	17
JPN	17
USA	17
UKM	16
GER (FTFR)	15
HUN	11
SWE	10
DEN	9
ITA	9
OST	8

Upper secondary / *Secondaire 2e cycle*

GER (FTFR)	18
JPN	16
SWE	16
SPA	16
USA	15
UKM	15
HUN	14
TUR	13
OST	11
CZC	10
DEN	10
ITA	9

Countries are ranked in descending order by the ratio of students to teaching staff

Les pays sont classés par ordre décroissant du ratio élèves / enseignant

P33: Teaching time

NUMBER OF TEACHING HOURS PER YEAR

POLICY ISSUES

Teaching time is an important element of the working conditions of teachers. It affects the amount of time available for planning and other professional activities, and is also related to motivational aspects of the teaching profession. Is actual teaching time as the part of human resources in education that is directly involved in the process of teaching and learning given its rightful emphasis as the teacher's primary activity?

KEY RESULTS

There is considerable diversity among the countries surveyed in the number of teaching hours per year for the average public school teacher in primary and lower secondary education. In nearly all countries, the number of hours per year in public primary education is higher (a mean of 858) than in public lower secondary education (a mean of 781).

DESCRIPTION AND INTERPRETATION

This indicator shows the number of hours per year a teacher is responsible for teaching students according to formal policy in his/her country. It gives no information regarding the hours devoted to other activities, such as lesson preparation, in-service training or staff meetings. It is thus important not to interpret this indicator as a measure of total workload, because it only reflects that portion associated with teaching hours.

Table P33 and Chart P33 show the number of teaching hours per year in primary, lower and upper secondary public education. In the Netherlands, Turkey and the United States, the number is relatively high for all levels reported, in Sweden it is relatively low. The high figure for primary level in the Netherlands can be explained partly by the fact that figures are based on the four highest grades only.

At the primary level the number of teaching hours per year varies from 624 in Sweden to 1 093 in the United States; the mean is 858 hours. In lower secondary education, it varies from 576 in Sweden to 1 042 in the United States. At the upper secondary level (general, not vocational), the variation is between 528 in Sweden to 1 019 in the United States, and the mean is 745 hours. Turkey has even higher figures (1 080) than the United States at the secondary levels, but it should be noted that those figures include additional teaching hours not counted as part of the standard number, for which teachers receive extra pay.

Countries with a relatively high number of hours at primary level also tend to have a high number at lower secondary level. At primary level the number of teaching hours per year is above the mean in France, Finland, Ireland, the Netherlands, Portugal, Spain, Turkey and the United States. The list is almost the same at the lower secondary level: Finland, Ireland, the Netherlands, New Zealand, Spain, Turkey and the United States. The difference in hours between the two levels is highest in Portugal and France.

DEFINITIONS

Teaching time is defined as the total number of hours per year (1 hour = 60 minutes) a full-time appointed teacher teaches students, according to the formal policy in the specific country.

Data are from the Network C survey on Teachers and the Curriculum.

If no formal data were available, it was acceptable to estimate the number of teaching hours from survey data. This was done for the United States.

P33: Teaching time

P33 : Temps d'enseignement

Table P33:
Number of teaching hours per year,
by level of public education (1992)

Tableau P33 :
Nombre annuel d'heures de cours
dispensées par les enseignants,
par niveau d'enseignement public (1992)

	Primary education / *Enseignement primaire*	Lower secondary education / *Enseignement secondaire 1er cycle*	Upper secondary education (general) / *Enseignement secondaire 2e cycle (général)*	Upper secondary education (vocational) / *Enseignement secondaire 2e cycle (professionnel)*	
Austria	780	747	664	714	*Autriche*
Belgium	840	720	660	849	*Belgique*
Finland	874	798	760	855	*Finlande*
France	944	632	...	...	*France*
Germany (FTFR)	790	761	673	679	*Allemagne (ex- terr. de la RFA)*
Ireland	951	792	792	792	*Irlande*
Italy	748	612	612	612	*Italie*
Netherlands	1 000	954	954	...	*Pays-Bas*
New Zealand	790	897	813	...	*Nouvelle-Zélande*
Norway	749	666	627	627	*Norvège*
Portugal	882	648	612	612	*Portugal*
Spain	900	900	630	630	*Espagne*
Sweden	624	576	528	612	*Suède*
Turkey	900	1 080	1 080	1 692	*Turquie*
United Kingdom	...	669	...	...	*Royaume-Uni*
United States	1 093	1 042	1 019	...	*Etats-Unis*
Country mean	**858**	**781**	**745**	**789**	*Moyenne des pays*

See Annex 1 for notes

Voir notes en annexe 1

P33: Teaching time

P33 : Temps d'enseignement

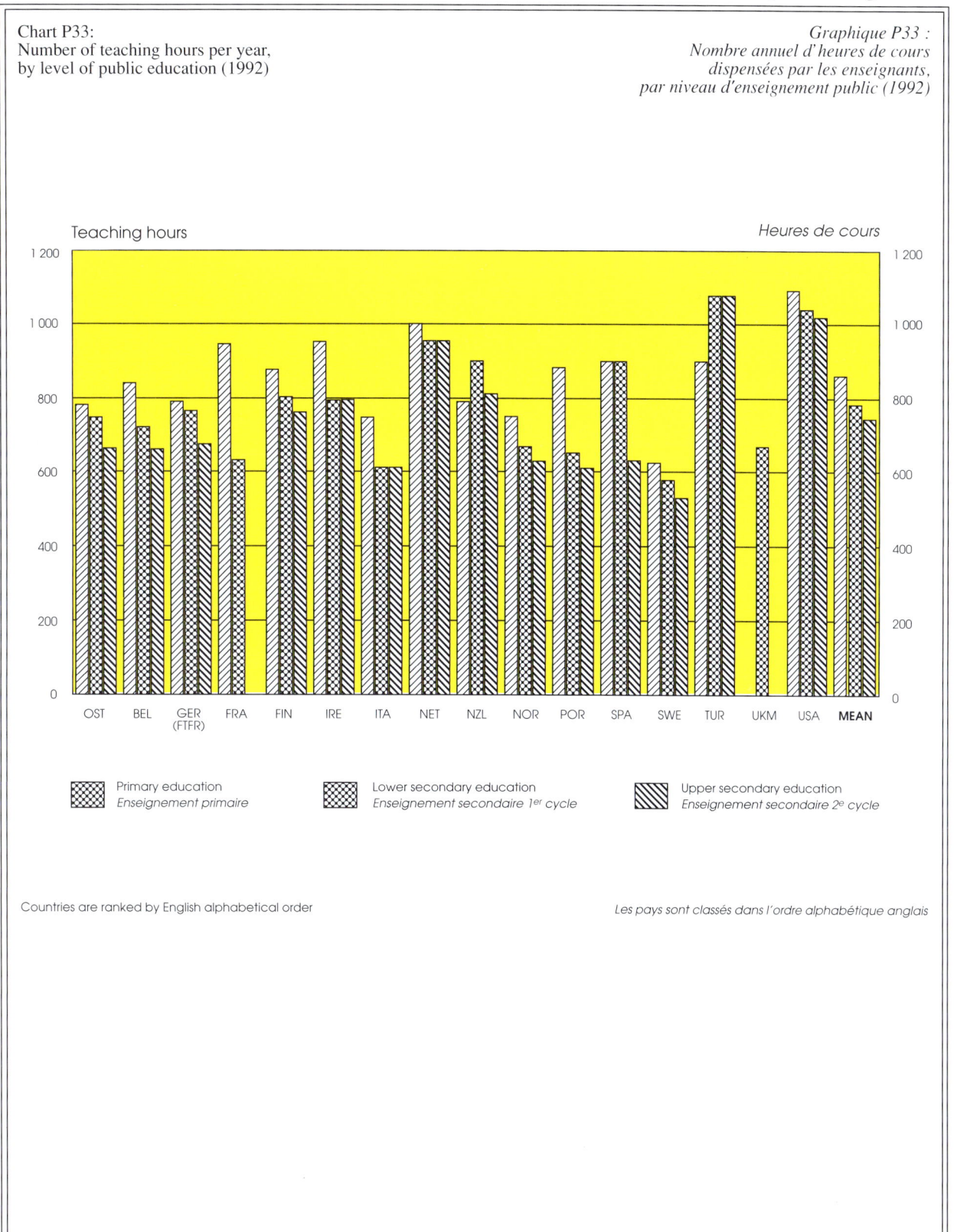

Chart P33:
Number of teaching hours per year,
by level of public education (1992)

*Graphique P33 :
Nombre annuel d'heures de cours
dispensées par les enseignants,
par niveau d'enseignement public (1992)*

Teaching hours / *Heures de cours*

Countries: OST, BEL, GER (FTFR), FRA, FIN, IRE, ITA, NET, NZL, NOR, POR, SPA, SWE, TUR, UKM, USA, **MEAN**

- Primary education / *Enseignement primaire*
- Lower secondary education / *Enseignement secondaire 1er cycle*
- Upper secondary education / *Enseignement secondaire 2e cycle*

Countries are ranked by English alphabetical order

Les pays sont classés dans l'ordre alphabétique anglais

P34: Teacher education

DURATION OF TEACHER EDUCATION

POLICY ISSUES

Is teacher training making its (expected) contribution to maintaining quality standards in education? What does its duration represent in the way of national investment in the training of new teachers?

KEY RESULTS

OECD countries are quite similar with respect to the duration of teacher education. To become a qualified teacher at early childhood, primary and lower secondary levels, education lasts 15 to 17 years in most countries (including the years in primary, secondary and tertiary education). Germany requires the highest number of years of education for teaching at primary, lower and upper secondary levels. In most countries, the formal requirements for teaching in public education are the same as those for teaching in private education.

DESCRIPTION AND INTERPRETATION

This indicator shows the number of years of education required to begin work as a fully qualified teacher according to the formal policy of the country. In most cases, the number varies slightly within countries. For all countries, the minimum number has been reported.

Table P34 shows the total number of years of education required to become a teacher in various levels of education. The duration of formal education (i.e. excluding pre-primary) varies from 12 years for public early childhood education in Italy, to 20 for teaching at upper secondary level in Germany. The requirements for teaching in public primary and secondary education are highest in Germany, i.e. 19 and 20 years, respectively. Part of the explanation for these high figures for Germany lies in the fact that the time new teachers are required to work in practice (i.e. in the classroom) as part of their training has been included.

Chart P34 shows clearly that in seven countries (France, the Netherlands, Portugal, Sweden, Turkey, the United Kingdom and the United States), the requirements for becoming a fully qualified teacher for primary education equal those for the other levels of education considered in the survey.

DEFINITIONS

The total number of years of teacher education refers to the total (minimum) number of years of primary, secondary and tertiary education required to start working as a fully qualified teacher according to the formal policy in a country.

Data are from the Network C survey on Teachers and the Curriculum.

In systems where the teacher has to work in the classroom before being qualified, these years of practice have been included.

P34: Teacher education

P34 : Formation des enseignants

Table P34:
Total number of years of education required by level of education (1992)

Tableau P34 :
Nombre d'années d'études requises pour devenir enseignant, par niveau scolaire (1992)

	Early childhood education *Education préscolaire*			Primary education *Enseignement primaire*			Lower secondary education *Enseignement secondaire 1er cycle*			Upper secondary education (general) *Enseignement secondaire 2e cycle (général)*			Upper secondary education (vocational) *Enseignement secondaire 2e cycle (professionnel)*			
	Public	Gov.-dep. private	Indep. private	Public	Gov.-dep. private	Indep. private	Public	Gov.-dep. private	Indep. private	Public	Gov.-dep. private	Indep. private	Public	Gov.-dep. private	Indep. private	
Austria	...	...	-	15	15	-	15	15	-	16	16	-	15	15	-	Autriche
Belgium	15	15	-	15	15	-	15	15	-	16	16	-	15	15	-	Belgique
Finland	15	.	.	17	.	.	18	.	.	18	.	.	17	17	.	Finlande
France	16	...	...	16	...	...	16	...	...	16	...	...	16	...	...	France
Germany (FTFR)	15	15	.	19	19	.	19	19	.	20	20	.	20	20	.	Allemagne (ex-terr. de la RFA)
Ireland	16	...	...	16	...	...	17	17	...	17	17	...	17	17	...	Irlande
Italy	12	.	11	13	.	12	17	.	16	17	.	16	17	.	16	Italie
Netherlands	17	17	.	17	17	.	17	17	.	17	17	.	...	...	...	Pays-Bas
New Zealand	17	17	17	17	17	17	17	17	17	19	19	19	...	...	...	Nouvelle-Zélande
Norway	15	15	...	15	15	...	15	15	...	16	16	...	15	15	...	Norvège
Portugal	16	16	16	17	17	17	17	17	17	17	17	17	17	17	17	Portugal
Spain	15	15	15	15	15	15	15	15	15	17	17	17	13	13	13	Espagne
Sweden	14	-	.	16	-	.	16	-	.	16	-	.	17	-	.	Suède
Turkey	15	.	15	15	.	15	15	.	15	15	.	15	15	.	15	Turquie
United Kingdom	17	...	17	...	...	17	...	...	17	...	...	...	...	...	...	Royaume-Uni
United States	16	.	16	16	.	16	16	.	16	16	.	16	16	.	16	Etats-Unis
Country mean	**15.4**	...	...	**15.9**	...	...	**16.3**	...	...	**16.9**	...	...	**16.2**	...	...	*Moyenne des pays*

See Annex 1 for notes

Voir notes en annexe 1

P34: Teacher education

P34 : Formation des enseignants

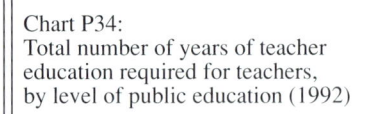

Chart P34:
Total number of years of teacher education required for teachers, by level of public education (1992)

Graphique P34 :
Nombre d'années d'études requises pour les enseignants de l'enseignement public, par niveau scolaire (1992)

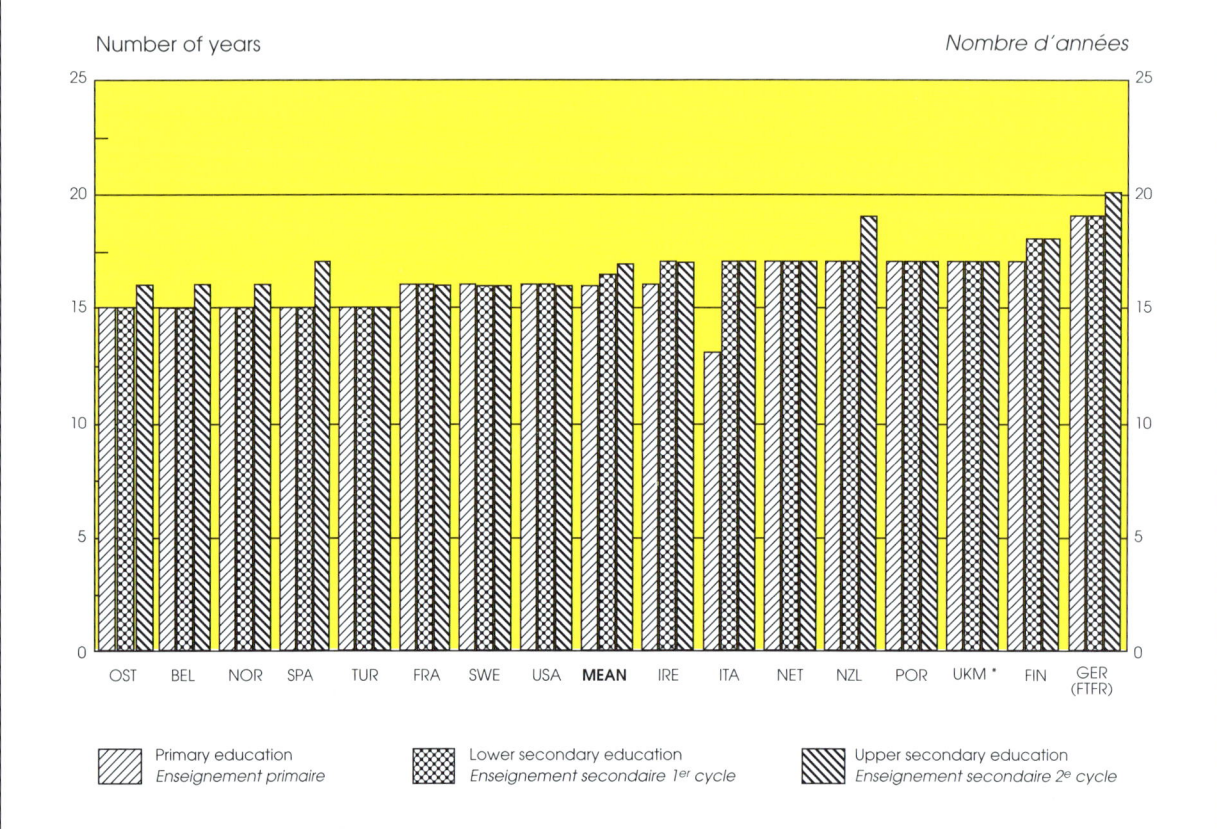

Number of years / *Nombre d'années*

Countries (x-axis): OST, BEL, NOR, SPA, TUR, FRA, SWE, USA, **MEAN**, IRE, ITA, NET, NZL, POR, UKM*, FIN, GER (FTFR)

Legend:
- Primary education / *Enseignement primaire*
- Lower secondary education / *Enseignement secondaire 1er cycle*
- Upper secondary education / *Enseignement secondaire 2e cycle*

* Private sector only.
Countries are ranked by ascending order of years required to teach in upper secondary general education

* Secteur privé seulement.
Les pays sont classés par ordre croissant d'années d'études requises pour enseigner au niveau du secondaire 2e cycle général

186

P35: Teacher compensation

STARTING AND MAXIMUM SALARIES OF TEACHERS IN PUBLIC PRIMARY AND LOWER SECONDARY EDUCATION

POLICY ISSUES

Salary is one of the malleable rewards of the teaching profession, and represents a high percentage of total expenditures in education. When and to what extent is it appropriate to increase teachers' remuneration?

KEY RESULTS

There are large salary differences across OECD countries, particularly with respect to maximum salaries in lower secondary education. Both starting and maximum salaries are somewhat higher for lower secondary school teachers than for primary school teachers.

The average number of years it takes teachers in public primary and lower secondary education to progress from their minimum to their maximum salary varies from 8 to 45 years. The average number of years is 25 for primary, and 24 for lower secondary education.

DESCRIPTION AND INTERPRETATION

This indicator shows the average starting and maximum salaries of teachers in public primary and lower secondary education. Salaries have been converted to purchasing power parity (PPP) rates (at the January 1992 price level). This basis for measurement allows meaningful comparisons among countries with respect to teacher salaries.

The gross domestic product per capita of the population (per capita GDP) can be regarded as an index of the welfare level of a country's population. Relating teacher salaries to per capita GDP provides some information on the status of the teaching profession in a country.

Tables P35(A) and P35(B) and Chart P35(A) provide an overall picture of the relationship between gross domestic product per capita and the minimum and maximum salaries of the teaching force at primary and secondary level. In general, they show that teachers' starting levels are similar to or slightly above per capita GDP in most countries. Starting salaries in Spain and Turkey are substantially higher than per capita GDP, which may indicate a relatively high standing of the teaching profession in those countries. Starting salaries are lowest relative to the GDP per capita in Sweden and the United States.

For both primary and lower secondary, starting salaries are highest in the former FTFR Germany ($23 627 for primary and $27 444 for lower secondary education) and maximum salaries are highest in Austria ($38 962 and $42 448 for primary and lower secondary education, respectively).

Differences between minimum and maximum salaries are largest in Austria, Portugal and the United Kingdom and smallest in Norway and Sweden. Also in Norway and Sweden, maximum teacher salaries are not substantially different from per capita GDP.

The far right column of the tables shows the average yearly increase in teacher salaries (maximum minus minimum divided by years to progress from minimum to maximum). It shows that the largest yearly increases in teacher salaries are found in the United Kingdom (lower secondary education) and the United States (primary and lower secondary education), and the smallest in Spain and Turkey (primary and lower secondary education). These figures should be interpreted with caution, because they assume an equal yearly salary increase.

DEFINITION

The starting salaries reported refer to the average scheduled gross salary per year of a full-time appointed teacher with the minimum level of training to be fully qualified at the beginning of his or her teaching career (school year of reference: 1991/92).

The gross salary is defined as the sum of wages (total sum of money paid by the employer for the labour supplied) minus the employer's premium for social security and pension funding (according to existing salary scales). Bonuses that constitute a regular part of the salary such as the 13th month, or holiday or regional bonuses, are included in the gross salary.

The maximum salaries reported refer to the average scheduled maximum gross salary (top of the salary scale) per year of a full-time teacher with the minimum level of training to be fully qualified for his or her job (school year of reference: 1991/92).

Data are from the Network C survey on Teachers and the Curriculum.

P35: Teacher compensation

P35 : Rémunération des enseignants

Table P35(A):
Primary teacher salaries:
starting and maximum salaries
in equivalent US dollars converted using PPPs (1992)

Tableau P35(A) :
Traitements des enseignants du primaire :
traitement de départ et traitement maximum
en équivalents dollars E-U convertis en PPA (1992)

	Per capita GDP / *PIB par habitant*	Starting salary / *Traitement de départ*	Maximum salary / *Traitement maximum*	Ratio of starting salary to per capita GDP / *Ratio traitement de départ / PIB par habitant*	Ratio of maximum salary to per capita GDP / *Ratio traitement maximum / PIB par habitant*	Ratio of maximum salary to starting salary / *Ratio traitement maximum / traitement de départ*	Years from starting to maximum salary / *Nombre d'années entre le traitement de départ et le traitement maximum*	Average yearly increase / *Variation annuelle moyenne*	
North America									*Amérique du Nord*
Canada	...	...	...	...	...	...	...	...	*Canada*
United States	23 215	21 240	35 394	0.9	1.5	1.7	16	885	*Etats-Unis*
Pacific Area									*Pays du Pacifique*
Australia	...	...	...	...	...	...	...	...	*Australie*
Japan	...	...	...	...	...	...	...	...	*Japon*
New Zealand	14 434	14 289	20 882	1.0	1.4	1.5	9	733	*Nouvelle-Zélande*
European Community									*Communauté européenne*
Belgium	18 195	17 531	28 582	1.0	1.6	1.6	27	409	*Belgique*
Denmark	...	...	...	...	...	...	...	...	*Danemark*
France	...	...	...	...	...	...	...	...	*France*
Germany (FTFR)	20 435	23 627	32 464	1.2	1.6	1.4	22	402	*Allemagne (ex-terr. de la RFA)*
Germany	...	...	...	...	...	...	...	...	*Allemagne*
Greece	...	...	...	...	...	...	...	...	*Grèce*
Ireland	12 391	17 748	32 624	1.4	2.6	1.8	24	620	*Irlande*
Italy	17 482	18 161	27 852	1.0	1.6	1.5	40	242	*Italie*
Luxembourg	...	...	...	...	...	...	...	...	*Luxembourg*
Netherlands	17 023	16 819	30 969	1.0	1.8	1.8	25	566	*Pays-Bas*
Portugal	9 766	13 784	36 078	1.4	3.7	2.6	29	769	*Portugal*
Spain	12 853	22 964	30 632	1.8	2.4	1.3	45	170	*Espagne*
United Kingdom	16 340	16 551	34 081	1.0	2.1	2.1	...	...	*Royaume-Uni*
Other Europe - OECD									*Autres pays d'Europe - OCDE*
Austria	18 096	17 309	38 962	1.0	2.2	2.3	34	637	*Autriche*
Finland	14 545	17 481	22 046	1.2	1.5	1.3	20	228	*Finlande*
Iceland	...	...	...	...	...	...	...	...	*Islande*
Norway	17 756	17 436	21 336	1.0	1.2	1.2	14	279	*Norvège*
Sweden	16 590	13 999	18 099	0.8	1.1	1.3	15	273	*Suède*
Switzerland	...	...	...	...	...	...	...	...	*Suisse*
Turkey	3 728	6 994	12 409	1.9	3.3	1.8	29	187	*Turquie*
Country mean	**15 523**	**17 062**	**28 161**	**1.2**	**2.0**	**1.7**	**25**	**457**	*Moyenne des pays*

See Annex 1 for notes

Voir notes en annexe 1

P35: Teacher compensation

P35 : Rémunération des enseignants

Table P35(B):
Lower secondary teacher salaries:
Starting and maximum salaries
in equivalent US dollars converted using PPPs (1992)

Tableau P35(B) :
Traitements des enseignants du secondaire 1er cycle :
traitement de départ et traitement maximum
en équivalents dollars E-U convertis en PPA (1992)

	Per capita GDP / PIB par habitant	Starting salary / Traitement de départ	Maximum salary / Traitement maximum	Ratio of starting salary to per capita GDP	Ratio of maximum salary to per capita GDP	Ratio of maximum salary to starting salary	Years from starting to maximum salary / Nombre d'années entre le traitement de départ et le traitement maximum	Average yearly increase / Variation annuelle moyenne	
North America									*Amérique du Nord*
Canada	...	...	...	...	...	...	...	...	*Canada*
United States	23 215	21 787	37 146	0.9	1.6	1.7	16	960	*Etats-Unis*
Pacific Area									*Pays du Pacifique*
Australia	...	...	...	...	...	...	...	...	*Australie*
Japan	...	...	...	...	...	...	...	...	*Japon*
New Zealand	14 434	15 108	21 950	1.0	1.5	1.5	8	855	*Nouvelle-Zélande*
European Community									*Communauté européenne*
Belgium	18 195	17 955	31 308	1.0	1.7	1.7	27	495	*Belgique*
Denmark	...	...	...	...	...	...	...	...	*Danemark*
France	...	...	...	...	...	...	...	...	*France*
Germany (FTFR)	20 435	27 444	36 119	1.3	1.8	1.3	20	434	*Allemagne (ex-terr. de la RFA)*
Germany	...	...	...	...	...	...	...	...	*Allemagne*
Greece	...	...	...	...	...	...	...	...	*Grèce*
Ireland	12 391	17 748	32 624	1.4	2.6	1.8	24	620	*Irlande*
Italy	17 482	19 708	30 927	1.1	1.8	1.6	40	280	*Italie*
Luxembourg	...	...	...	...	...	...	...	...	*Luxembourg*
Netherlands	17 023	16 855	33 454	1.0	2.0	2.0	25	664	*Pays-Bas*
Portugal	9 766	13 784	36 078	1.4	3.7	2.6	29	769	*Portugal*
Spain	12 853	22 964	30 632	1.8	2.4	1.3	45	170	*Espagne*
United Kingdom	16 340	16 551	39 259	1.0	2.4	2.4	9	2 523	*Royaume-Uni*
Other Europe - OECD									*Autres pays d'Europe - OCDE*
Austria	18 096	18 415	42 448	1.0	2.3	2.3	34	707	*Autriche*
Finland	14 545	20 033	25 677	1.4	1.8	1.3	20	282	*Finlande*
Iceland	...	...	...	...	...	...	...	...	*Islande*
Norway	17 756	17 436	21 336	1.0	1.2	1.2	14	279	*Norvège*
Sweden	16 590	15 699	19 698	0.9	1.2	1.3	15	267	*Suède*
Switzerland	...	...	...	...	...	...	...	...	*Suisse*
Turkey	3 728	7 053	12 409	1.9	3.3	1.8	27	198	*Turquie*
Country mean	**15 523**	**17 903**	**30 071**	**1.2**	**2.1**	**1.7**	**24**	**634**	*Moyenne des pays*

See Annex 1 for notes

Voir notes en annexe 1

P35: Teacher compensation

P35 : Rémunération des enseignants

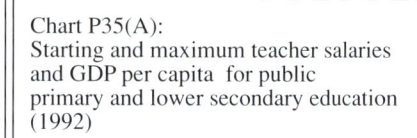

Chart P35(A):
Starting and maximum teacher salaries and GDP per capita for public primary and lower secondary education (1992)

Graphique P35(A) :
Traitements de départ et traitements maximum des enseignants et PIB par habitant dans l'enseignement public primaire et secondaire 1er cycle (1992)

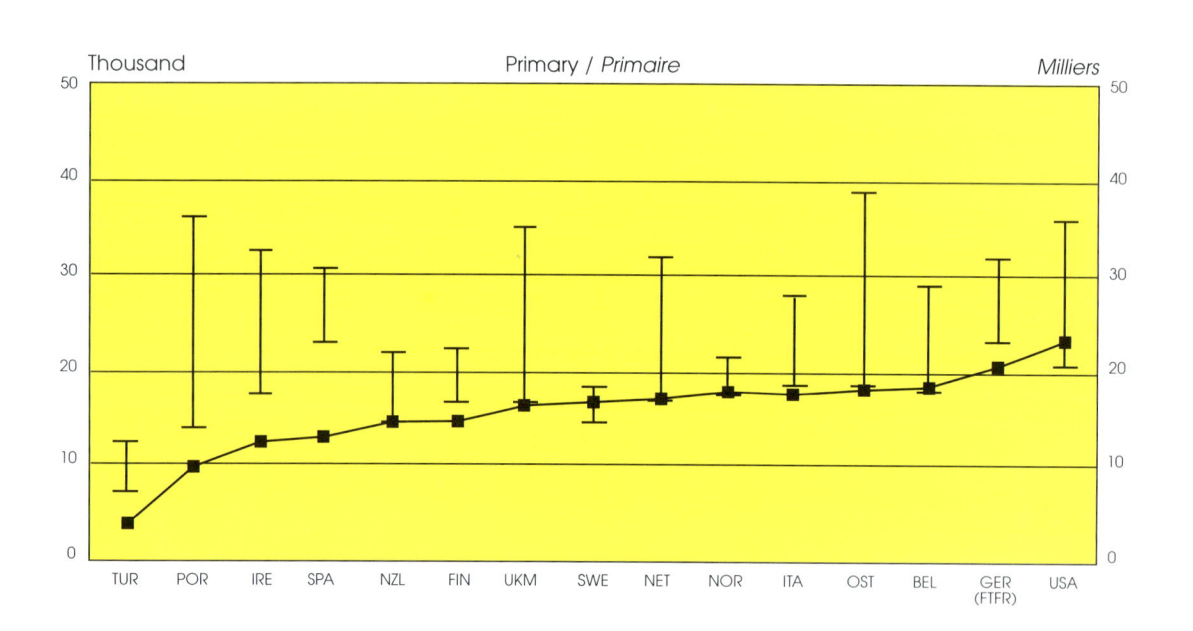

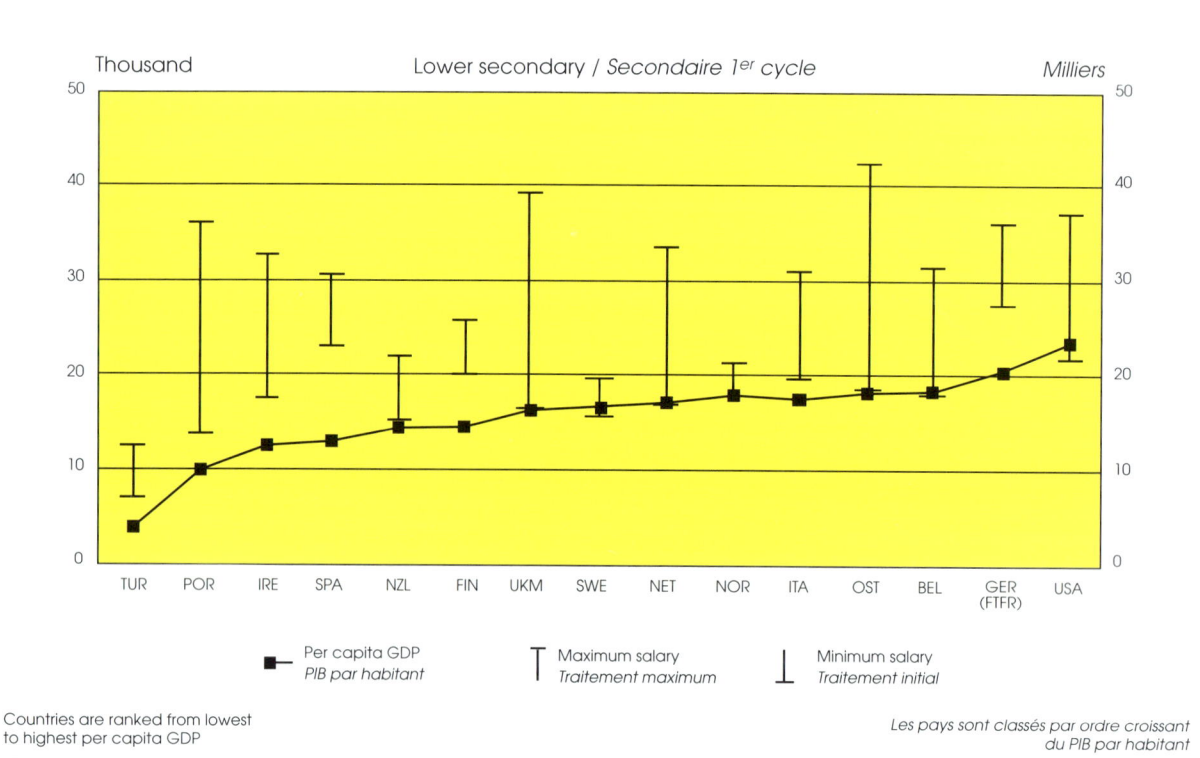

Countries are ranked from lowest to highest per capita GDP

Les pays sont classés par ordre croissant du PIB par habitant

- Per capita GDP / *PIB par habitant*
- Maximum salary / *Traitement maximum*
- Minimum salary / *Traitement initial*

P35: Teacher compensation

P35 : Rémunération des enseignants

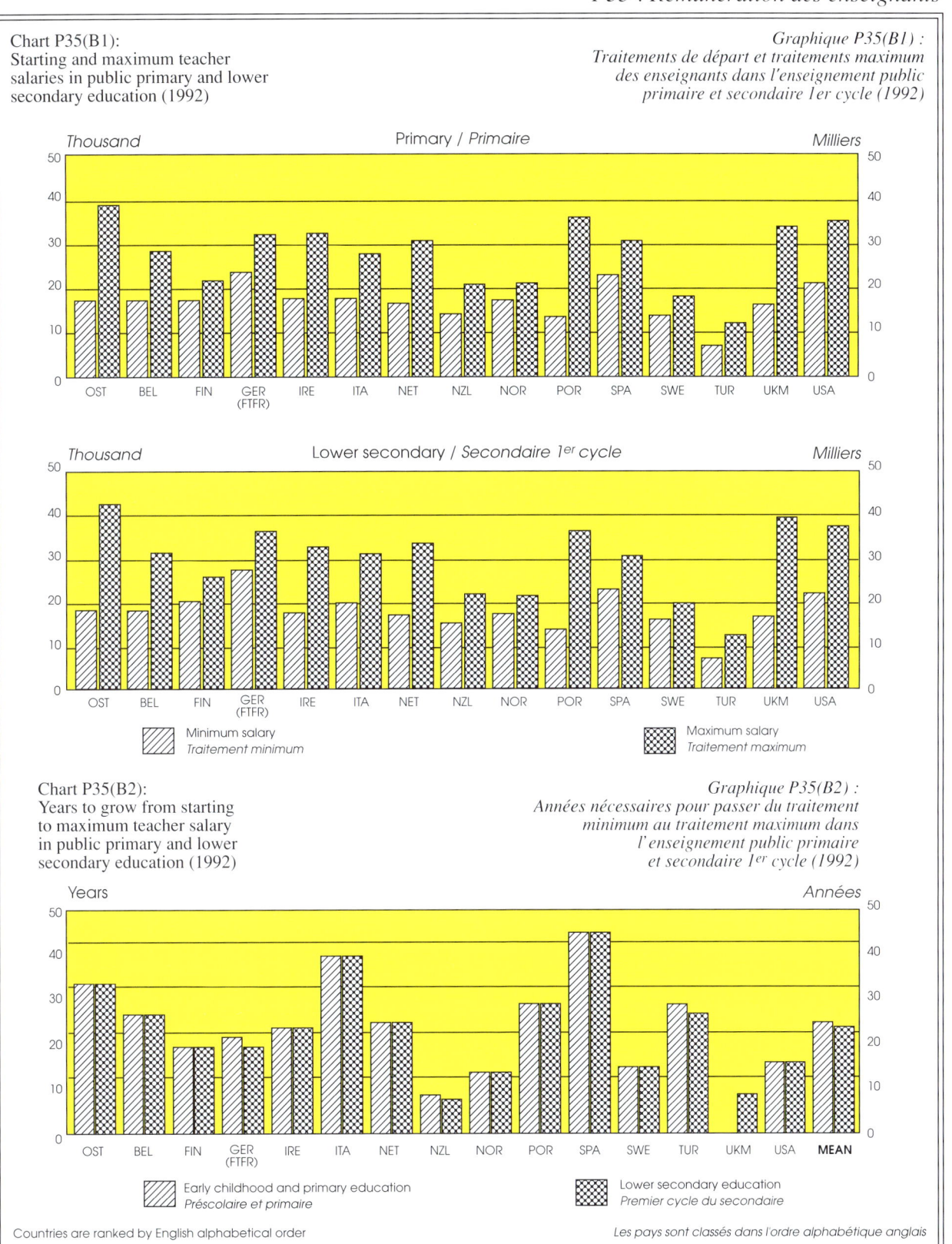

Chart P35(B1):
Starting and maximum teacher salaries in public primary and lower secondary education (1992)

Graphique P35(B1) :
Traitements de départ et traitements maximum des enseignants dans l'enseignement public primaire et secondaire 1er cycle (1992)

Primary / *Primaire*

Lower secondary / *Secondaire 1er cycle*

Minimum salary / *Traitement minimum*
Maximum salary / *Traitement maximum*

Chart P35(B2):
Years to grow from starting to maximum teacher salary in public primary and lower secondary education (1992)

Graphique P35(B2) :
Années nécessaires pour passer du traitement minimum au traitement maximum dans l'enseignement public primaire et secondaire 1er cycle (1992)

Early childhood and primary education / *Préscolaire et primaire*
Lower secondary education / *Premier cycle du secondaire*

Countries are ranked by English alphabetical order
Les pays sont classés dans l'ordre alphabétique anglais

P36: Teacher characteristics

AGE AND GENDER DISTRIBUTION OF TEACHERS

POLICY ISSUES

Is there a need to influence the composition of the future supply of teachers? Age characteristics are especially important because they are related to the issue of replacing retired teachers, and retaining both young and experienced teachers.

KEY RESULTS

Most teachers in most countries are in the age category of 40 to 49. There is considerable variation among countries in the percentage of teachers in the lowest age category, younger than 30.

A large majority of the teachers are female, especially at early childhood and primary education levels. At the upper secondary level, the figures for men and women are generally equal.

DESCRIPTION AND INTERPRETATION

This indicator shows the age distribution of teachers for public primary and lower secondary levels, and the gender distribution for public early childhood, primary and secondary education. It should be noted that within the broad categories used for reporting age distribution, some ages may be represented more heavily than others.

Austria, Ireland and the Netherlands have higher shares of young teachers at the primary level than the other OECD countries; Austria and Portugal have a relatively young teacher population at the lower secondary level. Table P36(A) shows that 62 per cent of the primary education teachers in Austria, 57 per cent in the Netherlands and 54 per cent in Ireland are younger than 40; 23 per cent in Austria, younger than 30. In lower secondary education, 67 per cent of the teachers in Austria and 63 per cent Portugal are younger than 40.

The largest percentages of teachers over 60 are found in Portugal for the primary level (16 per cent) and in Sweden for the lower secondary level (11 per cent).

With respect to the gender distribution, it can be seen from Table P36(B) that in all countries, teachers in early childhood and primary education are predominantly female. This over-representation of female teachers in primary education is reflected in all age categories [see Table P36(C)]. Although females continue to outnumber males in lower secondary education, the latter percentage of males range from 29 per cent in Italy to about half in Spain and the United Kingdom. In upper secondary education the percentages of male and female teachers are more similar. Portugal has the lowest percentage of male teachers (29 per cent) at this level.

DEFINITIONS

The teacher characteristics reported are age and gender, measured as the percentage of teachers per education level, within each of five age categories, and the percentage of males/females per education level.

Data are from the Network C survey on Teachers and the Curriculum.

P36: Teacher characteristics / P36 : Spécificités des enseignants

Table P36(A):
Percentage of teachers in public primary and lower secondary education, by age group (1992)

Tableau P36(A) :
Pourcentage d'enseignants dans l'enseignement public primaire et secondaire 1er cycle par tranche d'âge (1992)

	Ages < 30 Primary	Ages < 30 Lower sec.	Ages 30-39 Primary	Ages 30-39 Lower sec.	Ages 40-49 Primary	Ages 40-49 Lower sec.	Ages 50-60 Primary	Ages 50-60 Lower sec.	Age > 60 Primary	Age > 60 Lower sec.	
Austria	23	19	39	48	27	26	9	7	2	.	Autriche
Belgium	16	10	32	30	38	37	14	23	.	1	Belgique
Finland	5	3	29	22	29	36	30	34	7	4	Finlande
France	13	11	32	26	39	44	17	19	.	1	France
Germany (FTFR)	4	2	25	26	46	46	23	24	2	2	Allemagne (ex- terr. de la RFA)
Ireland	19	...	35	...	25	...	18	...	3	...	Irlande
Italy	10	1	30	27	33	50	21	17	7	5	Italie
Netherlands	17	7	40	30	32	43	11	20	.	.	Pays-Bas
New Zealand	14	14	28	26	37	38	19	21	2	2	Nouvelle-Zélande
Portugal	9	26	29	37	26	21	20	8	16	8	Portugal
Sweden	6	6	19	17	43	36	23	29	9	11	Suède
United Kingdom	15	11	23	30	42	42	19	16	1	1	Royaume-Uni
United States	7	7	23	22	40	42	24	24	6	5	Etats-Unis
Country mean	12.2	9.8	29.5	28.4	35.2	38.4	19.1	20.2	4.2	3.3	Moyenne des pays

See Annex 1 for notes / Voir notes en annexe 1

P36: Teacher characteristics

P36 : Spécificités des enseignants

Table P36(B):
Gender distribution of teachers by level of public education (1992)

Tableau P36(B) :
Répartition par sexe des enseignants, par niveau de l'enseignement public (1992)

	Early childhood education *Education préscolaire*		Primary education *Enseignement primaire*		Lower secondary education *Enseignement secondaire 1er cycle*		Upper secondary education (general) *Enseignement secondaire 2e cycle (général)*		Upper secondary education (vocational) *Enseignement secondaire 2e cycle (professionnel)*		
	Male *Hommes*	Female *Femmes*	Male *Hommes*	Female *Femmes*	Male *Hommes*	Female *Femmes*	Male *Hommes*	Female *Femmes*	Male *Hommes*	Female *Femmes*	
Austria	...	...	18	82	39	61	45	55	58	42	*Autriche*
Belgium	3	98	38	62	x	x	50	50	x	x	*Belgique*
Finland	...	...	35	65	32	68	39	61	...	...	*Finlande*
France	x	x	24	76	45	55	x	x	x	x	*France*
Ireland	x	x	24	76	...	...	...	...	...	...	*Irlande*
Italy	.	100	8	93	29	71	46	54	x	x	*Italie*
New Zealand	...	...	20	80	37	63	49	51	...	...	*Nouvelle-Zélande*
Portugal	...	...	9	91	x	x	29	71	x	x	*Portugal*
Spain	5	95	26	74	49	51	46	54	58	42	*Espagne*
United Kingdom	x	x	19	81	50	50	x	x	x	x	*Royaume-Uni*
United States	17	83	15	85	43	57	52	48	x	x	*Etats-Unis*

Table P36(C):
Gender distribution of teachers within age groups (public primary education) (1992)

Tableau P36(C) :
Répartition par sexe des enseignants dans les différentes tranches d'âge, enseignement primaire public (1992)

	Age < 30 *< 30 ans*		Age 30-39 *30-39 ans*		Age 40-49 *40-49 ans*		Age 50-60 *50-60 ans*		Age > 60 *> 60 ans*		Total *Total*		
	Male *Hommes*	Female *Femmes*	Male *Hommes*	Female *Femmes*	Male *Hommes*	Female *Femmes*	Male *Hommes*	Female *Femmes*	Male *Hommes*	Female *Femmes*	Male *Hommes*	Female *Femmes*	
Austria	2	21	5	34	7	20	3	6	1	1	18	82	*Autriche*
Belgium	3	13	9	23	18	20	8	6	.	.	38	62	*Belgique*
Finland	1	4	9	20	9	20	12	18	3	4	35	65	*Finlande*
France	...	...	...	...	...	...	...	...	...	...	24	76	*France*
Italy	2	8	1	29	3	30	3	18	1	5	8	93	*Italie*
New Zealand	2	12	5	24	21	16	5	14	.	2	20	80	*Nouvelle-Zélande*
Portugal	1	8	3	25	2	24	2	18	1	15	9	91	*Portugal*
United States	1	6	4	19	6	34	4	20	.	6	15	85	*Etats-Unis*

See Annex 1 for notes

Voir notes en annexe 1

P36: Teacher characteristics

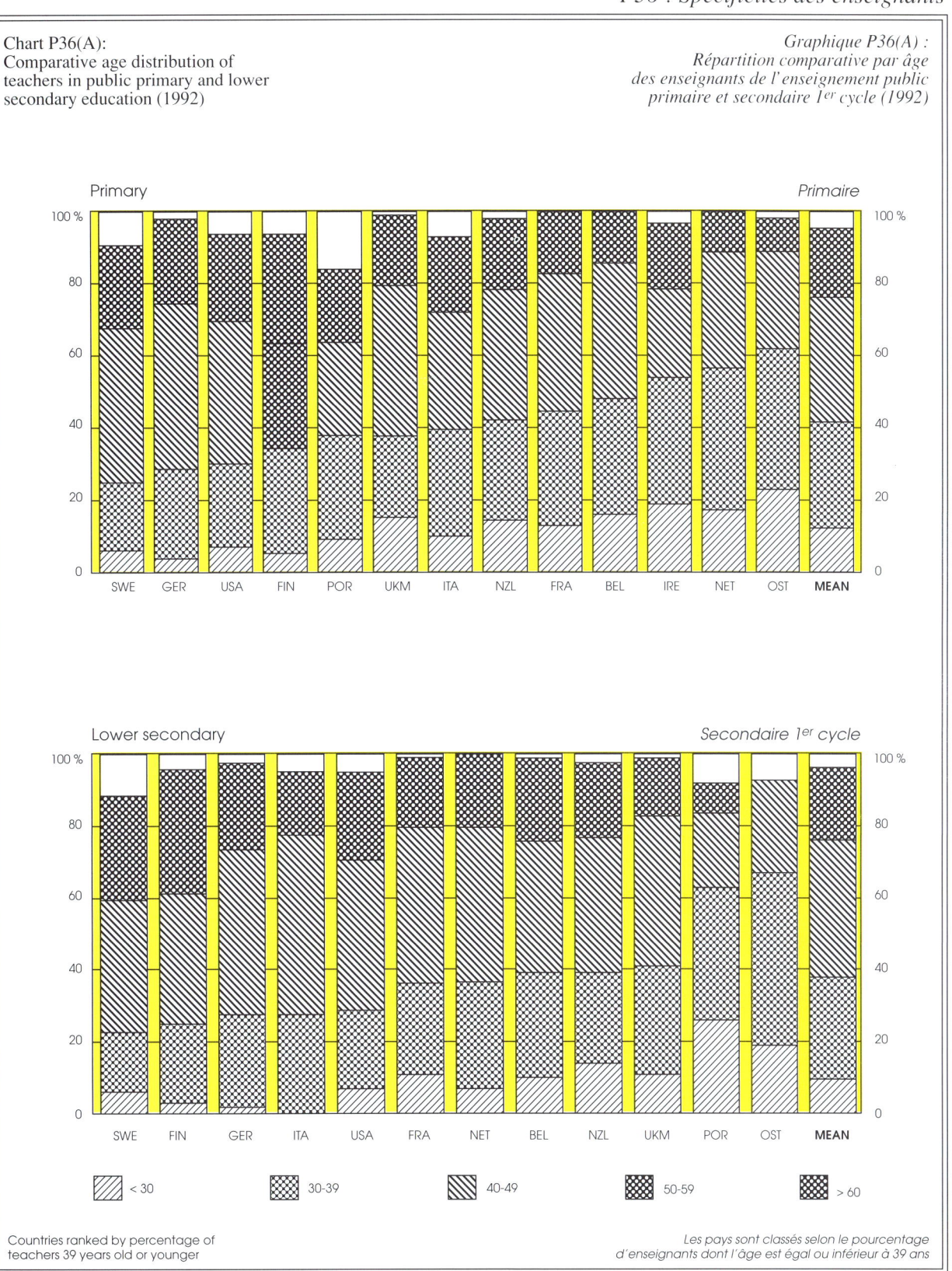

P36 : Spécificités des enseignants

Chart P36(A):
Comparative age distribution of teachers in public primary and lower secondary education (1992)

Graphique P36(A) :
Répartition comparative par âge des enseignants de l'enseignement public primaire et secondaire 1er cycle (1992)

Primary — *Primaire*

(SWE, GER, USA, FIN, POR, UKM, ITA, NZL, FRA, BEL, IRE, NET, OST, **MEAN**)

Lower secondary — *Secondaire 1er cycle*

(SWE, FIN, GER, ITA, USA, FRA, NET, BEL, NZL, UKM, POR, OST, **MEAN**)

Legend: < 30 | 30-39 | 40-49 | 50-59 | > 60

Countries ranked by percentage of teachers 39 years old or younger

Les pays sont classés selon le pourcentage d'enseignants dont l'âge est égal ou inférieur à 39 ans

195

P36: Teacher characteristics

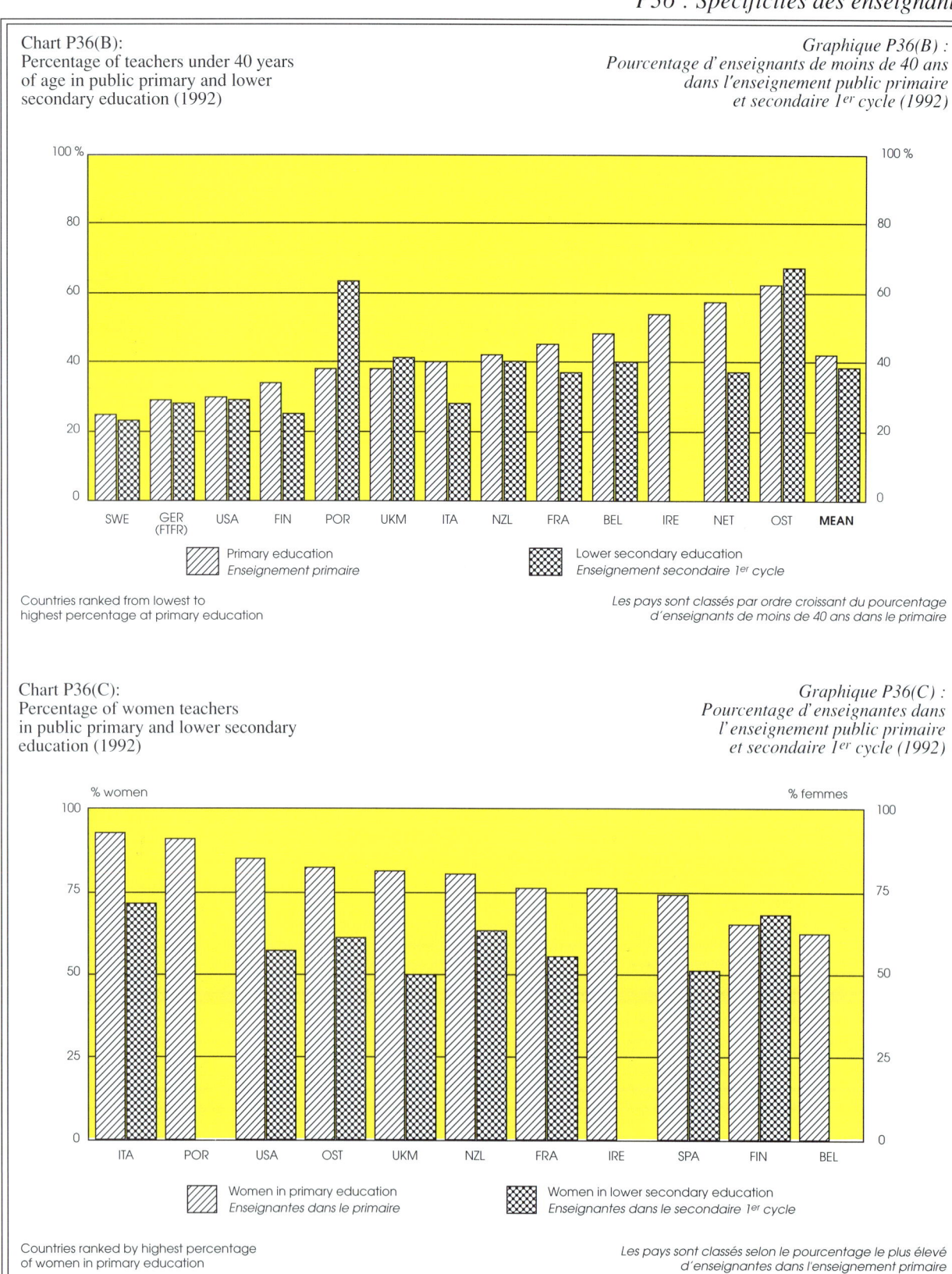

P36 : Spécificités des enseignants

Chart P36(B):
Percentage of teachers under 40 years of age in public primary and lower secondary education (1992)

Graphique P36(B) :
Pourcentage d'enseignants de moins de 40 ans dans l'enseignement public primaire et secondaire 1er cycle (1992)

- Primary education / *Enseignement primaire*
- Lower secondary education / *Enseignement secondaire 1er cycle*

Countries ranked from lowest to highest percentage at primary education

Les pays sont classés par ordre croissant du pourcentage d'enseignants de moins de 40 ans dans le primaire

Chart P36(C):
Percentage of women teachers in public primary and lower secondary education (1992)

Graphique P36(C) :
Pourcentage d'enseignantes dans l'enseignement public primaire et secondaire 1er cycle (1992)

- Women in primary education / *Enseignantes dans le primaire*
- Women in lower secondary education / *Enseignantes dans le secondaire 1er cycle*

Countries ranked by highest percentage of women in primary education

Les pays sont classés selon le pourcentage le plus élevé d'enseignantes dans l'enseignement primaire

P41: Educational R&D personnel

PERSONNEL RESOURCES ALLOCATED TO EDUCATIONAL RESEARCH AND DEVELOPMENT

POLICY ISSUES

The quantity of personnel resources allocated to educational R&D – a highly labour-intensive process – gives a good indication of national commitment to strengthening education through R&D. How firm is that commitment, especially as measured against the total R&D effort?

KEY RESULTS

In the eight countries for which relevant data are available, educational R&D personnel comprise on average a little over 1 per cent of all R&D personnel. This suggests that research on education has a relatively low priority within countries' total R&D effort. About four-fifths of educational R&D personnel are classified as researchers, and the rest are support personnel.

DESCRIPTION AND INTERPRETATION

The proportion of total R&D personnel involved in research on education is relatively high in Australia (2.3 per cent) and the United Kingdom (1.3 per cent), although this may be partly due to the fact that both countries include a comparatively wide range of post-graduate students in the measurement of R&D personnel. The proportion appears to be relatively low in Austria (0.7 per cent) and Sweden (0.4 per cent).

In the eight countries concerned, on average, about 75 per cent of educational R&D personnel are based in the university education sector, 20 per cent are located in the government sector, and 5 per cent are employed in private non-profit institutions (see additional data in Annex 3). The major exceptions to this pattern are Ireland (29.3 per cent), the Netherlands (50 per cent) and New Zealand (55.8 per cent). The concentration of educational R&D personnel in the university education sector may have an important bearing on the character of educational research in most countries. Educational R&D personnel are more heavily concentrated in higher education than are R&D personnel as a whole. However, the fact that in these eight countries educational R&D personnel in university education average just 3 per cent of all R&D personnel in university education suggests that educational R&D is under-represented even in the university education sector.

On average, only about 20 per cent of educational R&D personnel are employed in the government sector despite the fact that governments typically have the major responsibility for financing and providing education. Among the eight countries concerned, about 5 per cent of educational R&D personnel are employed in private, non-profit institutions. Only in Austria and the Netherlands are more than 10 per cent of educational R&D personnel located in the private non-profit sector.

Educational R&D generally has a higher proportion of personnel classified as researchers – about 80 per cent – than R&D as a whole. (Researchers refers to professional staff engaged in the design, implementation and management of research projects.) The remaining 20 per cent are technicians and support staff who normally work under the supervision of researchers. Across R&D activities as a whole, researchers constitute about 50 per cent of R&D personnel. In Australia and the United Kingdom, post-graduate students are estimated to constitute the majority of the full-time-equivalent researchers engaged in educational R&D. In the United Kingdom, only paid students are counted as researchers.

DEFINITIONS

The focus of these data is R&D *on* education, and not R&D *in* education. R&D on education comprises activities directed towards improved understanding of educational processes and institutions, and the development of materials to assist teaching and learning. In normal circumstances research on education will constitute only a small part of all the research conducted in educational institutions, especially universities.

Data are based on the OECD's *Standard Practice for Surveys of Research and Experimental Development, Parts 1 and 2* (the "Frascati Manual"). In some of the OECD countries covered in these collections, education is defined as a separate field of science. In others, educational R&D activities have to be inferred from knowledge of the institutions concerned. The data reported here have generally been extracted from national statistics on R&D

P41: Educational R&D personnel

as a whole. In some cases these data have been supplemented by special surveys of institutions known to conduct educational R&D.

The key distinguishing characteristics of R&D are originality and investigation; research and development ends when the work is no longer experimental or investigative. The following definition of educational R&D was developed for this project:

> Educational R&D is systematic, original investigation or inquiry and associated developmental activities concerning the social, cultural, economic and political context within which educational systems operate; the purposes of education; the processes of teaching, learning and personal development; the work of educators; the resources and organisational arrangements to support educational work; the policies and strategies to achieve educational objectives; and the social, cultural, political and economic outcomes of education.

In terms of measuring the personnel engaged in R&D, the "Frascati Manual" recommends that all persons employed directly on R&D projects be counted, as well as those providing direct services such as R&D managers, administrators and clerical staff. The supervision of post-graduate study by academic staff should be included, as should those parts of post-graduate study relating to independent research. In practice, however, some countries include only those post-graduate students employed by universities to work on research projects, or who receive research scholarships.

R&D personnel are classified by occupation into the categories of researchers (including post-graduate students), technicians and other support staff. Full-time-equivalence (FTE) is based on total working time; no one person can be working more than 1.0 FTE on R&D activities in any year. The estimation of FTE personnel allocated to R&D activities is particularly problematic in the university education sector. Some countries have used special surveys to estimate the proportion of university staff time allocated to research; in other countries, more *ad hoc* estimations have been used. Since most R&D on education is generally conducted by academics in the university sector, estimates of the proportion of time allocated by university staff to R&D have a considerable impact on the aggregate estimates of personnel resources.

Since this is the first time that indicators of the resources used in educational R&D have been reported on an international basis, and the estimation of R&D activities generally is a difficult process, caution is advised in interpreting the results. It is especially important to consult the country-specific notes in Annex 1. Additional data are presented in Annex 3.

P41: Educational R&D personnel

P41 : Personnel de R-D pédagogique

Table P41:
Personnel engaged in educational R&D
(full-time equivalents), total and as a percentage
of all R&D personnel and of all R&D personnel
in the higher education sector

*Tableau P41 :
Personnel de R-D pédagogique
(en équivalents plein temps), total et pourcentage
de tout le personnel de R-D et du personnel
de R-D dans l'enseignement supérieur*

	Year / Année	Total R&D personnel / Ensemble du personnel de R-D	Educational R&D personnel / Personnel de R-D pédagogique	Ratio of educational R&D personnel to total R&D personnel / Ratio personnel de R-D pédagogique / ensemble du personnel de R-D	Total R&D personnel in higher education / Ensemble du personnel de R-D dans l'enseignement supérieur	Educational R&D personnel in higher education / Personnel de R-D pédagogique dans l'enseignement supérieur	Ratio of educational R&D personnel to total R&D personnel in higher education / Ratio personnel de R-D pédagogique / ensemble du personnel de R-D dans l'enseignement supérieur	Ratio of educational R&D personnel in higher education to total R&D personnel / Ratio personnel de R-D pédagogique dans l'enseignement supérieur / ensemble du personnel de R-D	
North America									*Amérique du Nord*
Canada	...	...	...	...	...	...	...	...	*Canada*
United States	...	...	...	...	...	...	...	...	*Etats-Unis*
Pacific Area									*Pays du Pacifique*
Australia	1990/91	67 796	1 536	2.27	27 082	1 387	5.12	90.3	*Australie*
Japan	...	...	...	...	...	...	...	...	*Japon*
New Zealand	1991/92	8 837	95	1.08	2 326	53	2.28	55.8	*Nouvelle-Zélande*
European Community									*Communauté européenne*
Belgium	...	...	...	...	...	...	...	...	*Belgique*
Denmark	...	...	...	...	...	...	...	...	*Danemark*
France	...	...	...	...	...	...	...	...	*France*
Germany (FTFR)	...	...	...	...	...	...	...	...	*Allemagne (ex-terr. de la RFA)*
Germany	...	...	...	...	...	...	...	...	*Allemagne*
Greece	...	...	...	...	...	...	...	...	*Grèce*
Ireland	1991/92	8 799	75	0.85	3 010	22	0.73	29.3	*Irlande*
Italy	...	...	...	...	...	...	...	...	*Italie*
Luxembourg	...	...	...	...	...	...	...	...	*Luxembourg*
Netherlands	1991	66 710	720	1.08	20 090	360	1.79	50.0	*Pays-Bas*
Portugal	...	...	...	...	...	...	...	...	*Portugal*
Spain	...	...	...	...	...	...	...	...	*Espagne*
United Kingdom	1991/92	255 000	3 322	1.30	62 000	3 117	5.03	93.8	*Royaume-Uni*
Other Europe - OECD									*Autres pays d'Europe - OCDE*
Austria	1989	23 084	160	0.69	6 058	112	1.85	70.0	*Autriche*
Finland	1991	29 575	347	1.14	7 662	337	4.40	97.1	*Finlande*
Iceland	...	...	...	...	...	...	...	...	*Islande*
Norway	...	...	...	...	...	...	...	...	*Norvège*
Sweden	1991/92	53 604	236	0.44	16 810	236	1.40	100.0	*Suède*
Switzerland	...	...	...	...	...	...	...	...	*Suisse*
Turkey	...	...	...	...	...	...	...	...	*Turquie*

See Annex 1 for notes

Voir notes en annexe 1

P41: Educational R&D personnel

P41 : Personnel de R-D pédagogique

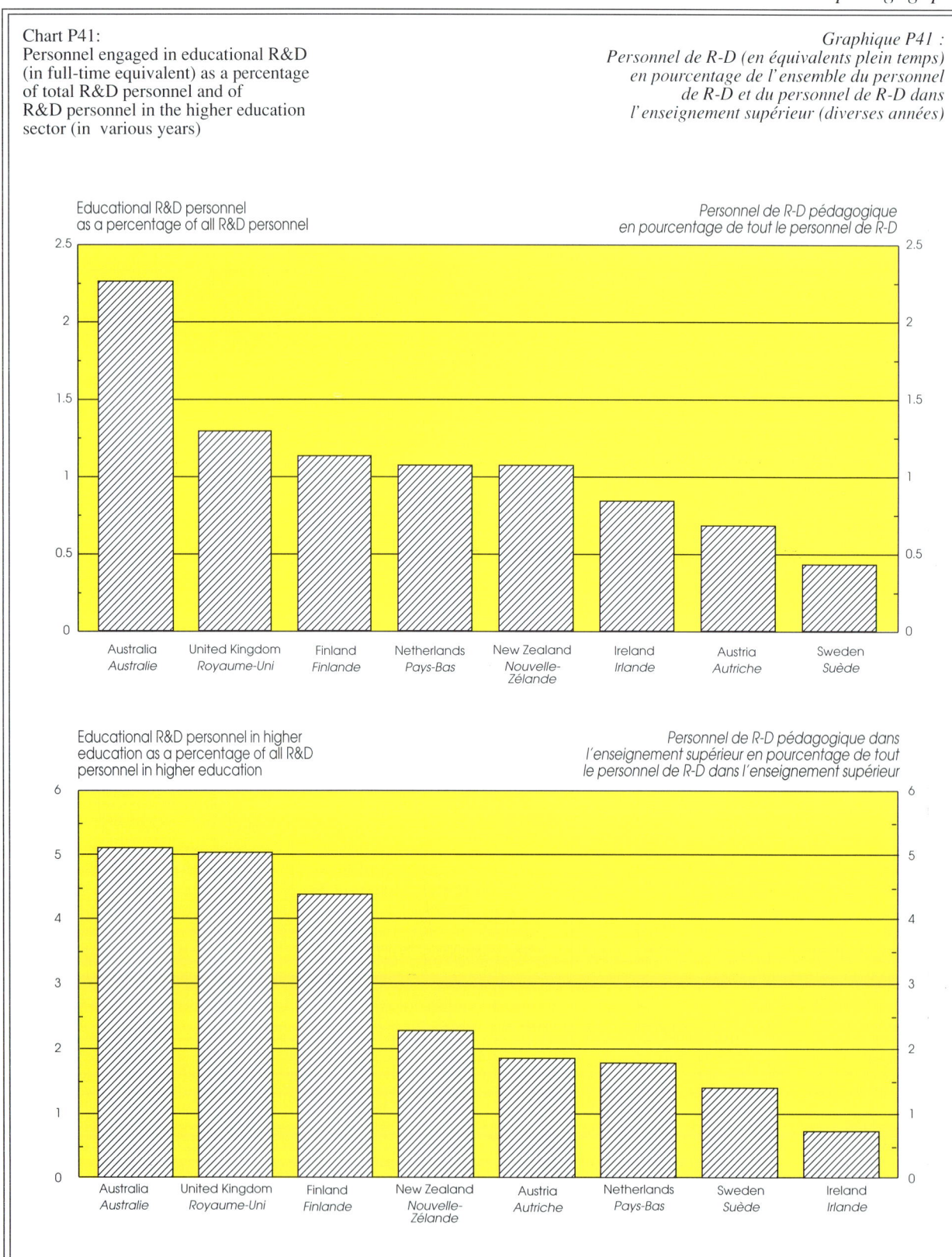

Chart P41:
Personnel engaged in educational R&D (in full-time equivalent) as a percentage of total R&D personnel and of R&D personnel in the higher education sector (in various years)

Graphique P41 :
Personnel de R-D (en équivalents plein temps) en pourcentage de l'ensemble du personnel de R-D et du personnel de R-D dans l'enseignement supérieur (diverses années)

Educational R&D personnel as a percentage of all R&D personnel

Personnel de R-D pédagogique en pourcentage de tout le personnel de R-D

Australia / Australie	~2.25
United Kingdom / Royaume-Uni	~1.30
Finland / Finlande	~1.13
Netherlands / Pays-Bas	~1.07
New Zealand / Nouvelle-Zélande	~1.07
Ireland / Irlande	~0.83
Austria / Autriche	~0.67
Sweden / Suède	~0.43

Educational R&D personnel in higher education as a percentage of all R&D personnel in higher education

Personnel de R-D pédagogique dans l'enseignement supérieur en pourcentage de tout le personnel de R-D dans l'enseignement supérieur

Australia / Australie	~5.1
United Kingdom / Royaume-Uni	~5.0
Finland / Finlande	~4.4
New Zealand / Nouvelle-Zélande	~2.3
Austria / Autriche	~1.8
Netherlands / Pays-Bas	~1.75
Sweden / Suède	~1.35
Ireland / Irlande	~0.7

P42: Educational R&D expenditure

EXPENDITURE ON EDUCATIONAL RESEARCH AND DEVELOPMENT

POLICY ISSUES

How important is R&D within education? Or education within total R&D? Is the correct allocation of expenditure an accurate indication of priorities?

KEY RESULTS

Among the six countries that supplied data, educational R&D on average accounts for less than 0.3 per cent of total educational expenditure. Educational R&D accounts for just under 1 per cent of total R&D expenditure – an allocation that appears to be lower than the size and importance of the education sector.

DEFINITION AND INTERPRETATION

Educational R&D is only a minor activity within the education sector. In the six countries for which relevant data are available, on average only 0.27 per cent of total education expenditure is allocated to educational R&D. The range among countries is from 0.37 per cent in Australia to 0.18 per cent in Ireland.

In line with the distribution of the educational R&D personnel, most educational R&D expenditure is incurred in the university education sector (65 per cent, on average). The major exceptions to this pattern are Ireland (35 per cent), the Netherlands (30 per cent) and New Zealand (47 per cent). In the case of Ireland, the remaining expenditure is incurred on R&D activities in the government sector. In the Netherlands, the remaining expenditure is more evenly spread between the government sector (40 per cent) and institutions in the private non-profit sector (30 per cent). In New Zealand the government sector portion is 43 per cent and the private non-profit sector portion 10 per cent). Austria is the only other country with substantial educational R&D activity in the private non-profit sector: 15 per cent of expenditure (see additional data in Annex 3).

In all countries, government is the principal source of funds for educational R&D either directly through its own research or, more significantly, through research financed from universities' general operating grants. Some countries also appear to place a relatively strong emphasis on research commissioned by government. In countries for which data are available, there is little funding for educational R&D from non-government sources.

Educational R&D, as mentioned in indicator P41, is a highly labour-intensive process. On average, labour costs account for almost 75 per cent of educational R&D expenditure in the countries having supplied data – which underscores the need to ensure high-quality research training, and to ensure that researchers' time is used productively.

There is little information on the types of research to which expenditure is directed. Three countries (Australia, Austria and Ireland) provided separate data for basic research, applied research, and experimental development. Such classifications tend to be highly subjective. In the case of Ireland, almost all educational R&D was classified as applied, and in Austria and Australia about one-half was classified as such.

Additional estimates of R&D expenditure in education are shown in Annex 3. The country-specific notes in Annex 1 should be consulted when interpreting the findings.

DEFINITIONS

The general issues associated with defining and measuring educational R&D were discussed in indicator P41. With regard to expenditure, the "Frascati Manual" focuses on the intramural expenditure on R&D conducted by each research-performing unit. Both capital and recurrent costs and administrative and other overhead expenditures necessary for the performance of R&D are included. Capital expenditures (including land and buildings) are reported in full for the period in which they occur; depreciation is excluded. Expenditure on labour includes all associated costs or fringe benefits, as well as the wages and salaries of R&D personnel. Only those post-graduate students who are employed by the university, and/or receiving external funds for R&D, are included in the R&D expenditures.

P42: Educational R&D expenditure

P42 : Dépenses afférentes à la R-D pédagogique

Table P42:
Expenditure on educational R&D as a percentage of public and private expenditure on education and of total public and private R&D expenditure (in millions of local currency and at current prices)

Tableau P42 :
Dépenses de R-D pédagogique en pourcentage des dépenses d'éducation publiques et privées et de l'ensemble des dépenses de R-D publiques et privées (en millions de monnaie locale et aux prix courants)

	Year / Année	Total public and private educational R&D expenditure / Ensemble des dépenses publiques et privées de R-D pédagogique	Total public and private educational expenditure / Ensemble des dépenses d'éducation publiques et privées	Total public and private R&D expenditure / Ensemble des dépenses de R-D publiques et privées	Ratio of public and private educational R&D expenditure to total public and private educational expenditure / Ratio dépenses publiques et privées de R-D pédagogique / dépenses publiques et privées d'éducation	Ratio of public and private educational R&D expenditure to total public and private R&D expenditure / Ratio dépenses publiques et privées de R-D pédagogique / dépenses de R-D publiques et privées	
North America							*Amérique du Nord*
Canada	1991/92	118	49 022	10 289	0.24	1.15	*Canada*
United States	...	...	...	...	...	...	*Etats-Unis*
Pacific Area							*Pays du Pacifique*
Australia	1990/91	78	21 043	5 091	0.37	1.53	*Australie*
Japan	...	...	...	...	...	...	*Japon*
New Zealand	1991/92	7	...	644	...	1.09	*Nouvelle-Zélande*
European Community							*Communauté européenne*
Belgium	...	...	...	...	...	...	*Belgique*
Denmark	...	...	...	...	...	...	*Danemark*
France	...	...	...	...	...	...	*France*
Germany (FTFR)	...	...	...	...	...	...	*Allemagne (ex-terr. de la RFA)*
Germany	...	...	...	...	...	...	*Allemagne*
Greece	...	...	...	...	...	...	*Grèce*
Ireland	1991/92	3	1 638	318	0.18	0.94	*Irlande*
Italy	...	...	...	...	...	...	*Italie*
Luxembourg	...	...	...	...	...	...	*Luxembourg*
Netherlands	1991	98	31 340	10 381	0.31	0.94	*Pays-Bas*
Portugal	...	...	...	...	...	...	*Portugal*
Spain	...	...	...	...	...	...	*Espagne*
United Kingdom	1991/92	53	...	12 619	...	0.42	*Royaume-Uni*
Other Europe - OECD							*Autres pays d'Europe - OCDE*
Austria	1989	143	...	22 967	...	0.62	*Autriche*
Finland	1991	120	41 455	10 171	0.29	1.18	*Finlande*
Iceland	...	...	...	...	...	...	*Islande*
Norway	...	...	...	...	...	...	*Norvège*
Sweden	1991/92	231	100 286	41 352	0.23	0.56	*Suède*
Switzerland	...	...	...	...	...	...	*Suisse*
Turkey	...	...	...	...	...	...	*Turquie*

See Annex 1 for notes

Voir notes en annexe 1

P42: Educational R&D expenditure

P42 : Dépenses afférentes à la R-D pédagogique

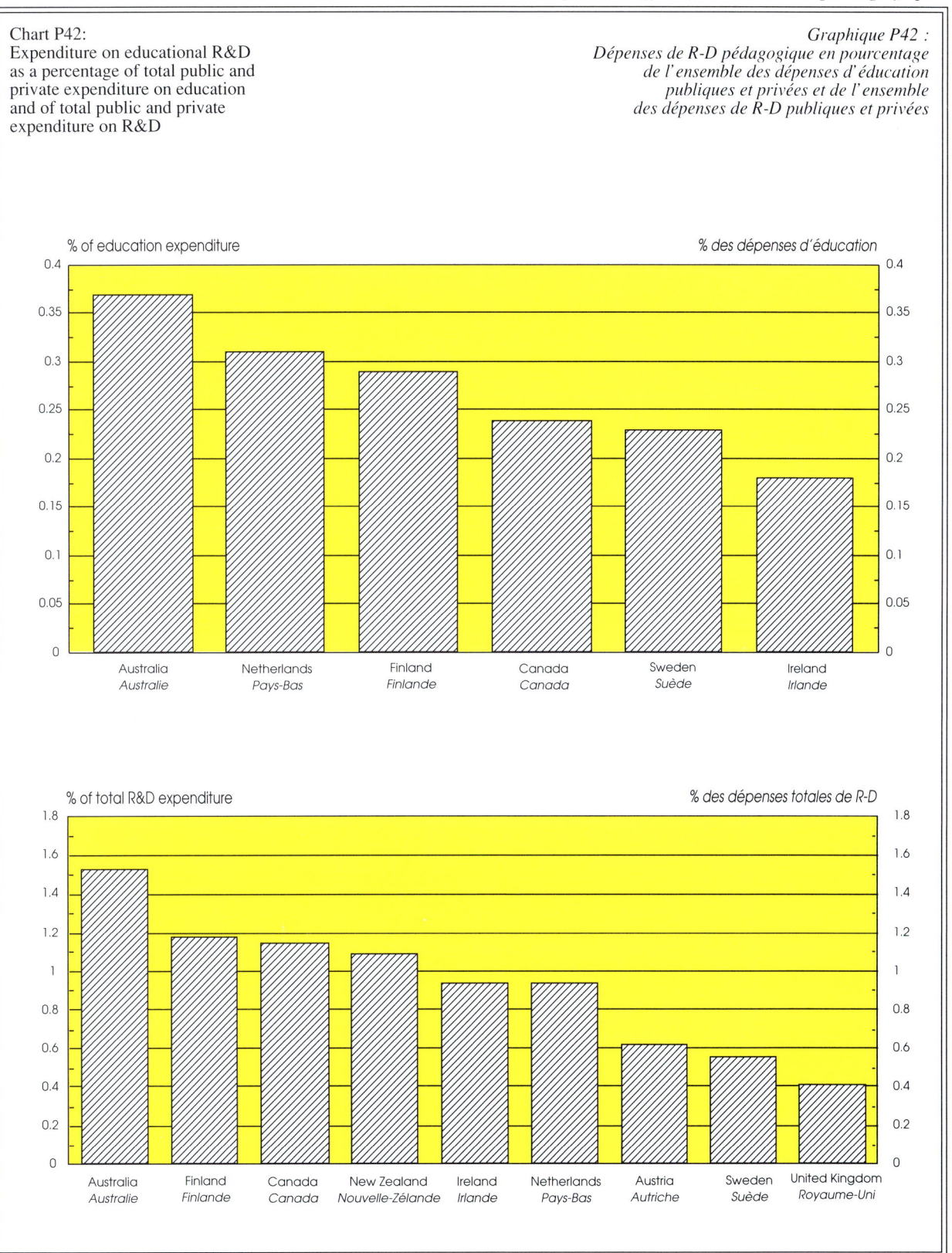

Chart P42:
Expenditure on educational R&D as a percentage of total public and private expenditure on education and of total public and private expenditure on R&D

Graphique P42 :
Dépenses de R-D pédagogique en pourcentage de l'ensemble des dépenses d'éducation publiques et privées et de l'ensemble des dépenses de R-D publiques et privées

% of education expenditure / % des dépenses d'éducation

Australia / Australie	0.37
Netherlands / Pays-Bas	0.31
Finland / Finlande	0.29
Canada / Canada	0.24
Sweden / Suède	0.23
Ireland / Irlande	0.18

% of total R&D expenditure / % des dépenses totales de R-D

Australia / Australie	1.53
Finland / Finlande	1.18
Canada / Canada	1.15
New Zealand / Nouvelle-Zélande	1.10
Ireland / Irlande	0.94
Netherlands / Pays-Bas	0.94
Austria / Autriche	0.62
Sweden / Suède	0.56
United Kingdom / Royaume-Uni	0.41

III

RESULTS OF EDUCATION

R04: Progress in reading achievement

DIFFERENCES IN READING LITERACY BETWEEN 9 AND 14 YEAR-OLDS

POLICY ISSUES

How much does reading literacy improve between the ages of 9 and 14? If progress is deemed insufficient, what factors are at work? Is education policy one of them?

KEY RESULTS

On average, across all OECD countries, the reading literacy of 14 year-olds exceeds that of 9 year-olds by more than 150 points, or approximately 1.5 standard deviations of the 14 year-olds' literacy score. The finding is of significance because it is the first estimate of how much, on average, is learned in reading over five years. Thus, this is the best approximation of a value-added indicator available to date.

Apart from cases where tests were probably very easy (ceiling effect) or very difficult (floor effect) for the whole population (e.g. Denmark and Finland), seven countries have very high five-year gains (above 160 points) – Canada (British Columbia), Germany (TFGDR), Germany (FTFR), Iceland, the Netherlands, New Zealand and Switzerland. In contrast, eight countries have rather low five-year gains – Belgium, Greece, Ireland, Italy, Norway, Spain, Sweden and the United States (150 points or less).

DESCRIPTION AND INTERPRETATION

The results can be interpreted in a number of ways. It is possible that reading development could be slower in the less wealthy countries (i.e. countries with a low development index). Another possibility is that the education systems of certain European countries [e.g. Germany (TFGDR), Germany (FTFR), the Netherlands and Switzerland] positively influence reading development.

A country's particular education policies may affect the reading scores of the two populations in different ways – that is, an education policy may be beneficial to only one population of students. It could, for example, emphasize reading literacy at earlier ages as opposed to later. This may account for differences in the mean reading literacy scores among the countries, as well as in the five-year difference scores among them.

The fact that children do not all begin school at the same age may furnish another explanation for the differences among countries in reading progress, especially for 9 year-olds. For example, the children starting school at age 7 in Denmark had scores below the country mean at age 9, while children in the United States, whose 9 year-olds' score was above the country mean, begin at age 6. Another possible reason is that countries which prepare children for school, either formally (through early childhood education in nursery school, kindergartens or similar institutions) or informally (e.g. through at-home instruction) have higher reading literacy scores. For example, children in Italy begin early childhood schooling at age 3 and France has extensive early childhood education that begins at age 2, while children in the Netherlands have no formal early childhood education and begin school at age 4. Informal preparation activities, such as parents teaching children the alphabet at home, may be expected in certain societies, while in others parents may emphasize other activities, such as socialisation. Finally, the type of language and the number of languages taught may have an influence.

Chart R04 provides mean reading literacy scores for 9 and 14 year-olds showing the confidence interval for each country. See Annex 3 for further explanations.

DEFINITIONS

This indicator is based on data collected between October 1990 and April 1991 for an IEA study on the reading literacy of pupils in the grade with the most 9 year-olds (Population A), and that of students in the grade level containing the majority of all 14 year-olds (Population B).

To calculate reading literacy, the mean scores of the two groups are computed and scaled so that the overall mean score of the participating OECD countries is 500 and the standard deviation 100 in Population B. Thirteen items administered to both student samples allow the alignment of Population A with Population B.

The "five-year difference in reading" indicator is obtained by subtracting the reading literacy of Population A from that of Population B, dividing by the age difference (in years and months) of the two populations, and multiplying by five.

R04: Progress in reading achievement

R04 : Progrès en lecture

Table R04:
Difference in reading literacy of 9 and
14 year-old students (1991)

*Tableau R04 :
Différence de maîtrise de la lecture
entre élèves de 9 et 14 ans (1991)*

	Mean reading literacy score of 9 year-olds / *Note moyenne de lecture des enfants de 9 ans*	Mean reading literacy score of 14 year-olds / *Note moyenne de lecture des enfants de 14 ans*	Difference in mean score between 9 and 14 year-olds / *Différence entre les notes moyennes des enfants de 9 et 14 ans*	
Denmark	291.2	500.4	209.1	*Danemark*
Germany (TFGDR)	321.7	500.8	180.4	*Allemagne (ex-RDA)*
Netherlands	303.8	486.3	178.3	*Pays-Bas*
Switzerland	339.7	515.5	171.6	*Suisse*
British Columbia (Canada)	324.5	494.3	168.3	*Colombie-Britannique (Canada)*
Germany (FTFR)	328.7	497.6	164.2	*Allemagne (ex-terr. de la RFA)*
Iceland	350.2	513.7	163.2	*Islande*
New Zealand	363.9	527.8	162.8	*Nouvelle-Zélande*
France	367.0	531.3	154.0	*France*
Spain	329.6	455.8	150.3	*Espagne*
Sweden	379.2	528.7	149.7	*Suède*
Greece	331.9	482.0	146.5	*Grèce*
Italy	365.4	488.4	146.3	*Italie*
Ireland	337.3	483.9	142.3	*Irlande*
Norway	357.9	489.4	131.3	*Norvège*
Finland	418.8	545.0	125.6	*Finlande*
Belgium	334.4	445.6	125.6	*Belgique*
United States	388.6	514.2	124.9	*Etats-Unis*
Country mean	**346.3**	**500.0**	**155.2**	*Moyenne des pays*

See Annex 1 for notes

Voir notes en annexe 1

R04: Progress in reading achievement

R04 : Progrès en lecture

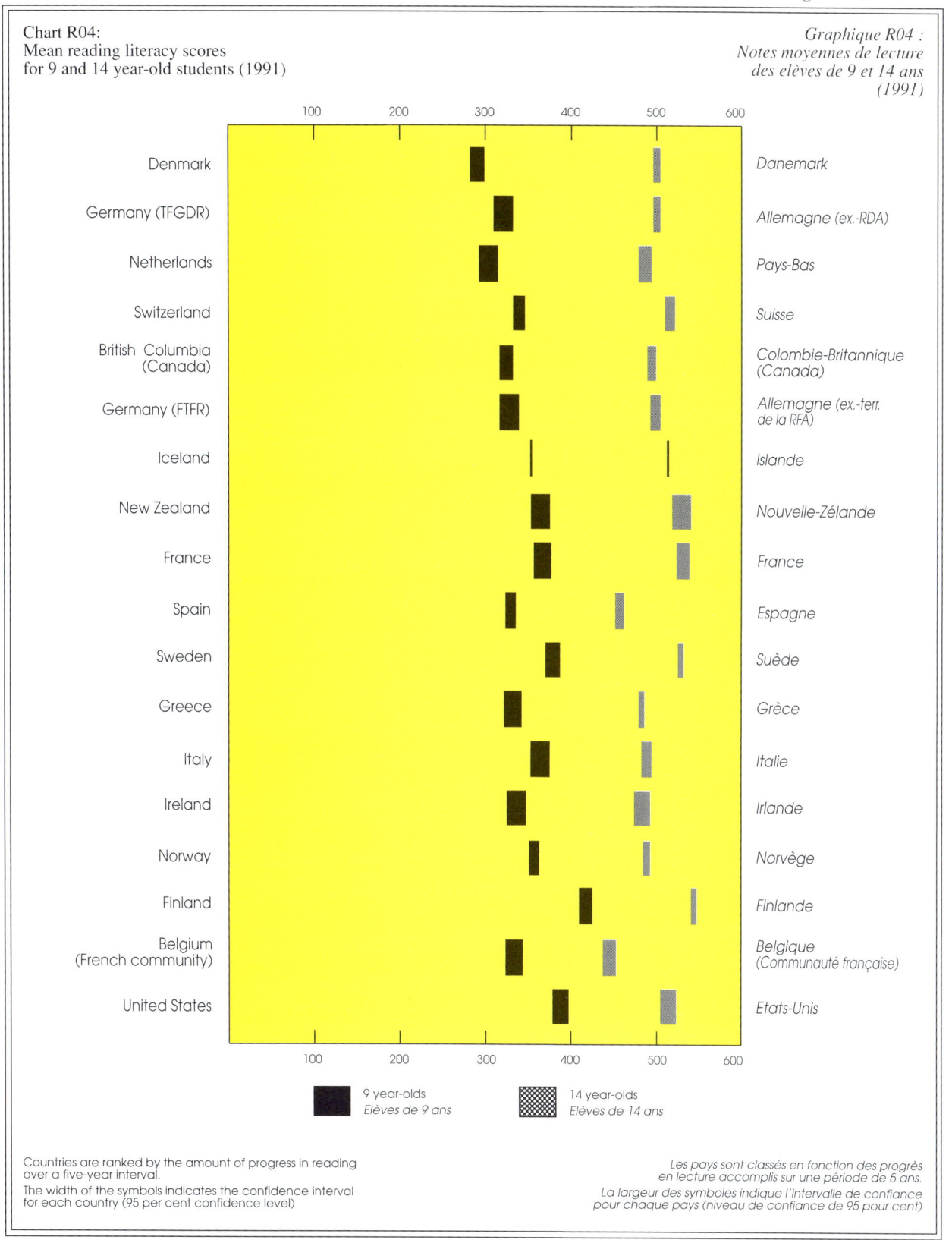

Chart R04:
Mean reading literacy scores for 9 and 14 year-old students (1991)

Graphique R04 :
Notes moyennes de lecture des elèves de 9 et 14 ans (1991)

Denmark		Danemark
Germany (TFGDR)		Allemagne (ex.-RDA)
Netherlands		Pays-Bas
Switzerland		Suisse
British Columbia (Canada)		Colombie-Britannique (Canada)
Germany (FTFR)		Allemagne (ex.-terr. de la RFA)
Iceland		Islande
New Zealand		Nouvelle-Zélande
France		France
Spain		Espagne
Sweden		Suède
Greece		Grèce
Italy		Italie
Ireland		Irlande
Norway		Norvège
Finland		Finlande
Belgium (French community)		Belgique (Communauté française)
United States		Etats-Unis

■ 9 year-olds / Elèves de 9 ans
▦ 14 year-olds / Elèves de 14 ans

Countries are ranked by the amount of progress in reading over a five-year interval.
The width of the symbols indicates the confidence interval for each country (95 per cent confidence level)

Les pays sont classés en fonction des progrès en lecture accomplis sur une période de 5 ans.
La largeur des symboles indique l'intervalle de confiance pour chaque pays (niveau de confiance de 95 pour cent)

R05: Amount of reading

STUDENT-REPORTED FREQUENCY OF READING

POLICY ISSUES

How often do students read? This indicator raises the issue of whether promoting reforms that increase the frequency with which students read results in improved reading literacy.

KEY ISSUES

In all countries, the students reporting a high reading frequency tend to score significantly higher on a test of reading comprehension than those reporting low reading frequency. Nevertheless, it cannot reveal the direction of the relationship – do good readers read well because they read so much? Or do they read so much because they are good readers?

Students in OECD countries vary substantially in terms of their reported frequency of reading. Whereas more than one in four students (14 year-olds) in Finland report a high reading frequency, fewer than one in ten students in the Netherlands do so. In addition, the mean reading literacy scores, regardless of the reported frequency of reading, vary substantially. Students in Finland report a high frequency of reading and perform well on the test. Students in the French community in Belgium report a low frequency of reading and obtain poor results compared with Finnish students.

DESCRIPTION AND INTERPRETATION

The data indicate that within each country, the mean reading literacy score is higher for students who report a high frequency of reading than for those who report a low frequency. In all countries except Finland, the students with "low frequency" have a mean reading literacy score below the international country mean (less than 500); in all countries except Spain and the French community in Belgium, the students who read frequently score above that mean (greater than 500).

The same trend occurs across countries. In seven of the nine countries where more than 15 per cent of the students report high reading frequency, the average reading score tends to be higher than the international country mean; the two exceptions are Greece and Ireland. In again seven of the nine countries where the proportion of frequent readers is the lowest (fewer than 15 per cent), the average reading score is consistently lower than the international country mean; the two exceptions in this case are Denmark and Iceland.

Overall, the data show a reasonably consistent relationship between reading literacy and reading frequency. However, the few exceptions are of interest. The average score of the "low frequency" readers in Finland is better than that of "high frequency" readers in the French community in Belgium, Greece and Spain. Also, the "high frequency" readers in Belgium and Spain have average reading literacy scores lower than those of "low frequency" readers in Finland, France and Sweden.

The data express neither the causality of the relationship, nor the extent to which these factors influence each other. Thus, while it may be likely that more frequent reading plays a role in enhancing reading comprehension, it may be equally likely that higher levels of reading comprehension play a role in encouraging a greater frequency of reading. Furthermore, both factors may depend on a number of others, such as social background; the general availability of books in students' homes, schools and communities, and students' proximity to public libraries and bookshops.

DEFINITIONS

This indicator is based on data collected between October 1990 and April 1991 for an IEA study on the reading performance of pupils in the grade with the most 14 year-old students (see Annex 1).

The frequency component was taken from the Reading Activity Inventory, which asked students to indicate the frequency with which they read various types of materials, such as books, magazines and newspapers. The accumulated frequency scores (for all types of materials) that were unreasonably high – and thus open to doubt – have been excluded from the computations; these represented about 4 per cent of the data.

Students scoring more than one standard deviation below the international country mean were designated as reporting a low frequency of reading; those scoring more than one standard deviation above that mean were designated as reporting a high frequency of reading. The percentage reporting a low reading frequency represents the weighted percentage of all students indicating a low amount of reading and *vice versa*.

R05: Amount of reading

R05 : Fréquence de la lecture

Table R05:
Student-reported frequency of reading
of 14 year-olds (1991)

Tableau R05 :
Fréquence des lectures
rapportée par les élèves (1991)

	Percentage of students reporting a low reading frequency / *Pourcentage d'élèves qui disent lire rarement*	Mean reading literacy score of reporting a low reading frequency student / *Note moyenne de lecture des élèves qui disent lire rarement*	Percentage of students reporting a high reading frequency / *Pourcentage d'élèves qui disent lire souvent*	Mean reading literacy score of reporting a high reading frequency students / *Note moyenne de lecture des élèves qui disent lire souvent*	Mean total score / *Note totale moyenne*	
Finland	10.4	508.2	25.9	567.6	545	*Finlande*
Greece	11.2	441.6	24.8	500.2	482	*Grèce*
Germany (TFGDR)	10.0	451.2	21.7	519.2	501	*Allemagne (ex-RDA)*
France	9.1	494.5	18.1	557.2	531	*France*
United States	14.5	467.5	17.2	534.4	514	*Etats-Unis*
Switzerland	12.7	471.2	16.9	539.4	515	*Suisse*
Ireland	13.7	432.2	16.7	508.6	484	*Irlande*
Sweden	14.1	491.4	15.9	552.3	529	*Suède*
New Zealand	12.7	467.6	15.8	563.6	528	*Nouvelle-Zélande*
Germany (FTFR)	13.2	449.8	14.7	513.7	498	*Allemagne (ex-terr. de la RFA)*
Italy	20.0	459.3	14.2	510.5	488	*Italie*
British Columbia (Canada)	17.2	452.2	13.6	514.7	494	*Canada (Colombie-Britannique)*
Spain	18.0	426.3	13.4	470.6	456	*Espagne*
Norway	16.8	444.6	13.1	516.3	489	*Norvège*
Denmark	17.4	455.2	12.3	527.1	500	*Danemark*
Iceland	20.4	480.0	11.1	541.1	514	*Islande*
Belgium (French community)	21.4	404.8	10.0	489.9	446	*Belgique (Communauté française)*
Netherlands	19.1	451.7	9.1	508.2	486	*Pays-Bas*
Country mean	**15.1**	**458.3**	**15.8**	**524.1**	**500**	*Moyenne des pays*

See Annex 1 for notes

Voir notes en annexe 1

R05: Amount of reading

R05 : Fréquence de la lecture

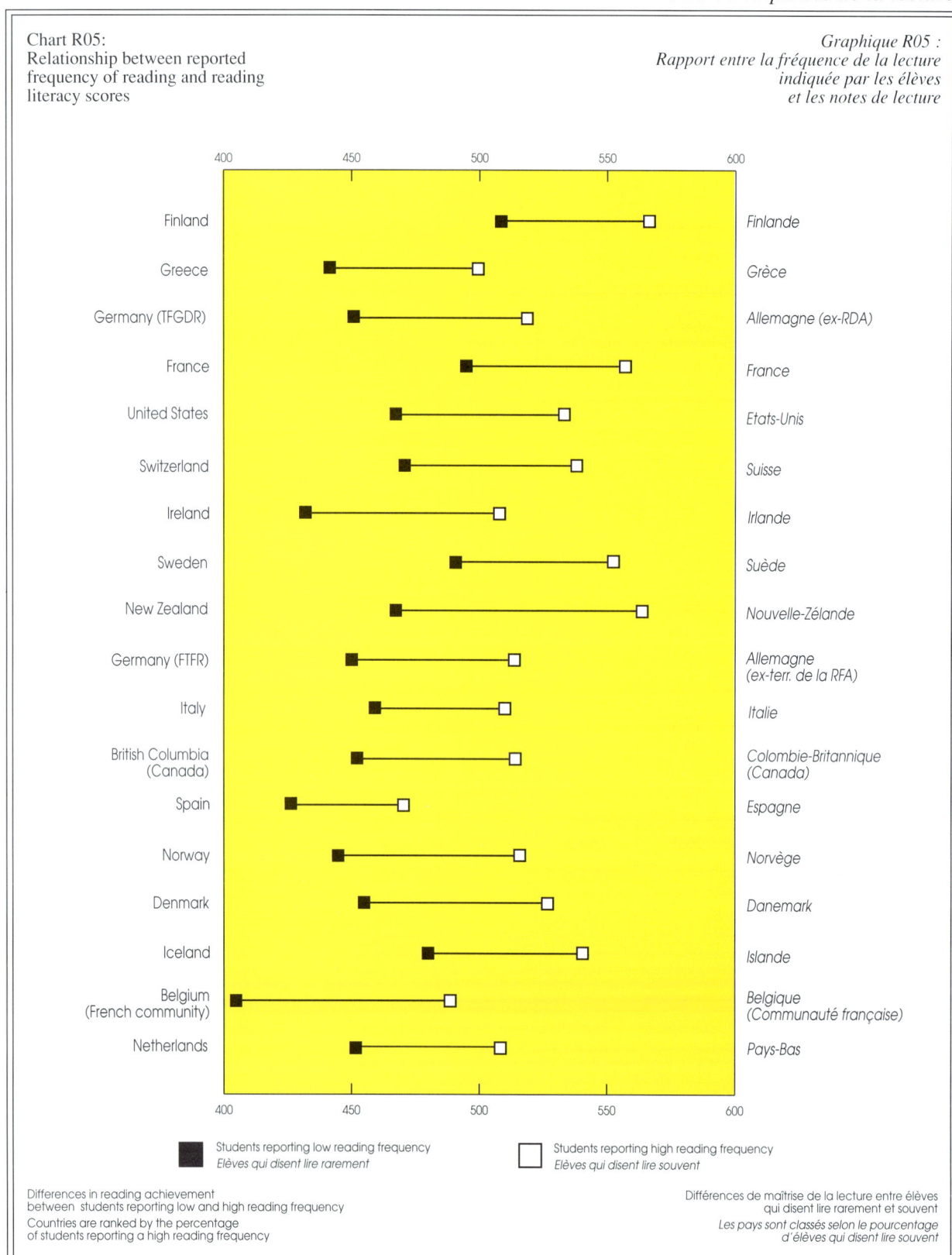

Chart R05:
Relationship between reported frequency of reading and reading literacy scores

*Graphique R05 :
Rapport entre la fréquence de la lecture indiquée par les élèves et les notes de lecture*

Finland	Finlande
Greece	Grèce
Germany (TFGDR)	Allemagne (ex-RDA)
France	France
United States	Etats-Unis
Switzerland	Suisse
Ireland	Irlande
Sweden	Suède
New Zealand	Nouvelle-Zélande
Germany (FTFR)	Allemagne (ex-terr. de la RFA)
Italy	Italie
British Columbia (Canada)	Colombie-Britannique (Canada)
Spain	Espagne
Norway	Norvège
Denmark	Danemark
Iceland	Islande
Belgium (French community)	Belgique (Communauté française)
Netherlands	Pays-Bas

■ Students reporting low reading frequency
Elèves qui disent lire rarement

□ Students reporting high reading frequency
Elèves qui disent lire souvent

Differences in reading achievement between students reporting low and high reading frequency
Countries are ranked by the percentage of students reporting a high reading frequency

*Différences de maîtrise de la lecture entre élèves qui disent lire rarement et souvent
Les pays sont classés selon le pourcentage d'élèves qui disent lire souvent*

R11: Upper secondary graduation

GRADUATION RATE IN UPPER SECONDARY EDUCATION

POLICY ISSUES

Is there anything countries can do to increase the rate at which youth complete upper secondary education, especially first programmes? If the rate at which youth complete upper secondary education is not satisfactory, to what extent might the problem lie in the distribution between general and vocational/apprenticeship programmes? Do graduates from second programmes have an advantage in the labour market?

KEY RESULTS

The proportion of students completing their first upper secondary programme range widely among the reporting countries. Although one country has a graduation rate below 30 per cent for persons at the typical graduation age, 13 out of 20 OECD countries providing data show rates above 80 per cent for persons at that same age. The majority of first programme graduates are in general education in half the countries, and in vocational and apprenticeship programmes (combined) in the other half. In a small number of countries, students who have graduated from upper secondary education re-enrol and graduate a second (or subsequent) time, almost always from vocational institutions or apprenticeship programmes.

DESCRIPTION AND INTERPRETATION

First programme upper secondary graduation rates vary widely among OECD countries. For 1992, the rates range from 29 to 96 per cent of persons at the typical age for graduation. Of the 20 countries providing information, all but two have a graduation rate of at least 60 per cent of persons at the typical age for graduation. Seven countries have graduation rates ranging between 60 and 80 per cent, and seven countries have rates between 80 and 90 per cent. Only Finland, Germany (FTFR), Japan and Norway have first programme upper secondary graduation rates above 90 per cent.

The distribution between general education and vocational education and apprenticeship combined also differs widely. Of the 17 OECD countries whose data make the distinction, eight report that the majority of first programme graduates come from institutions with general programmes and nine report that they come from vocational institutions or apprenticeship programmes.

Seven countries – Australia, Denmark, Germany (FTFR), Hungary, Ireland, the Netherlands and Spain – report that persons who have graduated from upper secondary education have re-enrolled and graduated from a second (or subsequent) upper secondary programme. Such graduates appear most common in Germany (FTFR) and Ireland, where they account for 19 and 18 per cent of persons at the typical completion age, respectively. Most second-programme completions occur in vocational education or apprenticeship.

DEFINITIONS

Upper secondary education graduates are persons who successfully complete the final year of upper secondary education. In some countries, successful completion requires a final examination; in others it does not. The graduation rates shown in this indicator are separated into first and second upper secondary programmes. In some countries, students may enrol in and complete additional programmes at the same level of education after completing the first. To obtain the graduation rates, the number of first-time (or second-time) upper secondary graduates is divided by the number of persons in the population who are the typical age at which persons in that country complete a first or second upper secondary programme.

To obtain the data on graduation rates for general and vocational or apprenticeship programmes, countries with differentiated upper secondary institutions – general or vocational – have reported the numbers of graduates by type of institution attended. A few countries with comprehensive upper secondary institutions offering multiple types of programmes have reported on the types of qualifications (general or vocational) obtained by the students attending, but most countries with comprehensive institutions are unable to provide this information.

R11: Upper secondary graduation

R11 : Réussite à la fin du deuxième cycle du secondaire

Table R11(A):
Ratio of public and private upper secondary education graduates to population at theoretical age of graduation by type of educational programmes, men and women (1992)

Tableau R11(A) :
Taux d'obtention d'un diplôme de l'enseignement secondaire du deuxième cycle, public et privé, par rapport à la population d'âge théorique de sortie, par type de programme, hommes et femmes (1992)

	Upper secondary education / Secondaire 2ᵉ cycle M+W H+F	Men Hommes	Women Femmes	General / Général M+W H+F	Men Hommes	Women Femmes	Vocational and apprenticeship / Professionnel et apprentissage M+W H+F	Men Hommes	Women Femmes	
North America										*Amérique du Nord*
Canada	68.4	64.2	72.9	...	...	...	...	...	...	*Canada*
United States	75.7	74.9	76.5	...	...	...	...	...	...	*États-Unis*
Pacific Area										*Pays du Pacifique*
Australia	87.8	93.6	81.8	...	...	...	...	...	...	*Australie*
Japan	92.2	89.0	95.5	67.4	64.2	70.7	24.8	24.8	24.8	*Japon*
New Zealand	...	...	...	...	...	...	27.6	28.6	26.6	*Nouvelle-Zélande*
European Community										*Communauté européenne*
Belgium	76.1	72.0	80.4	34.9	30.4	39.5	41.2	41.5	40.9	*Belgique*
Denmark	99.1	92.3	106.3	48.7	39.9	58.0	50.4	52.4	48.2	*Danemark*
France	78.2	74.7	82.0	32.3	27.1	37.9	45.9	47.6	44.1	*France*
Germany (FTFR)	109.6	111.3	107.9	24.3	23.4	25.3	85.5	88.1	82.8	*Allemagne (ex-terr. de la RFA)*
Germany	...	...	...	...	...	...	...	...	...	*Allemagne*
Greece	84.3	88.5	79.8	60.1	55.5	65.1	24.2	33.0	14.7	*Grèce*
Ireland	103.7	93.4	114.5	76.5	70.1	83.3	27.1	23.3	31.3	*Irlande*
Italy	58.9	56.0	61.9	21.8	15.3	28.6	37.1	40.7	33.3	*Italie*
Luxembourg	...	...	...	...	...	...	...	...	...	*Luxembourg*
Netherlands	95.6	97.1	94.0	35.3	32.8	38.0	60.2	64.3	56.0	*Pays-Bas*
Portugal	...	...	...	...	...	...	...	...	...	*Portugal*
Spain	74.8	67.8	82.2	43.6	37.9	49.6	31.2	29.9	32.7	*Espagne*
United Kingdom	80.1	76.6	83.8	63.6	58.6	68.8	16.6	18.1	15.1	*Royaume-Uni*
Other Europe - OECD										*Autres pays d'Europe - OCDE*
Austria	91.6	97.8	85.1	15.0	12.2	17.9	76.6	85.5	67.1	*Autriche*
Finland	129.5	104.2	156.3	45.4	35.7	55.7	84.1	68.5	100.6	*Finlande*
Iceland	...	...	...	...	...	...	...	...	...	*Islande*
Norway	95.6	108.2	82.6	40.3	35.6	45.2	55.4	72.6	37.4	*Norvège*
Sweden	83.0	80.7	85.3	21.8	14.9	29.1	61.1	65.8	56.2	*Suède*
Switzerland	82.6	86.5	78.6	16.1	14.5	17.7	66.6	72.0	60.9	*Suisse*
Turkey	29.2	34.6	23.4	16.8	18.3	15.1	12.5	16.3	8.4	*Turquie*
Country mean	**84.8**	**83.2**	**86.5**	**39.1**	**34.5**	**43.8**	**46.0**	**48.5**	**43.4**	***Moyenne des pays***
Central and Eastern Europe										*Europe centrale et orientale*
Czech Republic	97.1	97.9	96.2	37.1	27.2	47.5	60.0	70.7	48.6	*République tchèque*
Hungary	77.9	79.1	76.7	17.4	11.6	23.4	60.6	67.5	53.3	*Hongrie*
Poland	81.2	80.9	81.5	17.6	9.4	26.2	63.6	71.5	55.3	*Pologne*
Russia	109.2	...	...	53.1	...	...	56.1	...	...	*Russie*

See Annex 1 for notes   *Voir notes en annexe 1*

R11: Upper secondary graduation

R11 : Réussite à la fin du deuxième cycle du secondaire

Chart R11:
Number of public and private upper secondary education graduates per 100 persons in the population at theoretical age of graduation, men and women (1992)

Graphique R11 :
Taux d'obtention d'un diplôme de l'enseignement secondaire du deuxième cycle, public et privé, pour 100 personnes de la population d'âge théorique de sortie, hommes et femmes (1992)

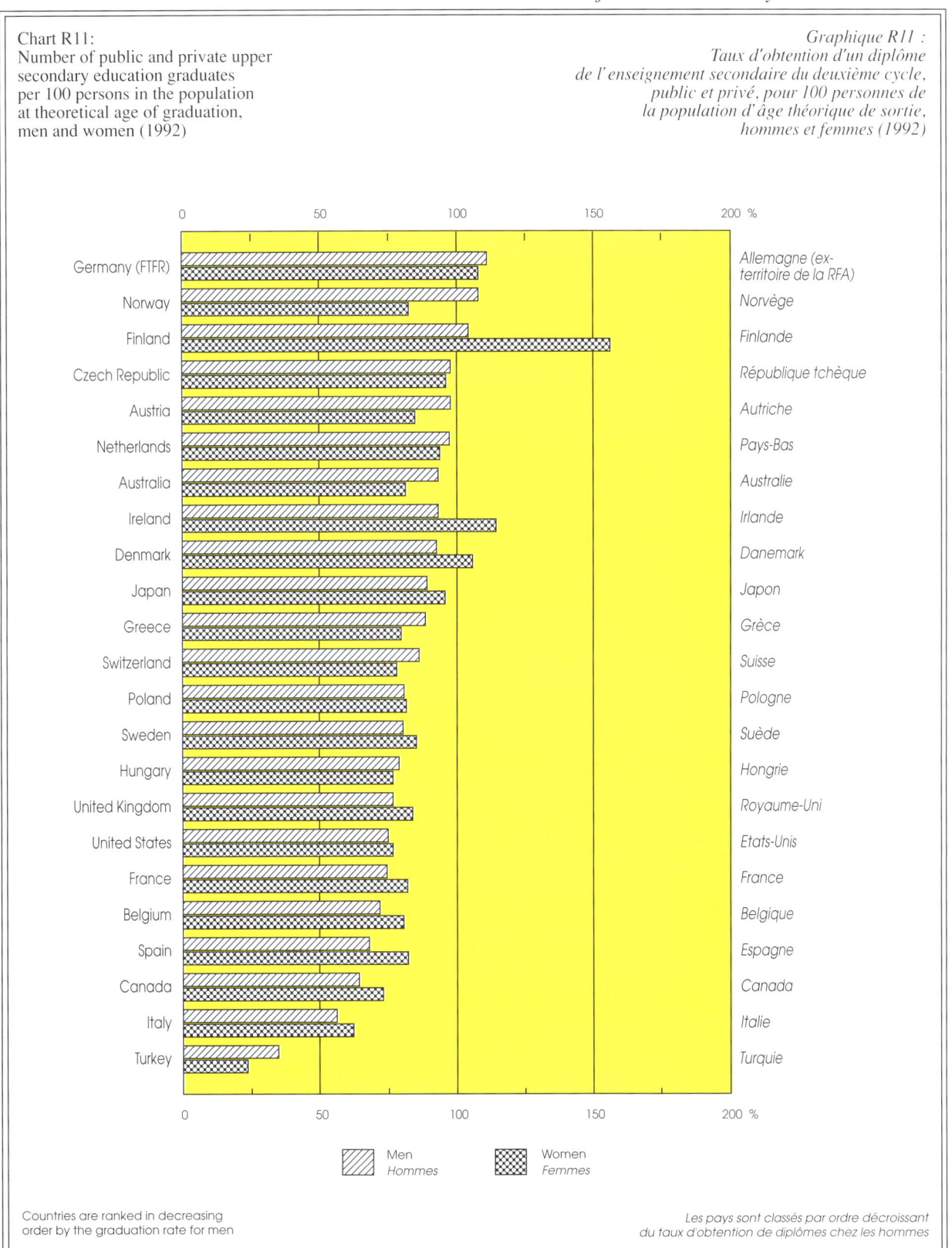

Germany (FTFR)		Allemagne (ex-territoire de la RFA)
Norway		Norvège
Finland		Finlande
Czech Republic		République tchèque
Austria		Autriche
Netherlands		Pays-Bas
Australia		Australie
Ireland		Irlande
Denmark		Danemark
Japan		Japon
Greece		Grèce
Switzerland		Suisse
Poland		Pologne
Sweden		Suède
Hungary		Hongrie
United Kingdom		Royaume-Uni
United States		Etats-Unis
France		France
Belgium		Belgique
Spain		Espagne
Canada		Canada
Italy		Italie
Turkey		Turquie

Men / *Hommes* Women / *Femmes*

Countries are ranked in decreasing order by the graduation rate for men

Les pays sont classés par ordre décroissant du taux d'obtention de diplômes chez les hommes

R11: Upper secondary graduation

R11 : Réussite à la fin du deuxième cycle du secondaire

Table R11(B):
Ratio of public and private upper secondary education graduates from first and second programmes to population at theoretical age of graduation (1992)

Tableau R11(B) :
Taux d'obtention d'un diplôme de l'enseignement secondaire du deuxième cycle, public et privé (premier et second cursus de formation) par rapport à la population d'âge théorique de sortie (1992)

	First educational programme / *Premier cursus de formation*			Second educational programme / *Second cursus de formation*			
	Upper secondary education / *Enseignement secondaire 2ᵉ cycle*	General / *Général*	Vocational and apprenticeship / *Professionnel et apprentissage*	Upper secondary education / *Enseignement secondaire 2ᵉ cycle*	General / *Général*	Vocational and apprenticeship / *Professionnel et apprentissage*	
North America							*Amérique du Nord*
Canada	68.4	...	...	.	.	.	*Canada*
United States	75.7	...	...	.	.	.	*Etats-Unis*
Pacific Area							*Pays du Pacifique*
Australia	73.3	...	...	14.5	.	13.3	*Australie*
Japan	92.2	67.4	24.8	-	-	-	*Japon*
New Zealand	66.4	38.7	27.6	...	...	.	*Nouvelle-Zélande*
European Community							*Communauté européenne*
Belgium	76.1	34.9	41.2	.	.	.	*Belgique*
Denmark	82.2	45.1	37.1	16.8	3.6	13.2	*Danemark*
France	78.2	32.3	45.9	.	.	.	*France*
Germany (FTFR)	92.6	24.3	68.3	18.8	.	18.8	*Allemagne (ex-terr. de la RFA)*
Germany	...	...	...	...	...	...	*Allemagne*
Greece	84.3	60.1	24.2	.	.	.	*Grèce*
Ireland	85.6	76.5	9.1	18.0	-	18.0	*Irlande*
Italy	58.9	21.8	37.1	-	-	-	*Italie*
Luxembourg	...	...	...	...	...	...	*Luxembourg*
Netherlands	89.6	33.6	56.1	5.9	1.8	4.1	*Pays-Bas*
Portugal	...	...	...	...	...	...	*Portugal*
Spain	63.1	43.6	19.5	11.7	.	11.7	*Espagne*
United Kingdom	80.2	63.6	16.6	x	x	x	*Royaume-Uni*
Other Europe - OECD							*Autres pays d'Europe - OCDE*
Austria	...	...	...	...	...	...	*Autriche*
Finland	92.8	43.3	49.5	...	...	...	*Finlande*
Iceland	...	...	...	...	...	...	*Islande*
Norway	95.6	40.3	55.4	.	.	.	*Norvège*
Sweden	83.0	21.8	61.1	.	.	.	*Suède*
Switzerland	82.6	16.1	66.6	-	-	-	*Suisse*
Turkey	29.2	16.8	12.5	.	.	.	*Turquie*
Country mean	**77.5**	**40.0**	**38.4**	...	...	...	***Moyenne des pays***
Central and Eastern Europe							*Europe centrale et orientale*
Czech Republic	97.1	37.1	60.0	.	.	.	*République tchèque*
Hungary	75.8	17.4	58.4	2.1	-	2.1	*Hongrie*
Poland	...	...	...	...	...	...	*Pologne*
Russia	...	...	...	...	...	...	*Russie*

See Annex 1 for notes

Voir notes en annexe 1

R12: University graduation

GRADUATION RATE IN FIRST-DEGREE UNIVERSITY EDUCATION

POLICY ISSUES

What conclusions can be drawn concerning the economy's skills pool, as measured by that proportion of young people who are the most highly qualified?

KEY RESULTS

In just over half the countries shown, the Bachelor is the first degree in the sequence of university degrees; the Master's would normally be a second degree, taken after the Bachelor. This group includes all the English-speaking countries and Japan. For other countries, all in Europe, the first degree is the Master's.

Graduation rates vary widely from 6-10 per cent (Austria, Hungary, Italy, Switzerland and Turkey) to 25 per cent or more (Australia, Canada and the United States), with the other countries spread fairly in the percentage range. The graduation rate in first degree is higher in the group of countries having the Bachelor as a first degree.

Women's graduation rates are generally higher at Bachelor level than those for men; Japan is the major exception and Finland, Ireland, Turkey and the United Kingdom are minor ones. Higher graduation rates for women also tend to be a feature of countries where the main first degree is the Bachelor degree. This tendency is much less marked, and sometimes reversed, where the Master's is the main degree.

DESCRIPTION AND INTERPRETATION

This indicator offers an approximate measure of the proportion of young people who obtain a first degree (whether Bachelor- or Master-level qualification). This rate is of interest because it shows the proportion of the age group who have participated in higher education and who have achieved a degree. It is important also as a measure of the skills available to national economies.

This indicator is closely linked to the extent the theoretical graduation age is representative of the actual average. Differences in graduation rates between men and women might partly reflect their choices; for example, women are more likely than men to opt for relatively shorter courses.

DEFINITIONS

The graduation rate relates the number of people with Bachelor (or Master's) degrees to the number in the population corresponding to the typical age of graduation.

The *university* graduation rate relates the number of people with Bachelor and, *separately*, Master's degrees to the number in the population corresponding to the typical age of graduation.

The theoretical graduation age by type of degree is reported in Annex 3.

R12: University graduation

R12 : Niveau de formation supérieure

Table R12:
Ratio of public and private university education graduates to population at theoretical age of graduation by type of degree, men and women (1992)

Tableau R12 :
Taux d'obtention d'un diplôme universitaire par rapport à la population d'âge théorique par type de diplôme, établissements publics et privés, hommes et femmes (1992)

	Bachelor or equivalent *Licence ou équivalent*			Master or equivalent *Maîtrise ou équivalent*			
	M + W *H + F*	Men *Hommes*	Women *Femmes*	M + W *H + F*	Men *Hommes*	Women *Femmes*	
North America							*Amérique du Nord*
Canada	32.2	26.9	37.7	4.8	4.9	4.7	*Canada*
United States	27.4	24.7	30.3	9.1	8.2	10.0	*Etats-Unis*
Pacific Area							*Pays du Pacifique*
Australia	26.3	22.0	30.8	...	...	...	*Australie*
Japan	23.4	32.3	14.1	1.6	2.7	0.5	*Japon*
New Zealand	18.0	17.7	18.3	7.3	7.9	6.6	*Nouvelle-Zélande*
European Community							*Communauté européenne*
Belgium	-	-	-	13.6	15.1	12.0	*Belgique*
Denmark	22.1	17.6	26.9	7.9	8.4	7.4	*Danemark*
France	...	...	...	14.5	13.3	15.6	*France*
Germany (FTFR)	.	.	.	13.0	15.4	10.3	*Allemagne (ex-terr. de la RFA)*
Germany	...	...	...	...	...	...	*Allemagne*
Greece	11.8	9.9	13.7	0.1	0.2	0.1	*Grèce*
Ireland	17.4	17.7	17.1	3.5	3.8	3.2	*Irlande*
Italy	0.7	0.5	0.8	9.8	9.4	10.1	*Italie*
Luxembourg	...	...	...	...	...	...	*Luxembourg*
Netherlands	17.8	17.6	18.0	8.6	9.6	7.5	*Pays-Bas*
Portugal	...	...	...	...	...	...	*Portugal*
Spain	8.0	5.8	10.4	12.1	10.8	13.4	*Espagne*
United Kingdom	20.4	21.1	19.7	7.2	7.8	6.7	*Royaume-Uni*
Other Europe - OECD							*Autres pays d'Europe - OCDE*
Austria	.	.	.	7.9	8.5	7.2	*Autriche*
Finland	6.5	7.8	5.2	11.8	10.5	13.2	*Finlande*
Iceland	...	...	...	...	...	...	*Islande*
Norway	19.4	14.8	24.2	6.4	7.3	5.4	*Norvège*
Sweden	11.4	9.6	13.3	.	.	.	*Suède*
Switzerland	x	x	x	8.0	10.4	5.7	*Suisse*
Turkey	6.0	7.4	4.4	0.4	0.5	0.3	*Turquie*
Country mean	**13.4**	**12.7**	**14.3**	**7.4**	**7.7**	**7.0**	*Moyenne des pays*
Central and Eastern Europe							*Europe centrale et orientale*
Czech Republic	.	.	.	13.4	13.9	12.9	*République tchèque*
Hungary	2.6	1.6	3.7	6.2	7.4	4.9	*Hongrie*
Poland	...	...	...	...	...	...	*Pologne*
Russia	.	.	.	21.1	...	...	*Russie*

See Annex 1 for notes

Voir notes en annexe 1

R12: University graduation

R12 : Niveau de formation supérieure

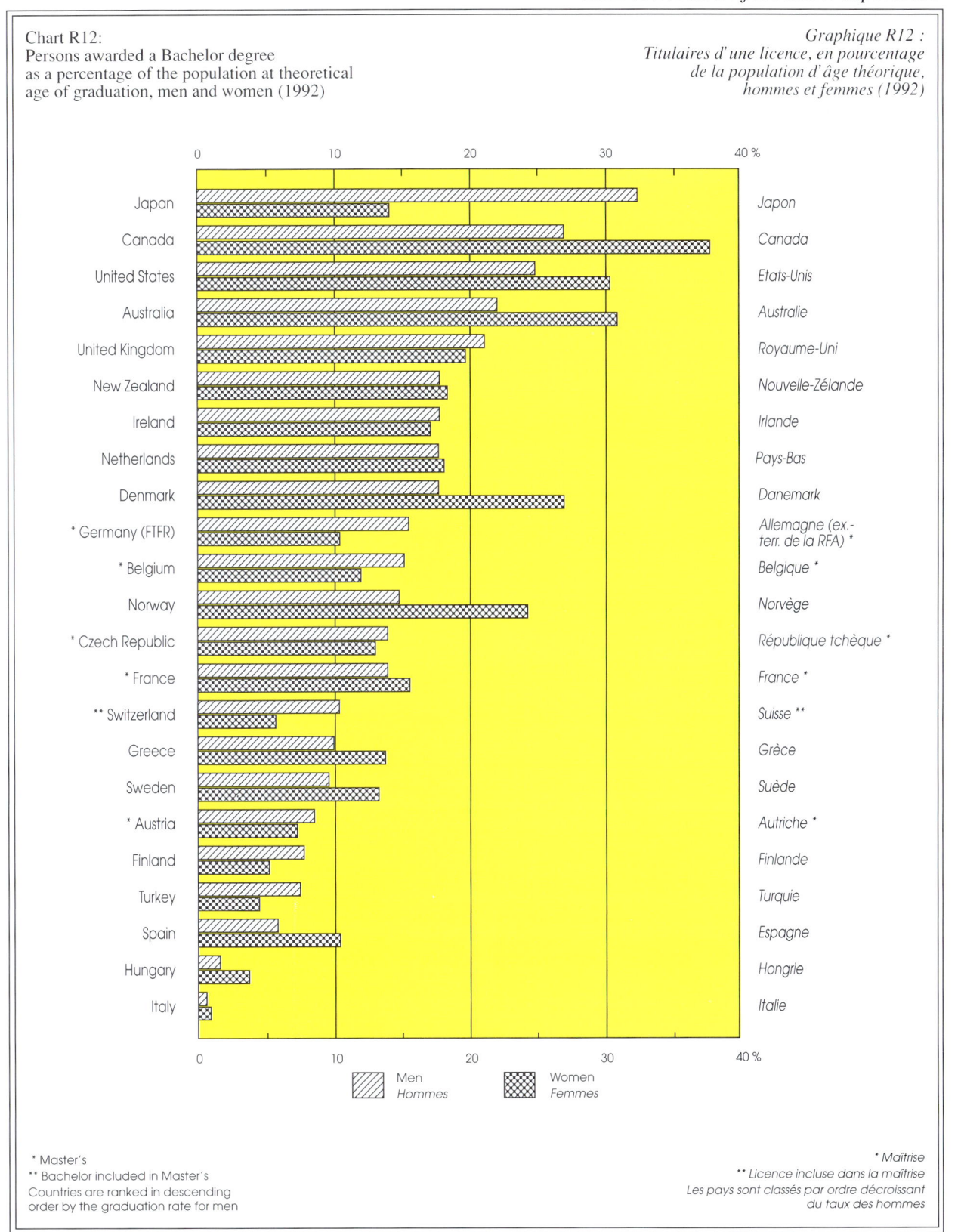

Chart R12:
Persons awarded a Bachelor degree as a percentage of the population at theoretical age of graduation, men and women (1992)

Graphique R12 :
Titulaires d'une licence, en pourcentage de la population d'âge théorique, hommes et femmes (1992)

Japan		Japon
Canada		Canada
United States		Etats-Unis
Australia		Australie
United Kingdom		Royaume-Uni
New Zealand		Nouvelle-Zélande
Ireland		Irlande
Netherlands		Pays-Bas
Denmark		Danemark
* Germany (FTFR)		Allemagne (ex.-terr. de la RFA) *
* Belgium		Belgique *
Norway		Norvège
* Czech Republic		République tchèque *
* France		France *
** Switzerland		Suisse **
Greece		Grèce
Sweden		Suède
* Austria		Autriche *
Finland		Finlande
Turkey		Turquie
Spain		Espagne
Hungary		Hongrie
Italy		Italie

Men / Hommes
Women / Femmes

* Master's
** Bachelor included in Master's
Countries are ranked in descending order by the graduation rate for men

* Maîtrise
** Licence incluse dans la maîtrise
Les pays sont classés par ordre décroissant du taux des hommes

R14: University degrees

FIRST DEGREES BY SUBJECT CATEGORY AS A PERCENTAGE OF TOTAL UNIVERSITY DEGREES

POLICY ISSUES

How strong is the link between the numbers of graduates holding degrees in a given field, and the level of demand for highly qualified labour in that same field?

KEY RESULTS

In general, the distribution pattern is very similar across countries. Among the five subject categories, the single biggest is human sciences, with law and business next; on the other hand, most countries have between 30 and 40 per cent of students graduating from the three other groups of medical science, natural science and engineering, taken together. Belgium, Germany (FTFR), Italy, Japan and Switzerland differ in having higher proportions graduating from law and business than from human sciences.

There are some exceptions to this pattern. The top subject area in the Czech Republic is engineering and architecture, with a degree share that is higher than in any other country shown: 33 per cent. Australia, Canada, New Zealand, Spain and the United States stand out for their relatively low proportion of graduates in engineering, which is seemingly correlated with these same countries having above-average proportions of graduates in law and business studies.

Separate figures for men and women show that there is a general pattern for a higher proportion of men to graduate in science, engineering, law and business, and for women to graduate in medical science and human sciences. These patterns of gender differentiation hold with very few exceptions, although the extent to which either gender is over-represented does vary across countries.

DESCRIPTION AND INTERPRETATION

The percentage of graduates in medical or natural science and engineering fields is slightly higher than 40 in many countries. However, the balance between these three subject groups varies markedly. Italy stands out as having the highest proportion of graduates in medicine, but the range across the rest of countries is very wide. More detailed figures show that countries also differ in the division of their medical graduates between medical and paramedical subjects (i.e. between training doctors and training medical support staff). See *OECD Education Statistics, 1985-1992*.

There are also wide differences between countries in the proportions of graduates in the various branches of science and mathematics. There is thus no general pattern for there to be, say, more biological science graduates than physical science graduates.

DEFINITIONS

The results rely heavily on how far countries have used consistent subject definitions. The inclusion of higher degrees will influence the distributions because the proportions of students pursuing such degrees will vary from subject to subject. The comments in Annex 1 should be taken into consideration when interpreting the findings.

The grouping of subjects is described more fully in Annex 3.

R14: University degrees

R14 : Diplômes universitaires

Chart R14:
University degrees as a percentage
of total degrees by subject
category, men and women (1992)

*Graphique R14 :
Diplômés par groupe de disciplines en proportion
du total des diplômés de l'enseignement
supérieur universitaire, hommes et femmes (1992)*

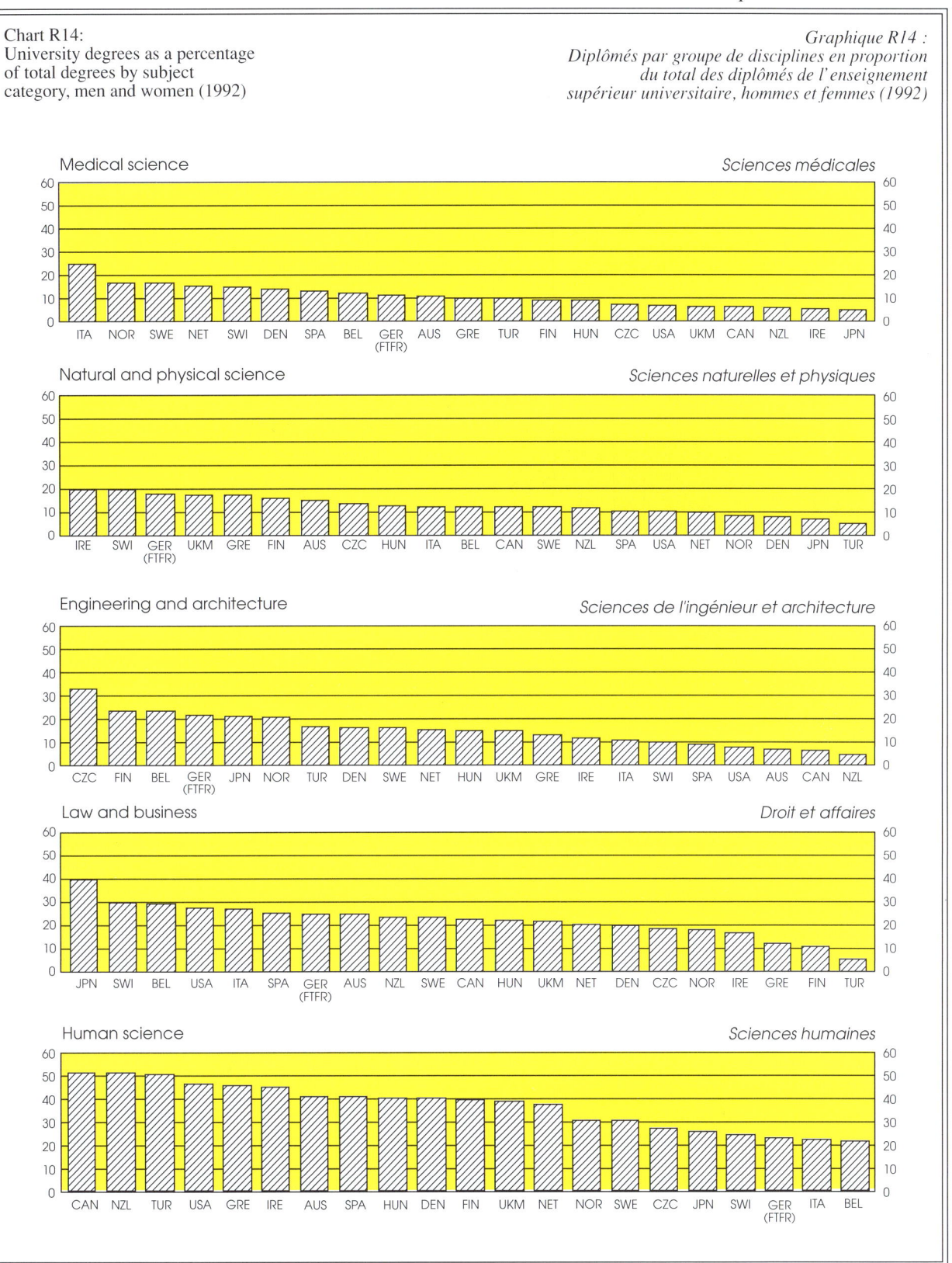

Medical science — *Sciences médicales*

Natural and physical science — *Sciences naturelles et physiques*

Engineering and architecture — *Sciences de l'ingénieur et architecture*

Law and business — *Droit et affaires*

Human science — *Sciences humaines*

221

R14: University degrees

R14 : Diplômes universitaires

Table R14:
University degrees as a percentage
of total degrees by subject category,
men and women (1992)

Tableau R14 :
Diplômés par groupe de disciplines
en proportion du total des diplômés
de l'enseignement supérieur universitaire,
hommes et femmes (1992)

	Medical science / Sciences médicales M+W	Men Hommes	Women Femmes	Natural and physical science / Sciences naturelles et physiques M+W	Men Hommes	Women Femmes	Engineering and architecture / Sciences de l'ingénieur et architecture M+W	Men Hommes	Women Femmes	
North America										**Amérique du Nord**
Canada	6.7	4.5	8.6	12.0	15.8	9.0	7.0	13.3	2.1	Canada
United States	7.1	4.4	9.5	10.3	13.3	7.6	8.1	14.4	2.4	Etats-Unis
Pacific Area										**Pays du Pacifique**
Australia	11.5	6.0	15.9	14.9	20.5	10.6	7.3	13.7	2.3	Australie
Japan	5.3	4.6	7.1	7.3	8.3	4.7	21.6	29.1	2.9	Japon
New Zealand	6.2	5.7	6.8	11.7	13.5	9.6	5.1	7.4	2.6	Nouvelle-Zélande
European Community										**Communauté européenne**
Belgium	12.8	10.1	16.5	12.1	13.1	10.7	23.9	34.1	10.2	Belgique
Denmark	14.2	4.2	22.3	8.2	12.4	4.9	16.6	29.2	6.4	Danemark
France	...	...	...	...	...	...	...	...	...	France
Germany (FTFR)	11.7	10.7	13.3	17.6	19.2	14.9	22.2	31.1	7.2	Allemagne (ex-terr. de la RFA)
Germany	...	...	...	...	...	...	...	...	...	Allemagne
Greece	10.5	6.0	14.1	16.8	21.1	13.3	13.7	22.8	6.5	Grèce
Ireland	5.8	5.4	6.3	19.2	21.3	16.9	12.4	20.1	3.8	Irlande
Italy	25.1	27.0	23.1	12.2	12.7	11.7	11.4	18.0	4.8	Italie
Luxembourg	...	...	...	...	...	...	...	...	...	Luxembourg
Netherlands	15.6	9.6	22.6	9.7	13.8	5.1	16.0	26.3	4.3	Pays-Bas
Portugal	...	...	...	...	...	...	...	...	...	Portugal
Spain	13.4	10.8	15.3	10.4	13.5	8.1	9.7	18.7	3.0	Espagne
United Kingdom	6.8	6.1	7.7	17.1	19.4	14.4	15.2	20.4	9.2	Royaume-Uni
Other Europe - OECD										**Autres pays d'Europe - OCDE**
Austria	...	...	...	...	...	...	...	...	...	Autriche
Finland	9.5	7.3	11.9	15.6	21.5	9.4	23.9	39.3	7.3	Finlande
Iceland	...	...	...	...	...	...	...	...	...	Islande
Norway	17.2	6.6	25.8	8.7	11.5	6.4	21.1	36.2	8.8	Norvège
Sweden	17.1	10.7	22.4	12.0	16.9	7.9	16.6	28.5	6.7	Suède
Switzerland	15.2	13.6	18.2	19.1	21.6	14.2	10.3	14.1	2.7	Suisse
Turkey	10.4	9.2	12.5	5.5	4.9	6.7	17.2	20.4	11.5	Turquie
Country mean	**11.7**	**8.5**	**14.7**	**12.7**	**15.5**	**9.8**	**14.7**	**23.0**	**5.5**	**Moyenne des pays**
Central and Eastern Europe										**Europe centrale et orientale**
Czech Republic	7.9	6.0	10.1	13.2	14.2	12.1	33.0	48.2	15.9	République tchèque
Hungary	9.5	8.0	11.1	12.4	17.2	6.9	15.2	23.1	6.1	Hongrie
Poland	...	...	...	...	...	...	...	...	...	Pologne
Russia	...	...	...	...	...	...	...	...	...	Russie

See Annex 1 for notes

Voir notes en annexe 1

R14: University degrees

R14 : Diplômes universitaires

Table R14:
University degrees as a percentage of total degrees by subject category, men and women (1992)

Tableau R14 :
Diplômés par groupe de disciplines en proportion du total des diplômés de l'enseignement supérieur universitaire, hommes et femmes (1992)

	Law and business / Droit et affaires M+W (H+F)	Men / Hommes	Women / Femmes	Human sciences / Science humaines M+W (H+F)	Men / Hommes	Women / Femmes	
North America							*Amérique du Nord*
Canada	22.6	27.5	18.8	51.7	38.9	61.7	*Canada*
United States	27.3	33.0	22.3	47.3	35.0	58.2	*Etats-Unis*
Pacific Area							*Pays du Pacifique*
Australia	24.7	32.4	18.7	41.5	27.5	52.5	*Australie*
Japan	39.4	44.6	26.4	26.3	13.4	58.9	*Japon*
New Zealand	23.4	27.8	18.6	51.6	43.4	60.3	*Nouvelle-Zélande*
European Community							*Communauté européenne*
Belgium	29.3	28.7	30.3	21.9	14.0	32.4	*Belgique*
Denmark	20.0	28.6	13.0	40.9	25.6	53.4	*Danemark*
France	...	...	...	...	...	...	*France*
Germany (FTFR)	24.7	24.7	24.7	23.7	14.2	39.8	*Allemagne (ex-terr. de la RFA)*
Germany	...	...	...	...	...	...	*Allemagne*
Greece	12.4	12.7	12.2	46.6	37.4	53.9	*Grèce*
Ireland	16.8	18.1	15.4	45.8	35.1	57.8	*Irlande*
Italy	27.1	30.1	24.2	22.8	10.5	35.0	*Italie*
Luxembourg	...	...	...	...	...	...	*Luxembourg*
Netherlands	20.5	24.6	15.7	38.1	25.7	52.4	*Pays-Bas*
Portugal	...	...	...	...	...	...	*Portugal*
Spain	25.3	28.6	22.7	41.2	28.4	50.9	*Espagne*
United Kingdom	21.8	22.1	21.5	39.1	32.1	47.2	*Royaume-Uni*
Other Europe - OECD							*Autres pays d'Europe - OCDE*
Austria	...	...	...	...	...	...	*Autriche*
Finland	11.0	10.6	11.4	40.0	21.4	60.0	*Finlande*
Iceland	...	...	...	...	...	...	*Islande*
Norway	18.3	24.8	13.1	31.3	17.6	42.4	*Norvège*
Sweden	23.4	24.6	22.4	31.0	19.2	40.7	*Suède*
Switzerland	29.8	31.3	26.8	24.8	18.1	38.1	*Suisse*
Turkey	5.6	6.0	4.9	51.3	44.5	63.5	*Turquie*
Country mean	**22.3**	**25.3**	**19.1**	**37.7**	**26.4**	**50.5**	**Moyenne des pays**
Central and Eastern Europe							*Europe centrale et orientale*
Czech Republic	18.4	13.9	23.6	27.3	16.4	39.6	*République tchèque*
Hungary	21.9	21.9	21.9	41.0	29.7	53.9	*Hongrie*
Poland	...	...	...	...	...	...	*Pologne*
Russia	...	...	...	...	...	...	*Russie*

See Annex 1 for notes

Voir notes en annexe 1

R15: Science and engineering personnel

SCIENCE AND ENGINEERING DEGREES AS A PERCENTAGE OF TOTAL UNIVERSITY DEGREES, AND OF SCIENTIFIC PERSONNEL IN THE LABOUR FORCE

POLICY ISSUES

Are the proportions of university students graduating with science degrees sufficient to warrant a confident outlook with regard to the generation of scientific research and technological innovation?

KEY RESULTS

There is a degree of similarity among the countries with regard to the percentage of university graduates awarded degrees in science, mathematics, computing and engineering subjects: most report between 15 and 30 per cent. Canada, Italy, New Zealand, Spain and the United States are at the lower end of the range, while the Czech Republic, Finland and Germany (FTFR) have rates over 30 per cent.

In almost all countries, engineering (including architecture) is by far the single biggest subject group within the total; for eleven out of the 21 countries shown, it accounts for more than half of all science degrees.

Countries tend to have more graduates in physical than in biological science, and more in mathematics and computing than in physical science, but the differences are not very great.

Countries differ with regard to the proportion of science, mathematics, computing and engineering graduates in the labour force; the variation is between 0.6 and 1 per cent of the 25-34 age group. Country proportions are not always in line with their relative proportions of new graduates qualifying in these subjects (as, for example, for Australia and the United States) – a result reflecting, *inter alia*, differences in the overall graduation rate.

DESCRIPTION AND INTERPRETATION

This indicator offers information about first- and higher-degree graduates in the biological sciences, physics, mathematics and engineering as a proportion of all first- and higher-degree graduates, and shows the number of graduates aged 25-34 in the labour force as a proportion of the total labour force in that age range.

As with indicator R14, the results depend heavily on the extent to which subject definitions are consistent between countries. The comments in Annex 1 should be taken into consideration when interpreting the findings.

The indicator does not show the number of graduates actually employed in scientific or engineering occupations or, more generally, those using their degree skills and knowledge in their employment. It therefore measures a potential supply of skills rather than their utilisation.

DEFINITIONS

This indicator shows the percentage of all university degrees awarded that are in science, including the natural sciences, mathematics and computer science, and engineering. It also shows the number of such degrees per 100 000 persons in the labour force who are 25 to 34 years of age.

R15: Science and engineering personnel

R15 : Personnel scientifique

Table R15:
Scientific degrees by subject as a percentage of total scientific degrees awarded in university education, and science graduates as a proportion of the labour force 25 to 34 years of age (1992)

*Tableau R15 :
Diplômés scientifiques par discipline en proportion du total des diplômés scientifiques de l'enseignement supérieur universitaire et en proportion de la population active âgée de 25 à 34 ans (1992)*

	Biological science and related	Physical science	Mathematics and computing	Engineering	All scientific subjects	Science graduates per 100 000 persons aged 25-34	
North America							*Amérique du Nord*
Canada	3.9	2.6	3.5	6.1	16.2	667.7	*Canada*
United States	3.4	1.8	3.6	7.2	16.0	688.0	*Etats-Unis*
Pacific Area							*Pays du Pacifique*
Australia	8.4	1.1	3.9	5.1	18.5	921.7	*Australie*
Japan	x	3.8	x	21.6	25.4	974.3	*Japon*
New Zealand	5.8	x	3.3	3.7	12.9	453.0	*Nouvelle-Zélande*
European Community							*Communauté européenne*
Belgium	2.0	3.2	2.3	22.0	29.4	...	*Belgique*
Denmark	3.7	0.2	1.5	15.8	21.2	682.5	*Danemark*
France	...	...	...	...	...	...	*France*
Germany (FTFR)	3.3	6.2	4.2	19.2	32.9	650.3	*Allemagne (ex-terr. de la RFA)*
Germany	...	...	...	...	...	...	*Allemagne*
Greece	1.3	5.8	5.7	12.8	25.6	500.3	*Grèce*
Ireland	3.2	8.6	5.0	11.8	28.6	950.9	*Irlande*
Italy	3.4	2.7	3.4	7.1	16.6	187.4	*Italie*
Luxembourg	...	...	...	...	...	...	*Luxembourg*
Netherlands	0.7	1.9	3.0	15.0	20.6	691.0	*Pays-Bas*
Portugal	...	...	...	...	...	...	*Portugal*
Spain	2.5	3.3	3.4	8.0	17.2	557.7	*Espagne*
United Kingdom	4.1	5.8	6.1	13.0	29.0	989.4	*Royaume-Uni*
Other Europe - OECD							*Autres pays d'Europe - OCDE*
Austria	...	...	...	...	...	...	*Autriche*
Finland	1.6	3.4	6.7	23.2	35.0	792.0	*Finlande*
Iceland	...	...	...	...	...	...	*Islande*
Norway	1.2	1.6	3.2	20.6	26.7	854.8	*Norvège*
Sweden	2.1	3.2	5.4	15.9	26.6	457.5	*Suède*
Switzerland	6.5	6.9	3.1	7.4	23.9	302.3	*Suisse*
Turkey	1.7	1.2	1.6	15.2	19.6	...	*Turquie*
Country mean	**3.1**	**3.3**	**3.6**	**13.2**	**23.3**	**665.9**	*Moyenne des pays*
Central and Eastern Europe							*Europe centrale et orientale*
Czech Republic	2.0	0.7	0.8	32.5	36.0	...	*République tchèque*
Hungary	3.2	x	x	15.2	18.4	...	*Hongrie*
Poland	...	...	...	...	...	...	*Pologne*
Russia	...	...	...	...	...	...	*Russie*

See Annex 1 for notes

Voir notes en annexe 1

R15: Science and engineering personnel

R15 : Personnel scientifique

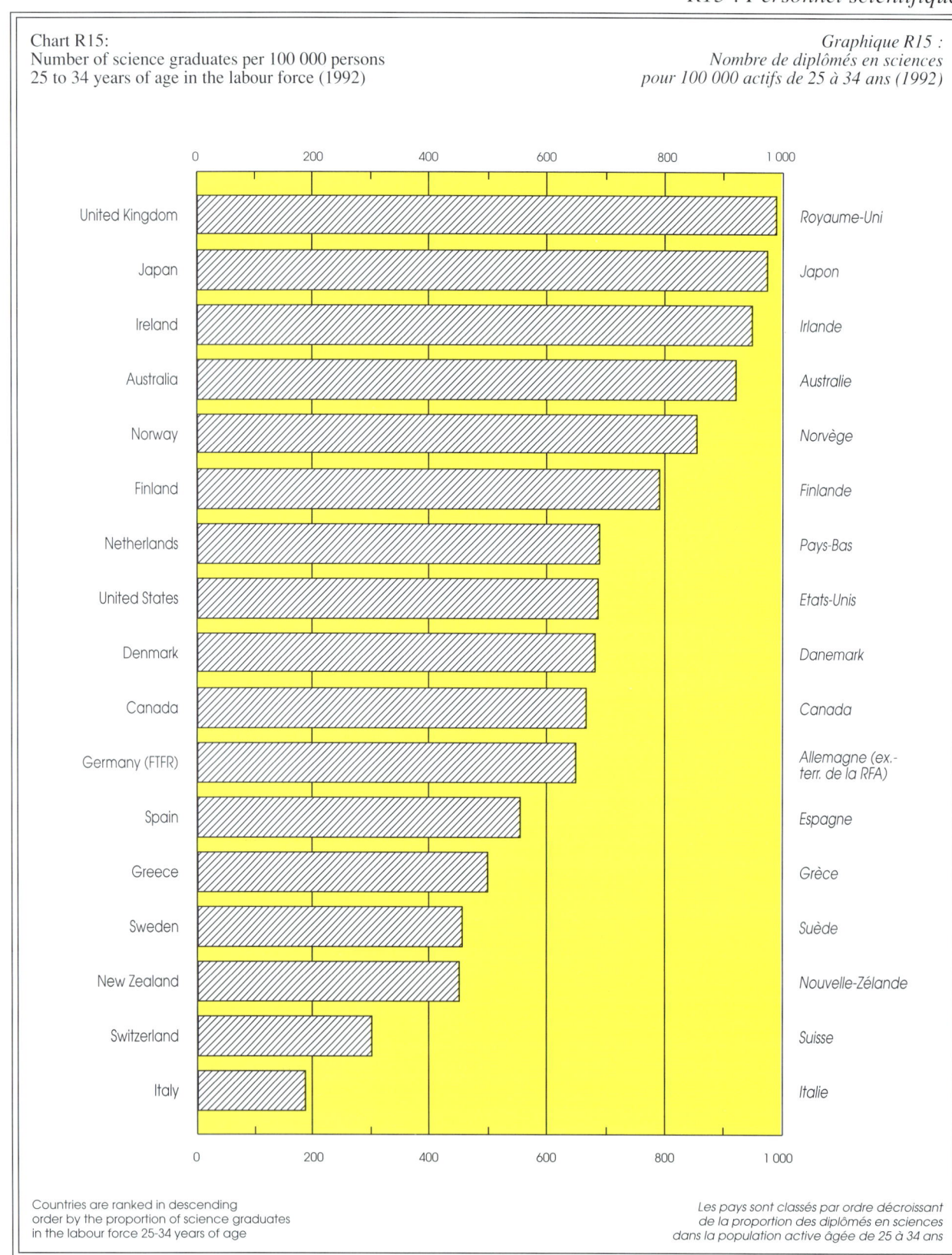

Chart R15:
Number of science graduates per 100 000 persons 25 to 34 years of age in the labour force (1992)

Graphique R15 :
Nombre de diplômés en sciences pour 100 000 actifs de 25 à 34 ans (1992)

Country	Value (approx.)	Pays
United Kingdom	~980	Royaume-Uni
Japan	~960	Japon
Ireland	~940	Irlande
Australia	~910	Australie
Norway	~850	Norvège
Finland	~780	Finlande
Netherlands	~690	Pays-Bas
United States	~680	Etats-Unis
Denmark	~670	Danemark
Canada	~660	Canada
Germany (FTFR)	~640	Allemagne (ex.-terr. de la RFA)
Spain	~560	Espagne
Greece	~500	Grèce
Sweden	~460	Suède
New Zealand	~450	Nouvelle-Zélande
Switzerland	~300	Suisse
Italy	~190	Italie

Countries are ranked in descending order by the proportion of science graduates in the labour force 25-34 years of age

Les pays sont classés par ordre décroissant de la proportion des diplômés en sciences dans la population active âgée de 25 à 34 ans

R21: UNEMPLOYMENT RATES BY LEVEL OF EDUCATIONAL ATTAINMENT

POLICY ISSUES

How do the various educational groups fare in the labour market? Does age play a role?

KEY RESULTS

People with a lower level of educational attainment are more likely to be unemployed than those with a higher level of attainment. Unemployment rates are therefore generally much higher for those with a primary, lower secondary or upper secondary education than for those with a university or non-university tertiary education.

As regards the risk of unemployment, the level of educational attainment seems to be of special importance to those who have recently entered the labour market. The differences in average unemployment rates between the lowest and highest levels of educational attainment are larger among the 25 to 34 year-olds than among the total labour force. In a longer perspective, professional experience can reduce the risk of unemployment. Older persons with long professional experience but a low level of educational attainment sometimes have as good or even better job opportunities than more highly educated newcomers to the labour market. The 1992 data show that the average unemployment rate for 45 to 54 year-olds with upper secondary education was about the same as that for 25 to 34 year-olds with a university degree.

DESCRIPTION AND INTERPRETATION

In 1992, the overall rate of unemployment was on average 7.6 per cent for 25 to 64 year-olds in OECD countries. The corresponding rate for 25 to 34 year-olds was two percentage points higher, 9.6 per cent. In ten countries, the overall unemployment rate for the latter age group was 10 per cent or above; in Spain it was over 20 per cent.

The average unemployment rate for 25 to 34 year-olds educated at levels below upper secondary was 14.8 per cent, two-and-a-half times as much as for the university-educated in the same age group. In Ireland, the United Kingdom and the United States, those with lower levels of educational attainment had unemployment rates five to six times as high as those for university graduates.

On average, those aged 25 to 34 had an unemployment rate one-and-a-half times as high as that for 45 to 54 year-olds. In Italy, the younger group's rate was almost four times as high. At each educational level, the unemployment rate was higher for the 25 to 34 year-olds than for the 45 to 54 year-olds in practically all countries. (See tables in *OECD Education Statistics, 1985-1992*.)

The two exceptions are Austria and the Netherlands, where the 25-34 age group had a lower unemployment rate than the 45-54 group, both overall and at certain educational levels.

The comparatively high unemployment rates for the 25 to 34 year-olds at each educational level indicate that lack of professional experience weakens the position of this group in the labour market, especially in periods of economic recession with weak labour demand.

DEFINITIONS

The unemployed are defined as persons who are without work, seeking work and currently available for work. The unemployment rate is the number of unemployed as a percentage of the labour force.

R21: Unemployment and education

R21 : Chômage et niveau d'instruction

Table R21(A):
Unemployment rates by level of educational attainment for persons 25 to 64 years of age (1992)

*Tableau R21(A) :
Taux de chômage par niveau d'instruction de la population âgée de 25 à 64 ans (1992)*

	Early childhood, primary and lower secondary education / *Education préscolaire, enseignement primaire et secondaire 1er cycle*	Upper secondary education / *Enseignement secondaire 2e cycle*	Non-university tertiary education / *Enseignement supérieur non universitaire*	University education / *Enseignement supérieur universitaire*	Total / *Total*	
North America						*Amérique du Nord*
Canada	15.1	9.7	9.0	5.2	10.0	*Canada*
United States	13.5	7.2	4.6	2.9	6.6	*Etats-Unis*
Pacific Area						*Pays du Pacifique*
Australia	11.2	8.9	5.7	4.4	8.8	*Australie*
Japan	...	...	...	...	...	*Japon*
New Zealand	11.2	7.5	4.6	3.7	8.0	*Nouvelle-Zélande*
European Community						*Communauté européenne*
Belgium	13.0	4.7	2.3	2.2	7.8	*Belgique*
Denmark	15.6	9.2	5.8	4.8	10.6	*Danemark*
France	12.1	7.4	4.6	4.4	8.8	*France*
Germany	8.9	6.4	4.5	3.7	6.2	*Allemagne*
Greece	...	...	...	...	...	*Grèce*
Ireland	19.8	9.3	5.8	3.3	13.5	*Irlande*
Italy	7.3	8.2	x	6.0	7.4	*Italie*
Luxembourg	...	...	...	...	...	*Luxembourg*
Netherlands	8.0	4.7	x	3.9	5.6	*Pays-Bas*
Portugal *	5.3	4.5	1.9	1.8	4.9	** Portugal*
Spain	16.0	14.1	12.5	9.9	14.7	*Espagne*
United Kingdom	12.3	8.3	3.3	3.6	8.4	*Royaume-Uni*
Other Europe - OECD						*Autres pays d'Europe - OCDE*
Austria	5.6	3.2	x	1.3	3.6	*Autriche*
Finland	14.9	12.1	5.7	3.4	11.4	*Finlande*
Iceland	...	...	...	...	...	*Islande*
Norway	7.1	4.9	2.8	1.8	4.6	*Norvège*
Sweden	4.6	4.3	2.3	2.0	3.8	*Suède*
Switzerland	3.5	2.2	2.3	3.0	2.5	*Suisse*
Turkey	5.1	6.7	x	4.1	5.2	*Turquie*
Country mean	**10.5**	**7.2**	**4.9**	**3.8**	**7.6**	***Moyenne des pays***

See Annex 1 for notes
* 1991 data

Voir notes en annexe 1
* données 1991

R21: Unemployment and education

R21 : Chômage et niveau d'instruction

Chart R21(A):
Unemployment rates by level of educational attainment, both genders (age: 25 to 64) (1992)

Graphique R21(A):
Taux de chômage par niveau d'instruction, hommes et femmes (25 à 64 ans) (1992)

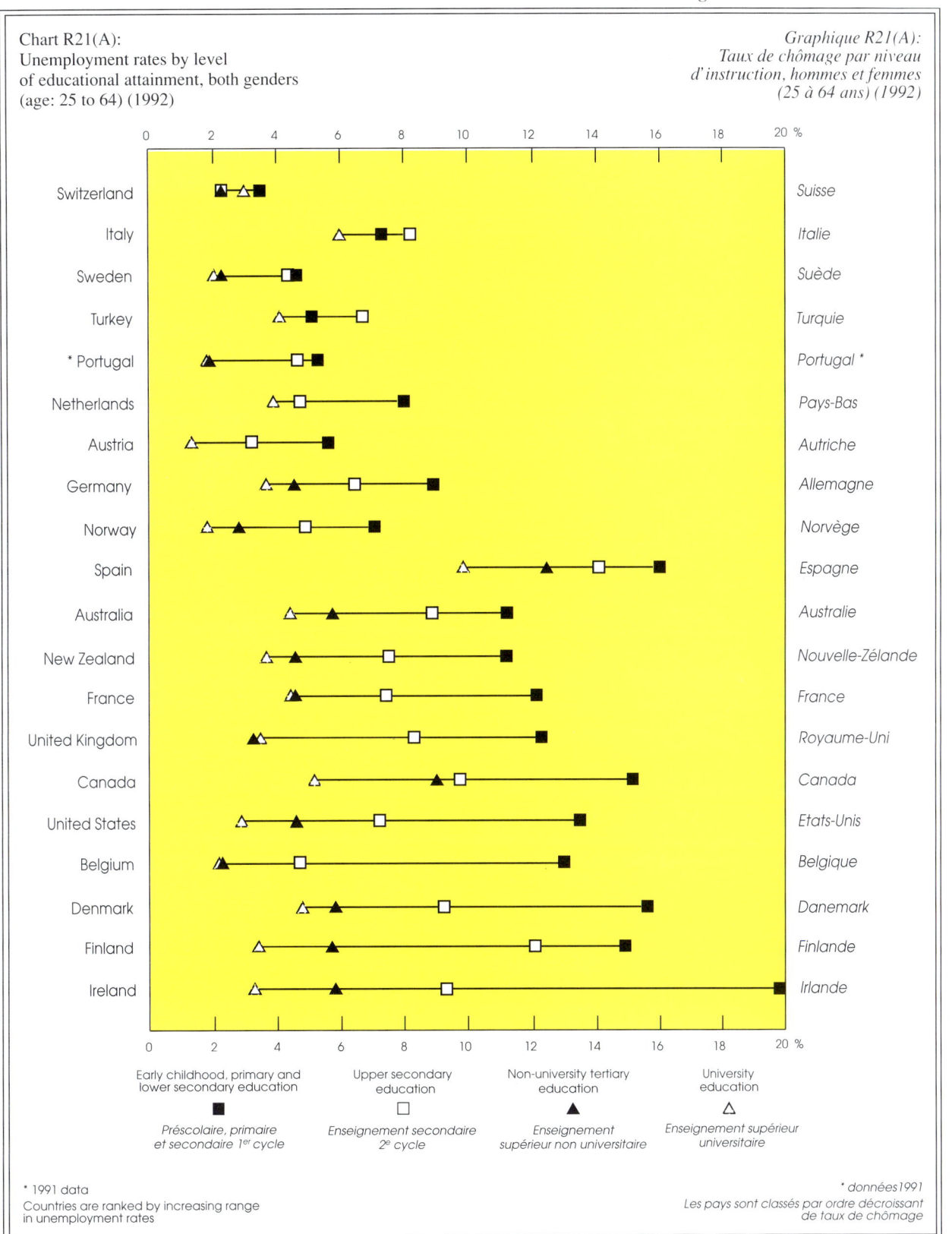

Switzerland		Suisse
Italy		Italie
Sweden		Suède
Turkey		Turquie
*Portugal		Portugal*
Netherlands		Pays-Bas
Austria		Autriche
Germany		Allemagne
Norway		Norvège
Spain		Espagne
Australia		Australie
New Zealand		Nouvelle-Zélande
France		France
United Kingdom		Royaume-Uni
Canada		Canada
United States		Etats-Unis
Belgium		Belgique
Denmark		Danemark
Finland		Finlande
Ireland		Irlande

■ Early childhood, primary and lower secondary education
□ Upper secondary education
▲ Non-university tertiary education
△ University education

■ *Préscolaire, primaire et secondaire 1er cycle*
□ *Enseignement secondaire 2e cycle*
▲ *Enseignement supérieur non universitaire*
△ *Enseignement supérieur universitaire*

* 1991 data
Countries are ranked by increasing range in unemployment rates

* *données 1991*
Les pays sont classés par ordre décroissant de taux de chômage

R21: Unemployment and education

R21 : Chômage et niveau d'instruction

Table R21(B):
Unemployment rates by level
of educational attainment for persons
25 to 34 years of age (1992)

*Tableau R21(B) :
Taux de chômage par niveau
d'instruction de la population âgée
de 25 à 34 ans (1992)*

	Early childhood, primary and lower secondary education / *Education préscolaire, enseignement primaire et secondaire 1er cycle*	Upper secondary education / *Enseignement secondaire 2e cycle*	Non-university tertiary education / *Enseignement supérieur non universitaire*	University education / *Enseignement supérieur universitaire*	Total / *Total*	
North America						*Amérique du Nord*
Canada	20.9	11.9	10.3	6.5	11.9	*Canada*
United States	17.9	8.9	5.7	3.0	8.2	*Etats-Unis*
Pacific Area						*Pays du Pacifique*
Australia	14.7	8.7	5.8	3.7	10.0	*Australie*
Japan	...	...	...	...	...	*Japon*
New Zealand	16.0	8.2	5.6	5.0	10.3	*Nouvelle-Zélande*
European Community						*Communauté européenne*
Belgium	14.8	6.3	3.1	3.4	8.6	*Belgique*
Denmark	23.0	10.5	7.2	7.8	13.6	*Danemark*
France	18.0	9.5	5.6	6.8	11.3	*France*
Germany	10.2	6.1	4.6	4.3	6.1	*Allemagne*
Greece	...	...	...	...	...	*Grèce*
Ireland	25.6	9.7	6.4	5.0	15.0	*Irlande*
Italy	12.9	14.1	x	17.2	13.7	*Italie*
Luxembourg	...	...	...	...	...	*Luxembourg*
Netherlands	8.8	4.2	x	5.2	5.8	*Pays-Bas*
Portugal *	6.6	6.0	2.7	2.5	6.1	** Portugal*
Spain	23.7	18.7	16.7	17.5	21.1	*Espagne*
United Kingdom	21.2	9.8	3.8	3.8	10.2	*Royaume-Uni*
Other Europe - OECD						*Autres pays d'Europe - OCDE*
Austria	6.6	2.6	x	2.2	3.3	*Autriche*
Finland	21.5	13.3	8.1	6.6	13.4	*Finlande*
Iceland	...	...	...	...	...	*Islande*
Norway	12.5	7.4	4.1	2.8	6.8	*Norvège*
Sweden	9.6	6.4	3.2	3.7	6.1	*Suède*
Switzerland	4.5	2.7	2.7	4.8	3.1	*Suisse*
Turkey	7.7	8.0	x	6.9	7.7	*Turquie*
Country mean	**14.8**	**8.7**	**6**	**5.9**	**9.6**	*Moyenne des pays*

See Annex 1 for notes
* 1991 data

Voir notes en annexe 1
* données 1991

R21: Unemployment and education

R21 : Chômage et niveau d'instruction

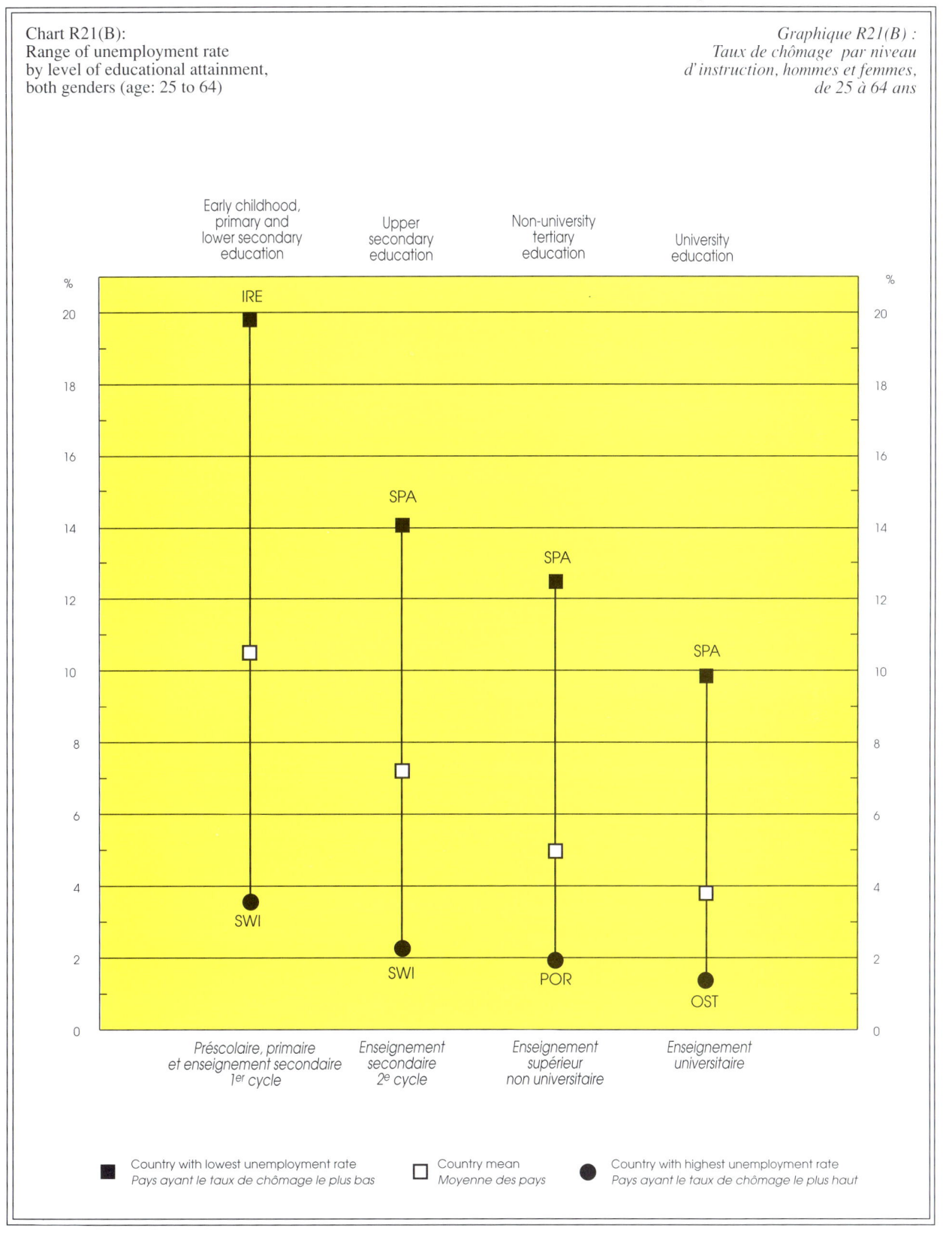

Chart R21(B):
Range of unemployment rate by level of educational attainment, both genders (age: 25 to 64)

Graphique R21(B) :
Taux de chômage par niveau d'instruction, hommes et femmes, de 25 à 64 ans

Level	Country with lowest unemployment rate	Country mean	Country with highest unemployment rate
Early childhood, primary and lower secondary education	IRE ~20	~10.5	SWI ~3.5
Upper secondary education	SPA ~14	~7.2	SWI ~2.3
Non-university tertiary education	SPA ~12.5	~5	POR ~2
University education	SPA ~10	~3.8	OST ~1.5

■ Country with lowest unemployment rate / *Pays ayant le taux de chômage le plus bas*
□ Country mean / *Moyenne des pays*
● Country with highest unemployment rate / *Pays ayant le taux de chômage le plus haut*

R22: Education and earnings

R22(A): EDUCATION AND RELATIVE EARNINGS FROM WORK

POLICY ISSUES

Are the individual and social returns on investment in education satisfactory?

KEY RESULTS

The average annual earnings from work of individuals tend to increase with educational attainment. The earnings advantage of those with higher education and disadvantage of those with less education differ greatly across countries. These findings apply to both men and women.

DESCRIPTION AND INTERPRETATION

Earnings can be considered an outcome of education and a measure of the extent to which it enables the recipient to find and hold gainful employment. Earnings also represent a useful indicator of the value of education, since they are closely associated with other important social outcomes such as health, crime, dependence on social assistance, education of offspring, etc.

University education normally offers a substantial earnings advantage in comparison with upper secondary education. Among men aged 25 to 64, the average earnings of university graduates are normally 45 to 75 per cent higher than the average earnings of those whose highest level of attainment is upper secondary education. In Italy, the Netherlands and New Zealand, however, the earnings advantage of university graduates is much smaller – and in Finland, much larger – than that percentage range.

The earnings advantage for women also lies in the range of 45 to 75 per cent in most countries. It is, however, much smaller in Austria, Denmark and Italy, and considerably larger in Portugal and the United Kingdom. In the United Kingdom many female university graduates earn over twice as much as women educated at the upper secondary level and about three times as much as women with pre-upper secondary education.

In all countries, non-university tertiary education leads to a considerably smaller earnings advantage than university education. Indeed, for men in New Zealand, non-university tertiary education results in a clear earnings *disadvantage* in relation to the earnings of persons educated at upper secondary level.

Women with non-university tertiary education earn on average around 25 per cent more than women with upper secondary education as their highest level. This is not the case in New Zealand, however, where women in the two educational groups receive on average practically the same annual earnings. In the United Kingdom, on the other hand, women with non-university tertiary education earn on average between 50 and 60 per cent more than those educated at upper secondary level.

Persons lacking an upper secondary qualification have on average considerably lower earnings than those educated at upper secondary or higher levels. Men aged 25 to 64 with less than upper secondary qualifications typically earn 10 to 25 per cent less than those who have attained that level. In Portugal and the United States, this difference is as large as around 35 per cent. In Finland, it is as small as 7 per cent.

Among women as well, the typical earnings disadvantage of those lacking upper secondary education is 10 to 25 per cent. As is the case with men, women in Portugal and the United States with pre-upper secondary education earn around 35 per cent less than those educated at upper secondary level; the figure for women in Switzerland is the same.

Portions of these disparities are due to differences in the number of working hours between the educational groups. On average, persons with higher levels of educational attainment tend to have more working hours per year than those with lower levels, which may have to do with these groups' difference in propensity to take on and ability to find full-time work.

DEFINITIONS

Relative earnings from work is defined as the mean annual earnings from work of individuals with a certain level of educational attainment divided by the mean annual earnings from work of individuals whose highest level of education is the upper secondary level. This quotient is then multiplied by 100. Calculations are based solely on persons with incomes from work during the reference period.

R22: Education and earnings

R22 : Niveau d'instruction et salaires

Table R22(A):
Ratio of mean annual earnings by level of educational attainment to mean annual earnings at upper secondary level (times 100) in the population 25 to 64 years of age, by gender (1992)

Tableau R22(A) :
Salaire annuel moyen par niveau d'instruction et par sexe par rapport au salaire annuel moyen de la population âgée de 25 à 64 ans ayant un niveau secondaire du 2ᵉ cycle (×100) (1992)

	Men / Hommes			Women / Femmes			
	Early childhood, primary and lower secondary education	Non-university tertiary education	University education	Early childhood, primary and lower secondary education	Non-university tertiary education	University education	
North America							*Amérique du Nord*
Canada *	81	107	162	72	116	174	* Canada
United States	66	120	164	65	130	170	Etats-Unis
Pacific Area							*Pays du Pacifique*
Australia *	88	121	158	90	124	175	* Australie
Japan	...	...	...	...	...	...	Japon
New Zealand	74	85	118	73	98	154	Nouvelle-Zélande
European Community							*Communauté européenne*
Belgium	86	115	149	78	137	164	Belgique
Denmark *	86	110	146	86	111	135	* Danemark
France	87	127	174	81	131	142	France
Germany	88	116	170	84	114	175	Allemagne
Greece	...	...	...	...	...	...	Grèce
Ireland	...	...	...	...	...	...	Irlande
Italy *	84	x	134	86	x	116	* Italie
Luxembourg	...	...	...	...	...	...	Luxembourg
Netherlands	84	x	132	73	x	147	Pays-Bas
Portugal **	65	124	179	67	117	188	** Portugal
Spain *	78	x	138	71	x	149	* Espagne
United Kingdom	80	121	171	70	156	206	Royaume-Uni
Other Europe - OECD							*Autres pays d'Europe - OCDE*
Austria	85	x	146	81	x	134	Autriche
Finland *	93	132	192	94	132	176	* Finlande
Iceland	...	...	...	...	...	...	Islande
Norway	80	131	165	76	131	157	Norvège
Sweden	88	118	160	92	119	156	Suède
Switzerland	76	127	152	67	126	152	Suisse
Turkey	...	...	...	...	...	...	Turquie

See Annex 1 for notes
* 1991 data
** 1993 data

Voir notes en annexe 1
* données 1991
** données 1993

R22: Education and earnings

R22 : Niveau d'instruction et salaires

Chart R22(A1):
Relative earnings by level of educational attainment for men 25 to 64 years of age (1992)

Graphique R22(A1) :
Salaires relatifs selon le niveau d'instruction des hommes de 25 à 64 ans (1992)

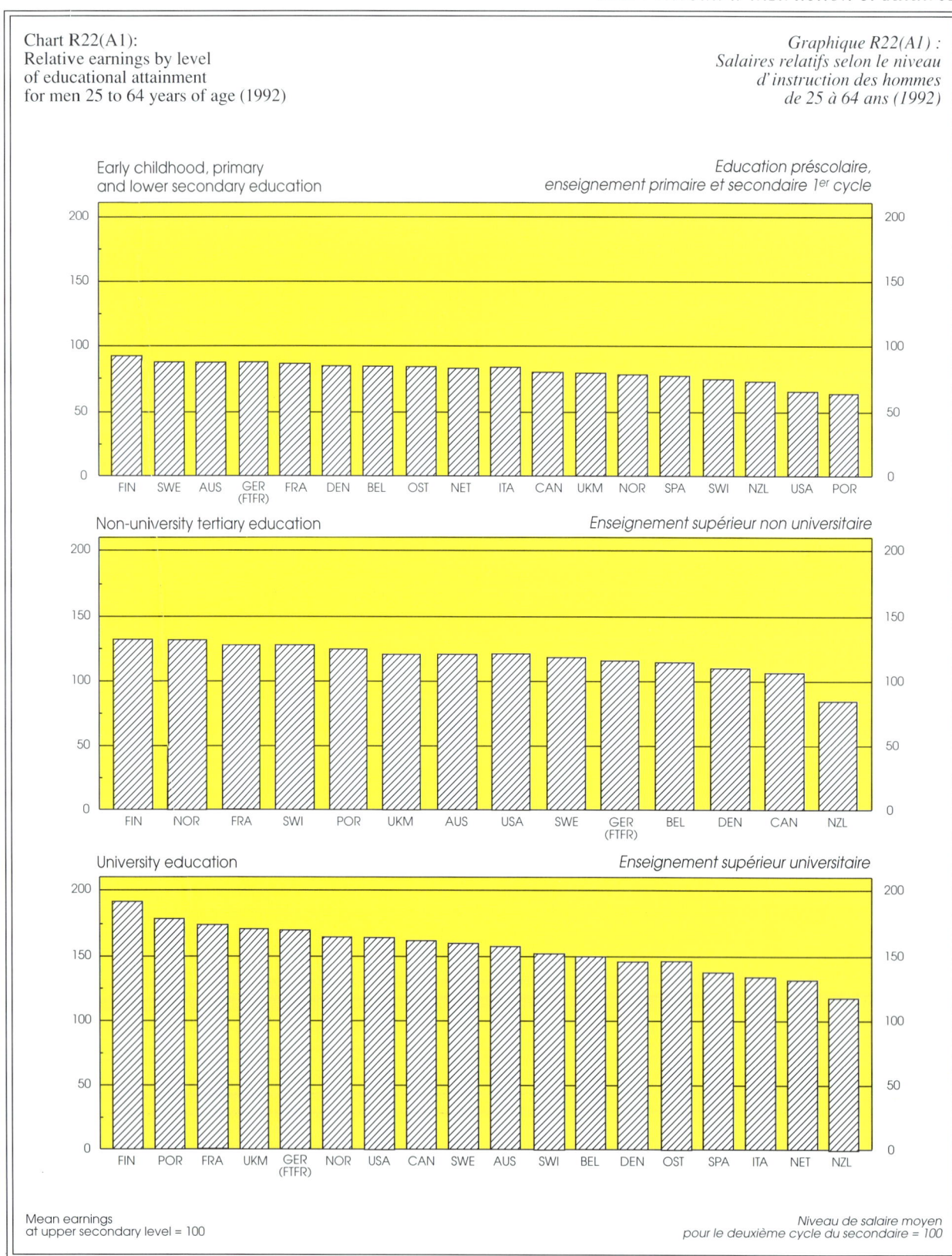

Early childhood, primary and lower secondary education
Education préscolaire, enseignement primaire et secondaire 1er cycle

FIN, SWE, AUS, GER (FTFR), FRA, DEN, BEL, OST, NET, ITA, CAN, UKM, NOR, SPA, SWI, NZL, USA, POR

Non-university tertiary education
Enseignement supérieur non universitaire

FIN, NOR, FRA, SWI, POR, UKM, AUS, USA, SWE, GER (FTFR), BEL, DEN, CAN, NZL

University education
Enseignement supérieur universitaire

FIN, POR, FRA, UKM, GER (FTFR), NOR, USA, CAN, SWE, AUS, SWI, BEL, DEN, OST, SPA, ITA, NET, NZL

Mean earnings at upper secondary level = 100

Niveau de salaire moyen pour le deuxième cycle du secondaire = 100

R22: Education and earnings

R22 : Niveau d'instruction et salaires

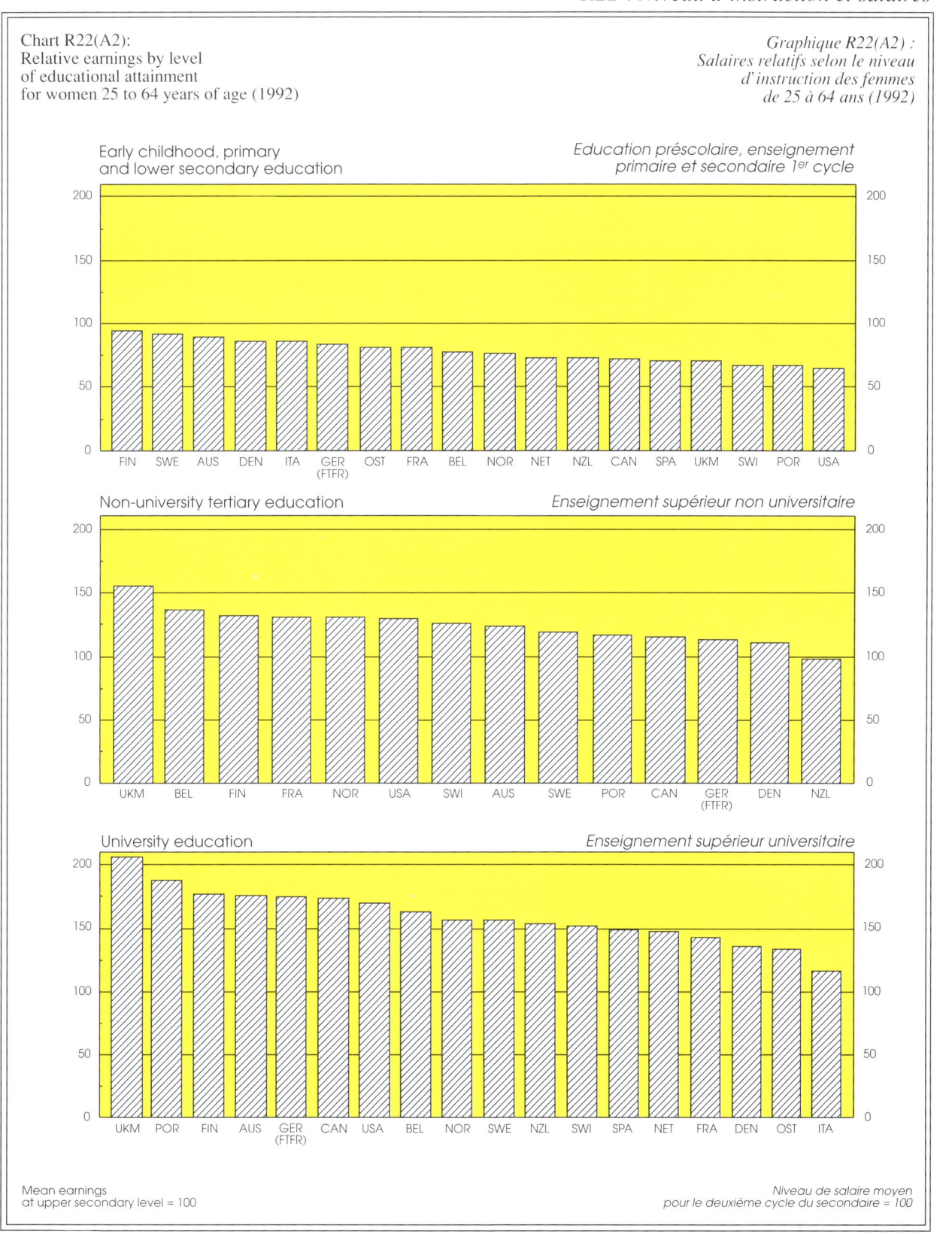

Chart R22(A2):
Relative earnings by level
of educational attainment
for women 25 to 64 years of age (1992)

*Graphique R22(A2) :
Salaires relatifs selon le niveau
d'instruction des femmes
de 25 à 64 ans (1992)*

Early childhood, primary and lower secondary education

Education préscolaire, enseignement primaire et secondaire 1er cycle

Non-university tertiary education

Enseignement supérieur non universitaire

University education

Enseignement supérieur universitaire

Mean earnings at upper secondary level = 100

Niveau de salaire moyen pour le deuxième cycle du secondaire = 100

R22: Education and earnings

R22(B): WOMEN'S EARNINGS FROM WORK COMPARED TO MEN'S EARNINGS FROM WORK

POLICY ISSUES

To what extent do such factors as tradition and bargaining power play a role in the setting of wage rates – and the establishment of earnings differentials?

KEY RESULTS

Women's annual earnings from work are less than those of men. Between the ages of 25 and 64, women earn around 50 to 75 per cent of what men earn. Part of this difference is due to the incidence of part-time work, which is higher among women than among men. There is a slight tendency for the difference to be somewhat smaller among those educated at upper secondary or tertiary level than among those educated at levels below upper secondary. Again, part-time work may be a factor; the proportion of those working part-time is normally smaller among those with upper secondary or tertiary education than among those with lower levels.

DESCRIPTION AND INTERPRETATION

All employed women aged 25 to 64 earn on average annually around 60 per cent of the earnings of men in the same age group, in the reporting countries. In three countries – the Netherlands, Switzerland and the United Kingdom – the average earnings of women are just below 50 per cent of the earnings of men. At the upper end, this percentage is around 75 per cent in four countries – Austria, Finland, France and Italy.

Differences tend to be greater at lower levels of education than at higher levels. This is best illustrated in the figures for New Zealand and the United Kingdom. In New Zealand the annual earnings of women are 51 per cent of those of men at educational levels below upper secondary, whereas the corresponding figure for university graduates is 68 per cent. In the United Kingdom the respective figures are 43 and 59 per cent.

Exceptions to this general pattern can be seen in Austria, Denmark, Finland, France, Italy and Sweden, where the relative earnings of women are the lowest among those who have attained a university education.

In examining these data, it is important to remember that total earnings differentials are not influenced solely by pay rates. Differences in the proportions of the population working either part-time or part-year are also a major factor. To a significant extent, differences in the earnings of men and women reflect different levels of participation in the labour market.

DEFINITIONS

The relative earnings of women compared to the earnings of men are calculated by dividing the average earnings of women with a given level of educational attainment by the average earnings of men with the same educational level, and then multiplying by 100. The earnings data refer solely to incomes from work and solely to persons with such incomes during the reference period.

R22: Education and earnings

R22 : Niveau d'instruction et salaires

Table R22(B):
Ratio of mean annual earnings of women
to those of men (times 100)
for the age group 25 to 64,
by level of educational attainment (1992)

*Tableau R22(B) :
Salaire annuel moyen des femmes
par rapport à celui des hommes (×100)
par niveau d'instruction, population âgée
de 25 à 64 ans (1992)*

	Early childhood, primary and lower secondary education / *Education préscolaire, enseignement primaire et secondaire 1er cycle*	Upper secondary education / *Enseignement secondaire 2e cycle*	Non-university tertiary education / *Enseignement supérieur non universitaire*	University education / *Enseignement supérieur universitaire*	Total / *Total*	
North America						*Amérique du Nord*
Canada *	53	59	64	63	61	** Canada*
United States	59	60	65	62	61	*Etats-Unis*
Pacific Area						*Pays du Pacifique*
Australia *	57	56	57	62	57	** Australie*
Japan	...	...	...	...	...	*Japon*
New Zealand	51	52	60	68	55	*Nouvelle-Zélande*
European Community						*Communauté européenne*
Belgium	50	55	66	61	58	*Belgique*
Denmark *	71	71	72	66	70	** Danemark*
France	72	77	79	63	74	*France*
Germany	58	62	60	63	58	*Allemagne*
Greece	...	...	...	...	...	*Grèce*
Ireland	...	...	...	...	...	*Irlande*
Italy *	75	74	x	64	76	** Italie*
Luxembourg	...	...	...	...	...	*Luxembourg*
Netherlands	42	49	x	54	49	*Pays-Bas*
Portugal **	72	69	66	73	72	*** Portugal*
Spain *	58	64	x	69	67	** Espagne*
United Kingdom	43	49	63	59	49	*Royaume-Uni*
Other Europe - OECD						*Autres pays d'Europe - OCDE*
Austria	80	83	x	76	77	*Autriche*
Finland *	80	78	78	72	76	** Finlande*
Iceland	...	...	...	...	...	*Islande*
Norway	58	61	61	58	59	*Norvège*
Sweden	70	68	68	66	68	*Suède*
Switzerland	47	53	53	53	48	*Suisse*
Turkey	...	...	...	...	...	*Turquie*

See Annex 1 for notes
* 1991 data
** 1993 data

*Voir notes en annexe 1
* données 1991
** données 1993*

R22: Education and earnings

R22 : Niveau d'instruction et salaires

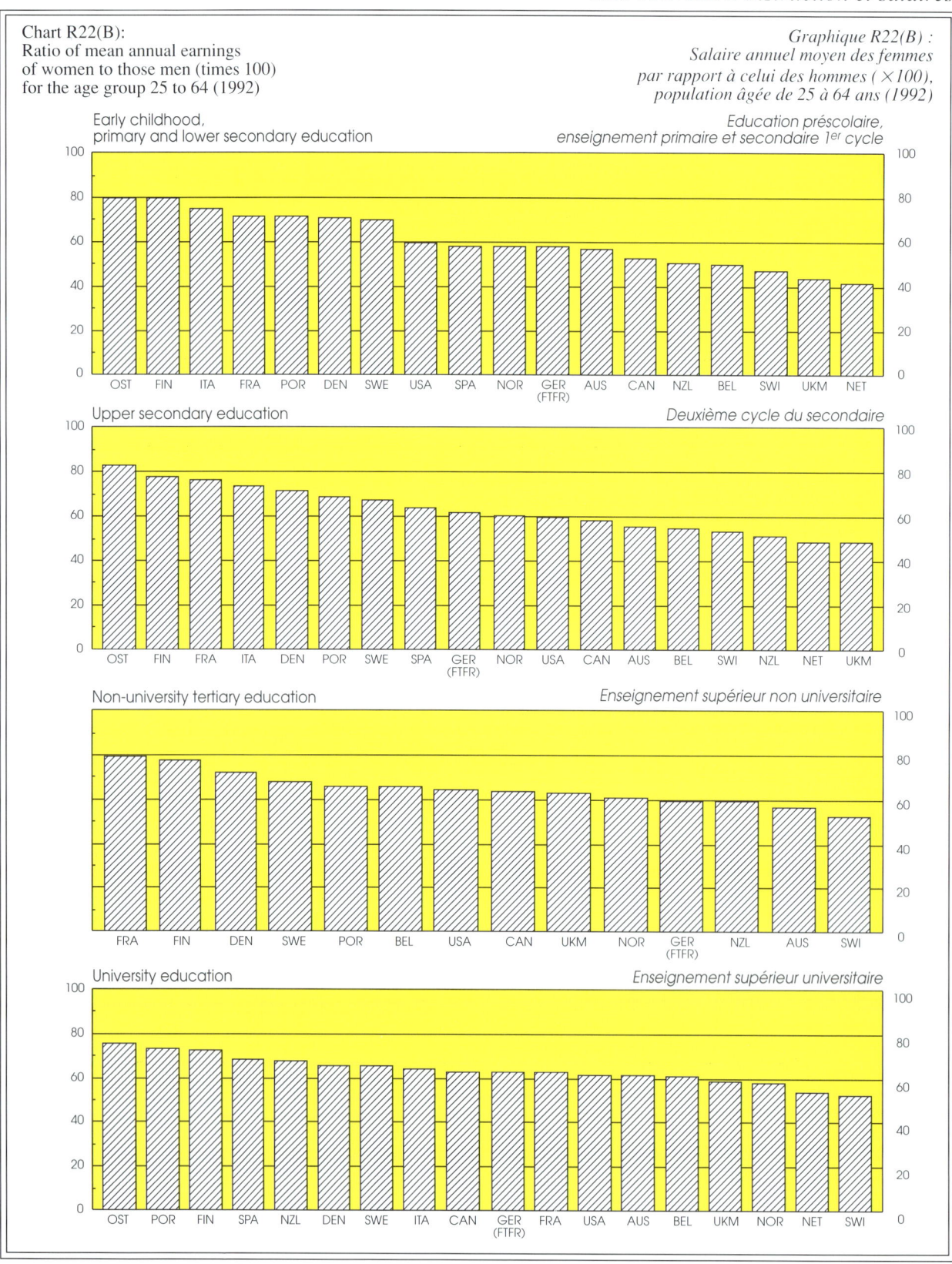

Chart R22(B):
Ratio of mean annual earnings of women to those men (times 100) for the age group 25 to 64 (1992)

Graphique R22(B) :
Salaire annuel moyen des femmes par rapport à celui des hommes (×100), population âgée de 25 à 64 ans (1992)

Early childhood, primary and lower secondary education — *Education préscolaire, enseignement primaire et secondaire 1er cycle*

OST, FIN, ITA, FRA, POR, DEN, SWE, USA, SPA, NOR, GER (FTFR), AUS, CAN, NZL, BEL, SWI, UKM, NET

Upper secondary education — *Deuxième cycle du secondaire*

OST, FIN, FRA, ITA, DEN, POR, SWE, SPA, GER (FTFR), NOR, USA, CAN, AUS, BEL, SWI, NZL, NET, UKM

Non-university tertiary education — *Enseignement supérieur non universitaire*

FRA, FIN, DEN, SWE, POR, BEL, USA, CAN, UKM, NOR, GER (FTFR), NZL, AUS, SWI

University education — *Enseignement supérieur universitaire*

OST, POR, FIN, SPA, NZL, DEN, SWE, ITA, CAN, GER (FTFR), FRA, USA, AUS, BEL, UKM, NOR, NET, SWI

R23: Educational attainment of workers

R23(A): YEARS OF EDUCATION COMPLETED BY WORKERS IN SELECTED OCCUPATIONS

POLICY ISSUES

Is the productivity of a worker employed in a particular occupation partly influenced by the amount and type of his or her education? Are workers with more education able to adapt to changing technology more quickly than those with less education, thus reducing the cost to employers of change-overs to new technology?

KEY RESULTS

Occupations differ substantially in the amount of education they require, as measured by the years of education index. For four of the nine occupations for which data were collected, this index varies by 5.7 or more years across the 14 OECD countries. For example, the index for life science and health associate professionals ranges from 11 years in Italy to 17 years in Spain. For workers in precision, handicraft, printing and related trades, the index ranges from 6.5 years in Spain to 12.3 in Switzerland. While this variation may indicate substantial differences across countries in the mix of specific occupations within the broader categories listed, it more likely relates to differences in the duration of education required to prepare for specific occupations.

Generally, the years of education index varies less across countries for a particular occupation than across occupations either within a country or for the OECD countries as a whole. For example, the years index for corporate managers varies from 11.8 years in New Zealand to 16.0 years in Italy, a range of 4.2 years. However, for 12 OECD countries the average index varies from 9.4 for plant and machine operators and assemblers to 15.5 for architects, engineers and related professionals, a range of 6.1 years.

Some countries show little variation in years of education across the occupation groups; others show a great deal. In Sweden, for example, the index varies by 3.8 years: from 10.5 for drivers and mobile plant operators to 14.3 for computing professionals. On the other hand, in Spain the index varies by 11.1 years from 5.9 for drivers, mobile plant operators and workers in extraction and building trades, to 17 for computing professionals, architects, engineers and life science and health associate professionals. These differences may be due to the fact that in countries such as Sweden, a higher proportion of working adults have completed at least compulsory education – thus reducing the gap in years of schooling for workers in different occupations.

DESCRIPTION AND INTERPRETATION

A variety of factors may give rise to variations in the average years of schooling for different occupations, including the general educational attainment of the population, the period of study and the intensity of the curriculum for specific occupations. These factors need to be considered if the indicator is to be interpreted accurately.

There may be comparability problems in the way occupations are defined across countries. Many OECD countries do not use the International Standard Classification of Occupations (ISCO) in their labour force surveys, relying instead on rough classification equivalents. This invariably leads to difficulties: occupations are grouped together even in the most detailed categories of the national taxonomy and cannot be separated to meet ISCO group requirements, even the aggregated ones used here. The resulting degree of error is likely to vary across countries.

DEFINITIONS

This indicator summarises the amount of education workers have completed in an index of years; it is thus a measure of the time investment workers have made to acquire their education credentials. For each country and occupation group, the index is calculated by multiplying the fraction of workers in the occupation group who have completed a particular level of education by the typical years required to complete that level, adding the totals across the levels of the International Standard Classification of Education (ISCED).

R23: Educational attainment of workers

R23 : Niveau d'instruction des travailleurs

Table R23(A1):
Years of education index of 35 to 54 year-old employed workers in selected occupations (1992)

Tableau R23(A1) :
Indice des années d'études des travailleurs de 35 à 54 ans occupés dans certains métiers (1992)

	Corporate managers (ISCO 12)	Computing professionals (ISCO 213)	Architects, engineers and related professionals (ISCO 214)	Physical and engineering science associate professionals (ISCO 31)	Life science and health associate professionals (ISCO 32)	Extraction and building trade workers (ISCO 71)	Precision, handicraft, printing and related trades workers (ISCO 73)	Plant and machine operators and assemblers (ISCO 80)	Drivers and mobile-plant operators (ISCO 83)	
North America										*Amérique du Nord*
Canada	13.6	14.9	16.1	13.0	13.7	11.4	10.5	...	10.5	*Canada*
United States	15.1	15.4	16.0	13.7	14.7	11.8	11.5	11.2	11.5	*Etats-Unis*
Pacific Area										*Pays du Pacifique*
Australia	...	...	...	...	...	...	...	...	...	*Australie*
Japan	...	...	...	...	...	...	...	...	...	*Japon*
New Zealand	11.8	14.7	15.0	13.3	14.3	11.2	10.5	8.8	8.5	*Nouvelle-Zélande*
European Community										*Communauté européenne*
Belgium	...	...	...	...	...	...	...	...	...	*Belgique*
Denmark	12.8	12.8	15.4	12.2	13.8	11.7	11.4	9.5	9.9	*Danemark*
France	13.1	14.8	14.4	11.4	13.3	8.9	10.2	7.5	8.4	*France*
Germany	14.5	16.6	16.4	13.2	12.8	11.7	11.6	10.2	11.1	*Allemagne*
Germany (FTFR)	...	...	...	...	...	...	...	...	...	*Allemagne (ex-terr. de la RFA)*
Greece	...	...	...	...	...	...	...	...	...	*Grèce*
Ireland	12.0	...	13.7	...	12.9	8.4	9.0	8.0	7.7	*Irlande*
Italy	16.0	16.0	16.0	12.3	11.0	7.8	8.7	...	8.2	*Italie*
Luxembourg	...	...	...	...	...	...	...	...	...	*Luxembourg*
Netherlands	12.7	14.2	14.2	12.0	12.5	9.9	9.5	9.0	9.1	*Pays-Bas*
Portugal	...	...	...	...	...	...	...	...	...	*Portugal*
Spain	12.0	17.0	17.0	12.1	17.0	5.9	6.5	6.2	5.9	*Espagne*
United Kingdom	13.4	15.5	15.6	14.1	12.7	12.1	11.8	11.2	11.6	*Royaume-Uni*
Other Europe - OECD										*Autres pays d'Europe - OCDE*
Austria	...	...	...	...	...	...	...	...	...	*Autriche*
Finland	14.3	14.3	17.4	13.0	12.4	10.4	10.4	10.0	9.9	*Finlande*
Iceland	...	...	...	...	...	...	...	...	...	*Islande*
Norway	...	...	...	...	...	...	...	...	...	*Norvège*
Sweden	12.9	14.3	12.8	11.3	13.6	10.9	11.0	10.6	10.5	*Suède*
Switzerland	13.7	14.7	16.8	13.3	13.4	11.7	12.3	10.7	10.6	*Suisse*
Turkey	...	...	...	...	...	...	...	...	...	*Turquie*
Country mean	**13.4**	**15.0**	**15.5**	**12.7**	**13.4**	**10.3**	**10.3**	**9.4**	**9.5**	*Moyenne des pays*

See Annex 1 for notes

Voir notes en annexe 1

R23: Educational attainment of workers

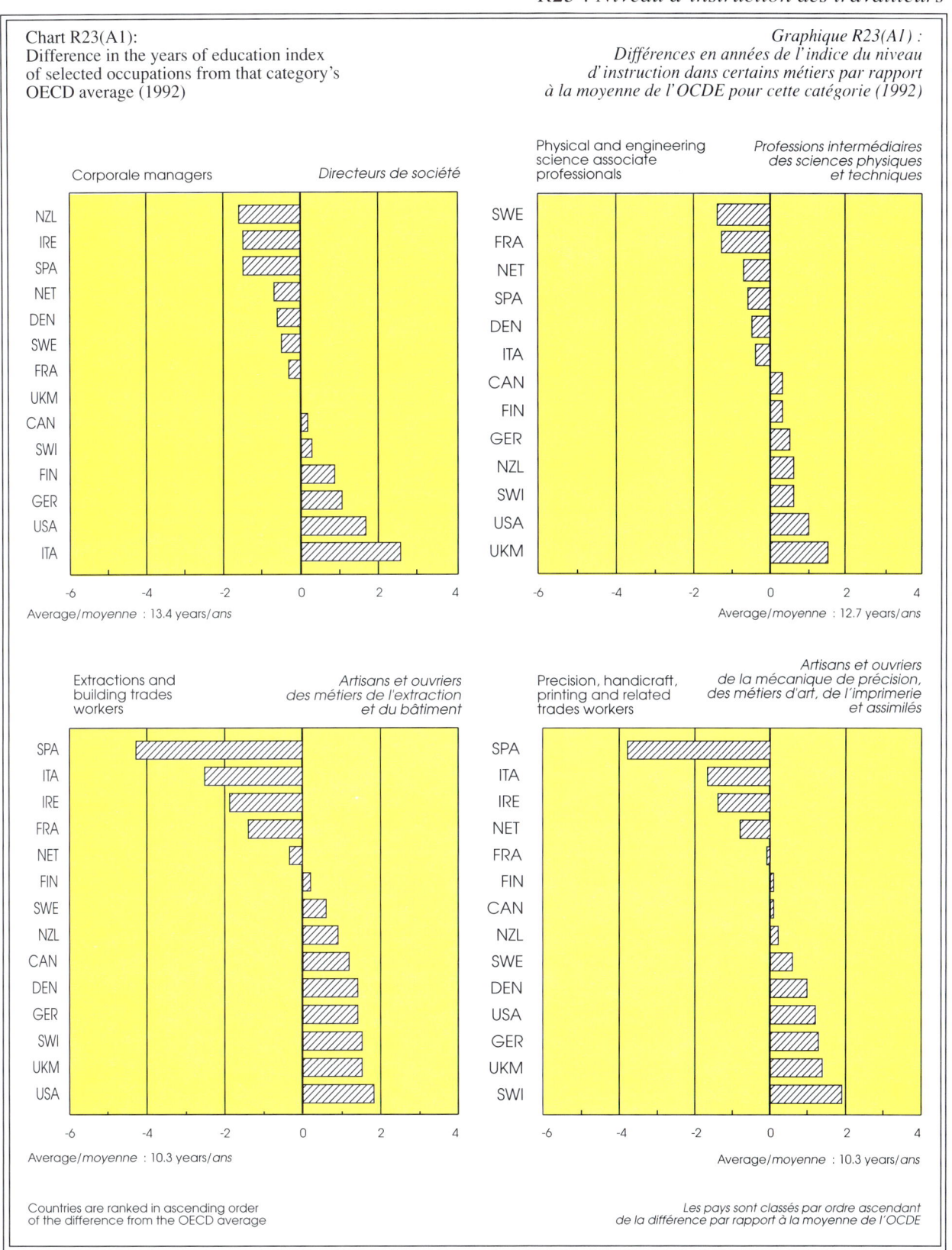

R23 : Niveau d'instruction des travailleurs

Chart R23(A1):
Difference in the years of education index of selected occupations from that category's OECD average (1992)

Graphique R23(A1) :
Différences en années de l'indice du niveau d'instruction dans certains métiers par rapport à la moyenne de l'OCDE pour cette catégorie (1992)

Corporate managers — *Directeurs de société*

Average/*moyenne* : 13.4 years/*ans*

Physical and engineering science associate professionals — *Professions intermédiaires des sciences physiques et techniques*

Average/*moyenne* : 12.7 years/*ans*

Extractions and building trades workers — *Artisans et ouvriers des métiers de l'extraction et du bâtiment*

Average/*moyenne* : 10.3 years/*ans*

Precision, handicraft, printing and related trades workers — *Artisans et ouvriers de la mécanique de précision, des métiers d'art, de l'imprimerie et assimilés*

Average/*moyenne* : 10.3 years/*ans*

Countries are ranked in ascending order of the difference from the OECD average

Les pays sont classés par ordre ascendant de la différence par rapport à la moyenne de l'OCDE

R23: Educational attainment of workers

R23 : Niveau d'instruction des travailleurs

Table R23(A2):
Percentage of 35 to 54 year-old employed workers in selected occupations (1992)

Tableau R23(A2) : Pourcentage de travailleurs de 35 à 54 ans occupés dans certains métiers (1992)

	Corporate managers (ISCO 12)	Computing professionals (ISCO 213)	Architects, engineers and related professionals (ISCO 214)	Physical and engineering science associate professionals (ISCO 31)	Life science and health associate professionals (ISCO 32)	Extraction and building trade workers (ISCO 71)	Precision, handicraft, printing and related trades workers (ISCO 73)	Plant and machine operators and assemblers (ISCO 80)	Drivers and mobile-plant operators (ISCO 83)	
North America										*Amérique du Nord*
Canada	6.2	1.0	1.1	3.6	5.4	4.0	3.0	...	3.6	*Canada*
United States	4.7	1.3	1.9	2.5	6.5	3.9	1.9	6.3	4.1	*Etats-Unis*
Pacific Area										*Pays du Pacifique*
Australia	...	...	...	...	...	...	...	...	...	*Australie*
Japan	...	...	...	...	...	...	...	...	...	*Japon*
New Zealand	14.5	0.2	1.3	2.8	1.0	4.3	1.3	5.7	3.2	*Nouvelle-Zélande*
European Community										*Communauté européenne*
Belgium	...	...	...	...	...	...	...	...	...	*Belgique*
Denmark	3.5	0.4	2.2	3.8	3.2	4.3	1.0	1.1	3.2	*Danemark*
France	5.3	0.7	2.2	3.6	2.5	6.2	0.5	0.5	4.0	*France*
Germany	3.4	0.3	3.0	4.7	2.3	6.1	1.2	4.4	4.1	*Allemagne*
Germany (FTFR)	...	...	...	...	...	...	...	...	...	*Allemagne (ex-terr. de la RFA)*
Greece	...	...	...	...	...	...	...	...	...	*Grèce*
Ireland	...	...	...	...	...	...	...	...	...	*Irlande*
Italy	0.2	...	0.8	2.9	1.9	5.9	1.2	...	4.0	*Italie*
Luxembourg	...	...	...	...	...	...	...	...	...	*Luxembourg*
Netherlands	7.2	1.1	2.3	3.3	3.1	4.4	0.8	7.1	3.8	*Pays-Bas*
Portugal	...	...	...	...	...	...	...	...	...	*Portugal*
Spain	2.3	0.2	1.3	1.1	0.1	8.4	1.1	12.3	3.2	*Espagne*
United Kingdom	17.2	0.8	2.7	2.0	1.4	5.5	1.0	8.6	4.0	*Royaume-Uni*
Other Europe - OECD										*Autres pays d'Europe - OCDE*
Austria	...	...	...	...	...	...	...	...	...	*Autriche*
Finland	3.4	0.6	2.3	5.9	3.4	3.6	1.2	8.8	5.2	*Finlande*
Iceland	...	...	...	...	...	...	...	...	...	*Islande*
Norway	...	...	...	...	...	...	...	...	...	*Norvège*
Sweden	1.4	0.1	0.8	0.1	1.0	0.4	0.1	1.5	0.5	*Suède*
Switzerland	8.9	1.1	1.7	3.7	2.4	5.3	1.1	4.8	2.5	*Suisse*
Turkey	...	...	...	...	...	...	...	...	...	*Turquie*
Country mean	**6.0**	**0.7**	**1.8**	**3.1**	**2.6**	**4.8**	**1.2**	**5.6**	**3.5**	***Moyenne des pays***

See Annex 1 for notes

Voir notes en annexe 1

R23: Educational attainment of workers

R23(B): YEARS OF EDUCATION COMPLETED BY WORKERS IN SELECTED INDUSTRIES

POLICY ISSUES

The increasing globalisation of markets will likely lead to faster employment growth in industries using sophisticated technology – and therefore requiring more highly skilled workers. If more years of education are a key element in building the skills pool behind these industries, what conclusions can be drawn from index comparisons with the same industries in other countries? Do gaps suggest shifts in comparative economic advantage?

KEY RESULTS

Among industry groups, the years of education index shows the highest degree of variation in computers and related activities: from 9.7 in Spain to 15.5 in the United Kingdom. The group category of health and social work shows the least variation: from 11.2 in Ireland to 14.1 in the United States. Both of these groups have workers with high average years of education.

The computers and related activities industry group is relatively young – that is, the firms involved are relatively young. In both Spain and the United Kingdom, however, the industry has an above-average share of total employment (3.3 and 2.1 per cent, respectively). Because firms in this group are relatively new, education credentials for their workers are not yet well established. In contrast, health and social work is a mature industry group, and education credentials are well established.

Among the five industries presented in this indicator, the variation in the years of education index is only 0.7 years in Denmark, but 4.3 in Portugal. This difference may be due to a variety of factors, including the fact that in countries such as Denmark a higher proportion of working adults have completed at least compulsory education.

DESCRIPTION AND INTERPRETATION

See R23(A).

DEFINITIONS

The definition of industries is based upon the International Standard Classification of Industries.

R23: Educational attainment of workers

R23 : Niveau d'instruction des travailleurs

Table R23(B1):
Years of education index
of 35 to 54 year-old employed
workers in selected industries (1992)

*Tableau R23(B1) :
Indice des années d'études
des travailleurs de 35 à 54 ans
occupés dans certains secteurs d'activité (1992)*

	Manufacture of chemicals and chemical products (ISIC 24) / *Fabrication de produits chimiques*	Manufacture of office, accounting and computing machinery (ISIC 30) / *Fabrication de machines et de matériel NCA*	Computers and related activities (ISIC 72) / *Activités informatiques et activités connexes*	Public administration and defence (ISIC 75) / *Administration publique et défense*	Health and social work (ISIC 85) / *Santé et action sociale*	
North America						*Amérique du Nord*
Canada	13.7	14.0	15.0	13.5	13.5	*Canada*
United States	13.7	14.7	13.0	14.1	14.1	*Etats-Unis*
Pacific Area						*Pays du Pacifique*
Australia	...	...	...	...	...	*Australie*
Japan	...	...	...	...	...	*Japon*
New Zealand	10.9	12.6	13.4	12.6	13.0	*Nouvelle-Zélande*
European Community						*Communauté européenne*
Belgium	...	...	...	...	...	*Belgique*
Denmark	11.9	12.3	12.6	12.4	12.1	*Danemark*
France	10.8	13.1	14.1	10.8	11.8	*France*
Germany	12.5	12.0	13.0	13.1	13.6	*Allemagne*
Germany (FTFR)	...	...	...	...	...	*Allemagne (ex-terr. de la RFA)*
Greece	...	...	...	...	...	*Grèce*
Ireland	10.6	9.5	...	10.7	11.2	*Irlande*
Italy	10.1	11.0	12.8	11.4	12.3	*Italie*
Luxembourg	...	...	...	...	...	*Luxembourg*
Netherlands	12.0	12.2	13.4	12.8	12.9	*Pays-Bas*
Portugal	8.9	9.8	13.2	9.4	11.3	*Portugal*
Spain	9.6	12.9	9.7	10.3	12.0	*Espagne*
United Kingdom	12.8	12.7	15.5	13.3	13.3	*Royaume-Uni*
Other Europe - OECD						*Autres pays d'Europe - OCDE*
Austria	...	...	...	...	...	*Autriche*
Finland	12.2	12.9	13.8	13.1	12.7	*Finlande*
Iceland	...	...	...	...	...	*Islande*
Norway	...	...	...	...	...	*Norvège*
Sweden	...	...	...	...	...	*Suède*
Switzerland	13.1	13.1	14.7	13.6	13.3	*Suisse*
Turkey	...	...	...	...	...	*Turquie*
Country mean	**11.6**	**12.3**	**13.4**	**12.2**	**12.7**	*Moyenne des pays*

See Annex 1 for notes

Voir notes en annexe 1

R23: Educational attainment of workers

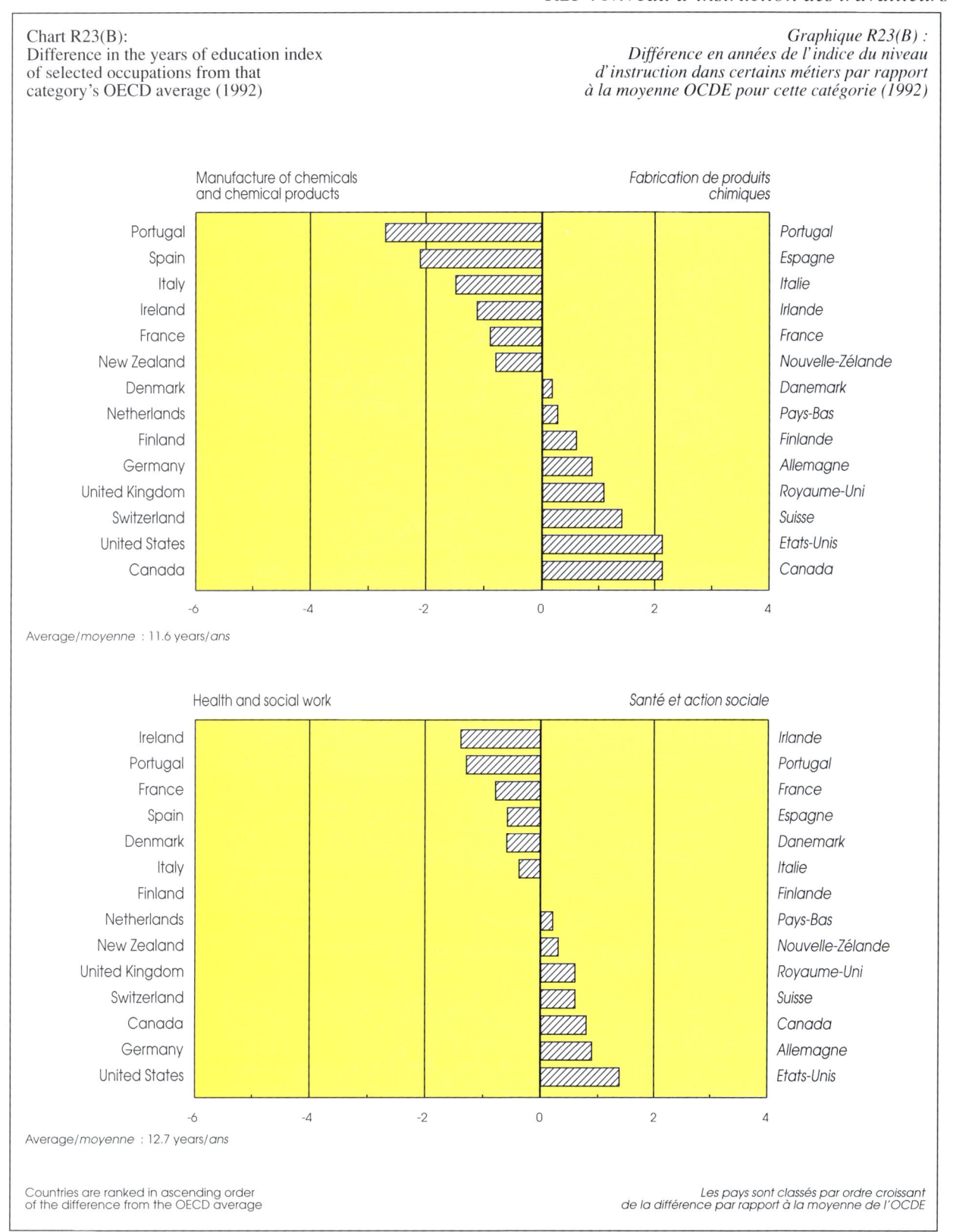

R23 : Niveau d'instruction des travailleurs

Chart R23(B):
Difference in the years of education index of selected occupations from that category's OECD average (1992)

Graphique R23(B) :
Différence en années de l'indice du niveau d'instruction dans certains métiers par rapport à la moyenne OCDE pour cette catégorie (1992)

Manufacture of chemicals and chemical products / Fabrication de produits chimiques

Portugal	Portugal
Spain	Espagne
Italy	Italie
Ireland	Irlande
France	France
New Zealand	Nouvelle-Zélande
Denmark	Danemark
Netherlands	Pays-Bas
Finland	Finlande
Germany	Allemagne
United Kingdom	Royaume-Uni
Switzerland	Suisse
United States	Etats-Unis
Canada	Canada

Average/*moyenne* : 11.6 years/*ans*

Health and social work / Santé et action sociale

Ireland	Irlande
Portugal	Portugal
France	France
Spain	Espagne
Denmark	Danemark
Italy	Italie
Finland	Finlande
Netherlands	Pays-Bas
New Zealand	Nouvelle-Zélande
United Kingdom	Royaume-Uni
Switzerland	Suisse
Canada	Canada
Germany	Allemagne
United States	Etats-Unis

Average/*moyenne* : 12.7 years/*ans*

Countries are ranked in ascending order of the difference from the OECD average

Les pays sont classés par ordre croissant de la différence par rapport à la moyenne de l'OCDE

R23: Educational attainment of workers

R23 : Niveau d'instruction des travailleurs

Table R23(B2):
Percentage of 35 to 54 year-old employed workers in selected industries (1992)

Tableau R23(B2) :
Pourcentage de travailleurs de 35 à 54 ans occupés dans certains secteurs d'activité (1992)

	Manufacture of chemicals and chemical products (ISIC 24)	Manufacture of office, accounting and computing machinery (ISIC 30)	Computers and related activities (ISIC 72)	Public administration and defence (ISIC 75)	Health and social work (ISIC 85)	
North America						*Amérique du Nord*
Canada	0.9	0.3	0.5	7.6	11.3	*Canada*
United States	1.4	0.6	0.3	5.8	11.3	*Etats-Unis*
Pacific Area						*Pays du Pacifique*
Australia	...	...	...	...	...	*Australie*
Japan	...	...	...	...	...	*Japon*
New Zealand	0.6	0.1	0.5	5.5	8.0	*Nouvelle-Zélande*
European Community						*Communauté européenne*
Belgium	...	...	...	...	...	*Belgique*
Denmark	1.0	0.1	0.7	7.6	17.9	*Danemark*
France	1.4	0.2	0.5	10.8	10.1	*France*
Germany	2.6	1.7	1.1	9.1	13.4	*Allemagne*
Germany (FTFR)	...	...	...	...	...	*Allemagne (ex- terr. de la RFA)*
Greece	...	...	...	...	...	*Grèce*
Ireland	...	...	...	...	...	*Irlande*
Italy	1.4	0.4	0.5	8.4	6.1	*Italie*
Luxembourg	...	...	...	...	...	*Luxembourg*
Netherlands	2.0	1.8	5.3	8.7	13.3	*Pays-Bas*
Portugal	...	...	...	...	...	*Portugal*
Spain	1.2	0.1	3.3	6.5	4.7	*Espagne*
United Kingdom	2.1	0.1	2.1	4.7	13.4	*Royaume-Uni*
Other Europe - OECD						*Autres pays d'Europe*
Austria	...	...	...	...	...	*Autriche*
Finland	1.0	...	0.6	5.7	12.1	*Finlande*
Iceland	...	...	...	...	...	*Islande*
Norway	...	...	...	...	...	*Norvège*
Sweden	...	...	...	...	...	*Suède*
Switzerland	1.7	0.1	0.5	4.5	7.4	*Suisse*
Turkey	...	...	...	...	...	*Turquie*
Country mean	**1.4**	**0.5**	**1.3**	**7.1**	**10.8**	***Moyenne des pays***

See Annex 1 for notes

Voir notes en annexe 1

R24: Labour force status for leavers from education

UNEMPLOYMENT RATES FOR LEAVERS FROM EDUCATION

POLICY ISSUES

Are education and training truly effective in reducing youth unemployment? What do unemployment rates reveal about the relation between supply and demand for different types of education in the labour market?

KEY RESULTS

In almost all reporting countries, unemployment rates one and five years after leaving education are very high for those leaving lower secondary level. The rate is highest in France, where almost 60 per cent of this group are unemployed one year after leaving school. In the same time perspective and for the same educational group, Denmark is an exceptional case: the relatively low unemployment rate – 9 per cent – is in fact lower than the rate for those completing upper secondary education.

In general, the unemployment rates recorded for leavers from upper secondary education one year after having left are relatively high compared to the average for the labour force in the same age group. In a longer perspective (five years), the rates for upper secondary school-leavers are lower than the average for the corresponding age group, with the exception of Denmark, but still higher than the average for the total labour force, with the exception of Finland.

Leavers from tertiary education meet a different situation. As early as one year after leaving, the unemployment rates for these groups are lower than the average for the corresponding age group, and after five years they are also well below the average for the total labour force.

DESCRIPTION AND INTERPRETATION

When about 90 per cent of an age cohort enter upper secondary education, which is the case now in many OECD countries, leavers from lower secondary education constitute a vulnerable group. They have lower rates of participation in the labour force and significantly higher rates of unemployment than leavers from upper secondary education. In addition, after five years, leavers from lower secondary level still have higher unemployment rates than the average for the total labour force.

In France, Ireland and Spain, the unemployment rates for leavers from upper secondary education were above 20 per cent one year after leaving education. High unemployment rates for leavers from university education one year after leaving education are reported for Italy (39 per cent) and Spain (26 per cent).

Follow-up surveys for leavers from education offer useful information about the transition from education to work. Unemployment rates for leavers give an indication of the relation between the supply and demand for different types of education in the labour market. Data suggest that there is not much demand for youth with low educational level.

Differences in unemployment benefits for the young unemployed will also have to be considered. In some (but not all) countries, these benefits are available only after a minimum duration of employment. Finally, there are also differences among countries in the degree of access to the next level in the education system. Limited access may to some extent help explain high unemployment rates for leavers.

Follow-up surveys of leavers are not pursued annually, which means that the latest available data refer to different years for different countries and levels of education. Consequently, changes in the labour market situation need to be considered in interpreting the data.

DEFINITIONS

Leavers from education are defined as students who have successfully completed a programme at one level of education but no higher and are, at the beginning of the school reference year, not enrolled in full-time education or training.

R24: Labour force status for leavers from education

R24 : Situation au regard de l'emploi des jeunes qui sortent du système éducatif

Table R24:
Unemployment rates after leaving education
for leavers from different school levels
(according to follow-up surveys for leavers)
and unemployment rates for the total labour force
(1992)

*Tableau R24 :
Taux de chômage des jeunes sortant
de différents niveaux du système éducatif
(selon les enquêtes de suivi)
et taux de chômage de la population active totale
(1992)*

	Year / Age	Lower secondary education / *Enseignement secondaire 1er cycle*	Upper secondary education / *Enseignement secondaire 2e cycle*	Non-university tertiary education / *Enseignement supérieur non universitaire*	University education / *Enseignement supérieur universitaire*	Age 15-24 / *15-24 ans*	Age 25-64 / *25-64 ans*	
One year after leaving education								*Un an après la sortie du système éducatif*
Australia	1992	33	...	...	...	18	9	*Australie*
Canada	1988	...	...	8	9	18	10	*Canada*
Denmark	1991	9	15	11	12	11	11	*Danemark*
Finland	1990	18	10	3		23	11	*Finlande*
France	1992	57	24	8	12	2	19	*France*
Ireland	1992	35	24	21	10	23	14	*Irlande*
Italy	1992	...	...	...	39	33	7	*Italie*
Spain	1991	34	36	13	26	34	15	*Espagne*
Sweden	1992	8	13	...	...	11	4	*Suède*
Switzerland	1993	...	...	12	8	7	3	*Suisse*
United Kingdom *	1993	15	13	...	...	15	8	** Royaume-Uni*
United States	1991	37	12	6	8	14	7	*Etats-Unis*
Five years after leaving education								*Cinq ans après la sortie du système éducatif*
Canada	1991	...	...	8	6	18	10	*Canada*
Denmark	1991	23	12	5	6	11	11	*Danemark*
Finland	1990	17	6	2	1	23	11	*Finlande*
France	1992	34	18	4	5	21	9	*France*
Spain	1991	34	21	7	13	34	15	*Espagne*
Sweden	1992	16	5	...	...	11	4	*Suède*
Switzerland	1993	...	...	...	3	7	3	*Suisse*

Se Annex 1 for notes
* England and Wales

Voir notes en annexe 1
* Angleterre et Pays de Galles

R24: Labour force status for leavers from education

R24 : Situation au regard de l'emploi des jeunes qui sortent du système éducatif

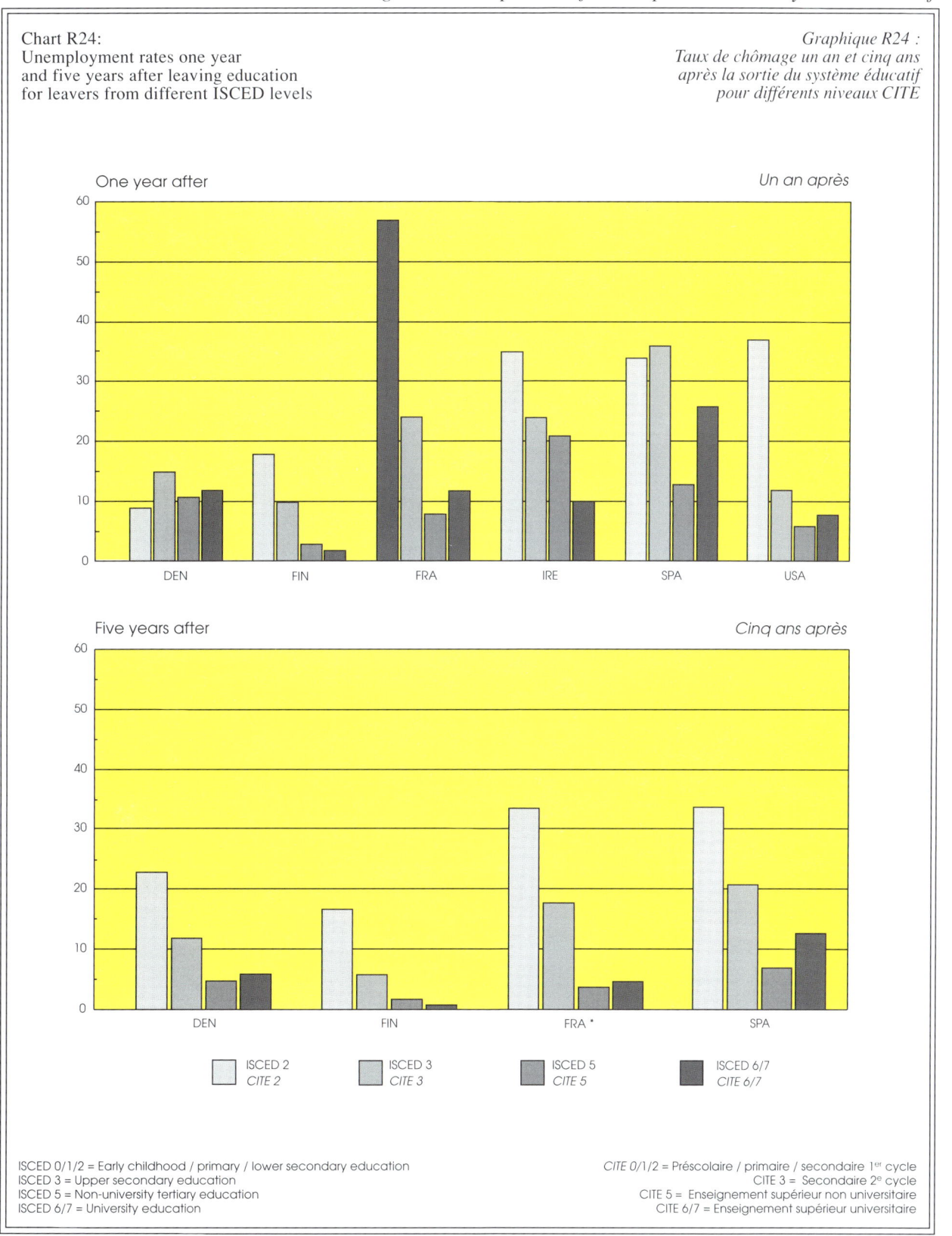

Chart R24:
Unemployment rates one year
and five years after leaving education
for leavers from different ISCED levels

Graphique R24 :
Taux de chômage un an et cinq ans
après la sortie du système éducatif
pour différents niveaux CITE

One year after — *Un an après*

Five years after — *Cinq ans après*

- ISCED 2 / CITE 2
- ISCED 3 / CITE 3
- ISCED 5 / CITE 5
- ISCED 6/7 / CITE 6/7

ISCED 0/1/2 = Early childhood / primary / lower secondary education
ISCED 3 = Upper secondary education
ISCED 5 = Non-university tertiary education
ISCED 6/7 = University education

CITE 0/1/2 = Préscolaire / primaire / secondaire 1er cycle
CITE 3 = Secondaire 2e cycle
CITE 5 = Enseignement supérieur non universitaire
CITE 6/7 = Enseignement supérieur universitaire

Legal compulsory school leaving age (1992)

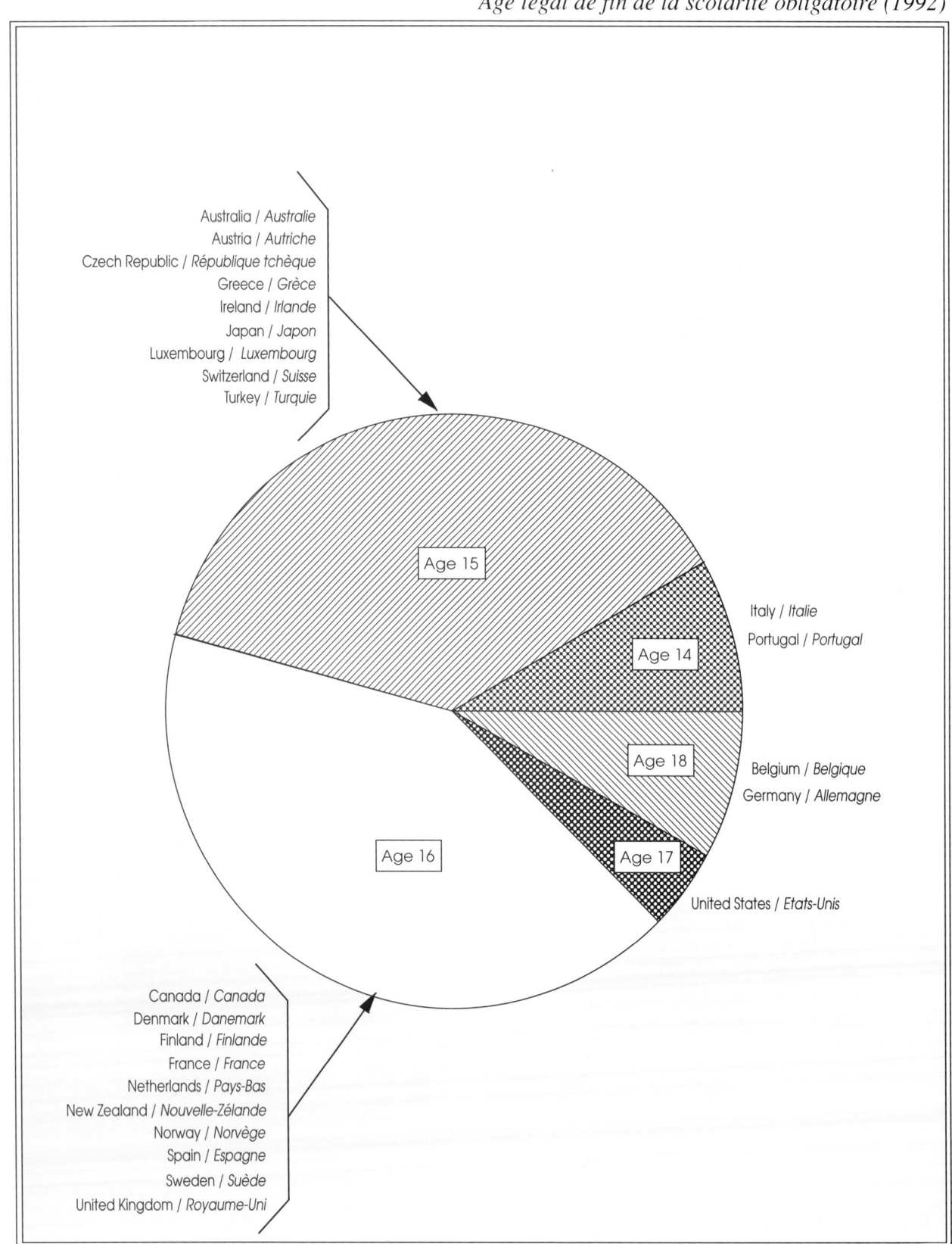

Age légal de fin de la scolarité obligatoire (1992)

Age 15:
- Australia / *Australie*
- Austria / *Autriche*
- Czech Republic / *République tchèque*
- Greece / *Grèce*
- Ireland / *Irlande*
- Japan / *Japon*
- Luxembourg / *Luxembourg*
- Switzerland / *Suisse*
- Turkey / *Turquie*

Age 14:
- Italy / *Italie*
- Portugal / *Portugal*

Age 18:
- Belgium / *Belgique*
- Germany / *Allemagne*

Age 17:
- United States / *Etats-Unis*

Age 16:
- Canada / *Canada*
- Denmark / *Danemark*
- Finland / *Finlande*
- France / *France*
- Netherlands / *Pays-Bas*
- New Zealand / *Nouvelle-Zélande*
- Norway / *Norvège*
- Spain / *Espagne*
- Sweden / *Suède*
- United Kingdom / *Royaume-Uni*

IV

ANNOTATED ORGANISATION CHARTS OF EDUCATION SYSTEMS

The notes accompanying these charts have been prepared and approved by the education authorities of the respective countries and not by the OECD. The terms used may vary from country to country. It should also be noted that the terms pertain strictly to the charts and not to the indicators.

It must be remembered that the relative size of the different blocks in the diagrams in no way represent the proportion of enrolments in a sector. Space considerations are determined by the complexity of what must be described rather than by the relative importance of specific programmes. Data on enrolments by programme are available in *OECD Education Statistics, 1985-1992*, Chapter 4.

Note: Each level of education is represented by a different colour. Part-time programmes within a level are indicated in *pink*. Vocational education is indicated in *mauve*.

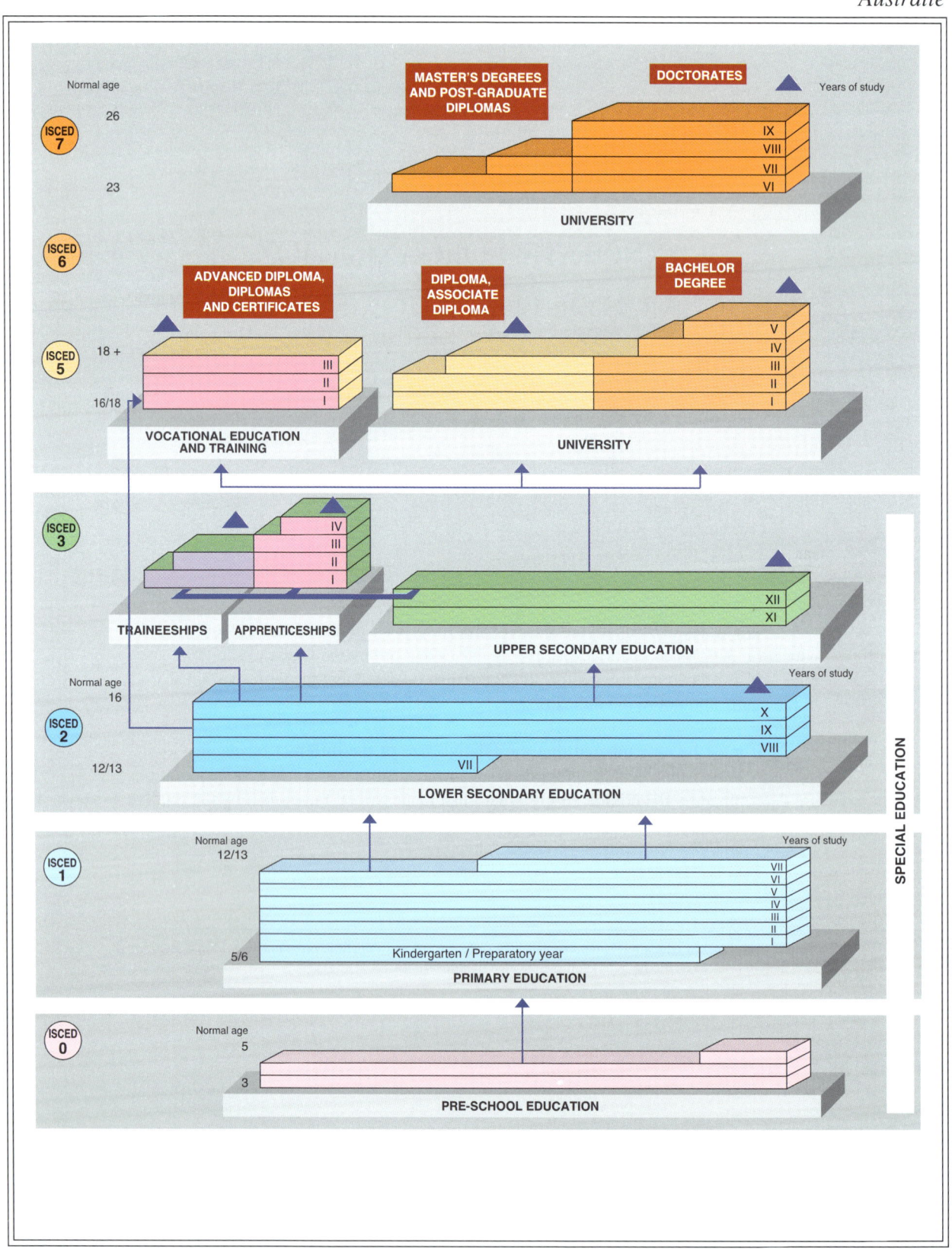

Australia

Australie

Australia

PRIMARY EDUCATION

Schooling is compulsory between the ages of 6 and 15 (16 in Tasmania). In most of Australia's six states and two territories children start primary school at around the age of 5, when they enrol in a preparatory or kindergarten year. After that, primary education lasts either six or seven years, depending on the state concerned. The scattered rural population in most states has necessitated a large number of very small primary schools, although this number is declining. All government and most non-government primary schools are co-educational.

SECONDARY EDUCATION

Secondary education is available for either five or six years, depending on the length of primary school in the state concerned. Students normally commence secondary school at about age 12. Most government secondary schools are co-educational, but a significant number of non-government secondary schools are single-sex.

Government schools, which enrol the majority of both primary and secondary students, operate under the direct responsibility of the State Education Minister. Non-government schools, which operate under conditions determined by government registration authorities, are required to provide certain minimum education standards and satisfactory premises. Almost all non-government schools have some religious affiliation, with the Catholic Church having the largest non-government school system. Each state has a substantial system of Catholic schools. Approximately 800 non-government schools are independent, that is, they do not belong to a system.

TERTIARY EDUCATION

Tertiary education includes higher education and vocational education and training. Higher education is provided in universities, and vocational education and training in Technical and Further Education (TAFE) institutions and private institutions such as business colleges. Universities are autonomous bodies that make their own decisions on, for example, matters of funding allocation, staffing and academic courses. The TAFE system is administered by state and territory governments.

Vocational education and training (VET). Most vocational education and training is provided by the TAFE system. There are also a growing number of private sector bodies offering accredited training, and less formal adult and community education providers.

TAFE institutions provide a full range of training, including entry level, pre-vocational, operator, trade, post-trade, technician (or paraprofessional) and (in some fields) certain professional levels. A typical student completes a one-year course, while apprentices complete a three- or four-year course part-time. Courses are open to all age groups. Ninety per cent of students in VET are part-time.

Higher education. Students commencing higher education courses will have completed a full secondary education or will have demonstrated that they have a high probability of successfully completing such a course. There is keen demand for places at many institutions, and quotas are often placed on new enrolments. Students are able to study on a full-time or part-time basis and external studies are offered by a large number of institutions. Some institutions offer full-time courses during breaks from full-time employment.

There are 43 publicly funded higher education institutions and private universities. Australian undergraduate students at the publicly funded institutions pay part of their education costs through the Higher Education Contribution Scheme (HECS).

The basic undergraduate course at most institutions is a Bachelor degree course of three or four years' duration, although at some institutions courses may be offered at the diploma or associate diploma level. Most institutions also offer post-graduate levels of study. The equivalent of one or two years of full-time post-graduate study is required for a Master's degrees, and the equivalent of three to five years of full-time study for a doctoral degree. Post-graduate diplomas are offered in some disciplines.

OTHER EDUCATION

Traineeships and apprenticeships are the two main forms of structured training allowing entry to the workforce, widely available.

Traineeships provide an avenue for people to gain structured entry to occupations not covered by the apprenticeship system. They provide either planned and structured on-the-job training or a combination of on- and off-the-job training; the latter instruction is provided by a TAFE college or other approved training provider. Traineeships, in which employers and unions participate, aim to assist trainees to gain a foothold in the workforce and add to the stock of skills in the economy.

Apprenticeships provide young people with an entry point into the trades. They typically involve a combination of on- and off-the-job training at a TAFE college or other training institution. While an apprenticeship typically lasts four years, durations are progressively becoming more flexible.

Traineeships and apprenticeships are administered through a Vocational Training Authority or a similar body in each state or territory.

From 1995, Australia will commence a new national entry-level training system called the Australian Vocational Training System (AVTS). The AVTS provides a broad range of articulated pathways combining education, training and experience in workplaces. It is based on competency rather than time served, and will eventually subsume the existing system of apprenticeships and traineeships.

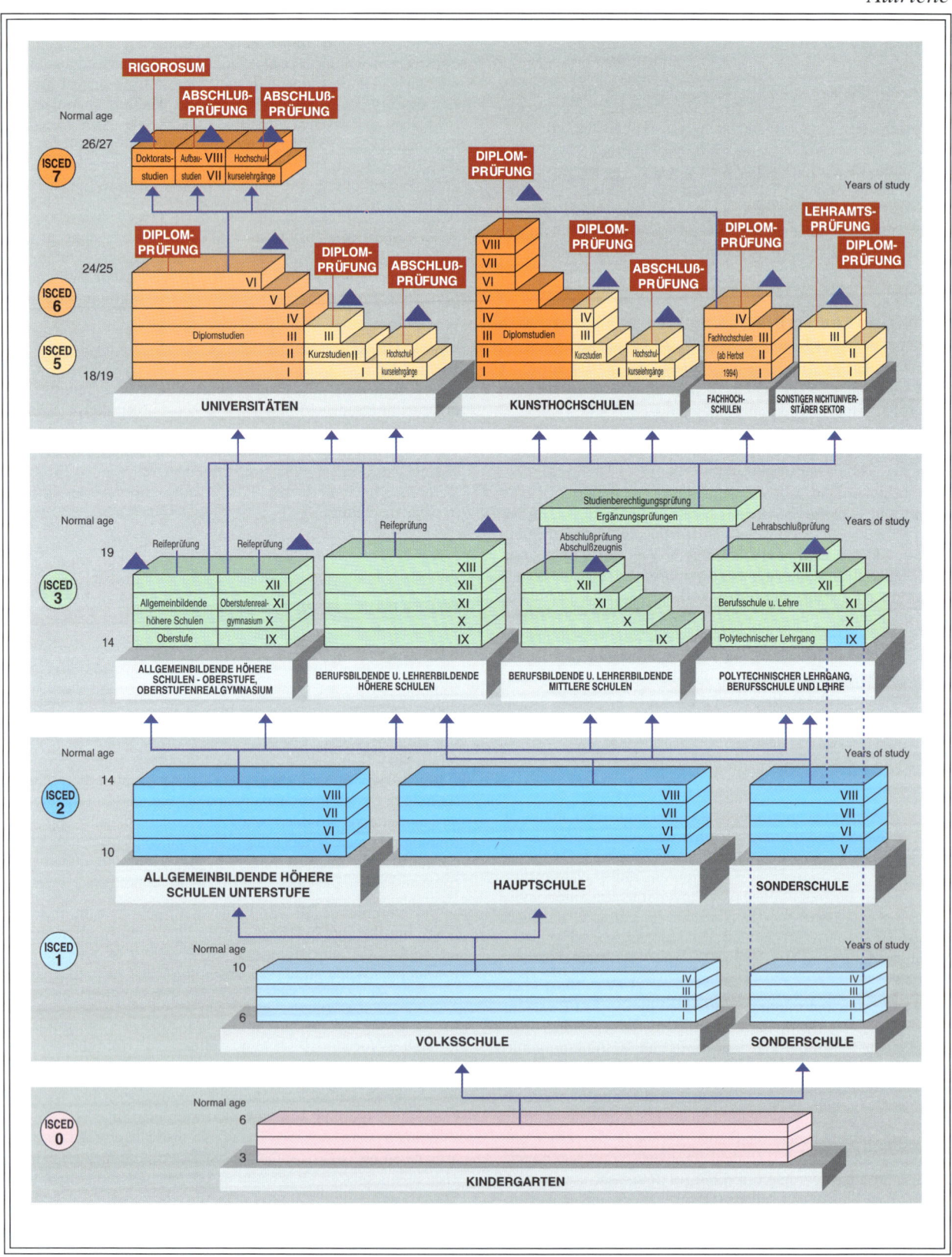

Austria

Autriche

Austria

PRE-PRIMARY EDUCATION

This sector (with private and public institutions) is non-compulsory, and consists of *crèches* for the very young (up to 1 year old), day nurseries (1 and 2 year-olds) and kindergartens (3 to 6 year-olds). Children of school age whose enrolment for the first school year would be premature in the light of their educational development attend a pre-primary stage (*Vorschulstufe*) to facilitate transfer to primary school proper. In administrative terms, the pre-primary stage forms part of the primary school.

PRIMARY AND LOWER SECONDARY EDUCATION

Compulsory education in Austria is predominantly supplied by public institutions (there are a few dependent denominational schools) and comprises nine years of school. As a rule, children commence school at 6 years of age, attending primary school (*Volksschule*) for four years. Special schools (*Sonderschule*) exist for the physically or mentally disadvantaged where enrolment in a mainstream school is not feasible. On completion of the fourth *Volksschule* year, the choice is between:

- the four-year main general secondary school (*Hauptschule*) – the majority choice outside large cities; and
- the four-year first stage of a higher general secondary school (*allgemeinbildende höhere Schule- AHS-Unterstufe*).

Choices must again be made prior to enrolment in the ninth year. A substantial proportion of the pupils in this age bracket – chiefly those from the *Hauptschulen* – opt for the pre-vocational year (*polytechnischer Lehrgang*), which becomes their last year of compulsory full-time schooling before entering apprenticeship training.

The primary, special, main secondary general schools and the pre-vocational year are referred to as general compulsory schools (*allgemeinbildende Pflichtschulen*).

UPPER SECONDARY SCHOOL

Apprenticeship (*Berufsschule und Lehre*)

Completion of compulsory general education (i.e. nine years of schooling) is obligatory to enter this path. Apprentice training college (*Berufsschule*) attendance is compulsory for all apprentices throughout their term of apprenticeship (i.e. up to four years) and is on a block- or day-release basis. Training at work is given by qualified instructors and takes place according to national syllabi. This so called "dual" educational path ends in a final formal examination (*Lehrabschlußprüfung*) and culminates in a vocational or craft qualification, such as a *Gesellenbrief* (Journeyman's Certificate).

Intermediate and higher technical and vocational education

Intermediate and higher technical and vocational colleges (*Berufsbildende mittlere Schulen – BMS* and *Berufsbildende höhere Schulen – BHS*) and intermediate and higher teacher training colleges (*lehrerbildende mittlere und höhere Schulen*), e.g. for kindergarten teachers, represent an alternative route to vocational qualifications from the ninth year (grade) onwards. The sector which provides formal education and training is almost all public, or dependent when run by trades or denominational organisations. The colleges offer programmes of up to five years and, on completion, award qualifications equivalent to those gained in the "dual" system, with well-defined paths to self-employment. The technical and vocational programmes train students for skilled industrial, commercial, business and agricultural occupations, and all higher programmes which terminate in final Matriculation Examinations (*Reifeprüfung*) qualify for university and most non-university tertiary admission. Their formal intermediate programmes terminate in an *Abschlußprüfung/Abschlußzeugnis*.

Higher general (or academic) secondary school

Second stage (ISCED level 3) programmes (*AHS-Oberstufe*) are mainly for pupils from the first stage, who continue on the premises. There are few private denominational, yet dependent schools; the vast majority are state institutions. Three prime *AHS* categories are distinguished: *Gymnasium, Realgymnasium*; and *wirtschaftskundliches Realgymnasium.* The *Realgymnasium* also exists as a separate second stage institution (*Oberstufenrealgymnasium*), designed as a special programme for main general secondary school leavers. All *AHS* programmes culminate in the Matriculation Examination (*Reifeprüfung*).

Public sector adult education (*Zweiter Bildungsweg für Berufstätige*)

In the public sector there are part-time (mostly evening) classes based on approved syllabi for technical trades, business, social work and *AHS* programmes. These are either second chance programmes for adults or modular programmes for qualified workers after their apprenticeship and offered by special adult education departments at intermediate/higher technical and vocational colleges, or at higher general secondary schools in the case of higher general education. These courses result in qualifications corresponding to those of their formal education equivalents (in terms of ISCED the higher of the technical and vocational programmes are located at the border of upper secondary and tertiary education and a few higher ones are in the tertiary bracket or distinctly transgress into tertiary education). A substantial proportion of the intermediate modular programmes are offered by the private technical and vocational colleges of the social partners.

TERTIARY EDUCATION

Tertiary education in Austria takes place at Universities (*Universitäten*), Colleges of Music and Arts (*Kunsthochschulen*), *Fachhochschulen* (as from 1994), and other non-university institutions (*sonstiger nichtuniversitärer Sektor*). Universities and

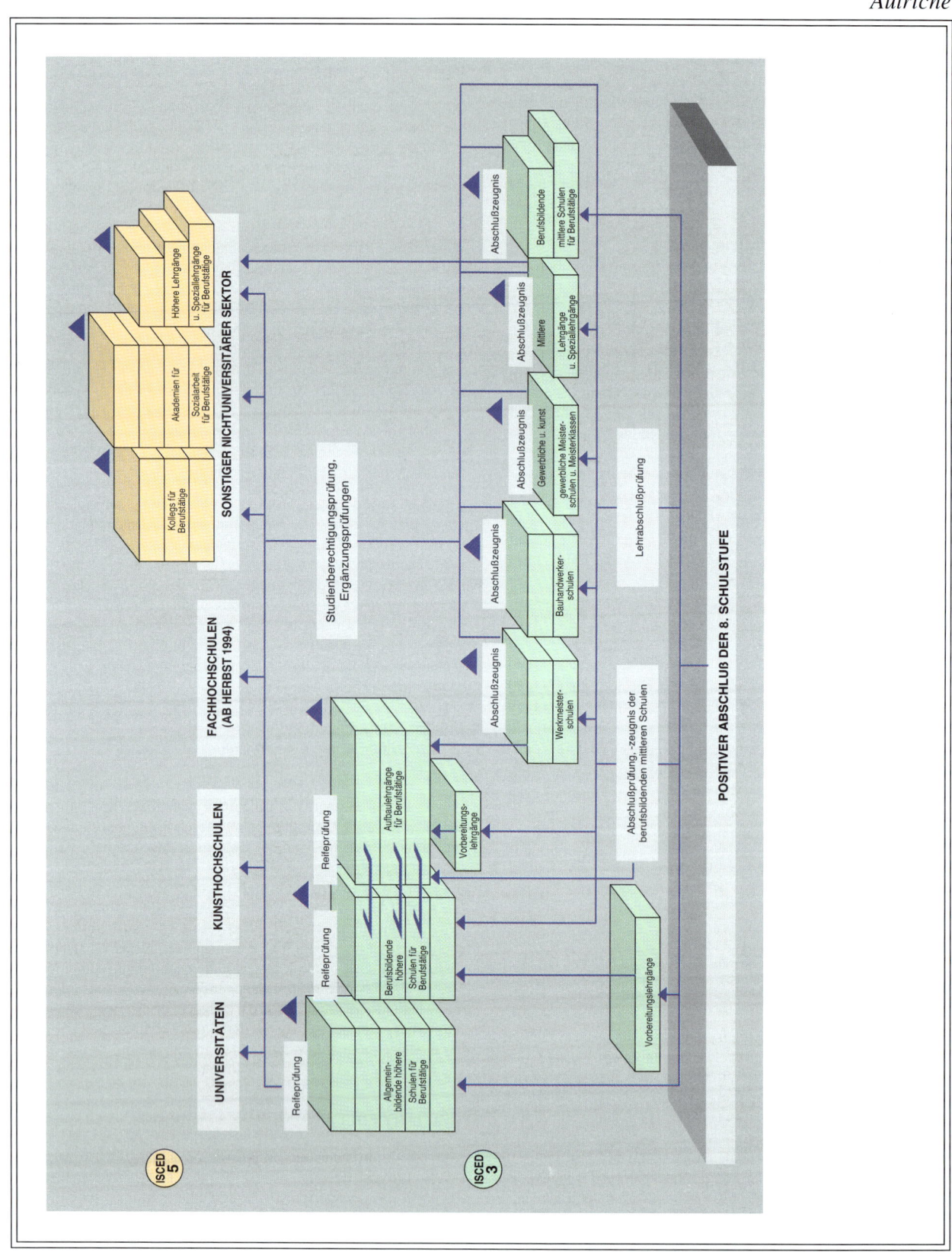

Austria

Autriche

Austria

Colleges of Music and Arts are state institutions, while *Fachhochschulen* are constructed as private, largely publicly subsidised establishments.

1. Entrance requirements

University education is open to all candidates who have successfully completed their secondary studies at a higher general or higher technical and vocational institution, i.e. passed the Matriculation Examination (*Reifeprüfung*). For adults without this formal qualification, an alternative route is offered by a set of preparatory courses and a special examination (*Studienberechtigungsprüfung*) leading to university admission in a certain field of study.

Colleges of Music and Arts: entrance examinations to test the artistic ability of the candidates are obligatory for admission; an additional Matriculation Examination is required for some study courses.

Fachhochschulen (as from 1994 onwards): the same entrance requirements as for universities apply. Admission is also possible for young people who have completed a vocational training pertinent to the field of study; to ascertain their educational level, additional examinations (*Ergänzungsprüfungen*) may be required.

Other non-university institutions: the main areas of education and training in this field are the training colleges for teachers of compulsory schools and for social workers (*Akademien*) and the *Kollegs* (the shorter tertiary version of the higher technical and vocational, and higher social and teacher training programmes). In principle the same entrance requirements as for universities apply. The training of paramedical staff at this level is usually attached to hospitals.

2. Types and duration of courses

Most courses offered at **universities** are degree courses which are completed by a final diploma examination after submission of a thesis (*Diplomstudien*, ISCED 6); graduates are awarded a Master's degree (*Magister/Magistra, Diplomingenieur*). A course in medicine leads to a doctor's degree. In the case of continuing and adult education, there are also non-degree courses (*Kurzstudien*) and vocationally-oriented courses at post-secondary level (*Hochschulkurse, Hochschullehrgänge* at post-secondary level, ISCED 5). Students having successfully completed a non-degree course may continue in the corresponding degree course. Students with a Master's degree may enrol in doctoral studies (*Doktoratsstudien*, ISCED 7) or in continuation courses (*Aufbaustudien*, ISCED 7). Universities also offer vocationally-oriented courses at post-graduate level (*Hochschulkurse, Hochschullehrgänge* at post-graduate level, ISCED 7).

The minimum length of all the study courses is defined by law: *Diplomstudien* require between four and five years, a course in medicine six years, doctoral studies between one and two years. Duration of non-degree courses is between two-and-a-half and three years. A longer duration of study, however, is usual.

Colleges of Music and Arts: most of the courses offered are degree courses leading to a diploma (*Diplomstudien*, ISCED 6).

These institutions also offer non-degree courses (*Kurzstudien*, ISCED 5) and vocationally-oriented courses at post-secondary level (*Hochschulkurse, Hochschullehrgänge* at post-secondary level, ISCED 5). Students having successfully completed a non-degree course may continue in the corresponding degree course. Duration of degree courses is between four and eight academic years, that of non-degree courses between two and four years.

The corresponding age groups indicated in the diagram are not suitable for students of music, because they often begin their studies some years earlier.

Fachhochschulen: have been recently established; the first courses are offered in the academic year 1994/95.

Fachhochschulen will provide degree courses leading to an academic degree (ISCED 6). The minimum duration of the courses will be three years plus a period of practical work. Graduates of *Fachhochschulen* will be entitled to enrol in doctoral studies at universities.

Other non-university institutions: *Kolleg* in two years (three years for adult part-time programmes); Teacher training colleges (*Akademie*) for teachers at general compulsory schools, in three years.

Vorschulstufe	Pre-primary school
Volksschule	Primary school
Sonderschule	Special school
Hauptschule	General secondary school
Allgemeinbildende höhere Schulen Unterstufe	Higher general secondary school
Reifeprüfung	Matriculation examination
Polytechnischer Lehrgang	Pre-vocational year
Berufsschule und Lehre	Apprenticeship
Universitäten	Universities
Kunsthochschulen	Colleges of Music and Arts
Diplomstudien	Final Diploma
Sonstiger nichtuniversitärer Sektor	Non-university sector

Belgium (Flemish community)

Belgique (Commmunauté flamande)

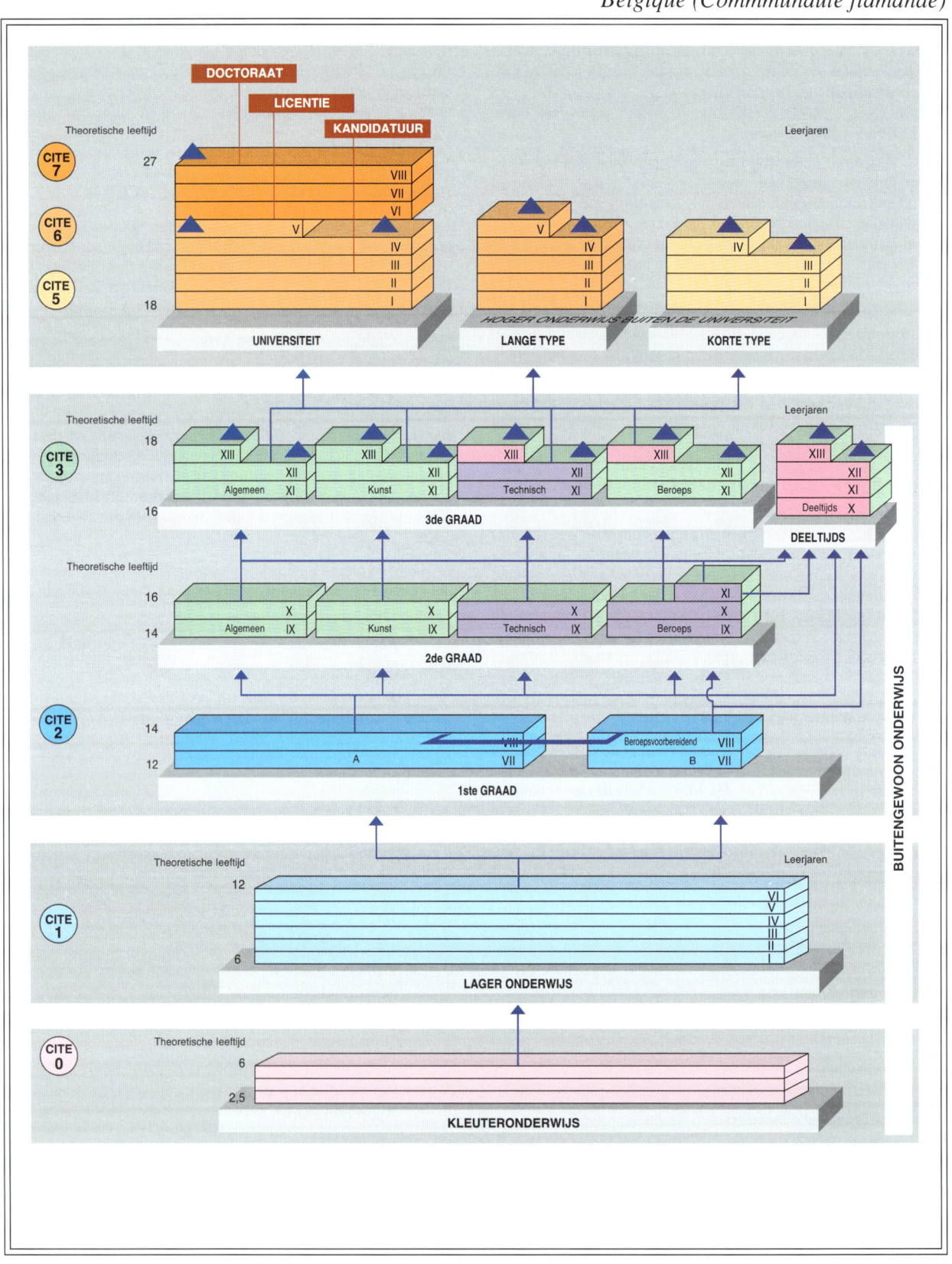

Belgium (Flemish community)

The present organisation of secondary education was adopted in 1989. In 1992 some schools still worked according to the old system with two cycles of three years, instead of the model with three stages of two years.

Education is compulsory from 6 to 18 years of age. In principle students complete at least secondary education before leaving school or continuing studies at (non-compulsory) higher levels. Since "compulsion" refers to age rather than education level, in practice may students leave formal education at the age of 18 without having successfully completed secondary education, due to the high percentage of repeaters.

Compulsory education is full-time until at least 14 years of age. From the age of 15 students can continue in part-time education until the age of 18. Students may still transfer to part-time education at the age of 16.

All forms of secondary education (general or *algemeen*, technical or *technisch*, arts or *kunst*, vocational or *beroeps*) give access to higher education. Students who complete vocational secondary education need to follow a seventh year of secondary education before entering higher education.

Students may move between different forms of secondary education, but there are some restrictions: for example a student in vocational secondary education may only move to technical education by repeating either one or two years. Nevertheless, most transfers between the different forms of the secondary education system occur from general to technical or arts, or from technical to vocational. Students may only continue in secondary education if they have successfully passed an examination in all subjects.

There are no entrance examinations for higher education (except for civil engineering). There are three types of higher education: Universities, short-type, and long-type higher education outside universities. Both universities and institutions for higher education outside universities (long type only) offer education at university level – ISCED 6.

There are different systems for teacher training depending on the initial diploma and the level of education the teacher will work in. Teachers for pre-primary, primary and lower secondary education follow a three-year full-time programme (ISCED 5). University students can obtain a certificate for teacher training in higher secondary education after completing their initial university programme.

There is a separate system for special education (*buitengewoon onderwijs*). Pupils with disabilities may also follow regular education while benefitting from special aid programmes.

Theoretische leeftijd	Normal age
Kleuteronderwijs	Pre-primary education
Lager onderwijs	Primary education
Buitengewoon onderwijs	Special education
Beroepsvoorbereidend	Pre-vocational education
Algemeen onderwijs	General education
Kunst	Arts
Technisch	Technical education
Beroeps	Vocational education
Deeltijds onderwijs	Part-time education
Universiteit	University
Kandidatuur	Candidate
Licentie	Licenciate
Doctoraat	Doctorate

Belgium (French community)

Belgique (Communauté française)

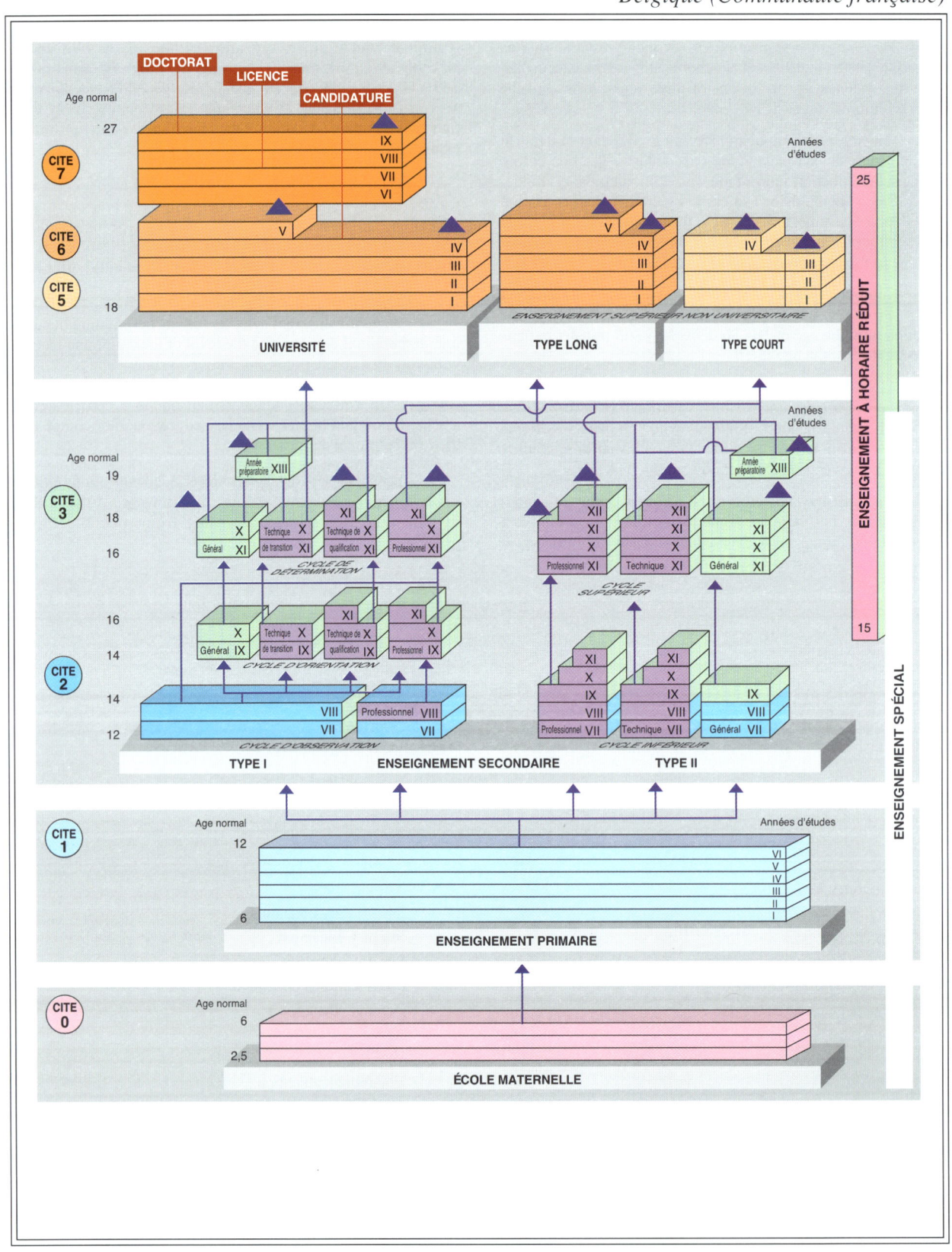

Belgium (French community)

The education system of the German-speaking community is similar to that of the French-speaking community.

GENERAL DESCRIPTION OF THE SCHOOL SYSTEM

Education is organised on four levels corresponding to the following age groups:

- **pre-primary education** for children aged 2-and-a-half to 6 years (ISCED 0);
- **primary education** for children aged 6 to 12 years (ISCED 1);
- **secondary education** for youngsters aged 12 to 18 years and above (ISCED 2 and 3);
- **higher education** of variable length according to the area of study for students aged 18 to 25 years and above.
  - **non-university education**, "short type", includes a single cycle of 3 to 4 years of study (ISCED 5);
  - **university level education**, "long type", includes at least four years of study divided into two cycles (ISCED 6);
  - **university education** includes from 4 to 7 years of study (ISCED 5 for the first diploma (*candidature*), equivalent to two or three years of study; ISCED 6 for the first degree (*licence*), equivalent to 2 to 5 years of study; and ISCED 7 for a doctorate which may vary greatly in length but is of at least two years' duration).

There are also two other types of education:

- **special education** designed for the handicapped from three to twenty-one years of age or above and organised at nursery, primary and secondary levels;
  - **social promotion education** designed for young people and adults who have left the school system and who feel the need to acquire new qualifications or to update their knowledge. This form of education may be at ISCED level 3, 5 or 6.

COMPULSORY SCHOOLING

The Compulsory Schooling Act of 29 June 1983 sets at 18 years of age the end of compulsory schooling, previously limited to 14 years of age. On his/her 18th birthday a pupil is no longer subject to compulsory schooling. However, compulsory **full-time** schooling ends as soon as a pupil has reached the age of 15 and has completed (without necessarily having passed) the first two years of full-time secondary education.

SECONDARY EDUCATION

It is at this level that the education systems of the French-speaking and Flemish-speaking communities differ.

In the French-speaking community secondary education is currently organised according to two different types.

The 1st type of secondary education (or new system) organised in three two-year cycles takes one of four forms:
- general education;
- technical education;
- artistic education;
- vocational education;

and one of two degrees of guidance:
- **the transitional phase**, the aim of which is preparation for higher education whilst allowing entry into the world of work;
- **the qualification phase**, the aim of which is entry into the world of work whilst retaining the possibility of further study in higher education.

Nevertheless, various bridges exist from the first year onwards allowing pupils who have chosen the "wrong" option to change course.

The 2nd type of secondary education (or traditional system) is organised in two three-year cycles.

Unlike the new system of education where the first two years are common to all four forms, in the traditional education system a differentiation is made in the lessons from the first year onwards between the general form (ancient humanities and modern humanities) and the technical, artistic and professional forms.

The first type of secondary education is becoming more widespread whilst the second type now covers only 3.7 per cent of the total number of pupils in secondary education.

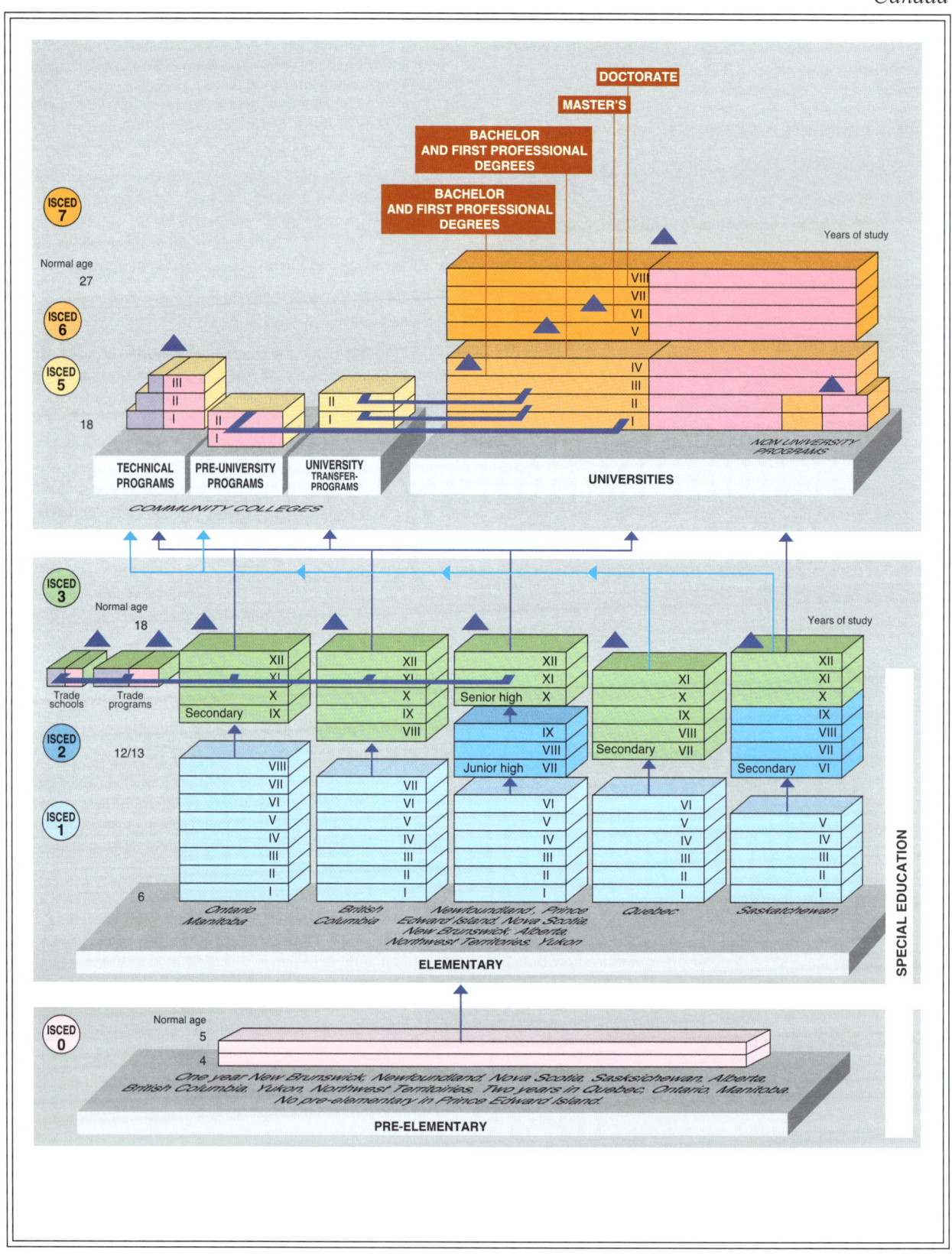

Canada

Canada

Canada is comprised of ten provinces and two territories, each of which, within the federative system of shared powers, is responsible for education. Therefore, each of the provinces and territories has developed its own educational structures and institutions; while these are similar in many ways, they reflect the circumstances of regions separated by great distances and the diversity of the country's historical and cultural heritage.

PRE-PRIMARY EDUCATION

Pre-school programmes or kindergartens, which are operated by the local education authorities and provide one year of pre-Grade One education for 5 year-olds, are offered by all provinces and territories with the exception of Prince Edward Island.

PRIMARY AND SECONDARY EDUCATION

In each province or territory, a ministry or department of education is responsible for primary and secondary education. Public education is provided free to all Canadian citizens and permanent residents until the end of secondary school – normally, age 18. The ages for compulsory schooling vary from one jurisdiction to another; generally, it is required from age 6 or 7 to age 16.

Primary education in most jurisdictions covers the first six to eight years of compulsory schooling. Afterwards, children proceed to a secondary education programme. A great variety of programmes – vocational (job training) as well as academic – are offered at the secondary level. The first years are devoted to compulsory subjects, with some optional subjects included. In the latter years, the number of compulsory subjects is reduced, permitting students to spend more time on specialised programmes that prepare them for the job market, or to take the specific courses they need to meet the entrance requirements of the college or university of their choice. Secondary school diplomas are granted to students who pass the compulsory and optional courses of their programmes.

Special-needs students, such as the physically or mentally disabled, the gifted, etc., are accommodated in the public schools in various ways. In some cases, separate programmes are available to meet their needs; in others, these students are integrated into the regular classroom and, to the extent possible, follow the regular programme of instruction.

Private or independent schools, which provide an alternative to publicly funded schools, may operate in any province or territory if they meet the general standards prescribed by that jurisdiction for primary and secondary schools. Although in most cases they closely follow the curriculum and diploma requirements of the Department or Ministry of Education, they function independently of the public system and charge fees. Five provinces – Alberta, British Columbia, Manitoba, Quebec and Saskatchewan – provide some form of financial assistance to these schools.

The point of transition from primary to secondary school may vary from jurisdiction to jurisdiction. Some school boards break up the primary-secondary continuum into schools that group together, for example, kindergarten to Grade Six, Grades Seven to Nine (junior high), and Ten to Twelve (senior level). In Quebec, secondary schooling ends at Grade Eleven.

TERTIARY EDUCATION

Once secondary school has been successfully completed, a student may apply to a college or a university, depending on the region and on whether he or she qualifies.

Quebec students – again, having completed secondary schooling in 11 as opposed to 12 years – must obtain a college diploma in order to be admitted into a university programme. The colleges, called *CÉGEPs* (*collèges d'enseignement général et professionnel*), offer both a general programme that leads to university admission, and a professional programme that prepares students for the labour force. In Ontario, students must complete six Ontario Academic Credit courses in order to be admitted to a university programme. This can be accomplished during the four-year secondary school programme, or during an additional year after completion of Grade Twelve.

Tertiary education is available in both government-supported and private institutions, some of which award degrees and some of which do not. Colleges such as technical and vocational institutions, community colleges, *CÉGEPs* and other institutes of technology offer programmes for continuing education and for developing skills for careers in business, the applied arts, technology, social services and some health sciences. Programmes vary in length from six months to three years. There are also private vocational or job training colleges in some provinces. In general, colleges award diplomas or certificates only; they do not award degrees.

Many colleges offer, in co-operation with industry and business partners, professional development services or specialised programmes in high-technology areas. Technical training and technology programmes prepare students for employment in the trades, industry or agriculture, or for a job as a professional technician or technologist. A certificate is granted for programmes requiring one year of study (24 to 30 weeks). Two-year or three-year programmes lead to a diploma. Some programmes last four years; these are made up of courses of an academic rather than job-training nature.

The British Columbia community college system allows students to complete two years of academic course work towards Bachelor degrees. Thus, while some students may decide not to continue, others have the opportunity to go on to complete the third and fourth years at a university-college or university and receive a degree. In many provinces, however, the transfer is not automatic. A student must apply for admission and have his or her college studies evaluated before being granted credit for completed college courses.

Canada

Programmes leading to degrees are offered in universities or, as they are sometimes known, degree-granting institutions. Most Canadian universities, especially those in the larger cities, offer a complete range of programmes. Others are more specialised, and have developed areas of excellence. There are also some specialised institutions that are not campus-based and offer university programmes through correspondence courses and distance education.

It is possible to study at three different levels, that lead to a Bachelor, Master's or doctoral (Ph.D.) degree. Not all universities offer graduate studies (Master's and doctorates). In addition to degree programmes, most universities offer diploma and certificate programmes. These can be either at the undergraduate or graduate level, and can range from one to three years in duration.

Bachelor degrees can take either three or four years of study, depending on the programme and the province. Universities in some provinces grant general pass degrees in three years and require a fourth year for an Honours degree. Other provinces require four years of study regardless of whether it is for a general or an Honours degree.

Master's degrees require one or two years of study after completion of an Honours Bachelor degree. Some may require a thesis or professional internship.

Doctoral degrees usually require three years of study after a Master's degree. Most students need much more time to complete a Ph.D., the average being four or five years. Doctoral degrees usually involve researching, writing, presenting and defending a thesis, in addition to attending seminars and a specified number of courses.

Czech Republic

PRE-SCHOOL EDUCATION

Kindergartens accept children from the age of 3. A child entering primary school must be judged sufficiently mature; otherwise entry (normally at age 6) is postponed a year.

PRIMARY AND LOWER SECONDARY EDUCATION

Compulsory education consists of two parts. General school lasts five years and provides primary education; the pupil receives the core knowledge of general polytechnical, physical and aesthetic education. The second level, from Grades Six to Nine, provides instruction in the mother tongue, mathematics, natural science, civics, supplemented by history, geography, physics, chemistry and other subjects including a foreign language. Each subject is taught by a different teacher. Talented students may attend a school with an extended curriculum of languages, mathematics, sport, etc. Pupils are tested in oral and written examinations.

UPPER SECONDARY EDUCATION

The upper secondary level prepares students directly for occupations or for further study at university or one of the newly established non-university schools.

There are three types of secondary schools:
- *gymnasia*;
- *secondary specialised schools and conservatoires*;
- *secondary vocational schools*.

Students are accepted for study on the basis of entrance examinations and their compulsory school results. The years since 1990 have seen the establishment of many private and church schools.

Gymnasia provide students with a broad and thorough general education in preparation for university. Studies conclude with a matriculatory final exam.

Secondary specialised schools and conservatoires compare with several non-university schools abroad, provide a broad general education as well as specialised study in a particular field (e.g. nursing, certain technical areas, tourism, library science, accounting, etc.). After four years, studies end with a matriculation exam.

Secondary vocational schools prepare students for occupations. Three-year programmes conclude with an apprenticeship exam. Students who have received high grades in compulsory education can choose a four-year programme ending with both general education and apprenticeship exams. These professional schools specialise mostly in engineering and technical areas. They provide also general education, including mother tongue, history, mathematics and sciences.

SPECIAL EDUCATION

Special schools have been established for handicapped children who cannot be integrated within the regular schools. Special education is available in kindergarten, primary, lower secondary and upper secondary levels. Those students who study at university are already integrated.

TERTIARY EDUCATION

Because of the existence of specialised secondary schools, there was no perceived need for non-university tertiary schools until 1990. Since that year, however, several new schools of this kind have been developing from the extension courses organised by secondary schools; their number is expected to grow.

Universities, the highest level within the Czech education system, are granted full autonomy by law. The typical length of programmes is five years (six for medicine, veterinary medicine and architecture; teacher training four to five). A three-year Bachelor degree has recently been established. Students are admitted on the basis of an entrance examination and the results of final exams at the end of secondary school.

Post-graduate study prepares graduates for independent scientific work.

ADULT EDUCATION

Adult education is provided by secondary schools and universities. Students study the same curricula as their young colleagues, take the same examinations and receive a degree of the same value.

Czech Republic

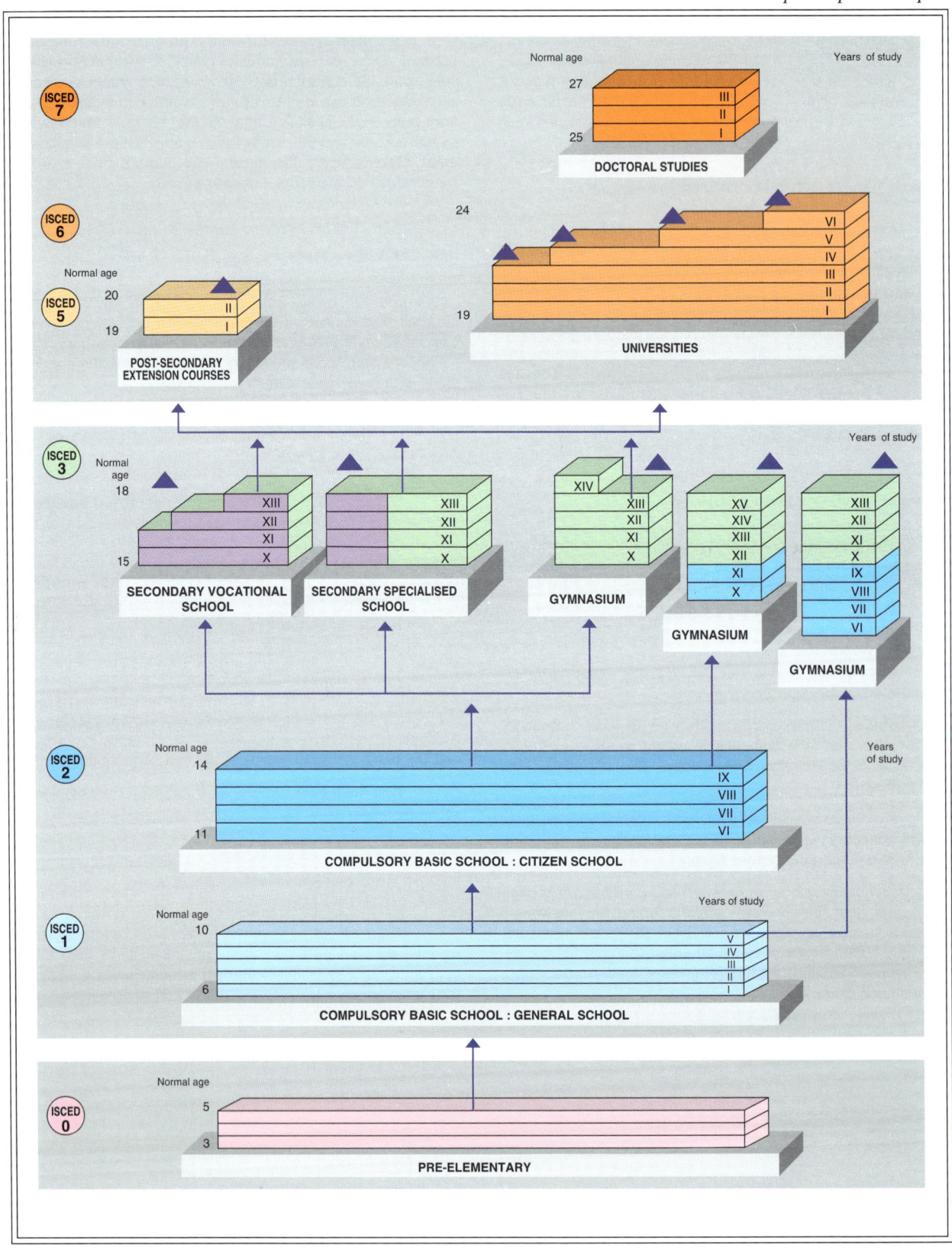

République tchèque

Denmark

PRE-PRIMARY, PRIMARY AND LOWER SECONDARY EDUCATION

Although pre-school education is voluntary, it must be offered by the municipalities; 96 per cent of all children are enrolled. Following on from this, the municipal *Folkeskole* provides a compulsory nine years of basic schooling between the ages of 7 and 16. Pupils are grouped in classes which remain together throughout the whole period of basic schooling. About half of a class stays on for 10th form, which is voluntary. Some pupils complete their final years of schooling in "continuation schools" (*efterskoler*) which are boarding schools.

The *Folkeskoler* are run by the municipalities, but there is also an independent sector which caters for 11 per cent of all pupils. Up to 80 per cent of the expenditure for private schools are covered by public funding.

UPPER SECONDARY EDUCATION

If students pass the leaving examination at the end of *Folkeskole* they are automatically qualified for general upper secondary education. This may mean three years of *Gymnasium* (upper secondary school), or a two-year higher preparatory examination course (the *HF*-course), or two years of adult upper secondary level courses. All these courses are academically oriented and both the upper secondary school leaving examination (the *studentereksamen*) and the higher preparatory examination (the *HF*-examination) qualify students for admission to higher education.

Students who have completed their basic schooling plus one year of vocational education and training can begin a course in general/vocational upper secondary education. These two-year courses lead to the Higher Commercial Examination (the *HHX*) and the Higher Technical Examination (the *HTX*), and qualify students for admission to certain higher education courses. The *HHX*, for instance, qualifies them for the humanities course in a university, and the *HTX* for degree courses in engineering.

Students who wish to proceed directly to the labour market as skilled workers can take three- and four-year vocational education and training courses. These consist of a mixture of theoretical education at a school and practical training in the workplace, and train commercial and clerical workers as well as skilled craft workers. Basic social and health education courses run parallel to the vocational education and training courses, and they also contain a mixture of practical training and theoretical education. There are also a number of specialist maritime courses at this level, and agricultural courses which lead to the award of the "green certificate" for farmers.

TERTIARY EDUCATION

Short-cycle higher education consists of courses at middle technician's level within the areas of food, construction, clothing, electronics and mechanical technology. There are also health education courses leading to qualifications such as laboratory technologist and dental technician, and maritime and home economics courses which lead to qualifications such as first mate and home economics technician. The admission requirements for some of these short-cycle courses are: an upper secondary school leaving examination; a higher preparatory examination; or a Higher Commercial or Technical Examination. Admission to other short-cycle courses requires a vocational education and training qualification.

Medium-cycle higher education consists of complete courses, which qualify people directly for the labour market as, for example, school teachers, nurses, or journalists. The *Bachelor degree* can also qualify individuals directly for the labour market, but usually from part of a long-cycle higher education course. The admission requirement for a medium-cycle course or a Bachelor degree course is the school leaving examination at general or general/vocational upper secondary level.

Master's degree courses consist of courses within the social sciences, the humanities, music, theology, psychology and the natural sciences, as well as degree courses in law and economics, courses for the *cand.mag.-degree* (degree with a minor and a major subject), the *cand.ling.merc.-degree* (degree in applied languages), for the *can.scient.-degree* (degree in the natural sciences), for doctors of medicine, dentists, veterinary surgeons and "civil" engineers (Master's degree in engineering). The admission requirement is a Bachelor degree or – for some courses – the leaving examination from general or general/vocational upper secondary level.

Courses for researchers build on the Master's degree. When they have passed their examinations, the graduates from these courses are entitled to be awarded the Ph. D. degree.

ADULT EDUCATION

In Denmark, there is a long and strong tradition of adult education and continuing training. There is a wide range of programmes for adults who want to learn general subjects such as Danish, mathematics, history and languages. There are also many examples of vocationally oriented continuing training for unskilled and skilled workers and for people with higher education qualifications. Finally – in step with the increasing unemployment of recent years– large-scale education, training and employment programmes have been developed.

Adult education and continuing training are financed from both public and private sources. The scope and depth may vary a great deal – from only one lesson a week for a short period to full-time courses lasting more than a year. Such courses take place at single-subject centres (*VUC*); at open education and vocational schools or universities and other higher education institutions; at *AMU* (labour market training) centres; in the workplace; at folk high schools and at non-residential folk high schools.

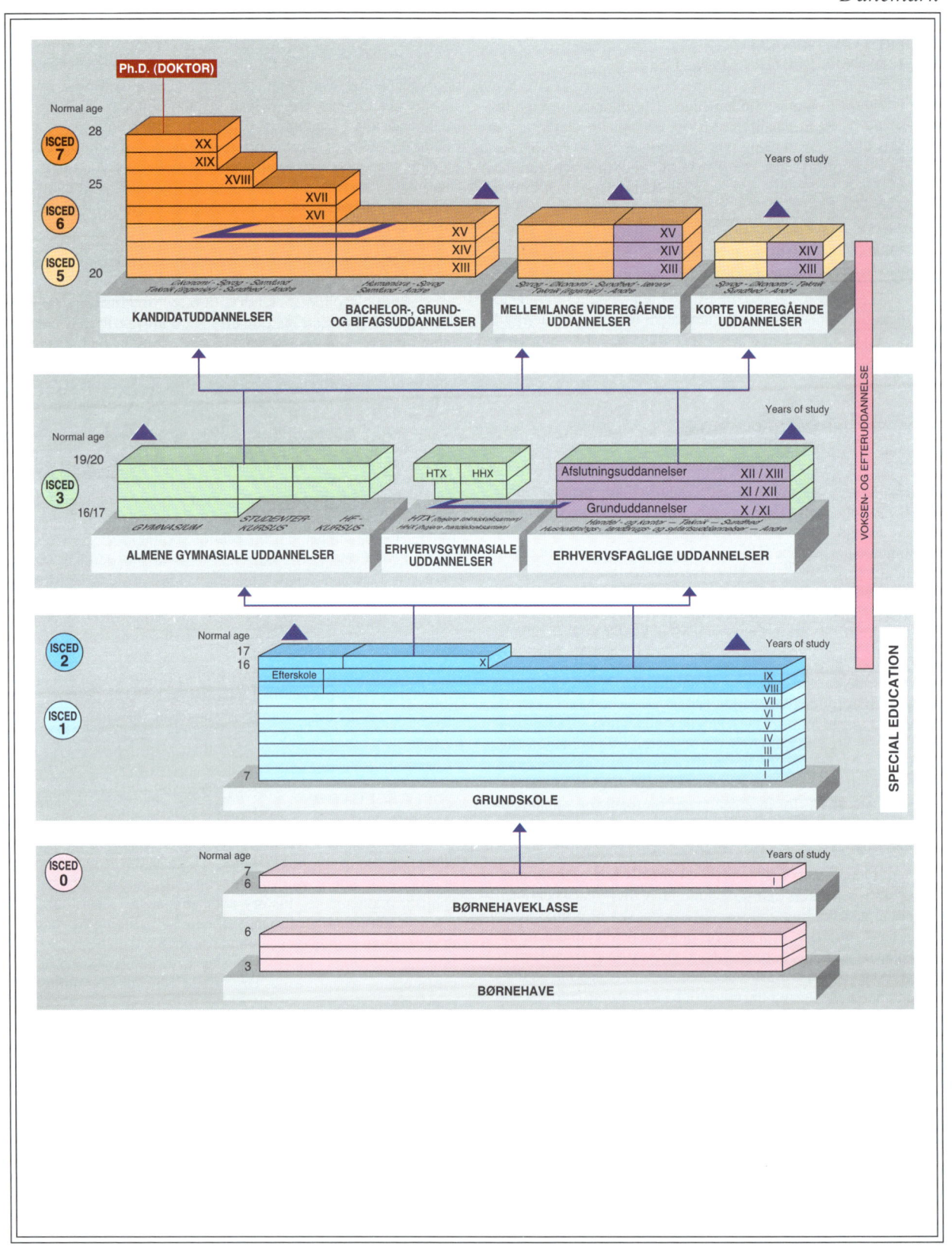

Denmark

Danemark

Denmark

Børnehave	Kindergarten
Børnehaveklasse	Pre-school class
Grundskole	Basic school
Efterskole	Continuation school
Almene gymnasiale uddannelser	General upper secondary education
Gymnasium	High school
Studenterkursus	(Adult) upper secondary level courses
HF-kursus	Higher preparatory examination course
Erhvervsgymnasiale uddannelser	General/vocational upper secondary education
HTX (højere tekniskeksamen)	Courses for higher technical examination
HHX (højere handelseksamen)	Courses for higher commercial examination
Erhvervsfaglige uddannelser	Vocational education and training
Afslutningsuddannelse	12/13 years of study
Grunduddannelse	10 years of study
Handel- og kontor	Commercial and clerical vocational courses
Teknik	Technical vocational courses
Sundhed	Health-related auxiliary programmes
Husholdnings-, landbrugs- og søfartsuddannelser	Domestic, agricultural and fishery programmes
Andre	Other
Korte videregående uddannelser	Short-cycle higher education
Mellemlange videregående uddannelser	Medium-cycle higher education
Bachelor-, grund- og bifagsuddannelser	Bachelor degree courses
Kandidatuddannelser	Master's degree courses
Voksen - og efteruddannelse	Adult education and further training

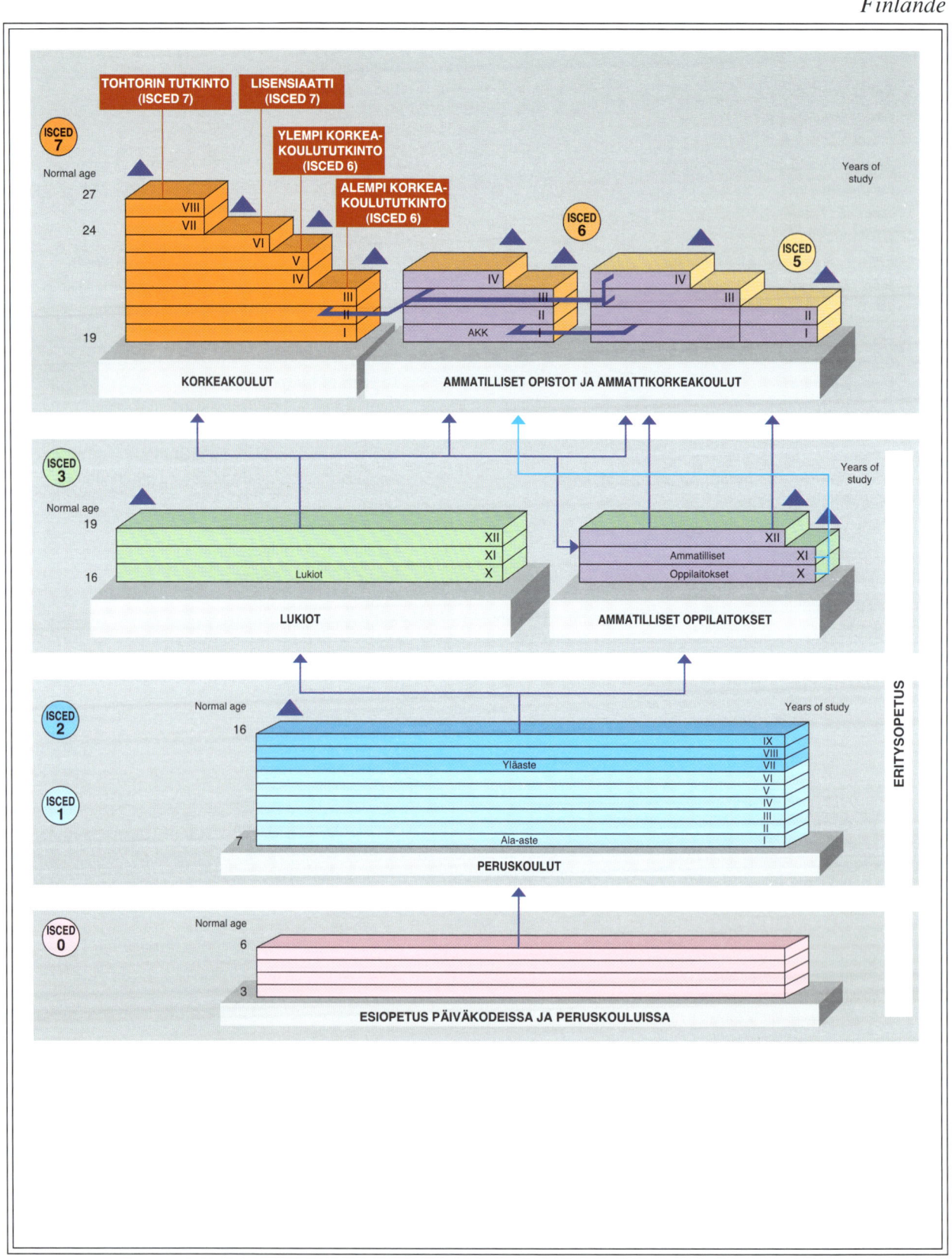

Finland

Finlande

ISCED 7

- TOHTORIN TUTKINTO (ISCED 7)
- LISENSIAATTI (ISCED 7)
- YLEMPI KORKEAKOULUTUTKINTO (ISCED 6)
- ALEMPI KORKEAKOULUTUTKINTO (ISCED 6)

Normal age: 19, 24, 27

KORKEAKOULUT

AMMATILLISET OPISTOT JA AMMATTIKORKEAKOULUT

AKK

ISCED 3

Normal age: 16–19

LUKIOT — Lukiot (X, XI, XII)

AMMATILLISET OPPILAITOKSET — Ammatilliset Oppilaitokset (X, XI, XII)

ISCED 2 / ISCED 1

Normal age: 7–16

PERUSKOULUT
- Ala-aste (I–)
- Yläaste (–IX)

ERITYSOPETUS

ISCED 0

Normal age: 3–6

ESIOPETUS PÄIVÄKODEISSA JA PERUSKOULUISSA

Finland

PRE-PRIMARY EDUCATION

Pre-school education (ISCED 0), in the main, is handled by the Social Welfare authorities and organised in conjunction with the day care of children below regular school age. For 6 year-olds, pre-school education may also take place in conjunction with comprehensive school. This alternative, however, requires a permit from the Ministry of Education, and is designed mainly to take care of the needs of the children in the country's sparsely-populated areas. Approximately 60 per cent of all 6 year-olds partake in pre-school education.

PRIMARY AND LOWER SECONDARY EDUCATION

Comprehensive schooling is nine years of compulsory education. It is divided up into a lower stage (ISCED 1) comprising six years and an upper stage (ISCED 2) comprising three years of education. It may also contain a tenth optional school year. Comprehensive schools, with very few exceptions, are maintained by the municipalities.

A child becomes subject to compulsory school attendance from age 7. Compulsory school attendance is ten years; for certain groups of seriously disabled children, it begins when they are 6 and extends for eleven years.

Special education is arranged in special schools annexed to comprehensive schools, in special classes as part of normal education, or as integrated teaching in normal education. The general trend is to decrease segregation and to increase integration. For some special groups, there are state-owned special schools (e.g. schools for pupils with impaired hearing and vision).

UPPER SECONDARY EDUCATION

Post-comprehensive education is given by senior secondary schools and vocational schools. Approximately 90 per cent of the comprehensive school leavers continue their studies in upper secondary education and 60 per cent of these in senior secondary schools. The senior secondary schools are mainly run by the municipalities. The senior secondary schools (ISCED 3) offer a general education of three years' duration, at the end of which the pupil takes the national matriculation examination, which is the general eligibility criterion for university admission. Senior secondary education has traditionally been the main channel to higher education. Special education, as a rule, is integrated into normal education.

Initial vocational education and training is given mainly in educational institutions run and aided by the State or municipalities. The share of apprenticeship training is very small (in 1992 less than 1 per cent of the admission places). There are special institutions of vocational education for the seriously disabled.

Post-comprehensive vocational education extends for two or three years after comprehensive schooling.

At present, vocational education comprises 26 comprehensive basic programmes and approximately 250 specialisation programmes which represent all occupational sectors (part of the 250 programmes belong to the advanced vocational education level). From 1995, on there will be no more basic programmes and the number of specialisation programmes will be reduced to about 160. In lieu, programmes will become more comprehensive and elective. Students will also be more free to make selections, allowing for a more personal study programme. In future, it will also be possible to combine general education studies with vocational studies which is even now a reality in experimental programmes.

TERTIARY EDUCATION

Tertiary education consists of *higher education* and *advanced vocational education*. Most institutions of vocational education impart both academic and vocational subjects in vocational training at all levels (ISCED 5 and 6).

Advanced vocational education

At advanced vocational level, students are offered college-level diplomas and higher vocational diplomas. College-level qualifications take three to five years, and higher vocational five to six years. The entry requirement is the leaving certificate of either comprehensive or upper secondary education.

The structure and diplomas of vocational education will be reformed in 1995. Education will be arranged linearly so that students at the tertiary level are required to have attained either the senior secondary or the secondary vocational school. There is currently an experimental project in which part of the institutions giving advanced vocational education have been changed into temporary polytechnics (see higher education).

Higher education

The Finnish higher education is divided into two sectors: the *university sector* and the *non-university sector*.

The *university sector* consists of 21 institutions of higher education. These institutions are financed by the State and are free for the students. The basic degree, corresponding to a Master's degree, ideally takes from five to five-and-a-half years to complete. In some fields, it is possible to sit for a lower examination, corresponding to a Bachelor degree, the foregoing studies take from three to three-and-a-half years to complete. During the years 1994 and 1995, the lower university degree will be extended to almost all fields of study. Post-graduate studies lead to a licentiate's degree followed by a doctorate, both of which take several years to complete.

Finland

A student who passes the matriculation examination is eligible for university studies. Since 1991, higher vocational level diplomas awarded by vocational institutions give the same eligibility.

The *non-university sector* consists of 22 temporary, experimental polytechnics formed out of 85 institutions providing advanced vocational education. The experiment began in 1991 and the target is to improve the standard and quality of vocational education. Diplomas of these polytechnics are classified on a level with university degrees. Studies generally take three to four years to complete.

A prerequisite for admission into polytechnics is a senior secondary school leaving certificate, either a matriculation certificate or a vocational certificate in the same branch of education. From 1995 on, a prerequisite for admission to higher educational institutions (ISCED levels 5 and 6) other than the polytechnics is that the candidates have a matriculation certificate or a vocational certificate.

Esiopetus päiväkodeissa ja peruskouluissa	Early childhood education in day-care centres (kindergartens) and comprehensive schools
Peruskoulut	Comprehensive schools
Ala-aste	Lower stage
Yläaste	Upper stage
Ammatilliset oppilaitokset	Vocational education
Lukiot	General education
Korkeakoulut	Universities
Ammatilliset opistot ja ammattikorkeakoulut	Higher vocational institutions and polytechnics
Alempi korkeakoulututkinto	Bachelor degree
Ylempi korkeakoulututkinto	Master's degree
Lisensiaatti	Licentiate degree
Tohtorin tutkinto	Doctor's degree

France

The French education system continues to be largely state-controlled in spite of the radical changes it underwent in the 1980s. A number of basic powers are still held by the State, including teacher recruitment, the setting of national curricula, the conferment of university diplomas of which the *baccalauréat* is taken to be the first level. The conferment of these diplomas is under full State control. Since the decentralisation acts were introduced however (1982-1985), many of the powers formerly held by the State have been passed on to the regional authorities. Vocational training, for instance, is now fully under regional control. Meanwhile, secondary education establishments have become more independent and their legal status has been adjusted accordingly. Universities have already been autonomous to a large extent since 1968, and even more so since 1984.

GENERAL ORGANISATION OF THE EDUCATION SYSTEM

Education is divided into **three main levels**:

- **primary education** (first level): pre-primary and primary education provided in nursery schools and primary schools. In the first cycle starting skills are taught, in the second basic skills, and in the third further skills;
- **secondary education** (or second level): the first cycle is provided in *collèges* and the second cycle in vocational *lycées* (vocational training) or in general or technical *lycées* (for these two types of education). It is sanctioned by the award of the *baccalauréat* (general, technical or vocational), which still enjoys considerable status. The implementation of the vocational option in 1985 led to a very high increase in access to the *baccalauréat* by creating an opening via vocational training. Thirty-four per cent of a generation obtained the *baccalauréat* in 1980, and 65.5 per cent in 1992, of which 8.6 per cent via vocational training;
- **higher education**: provided in universities, including University Institutes of Technology (*IUT*), or by *grandes écoles* but also by *post-baccalauréat* classes in *lycées*: higher technician sections (*STS*) and preparatory classes for the entrance examinations to the *grandes écoles*. The latter recruit through competitive examination following a preparation of one to three years depending on the case. By contrast the *baccalauréat* is a sufficient entrance requirement for university.

In 1992/93 the school and university population accounted for over one-quarter of the total French population.

The share of private education varies depending on the levels concerned: 13.8 per cent of pupils in the first level, 20 per cent in the first cycle of secondary education, 22.3 per cent in the second vocational cycle, 21.3 per cent in general and technical secondary education, and 29.3 per cent in upper *lycée* classes. At the first and second levels, most private schools are under State contract with majority public funding. In higher education not provided by universities, the share of private funding without contracts is much larger. There are no private universities without contracts.

In the first and second cycle of secondary education, pupils are channelled (repeating, moving up to the next class, changing streams) according to a procedure involving the teachers, management and parents of pupils within each school. While teachers' opinions come first, parents may appeal if the decision does not suit them and may insist on their children moving up to the next class instead of repeating, or repeating instead of changing streams, depending on the educational level. At each school a specialised team of advisors helps pupils, parents and teachers to settle any problems.

Apprenticeship training mostly concerns those who have completed compulsory education (age 16) and are learning a trade, partly in employment under the responsibility of an apprenticeship trainer and partly in educational centres referred to as *Centres de formation d'apprentis* (*CFA*). They are bound by a special type of work contract allowing them to follow courses at *CFA*s. Over three-quarters of apprentices are enrolled at *CFA*s run by trade chambers, chambers of commerce and industry or vocational company or joint bodies. The other *CFA*s are run by vocational *lycées* or regional authorities. Apprenticeship training leads to the first vocational training diplomas of upper secondary education. Since 1987 it leads to the award of the vocational *baccalauréat*, short higher education diplomas (higher technician diplomas, technology university diplomas) and even engineering diplomas. It concerns just over 10 per cent of a generation.

Special education is mostly provided in primary and secondary schools but also in special institutions under the control of the Ministry of National Education or the Ministry of Health. It caters for students with various types of disability.

Adult training is an important activity of the public education sector. It has long been established, especially through social promotion action. Since the 1989 orientation act, it forms an integral part of the schools' functions. Public education accounts only for a small share of adult training however: 1.9 million out of 7.8 million adults who received training in 1992. There are three main sources of funding: the State, regional authorities and business. The latter must allocate 1.4 per cent of total wage costs to adult training. Each year one out of five wage-earners obtains training courses, with management staff in the lead. The government provides most of the funding for training courses offered to job-seekers.

Second level educational institutions are grouped into *GRÉTA*s (*Groupement d'établissements*) to co-ordinate this training. They are more concerned by public-funded courses than company-funded ones. In the case of universities, the opposite is true. Overall, *GRÉTA*s and universities received FF 4.1 billion in 1992 for adult training activities.

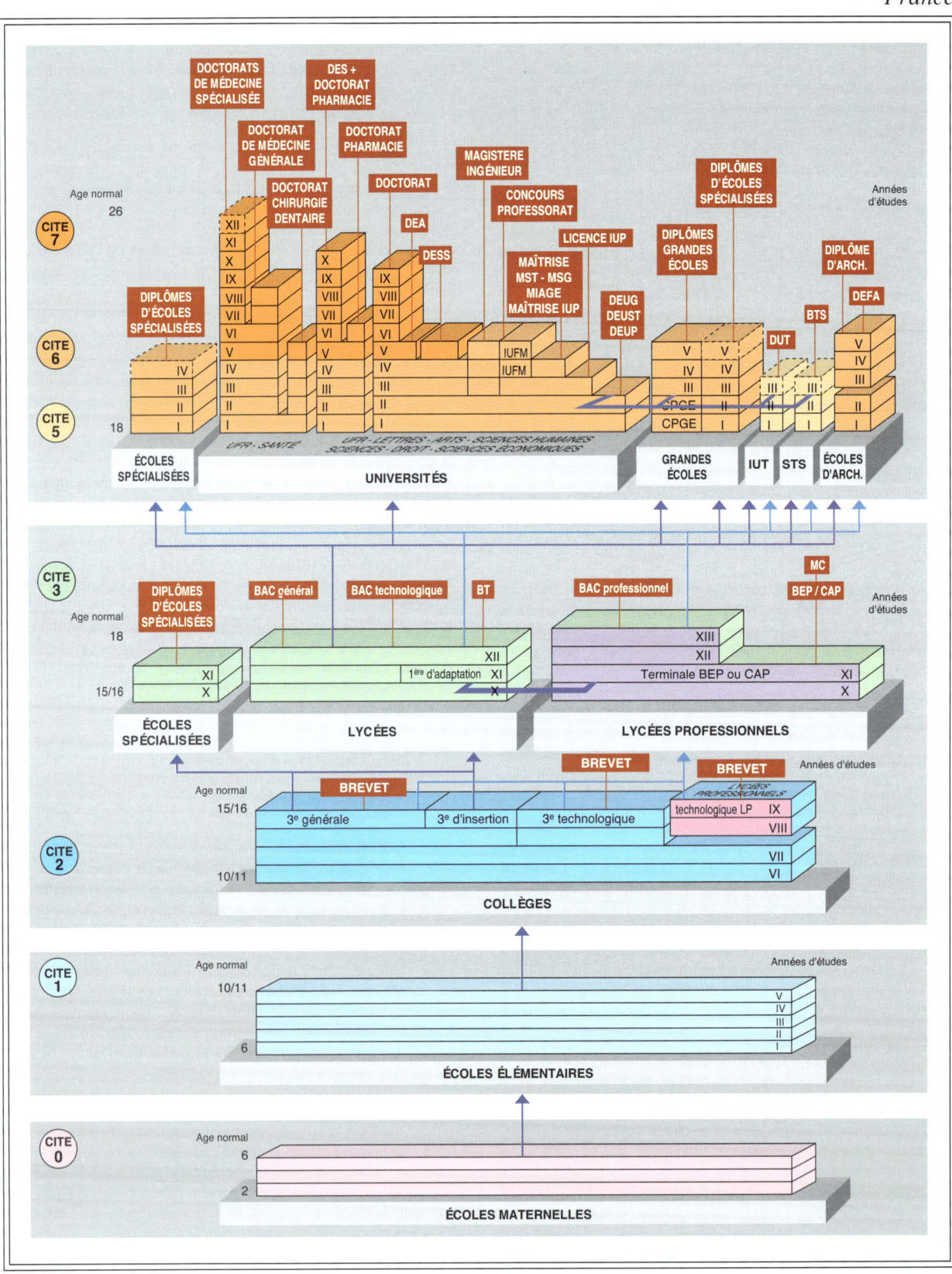

France

France

Age and school attendance

While education is compulsory from the age of 6 to 16, practically all children attend school by the age of 3 and 35 per cent of children at the age of 2 (53 per cent of children aged 2 at the start of the school year). After the age of 16, more and more students go on to the second cycle of secondary education, higher education or apprenticeship training.

Although it is difficult to draw parallels between the age and the level of achievement of students owing to the introduction of pluriannual cycles in primary education, to differing syllabuses and rates of progress at secondary level and to possible repeating in all cycles, the most common pattern for a student who has not repeated any year is as follows:

- elementary education for five years from the age of 6 to 10;
- first cycle of secondary education for four years from the age of 11 to 14;
- second cycle for two or four years for vocational training, three years for general technological training (from the ages of 15 to 16, 15 to 18 or 15 to 17 depending on the case);
- higher education includes short two-year courses (*IUT* or *STS*). Universities award diplomas after two years of study (*DEUG*); degrees usually correspond to three years of study and Master's degrees to four years. To obtain a doctorate or certain medical specialisations, training may take nine to ten years. For the *grandes écoles*, prior preparation of two years at *lycées* is followed by three or four years of study at the schools concerned. Engineering diplomas awarded by universities and *grandes écoles* correspond on the whole to the *baccalauréat* level plus five years of study.

Germany

Responsibility and competence for educational policy and planning are determined by the federative state structure. Accordingly, competence in education and science are divided up between the Federal and *Länder* governments. The *Länder* are predominantly in charge of legislation and administration.

PRE-PRIMARY AND PRIMARY EDUCATION

Pre-school education caters for children between the ages of 3 and 6 (mostly kindergartens, but also pre-school classes) as well as for children who are of school age but not yet ready for school (school kindergartens, pre-school classes and other, similar forms of pre-primary education, remedial classes).

Primary education. Compulsory schooling begins for all children at the age of 6. All children of compulsory school age attend the common primary school, which comprises the age levels 1 to 4 (in Berlin and Brandenburg the age levels 1 to 6).

LOWER SECONDARY EDUCATION

Secondary education stage I (*Sekundarbereich I*) comprises school provision from age level 5 (or 7) to 10 and is subdivided into various school types. In the sphere of general education most *Länder* have secondary general schools (*Hauptschulen*), intermediate schools (*Realschulen*), grammar schools (*Gymnasien*), and comprehensive schools (*Gesamtschulen*). A few *Länder* have so-called *Mittel-*, *Regel-* and *Sekundarschulen*. In some *Länder*, the age levels 5 and 6 of all general education schools are organised as an orientation stage.

UPPER SECONDARY EDUCATION

Secondary education stage II (*Sekundarbereich II*) comprises all educational provision which builds on secondary education stage I, that is to say, mainly age levels 11 to 13. It provides both general and vocational education courses leading to vocational qualifications or the right to enter the higher education sector.

In 1992, at general education schools, approximately 21.7 per cent of the relevant age group acquired either general university entrance qualifications or entrance qualifications for studies at *Fachhochschulen*.

Vocational education is characterised by a great variety of educational institutions. Their very number testifies to the special significance of vocational education in Germany. Vocational education comprises – sometimes with special forms in some *Länder* – the following types of secondary education stage II: part-time vocational school (*Berufsschule*), which is offered in combination with in-company training (the dual system), the basic vocational training year (*Berufsgrundbildungsjahr*), full-time vocational school (*Berufsfachschule*), vocational extension school (*Berufsaufbauschule*), *Fachoberschule*, specialised grammar school (*Fachgymnasium*) and trade and technical school (*Fachschule*).

Vocational education and training in the dual system are provided both in the company and at part-time vocational school. Training in individual occupations is based on training regulations. The dual system constitutes the core of vocational education and training in Germany. Approximately 70 per cent of an age group are provided with vocational education and training under this system.

The *Berufsgrundbildungsjahr* (basic vocational training year) provides students with a general or occupational field-related basic education either full-time or part-time. The *Berufsfachschulen* are full-time vocational schools to be attended for at least one year. The certificate awarded after two years' schooling qualifies its holder for admission to a *Fachschule* and is equivalent to an intermediate school certificate.

The *Berufsaufbauschulen* (vocational extension schools) are attended by adolescents who are at the same time undergoing vocational training or pursuing an occupation. The certificate awarded by these schools provides holders with *Fachschule* entrance qualification and is equivalent to an intermediate school certificate.

Fachoberschulen provide either full-time or part-time instruction. The certificate they award provides entrance qualification for studies at *Fachhochschulen*. *Fachgymnasien* (specialised grammar schools) are vocational grammar schools providing general higher education entrance qualification.

In 1992, approximately 11 per cent of the corresponding age group acquired entrance qualifications for general higher education or for studies at *Fachhochschulen* (higher vocational schools).

Health sector schools (for nurses, midwives, etc.) occupy a special position. They provide training for non-academic health-sector occupations, beginning at the level of secondary education II and overlapping into the higher education sector. In terms of organisation and location, many of these schools are associated with hospitals where training is provided in theory and practice.

SPECIAL EDUCATION

For pupils who, owing to a mental or physical handicap, are unable to attend general schools, various types of special schools are available in the sector of general and vocational education.

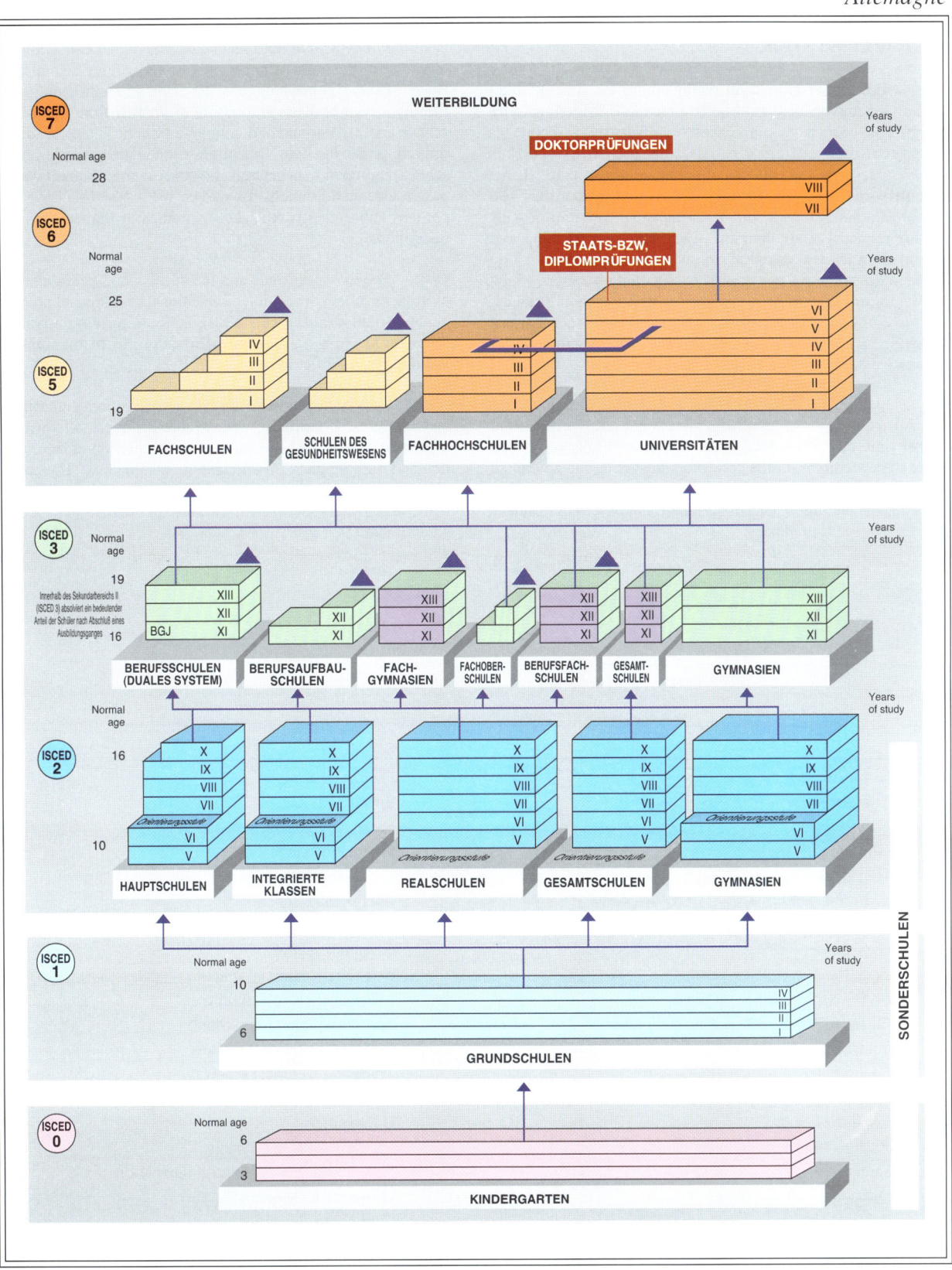

Germany

Allemagne

Germany

TERTIARY EDUCATION

The **higher education sector** comprises state or state-recognised universities and higher education institutions with comparable goals (e.g. comprehensive universities and colleges of education), colleges of art and music as well as *Fachhochschulen* and colleges of public administration. There are only few private higher education institutions and *Fachhochschulen* for specific disciplines. Universities provide a wide range of study courses. They combine teaching and research and are entitled to award doctorates. The *Fachhochschulen* and colleges of public administration, which are increasingly gaining significance, provide their students with a strongly application-oriented education for occupations requiring the application of scientific knowledge and methods or of creative design abilities.

In 1992, the share of first-year students at universities – as a percentage of the number of all new entrants – was around 68 per cent, that of *Fachhochschulen* around 32 per cent. The share of new entrants of the corresponding age group amounted to approximately 32.8 per cent. There are also institutions offering courses leading to vocational qualifications for secondary education stage II graduates.

It is typical of both secondary and higher education sectors to offer the possibility not only of vertical but also of cross flows. Thus, it is possible to go on to vocational training under the dual system after graduating from full-time vocational school and to continue and complete training there, or to start training under the dual system after graduating from grammar school (equipped with general university entrance qualifications or entrance qualifications for studies at *Fachhochschulen*) and, perhaps subsequently, to take up studies at higher education institutions.

Fachschulen (trade and technical schools) are attended by students after completion of vocational training and practical occupational experience. These schools provide advanced vocational training (leading for example to masters' or technicians' qualifications).

Continuing education comprises general, vocational and academic continuing education. It covers all forms of organised and informal learning after completion of the education and training phase. Participation is voluntary. The continuing education sector is characterised by a multitude of offerings, a plurality of providers and the subsidiary role of government.

Grundschulen	Primary schools
Sonderschulen	Special schools
Hauptschulen	Secondary general schools
Orientierungsstufe	Orientation stage
Integrierte Klassen	Integrated classes
Realschulen	Intermediate schools
Gesamtschulen	Comprehensive schools
Gymnasien	Grammar schools
Berufsschulen (duales System)	Part-time vocational schools
Berufsaufbauschulen	Vocational extension schools
Fachgymnasien	Specialised grammar schools
Berufsfachschulen	Full-time vocational schools
Fachschulen	Trade and technical schools
Schulen des Gesundheitswesens	Schools for nurses and midwives
Universitäten	Universities
Fachhochschulen	Higher vocational schools
Staats-bzw. Diplomprüfungen	State University Diploma Examinations
Doktorprüfungen	Doctorate Examination
Weiterbildung	Continuing Education

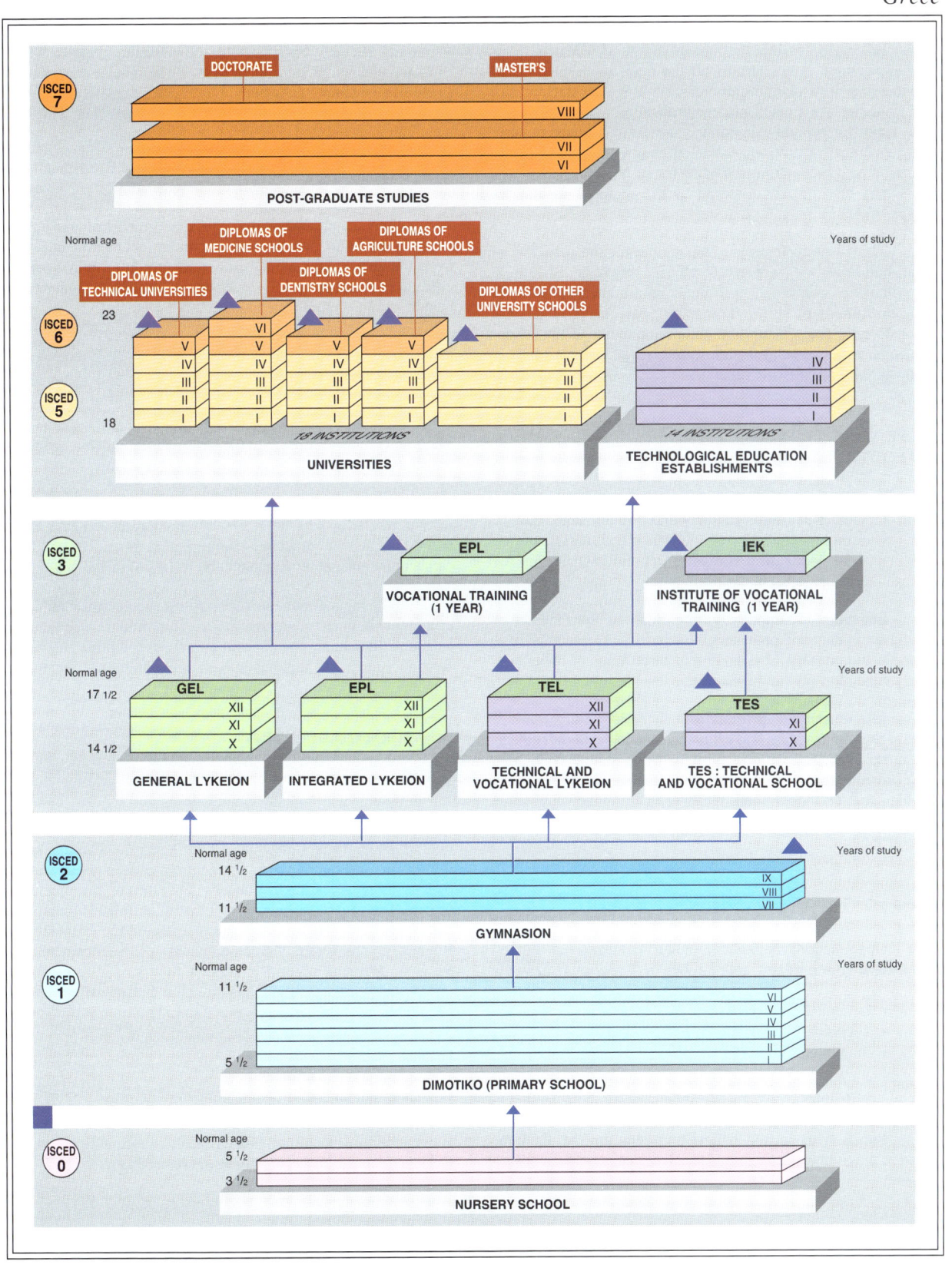

Greece

Grèce

Greece

Education is the responsibility of the Ministry of Education which issues almost all the decisions that concern educational policy, planning of curricula, teaching staff, school operation, etc. As a result of decentralisation over the past ten years, funds for general expenditure may be transferred directly to the prefectures (*Nomarchia*) through the Ministry of Education or directly from the Ministry of National Economy. Funds may also be administered by the regional authorities (*Peripheries*).

The 54 prefectures are responsible for the planning of school buildings. At the prefectural level there are also education authorities concerned with the school administration and the appointment of staff. The municipalities (*Demos*) are responsible for the construction and maintenance of the school buildings, and the school committee at the school level is responsible for small-scale repairs.

PRE-PRIMARY, PRIMARY AND LOWER SECONDARY EDUCATION

The Greek education system consists of three levels:
- primary education (nursery and primary schools);
- secondary education (in *gymnasia* and *lykeia*);
- higher education (universities and institutions for technological education).

Education is compulsory for children as from the age of 5-and-a-half years and consists of six years of elementary education (in the primary schools) and of three years of lower secondary education (in the *gymnasia*).

The schools for primary and secondary education are mostly state-run (public), and exclusively so at the higher education level. Public education is provided free at all levels, there being no registration or tuition fees and pupils/students are provided with textbooks without charge. During the six years of elementary education, all pupils are promoted automatically to the next grade.

UPPER SECONDARY EDUCATION

Upper secondary non-compulsory education is divided into *Lykeia* (three years) and *Technical Vocational Schools* (*TES*, two years). There are three types of *Lykeia*:
- General *Lykeia* (GEL);
- Technical and vocational *Lykeia* (TEL);
- Integrated *Lykeia* (EPL).

Special education

Pupils with special education needs are mainly integrated in the ordinary schools and receive special help according to individual cases. Such help may be given individually, within ordinary classes, as additional help, or in special classes integrated in ordinary schools. There are special schools for severely handicapped pupils and for blind and deaf children.

Private education

Private education is regulated in all aspects by the Ministry of Education (curricula, building standards, etc.) and even the annual fees are subject to State control. The private education sector is steadily decreasing and only roughly 6 per cent of primary pupils attend private schools.

TERTIARY EDUCATION

Entrance examinations to higher education are divided into four groups according to the streams that students choose in their *Lykeia* studies.

There are special provision of training centres (*IEKs*) for *Lykeia* graduates who do not follow higher general education, and do not wish to enter the labour market immediately. They can acquire special professional and technical skills.

The higher education institutions (universities and technology institutions) are autonomous. The Ministry of Education finances their main current and capital expenditure, confirms their decisions, and supervises them in general.

NON-FORMAL EDUCATION

Public

Non-formal education consists mainly of adult education which comprises programmes in literacy, vocational training, in-service training, etc. These programmes are sponsored by various agencies and institutions under the various ministries, organisations, associations, etc. Two of the most important of these agencies are the following: under the Ministry of Education, the General Secretariat of Adult Education and Services offering reception classes for immigrant children; under the Ministry of Agriculture, the Organisation for the Employment of the Labour Force (OAED).

Private

In the private sector there are a large number of institutes and schools for foreign languages, centres for liberal studies, special tuition (cramming) schools, music schools, dance schools, etc., which are mostly found in urban areas.

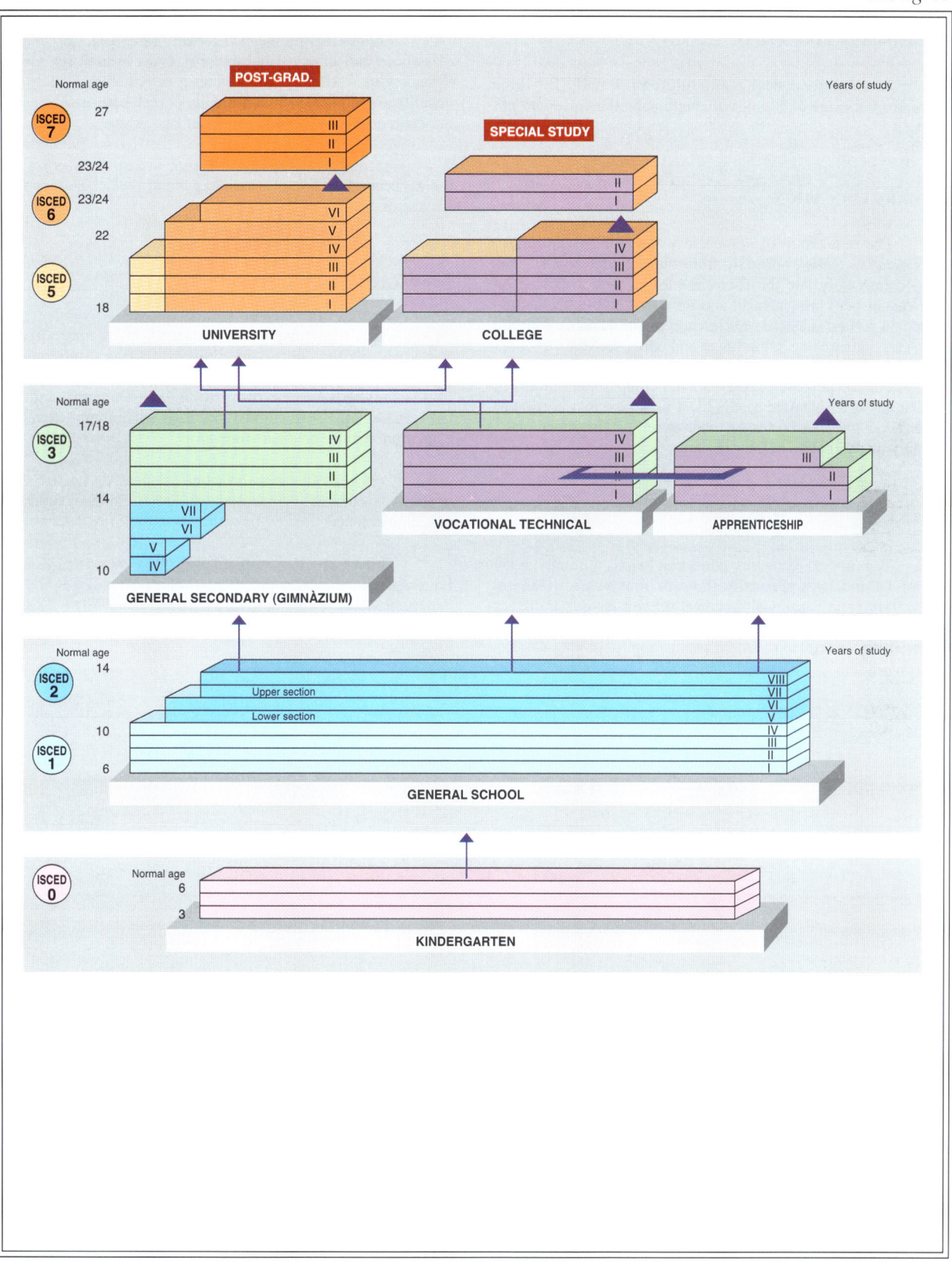

Hungary

Hongrie

Hungary

PRE-PRIMARY EDUCATION

Kindergartens deal with children normally for three years, from the age of 3 to 6, but length and boundaries are not strict.

PRIMARY EDUCATION

The main form of compulsory schooling is the *eight-class general school*, normally from the age of 6 to 14. It is divided internally into the four-class lower section (based on one teacher per class, mainly) and the four-class upper section (based on special subjects). Different types of qualifications are necessary for teaching in the lower and upper section.

For the purpose of international comparison, the lower section has been reported as ISCED 1 and the upper section as ISCED 2. This division can be made exactly in enrolment data, but only by estimation in finance data.

SECONDARY EDUCATION

The (upper) secondary education begins normally at the age of 14 and lasts generally three or four years. General (*gimnàzium*) and vocational-technical schools have four classes and after a final exam they give a certificate (*matura*), which is necessary for several jobs and for application for tertiary studies.

Apprenticeship means normally three years of study in classroom and after a final exam it gives a qualification for skilled work. After apprenticeship it is possible to study in a vocational-technical school normally or on a part-time basis and to obtain a secondary certificate after two years.

As new developments, there are some 8-class and 6-class secondary schools (mainly general), which start as from the age of 10 or 12.

TERTIARY EDUCATION

Universities offer theory-based studies normally, for five years, giving a university diploma. Doctoral programmes were formerly organised by separate research institutes. Since 1993, they have been integrated into the universities. Universities offer special post-graduate programmes as further education, mainly on a part-time basis.

Colleges offer more practice-oriented studies for three or four years and deliver a college diploma. Colleges offer special supplemental courses, as well, normally for two years.

Three-year courses of colleges are reported as ISCED 5. Four-year courses and supplemental courses of colleges and university graduate programmes are reported as ISCED 6. Special part-time post-graduate programmes of universities are reported as ISCED 7.

Ireland

PRE-PRIMARY EDUCATION

Pre-primary education is provided in the same schools as primary level education. These schools are called National Schools. Pre-primary education in National Schools is defined to cover two grade-years – junior and senior infant classes.

National Schools (with a few exceptions) are privately owned and controlled but are publicly aided and are subject to public regulation and inspection. All National Schools at both this level and primary (ISCED 1) follow a national curriculum. Teachers in National School are employed by the School Board of Management of each school but are paid directly by the Department of Education.

PRIMARY EDUCATION

For the purposes of reporting data on ISCED level 1 (primary), pupils enrolled in all classes above infant classes in National Schools are included under this ISCED level. The only exception is special schools (which are in all cases counted as National Schools) where pupils aged 13 and over are allocated ISCED level 9. Corresponding amounts of expenditure and numbers of teachers in special schools are allocated to ISCED 9. There are six standards (or grade-years) corresponding to primary level within National Schools.

LOWER SECONDARY EDUCATION

This level corresponds to junior cycle of second level. Junior cycle consists of three years leading to the Junior Certificate examination taken usually at the age of 15 or 16. The Junior Certificate is a written public examination assessed by teachers outside the pupils' school.

The main types of second level schools are voluntary secondary, vocational, community and comprehensive schools. Despite the title of these schools, in recent years the range of subjects and curriculum provided at this level is broadly similar across the different school types. All of the above-mentioned types of schools are publicly aided. Voluntary secondary schools are privately owned and controlled although subject to similar regulations as other types of second level schools. Vocational schools are administered by local education authorities called Vocational Education Committees.

UPPER SECONDARY EDUCATION

This level corresponds to senior cycle of second level education. This level comprises two years of a Leaving Certificate programme preceded by an optional transition year which is also part of upper secondary education. The Leaving Certificate is a general programme leading to the Leaving Certificate examination, usually at the age of around 17 or 18. There are a number of vocational modules within the Leaving Certificate programme as special pre-employment vocational programmes to facilitate transfer from senior cycle to the labour market. The latter are known as Vocational Preparation and Training Programmes (VPT1 and VPT2).

Also included in statistics of education at this level are courses in agricultural and second level private commercial colleges. In a limited number of cases, courses of second level standard are provided in third level institutions (for example apprenticeship training courses).

A small but growing number of the long-term unemployed aged 21 or over are availing of the Vocational Training Opportunities Scheme (VTOS) which covers studies at both lower and upper secondary level.

TERTIARY EDUCATION

Sub-degree level

Education at the third level of a type that leads to an award not equivalent to a first university degree (ISCED 5) takes place mainly in Regional Technical Colleges and the Dublin Institute of Technology. These institutions are publicly controlled and financed. The National Council for Education Awards validates most sub-degree and some degree courses in the Technological Colleges.

Primary university degree level

Education at this level includes all Primary or Bachelor Degree programmes, whether they are taken in university or non-university institutions. All post-graduate diplomas or certificates (but not degrees) are classified under ISCED 6. All primary degrees take at least three years; many take four years; and certain disciplines such as medicine, architecture and engineering take longer. Post-graduate diplomas and certificates take one year.

Students in Regional Technical Colleges or in the Dublin Institute of Technology can obtain a Bachelor Degree in either of two ways – through following what is termed an *ab-initio* degree programme lasting for four years leading to a Bachelor Degree awarded by an external university. This is equivalent in academic terms to a three- or four-year Bachelor programme in a university institution. Alternatively, students may complete a three-year diploma course leading to a National Diploma after which they complete one further year of study leading to a Bachelor Degree awarded externally. The latter type of award is referred to as an "add-on" degree.

University institutions are publicly funded and are managed by governing bodies whose composition varies from institution to institution. All universities are influenced by public policy with regard to the numbers recruited. The total budget of the universities is set by the Higher Education Authority which is a public funding body for the universities. The universities are free to attract private sources of funding for research and teaching.

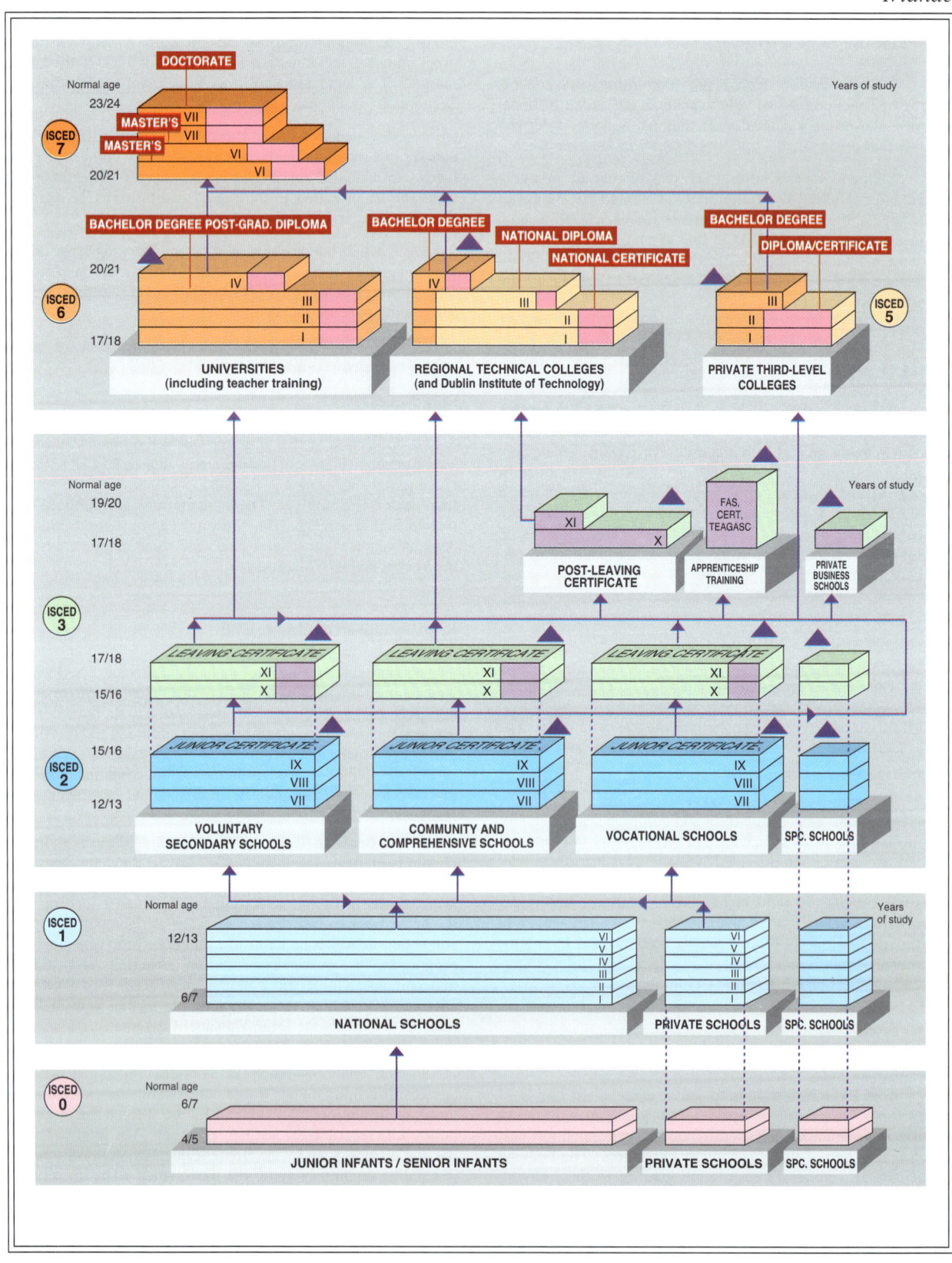

Ireland

Irlande

Ireland

Post-graduate degree level

Education at this level includes all Master's degree programmes as well as Ph.D. programmes. Master's degree programmes generally take one to two years on a full-time basis after completion of the Primary Degree or longer if taken on a part-time basis. Post-graduate diplomas or certificates are **not** classified under ISCED 7. A small number of Bachelor Degree graduates in Technical Colleges proceed to Master's degree programmes in these institutions.

ADULT EDUCATION

Adult education is defined in terms of second-chance education where an individual returns to education (full-time or part-time) after a break in studies since leaving school or college. The term includes both vocational education and training taking place in educational institutions and training centres as well as general courses of a short duration (such as personal development). In most cases adult education takes place in regular educational institutions (or centres attached to the regular school system). Most of adult education is allocated to ISCED levels 3, 5, and 6.

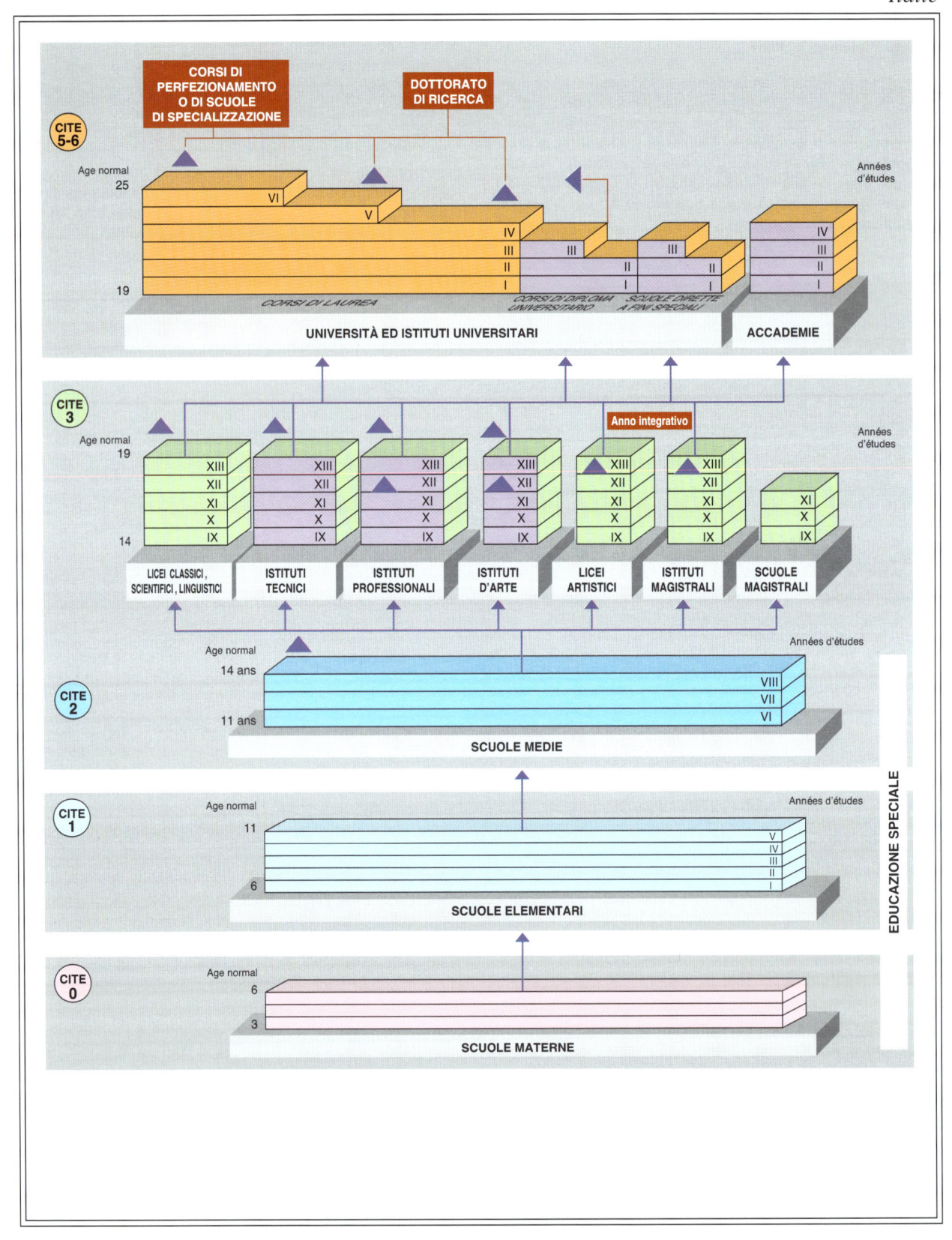

Italy

Italie

Italy

PRE-SCHOOL EDUCATION

Pre-schools accept all children between the ages of 3 and 6, including those with adjustment and learning difficulties. Children attending pre-school are organised into groups (sections), with a minimum of 14 and a maximum of 28 children. The sections can be comprised of children of the same age or of mixed ages. Attendance at State pre-schools is free of charge; a contribution is requested from families for transportation and meal services provided by the municipality.

PRIMARY EDUCATION

Between 1985 and 1990, primary education in Italy underwent a process of profound renewal which was completed by the *new programmes*, approved in 1985, and the *new system* set out in a 1990 law. Primary school attendance is compulsory for children aged between 6 and 11 years.

Primary schools are made up of five classes divided into two cycles according to the developmental levels of the children: the first cycle is comprised of the initial two classes in which basic skills predominate; the second cycle gradually introduces pupils to concepts. Classes are made up of no more than 25 pupils, with a limit of 20 pupils for classes containing a handicapped pupil for whom the presence of a support teacher is provided, in order to foster integration and learning.

With regard to organisation, a system of more than one teacher for each class is used according to a structure called a *module*. The law provides for the presence of three teachers for every two classes or four teachers for every three classes.

LOWER SECONDARY EDUCATION

The lower secondary school, or *scuola media*, is compulsory, free of charge and lasts three years. It represents the next step after primary education and is the only possible way of completing compulsory education. The requisite for admission is the possession of the primary school leaving certificate which is normally obtained at the age of 11.

The timetable of compulsory education is 30 hours a week (five hours each morning from Monday to Saturday), distributed among the various subjects of study; each lesson lasts 60 minutes.

UPPER SECONDARY SCHOOLS

After finishing the period of compulsory education and passing the lower secondary school examination, students may undertake courses of study lasting for five, four or three years. At the end of these courses they may go on to higher education or enter the job market.

All schools that offer post-compulsory instruction are part of upper secondary education and are comprised by the following categories:

- classical, scientific and primary and pre-school teacher training (commonly designated as the "Classical" category);
- artistic education: artistic *licei* and art schools;
- technical education: technical schools;
- vocational education: includes all vocational schools.

The classical *liceo* offers a course of humanistic study and aims to prepare students for university and other forms of higher education. It consists of five years of study divided into two cycles: one two-year period called *ginnasio* and another three-year period called *liceo*.

The scientific *liceo* develops and deepens the education of those intending to follow university studies in the faculties of science, medicine and surgery. Since 1969, the year which brought about the liberalisation of university admission, this *liceo*, like the "classical" one, gives access to all types of university training and higher education.

The primary teacher training school (*Istituto Magistrale*) and the pre-school teacher training school (*Scuola Magistrale*) prepares pre-school and primary teachers.

Technical education is directed towards students aged between 14 and 19 years. Technical schools aim to prepare students to practise professions, or technical or administrative services, in the agricultural, industrial and commercial sectors. The study programmes for technical schools include, in the first two-year period, cultural subjects which are common to all the sectors and specialisations.

Vocational schools accept students from 14 to 17 years of age, offering the possibility of extending studies until the age of 19 for those attending experimental five-year courses. Vocational schools were created in the 1950s in order to train qualified entry-level technicians.

At the end of the upper secondary school courses offered by the classical and artistic school categories, students must take the upper secondary school leaving certificate examination (*Maturità*). Only those who have received a positive assessment of their previous year's results are admitted to this examination. The examination is comprised of two written tests and an oral examination which is held before a Board of Examiners appointed by the Ministry of Education.

The final examinations for the two- or three-year courses offered by vocational schools are called qualification examinations and are held before commissions composed of teachers of cultural, technical and practical subjects from the school plus two external experts delegated by business and industry who have an interest in a particular school.

Artistic education is composed of schools belonging to the upper secondary school system as well as institutes of non-university higher education.

Italy

Art schools provide suitable cultural education in order to develop the creative qualities of students and to train them for employment and artistic production, while taking into account specific local traditions. The study programmes of these schools last for five years, divided into a three-year cycle followed by a two-year cycle.

The three-year study cycle ends with a final examination for obtaining the "Master of Art Diploma" and the following two-year cycle ends with a State examination for obtaining the "applied arts upper secondary school leaving certificate". Artistic *licei* aim to give students cultural training which is specifically oriented towards the sector of visual arts and relevant forms of expression.

Courses normally last four years and are divided into one two-year cycle which is common to both sections, followed by another two-year period which differs for each section. At the end of these four years, students take a State examination in order to obtain the artistic upper secondary school leaving certificate (*Maturità Artistica*).

TERTIARY EDUCATION

Article 33 of the Italian Constitution recognises the right of universities and academies to act autonomously within the limits set by law. Both public and private organisations have the right to establish schools and educational institutes. Therefore, institutes of higher education are divided into State and non-state establishments.

It is also possible to distinguish between universities and non-university institutes. In the former category, for example, in addition to universities, there are the Institutes of Higher Physical Education and special types of Institutes of Higher Education including the *Istituto Orientale*, the *Istituto superiore navale* of Naples and the *Scuola normale superiore* of Pisa.

Artistic higher education institutes belong instead to the non-university higher education category.

The *Ministry of Universities and Scientific and Technological Research* has general responsibility for university education. It also distributes available funds among State universities and those private universities that have conformed to the structure of the public sector and that have obtained the authorisation to issue legally recognised qualifications. Private universities, moreover, also receive financial resources from local organisations, associations or foundations. In the context of university autonomy, State universities are allowed to accept financing and contributions for research and activities for different users. Additional income for the university comes from contributions paid by students for services (laboratories and libraries).

Universities issue the following qualifications:

- university diploma (*laurea breve*);
- degree certificate (*laurea*);
- specialisation certificate;
- research doctorate (*dottorato di ricerca*).

Scuola materna	Pre-school education
Scuola elementare	Primary education
Scuola media	Lower secondary education
Liceo classico	Classical high school
scientifico	Scientific
linguistico	Language
Licei artistici	Art high schools
Istituti tecnici	Technical institutes
Istituti professionali	Professional institutes
Istituti d'arte	Art institutes
Istituti magistrali	Teacher training institutes
Scuole magistrali	Pre-school teacher training institutes
Anno integrativo	Additional complementary year
Università ed Istituti universitari	University and higher education centres
Corsi de laurea	Master's degree programmes
Corsi di diploma universitario	Higher education degree programmes
Scuole dirette a fini speciali	Specialised schools
Accademie di belle arti	Fine arts academies
Dottorato di ricerca	Ph.D. degree
Corsi di perfezionamento o Scuole di specializzazione	In-service training centres

Japan

It is compulsory to attend both an elementary school and lower secondary school or to attend a special education school for a period of nine years, from the age of 6 to 15.

Private education. There are national, local public and private institutions at all levels of education. The percentage of enrolments in private educational institutions at each level of education is as follows:

Pre-primary education (kindergartens):	about 80%
Compulsory education (elementary and lower secondary schools):	less than 1%
Upper secondary education (upper secondary schools):	about 30%
Higher education (universities):	about 70%
(junior colleges):	about 90%
(colleges of technology):	about 5%
Others (special training colleges):	about 95%
(miscellaneous schools):	about 98%

PRE-PRIMARY AND PRIMARY EDUCATION
(Yochien)

Kindergartens cater for children aged 3, 4 and 5 and provide them with one- to three-year courses. Elementary schools (*Shogakko*) aim at giving children between the ages of 6 and 12 elementary general education suited to the stage of their mental and physical development.

SECONDARY EDUCATION

Lower secondary schools (*Chugakko*) give children between the ages of 12 and 15 general secondary education suited to the stage of their mental and physical development, continuing on the basis of work done in elementary school. Upper secondary schools (*Koto gakko*) offer, in addition to full day courses (*Zennichisei katei*), day/evening (*Teijisei katei*) and correspondence courses (*Tsushinsei katei*). Full-day courses last three years, while both day/evening and correspondence courses last three years or more. The latter two courses are mainly intended for young workers who wish to pursue their upper secondary studies in a flexible manner. All these courses lead to a certificate of upper secondary education. Upper secondary school courses may be classified into two categories: general and specialised (vocational) courses.

Special education schools (*Tokushu-kyoiku-gakko*) exist for the blind, deaf and otherwise handicapped. They are divided into four levels: kindergarten, elementary, lower secondary and upper secondary departments. In addition, special classes in ordinary elementary and lower secondary schools cater for children with less severe handicaps.

TERTIARY EDUCATION

Institutions of higher education include universities, junior colleges and colleges of technology. In addition, special training colleges offering post-secondary courses may be regarded as another type of higher education institution.

Universities (*Daigaku*) require for admission the completion of upper secondary schooling or its equivalent, and offer courses of at least four years leading to a Bachelor degree (*Gakushi*). Universities may set up a graduate school offering advanced studies in a variety of fields leading to Master's (*Shushi*) and doctoral (*Hakushi*) degrees. Graduate schools normally last five years, consisting of the first two-year courses leading to a Master's degree and the following three-year courses leading to a doctoral degree.

Junior colleges (*Tanki-daigaku*) require for admission the completion of upper secondary schooling or its equivalent, and offer two- or three-year programmes in different fields of study which lead to the title of associate (*Jungakushi*). Those who have completed junior college may go on to university and their credits acquired at junior college may be counted as part of the credits leading to a Bachelor's degree.

Colleges of technology (*Koto senmongakko*) unlike universities or junior colleges, accept those who have completed lower secondary schooling, and offer five-year programmes leading to the title of associate. They teach specialised subjects in depth and prepare students for vocational life. Those who have completed college of technology may apply for admission to the upper division of university.

In addition to the above-mentioned institutions of elementary, secondary and higher education, there are educational institutions known as "special training colleges" (*Senshugakko*) and "miscellaneous schools" (*Kakushugakko*) which offer a variety of practical vocational and technical education programmes in response to diverse demands of people. The great majority of these schools are privately controlled.

Courses provided in special training colleges may be classified into three categories: upper secondary, post secondary and general courses. From 1986, on students who have completed an upper secondary course lasting three years or more in special training colleges designated by the Minister are entitled to apply for a university place.

Miscellaneous schools provide people with vocational and practical training in such fields as dress-making, cooking, book-keeping, typing, automobile driving and repairing, computer techniques, etc. Most courses in miscellaneous schools require for admission the completion of lower secondary schooling. These courses normally last one year or more with at least 680 class hours per year, but there are also shorter courses of three months or more.

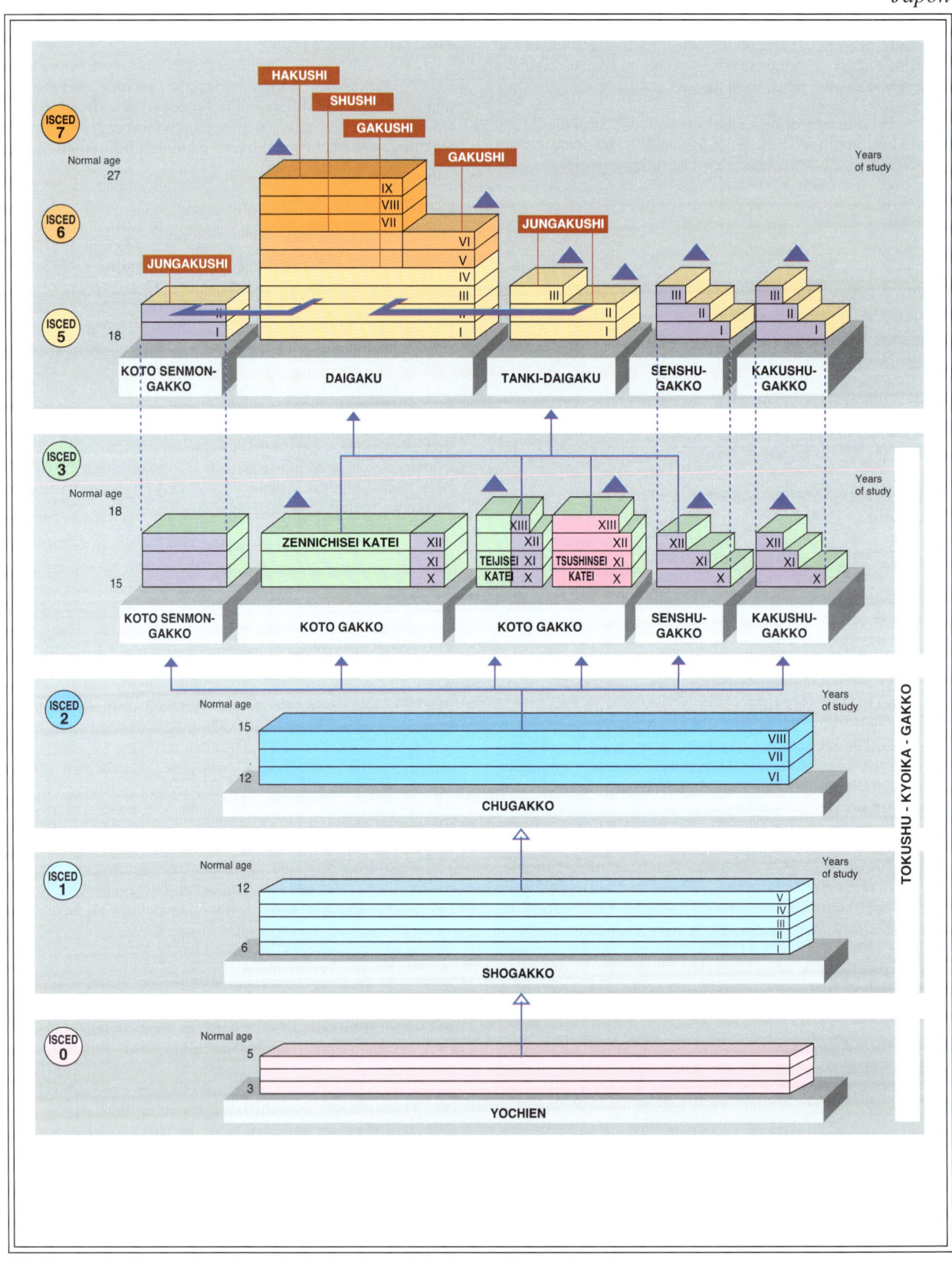

Japan

Japon

ISCED 7
- Normal age 27
- HAKUSHI
- SHUSHI
- GAKUSHI
- GAKUSHI
- JUNGAKUSHI
- JUNGAKUSHI

ISCED 6 / ISCED 5
- Normal age 18
- KOTO SENMON-GAKKO
- DAIGAKU (I–IX)
- TANKI-DAIGAKU (I–III)
- SENSHU-GAKKO (I–III)
- KAKUSHU-GAKKO (I–III)

ISCED 3
- Normal age 15–18
- KOTO SENMON-GAKKO
- KOTO GAKKO — ZENNICHISEI KATEI (X–XII)
- KOTO GAKKO — TEIJISEI KATEI / TSUSHINSEI KATEI (X–XIII)
- SENSHU-GAKKO (X–XII)
- KAKUSHU-GAKKO (X–XII)

ISCED 2
- Normal age 12–15
- CHUGAKKO (VI–VIII)

ISCED 1
- Normal age 6–12
- SHOGAKKO (I–V)

ISCED 0
- Normal age 3–5
- YOCHIEN

TOKUSHU - KYOIKA - GAKKO

Japan

Yochien	Kindergarten
Shogakko	Elementary school
Chugakko	Lower secondary school
Koto gakko	Upper secondary school
Zennichisei katei	Full day course
Teijisei katei	Day/evening course
Tsushinsei katei	Correspondence course
Daigaku	University
Gakushi	Bachelor
Daigakuin	Graduate school
Shushi	Master
Hakushi	Doctor
Tanki-daigaku	Junior college
Jungakushi	Associate
Koto senmongakko	College of Technology
Jungakushi	Associate
Senshugakko	Special Training College
Kakushugakko	Miscellaneous school
Tokushu-kyoiku-gakko	Special education schools

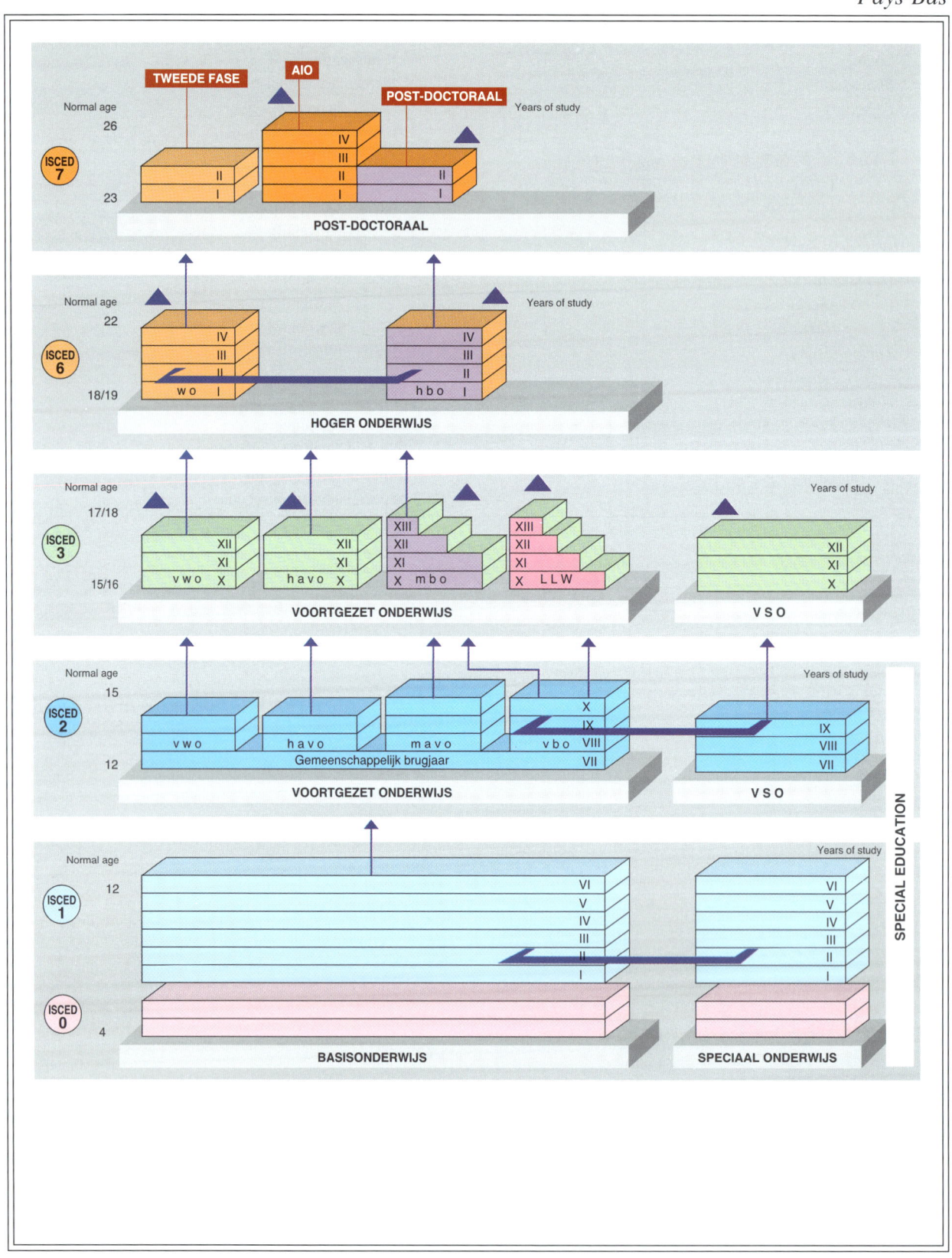

The Netherlands

Pays-Bas

The Netherlands

Freedom of education, which is laid down in the Constitution, finds expression in virtually all facets of the Dutch education system. The threefold freedom – to found schools, to organise them and to determine the principles on which they are based – is the reason for the wide variety of schools in the Netherlands. Under the terms of the Constitution, the government funds public and private schools on an equal basis. Freedom of education is subject to restrictions laid down in the Compulsory Education Act, which stipulates that, until they reach the age of 16, children must attend an educational establishment which complies with statutory requirements.

The diagram reflects the situation in 1992.

PRIMARY EDUCATION

Primary education (*basisonderwijs*) caters for children from 4 to about 12 years of age and provides in principle 8 consecutive years of schooling. All children must attend school from the first day of the month following their 5th birthday. However, almost all children attend primary school from the age of 4.

SPECIAL EDUCATION

Special and secondary special education is intended for children who require extra educational help beyond what normal education can offer. To provide such students which a suitable education, there are various types of (secondary) special education. Each type specialises in education for specific types of students, such as those with hearing, visual or physical handicaps, or those with (severe) learning difficulties or maladjusted children.

In principle, special education (*SO*) aims at the same age group as normal primary education. The age at which children may enter special education differs, varying from 3 to 6 years, depending on the type of school. Secondary special education (*VSO*) is for children starting at age twelve. There is a maximum of twenty years of age for special education. After following special education, students usually move to secondary special education or to one type of individual vocational education. Students may also pursue a *VWO*, *HAVO*, *MAVO* or *VBO* education.

SECONDARY EDUCATION *(voortgezet onderwijs)*

General secondary education follows on from primary education and caters for pupils from 12 to about 18 years of age. Secondary education is provided in the following forms:

- pre-vocational education (*VBO*) for age 12 to 16, a four-year course;
- junior general secondary education (*MAVO*) for age 12 to 16, a four-year course;
- senior general secondary education (*HAVO*) for age 12 to 17, a five-year course;
- pre-university education (*VWO*) for age 12 to 18, a six-year course.

Most secondary school pupils spend one or more years in a transition class (*gemeenschappelijke brugklas*), after which they are referred to the type of schools best suited to their needs.

VBO, MAVO, and the first three years of HAVO and VWO are part of the first phase of secondary education. The fourth and fifth years of HAVO and the fourth to sixth year inclusive of VWO belong to the second phase. Schools for secondary education start with a basic education period, effective for the 1993/94 school year. This is a three-to-five-year period. It concerns substantive innovation within existing types of schools.

Senior secondary vocational education (*MBO*) currently falls under the Secondary Education Act. In future, however, these forms will be incorporated in the Education and Vocational Education Act (*WEB*). MBO is vocationally oriented, leading to middle management positions in industry, service industries and government. MBO, for age 16 to 18-20, is a continuation of *VBO* or *MAVO* and lasts a maximum of four years. Longer courses (three and four years) lead to middle management jobs and are contiguous to *HBO*. Interim courses (maximum three years) lead to an independent profession and short training courses (maximum two years) lead to a starting profession, possibly moving on to the long MBO.

The **apprenticeship system** (*LLW*) is general vocational training under the joint responsibility of education, government and the social partners. Following one or two days at school, the other days comprise practical training in industry or trainee workshop. This combination of practical and theoretical training forms the basis of the apprenticeship system. It is for young people from 16 years of age, with or without VBO or MBO certificates. It lasts one to three years. The Ministry of Education and Science provides the financing.

The apprenticeship system has three levels: *primary training* leads to a starting profession, linked to MAVO and VBO; it lasts two to three years; *secondary training* leads to an independent profession, linked to primary apprenticeship system training and to the short *MBO* training, duration one to two years; *tertiary training* leads to specialists profession, linked to secondary apprenticeship system training and to the interim *MBO* training, duration one to two years.

TERTIARY EDUCATION

Tertiary education comprises higher professional education (*HBO*) university education (*WO*) (universities). As of 1993, these sectors are part of a single law, the Higher Education and Research Act (*WHW*). *HBO* and *WO* have a two-tier system. The first phase, or undergraduate level, may last up to four years, the propaedeutic stage of which lasts no longer than one year.

The Netherlands

Higher professional education (*HBO*) provides theoretical and practical training for occupations which require a higher vocational qualification, and is taught at *HBO* colleges. It follows on from the higher types of secondary education (i.e. *HAVO*, *VWO* and *MBO*). Besides initial education (directly related to secondary education), the *HBO* also provides – in its second phase – several secondary training courses, among others for the arts. To follow a secondary training course, students must have higher educational training. *HBO* colleges can carry out research to the extent that it relates to the institutions' training courses. Graduates of a four-year technical or agricultural course earn the title of *ingenieur* (*ing.*), for the other branches of study, the title is that of *baccalaureus* (*bc*). Internationally, the title of Bachelor (B) may be used.

University education (*WO*) comprises training in the independent pursuit of scholarship and preparation of positions in the community for which a university degree is required. A university also has the function of transmitting the knowledge obtained in the pursuit of scholarship for the benefit of the community, as a service to society. A *VWO*-certificate, a special entrance examination or a foundation course from a higher professional course provides admission to university studies.

Following the undergraduate exam, one earns the title of *doctorandus* (*drs.*), *meester* (*mr*; law) of *ingenieur* (*ir*; science). The title of Master may be used internationally.

The second stage, to which a limited number of students is admitted, provides academic training at post-graduate level. Students in these courses, who are known as trainee research assistants or AIOs, are trained as researchers or design engineers. The courses vary in length from 1 to 4 years and are open to HBO as well as university graduates. In addition, universities provide post-graduate vocational courses, including, for example, those for doctors, veterinary surgeons and dentists).

Teacher training courses for the various fields of education form part of higher education and can be subdivided into:

- Teacher training for full competence in primary education in all subjects and for all age groups (*HBO*).
- General teacher training for a second degree and a first degree qualification in secondary education. Second degree teachers may give lessons in the first three years of HAVO and *VWO* and in all years of *VBO*, *MAVO* or *MBO*, first degree teachers in the complete secondary education system. Full-time training for second-degree qualification lasts four years, with special training in a single subject. A first degree can then be attained by taking three-year, part-time training (*HBO*).
- Teacher training in the technical subjects for a second-degree qualification at the Netherlands Pedagogic Technical College. The course lasts five (full-time) or seven (part-time) years (*HBO*).
- Teacher training for physical education for a first-degree qualification, at five colleges. The course lasts four years (*HBO*).
- University teacher training for a first-degree qualification in secondary education in the subject completed at the university. It is a one-year course. Passing an undergraduate exam, in which a two-month orientation towards the teaching profession is part of the study programme, is a requirement for admission (*WO*).

	Basisonderwijs	Pre-primary education
O	*Speciaal onderwijs*	Special education
VO	*Voortgezet onderwijs*	Secondary education
VSO	*Voortgezet speciaal onderwijs*	Secondary special education
	Gemeenschappelijk brugjaar	Transition class
VBO	*Voorbereidend beroepsonderwijs*	Pre-vocational education
MAVO	*Middelbaar algemeen voortgezet onderwijs*	Junior general secondary education
HAVO	*Hoger algemeen voortgezet onderwijs*	Senior general secondary education
VWO	*Voorbereidend wetenschappelijk onderwijs*	Pre-university education
MBO	*Middelbaar beroepsonderwijs*	Senior secondary vocational education
LLW	*Leerlingwezen*	Apprenticeship system
HO	*Hoger onderwijs*	Higher education
WO	*Wetenschappelijk onderwijs (universiteiten)*	University education
HBO	*Hoger beroepsonderwijs (Hogescholen)*	Higher professional education
	Post-doctoraal	Post-graduate level
	Tweede fase	Second-phase courses
AIO	*Assistent-in-opleiding*	Trainee research assistant

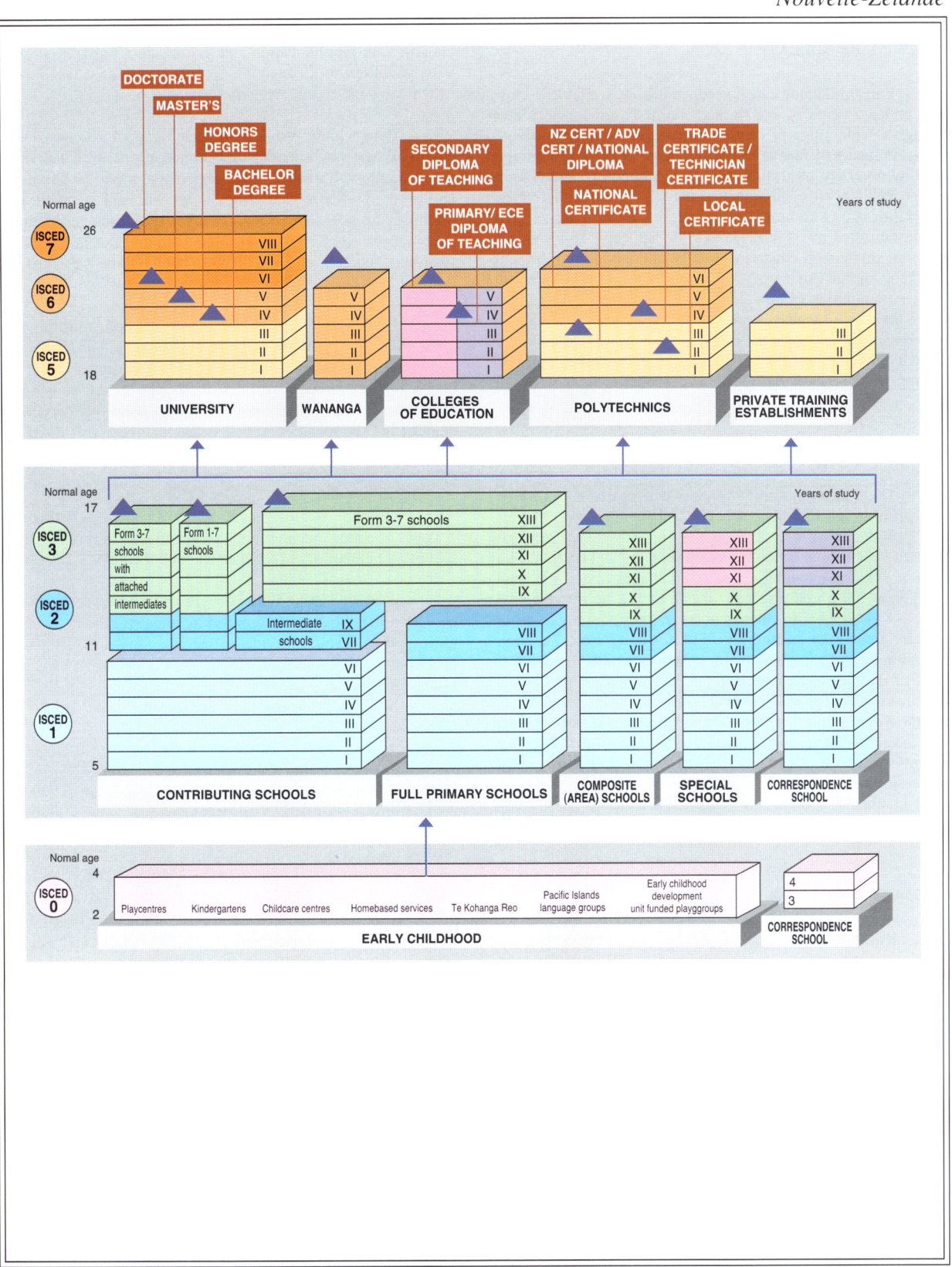

New Zealand

Nouvelle-Zélande

New Zealand

PRE-PRIMARY EDUCATION

Early childhood care and education are available to children under 6 years of age through home-based services and through a wide range of centre-based services which provide both sessional and full-day programmes. These are administered by a variety of groups including community and church groups, voluntary agencies (such as playcentre and kindergarten associations) and commercial operators. *Kohanga reo* have been established by New Zealand's Maori people to provide a language immersion educational early childhood environment in which children can learn Maori language and culture. Pacific Island communities are also establishing early childhood centres where their own languages are used. All early childhood care and education services must meet minimum requirements laid down by government. To be eligible for a government general funding grant, services must also have a negotiated charter.

PRIMARY AND SECONDARY EDUCATION

The Education Act (1989) provides for free education in State primary and secondary schools, and attendance is compulsory from the age of 6 until the age of 16. However, almost all children start formal schooling at the age of 5. The final two years of primary schooling, forms 1 and 2 (ages 11 and 12), may be taken at full primary school (ages 5 to 12), an intermediate school (which caters for those two years only), an area school (which caters for all students ages 5 to 17), or a form 1-7 school, depending on the schools available within the child's neighbourhood or district. The majority of children begin secondary school at age 13 (form 3). A smaller number (about 12 per cent) remain within either the area school or form 1-7 school they have been attending. Maori medium education in the school sector is supported through the provision of bilingual and immersion programmes in mainstream schools or through a small number of schools (currently 34) which are specifically designated Maori medium schools (*kura kaupapa Maori*).

TERTIARY EDUCATION

Beyond secondary school level, which may be completed at either forms 5, 6 or 7 (ages 15 to 17), students may undertake further education and training in a polytechnic, university, college a of education, a private training establishment or with an employer in industry.

Polytechnics provide a diverse range of vocational education. Programmes are generally concentrated at ISCED levels 3 and 5, although a broad range of personal growth, community and general, bridging and professional skills enhancement programmes are also catered for. Courses span from certificate to degree level. Subjects range from trade training, in areas such as plumbing and carpentry, to secretarial and business courses and training for nurses.

Universities in New Zealand offer education ranging from ISCED level 3 (a very small number of programmes) through ISCED 7. The majority of programmes are at the degree or postgraduate level (ISCED 6 and 7). All universities offer arts, science and commerce, while others offer specialist degrees in law, music, veterinary science, medicine, dentistry, agriculture, horticulture, architecture, planning, engineering, optometry and fine arts.

Teacher training (ISCED 5) is provided through colleges of education, although teacher education is also offered in a small number of universities and polytechnics.

Wananga are tertiary education providers, set up by tribal authorities, that are recognised by the government for funding purposes. They provide polytechnic and university level programmes specifically for Maori and with an emphasis on Maori language and culture. This is a relatively new development with only two institutions recognised to date and student numbers are still small.

Education and training are also provided through a range of private and commercial training establishments, through government training establishments and by industry. The largest group of private training establishments are fully funded by government to provide education and training for school leavers with low or no qualifications and for the long-term unemployed with low qualifications. Other private training providers are privately funded and offer courses in a broad range of specialist fields. Some industries may also receive support from government for the provision of training.

Norway

PRE-PRIMARY, PRIMARY AND LOWER SECONDARY EDUCATION

At present Norwegian children start school during the calendar year they reach the age of 7. From 1997 they will start at the age of 6 and compulsory education will be extended from nine to ten years. Today voluntary pre-school education at school or at a child-care institution is available to 90 per cent of all 6 year-olds.

Handicapped children are, as far as possible, integrated into regular classes. However, for certain groups of severely handicapped pupils, national centres of competence assist municipalities and schools.

Compulsory education consists of primary school, grades 1-6 (age 7 to 13) and lower secondary school, grades 7-9 (age 13 to 16). Compulsory education is completely comprehensive. The aim is to offer all children an education which is adapted to the individual's abilities. Each class is kept together as a heterogeneous unit, at least from the first to the sixth grade. During the eighth and ninth grades, students can choose electives in addition to the required studies, but class units remain unchanged except for the elective courses. There is no repeating of grades.

UPPER SECONDARY EDUCATION

In the school year beginning August 1994, great changes are being introduced in upper secondary education. The reform (Reform '94) gives all young people aged 16 to 19 years the legal right (but not an obligation) to three years' full-time upper secondary education, extended to five years for disabled pupils. The regional authorities have to provide the adequate number of places to guarantee this right. The training will qualify for higher education or lead to a craft or journeyman's certificate or other occupational qualification. It will be easier for pupils with vocational training to qualify themselves for entry to a college or university.

During the first year of upper secondary education there are now 13 foundation courses to choose from. The new foundation courses have a more general educational content, leaving specialisation to the level of the advanced courses and/or apprenticeship training.

Training in trades that come under the Vocational Training Act takes the form of two years of vocational education at school followed by an apprenticeship period in an enterprise. The year of apprenticeship may be extended to two years if combined with actual participation in the work of the enterprise, in which case the apprentice is considered an employee and receives wages for the work. In special cases, all training may take place in working life. State grants are given to the enterprise to cover the cost of instruction.

In recent years, around 95 per cent of the 16 year-olds have continued their education after compulsory education. Although typically attended by students in the 16-19 age group, there has been a recent increase in the enrolment of older students who either wish to complete or continue their education. Today, approximately 25 per cent of the pupils in upper secondary education are more than 20 years old.

TERTIARY EDUCATION

A general qualification has been introduced for all higher education. The minimum qualification is as follows:

- completed three years' upper secondary education, including foundation course and advanced courses I and II, with pass marks or a craft or journeyman's certificate, *and*
- a specified level of knowledge in the subjects Norwegian, English, social studies, mathematics and natural sciences/environmental studies.

Reform '94 will provide better opportunities for recruitment to higher education from vocational training at school and in working life.

Norway has four universities and six specialised colleges at university level. These institutions offer degrees at several levels, requiring courses of study lasting four to seven years.

In 1994 the existing 98 public colleges were reorganised into 26 colleges. The basic idea was to link institutions of higher education together in an integrated "Norway Network" in order to create a structural framework for increased co-operation and communication among the institutions. These institutions offer programmes running for one to three years and, at some institutions, longer courses and graduate programmes of four to six years have also been introduced.

Degrees offered by the universities and other institutions of higher education may vary from one institution to the next. Questions concerning degrees, exams and normal time of study are to be decided by the government. Decisions on subject areas which could be included in an exam are taken by the Ministry.

Most programmes at the colleges are oriented towards specific professions, their graduates becoming professional or para-professional personnel in areas such as teaching in pre-schools and at the compulsory school level, engineering, social work, administration, economics, electronic based data, health professions, libraries, journalism, etc.

Many of the undergraduate programmes offered by the colleges and other non-university institutions of higher education can easily be transferred to undergraduate degree programmes at the universities. At the colleges, one-year programmes usually correspond to "foundation studies" at the universities. The more specialised "intermediate studies" also correspond to university programmes. The two- and three-year programmes give right to the title *Hogskole-kandidat* (college graduate). The *cand.mag.* degree may be conferred to students who, according to certain regulations, have successfully completed at least four years of study.

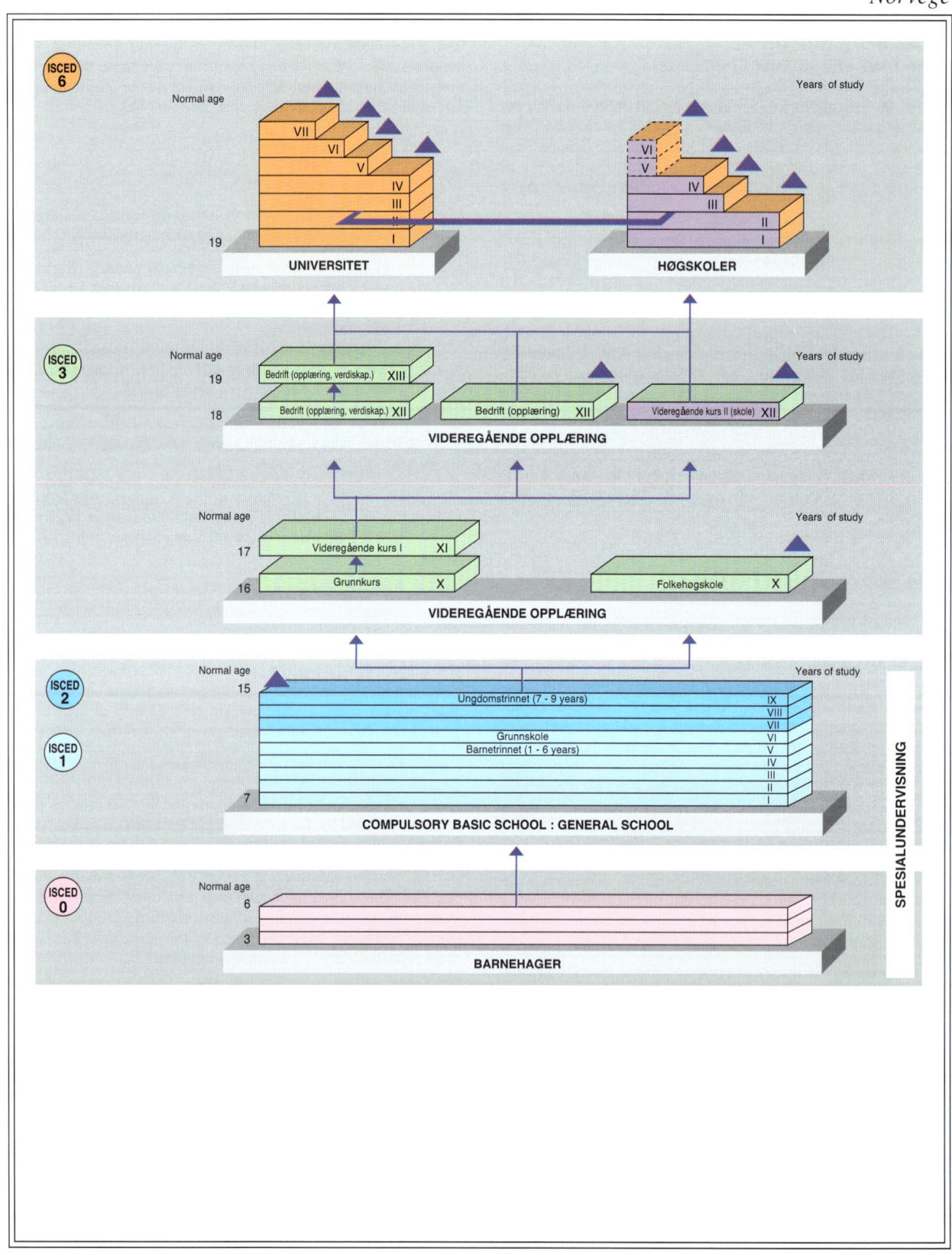

Norway

Norvège

Norway

Graduate degree studies may be expanded into a doctoral study programme (*dr.scient., dr.art., dr. polit., dr.med., dr.psychol., dr.odont., dr.juris*) over a three to four year study period. This presupposes the successful submission of an application to the doctoral programme, which is essentially a research training programme. In addition to completing a doctoral thesis under contract bound supervision, the candidate has to undergo obligatory training in scientific theory and method.

Adult education

The responsibility for adult education is divided between the authorities and the adult education associations, which have been jointly organised by non-government organisations with adult education as their main objective, such as *Friundervisningen* and the Workers' Educational Association. The State subsidises adult education in accordance with the provisions of the Adult Education Act.

The municipalities are responsible for adult education at primary and lower secondary level and the counties for the upper secondary level. The adult education associations and distance learning institutions also provide courses at this level, as well as courses in higher education and courses that are not offered by the public institutions.

The *folk high schools* with half-year and one-year courses as well as shorter courses provide education for young people and adults, primarily of 17-22 years, do not result in formal qualifications.

Labour market courses provide occupational qualifications. They are part of the government's labour market strategy and are fully financed by the State. The courses take place at upper secondary schools, in separate centres attached to the schools or in enterprises. They are run by the labour market authorities, the adult education associations and the school authorities in co-operation.

Private schools

There are few private schools in Norway. By the Act of State Grants to Private Schools implemented in 1985, the government established the conditions under which private schools can obtain public financing. About 98 per cent of all children in compulsory school and 96 per cent of those at upper secondary school attend State schools.

Barnehager	Kindergartens
Grunnskole	Compulsory school
Obligatorisk skole	Compulsory school
Barnetrinnet	Primary school
Ungdomstrinnet	Lower secondary school
Spesialundervisning	Education for handicapped pupils
Videregående opplæring	Upper secondary school
Grunnkurs	Foundation course
Videregående kurs I	Advanced course I
Folkehøgskole	Folk high school
Videregående kurs II (skole)	Advanced course II (school)
Bedrift (opplæring)	At the workplace (training)
Bedrift (opplæring, verdiskaping)	At the workplace (training and productive work)
Høgskole	College
Universitet	University

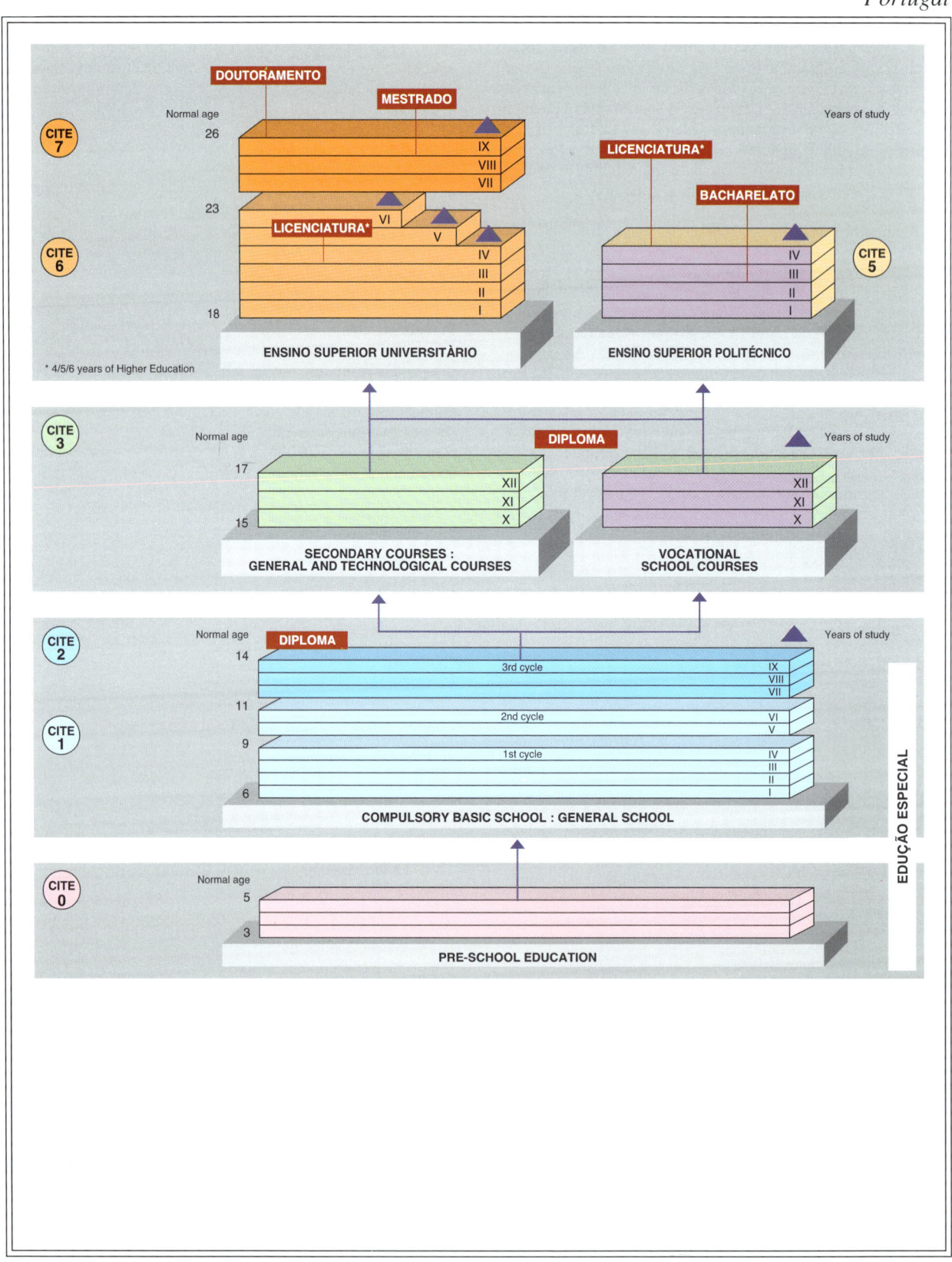

Portugal

CITE 7 / CITE 6
- DOUTORAMENTO
- MESTRADO
- LICENCIATURA*
- Normal age: 18–23–26
- ENSINO SUPERIOR UNIVERSITÀRIO
- * 4/5/6 years of Higher Education

CITE 5
- LICENCIATURA*
- BACHARELATO
- ENSINO SUPERIOR POLITÉCNICO

CITE 3
- DIPLOMA
- Normal age: 15–17
- SECONDARY COURSES: GENERAL AND TECHNOLOGICAL COURSES
- VOCATIONAL SCHOOL COURSES

CITE 2 / CITE 1
- DIPLOMA
- Normal age: 6–9–11–14
- 1st cycle / 2nd cycle / 3rd cycle
- COMPULSORY BASIC SCHOOL: GENERAL SCHOOL

CITE 0
- Normal age: 3–5
- PRE-SCHOOL EDUCATION

EDUCAÇÃO ESPECIAL

Portugal

The Comprehensive Law of Education (Law 46/86) establishes the general framework for the education system, covering pre-schooling education, schooling education and non formal schooling education. The education system, which covers all Portuguese territory – mainland and autonomous regions – and, in a flexible and diversified form, the needs of the Portuguese communities living abroad, comprises a set of facilities that ensure the right to education and guarantee equal opportunities to both access to schooling and success at school.

The State is responsible for the democratisation of education, but is not entitled to direct education and culture according to any philosophical, aesthetic, political or religious orientation. State education is not confessional, but the right to create private and co-operative schools is guaranteed.

PRE-PRIMARY EDUCATION

Pre-schooling education is not compulsory. The government's priority is to attain an enrolment rate of 90 per cent at this level by the end of the century.

PRIMARY AND LOWER SECONDARY EDUCATION

Universal, free and compulsory basic education lasts nine years. It comprises three cycles: the first cycle (four years) covers general education, taught by one teacher in first cycle schools (former primary schools).

The second cycle (two years) is organised as a basic introduction to interdisciplinary subject areas, usually with one teacher per area. It is taught in second cycle schools (former preparatory: "C" schools) in comprehensive "C+S" (preparatory and secondary) schools and in the experimental Basic Comprehensive Schools (EB 1, 2, 3).

The third cycle (three years) is taught according to a standard curriculum, covering different technological subject areas, with one teacher per subject or group of subjects. It is taught in third cycle schools, in comprehensive "C+S" schools, in secondary schools and in the experimental Basic Comprehensive Schools (EB 1, 2, 3).

UPPER SECONDARY EDUCATION

Upper secondary education is optional and consists of a single cycle of three years (the 10th, 11th and 12 years), comprising both general courses leading to the further pursuit of studies, and technological courses geared more to vocational preparation. Transferability between the two types of courses is guaranteed. In secondary education students have several teachers, each teacher being responsible for one subject area. Secondary education is taught in secondary schools.

TERTIARY EDUCATION

Higher education includes university and polytechnic higher education. The private sector in higher education is more important than in basic and secondary education. Forty-five per cent of students are enrolled in private tertiary institutions against 6 per cent at primary and secondary levels.

Educação pré-escolar	Pre-school education
Educação especial	Special education
Ensino secundário	Secondary courses
Cursos de carácter geral	General courses
Cursos tecnológicos	Technological courses
Escolas profissionais	Vocational school courses
Ensino superior universitário	University higher education
Ensino superior politécnico	Polytechnic higher education
Bacharelato	Bachelor degree
Licenciatura	4/5/6 years of higher education
Mestrado	Master's degree
Doutoramento	Ph.D.

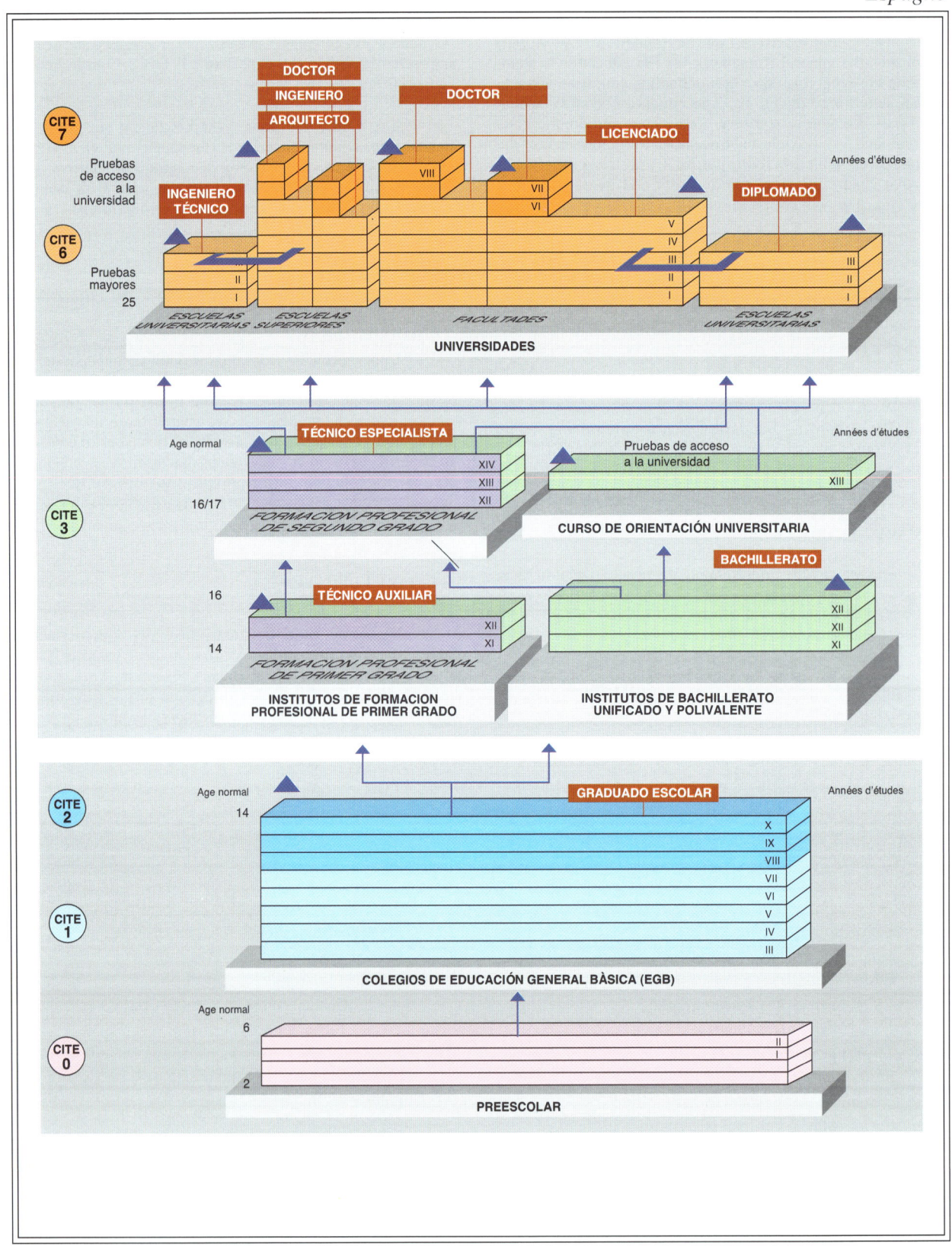

Spain

Espagne

Spain

The structure of the Spanish education system was recently reformed by the Organic Act on General Management of the Education System (*LOGSE*), passed in October 1990. A ten-year period is provided for full implementation of the new Act, and at the majority of educational levels, the structure laid down by the earlier General Education Act (*LGE*) of 1970 remains in force to be progressively replaced as the new levels and cycles are brought into effect. So, the diagram reflects the structure of the Spanish education system according to the 1970 Act, as it was the rule in 1992.

The structural system under the General Education Act (*LGE*) consists of four educational levels: pre-school, basic general education (*EGB*, equivalent to the new primary education and lower secondary stages), the Baccalaureate (*Bachillerato Unificado Polivalente*, *BUP*, or *Bachillerato*) and university education. Vocational training, although not included in the 1970 Act as an "educational level" in the strict sense (as it is specifically concerned with job training), forms part, together with the *Bachillerato*, of what is known in Spain as "middle level education" (equivalent to upper secondary education in other countries).

PRE-PRIMARY EDUCATION

Pre-school education is the first stage of the education system mapped out by the *LGE* and is not compulsory. It is divided into two stages: kindergarten, for children aged two and three years, and infant school, for four and five-year-olds.

PRIMARY AND LOWER SECONDARY EDUCATION

General basic education (*EGB*) is eight-year, compulsory, basic education for all pupils aged between 6 and 14 years. At its end, pupils who satisfactorily achieve the stipulated objectives are awarded the *Graduado Escolar* and may go on to both vocational training (*FP*) and the *Bachillerato*. Pupils who do not achieve the objectives receive the *Certificado de Escolaridad*, which means that the only option open to them is vocational training. *EGB* is divided into three cycles: lower, intermediate and higher.

UPPER SECONDARY EDUCATION

The *Bachillerato* (*BUP*) is composed of two core courses and a third in which pupils opt for the "sciences" or the "arts". Pupils who wish to go on to higher education after the Baccalaureate have to complete the *Course of University Guidance* (*COU*) in one of the four possible areas: science and technology, biology and health, social sciences and the humanities, and languages. Once they have passed *COU*, pupils may take university entrance examinations.

Vocational training is divided into two levels: first-grade and second-grade. First-grade vocational training (*FP I*) is a two-year course and is compulsory and free for all pupils who do not take the Baccalaureate. There are more than 20 different branches, divided in turn into specialities. Pupils who complete *FP I* or have the *Bachillerato* can go on to second-grade vocational training (*FP II*) which lasts two or three years, depending on how the courses are structured, and there are more than 60 specialities.

TERTIARY EDUCATION

Higher education is organised in three cycles (first and second ISCED 6 and third ISCED 7). It may be completed at university schools, faculties and higher technical schools. University schools offer first-cycle (3-year) studies and award the degrees of *Diplomado*, Architectural Technician and Engineering Technician. Courses at faculties and higher technical schools offer first and second cycles (5 or 6 years) studies. These institutions award the degrees of Licenciate, Architect or Engineer, after completion of second-cycle courses. The third cycle leads to a doctorate degree, after the doctorate courses (usually two years) have been completed and a Ph.D. dissertation has been passed.

OTHER EDUCATION

The General Education Act also referred to alternative types and kinds of education to be encompassed by the continuing education system which the Act aimed to establish: *Lifelong adult education*, providing people who, for one reason or another, were unable to complete the different educational levels at the right time with the chance to do so, and giving them the opportunity of further training and to build on their culture at different levels, etc.; *specialised education*, encompassing arts and language teaching which are not, due to their characteristics, integrated into the levels, cycles and grades of the regular system; *distance education* and *special education*. There have been profound changes in the structure of *special education* over recent years, as the scheme for integrating pupils with special needs into regular schools was introduced.

The system laid down by the *LOGSE* provides for a general education system with the following educational levels: infant education, primary education, secondary education (made up of the compulsory secondary education (*ESO*), the Baccalaureate and medium level vocational training), higher level vocational training and university education.

Spain

General timetable for implementing the *LOGSE*

Academic Year	New System	Replacing
1991-1992	Infant education	
1992-1993	1st and 2nd primary	1st and 2nd *EGB*
1993-1994	3rd and 4th primary	3rd and 4th *EGB*
1994-1995	5th primary	5th *EGB*
1995-1996	6th primary	6th *EGB*
1996-1997	1st *ESO*	7th *EGB*
1997-1998	2nd *ESO*	8th *EGB*
1998-1999	3rd *ESO* 1st Baccalaureate	1st *BUP* 1st *FP I* 3rd *BUP* 1st *FP II* (specialised studies system)
1999 - 2000	4th *ESO* 2nd Baccalaureate specific vocational training at middle level	2nd *BUP* 2nd *FPI* *COU* (university preparatory year) 1st *FP II* (general system) 2nd *FP I* (specialised studies system)
2000-2001		2nd *FP II* (general system) 3rd *FP II* (specialised studies system)

Note: Specific vocational training at higher level (ISCED 5) will be progressively brought in throughout this period and is therefore not included in the table.

Early implementation of some levels in a specific number of schools has been planned in parallel with the gradual implementation of the system. This is the case for compulsory secondary education and Baccalaureate.

Pre-escolar	Pre-primary education
Educación general básica	General basic education
Institutos de formación profesional de primer grado	Vocational training schools
Institutos de Bachillerato Unificado y polivalente	Baccalaureate schools
Bachillerato	Baccalaureate
Técnico auxiliar	Technician
Curso de orientación universitaria	University guidance course
Técnico especialista	Specialist technician
Universidades	Universities
Escuelas universitarias	University schools
Escuelas superiores	Higher technical schools
Facultades	University faculties
Colegios universitarios	University colleges
Diplomado	Diploma
Licenciado	Licentiate
Doctor	Doctorate
Ingeniero técnico	Technical engineer
Arquitecto	Architect

Sweden

BASIC PRINCIPLES

Compulsory school and upper secondary school are both comprehensive schools, designed to accommodate all members of the rising generation. All schools are co-educational and free of charge. Education for adults equivalent to the education conferred by the compulsory and upper secondary school is part of the public school system. Swedish education is thus a structurally uniform education system from elementary level via upper secondary schooling to adult education.

The government lays down national curricula and syllabi for the school system. Since 1991 municipalities and county councils have an undivided responsibility for organising and implementing school activities. Since 1993 the role of the State has been further limited by a radical reform of the higher education system.

Another guiding principle of the education policy is to create scope for diversity within the education system. The percentage of private compulsory and private upper secondary schools is 1.5 per cent. There are very few private institutions within higher education.

PRE-SCHOOL EDUCATION

Child-care services mainly take the following forms:
- day-care centres (*daghem*) for children aged 1–6 years;
- open pre-school (*öppen förskola*) targeted on pre-school children without any other kind of pre-school place.

Pre-school teachers co-operate in various ways with teachers at the lower level of compulsory school. By 1991 all pre-school children over the age of 18 months would be provided for.

COMPULSORY SCHOOLING – PRIMARY AND LOWER SECONDARY EDUCATION

The compulsory school system comprises compulsory school (*grundskolan*), special schools (*specialskolan*) for children with certain handicaps and compulsory school for the mentally disabled (*särskola*). There is also a Sami school for Sami-speaking children in the north of the country. Almost all pupils (over 98 per cent) attend schools run by the municipalities.

Compulsory school is divided into three levels:

- *Lågstadium*
    (lower level)   1st–3rd year (ISCED 1)
- *Mellanstadium*
    (intermediate level)   4th–6th year (ISCED 1)
- *Högstadium*
    (upper level)   7th–9th year (ISCED 2)

Education at lower and intermediate levels could be classified as primary education and upper level education as lower secondary education.

The curriculum lays down goals and guidelines of a more general nature. It also includes time-schedules specifying the number of periods per week (lessons) at each three-year level for each subject. The curriculum puts a great deal of emphasis on training the pupils in basic skills – reading, writing and arithmetic – all the way through school. Similarly, a great deal of attention has to be paid to supplying the pupils with a basic knowledge of civics, natural science and technology. At lower and intermediate levels all pupils take the same subjects. Pupils at the upper level have a certain choice in optional courses.

There are no examinations in compulsory school. Marks are awarded in Grades Eight and Nine, as information and as a basis for upper secondary school entrance. Compulsory schools also inform parents of their children's progress and difficulties by means of interviews. A leaving certificate on completion of nine years compulsory education confers general eligibility for upper secondary education.

In 1993 Parliament adopted legislation laying down new curricular guidelines for the whole school system, geared to the new goal and result-related governing system for schools. This will mean extensive changes in the curriculum, syllabi and time-schedules as well and in the marking system in the next few years. The new system will take effect in the 1995/96 school year for Grades One to Seven. The reform will be fully implemented as from the 1997/98 school year.

UPPER SECONDARY EDUCATION

Since 1970 upper secondary school (*gymnasieskolan*) was divided into about 25 different lines (*linjer*) and some 500 specialised courses (*specialkurser*). Most lines were practical/vocational lines of two years' duration (*2-åriga linjer*). Five three-year lines (*3-åriga linjer*) were in principle preparatory for university level studies. The one and only four-year line (now abandoned) conferred, after three years, eligibility for admission to higher technical studies. The lines were subdivided in subsequent grades into several "branches" and "variants". The specialised courses ranged in duration from a week to a couple of years, providing vocational education in a wide variety of fields.

All lines and specialised courses had their own time-schedules and syllabi. Swedish, English, physical education and civics or working-life orientation were compulsory in all study programmes. The two-year vocational lines had only a few general subjects. There were no examinations and students were awarded marks for all subjects every term. Centrally compiled achievement tests were used in order to achieve a nation-wide uniformity in the marking system. An upper secondary school leaving certificate after at least two years of study including a specified amount of Swedish and English conferred general eligibility for tertiary education.

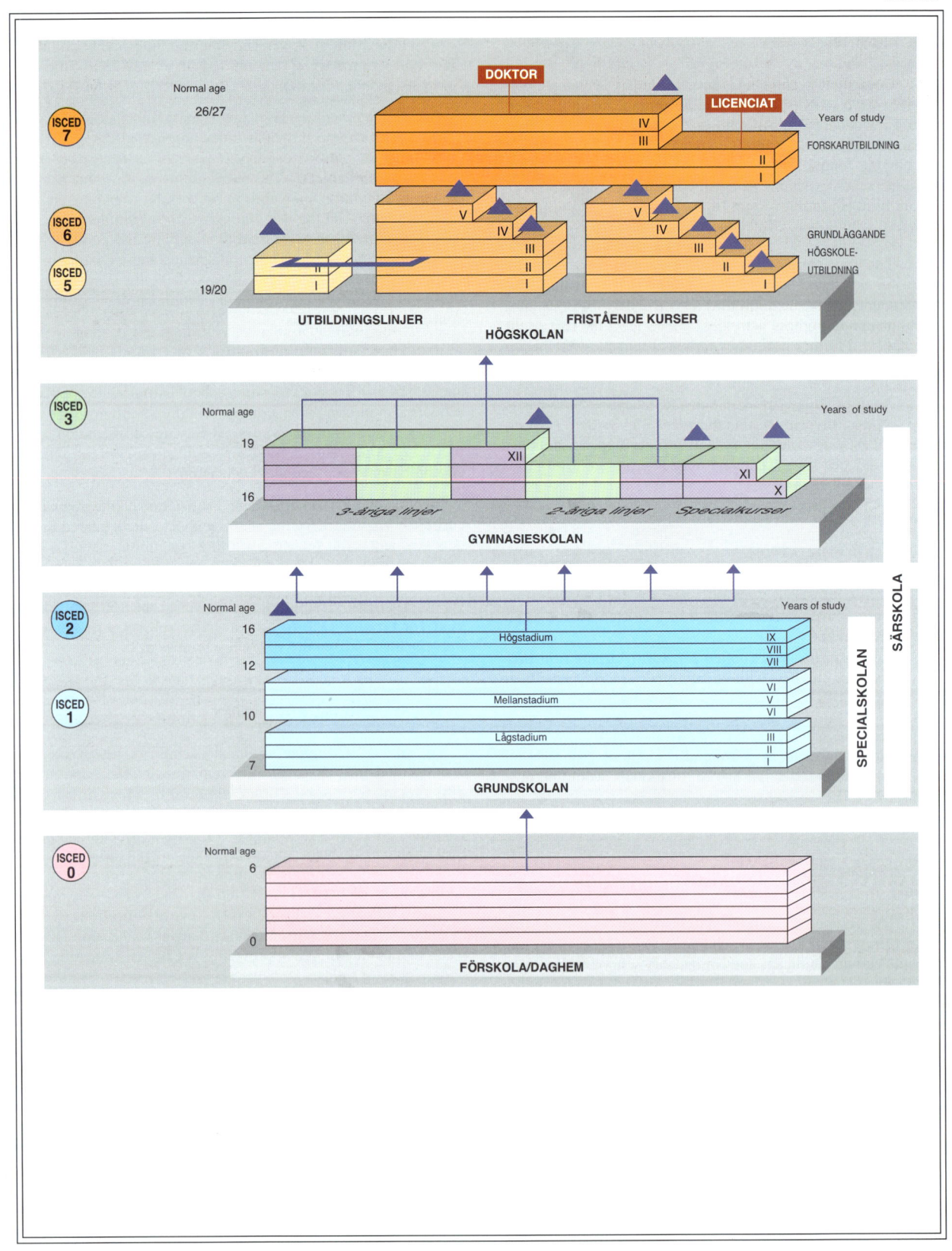

Sweden

Suède

ISCED 7 — Normal age 26/27

- DOKTOR
- LICENCIAT
- FORSKARUTBILDNING

ISCED 6 / ISCED 5 — Normal age 19/20

- GRUNDLÄGGANDE HÖGSKOLEUTBILDNING
- UTBILDNINGSLINJER
- FRISTÅENDE KURSER
- HÖGSKOLAN

ISCED 3 — Normal age 16–19

- 3-åriga linjer
- 2-åriga linjer
- Specialkurser
- GYMNASIESKOLAN

ISCED 2 / ISCED 1 — Normal age 7–16

- Högstadium (VII, VIII, IX)
- Mellanstadium (IV, V, VI)
- Lågstadium (I, II, III)
- GRUNDSKOLAN
- SPECIALSKOLAN
- SÄRSKOLA

ISCED 0 — Normal age 0–6

- FÖRSKOLA/DAGHEM

Sweden

Since 1 July 1992 municipalities are obliged to provide three years of upper secondary schooling for all pupils leaving compulsory school. The new system of upper secondary education will be fully implemented by the school year 1995/96. In the new upper secondary school, all education is organised in 16 national study programmes (*program*) of three years' duration, 14 of which are primarily vocationally oriented and two preparing primarily for university studies. Students who have requirements other than those provided for within the national programmes can opt to follow a specially designed programme, an individual programme or apprenticeship training. In all programmes, time is set aside for local supplements or practical work connected with subjects, as well as for individual choice to allow students to choose additional subjects and courses within the national programmes. The new curriculum came into effect 1 July 1994. Marks will be awarded on a four-category scale: Failed, Passed, Passed with distinction and Passed with exceptional distinction. The criteria for awarding marks will be specified in the different syllabi. All three-year programmes will meet with the general eligibility requirements for pursuing tertiary education.

TERTIARY EDUCATION

Tertiary education is divided into undergraduate studies (*Grundläggande högskoleutbildning* - ISCED 5 and 6) and postgraduate studies and research (*Forskarutbildning* - ISCED 7). All tuition within tertiary education is free of charge.

To be admitted to tertiary education, a student must first fulfil the general eligibility requirements which are common to all programmes or courses, and then meet the specific eligibility requirements which are usually imposed on applicants by the individual university or university college. For the selection of students one or more of the following criteria are applicable: school marks; results on the university aptitude test (a national, non-compulsory test) which is common for all institutions of higher education, or a special test (e.g. interviews), or previous education and work experience.

Roughly 30 per cent of young persons go on to tertiary education after completion of their upper secondary schooling. Apart from students coming straight from school, the tertiary student population includes a relatively large proportion of mature students, i.e. students who have previously acquired various amounts of work experience.

Students are able freely to choose their study route and to combine different subject courses into a degree. All courses and educational programmes have to follow curricula, established by the individual university or university college. First degree programmes (*utbildningslinjer*) will generally take between two and five years to complete. The separate courses (*fristående kurser*) usually vary in length from five weeks to one-year-and-a-half.

All courses include continuous examination, written and/or oral. There are, however, no final examinations which cover an entire three- or five-year programme. Marks are generally awarded on a three-level scale: Fail, Pass and Pass with distinction.

In 1991 a major reform was initiated, aiming at a deregulation of the unitary system of higher education and greater autonomy for the individual institutions of higher education. In 1993 a new Higher Education Act came into effect. The dimensioning of different programmes and the allocation of grants between institutions has been made more dependent than before on the requirements of the individual students and the achievements of the individual institutions. The organisation of study and range of courses on offer are determined locally and students have been given increased freedom of choice over study route.

Förskola/daghem	Open pre-school/day-care centre
Grundskolan	Compulsory school
Lågstadium	Lower level
Mellanstadium	Intermediate level
Högstadium	Upper level
Specialskolan	Special school
Särskola	School for mentally disabled
Gymnasieskolan	Upper secondary school
Linjer	Lines (streams)
Specialkurser	Specialised courses
Högskolan	Universities
Grundläggande högskoleutbildning	Undergraduate studies
Forskarutbildning	Post-graduate and research studies
Utbildningslinjer	First-degree programmes
Fristående kurser	Separate courses

Switzerland

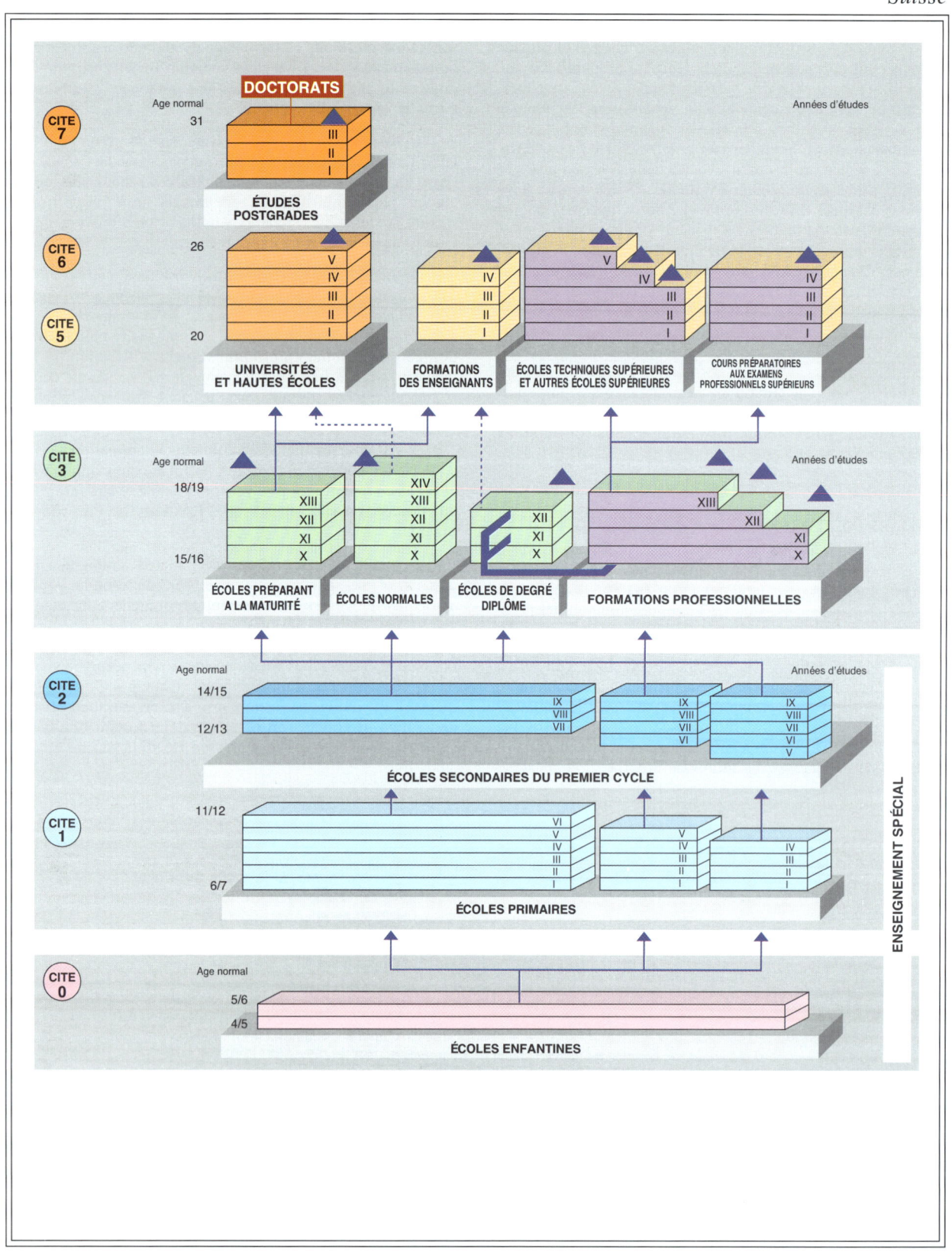

Suisse

Switzerland

The diagram outlines the situation of institutionalised education in 1992. It includes the many different structures and channels at secondary and higher levels as well as the specific features of the 26 cantonal education systems. It sets out the major training paths followed by the vast majority of students. Nevertheless, the various forms of training are not necessarily available in all cantons and their relative weights may differ.

There is no Federal Ministry of Education. Cantons are mainly responsible for education. However, the Confederation controls the organisation of compulsory and free education. It also controls vocational training and approves leaving certificates under an ordinance originally adopted for regulating access to polytechnical schools and medical faculties. Both at federal and at cantonal levels, powers are shared among various government departments (ministries). The Department of the Interior (federal level) and public education departments (cantonal level) have the responsibility for the compulsory, general and university education; the Departments of Economic Affairs, for vocational training.

PRE-SCHOOL EDUCATION

Pre-school attendance varies from one to three years. In most cantons, the duration is two years. Although pre-primary education is optional, 98 per cent of children receive it for at least one year.

FIRST LEVEL EDUCATION

In 1992, the duration of primary education was six, five and four years in eighteen, four and four cantons, respectively. Since then, reforms have been or are to be undertaken in several cantons to extend the period from four to six years. The aim of the reforms is to postpone school selection and to improve co-ordination among the various cantonal systems.

SECONDARY EDUCATION, FIRST CYCLE

The duration is three to five years and there are two or three types of requirements depending on the cantons. The duration of compulsory education, covering first level education and the first cycle of secondary education, is nine years in all cantons.

SECONDARY EDUCATION, SECOND CYCLE

The *écoles de maturité* lead to the award of school leaving certificates (*baccalauréat* or *maturité*) which give access to higher education.

The *écoles normales* train teachers for the pre-primary, primary and secondary-first cycle, levels in some cantons. The diploma awarded also gives access – subject to certain restrictions – to higher education. In 1995 a reform will introduce generalised intercantonal recognition of primary education diplomas, which will mean that all primary teachers will be allowed to teach in different cantons from where they actually graduated.

The *écoles de degré diplôme* provide general education. They prepare students for vocational training at secondary-second cycle, or higher education levels, especially in teaching, paramedical, social and administrative fields and the performance and visual arts.

Vocational training accounts for over two-thirds of students in the second cycle of secondary education. It includes full-time vocational schools and apprenticeships. In the latter case, full-time training is shared between vocation schools and the place of work (where apprentices are trained by official instructors). This dual system is supplemented by preparatory courses organised by trade associations. Federal certificates of aptitude are awarded following examinations. It is envisaged is to introduce a vocational *baccalauréat*, which will give access to future specialised higher education establishments without entrance examinations.

HIGHER EDUCATION

ISCED 5

The *écoles supérieures* and *écoles techniques* are open to holders of a federal certificate of aptitude provided they have passed the entrance competitive examination for the purpose of further studies. These are sanctioned by a diploma. A reform is planned to convert some *écoles supérieures* into specialised *hautes écoles*. Access will be open without restriction for those holding the vocational *baccalauréat*.

Preparatory courses for vocational examinations and higher vocational examinations are open to holders of a federal certificate of aptitude with several years of work experience. The education is provided in parallel with occupational activity. It is organised by trade associations to develop further skills and train future managers. After passing an examination, course participants are awarded a federal certificate or diploma.

Teacher training at tertiary level in some cantons is given at a teacher training school or an institution attached to the university. However, the certificate awarded is not regarded as a university degree.

ISCED 6

Switzerland has two federal institutes of technology and eight cantonal universities. These are public institutions. Students enroling at a Swiss university must hold a school-leaving certificate or a recognised equivalent diploma. The training is sanctioned by a first university degree, either a diploma or an actual degree.

ISCED 7

This education level concerns the holders of a university degree who are preparing a doctorate or following post-graduate courses.

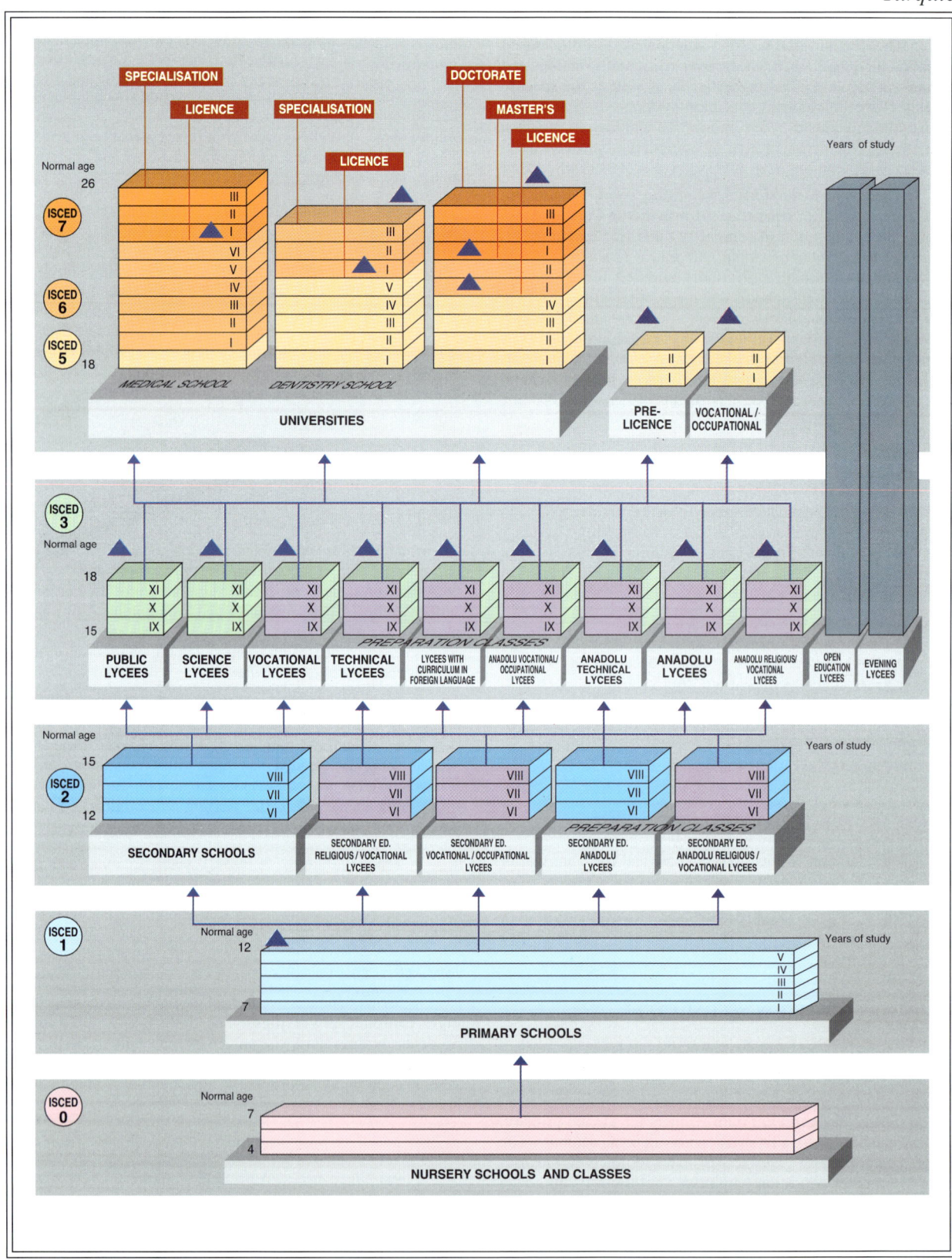

Turkey

Turquie

Turkey

The basic structure of the national education system is outlined in Basic Law No. 1739 on National Education. The education system is divided into two main sections: formal and non-formal.

FORMAL EDUCATION

Pre-school education, primary education, secondary education and higher education institutions are included in this group.

PRE-PRIMARY EDUCATION

The aims of pre-school education, which is optional, are to develop physical, mental and emotional abilities of children; to help them acquire good habits; to prepare them for basic education; to provide an atmosphere of growing together for children coming from poor areas, and to help them acquire an adequate knowledge of the Turkish language. Pre-school education can be organised as independent kindergartens, as well as kindergartens that are annexed to primary schools or other educational institutions.

PRIMARY EDUCATION

Primary education assures the education of children 6 to 14 years old. This includes five years of primary school and three years of middle school. Diplomas are given at the end of primary school and secondary education. In Turkey, the primary school forms the basis of the national education system. It is compulsory for all Turkish citizens who have reached the age of 6. This level of education is both compulsory and free of charge in public schools. There are also primary schools that are private and under State control.

SECONDARY EDUCATION

Secondary education encompasses general, vocational and technical education institutions, where a minimum of three years of schooling is implemented after primary education. After three years of middle school, secondary education is divided into three parts:

- *General Lycées* prepare students for institutions of higher education. They provide a three-year programme over and above middle school education, and comprise students in the 15-17 age group.
- *Vocational Lycées* provide a three-year programme that prepares students for active life in different occupations and in institutions of higher education.
- *Technical Lycées* prepare students for professions and institutions of higher education. They comprise a four-year programme, where the first year of education is similar to that of vocational *lycées*.

TERTIARY EDUCATION

This includes all educational institutions where a programme of at least two years over and above secondary education is implemented.

Higher education is organised as one whole, encompassing graduate, Bachelor's and Master's degrees. There is a tuition fee for higher education. Successful students who lack financial means are provided with full support by private persons, organisations, and the State. Higher institutions of learning comprise universities, faculties, institutes, higher schools, conservatories, higher vocational schools and implementation and research centres.

NON-FORMAL EDUCATION

Non-formal education comprises programmes which can take place alongside formal education or outside it. They include:

- General programmes that provide literacy courses and social-cultural courses.
- Vocational and technical education programmes open to persons with no formal education or vocational training for the purpose of teaching them a trade. These courses are offered at adult education centres.
- Programmes for apprentices, assistant masters and masters that offer training for persons in the 12-18 age group who have completed their basic education but have not attended middle schools and have not had a normal education. This training encompasses one day of theory in schools and four days of on-the-job training.

United Kingdom (England and Wales)

Royaume-Uni (Angleterre et Pays de Galles)

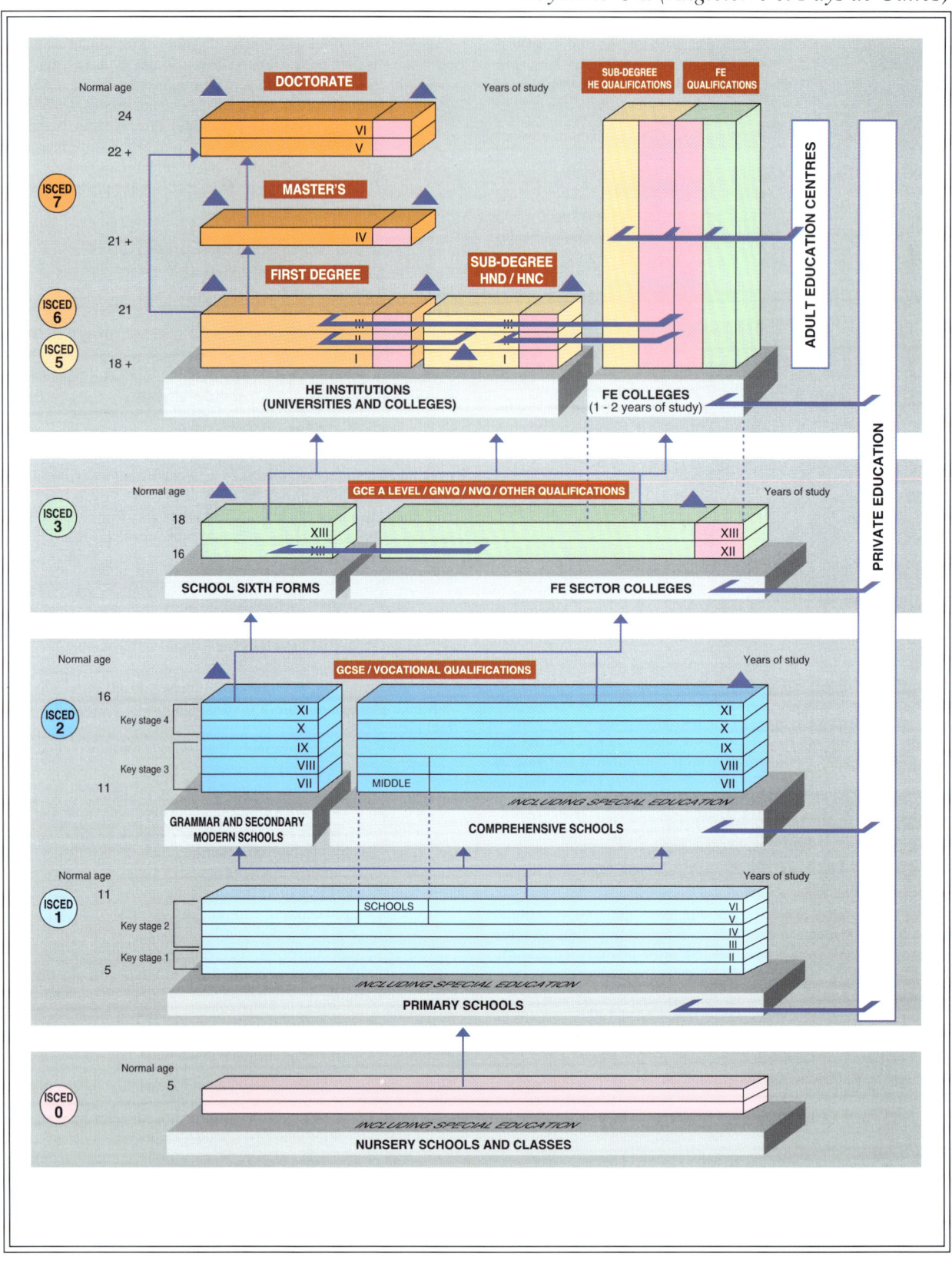

United Kingdom (England and Wales)

The diagram covers the academic year 1993/94. It reflects the structure of education provision in England and Wales. There are differences in Scotland and Northern Ireland.

PRE-PRIMARY EDUCATION

Over 90 per cent of 3 and 4 year-olds receive some form of pre-primary provision: 26 per cent are admitted to maintained nursery schools and classes; 24 per cent are admitted to infant classes in maintained primary schools (mainly 4 year-olds in reception classes); 4 per cent are admitted to special or independent schools, and 41 per cent attend playgroups.

COMPULSORY SCHOOLING

Children of statutory school age (5 to 16) in State schools must study the National Curriculum. It is divided into four "Key Stages" which correspond to different school year groups. Pupils start Key Stage 1 when they reach compulsory school age, that is, at age 5. Key Stages 1 and 2 constitute the primary phase, and Key Stages 3 and 4 the secondary phase.

The National Curriculum requires the regular assessment of pupils' progress. This includes the testing of English and maths at the end of Key Stage 1, and of English, maths and sciences at the end of Stages 2 and 3. The General Certificate of Secondary Education (GCSE) tests National Curriculum subjects at Key Stage 4.

Government policy promotes diversity in school provision. Although the majority of schools are comprehensive, some areas also have grammar and secondary modern schools which cater specifically for children in the higher and lower ability ranges, respectively. Similarly, in most areas a two-tier system of primary and secondary schools operates, with children transferring from one sector to the other, but some areas have a three-tier system of first, middle and upper or high schools. The development of secondary schools specialising in particular subject areas, such as technology, is encouraged. In some areas choice is enhanced by the existence of Grant-Maintained Schools and City Technology Colleges.

Standards of achievement and quality of education are monitored through the regular independent inspection of schools on a four-year cycle by the Office for Standards in Education (OFSTED).

State schools: funding and organisation

At both primary and secondary levels, there are four main categories of maintained (State) schools in England and Wales which are governed and funded in distinct ways:

County schools are funded wholly through the local education authority (LEA). The LEA delegates significant spending power and other responsibilities to the schools' governing bodies, but retains powers of oversight and funding for various services organised centrally.

Voluntary controlled schools are owned by charitable foundations, mostly the Churches. The LEA still retains most powers over the school but the governors have more discretion over the curriculum, reflecting the aims of the Church or voluntary body providing the school.

Voluntary aided schools are also owned by charitable organisations. They appoint the majority of the governing body and the governing body employs the staff of the school. The governors have discretion over certain aspects of the curriculum, in particular the teaching of religious education, and the handling of collective worship. Their recurrent funding comes from the LEA in the same way as for county schools. The LEA is responsible for part of the capital expenditure and repairs, but most is the responsibility of the schools that are eligible for grants of up to 85 per cent on this expenditure.

Grant-maintained schools are free from LEA control and funded by central government through a Funding Agency for Schools, an agency of the Department of Education. Each school controls its full budget and sets its own policies within the national framework of law applying to all maintained schools.

The proportions of these different categories of schools vary between the primary and secondary sectors and in different parts of the country.

Private schools

Parents are free to have their children educated in independent schools, in preference to State schools provided they are able to pay the fees. Independent schools range from small kindergartens to large day and boarding schools and from new experimental schools to ancient foundations.

The government has introduced an Assisted Places Scheme, which enables pupils from low-income families to attend selected independent schools by providing assistance with the cost of tuition fees and some incidental expenses. There are some 35 000 assisted places available in England and Wales.

Special education

Provision for most children with special educational needs is made in mainstream primary and secondary schools and further education colleges. Some children with special educational needs attend, for all or part of their schooling, special schools. Young people who have attended special schools may go on to colleges of further education and to higher education.

United Kingdom (England and Wales)

POST-COMPULSORY EDUCATION

Further education

Young people aged 16 to 19 may study in either the sixth form of a school or at a college in the Further Education sector. They are offered a framework of three kinds of qualifications: General Certificate of Education (GCE); broad-based General National Vocational Qualifications (GNVQs); and job-specific National Vocational Qualifications (NVQs). Students may study for one of these qualifications or a combination of them within the same programme.

Typically full-time courses last one or two years. Some colleges also offer sub-degree or degree level courses. These qualifications and others can also be studied by adults at colleges within the Further Education sector.

Higher education

In England, 130 universities and colleges of higher education receive public funds to provide higher education – i.e. study above Advanced level (GCE A level, the Scottish equivalent or advanced level GNVQ/NVQ level 3). In addition to 46 "old" university institutions, these include 34 "new" universities – mostly former polytechnics – and 50 colleges. Some FE colleges also provide higher education.

Universities and colleges are autonomous bodies, responsible for managing their own financial, administrative and academic affairs, including curricula, admissions and examinations. Universities award their own degrees; most colleges award degrees validated by universities.

Many undergraduate courses are Bachelor degree courses requiring three or so years' full-time study. Also offered are shorter undergraduate courses leading to diplomas; post-graduate courses leading to Master's degrees; and post-graduate research courses leading to doctorates. Part-time courses, taking longer to complete, are also offered at all levels.

In addition to traditional universities and higher education colleges, the Open University offers, through the medium of distance learning, a range of higher education courses to those over 18 who might otherwise be unable to take advantage of the education system.

Education of adults

Sixty-five per cent of higher education students and 60 per cent of further education students are aged over 21. Adults may resume their education at any age, and have access to a wide range of further and higher education courses, including appropriate short courses. Access courses facilitate the admission to undergraduate courses for mature students or those with non-traditional or non-formal qualification.

Key Stages 1-4	Different levels of the National Curriculum
GCSE	General Certificate of Secondary Education
NVQ	National Vocational Qualification
GNVQ	General National Vocational Qualification
GCE A Level	General Certificate of Education Advanced Level
HND/HNC	Higher National Diploma/Higher National Certificate
FE	Further education
HE	Higher education

United States

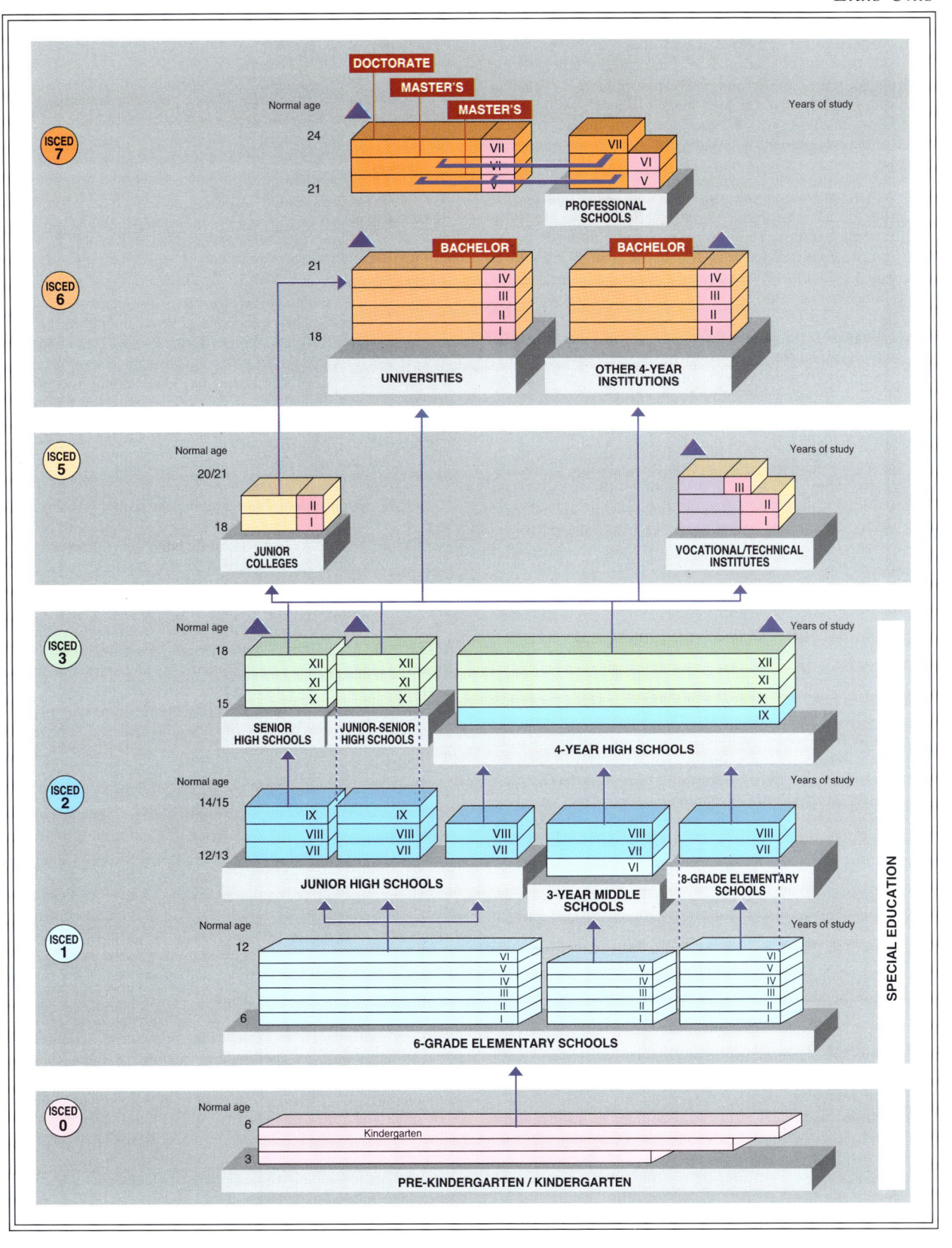

Etats-Unis

United States

Education is a highly decentralised activity. Since responsibility for education is not assigned to the federal government in the Constitution, the responsibility for education has been delegated to the states. Thus, the states organise and operate an education system as they deem appropriate – subject to constitutional guarantees of the rights and privileges of U.S. citizens.

State statutory provisions for establishing educational institutions and programmes vary greatly. Some are quite specific; others simply mention educational matters in broad terms. Local school districts are the next level of school governance below the state level and are normally the level at which financial decisions about specific expenditures are made. Districts generally have considerable authority to hire staff and establish curricula. School districts are subject to state regulations which cover the duration of the school year and day, graduation requirements, standards for teacher certification, school transportation, health services and fire protection. School districts vary in size from fewer than a dozen to nearly one million students.

Variations in the structure of elementary and secondary schools (ISCED 0 to 3) abound. Frequently, there are different grade patterns for schools within the same district and schools with every conceivable grade span exist within the United States. The accompanying chart provides some typical examples.

PRE-PRIMARY, PRIMARY AND SECONDARY EDUCATION

Pupils ordinarily spend from six to eight years in the elementary grades, which may be preceded by one or two years in nursery school and kindergarten. The elementary programme is frequently followed by a middle school or a junior high school programme, which generally lasts two or three years. Students then finish their compulsory schooling at the secondary or high school level, which may last from three to six years depending on the structure within their school district. The entire programme always requires 12 grades and is generally completed by age 17 or 18.

Schools are required to provide *special education* for all persons under 22 needing services. These special education services may be provided through regular schools or in special facilities.

Education in the United States is compulsory from age 6 or 7 to age 16, 17 or 18, depending on the state. Public education through completion of grade 12 is free. State legislation also provides for establishment of *private schools* at every level, subject to state licensing and accreditation requirements. At elementary and secondary level, these institutions parallel the public institutions in general structure, but more frequently have wider grade spans such as 1 to 8 and 9 to 12 or even 1 to 12. These institutions may receive limited government aid for specialised purposes, but are, for the most part, financially independent.

TERTIARY EDUCATION

High school graduates who decide to continue their education may enter a technical or vocational institution, a 2-year college, or a 4-year college or university. A 2-year college normally offers the first two years of a standard 4-year institution curriculum and a selection of terminal-vocational programmes. Academic courses completed at a 2-year college are usually transferable for credit at a 4-year college or university. A technical or vocational institution offers post-secondary technical training leading to a specific career.

Colleges may be publicly or privately controlled. They receive funds through a variety of sources, including tuition; federal, state and local appropriations; grants and contracts; endowment funds; private gifts; and revenue from auxiliary enterprises and university hospitals. Both public and private colleges receive funds from all of these sources, but the public colleges receive a higher proportion from government sources, while private colleges receive a higher proportion of their funds from tuition and other private sources.

An associate degree requires at least two years of college-level work, and a Bachelor's degree normally can be earned in four years. At least one year beyond the Bachelor's is necessary for a Master's degree, while a doctoral degree usually requires a minimum of three or four years beyond a Bachelor's.

Professional schools differ widely in admission requirements and in programme length. Medical students, for example, generally complete a 4-year programme of premedical studies at a college or university before they can enter the 4-year programme at a medical school. Law programmes normally require three years of course work beyond the Bachelor's degree level.

Post-secondary education in the United States is diverse; American colleges and universities offer a wide range of programmes. For example, a junior college may offer vocational training or the first two years of training at the college level. A university typically offers a full undergraduate course of study leading to a Bachelor's degree as well as first-professional and graduate programmes leading to advanced degrees. Vocational and technical institutions offer training programmes which are designed to prepare students for specific careers. Other types of educational opportunities for adults include community groups, churches, libraries and businesses.

In recent decades, post-secondary education has become more accessible to all segments of the population. The growth of community colleges and low-cost institutions means that the student can attend at minimum cost. Federal student financial aid and other aid programmes also have attracted many students who otherwise would have found it difficult to finance a college education. Businesses frequently provide financial support for their employees who are pursuing additional education. Post-secondary education involves students of all ages. Today, about half of the college students are over age 25.

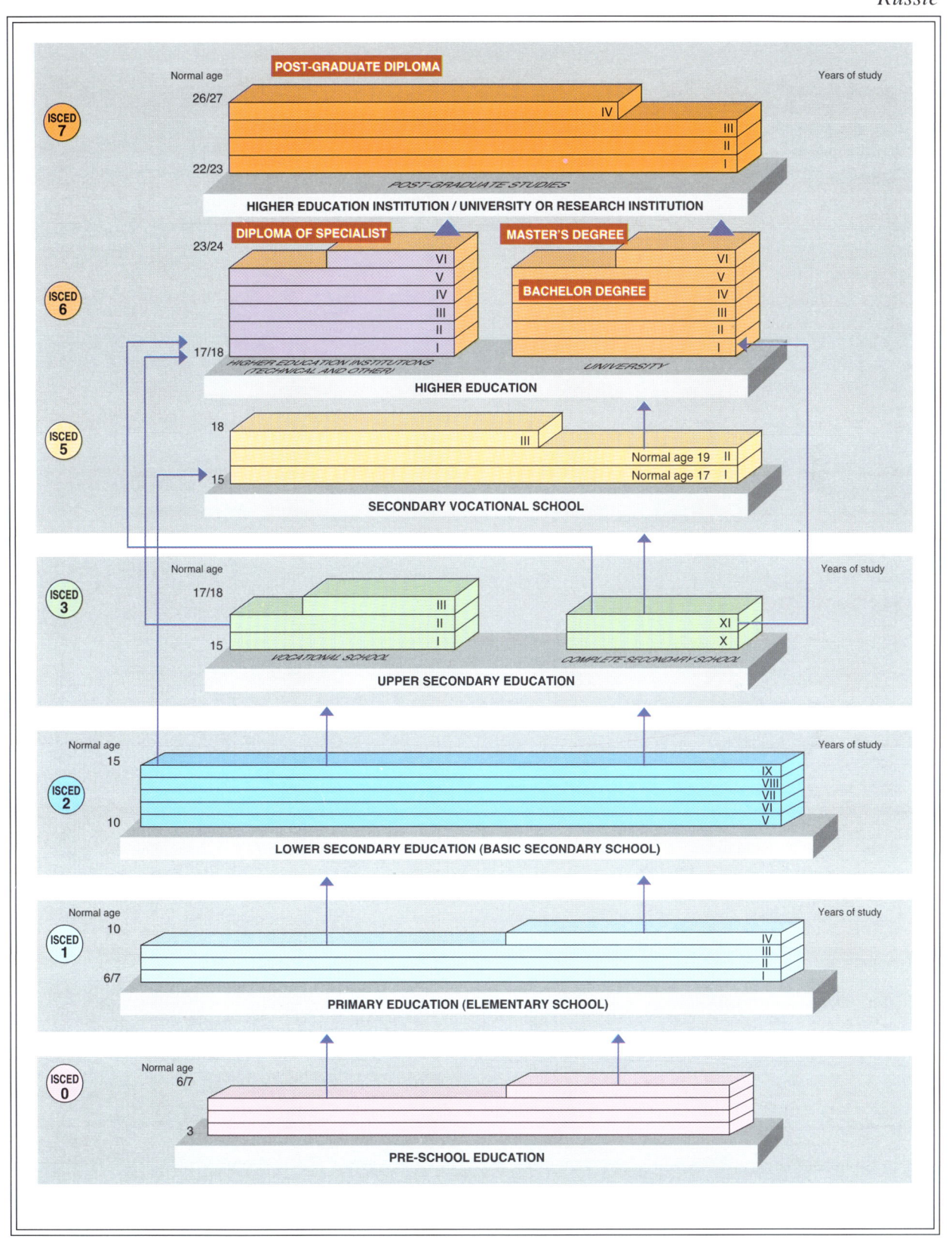

Russia

Russie

ISCED	Level	Normal age	Details	Years of study
7	POST-GRADUATE DIPLOMA	22/23 – 26/27	POST-GRADUATE STUDIES — HIGHER EDUCATION INSTITUTION / UNIVERSITY OR RESEARCH INSTITUTION	I, II, III, IV
6	DIPLOMA OF SPECIALIST / MASTER'S DEGREE / BACHELOR DEGREE	17/18 – 23/24	HIGHER EDUCATION INSTITUTIONS (TECHNICAL AND OTHER) / UNIVERSITY — HIGHER EDUCATION	I–VI
5	—	15 – 18	SECONDARY VOCATIONAL SCHOOL	I (Normal age 17), II (Normal age 19), III
3	UPPER SECONDARY EDUCATION	15 – 17/18	VOCATIONAL SCHOOL / COMPLETE SECONDARY SCHOOL	I, II, III / X, XI
2	LOWER SECONDARY EDUCATION (BASIC SECONDARY SCHOOL)	10 – 15		V, VI, VII, VIII, IX
1	PRIMARY EDUCATION (ELEMENTARY SCHOOL)	6/7 – 10		I, II, III, IV
0	PRE-SCHOOL EDUCATION	3 – 6/7		

V

ANNEXES

Annex 1 — Notes

INDICATOR C01

Australia

The classification of educations has been made according to the new ABS Classification of Qualifications, which corresponds better to ISCED than the old classification. In order to enable the use of this classification, data are reported for 1993 instead of 1992. The main difference compared to the data for 1991 is that some educational programmes have been reclassified from ISCED 5 to ISCED 3.

Belgium

The classification by ISCED levels is based on the highest level of diploma or degree obtained. The unemployed are defined as people who are "full-time" unemployed and who receive unemployment benefits.

Canada

The classification of educational programmes according to ISCED has changed compared to 1991. Allocation to ISCED 3 was previously based on the number of years of schooling. Now, ISCED 3 includes only those who report having received a secondary school certificate or diploma. The increase of the ratio of the population with ISCED 5 is partly a result of ongoing efforts to improve the classification of post-secondary educational programmes.

France

The ISCED classification is based on the highest diploma or degree obtained. To avoid underestimation of the number of people in the higher ISCED categories, the number of people with higher qualifications than suggested by their diploma has been estimated. The estimates have been adjusted accordingly.

Germany

The rate of non-response is 11.1 per cent. In the calculations, respondents and non-respondents are assumed to have the same distribution by educational attainment.

Ireland

Classification by ISCED level is made by level of certificate with the exception of ISCED 0 and ISCED 1, where the number of years of schooling is used. A certain proportion of the population classified as having attained ISCED 2 have completed apprenticeship training comparable to ISCED 3. These persons cannot be identified from the Labour Force Survey. Attainment of ISCED 3 refers to persons who have obtained the leaving certificate, usually at the age of 17 or 18. This is a general qualification that, in principle, offers access to tertiary education.

Norway

Persons for whom the level of educational attainment is unknown have been allocated to ISCED 0/1. The figures given for these categories are therefore equivalent to "unknown".

Switzerland

Apprentices have been defined as being in full-time education. In previous editions of *Education at a Glance*, they were defined as full-time employed.

United Kingdom

The retirement age for women is 60, and therefore 60-64 year-old women are not targeted by the Labour Force Survey. Women 60-64 years of age are estimated to have the same distribution by ISCED categories as women 55-59 years of age.

United States

In 1992, the educational attainment question in the Current Population Survey was changed. ISCED 3 now excludes a small number of individuals who have completed grade 12 but did not receive a diploma or its equivalent. In addition, ISCED 3 includes a large number of people with some tertiary education but no credential. ISCED 5 only includes individuals who received an Associate degree, a credential awarded in programmes normally requiring two years of full-time study. Compared to statistics published in earlier editions of this report, the change will increase the percentage of the population whose highest educational attainment is ISCED 3 and will decrease the percentage whose highest education attainment is ISCED 5.

INDICATOR C02

See notes to C01.

INDICATOR C11

See notes to C01.

INDICATOR C12

For the Czech Republic, Germany (FTFR), Greece, Hungary, Japan, Luxembourg, Poland and Russia the data were not supplied from Network B sources but were derived from the *OECD Labour Force Statistics* database.

Australia

C12(A): The unemployment rates are 1993 figures. Due to a strong recovery in the labour market, unemployment rates in Australia are now about 1.5 percentage points lower.

INDICATORS C21, C23 to C27

A difference of 3 or 4 percentage points is usually required before it can be regarded as significant.

Annex 1 – Notes

INDICATOR C21

All countries

"Social Subjects" = Geography and History.

Denmark

The subject *Technology* was not included in the Danish questionnaire.

Switzerland

The Swiss questionnaire was modified. *Foreign language* was taken as *English language*.

INDICATOR C22

United Kingdom

The item *Skills and knowledge that will help to continue studies or training* was added to the questionnaire after the commencement of the United Kingdom survey.

INDICATOR C23

Difference can be regarded as worthy of interest.

INDICATOR C24

Switzerland

The Swiss data have not been included because the question was not asked in the agreed upon form.

INDICATOR C25

Switzerland

The Swiss data have not been included because the question was not asked in the agreed upon form.

INDICATOR C27

Caution is advised when interpreting the results in some countries such as France as many people do not know how decisions are actually made in the present system.

INDICATOR F01

Austria, Belgium, Czech Republic, Italy

Figures on private expenditure have not been provided.

Austria

Expenditure for "not allocated by level" includes the main non-tertiary scholarships, schoolbooks and free travel arrangements for students and expenditure for adult and special education.

Belgium

Research expenditures are included to the extent that they are covered by funds provided by the community education authorities. Research funds from other public and private sources are excluded.

Finland

The percentage is affected by the decline in GDP between 1990 and 1992. Expenditure for "not allocated by level" includes expenditure for adult education and educational expenditure from the Ministry of Education and the National Board of Education. Research expenditure includes general university and business enterprise funds but not other separately identifiable R&D funds.

France

Expenditure for "not allocated by level" includes expenditure for special education in primary and lower secondary education and expenditure for arts education. All separately identifiable R&D expenditures are not taken into account; however, compensation of university teaching staff (and other regular university staff) is included, of which the portion of compensation attributable to research.

Germany (FTFR)

Total educational expenditures are not complete. The following expenditures are missing: private schools (however, public grants given to private schools are included); schools for nurses; agricultural training and research centres; German Research Foundation; Federal Institute for Employment (expenditure for retraining, better qualification, etc.); training of apprentices in the public service; support payments for dependent children made to persons undergoing education/training; allowances paid to teachers enjoying the status of public official for medical treatment and health insurance; scholarships granted by private institutions; households' purchases of commodities and services for education.

Public expenditures broken down by level of education and by type of expenditure are estimates.

Figures do not include the payments by private households and other private entities to government-dependent institutions.

Almost all expenditure on research is included: there are some minor omissions.

Annex 1 – Notes

Hungary

Expenditure for "not allocated by level" includes pedagogical services.

Ireland

Expenditure includes mainstream higher education research.

Expenditures of private entities other than households are underestimated because they are only provided for tertiary education. The expenditures for the other levels of education are not available.

Japan

Expenditures for "not allocated by level" include: expenditure for special education, special training colleges, miscellaneous schools, educational administration, scholarship and textbooks.

All separately identifiable research expenditure has not been taken into account but compensation of teaching staff (and other regular staff) in universities is included.

New Zealand

Expenditures for "not allocated by level" include: policy advice, management of contracts/administration of payments, provision and support of the curriculum, ministerial servicing, payment of salaries and allowances, provision of information, provision of teaching/learning accommodation, provision of teacher and caretaker housing, loss on sale of fixed assets, restructuring expenses, provision for retirement and long-service leave, capital investment.

Norway

Expenditures for early childhood education in government-dependent institutions (their amount is small) are included in expenditures for primary education.

Portugal

There is no distinction between public and private expenditures for public institutions.

Spain

Public expenditures on education are underestimated because an important part of the contributions paid by employees has not been taken into account.

Payments to independent privates institutions for tertiary education are underestimated because only the payments of private entities to universities for their activities of research and development are included.

Expenditure on research has been partly taken into account. Some higher education institutions have all R&D expenditure in their budgets; others have only general university funds and certain types of contracts.

United Kingdom

Expenditure by or on behalf of independent institutions at the tertiary level has been assumed to be negligible.

Only general university funds and grants from the Department of Education are included. All other separate R&D funds have not been taken into account.

United States

All research expenditures are included excepted for funds on major university-administered federal R&D centres.

INDICATOR F02

Austria, Netherlands

Expenditures for independent private institutions are included in expenditures for government-dependent private institutions.

Canada

Expenditure for pre-primary education is included in expenditure for primary and secondary education.

Denmark

Because some expenditures for independent private institutions are not available by level of education, some percentages broken down by school level are included in "all levels of education combined".

Finland

For early childhood, expenditures in government-dependent private institutions are included in expenditures for public institutions.

Germany (FTFR)

The expenditure share of government-dependent private institutions includes public transfers to government-dependent private institutions only.

Expenditures of government-dependent institutions for pre-primary education do not include private expenditures financed by private institutions and by parents (via the kindergarten fees). These expenditures account for a substantial amount of total expenditure. Unfortunately, there are no available data for these expenditure.

United Kingdom

See F01.

All pupils below compulsory school age in independent private schools are assumed to be receiving primary education rather than early childhood education.

Annex 1 – Notes

INDICATOR F03

Austria

Seventy per cent of full-time apprentices have been excluded from the total number of full-time equivalent enrolments. Subtracting this percentage that represents training in firms was required to adjust the figures to data on expenditure because figures on firms' expenditure were not available. It was assumed that apprentices spend about 30 per cent of their training in public schools and 70 per cent with the employers (these are approximate figures).

Canada

At tertiary level, for public institutions, expenditures are net of ancillary services.

Czech Republic

Costs per student cannot be calculated by distinguishing expenditures for primary and secondary levels because the data for lower secondary education have been included in primary and not in upper secondary education.

Data on expenditures for non-university tertiary education have been included in expenditures for upper secondary education but these expenditures are small.

Denmark

Because adult education is included in the expenditure, the following figures for full-time equivalent enrolments have been used to calculate the participation indicators:

Lower secondary education:	12 000
Upper secondary education:	21 000
Tertiary education:	15 000

Japan

Figures on expenditure by type of institutions do not include expenditure for textbooks and scholarships.

Sweden

Enrolments and expenditure for adult education have not been taken into account.

Switzerland

Costs per student in secondary education and in primary-secondary education have not been calculated because figures on apprentices and vocational education students do not correspond to the figures for expenditure at this level.

INDICATOR F04

Austria, Czech Republic

See F03.

Canada, Denmark, Finland

See F02.

Finland

Figures include day care and pre-school education (and meals) provided for 3-6 year-olds, in day-care centres, generally 8 to 10 hours a day, five days a week.

Germany (FTFR)

For pre-primary, primary and secondary levels, figures refer to public institutions only.

For tertiary education and all levels of education combined, shares of enrolments have not been calculated because enrolments cannot be distinguished between public and private institutions

New Zealand

Figures concern only public institutions.

INDICATOR F05

Finland

Early childhood education comprises only current expenditure.

Germany (FTFR)

Figures refer to public institutions only.

Japan

Expenditures for principals and vice-principals are included in expenditures for teachers.

INDICATOR F11

Canada

See F02.

Finland

Data concerning households and private organisations are not available.

Annex 1 – Notes

United Kingdom

See F01.

INDICATOR F12

Belgium

Figures on central funds are available for all levels of education combined but they cannot be broken down by level of education.

Canada

See F02.

Denmark, Ireland, Spain

Country mean. Totals include certain percentages of funds from international sources. For this reason, the country mean for the three levels of governments does not add up to 100 per cent.

Hungary

There are regional governments (counties) and municipalities as well but it is preferable to regard both as local governments because regional governments have no significant redistributive role.

Japan

Expenditure of prefectures and municipalities cannot be provided separately.

INDICATOR F13

Ireland, Norway, Spain

Figures on total public expenditure are estimates. They refer to fiscal year 1991 and are adjusted by inflation rate.

New Zealand, Portugal

Figures on total public expenditure from OECD National Accounts are not available either for 1991 or 1992.

INDICATOR P01

Australia

Lower secondary education includes ungraded secondary students.

The participation figures for non-university tertiary education, as indicated in the commentary, are on the high side. This is mainly due to difficulties in attaching the appropriate categories of school levels to TAFE enrolments: these numbers, currently classified as non-university tertiary education, could be reduced substantially. Many of these could either go into upper secondary education or be classified as "out of scope" (i.e. to be regarded as courses whose duration is not long enough to be included in *Education at a Glance*).

Czech Republic

Most part-time students are enrolled in adult education. Their age is unknown. They attend the same curricula as full-time students and take the same examinations.

Denmark

All formal regular education is classified as full-time education. Numbers of pupils and students refer to the number of persons enrolled on 1 October 1991. Adult education is excluded.

Hungary

Disabled students are included in primary and lower secondary education. Age distribution data are estimated for some age groups: at lower secondary education for 14 year-olds and over; at upper secondary education for 19 year-olds and over; at tertiary education for 24 year-olds and over.

Italy, Sweden

No distinction between full-time and part-time at tertiary education.

Japan

Table P01(A1): there are an additional 147 500 students, whose ages are unknown, who are not included.

Norway

Figures broken down by age are estimates for primary and lower secondary education.

United States

No distinction between full-time and part-time at upper secondary education.

INDICATOR P02

All countries

Participation rates are based on head counts of enrolments and do not differentiate between "full-time" and "part-time" enrolments.

Australia

At primary education, age 5 refers to ages 5 and under.

Austria

Figures refer only to kindergartens and pre-primary classes in primary schools. Day-care centres are generally excluded.

Annex 1 – Notes

Nearly all private institutions should be classified as "government-dependent" but there remains a very small number of independent private institutions with only a few pupils.

Belgium

Early childhood education starts at age 2 years and six months, so that the relevant population is only half the one taken into consideration. Taking this into account would bring the net enrolment rate for the 2 year-olds to 70.3 per cent.

Czech Republic

There are no kindergartens outside the public sector.

Denmark

Children in crèches (normally before 2 years of age) are excluded. Children in private day care/child-minding are excluded. Children in private kindergartens (receiving substantial public subsidies) are included in public education. A small number of children enrolled part-time in kindergartens are classed as full-time. A small number of children enrolled in both kindergartens and pre-primary classes in primary schools are classed as primary school pupils. Age groups for pupils in pre-primary classes in primary schools are estimated.

Germany (FTFR)

Table P02(B) shows a net enrolment rate of 115.1 for 6 years-old pupils. This overstated figure is due to the fact that the Microcensus, which is the source for these data, was conducted at the beginning of May while the population data are from 1st January.

Enrolments at 2 or 7 years of age occur only in exceptional cases for the new *Länder* and the Former Territory of the Federal Republic.

Hungary

Figures on early childhood and primary enrolments are estimates.

Japan

Only kindergartens are included. Day nurseries, which are social welfare institutions, are excluded.

Poland

In early childhood education, age 3 refers to ages 3-5.

Spain

Participation rates are higher than 100 because there are more registered pupils than children according to demographic projections from INE.

United Kingdom

Children in day-care facilities are excluded. Ages are recorded in August rather than in December.

The transition from early childhood to primary education can begin as early as age 2 or 3 but very frequently at age 4 (over three-quarters). The 1 per cent of 2 year-olds and 4 per cent of 3 year-olds who are in primary education have been excluded from this indicator.

INDICATOR P03

Australia

Figures on upper secondary enrolments at age 20 refer to ages 20 and over.

Data broken down by single age for part-time enrolments are not available.

Belgium

Some students in full-time vocational programmes are included in general programmes of lower secondary education.

Czech Republic, Denmark, Hungary, Norway

See P01.

Finland, Greece, Ireland

Figures broken down by single age are estimates.

Greece

In secondary education, age 21 refers to ages 21 and over.

Ireland

In upper secondary education (part-time) unknown ages include 24 and over.

Italy

Figures for "short courses" (3 years) are not reported.

Japan

In part-time upper secondary education, age 20 refers to ages 20-24; age 25 to ages 25-29 and age 30 to ages 30 and over.

Table P03(A): see P01(A1).

Norway

In lower secondary education, enrolments broken down by single age are estimates.

Annex 1 – Notes

Poland

In upper secondary education, age 20 refers to ages 20-23 and age 25 to ages 25 and over.

Russia

In secondary education (part-time), age 16 refers to ages 16-17; and age 29 to ages 18-29.

Spain

Participation rates do not take into account pupils whose age is unknown (about 3 per cent of full-time students in upper secondary education).

No distinction is made between full-time and part-time upper secondary education.

Sweden

See P01.

In upper secondary education, age 22 refers to ages 22 and over. Most of these students are enrolled in adult education.

United Kingdom

In general programmes, age 20 refers to ages 19-20.

Students in second educational programmes are included in first educational programmes.

Vocational course figures are normally only available for students in their last two years of upper secondary education.

Vocational course figures are inflated by large numbers of adults taking one or two courses at the upper secondary level who are much older than the typical age group.

Students in private further and tertiary education aged 19 and over are excluded to avoid possible double counting with public-sector provision.

Part-time enrolment data are shown here; comparable data by single age for other countries are not always available.

United States

See P01.

INDICATOR P04

All countries

See P03.

Australia

In tertiary education, age 16 refers to ages 15-16, age 27 to ages 25-27 and age 30 to ages 28 and over.

Austria

In non-university tertiary education, figures broken down by single age are not available.

In university education, age 17 refers to ages 16-17.

Austria is included in this indicator although it is excluded from most of the analysis because of its inability to provide upper secondary or non-university tertiary enrolments by age.

Belgium

University education corresponds to long tertiary courses and higher education in institutions other than universities; non-university tertiary education corresponds to short courses of higher education.

No distinction is made between first and second stages at university level.

Czech Republic

In non-university tertiary education, age 19 refers to ages 19 and over.

Germany (FTFR)

There is no distinction between first and second stages of tertiary education but there is a distinction between Master's degrees and Ph.D. degrees. Programmes to obtain a Ph.D. generally last from 3 to 5 years.

Italy

See P01.

Japan

In part-time tertiary education, age 18 refers to ages 18-22; age 23 to ages 23-24; age 25 to ages 25-29 and age 30 to ages 30 and over.

Poland

No distinction is made between first and second stages of tertiary education.

In non-university tertiary education, age 25 refers to ages 25 and over.

Russia

In tertiary education, age 24 refers to ages 21-24 and age 29 to ages 25-29.

Switzerland

In non-university tertiary education, part-time students are of different ages up to about 40 years.

Annex 1 – Notes

United Kingdom

In tertiary education, age 15 refers to ages 14-15.

INDICATOR P05

Austria

Austria reports equal male and female university enrolment rates.

Czech Republic

Unknown ages include ages 19 and over.

Denmark

See P03.

New entrants to university education second stage are excluded; 25 per cent of all students enter university education directly at second stage.

Germany, Italy, Poland, United Kingdom

See P04.

INDICATOR P06

Australia, Denmark, Italy

See P01.

Belgium, Czech Republic, Germany, Japan, Poland, Russia, United Kingdom

See P04.

Finland

See P03.

Hungary

Part-time students are estimates.

INDICATOR P08

France

The data on continuing education and training are related to training provided or financed by the employers. Due to employers' legal obligation to provide continuing education and training, there are administrative data sources available that give the number of employed who have participated in training during a given year. The Labour Force Surveys give data on the number of participants in continuing education and training on the day of the survey. The structural distribution by level of educational attainment, gender and age is not available in the administrative data sources, but has therefore been assumed to be the same as in the Labour Force Survey.

Germany

Training of students over 25 years old in vocational schools and in the dual system in the framework of initial training is *not* considered to be continuing vocational education. Forms of continuing vocational education other than courses are also not considered, e.g.: visits to occupational-related trade fairs or conventions, participation in short-duration events such as talks/lectures or half-day seminars, familiarisation-phases at the workplace, computer-aided learning at the workplace, quality circles, workshop circles and learning workshops.

Ireland

Job-related training for the employed includes training related to employment in the workplace and in an educational institution.

Sweden

The data refer to continuing education and training provided – or sponsored – by the employer. The data were collected in the Labour Force Survey of June 1993. The reference period in the survey was six months. The number of people involved in training during a 12-month period is assumed to be 150 per cent of the training rate during six months. Labour market training is not included.

United States

Respondents were asked to list up to four adult education activities or courses taken in the past 12 months, and indicate whether or not they were taken for credit towards a degree and whether or not they were completed. Then they were asked to indicate the main reason for taking each course. The data reported in the indicator are restricted to those who indicated that the main reason for participation was: *a)* to improve, advance, or keep up to date on the current job; *b)* to train for a new job or a new career; and *c)* for other employment- or career-related reasons. Examples of adult education activities or courses include: 1) continuing education or non-credit courses; 2) courses by mail, television, radio, or newspaper; 3) private instruction or tutoring; 4) educational or training activities organised by an employer, labour organisation, neighbourhood centre, church, or community group; 5) instruction in basic skills such as mathematics or reading or writing English; 6) instruction in English as a second language; 7) any other organised educational activity; 8) preparation for high-school equivalency examination; and 9) computer courses.

INDICATOR P11

Austria

1. Information technology not compulsory subject in 3rd and 4th grade with 2 hours per week; information technology not included in this figure.
2. Not compulsory.
3. Latin and descriptive geometry.

Annex 1 – Notes

Belgium

Schools have a high degree of freedom in designing their own schedule of lessons. Only the minimum hours (as fixed in the curriculum) are given in the table for each subject matter. The remaining hours for these subject matters (chosen by the school) are included in the category "other".

4. Orientation in technology is optional in the French community and a basic course in the Flemish community.
5. Could be any subject including remedial courses, Greek, Latin, technical activities, scientific work, socio-economic initiation, typing.

Finland

6. The Finnish data concern the obligatory subjects only. The first grade at ISCED level 2 education includes a total of 30 hours compulsory subjects per week. During the second and third years, there are 24 hours obligatory and 6 hours optional subjects per week. The optional subjects, which are not included in the Finnish figures, include altogether eleven subjects.
7. The national distribution of teaching hours combines biology and geography. Here, the hours have been divided between science and social studies.
8. Information technology is an optional subject. Technical work is included in other subjects.
9. Other subjects include: home economics, technical work, textile work, student counselling, the second language.

France

10. Latin and Greek.

Germany

11. Economics, technics, domestic science.

Ireland

12. The same amount of time is devoted to both Irish and English, and included in this figure
13. Technology as a core subject is under consideration.

Italy

Some middle schools (ISCED 2) have a longer timetable.

Netherlands

Reported in this table are figures for MAVO, including the transition class (4 years' secondary education in total); the figures reflect the minimum number of hours for the entire course. Dutch schools have a high degree of freedom in designing their own timetable.

New Zealand

In the first two years of ISCED 2, students follow the primary school curriculum, which is an integrated curriculum built around the core learning of language, mathematics, science, social studies, arts, physical education and health. Added to these are technology subjects and some electives. Because of the integrated nature of the curriculum at this stage of learning, the figures for each of the subjects listed are estimates, except for the more distinct subjects of technology, arts and physical education.

In Grades Three, Four and Five of ISCED 2, the curriculum is based on separate disciplines. Students follow a common core. In addition, several electives are offered, which invariably include a second language, technology subjects, vocational subjects, and more specialist options for some of the core subjects. In this table, only the percentages of the total time available for ISCED 2 Grades One, Two and Three have been reported;

14. English includes English, English as a second language, language studies, media studies, public speaking, and remedial reading.
15. Mathematics includes mathematics, mathematics with statistics, and remedial mathematics.
16. Science includes science, agriculture/horticulture/forestry, biology, chemistry, human biology, physical science, physics, and environmental studies.
17. Social studies includes social studies, classical studies, community studies, contemporary studies, economics, environmental studies, geography, history, humanities, legal studies, liberal studies, New Zealand studies, and social sciences.
18. Foreign languages include Chinese, French, German, Indonesian, Japanese, Maori, Russian, and Spanish.
19. Technology includes computer studies, construction/surveying, electronics, graphics and design, home economics, keyboard skills, technology, word-processing, and workshop technology/design technology.
20. The arts include art core, art elective, art history, practical art, dance and drama, core music, elective music, performance music, photography.
21. Physical education includes physical education, health, human biology, human relationships/parenting skills, outdoor education, and recreation and sport.
22. Religious education is generally not taught at state schools out of respect for the secular clause set out in the 1964 Education Act, which prohibits religious instruction and religious observance in state primary schools.
23. Vocational skills include accountancy, business studies, career education, clothing and textiles, LINK, polytechnic programmes, secretarial studies, shorthand and typing, tourism and hospitality, transition, and work experience.
24. *Other* includes form periods and assemblies.

Annex 1 – Notes

Norway

The figures reflect the minimum number of hours for the three-year block (Grades Seven to Nine).

25. Others includes home economics, pupil/class council, optional subjects (including a second foreign language).

Portugal

26. In Grade Three, time devoted to orientation in technology may attain 252 hours per year according to the specific study area and availability of school facilities.

27. Religion is optional.

Spain

ISCED 2 has only three grades. This table shows the minimum curriculum established for all schools in the country. The formal document indicates the time to be devoted to diverse subject matters in percentages which have been converted to lessons on the basis of 26 hours per week.

In some Autonomous Communities, a second mother tongue (Catalan, Valencian, Basque, Galician) other than Spanish is taught. In this case, the same amount of time is devoted to teach the proper language as is devoted to teach Spanish. That is, the time devoted to language teaching is doubled. In any case, neither the proper language nor Spanish should be considered a foreign language. The figures reported for reading and writing represent the minimum, assuming only one language.

Sweden

"Others" includes Sloyd (handicrafts), child studies, domestic science, and electives (French or German or local options).

INDICATOR P12

Belgium (French community)

10-20% of the data are missing.

Canada

10-20% of the data are missing.

France

10-20% of the data are missing.

Germany (FTFR)

10-20% of the data are missing.

Germany (TFGDR)

10-20% of the data are missing.

Ireland

Data have not been derived from the IEA study. The figure reflects the number of teaching hours per year for all schools. Calculation: 25 hours of instruction per week x 36.8 full-instruction weeks per year.

INDICATORS P31 and P32

Australia

Teachers include principals, deputy principals and senior teachers mainly involved in administrative tasks.

Denmark

Full-time and part-time teachers are estimates. Distribution by school level (pre-primary, primary and lower secondary levels) is also an estimate. Pre-primary level only includes teachers in pre-primary classes in primary schools.

Kindergartens are classified as public institutions.

France

The number of full-time equivalent teachers does not take into account the additional hours given by teachers. In public secondary education institutions, an increase of 6.6 per cent of total full-time equivalents would be observed if the additional hours were taken into account.

The number of teachers in private tertiary education institutions and in independent private secondary education institutions are entirely estimates.

An important part of pedagogical and support staff has been estimated, about 18 per cent of all the pedagogical and support staff, and about 7 per cent of all the staff employed in education.

Germany

Most figures are estimates.

Japan

Principals and vice-principals are included in "Teachers" while other staff is included in "Support staff". Full-time equivalents of part-time teachers are not calculated, since there are no valid and reliable data available on the basis of which such calculations can be made.

Netherlands

Teaching staff do not include direction staff.

Poland

No distinction is made between full-time and part-time early childhood education.

Annex 1 – Notes

United Kingdom

Pupil/teacher ratios are based on a head count of pupils aged under 5 rather than on full-time equivalents. Most pupils in early childhood education are enrolled part-time.

Figures on teachers at lower secondary education are included in upper secondary education.

United States

Figures on teachers in early childhood education are included in primary education.

INDICATOR P33

France

Figures for upper secondary education (general and vocational) are included in figures for lower secondary education.

Ireland

Children from 4 to 6 years of age spend two years in formal education in primary schools.

Netherlands

Figures for ISCED 0 include Grades Three and Four (ages 6 and 7).

New Zealand

There is no formal regulation specifying the minimum number of teaching hours per day/week/year for primary schools. However, there is a legal requirement for primary schools to provide a minimum of two hours of teaching before noon and two hours after noon to be deemed as sessions for one half-day respectively, and to be open for 394 or 396 half-days per annum (i.e. 39.5 weeks). In practice, all schools provide more than 4 hours per day, varying usually between 4.6 and 4.75 hours (i.e., on average, 23.5 hours per week), and are open for at least 40 weeks. The official number of hours (not the actual number) has been put in the table.

As with primary schools, there is no formal regulation requiring a minimum of teaching hours per day/week or year for secondary schooling. However, the regulation for funding schools staffing on the basis of weekly teaching half-days is used to indicate the minimum weekly total of 25 teaching hours for secondary schools. Secondary schools must be open for at least 38 weeks.

Sweden

ISCED 3: Different subgroups of teachers have different numbers of teaching hours. Teachers in general subjects like mathematics, languages, etc. have 14 teaching hours per week; teachers in arts, sports, etc. have more. This is a mean estimated from figures on the number of different types of teachers.

ISCED 3 Vocational: Many types of teachers teach at ISCED 3 vocational programmes, teachers in general subjects have 14 teaching hours per week; teachers in vocational subjects like welding have 18 hours per week. This is a mean (rough) estimated from the approximate number of different teachers in these programmes.

Turkey

Figures given are the ultimate hours a teacher instructs per week and include additional teaching hours which are paid accordingly.

For ISCED 3 vocational, the number of teaching hours refers only to vocational teachers.

United Kingdom

Only figures for England and Wales have been reported.

United States

Survey data, based on teachers' self-reported number of hours they are required to be in school in the most recent full week of teaching. Formula: hours required in the school year 1991 x (classroom teaching hours/hours required in the school year 1988).

Figures for upper secondary vocational education are included in figures for upper secondary general education.

INDICATOR P34

Austria

The number of years varies; the minimum number of years has been reported.

For ISCED 2, the number of years varies from three to four; the minimum number has been reported in the table.

For ISCED 3 vocational, the number of years varies from three to six; the minimum number has been reported in the table.

Finland

Vocational school teachers take four to six years of studies, including practice, and one to two years of requested work experience before being qualified. The total number of years of tertiary teacher education thus varies from five to eight; the minimum number is reported in the table.

France

The number of years varies; the minimum number of years has been reported.

In the independent private sector, there is no *a priori* regulatory requirement. In order to teach in public institutions controlled by the Ministry of Education, the precondition is to have attended:

Annex 1 – Notes

- primary education (5 years);
- secondary education (7 years);
- university education up to a first degree (3 years);
- one year of teacher training in a IUFM (*Institut universitaire de formation des maîtres*) after the teacher proficiency exam. Preparation for this exam also takes place in the IUFM. An increasing number of would-be teachers take advantage of this preparation year.

The duration of high-level training thus becomes five years.

This training pattern applies to primary and secondary teachers since 1992 when the external exams took place. In 1991/92, however, the prevailing system had the same number of study years (12+4), even if they did not correspond to the same level of higher education for pre-primary and primary teachers (ISCED levels 0 + 1). Auxiliary teachers, or teachers fully qualified by integration or by examination are exempted from attending the preparatory year in a IUFM if they are to teach in a secondary school (ISCED 2 + 3) and may thus not hold a university degree.

Ireland

Two years of formal education for children aged 4 to 6 have been included.

Italy

The number of years in primary and secondary education varies between 12 and 13; the minimum number is reported in the table for ISCED 2 and ISCED 3.

Netherlands

Two years of pre-primary education have been included.

The number of years in secondary education varies; the minimum number is included in the table.

New Zealand

Two years of formal education for children, ages 4 to 6, have been included.

The number of years for ISCED 2 varies; the minimum number has been put into the table.

Tertiary teacher education for teaching at ISCED 3 consists of three years (minimum) to complete a university degree, one year teacher training, and two years for registration.

Tertiary teacher education for teaching at ISCED levels 0 and 1 consists of three years to complete teacher training plus two years for registration. However, most early childhood educators and teachers currently are unregistered and have no tertiary teacher training.

Portugal

The number of years varies; the minimum number of years is included in the table.

Spain

The number of years varies; the minimum number of years is included in the table.

ISCED 3 vocational: with regard to their minimum initial training, teachers can be sorted in three categories: *a)* teachers whose initial training is ISCED 3 vocational; *b)* teachers with a short tertiary degree; and *c)* teachers with a long tertiary degree. They are distributed roughly as follows. Public: *a)* 3 per cent; *b)* 30 per cent; *c)* 66 per cent; and private *a)* 10 per cent; *b)* and *c)* 90 per cent. Accurate data are not available.

Sweden

The number of years varies; the minimum number is shown in the table.

The data are based on all students enrolled in 1991/92. For ISCED 3 vocational, the number of years for teachers in vocational subjects has been reported.

United Kingdom

Only figures for England and Wales have been reported.

United States

There is no published source; standard practice.

INDICATOR P35

Austria

Teachers' salaries depend exclusively on the training they have received (university training versus non-university training).

Germany

Figures are for unmarried teachers with no children.

Spain

Public: weighted means.

United Kingdom

Only figures for England and Wales have been reported.

United States

Teacher compensation is based on teacher assessment reports: includes basic academic salary, plus compensation from school for extra duty, and other job-related income (including bonuses).

Annex 1 – Notes

INDICATOR P36

Belgium

The data on the age distribution of teachers as percentages of the total teaching body at ISCED 1 public are based on an extrapolation of the data for the Flemish community.

Figures for ISCED 2 public include ISCED 3.

France

Figures for ISCED 1 pubic include ISCED 0. Figures for ISCED 2 public include ISCED 3. Percentages were computed on figures for full-time and part-time enrolments.

Germany

The percentage is for public and government-dependent private; for ISCED 0, *Praktikanten* are included.

Ireland

Figures for ISCED 1 public include ISCED 0.

Italy

Figures on the sex distribution of teachers do not always add up to 100 per cent due to rounding.

Netherlands

Figures for ISCED 2 public include ISCED 3.

New Zealand

Data for ISCED 2 apply only to teachers of Grades One and Two of ISCED 2 and are a percentage of area schoolteachers (i.e. teaching several subjects, and not only one subject). Secondary teachers are covered in ISCED 3.

Portugal

Figures for ISCED 2 public include ISCED 3.

Sweden

The data on ages are derived from the database on teachers. As teachers are not classified according to ISCED, their numbers have been estimated by using the levels at which different subgroups of teachers teach.

United Kingdom

Figures for ISCED 1 public include ISCED 0. ISCED 2 public includes ISCED 3. Figures for only England and Wales have been reported.

United States

School year 1990/91; vocational included with general.

INDICATOR P36(C)

Belgium and Portugal

Figures for lower and upper secondary education (figures for upper general secondary education include vocational education).

France

Figures for upper secondary education (general and vocational) are included in figures for lower secondary education.

France, Ireland and the United Kingdom

Figures for early childhood education are included in figures for primary education.

Italy and the United States

Figures for upper secondary vocational education are included in figures for upper secondary general education.

INDICATOR P41

See also notes to P42

Australia

The figures reflect the high proportion of R&D that takes place in the university sector as well as the availability of detailed Australian statistics on this area. Australia's high ranking on this indicator might be slightly lower if similar data were available for all OECD countries.

The data refer to 1990/91 for the government and private non-profit sectors, and to 1990 for the university education sector. The government sector includes state and federal government levels. In the university education sector, researchers comprise 491 person-years for academic staff and 727 person-years for post-graduate students. Only post-graduates obtaining their qualification solely through research (including those who are not employed by the university or in receipt of a research scholarship) are included in this estimate.

Austria

The government sector data refer to the federal or central government. In the university education sector, post-graduate students are not recorded separately but are included in the academic staff category when on the payroll of the university, or when they are employed as university assistants to work on particular research projects and paid for by research grants.

Finland

The government sector data refer to the central government. In university education category, the researchers comprise 245 person-years for academic staff and 31 person-years for post-graduate students. For post-graduate students, a person-year is included only when they are financed by grants amounting to a normal salary.

Annex 1 – Notes

Ireland

The government sector data refer to the central government. They include data on an agency that is concerned mainly with research on student assessment. The agency is nominally controlled by a teacher training college and could therefore be alternatively classified in the university education sector. In the university education category, researchers comprise 18 person-years for academic staff and 4 person-years for post-graduate students. Only PhD students are included. The educational research activities of non-profit organisations such as teacher unions and Church associations are not included, but these are likely to be very small.

Netherlands

The Netherlands R&D survey data are organised in terms of education as an area of relevance or as an objective, and therefore are likely to encompass a broader range of activities than in most other nations. R&D activities in the research institutes sector are surveyed using the Frascati methodology. In the university education sector estimates are derived from knowledge of the number of academics who are likely to be engaged in educational R&D and the proportion of their time devoted to research. The government sector data refer to the central government level and include staff employed at the National Curriculum Development Institute. Post-graduate students are not recorded separately but are included in the academic staff category when employed by the university. The university education category comprises 200 person-years in university departments and 160 person-years in research institutes.

New Zealand

The government sector data refer to the central government. In the government sector, the distribution of educational R&D personnel between researchers and other staff categories is assumed to be the same proportion as for government research as a whole. In the university education and private non-profit categories, staff numbers shown as researchers refer to all categories of staff – detailed breakdowns are not available. Post-graduate students engaged in educational R&D are not included in the data. However, they are included in the estimates of total R&D personnel when employed by universities.

Sweden

Government and private non-profit sectors conduct very little educational R&D although they do play a role in funding research. Since education is not included as a field of science in national R&D surveys, estimates for the university education sector are derived from data on the types of research performed in different universities. Information is not available on private and municipality-owned units in the university education sector, but the amount of educational R&D they perform is likely to be negligible. Researchers in the university education category comprise academic staff and those post-graduate students who are employed by the universities.

United Kingdom

The government sector data refer to the central government level. In the university education category, researchers comprise 977 person-years for academic staff and 1 163 person-years for post-graduate students. Post-graduates studying for a research-based qualification and paid as researcher assistants are included in the estimate. Data are not available on post-graduate students enrolled in non-university institutions.

INDICATOR P42

See also notes to P41

Australia

The government data include expenditure in the state and federal government sectors. In the university education sector, capital expenditure includes 4 million on land and buildings. Government funding for R&D in the university education sector comprises 59 million from the federal government and 3 million from state governments. In the private non-profit sector, government funding for R&D comprises 1 million from the federal government and 2 million from state governments. Data for total public and private R&D expenditure refer to 1990.

Total public and private R&D expenditure in Australia ($5 091 million) is not strictly correct: some data referring to 1990/91 and some others referring to the 1990 calendar year have been aggregated.

Austria

The government sector data refer to the federal government level except for the source of funds classification. In the university education sector, capital expenditure includes 7 million on land and buildings. Government funding for R&D in the university education sector comprises 108 million from the federal government, 0.5 million from provincial governments, and 1.5 million from local or municipal governments.

Canada

Total expenditure on educational R&D may be underestimated since only data for the university education sector are included. However, the lack of data from the government and private non-profit sectors is not viewed as a major problem since it appears that these sectors engage in relatively little educational R&D. The estimated level of expenditure on educational R&D in the university education sector is based on estimates of the consumption of university resources by different academic fields, and on the proportion of expenditure each field allocates to R&D in universities with different research profiles.

Annex 1 – Notes

Finland

The government sector data refer to the central government level. No data are available for the private non-profit sector, but it appears that little educational R&D occurs in that sector. Expenditure on land, buildings and other capital items is not included, except for the acquisition of equipment in the university education sector. "Other" expenditure includes the labour costs of staff other than researchers.

Ireland

The government sector data refer to the central government level. Data are not available for the private non-profit sector, but educational R&D activities in this sector are likely to be only minor. In the university education sector only the overheads associated with individual academic departments are included; central overheads of any kind are not included. Especially the latter may represent an important source of underestimation in the data.

Netherlands

The government sector data refer to the central government level and comprise 15 million for the National Curriculum Development Institute and 23 million for the research institutes sector. Detailed breakdowns are not available for the research institutes and private non-profit sectors. To construct the table, it has been assumed that two-thirds of the expenditure in those sectors are on labour costs and one-third on other expenditure.

New Zealand

The government sector data refer to the central government level. In the government sector the distribution of educational R&D expenditure between types of expenditure is assumed to be the same as for government research as a whole. Total public and private R&D expenditure is based on data for 1991.

Sweden

Data are not available for the government and private non-profit sectors, but it appears that very little educational R&D is conducted in these sectors, although they do fund some research. Government funding for R&D in the university education sector is supplied by the central government. The data include an estimated share of administrative and other overhead expenditures. Data for total public and private R&D expenditure refer to 1991.

United Kingdom

Data are not available for the private non-profit sector. The government sector data refer to the central government level.

INDICATOR R11

Denmark

See P01.

Classification has changed for basic vocational education (Higher Commercial Examination): before 1992, it was included in vocational upper secondary education. Now, it is classified as general upper secondary education.

Germany (FTFR)

All graduates in general education are first educational programme graduates. The relevant age is 19.

Some graduates in vocational/technical education are first educational programmes graduates (their graduation age is 19) while others are second educational programmes (their graduation age is 22). Therefore, a weighted average has been used to calculate the graduation rate.

Ireland

Around 86 per cent of the age cohort were shown under "first educational programmes" and a further 18 per cent of the age cohort under "second educational programmes". These latter graduates were from vocational programmes in 1991 and had previously obtained a qualification under upper secondary education. Therefore the combination of first and second programmes gives an equivalent of 104 per cent of the age cohort.

Italy

All vocational programme students who want to follow a full course (5 years) must obtain a preliminary degree after roughly 3 years. They are not reported in the table.

Spain

Figures on first general educational programmes are based only on students who finish the *Curso de orientacion universitaria (COU)*. Therefore, these rates are underestimated because they do not take into account students who obtain the *Titulo de bachiller* and do not continue to follow the *curso de orentacion universitaria (COU)*: they can leave the education system or study FPII-vocational training).

United Kingdom

Students on second educational programmes are included in first educational programmes.

Many students graduate from general education programmes after 2 rather than 4 years.

Annex 1 – Notes

INDICATOR R12

Australia
Some post-graduate degrees (as post-graduates qualified/preliminary, post-graduate diploma external/new, Bachelor post-graduate, graduate certificates) are included in Masters' or equivalent.

Belgium
To avoid double counting, 2 033 graduates in teacher training have been dropped since this is a part-time training mostly followed simultaneously with other studies.

Although a Bachelor degree exists in Belgium, it has no value on the labour market. Therefore the Master's degree is considered as a first degree.

Denmark
See P01.

Finland
The first degree is the Master's. But the introduction of a Bachelor degree is being planned in many fields. It takes 6-10 years to obtain a degree depending on the field. In practice, the median age is 27.

Greece
The first degree in medicine takes 12 semesters of studies. Engineering studies last 5 years and award a diploma (e.g. Diploma of architect engineer, of civil engineer); this diploma is a first degree but equivalent to a Master's. Post-graduate studies do not set limits to starting or ending ages and their minimum duration is 2 years for the equivalence to Master's and 3 years for the equivalence to Ph.D. degrees.

Hungary
Some Bachelor degrees (e.g. in teacher training and art colleges with 4 years of training) do not precede Master's degrees. The duration for obtaining them is equivalent to the typical duration for obtaining Master's degrees.

Italy
Less than 5 per cent of students aged 22 (theoretical graduation age) obtain a Master's degree. Around 20 per cent graduate at the age of 25.

Spain
Figures are estimates.

Switzerland
Bachelor degrees are included in Master's degrees.

INDICATOR R14

Belgium, Spain
See R12.

Denmark
See P01.

Italy
Ph.D. degrees by subject are not reported.

Netherlands
Some post-graduates in paramedical science are included in natural and physical science.

United Kingdom
Graduates in interdisciplinary subjects have been pro-rated across the five broad subject groups.

INDICATOR R15

Belgium
See R12.

Hungary
Physical science, mathematics and computing are included in biological science and related.

Japan
"Law and business" includes political science, sociology and other related fields as well.

United Kingdom
This indicator includes a pro-rated share of graduates in interdisciplinary subjects.

INDICATOR R21

See notes to C01.

INDICATOR R22

Austria
The self-employed are not included.

Annex 1 – Notes

Belgium

Net incomes (after taxes) from the survey have been weighted taking into account differences in tax rates. Data are based on a sample of 4 000 persons.

France

The French ISCED classification is based on the highest diploma obtained. To avoid underestimation of the number of people in the higher ISCED categories, the number of people with qualifications beyond the level of their diploma has been estimated.

Incomes refer to the main source of earnings for the employed persons. Incomes from other sources are not included. The self-employed are likewise not included.

Italy

Data for ISCED 0/1/2 refer only to ISCED 2.

Netherlands

The self-employed are not included. Incomes are reported without taking into consideration employers' contributions to social security and similar schemes.

Spain

ISCED 5 is included in the figures for ISCED 3.

Switzerland

Reported earnings refer to the month preceding the interview, not to the whole year.

INDICATOR R23

Australia

The occupational classification system used differs from ISCO. Some occupations have not been reported.

Canada

No official link exists between the Canadian Standard Occupation and Industry Coding Systems and the ISCO and ISIC systems. An attempt has been made to assign the Canadian codes to the ISCO and ISIC categories as best as possible. Canada has been unable to provide a reasonable link to ISCO-80 since these occupations are contained within a broad range of occupation codes in the Canadian system.

Full-time members of the Canadian armed forces are not eligible to take part in the Canadian Labour Force Survey, and so they are not included in the data for ISIC 75.

France

The French ISCED classification is based on the highest diploma obtained. To avoid underestimation of the number of people in the higher ISCED categories, the number of people with qualifications beyond the level of their diploma have been estimated in the data.

Ireland

In the case of occupations, data on the basis of ISCO-88 were not available for the 1992 Labour Force Survey. Consequently, occupational categories had to be approximated using the national occupation classification.

Due to the likelihood of too small samples underlying some of the grossed up figures for ISCO codes 213, 31 and 80 (computing professionals, physical and engineering science associate professionals, and machine and plant operators), these groups are not reported.

The data on completion of education by industry group were provided on the basis of NACE which is close to ISIC. Due to problems of sample size, ISIC 72 (computer and related activities) was not reported.

Netherlands

ISCED 5, 6 and 7 are considered as one category.

Sweden

The Labour Force Survey (LFS) was used as a source of information for the Swedish data in Table R23(A). It was not possible to make the Swedish data conform strictly to the ISCO-88 definition of occupational groups because of: *a)* the high level of aggregation of occupations in the LFS data; and *b)* the difficulty in converting the Swedish classification into the ISCO-88.

As a result of this it has not been possible to include in the Swedish data several occupations, which belong to the group of Corporate managers (sub-major group 12 of ISCO-88), such as: Department managers in Sales and marketing, Advertising and public relations, Supply and distribution, Computing services, and Research and development.

On the other hand, some occupations, which do not belong to the group of Corporate managers (such as assistant nurses, social workers, economists and statisticians) have been included in the reported data because it was not possible to separate them from the aggregated groups in the LFS statistics.

Owing to the same problems, Sweden has not been able to report data for the complete occupational group of Physical and engineering science associate professions (sub-major group 31 of ISCO-88). Thus, the data reported for this group do in fact only refer to the minor group of Computer associate professionals and to occupations which should not be included in group 31, such as Computer process workers, Repairer, Electronic equipment and Electrical line installers.

Annex 1 – Notes

Similar problems of delimitation are attached to all Swedish data reported for the occupational groups.

United States

R23(A): The household survey used as the source of information for the United States data does not use the ISCO system. It uses the United States Standard Occupational Classification (SOC). Also, no official link between ISCO and SOC exists. Nevertheless, for the purpose of providing US data, an attempt was made to assign SOC categories to ISCO categories. In some instances this was difficult because occupations grouped together in the SOC are not in the ISCO. For example, Computing professionals (ISCO-213) includes computing system designers. In the SOC, some of these occupations may be included in "Electrical or electronic engineers" and could not be separated from other engineers in this category.

R23(B): The household survey used as the source of information for the United States data does not use the ISIC system. It uses the United States Standard Industrial Classification (SIC). However, some work has been done to create a link between the two classification systems. Nevertheless, there may be some inaccuracies because sometimes in the SIC, an industry that belongs to a particular ISIC category has been grouped with other industries that do not belong or because the United States codes are not exhaustive enough to cover all related areas identified in the ISIC. For example, Computing and related activities (ISIC-72) identifies activities that cannot be identified in the SIC such as Hardware consultancy, Software consultancy and supply, and Maintenance and repair of office, accounting, and computing machinery.

INDICATOR R24

Australia

Data for all school-leavers have been used as the statistics on transition from education to work do not distinguish between those who obtained their Secondary School Certificate (ISCED 3) and those who did not (ISCED 2).

France

One year after leaving education: seven months after leaving education instead of one year. Data for tertiary education are from 1989.

Five years after leaving education: two years after leaving education instead of five. Data for tertiary education are from 1991.

Ireland

Leavers from ISCED 2 include both persons who left full-time education after having successfully completed ISCED 2 and persons who left school while attending ISCED 3, but who did not complete it.

The data relate in all cases to short-term perspectives, i.e. one year following departure from full-time education. Long-term perspective data are not available for any ISCED level.

1992 is the year of survey in all cases. Since submitting data for 1991, some minor adjustments have been made to the estimates over and above those arising from the reclassification of labour force status.

In the case of ISCED 2, data are shown that refer to the labour force status of persons who left full-time education at ISCED 2 one year prior to the survey. Persons who left school while attending ISCED 3 but who did not complete ISCED 3 are included in the total of ISCED 2-leavers.

Leavers from ISCED 3 refer to those who successfully completed ISCED 3 one year prior to the survey and who were not enrolled in full-time education at the time of the survey.

Leavers from both ISCED 5 and 6/7 relate to graduates at this level only.

For all ISCED levels, persons in employment include those on various publicly sponsored work experience and job training schemes for the unemployed. These persons receive an allowance and are regarded as being in employment in the reference period immediately prior to the survey. Persons who have emigrated after leaving school are classified according to their labour force status abroad.

School-leavers from ISCED 2 include those who commenced an ISCED 3 programme but dropped out before graduation. Data for leavers from ISCED 3 include ISCED 3 graduates but exclude those who entered tertiary education and subsequently dropped out. All of the data relate to persons leaving full-time education in the 1990/91 school year.

Sweden

One year after leaving education: data for lower secondary education are from 1990.

Five years after leaving education: data for lower secondary education are from 1988.

United Kingdom

Data refer to England and Wales only.

United States

Data from a household survey with retrospective information were used. The survey, fielded in October, asked respondents about their current level of educational attainment and their current enrolment in education. It also asked respondents about their enrolment in education one year earlier. The population of recent leavers was deduced from this information.

Annex 2 – Data sources

INDICATORS C01 and C02

Australia
Australian Bureau of Statistics, *Transition from Education to Work Survey*, 1993.

Austria
Micro-census of the Austrian Central Statistics Office, averages for 1992.

Belgium
Labour Force Survey 1992. The unemployment register in April 1992 has been used for data on the number of unemployed.

Canada
Canadian Labour Force Survey.

Denmark
Statistical register of the labour force and register of statistics on unemployment.

Finland
The register of completed educational programmes and degrees has been used for the indicators C01 and C02. The *Labour Force Survey* of 1992 has been used for C11 and R21.

France
Labour Force Survey, March 1992.

Germany
Labour Force Survey, 1992.

Ireland
Labour Force Survey, 1992.

Italy
Labour Force Survey, 1992.

Netherlands
Labour Force Survey, 1992.

New Zealand
Household Labour Force Survey, 1992.

Norway
Labour Force Survey, 1992.

Spain
Labour Force Survey, 1992.

Sweden
The register of educational attainment for the population has been used for the indicators C01 and C02. The *Labour Force Survey* of 1992 has been used for C11 and R21.

Switzerland
Enquête suisse population active, *Labour Force Survey*, 1992.

Turkey
Household Labour Force Survey, 1992.

United Kingdom
Labour Force Survey, 1992.

United States
Current Population Survey, March 1992.

INDICATOR C03

All countries
OECD demographic data base (SMEDUC), 1992.

INDICATOR C11

See notes to C01.

INDICATOR C12

All countries
OECD Labour Force Statistics, Part III, 1994.

INDICATOR C13

All countries
OECD, *National Accounts*, 1994.

INDICATORS F01 to F05 and F11 to F13

Australia
Department of Employment, Education and Training, Higher Education Division, Canberra.

Austria
Austrian Central Statistical Office, Vienna.

Belgium
SEDEP (*Service de Développement et d'Évaluation des Programmes de Formation*), University of Liège; and Katholieke Universiteit Leuven, Faculteit der Psychologie en Pedagogische Wetenschappen, Leuven.

Canada
Statistics Canada, Ottawa.

Czech Republic
Institute for Informatics in Education, Prague.

Denmark
Undervisnings Ministeriet, Datakontoret, Copenhagen.

Finland
Statistics Finland, Helsinki and Ministry of Education, Helsinki

France
Ministère de l'Éducation nationale et de la Culture, Direction de l'Évaluation et de la Prospective, Paris.

Annex 2 – Data sources

Germany

Statistiches Bundesamt, Wiesbaden.

Greece

Ministry of National Education and Religious Affairs, Directorate of Investment Planning and Operational Research, Athens.

Hungary

Pénzügyminisztérium, Budapest.

Ireland

Department of Education, Statistics Section, Dublin.

Italy

ISTAT, Roma; and Servizio Statistico, Ministero della Pubblica Istruzione, Rome.

Japan

Ministry of Education, Culture and Science, Research and Statistics Planning Division, Tokyo.

Netherlands

Centraal Bureau voor de Statistiek, Department for Statistics of Education, Voorburg; and Ministerie van Onderwijs en Wetenschappen, Zoetermeer.

New Zealand

Ministry of Education, Wellington.

Norway

Statistisk Sentralbyra, Division for Population, Education and Regional Conditions, Kongsvinger; and The Royal Norwegian Ministry of Education, Research and Church Affairs, Oslo.

Poland

Central Statistical Office, Republic of Poland, Warsaw.

Portugal

Ministerio de Educaçao, Gabinete de Estudos e Planeamento, Departamento de Programação, Lisboa.

Russia

Centre for Science Research and Statistics, Moscow.

Spain

Instituto Nacional de Estadistica, Subdireccion General de Estadisticas e Investigaciones Sociales, Madrid; and Ministerio de Educacion, Officina de Planificacion, Madrid.

Sweden

Swedish National Agency for Education *(Skolverket)*, Stockholm; and Statistics Sweden, Örebro.

Switzerland

Office fédéral de la statistique, Bern.

Turkey

State Institute of Statistics, Ankara.

United Kingdom

Department for Education, Darlington.

United States

Department of Education, Office of Educational Research and Improvement, National Center for Education Statistics, Washington, D.C.

INDICATORS P01 to P06

All countries

See notes to F01-F05 and F11-F13.

INDICATOR P08

Canada

Adult Education and Training Survey (AETS), which was a supplement to the *Labour Force Survey* fielded in January 1992.

France

Administrative data sources for continuing education and training (DARES - Ministère du Travail) and *Labour Force Survey* (INSEE), 1992.

Germany

Berichtssystem Weiterbildung (*BSW* report system on continuing education).

Ireland

Labour Force Survey.

Norway

Level of Living Survey (*Levekårsundersøkelsen*), 1991.

Spain

Survey of Active Population.

Sweden

Labour Force Survey, June 1993.

United States

National Household Education Survey, adult education component, 1991

Annex 2 – Data sources

INDICATOR P11

LEGEND

1. Data source, full reference
2. Type of data source:
   - law = law or policy document based on law (data on formal arrangements)
   - stat = national statistics (data on formal arrangements)
   - intsur = international survey (data on samples)
   - natsur = national survey (data on samples)
   - other = other
3. In case of data on formal arrangements:
   - 3a. Groups under concern
   - 3b. Year of reference
4. In case of data on populations:
   - 4a. Population under concern
   - 4b. Period of data collection
5. In case of data on samples:
   - 5a. Population from which sample was drawn
   - 5b. Period of data collection
   - 5c. Type and size of the sample
   - 5d. How were data collected?:
     - reg = use of register
     - inq = postal inquiry
     - pho = interview by phone
     - vis = interview by visit
     - oth = other
   - 5e. Sampling errors calculated and accessible?
   - 5f. Translation procedure (in case of international survey)
6. Deviation from definition of the indicator?
7. Other comments

AUSTRIA

1. Curriculum *Hauptschule*; 1-4 grade *Gymnasium* (RG, wkRG)
2. Ordinance, based on the School Organisation Act (*Schulorganisationsgesetz*)

BELGIUM

1. Flanders: Curriculum of the 3 educational networks
   Direction générale de l'enseignement secondaire du ministère de l'Éducation, de la Recherche et de la Formation de la Communauté française
2. Law

FINLAND

1. National curriculum / Basic lines of national curriculum
2. Decision of State Council

FRANCE

1. Les données transmises sont issues d'une exploitation spécifique
2. Les données mobilisées pour cette exploitation proviennent de deux types de sources:
   - le *Bulletin Officiel* (B.O.) du ministère de l'Éducation nationale dans lequel sont intégrés les arrêtés définissant les programmes officiels des différentes filières que peuvent suivre les élèves
   - des statistiques nationales exhaustives décomptant les élèves inscrits dans chaque filière, et les élèves qui suivent effectivement chacune des matières proposées
3. Les programmes officiels utilisés correspondent à ceux effectivement en vigueur dans toutes les filières proposées aux élèves en 1991/92. Ces programmes sont composés de matières obligatoires (tronc commun) et de matières optionnelles, obligatoires ou facultatives. A chacune de ces matières correspond un horaire théorique
4. Les effectifs des élèves scolarisés dans chaque filière et le décompte de ceux qui suivent effectivement chacune des matières optionnelles sont connus pour 1991/92 en 6e, 5e, 4e et 3e y compris 4e et 3e technologiques pour tous les établissements publics et privés sous contrat de France métropolitaine (les élèves scolarisés hors de métropole représentent 1.0% des effectifs France entière). Les résultats transmis ne tiennent pas compte des élèves de CPPN et CPA qui correspondent à 1.2% du total des élèves du premier cycle du second degré
7. Une leçon correspond à une heure, les programmes officiels étant les mêmes pour les établissements publics et pour les établissements privés sous contrat. Les résultats qui sont transmis correspondent à l'ensemble des élèves scolarisés dans ces deux types d'établissement de France métropolitaine

GERMANY

IRELAND

ITALY

2. Law
3a. See tables

NETHERLANDS

1. – Establishing Decree (ISCED 2)
   – 3 different investigations of 1987, 1992 and 1993 (ISCED 1)
2. Law (ISCED 2); natsur (ISCED 1)
3a. All students
3b. 1991/92
5a. Unknown
5b. 1987, 1992, 1993
5c. Unknown
5d. Unknown
5e. Unknown

Annex 2 – Data sources

NEW ZEALAND

1. *i)* 1975 Education (Secondary Instruction) Regulations, Education Act 1964 – regulations re. minimum hours per week for compulsory secondary school curriculum

   ii) *Education Gazette* 16 June 1992, Education Act 1989 65A – regulations re. length of 1993 school year

   iii) Assessment, Examination and Certification Regulations and School Qualifications Prescriptions, New Zealand Qualifications Authority, 1993 – regulations re. minimum annual hours for full-time secondary school students to complete courses for senior school examinations and certification

   iv) Education Statistics of New Zealand 1993, Ministry of Education, Oct. 1993 – numbers of students taking various courses

   v) Eleven Wellington secondary schools

2. Law *i)*, *ii)* and *iii)*

   Stat *iv)*

   Natsur *v)*

3a. Regulations apply to all New Zealand secondary schools, the administration of which is the responsibility of all boards of trustees, principals, and classroom teachers:

   i) relates to the common curriculum of all New Zealand school students in their first three years of secondary education

   ii) relates to the minimum hours of attendance required for all students to complete each level of secondary education

   iii) sets out the minimum annual hours of instruction for all students seeking to qualify for New Zealand senior secondary school awards

3b. See 1 above

4a. Data applies to the enrolments and staffing levels of all students and sectors of education of the New Zealand education system

4b. The data were collected following the March and July 1993 returns

5a. The sample consisted of a cross section of Wellington area secondary schools: co-educational, single sex (both male and female), state and private, large to medium-sized schools; the sample did not include an integrated school or a small-sized secondary school; it presented c. 4% of the total New Zealand secondary school population

5b. 2/1994

5c. N/A

5d. Interview by phone

5e. N/A

5f. N/A

6. N/A

NORWAY

1. Curriculum Guidelines for Compulsory Education in Norway 1987

PORTUGAL

1. National Curriculum, "preparing the schooling year". LAL document 1991/92

2. Law

3a. Students from Grade Seven up to Nine

3b. 1991/92

SPAIN

1. Orden Ministerial de 2-12-1970 (Orientaciones pedagógicas para la EGB).

2. Law

SWEDEN

1. National curriculum plan (*Läroplan för grundskolan*)

2. Law

7. Two instances given

TURKEY

UNITED KINGDOM

UNITED STATES

341

Annex 2 – Data sources

INDICATORS P31 and P32

All countries

See notes to F01-F05 and F11-F13.

INDICATOR P33

LEGEND

1. Data source, full reference

2. Type of data source:
   - law = law or policy document based on law (data on formal arrangements)
   - stat = national statistics (data on formal arrangements)
   - intsur = international survey (data on samples)
   - natsur = national survey (data on samples)
   - other = other

3. In case of data on formal arrangements:
   - 3a. Groups under concern
   - 3b. Year of reference
4. In case of data on populations:
   - 4a. Population under concern
   - 4b. Period of data collection
5. In case of data on samples:
   - 5a. Population from which sample was drawn
   - 5b. Period of data collection
   - 5c. Type and size of the sample
   - 5d. How were data collected?:
     - reg = use of register
     - inq = postal inquiry
     - pho = interview by phone
     - vis = interview by visit
     - oth = other
   - 5e. Sampling errors calculated and accessible?
   - 5f. Translation procedure (in case of international survey)

6. Deviation from definition of the indicator?

7. Other comments

AUSTRIA

1. Staff-service-code for teachers (Beamten-Dienstrechtsgesetz 1979)
2. Law
3a. Teachers employed by the Federation or by the provinces/cities
3b. 1991/92

BELGIUM

1. – Ministère de l'Éducation de la Recherche et de la Formation de la Communauté française
   – *Onderwijszakboekje*, Kluwer editorial
2. Law
3a. Preceptor (teacher) of special courses, religion, ethical thinking, physical education and second language education not included
3b. 1991/92

FINLAND

1. Agreements between the Ministry of Education and the teachers' unions on working hours and working conditions

FRANCE

1. – Obligation réglementaire de service (ISCED 0,1)
   – Enquêtes sur le service des enseignants rémunérés par le ministère de l'Éducation nationale (ISCED 2, 3)
2. – Law
   – Stat
3a. Ensemble des enseignants premier degré public + privé à financement public prédominant
3b. 1991/92
4a. Enseignants du second degré public des établissements relevant du ministère de l'Éducation nationale, environ 98% des enseignants du public
4b. 1991/92
7. Pour le second degré, le nombre d'heures d'enseignement est calculé sans heures supplémentaires ; ce nombre est rapporté a un nombre d'équivalents plein temps calculé également sans heures supplémentaires

GERMANY

IRELAND

1. Department of Education

ITALY

1. D.P.R. 399/88, L. 476/86, D.P.R. 417/74
2. Law
3a. Public schools

NETHERLANDS

1. Legal Status (education) Decree; WBO and RPBO
2. Law
3a. All
3b. 1991/92

NEW ZEALAND

1. – NZ law, regulations: *i)* Education Act 1989 sections 20, 25, 65b; *ii)* 1992 state collective contracts for primary teachers (section 2.9) and secondary teachers (sections 4.1 to 4.6))
   – National interpreters: *iii)* key staff from Ministry of Education, Catholic Schools' Council, Independent Schools' Association, New Zealand Education Institute
2. – Law: NZ law and regulations (*i* and *ii*)
   – Other (= national interpreters) *(iii)*
3a. Regulations apply to New Zealand state and integrated primary and/or secondary schools, the administration of which is the responsibility of all school boards of trustees and principals:
   i) relates to the attendance of students, the definition of a school day, the number of half-days schools must be opened for, and staffing allocations;
   ii) addresses the hours of work which teachers may reasonably be required to undertake, Monday to Friday
3b. *i)* 1989; *ii)* 1992

NORWAY

1. Agreements between the Ministry of Education and the teachers' unions on working hours and working conditions

342

Annex 2 – Data sources

PORTUGAL

1. Statute of the teaching career
2. Law
3a. All groups of teachers
3b. 1991/92

SPAIN

1. – Orden Ministerial de 31-7-1987
   – National Collective Labour Agreement for 1992
2. Law

SWEDEN

2. – Stat: number of subgroups of teachers (but there are no exact data on which programmes different subgroups teach)
   – Other: national agreements between labour market organisations
4. No exclusions (but approximations of breakdowns on ISCED levels)

TURKEY

UNITED KINGDOM

1. School Teachers Pay and Conditions Document 1994 and Secondary School Staffing Survey 1992
2. – Law
   – Natsur
3a. All teachers employed by local education authorities or the governing bodies of grant-maintained or voluntary-aided schools in the provision of primary and secondary education in England and Wales
3b. 1991/92
5a. Teachers in maintained secondary schools in England
5b. January 1992
5c. Stratified sample of schools (N=500, 10% of population). All teachers in sampled schools
5d. Inq
5e. No
7. See notes to tables

UNITED STATES

1. US Department of Education, National Center for Education Statistics, *Schools and Staffing Survey 1990/91* and *1987/88*
2. Natsur
5a. Teacher in Grades K-12, including public and private school teachers
5b. 1990/91 and 1987/88
5c. Stratified cluster sample (N=43, 125) for 1990/91 and (N=56, 242) for 1987/88
5d. – Inq
    – Pho
5e. Yes

INDICATOR P34

LEGEND

1. **Data source, full reference**

2. **Type of data source:**
   law   = law or policy document based on law (data on formal arrangements)
   stat = national statistics (data on formal arrangements)
   intsur = international survey (data on samples)
   natsur = national survey (data on samples)
   other = other

3. **In case of data on formal arrangements:**
   3a. **Groups under concern**
   3b. **Year of reference**

4. **In case of data on populations:**
   4a. **Population under concern**
   4b. **Period of data collection**

5. **In case of data on samples:**
   5a. **Population from which sample was drawn**
   5b. **Period of data collection**
   5c. **Type and size of the sample**
   5d. **How were data collected?:**
   reg = use of register
   inq = postal inquiry
   pho = interview by phone
   vis = interview by visit
   oth = other
   5e. **Sampling errors calculated and accessible?**
   5f. **Translation procedure (in case of international survey)**

6. **Deviation from definition of the indicator?**

7. **Other comments**

Annex 2 – Data sources

AUSTRIA
1. Federal law concerning university studies on humanities and sciences (*Bundesgesetz über geistes- und natürwissenschaftliche Studienrichtungen*); School Organisation Act (*Schulorganisationsgesetz*)
2. Law
3a. Teachers employed by the Federation or by the provinces/cities
3b. 1991/92

BELGIUM
1. – Ministère de l'Éducation de la Recherche et de la Formation de la Communauté française
   – *Education in Belgium: the diverging paths*, Ministerie van de Vlaamse gemeenschap, 1991
2. Law
3b. 1991

FINLAND
1. Teacher education curriculum (cf. law)
2. Law

FRANCE
1. Ministère de l' Éducation nationale IDEP
2. Law
3. Enseignants du secteur public
7. Une proportion croissante de futurs enseignants suit une année de préparation au concours de recrutement dans un Institut Universitaire de Formation des Maîtres (IUFM) – la durée de leurs études est alors de 17 ans.

GERMANY

IRELAND

ITALY
1. D.P.R. 417/74 D.H. 3.9.82 e succ. modifiche
2. Law
3a. See tables

NETHERLANDS
1. – WBO
   – Secondary Education Act
2. Law
3a. – Student teacher training courses
    – Post-graduate teacher training
3b. 1991/92

NEW ZEALAND
1. *i)* Education Act 1989, relevant sections from Education Acts, 1964, 1990, 1993
   ii) "Assessment, Examination, and Certification Regulations" handbook, New Zealand Qualifications Authority, 1993
   iii) Relevant pages from calendars of various colleges of education, and from brochures of New Zealand Teacher Registration Board
   iv) Registrars of the two major secondary colleges of education
   v) Key staff from New Zealand Council for Teacher Education, New Zealand Ministry of Education, and New Zealand Teacher Registration Board
2. – Law: NZ law, regulations, requirements *i), ii), iii)*
   – Other: regional survey *iv)*; national "interpreters" *v)*
3a. Regulations apply to New Zealand colleges of education, the administrations of which is the responsibility of the college councils and principals:
   i) relates to the entrance criteria, course requirements, and attendance of students; and gives power to the Teacher Registration Board to determine the requirements for teacher registration;
   ii) spells out the prerequisites and course requirements to complete successfully a nationally-approved diploma of teaching;
   iii) provides details prescribed by various colleges of education and by the New Zealand Teacher Registration Board
3b. *i)* 1989, 1964, 1990, 1993
    ii) 1993
5a. The two secondary colleges in Auckland and Christchurch service the training needs of most secondary teacher-trainees
5b. March 1994
5c. Data from the regional survey represent c. 80% of the national intake for 1994
5d. Pho

NORWAY
1. Law

PORTUGAL
1. Higher Education Curriculum Departamento de Programaçao e Gestâo Financeira
2. Stat
3a. Student teachers of all schooling levels entering the profession after professional qualification
3b. 1991/92

SPAIN
2. Law

SWEDEN
1. UTB Planer (law)
2. Law
3a. Formal requirements have been described. Requirements differ between different subgroups of teachers
3b. 1991/92
7. On each ISCED level, different types of teachers are teaching; here has been reported the educational background of the largest groups on each level

TURKEY

UNITED KINGDOM
1. Database for Teacher Records
2. Law
4a. All succesful completers of initial teacher training in 1992
4b. 1992

UNITED STATES
1. No published source; standard practice

Annex 2 – Data sources

INDICATOR P35

LEGEND

1. Data source, full reference

2. Type of data source:
- law = law or policy document based on law (data on formal arrangements)
- stat = national statistics (data on formal arrangements)
- intsur = international survey (data on samples)
- natsur = national survey (data on samples)
- other = other

3. In case of data on formal arrangements:
- 3a. Groups under concern
- 3b. Year of reference

4. In case of data on populations:
- 4a. Population under concern
- 4b. Period of data collection

5. In case of data on samples:
- 5a. Population from which sample was drawn
- 5b. Period of data collection
- 5c. Type and size of the sample
- 5d. How were data collected?:
    - reg = use of register
    - inq = postal inquiry
    - pho = interview by phone
    - vis = interview by visit
    - oth = other
- 5e. Sampling errors calculated and accessible?
- 5f. Translation procedure (in case of international survey)

6. Deviation from definition of the indicator?

7. Other comments

AUSTRIA
1. Staff-service-code for teachers "Salary and Wage Act (*Gehaltgesetz*)"
2. Law
3a. Teachers employed by the Federation or by the provinces/cities
3b. 1991/92
7. In Austria the salaries for civil servants and teachers are first negotiated between the government and the unions. The result of these negotiations are fixed by law

BELGIUM
1. – Ministère de l'Education, de la Recherche et de la Formation de la Communauté française
   – Direction générale des personnels, des statuts et de l'organisation administrative
2. Stat
4a. Full-time teachers
4b. 10/93 - 02/94

FINLAND
1. Teachers' Wage and Salary Agreement (TWSA) of Municipalities and Central Statistical Office of Finland
2. – Law
   – Stat
3b. 1992
4a. ISCED 1, 2: 98% included; ISCED 3 General: 98% included; ISCED 3 Vocational: 54% included, outside government and government-dependent vocational educational schools
4b. Central Statistical Office data were collected October 1992, TWSA 1991
7. Teachers' Wage and Salary Agreement (TWSA) of Municipalities is in force in the whole country. The basic salary is constructed from TWSA. Data from the national statistics are used to raise the basic salary with average regional compensations and with average compensation of teaching hours and other tasks which exceed hours of the basic salary

FRANCE

GERMANY

IRELAND

ITALY
1. Salaries: DPR 399/88, DPR. n° 13, art. 16, D.L. 19.9.92 n° 384 art. 7 (conv. L. n° 438/92)

   Benefits: DM 372/81, DM 55/93 (retroactive)
2. Law
3a. Public schools (see tables)

NETHERLANDS
1. Legal Status (education) Decree; and RPBO
2. Law
3a. All
3b. 1991/92

NEW ZEALAND
1. *i)* 1992 Primary and Secondary Teachers Collective Employment Contracts- award settlement statement
   ii) "Position of Women in the Education Services, 1991/92", Ministry of Education 1993
   iii) Key staff from Ministry of Education, Catholic Schools' Council, Independent Schools' Association, New Zealand Education Institute
2. – Law : regulations *i)*
   – Stat *ii)*
   – Other (= national interpreters) *(iii)*
3a. The Collective Employment Contract award governs the salaries of all New Zealand state and integrated teachers below the principal (whose salary is negotiated individually with the school's board of trustees) during the period the award specifies (often one or two years)
3b. *i)* 1992; *ii)* 1991, 1993
4a. The data are based on a survey of all teachers in the state and integrated system
4b. 1992

Annex 2 – Data sources

NORWAY

1. Agreements between the Ministry of Education and the teachers' unions on working hours and working conditions

PORTUGAL

1. – Statute of the Teaching career
   – Collective work contract for private schools employees
2. Law
3a. All levels of the system
3b. 1991/92

SPAIN

1. – Public salaries: *Ley de Presupuestos Generales del Estado de 1992*. Differences in salary structure in the Autonomous Communities have been taken into account
   – Private, government-dependent salaries: *Acuerdo Laboral parala Enseñanza Privada para los años 1992 y 1993, complementario del VIII Convenio Colectivo de la Enseñanza Privada*
   – Private, independent salaries: *III° Convenio Colectivo Nacional para Centros de Eseñanza Privada sin Ningún Nivel Concertado o Subvencionado*
2. Law

SWEDEN

2. Other: national agreements between labour market organisations (Swedish Association of Municipalities, Teachers' organisations)
7. According to agreements per 1/7/1991

TURKEY

UNITED KINGDOM

1. – School Teachers Pay and Conditions Document 1994
   – Database of Teacher Records March 1992
2. – Law
   – Stat
3a. All teachers employed by local education authorities or the governing bodies of grant-maintained or voluntary-aided schools in the provision of primary and secondary education in England and Wales
3b. 1991/92
4a. Teachers in maintained nursery, primary and secondary schools in England and Wales
4b. Information relating to March 1992, collected April-December 1992

UNITED STATES

1. US Department of Education, National Center for Education Statistics, *Schools and Staffing Survey 1990/91*
2. Natsur
5a. US Teachers in Grades K-12 public and private sectors
5b. 1990/91
5c. Stratified sample N= 43 125
5d. – Inq
    – Pho
5e. Yes

INDICATOR P36

LEGEND

1. **Data source, full reference**

2. **Type of data source:**

   law = law or policy document based on law (data on formal arrangements)
   stat = national statistics (data on formal arrangements)
   intsur = international survey (data on samples)
   natsur = national survey (data on samples)
   other = other

3. **In case of data on formal arrangements:**
   3a. Groups under concern
   3b. Year of reference

4. **In case of data on populations:**
   4a. Population under concern
   4b. Period of data collection

5. **In case of data on samples:**
   5a. Population from which sample was drawn
   5b. Period of data collection
   5c. Type and size of the sample
   5d. How were data collected?:
       reg = use of register
       inq = postal inquiry
       pho = interview by phone
       vis = interview by visit
       oth = other
   5e. Sampling errors calculated and accessible?
   5f. Translation procedure (in case of international survey)

6. **Deviation from definition of the indicator?**

7. **Other comments**

Annex 2 – Data sources

AUSTRIA	**NORWAY**
2. Stat	
BELGIUM	**PORTUGAL**
1. Service des statistiques du ministère de l'Éducation, de la Recherche et de la Formation de la Communauté française	1. Statistical Information for Education — INFORED
2. Stat	2. Stat
4b. 21/01/94	3a. All teachers for public; 25% for ISCED 1 private; 55% for ISCED 2 and 3 private
FINLAND	3b. 1991/92
FRANCE	**SPAIN**
GERMANY	2. Stat
IRELAND	4b. At the beginning of school year 1991/92
ITALY	**SWEDEN**
1. DL. 3.2.93 "Conto annuale scuola"	1. Database on teachers
2. Stat	2. Stat
4a. 100%	**TURKEY**
4b. 1992	**UNITED KINGDOM**
NETHERLANDS	1. Database for teacher records
2. CASO (Central Administration of Salaries for Education), IPTO (Integral Registration of the Teaching Staff) 1990/91	2. Stat
3. Stat	4a. All teachers in maintained nursery, primary and secondary schools
4a. – Teaching staff and non-teaching staff in the schools (ISCED 2) – All teachers in public and private education (ISCED 1)	4b. April-Dec. 1992
4b. 3/1992	**UNITED STATES**
NEW ZEALAND	1. US Department of Education, National Center for Education Statistics, *Schools and Staffing Survey*, 1990/91
1. Teachers Payroll Data: 1/3/92	2. Natsur
2. Stat	5a. US Teachers in Grades K-12, including public + private
4a. Data for schooling: primary, intermediate and secondary schools	5b. 1990/91 school year
4b. 1/3/92	5c. Stratified cluster sample; N = 43 125
7. State and state-integrated schools only	5d. Inq Pho
	5e. Yes

INDICATORS R04 and R05

Data derived from the *Reading Literacy Study* conducted by the International Association for the Evaluation of Educational Achievement (IEA) from October 1990 to April 1991, depending on the country.

INDICATORS R11, R12 and R14, R15

All countries

See notes to F01-F05 and F11-F13.

INDICATOR R21

See notes to C01.

INDICATOR R22

Australia

Australian Bureau of Statistics, *Transition from Education to Work Survey*, 1993.

Belgium

Survey on Poverty within the framework of the Second Community Action Programme to combat poverty, 1992.

Canada

Annual Survey of Consumer Finances, April 1992.

Denmark

Register-based personal income statistics, 1991.

Finland

Regional employment statistics.

France

Labour Force Survey, March 1992.

Germany

German Socio-economic Panel (SOEP), 1992.

Netherlands

Yearly Wage Survey, supplementary questionnaire for education.

Annex 2 – Data sources

Norway
Register of salaries and taxes and register of educational attainment.

New Zealand
Household Expenditure and Income Survey, 1991/92.

Spain
Family Budget Survey, 1990/91.

Sweden
The register of educational attainment for the population (January 1993) and the register of regional income distribution (ÅRSYS) 1992.

Switzerland
Enquête suisse population active (Labour Force Survey), 1992.

United Kingdom
General Household Survey, 1992.

United States
Current Population Survey, March 1992.

INDICATOR R23

Canada
Labour Force Survey.

France
Labour Force Survey, 1993.

Ireland
Labour Force Survey, 1992.

Italy
Labour Force Survey, October 1992.

Netherlands
Labour Force Survey, 1992.

New Zealand
Population Census, 1991.

Spain
Labour Force Survey, 1992 (for occupations) and *Socio-demographic Survey*, 1991 (for industries).

Sweden
Labour Force Survey, 1992 (occupations). The register of regional income distribution (ÅRSYS), 1992 (for industries).

Switzerland
Population Census, 1990.

United States
Current Population Survey, March 1992.

INDICATOR R24

Australia
Australian statistics on transition from education to work (cross-tabulation of school-leavers and labour market destinations).

Canada
The National Graduate Survey and follow-up of the National Graduate Survey.

France
Panel téléphonique du CEREQ (Centre d'études et de recherches sur les qualifications).

Ireland
ISCED 2 and 3: *The Economic Status of School-leavers 1991* (Department of Enterprise and Employment). For leavers from ISCED levels 5 and 6/7, the data source is the survey of *First Destination of Award Recipients in Higher Education 1991* (Higher Education Authority).

Spain
Socio-demographic Survey.

Sweden
Follow-up surveys for leavers from education. Data for leavers from ISCED level 3, short-term perspective, are derived from a long-term follow-up for leavers from ISCED level 2 (Grade Nine).

United States
Current Population Survey, October 1992.

Annex 3 – Technical notes

INDICATOR C02(B)

Calculation formula

The index of gender differences is calculated by subtracting the quotas among men in ISCED levels 0/1, 2, 5 and 6/7 from the quotas among women in the same categories. The result in category 0/1 is multiplied by 2 and then added to the result in category 2. The result in category 5 is added to the result in category 6/7 which is also multiplied by 2.

The result of this operation in the higher ISCED levels is subtracted from the result in the lower ISCED levels. To get an index that runs in theory from -100 to +100, the result is divided by 4 and multiplied by 100.

To present differences over time, data are calculated for the age groups 25-34 and 55-64 years.

The formula was adapted in accordance with the ISCED levels for which countries provided data.

INDICATORS C21 to C27

The indicators C21 to C27 are based on data collected by means of a questionnaire distributed to a sample of the general public in each of the participating OECD countries. The public were asked for their views on the importance of, and their confidence in, various aspects of education.

The questionnaire referred specifically to the final years of compulsory secondary education and a common set of questions were asked in all countries. The organisation of the survey was undertaken within each country and the surveys were administered by reputable national survey organisations. In some countries additional questions were asked to inform policy matters in these countries.

The recommended sample size was 1 000 individuals.

The following summary indicates sample type and effective sample size. The Network D Report to the INES General Assembly 1995 contains further evaluative analysis of the survey findings. The Network D Technical Report contains full details on sampling methods, calculation of weights and design effects, etc.

	Effective sample size	*Sample type*	*Survey agency*
Austria	1 757	Address-based probability sample.	GFK
Belgium (Flemish community)	808	Address-based probability sample.	Dimarso
Denmark	1 135	Population register-based probability sample.	Danish Research and Development Centre
Finland	1 283	Population register-based probability sample.	Statistics Finland
France	1 508	Address-based non-probability sample.	Research International
Netherlands	934	Address-based probability sample.	University of Twente
Portugal	1 271	Address-based probability sample.	National Institute of Statistics
Spain	1 399	Address-based non-probability sample.	CIS
Sweden	1 003	Population register-based probability sample.	Statistics Sweden
Switzerland	980	Address-based non-probability sample.	GIS
United Kingdom	1 242	Address-based probability sample.	SCPR
United States	1 281	Telephone-based probability sample.	Westat

Annex 3 – Technical notes

INDICATOR F03

Comparisons of expenditures for tertiary education, and especially per tertiary student, can be misleading because the figures for universities and other tertiary institutions include substantial expenditures for research.

The research share of total tertiary spending varies among countries partly because of differences in the share of total national research and development (R&D) performed by the higher education sector. As shown in the following table, the percentage of all such R&D varies from less than 17 per cent in Germany (FTFR) to over 26 per cent in Canada and nearly 27 per cent in Sweden.

Percentage of total national R&D performed by the higher education sector (1992)

Canada	26.4	Netherlands	24.7
Finland	22.0	Spain	24.3
Germany (FTFR)	16.6	Sweden	* 26.7
Ireland	22.9	United Kingdom	17.0
Japan	18.5	United States	17.2

* Figure for 1993

Source: OECD, *Main Science and Technology Indicators 1993, No. 2*, Paris, 1994, p. 22.

Another reason why research spending distorts comparison of expenditure per tertiary student is that research outlays have not been included to the same extent in the tertiary expenditure figures of all countries. For example, countries such as Canada, Germany (FTFR) and the United States have included essentially all research outlays of institutions of higher education in their tertiary expenditure statistics, whereas others such as Japan, and the United Kingdom excluded separately funded or separately budgeted research.

Recognising these problems, policy-makers in several countries have asked for an indicator that distinguishes between expenditures for research and expenditures for teaching, and compares countries with respect to expenditure per tertiary student net of the cost of research. Unfortunately, this request is difficult to satisfy. One obstacle is that some countries do not have complete data on the research outlays of their tertiary institutions. Another obstacle is conceptual: an important activity of universities, the "training by doing" of students (especially postgraduate) to be researchers can be described with equal validity as either teaching or research. It is therefore very difficult to measure those two components consistently.

The OECD does have at its disposal, however, a resource that can shed some light on the research-versus-teaching distinction: the statistics on national R&D expenditures compiled by the OECD Directorate of Science, Technology, and Industry (DSTI). These statistics include information on higher education R&D (HERD) expenditures, broken down by source of funds. Using the HERD figures, it is possible to illustrate how exclusion of the research component of tertiary expenditures might affect the international comparison of expenditure per student.

The following table covers the relatively small number of countries for which there is reasonable compatibility between the DSTI/HERD expenditure data and the research component of the country's reported spending for tertiary education. To the extent permitted by the data, the table shows:

1. Total expenditure per tertiary student — that is, before deducting any R&D expenditures (these figures are taken from indicator F03).

2. A corresponding estimate of expenditure per tertiary student, excluding R&D expenditure. These estimates have been calculated by reducing expenditure per tertiary student, as shown in indicator F03, by the percentage that DSTI/HERD expenditure (or, in some cases, only the appropriate part of HERD expenditure) makes up of total tertiary expenditure.

3. The percentage by which expenditure per student excluding R&D is less than expenditure per student including R&D.

Because the tertiary expenditure figures of Belgium, Finland and the United Kingdom in indicator F03 do not include all research spending of tertiary institutions, it is not possible to compare expenditure per student including and excluding R&D for these countries.

Annex 3 – Technical notes

Expenditure per tertiary student including and excluding expenditure for higher education research and development (HERD)

	Expenditure per student including R&D expenditure (US dollars)	*Estimated expenditure per student excluding R&D expenditure (US dollars)*	*Percentage by which estimated expenditure per student excluding R&D is less than expenditure per student including R&D*
Austria	5 820	3 653	37
Belgium	*a*	5 095	*a*
Canada	12 350	10 584	14
Denmark	6 710	4 865	28
Finland	*a*	7 408	*a*
Ireland	7 270	6 201	15
Netherlands	8 720	6 816	22
United Kingdom	*a*	8 533	*a*

a) Data not available on tertiary expenditures inclusive of all research spending in institutions of tertiary education.

The results shown in this table, though imprecise and only covering eight countries, suffice to demonstrate two points. First, research spending constitutes an important fraction of total expenditure for tertiary education. Secondly, the estimated research share of total tertiary expenditure varies among countries. For the handful of countries covered, the subtraction of R&D expenditures reduces estimated expenditure per student by amounts ranging from 14 to 37 per cent.

It follows that international differences in spending per tertiary student (shown in indicator F03) and in spending for tertiary education as a percentage of GDP (shown in indicator F01) reflect in part differences among countries in the research roles of institutions of higher education. The spending differentials do not necessarily, or exclusively, reflect differences in the amounts spent per student to support the teaching functions of tertiary institutions. The OECD will endeavour in the future to measure the research component of tertiary expenditures more comprehensively, more precisely, and for a larger number of countries.

Annex 3 – Technical notes

INDICATORS P01 to P06

Coefficients for full-time equivalents
2 part-time = 1 full-time

	Early childhood education	Primary education	Lower secondary education	Upper secondary education – General	Upper secondary education – Vocational	Upper secondary education – Apprenticeship	Upper secondary education – Total	Non-university tertiary education	University education – 1st stage	University education – 2nd stage	University education – Total	Not defined
Australia	1	1	1	1	4	3.33	3.37	4.66	2.15	2.26	3.89	1
Austria	1	1	1	1	1	1	1	2	2	2	2	1
Belgium	1	1	1	1	1	1	1	2	2	2	2	4
Canada	2	1	1	1	1	1	1	3	3	3	3	3
Czech Republic	1	1	1	1	1	1	1	2	2	2	2	1
Denmark **	1	1	1	1	1	1	1	1	1	1	1	1
Finland **	1	1	1	1	1	1	1	1	1	1	1	1
France **	1	1	1	1	1	1	1	1	1	1	1	1
Germany	1	1	1	1	1	1	1	2	2	2	2	1
Greece **	1	1	1	1	1	1	1	1	1	1	1	1
Hungary	1	1	1	1	1	1	1	1	1	1	1	1
Ireland	1	1	1	2	2	2	2	2	2	2	2	1
Italy **	1	1	1	1	1	1	1	1	1	1	1	1
Japan	1	1	1	1	1	1	1	2	2	2	2	1
Luxembourg *	1	1	1	1	1	1	1	2	2	2	2	1
Netherlands	1	1	2	2	2	2	2	2	2	2	2	2
New Zealand	2	1	2	2	2	2	2	2	2	2	2	1
Norway	1	1	1	1	1	1	1	2	2	2	2	1
Poland **	1	1	1	1	1	1	1	1	1	1	1	1
Portugal *	1	1	1	1	1	1	1	2	2	2	2	1
Russia *	1	1	1	1	1	1	1	2	2	2	2	1
Spain	1	1	1	2	2	2	2	2	2	2	2	1
Sweden	1	2	2	2	2	2	2	1	1	1	1	1
Switzerland	1	1	1	1	1	1	1	2	2	2	2	1
Turkey *	1	1	1	1	1	1	1	2	2	2	2	1
United Kingdom	1	1	1	2	2	2	2	2.86	2.86	2.86	2.86	1
United States	2	1	1	1	1	1	1	3	2.5	2.7	2.82	1

*   Coefficients determined by INES Secretariat.
** No part-time enrolments.

Annex 3 – Technical notes

Typical age ranges in early childhood, primary and lower secondary education

	\multicolumn{2}{c}{Early childhood education}	\multicolumn{2}{c}{Primary education}	\multicolumn{3}{c}{Lower secondary education}
	Starting age	Ending age	Starting age	Ending age	Starting age	Ending age	Graduation age
Australia	...	...	...	...	...	...	...
Austria	3	5	6	9	10	13	14
Belgium	2,5	5	6	11	12	13	.
Canada	4	5	6	11	12	14	.
Czech Republic	3	5	6	9	10	13 to 14	14 to 15
Denmark	3	6	7	12	13	14 to 15	16 to 17
Finland	3 to 6	3 to 6	7	12	13	15	16
France	2	5	6	10	11	14	.
Germany	3	5	6	9	10	15	16
Greece	3.5	4.5	5.5	10.5	11.5	13.5	14.5
Hungary	3	5	6	9	10	13	.
Ireland	4 to 5	5 to 6	6 to 7	11 to 12	12 to 13	14 to 15	15 to 16
Italy	3	5	6	10	11	13	14
Japan	3	5	6	11	12	14	15
Luxembourg	...	...	...	...	...	...	...
Netherlands	4	5	6	11	12	15	16
New Zealand	2	4	5	10	11	14	.
Norway	3	6	7	12	13	15	.
Poland	3	6	7	.	.	14	15
Portugal	3	5	6	11	12	14	15
Russia	3	5	6	8	9	14	15
Spain	2	5	6	10	11	13	14
Sweden	3	6	7	12	13	15	.
Switzerland *	4 to 5	5 to 6	6 to 7	10 to 12	11 to 13	14 to 15	.
Turkey	3	5	6	10	11	13	14
United Kingdom	2	5	5	10	11	13	.
United States	3	5	6	11	12	14	.

* The span age for theoretical and ending ages reflects the difference in the cantonal school systems. The duration for primary and lower secondary education is nine years for the whole country.

Annex 3 – Technical notes

Typical age ranges
Theoretical starting, ending and graduation ages at upper secondary education by type of programme

	General			Vocational/technical			Apprenticeship		
	Starting age	*Ending age*	*Graduation age*	*Starting age*	*Ending age*	*Graduation age*	*Starting age*	*Ending age*	*Graduation age*
Australia	16	17	18	16	19	20	16	19	20
Austria	14	17	18	14	15 to 18	16 to 19	15	17 to 18	18 to 19
Belgium	14	17	18	14	17 to 18	18 to 19	15 to 16	17 to 18	18 to 19
Canada	15	17	18	15	17	18	.	.	.
Czech Republic	14 to 15	17 to 18	18 to 19	14 to 15	17 to 18	18 to 19	14 to 15	16 to 17	17 to 18
Denmark	16 to 17	18 to 19	19 to 20	16 to 17	18 to 19	19 to 20	.	.	.
Finland	16	18	19	16	17 to 18	18 to 19	16	17 to 18	18 to 19
France	15	17	18	15	16 to 18	17 to 19	.	.	.
Germany (FTFR) *	16	18	19	16	18	19	.	.	.
Germany	16	17 to 18	18 to 19	16	18	19	.	.	.
Greece	14.5	16.5	17.5	14.5	16.5	17.5	14.5	15.5	16.5
Hungary	14	17	18	14	17	18	14	16	17
Ireland	15 to 16	16 to 17	17 to 18	15 to 16	16 to 17	17 to 18	16 to 17	19 to 20	20 to 21
Italy	14	18	19	14	18	19	.	.	.
Japan	15	17	18	15	17	18	.	.	.
Luxembourg	...	...	...	...	...	...	...	...	...
Netherlands	15	16 to 17	17 to 18	16	18	19	16	17 to 20	18 to 21
New Zealand	15	17	18	16	17	18	16	19	20
Norway	16	18	18	16	18	18	16	18	18
Poland	15	18	19	15	16 to 19	17 to 20	.	.	.
Portugal	15	17	18	15	17	18	15	18	.
Russia	15	17	18	15	17	18	.	.	.
Spain **	14	17	18	14	18	19	.	.	.
Sweden	16	18	19	16	17 to 18	18 to 19	.	.	.
Switzerland	15 to 16	17 to 19	18 to 20	15 to 16	17 to 19	18 to 20	.	.	.
Turkey	14	16	17	14	16 to 18	17 to 19	14	16	17 to 17.5
United Kingdom ***	14	17	16	16	17	18	.	.	.
United States	15	17	18	.	.	.	.	.	.

* Germany: first programmes: 16-18; second programmes: 19-21.
** Spain: first programmes for vocational and apprenticeship: 14-15 (graduation at 16); second programmes for vocational and apprenticeship: 16-18 (graduation at 19); for general programmes: 14-16
*** United Kingdom: many students graduate from general education programmes after 2 rather than 4 years.

Annex 3 – Technical notes

Typical age ranges
Theoretical starting, ending and graduation ages at non-university tertiary education

	Starting age	*Ending age*	*Graduation age*
Australia	17 to 18	18,5 to 20,5	...
Austria	18 to 19	19 to 24	20 to 25
Belgium	18	20 to 21	21 to 22
Canada	18	19	20
Czech Republic	18	19	20
Denmark	19 to 20	20 to 21	21 to 22
Finland	19	20 to 21	21 to 22
France	18	19	20
Germany (FTFR)	19	20	21
Germany	19	20	21
Greece	17.5	20.5	21.5
Hungary	18	20	21
Ireland	18	19	20
Italy	19	21	22

	Starting age	*Ending age*	*Graduation age*
Japan	18	19 to 20	20 to 21
Luxembourg	...	...	...
Netherlands *	.	.	.
New Zealand	18	20	21
Norway	19	19 to 20	21
Poland	19 to 20	19 to 22	20 to 23
Portugal	18	20 to 21	21 to 22
Russia	17 to 18	18 to 19	19 to 20
Spain	18	19 to 20	20 to 21
Sweden	19	20 to 20.5	21 to 21.5
Switzerland	20	22	23
Turkey	17	18	19
United Kingdom	18	19	20
United States	18	19	20

* Non-university tertiary education does not exist.

Annex 3 – Technical notes

Typical age ranges
Theoretical starting, ending and graduation ages at university education

		Name of degree	Starting age	Ending age	Graduation age
Australia	1	Bachelor	17 to 18	...	21
	2	...		...	...
	3	...		...	...
Austria	1	.	.	.	.
	2	Diplomingenieur or Magister	18 to 19	21 to 24	22 to 25
	3	Doktor	22 to 25	23 to 26	24 to 27
Belgium	1	Candidat or equivalent	18	19	20
	2	Licenciat or equivalent	20	21 to 22	22 to 23
	3	Doctorat or equivalent	22 to 23	25 to 26	26 to 27
Canada	1	Bachelor	18	21	22
	2	Master	22	23	24
	3	Doctorate	24	26	27
Czech Republic	1	Bakalar	18	20	21
	2	Magister, Inzenyr, MUDr., MVDr.	18	22	23
	3	Doktor	23	25	26
Denmark	1	Bachelor, MVU	19 to 20	21 to 22	22 to 23
	2	Kandidat	19 to 20	23 to 24	24 to 25
	3	Ph.D.	25	26	27
Finland	1	Bachelor or equivalent	19	21 to 22	22 to 23
	2	Master or equivalent	19	24	25
	3	Ph.D. and licenciate	25	28	29
France	1	Licence	18	20	21
	2	Maîtrise	21	21	22
	3	Doctorat	22	25	26
Germany (FTFR)	1				
	2	Staats-Diplomprüfung	19	25	26
	3	Doctor	26	28 to 30	29 to 31
Greece	1	Degree in all disciplines	17.5	20.5	21.5
	2	Master / Diplom	17.5	21.5	22.5
	3	Doctoral degree	22.5	24.5	25.5
Hungary	1	College diploma	18	20 to 21	21 to 22
	2	University diploma	18 or 21	22	23
	3	Doctorate	23	25	26
Ireland	1	Bachelor	18	20	21
	2	Master	21	21	22
	3	Doctorate (Ph.D.)	22	.	.
Italy	1	Laurea Breve	19	21	22
	2	Laurea	19	22	23
	3	Dottorato/Specializzazione post-laurea	23	24	25
Japan	1	Gakushi	18	21	22
	2	Shushi	22	23	24
	3	Hakushi	24	26	27

Annex 3 – Technical notes

		Name of degree	Starting age	Ending age	Graduation age
Luxembourg	1	...	...	...	...
	2	...	...	...	...
	3	...	...	...	...
Netherlands	1	HBO	18	21	22
	2	Doctoraal	18	21	22
	3	Doctor	22	25	26
New Zealand	1	Bachelor	18	20	21
	2	Bach. Itons/Masters	21	22	23
	3	Ph.D.	23	24	25
Norway	1	.	.	.	.
	2	Cand.mag.	19	21	22
	3	Embetseksamen	19 or 22	24	25
Poland	1	Licenjat or Inzynier	19 or 20	21 to 23	22 to 24
	2	Magister or Lekarz	19 or 20	23 to 25	24 to 26
	3	Doktor	24	26	27
Portugal	1	Bacharelato	18	18 to 21	22
	2	Licenciatura	18	21 to 23	22 to 24
	3	Mestrado/Doctor	22 to 24	23 to 25	24 to 26
Russia	1	.	.	.	.
	2	Specialist s vysshim obrazovaniem	18	21	22
	3	Kandidat Nauk	22	.	26
Spain	1	Diplomado o Ingenerio tecnico	18	20	21
	2	Licenciado, Arquitecto o Ing. superior	18 or 21	22	23
	3	Doctor	23	24	25
Sweden	1	Undergraduate bachelor	19	21 to 23,5	22 to 24,5
	2	.	.	.	.
	3	Licenciate	22	23 to 23,5	24 to 26,5
	3	Doctor	22	25 to 27,5	26 to 28,5
Switzerland	1	x	x	x	x
	2	Licence/diplôme	20	25	26 *
	3	Doctorat	26	31	31 *
Turkey	1	Lisans	17	20	21
	2	Yüksek Lisans	21	22	23
	3	Doktora	23	24 to 26	25 to 27
United Kingdom	1	Bachelor	18	20	21
	2	Master	21	21	22
	3	Doctorate	22	24	26
United States	1	Bachelor	18	21	22
	2	Master	22	23	24
	3	Ph.D.	24	26	27

* Median age of graduation

Annex 3 – Technical notes

INDICATOR P11

List of possible subjects that are taught under the headed subjects (a not exhaustive enumeration, derived from additional footnotes provided by some countries)

Reading and writing:
- reading and writing in the mother tongue
- reading and writing in a second "mother tongue"
- reading and writing in the mother tongue as a second language
- language studies
- media studies
- public speaking
- remedial reading

Mathematics:
- mathematics
- mathematics with statistics
- remedial mathematics

Science:
- science
- physics, physical science
- chemistry
- biology, human biology
- earth science
- agriculture/horticulture/forestry
- environmental studies
- geography

Social studies:
- social studies
- classical studies
- community studies
- contemporary studies
- economics
- environmental studies
- geography
- history
- humanities
- legal studies
- liberal studies
- studies of the own country
- social sciences

Foreign languages:
- foreign languages
- a second mother tongue

Technology:
- orientation in technology, including information technology
- computer studies
- construction/surveying
- electronics
- graphics and design
- home economics
- keyboard skills
- word processing
- workshop technology/design technology

Arts:
- arts
- music
- visual arts
- art history
- practical art
- dance and drama
- performance music
- photography

Physical education:
- physical education
- gymnastics
- dance
- health
- human biology
- human relationships/parenting skills
- outdoor education
- recreation and sport

Religion:
- religion
- history of religions
- religions and culture
- ethical thinking

Vocational skills:
- vocational skills (preparation for specific occupation)
- economics
- technics
- domestic science
- accountancy
- business studies
- career education
- clothing and textiles
- polytechnic programmes
- secretarial studies
- shorthand and typing
- tourism and hospitality
- transition
- work experience

Other:
- Latin
- descriptive geometry
- remedial courses
- Greek
- technical activities
- scientific work
- socio-economic initiation
- typing
- form periods
- assemblies
- home economics
- pupil/class council
- optional subjects
- Sloyd
- child studies
- domestic science
- electives (local options)
- elective foreign languages
- artistic activities
- study groups
- upgrading courses
- commercial subjects
- business studies

Annex 3 – Technical notes

Note that some subjects have been reported under multiple categories. This must be taken into account when interpreting the subject-categories under concern. This is the case for human biology (science and physical education), environmental studies (science and social studies), geography (science and social studies), economics (social studies and vocational skills), home economics/domestic science (technology, vocational skills, "other"), foreign languages (foreign languages and "other").

INDICATOR P21

Standard errors of sampling were calculated for all percentages and are shown in the table below. The coefficient of variation (standard error/estimate) should not exceed 0.2 according to OECD standards. This standard has been reached for most figures in P21, column 1 "no grouping". Only for Denmark, Germany (TFGDR), the Netherlands and New Zealand, the figures should be interpreted cautiously because of a relatively high coefficient of variation. Within the category "ability grouping" (second column Table P21), the coefficient of variation does not exceed 0.2 for most cases except for the figures of Finland, Greece and Spain, which allows for a proper interpretation of the figures of most countries. The coefficient of variation for the figures in the other three columns is relatively high for all countries.

Table P21: Most frequent type of grouping in percentages (standard errors between brackets)

	No grouping	Ability groups	Interest groups	Age groups	Other
Belgium (French community)	71 (4)	16 (3)	9 (2)	1 (1)	3 (1)
Canada (British Columbia)	57 (4)	19 (3)	7 (2)	2 (1)	15 (3)
Denmark	26 (3)	38 (3)	17 (3)	0 (0)	19 (3)
Finland	66 (6)	13 (4)	14 (4)	1 (1)	6 (3)
Germany (TFGDR)	24 (4)	55 (5)	9 (3)	0 (0)	12 (3)
Germany (FTFR)	63 (4)	32 (4)	3 (2)	0 (0)	2 (1)
Greece	84 (3)	9 (2)	4 (2)	1 (1)	2 (1)
Iceland	41 (3)	48 (3)	3 (1)	1 (1)	7 (2)
Ireland	49 (5)	49 (5)	1 (1)	1 (1)	0 (0)
Netherlands	9 (3)	87 (3)	0 (0)	2 (1)	2 (1)
New Zealand	6 (2)	83 (3)	4 (1)	0 (0)	7 (2)
Portugal	69 (4)	14 (3)	13 (3)	0 (0)	4 (2)
Spain	89 (2)	8 (2)	1 (1)	1 (1)	1 (1)
Switzerland	52 (3)	16 (2)	12 (2)	1 (1)	20 (3)
United States	31 (3)	45 (3)	4 (1)	12 (2)	7 (2)

INDICATORS P12 and P21

Data for the above-mentioned indicators come from the Reading Literacy Study, which was performed by the IEA (International Association for the Evaluation of Educational Achievement) in the school year 1990/91. One of the aims of the study was to compare the reading literacy performance of pupils in the modal grades of 9 year-olds (Population A) and 14 year-olds (Population B) in different countries. A further major aim of the study was to identify differences in policies and instructional practices in reading (W.B. Elley, *How in the World do Students Read?*, Grindeldruck GMBH, Hamburg, 1992) and this "influence" on differences in pupil achievement.

Description of the target populations and samples

The sample design for the Reading Literacy Study can generally be referred to as a two-stage cluster sample. The first stage sampling units mostly individual schools but sometimes areas (in which case there were three stages of sampling). The schools in each nationally defined target population were selected from an explicitly stratified national sampling frame of schools within explicit strata with a probability proportional to the estimated number of students in the target population grade or school who are in the respective nationally defined target populations (Denmark sampled classes and not schools; in Iceland the whole student target population was tested).

Annex 3 – Technical notes

Intact classes were chosen within each selected school with a probability proportional to the class size. The application of this design resulted in unequal selection probabilities which were compensated for by using sampling weights. The sum of weights was then adjusted so that it was equal to the total number of students in the country (Elley, 1992).

The target Population A was defined as follows: all students attending mainstream schools on a full-time basis at the grade level in which most students were aged 9 years and 0 months to 9 years and 11 months during the first week of the eighth month of the school year. Students in separate schools for special education thus were excluded from the desired target population. Most countries sampled from almost all age-eligible children (more than 90 per cent of students were included in the eligible population). The exceptions were France where students in private schools and overseas territories (16 per cent of the students) were excluded, and Finland, where students who participate in Swedish-speaking special education and teacher education colleges (9.2 per cent of students) were excluded. The participation rates were also high in most countries: the participation rate among sampled schools (or classes) was greater than 85 per cent in all OECD countries. The final response rates that were calculated for the study included the use of backup schools as replacements for non-participating original schools. In some systems the reported response rate may therefore overstate the actual level of response.

Samples with large population exclusions bear the risk that the exclusion could change the results. Some of the concerned countries therefore applied *a posteriori* studies to analyse the potential bias.

In the case of Finland, for example, such studies verified that despite a large excluded population the results were not likely to be biased. Such efforts to provide a reasonable explanation about potential bias should be commended and encouraged.

Excluded populations

The following provides a brief description of the achieved target populations.

Belgium

Pupils in the French community who received instruction in Flemish or German (3.6 per cent of 9 year-olds and 3.8 per cent of 14 year-olds) excluded.

Canada (British Columbia)

Pupils in Government Native Indian schools (1.2 per cent of 9 year-olds and 1.1 per cent of 14 year-olds) excluded. British Columbia is one of the ten provinces and two territories that make up Canada.

Denmark

All students in the designed target populations sampled.

Finland

Pupils in schools where the official language was Swedish, and students enrolled in special education and laboratory schools (9.2 per cent of 9 year-olds and 12.4 per cent of 14 year-olds) excluded.

France

Pupils in overseas territories and private schools in mainland France (16 per cent of the 9 year-olds and 21 per cent of the 14 year-olds) excluded.

Germany (TFGDR)

Special schools for the handicapped and those for gifted students (about 8 per cent of each population) excluded.

Germany (FTFR)

Special schools for the handicapped and non-graded private schools (8.3 per cent of the students in both target populations) excluded.

Greece

Four per cent of 14 year-olds attending evening school excluded.

Hungary

All data were excluded because of the high probability of socially desirable responses by the students.

Iceland

Schools with fewer than five students in the target populations (0.5 per cent of 9 year-olds and 2.6 per cent of 14 year-olds) excluded.

Ireland

Private schools and schools with fewer than five students in the target population (4.2 per cent of 9 year-olds) excluded.

Italy

Pupils in private schools (8.6 per cent of 9 year-olds and 4.8 per cent of 14 year-olds) excluded.

Norway

Schools for Lapps (0.3 per cent of 9 year-olds and 0.2 per cent of 14 year-olds) excluded.

Portugal

All data were excluded because of the high probability of socially desirable responses by the students.

Annex 3 – Technical notes

Spain

Students from schools with fewer than ten students in the defined grade and from schools where the medium of instruction was not Spanish (11.1 per cent of 9 year-olds and 6.5 per cent of 14 year-olds) excluded.

United States

Schools and students were sampled in 50 states (mainland states, Alaska and Hawaii). Students in eligible schools not capable of taking the reading test (4.9 per cent of each population) excluded.

Nineteen OECD countries participated in the IEA Reading Literacy Study. The following table provides an overview of the number of schools and teachers in OECD countries that participated in Population A (9 year-old students). The teachers are those who were teaching the sampled students in reading. They therefore do not represent the general population of teachers in the countries.

Participation overview

	Schools	*Teachers*
Belgium (French community)	149	150
Canada (British Columbia)	157	151
Denmark	164	209
Finland	136	134
France	136	134
Germany (TFGDR)	100	99
Germany (FTFR)	150	146
Greece	175	175
Iceland	180	281
Ireland	122	122
Italy *		
Netherlands	91	98
New Zealand	176	176
Norway *		
Portugal	145	162
Spain	324	324
Sweden *		
Switzerland	225	227
United States	165	300

* Italy, Norway and Sweden are not represented in *Education at a Glance 3* for these indicators because of doubts concerning the validity of the data for these comparisons.

Some of the figures reported differ slightly from the figures in earlier IEA publications. This is because missing data were treated differently in these analyses.

Design effects, standard errors and sampling weights

In the computation of means and standard errors of the means, both the selection probabilities and the stratification of the samples have been taken into account; the selection probabilities by assigning proper weights to each case, the stratification by treating the strata as fixed effects in an analysis of variance model. Using a fixed effects model caused that the computed standard errors were approximately 0 per cent to 20 per cent smaller (depending on the country and the variable involved) than when this would have been ignored. This also implies that the effective sample sizes are in fact slightly larger than the obtained sample sizes and the design effect per country is slightly smaller than 1.

The formula used for calculating the standard errors of the mean is:

SE = sqrt (mean square within strata/sum of weights).

The formula used for calculating the standard errors of percentages is: SE = sqrt (percentage)* (100-percentage/sum of weights).

It must be noted that for all indicators referring to teacher and school-level data of the Reading Literacy Study, the standard errors are relatively high. One reason for this is that the samples had been designed primarily to compare student achievement data and therefore the number of teachers associated with the students is usually relatively small. Furthermore, one should consider the fact that a large standard error could point at a really existing and possibly interesting variation for specific indicators within countries. This could be a motive for presenting figures and charts on the dispersions within countries.

INDICATOR P41

Estimates of the number of personnel engaged in educational research and development, measured in number of full-time-equivalent person-years, are shown in the table below. These estimates were provided by the national authorities of the countries concerned. The country-specific notes in Annex 1 should also be consulted.

Annex 3 – Technical notes

Personnel engaged in educational research and development
(Number of person-years)

	Year	Govt. sector Researchers	Govt. sector Other staff	University education Researchers	University education Other staff	Private non-profit Researchers	Private non-profit Other staff	Total
Australia	1990/91	90	27	1 218	165	25	12	1 536
Austria	1989	11	9	87	25	15	13	160
Finland	1991	5	5	276	61	-	-	247
Ireland	1991/92	36	16	22	...	2	...	75
Netherlands	1991	160	100	360	-	100	-	720
New Zealand	1991/92	17	17	53	-	9	-	95
Sweden	1991/92	-	-	193	43	-	-	236
United Kingdom	1991/92	84	121	2 140	977	-	-	3 322

INDICATOR P42

The table below shows additional data on expenditure on educational research and development (in millions in local currency and at current prices). The country-specific notes in Annex 1 should be consulted when interpreting the data.

Expenditure on educational research and development

(in millions in local currency and at current prices)

i) By type of expenditure

	Year	Govt. sector Capital	Govt. sector Labour	Govt. sector Other	University education Capital	University education Labour	University education Other	Private non-profit Capital	Private non-profit Labour	Private non-profit Other	
Australia	1990/91	1	5	3	9	44	14	0	2	1	78
Austria	1989	-	9	3	9	54	48	1	11	9	143
Finland	1991	-	2	1	7	70	40	-	-	-	120
Ireland	1991/92	-	2	-	-	1	-	-	-	-	3
Nether-lands	1991/92	-	25	13	-	20	10	-	20	10	98
New Zealand	1991/92	-	1	2	-	3	-	-	1	-	7
United Kingdom	1991/92	-	6	-	2	45	-	-	-	-	53

ii) By type of research

	Year	Govt. sector Capital	Govt. sector Labour	Govt. sector Other	University education Capital	University education Labour	University education Other	Private non-profit Capital	Private non-profit Labour	Private non-profit Other	
Australia	1990/91	2	3	3	25	32	8	1	1	1	78
Austria	1989	3	8	1	40	57	15	3	17	...	143
Ireland	1991/92	-	2	-	-	1	-	-	-	-	3

Annex 3 – Technical notes

INDICATORS R04 and R05

See comments for indicators P12 and P21.

Ages of students in the Reading Literacy Study

In order to compare students of different ages within the same grade, the IEA study used three independent approaches to produce an age adjustment. These methods were a regression adjustment, studies of academic growth from ages 9 to 14, and an empirical comparison of adjacent age groups. As all three approaches produced similar results, IEA considered this adjustment statistically valid.

The mean ages of the students sampled in different systems in the IEA Reading Literacy Study varied somewhat across countries. This is important because the average level of reading literacy of secondary students is correlated with their average age. This suggests that scores may be slightly overestimated in countries in which the mean age of the participating students is above the average. Similarly, scores in countries with younger participants may be slightly under-estimated. The average ages of students included in the study are given below:

	Grade tested	Mean age (in years)
Belgium (French community)	8	14.3
Canada (British Columbia)	8	13.9
Finland	8	14.7
France	9	15.4
Germany (TFGDR)	8	14.4
Germany (FTFR)	8	14.6
Greece	9	14.4
Iceland	8	14.8
Ireland	5	14.5
Netherlands	8	14.3
New Zealand	10	15.0
Norway	8	14.8
Spain	8	14.2
Sweden	8	14.8
Switzerland	8	14.9
United States	9	15.0

Measurement error in the Reading Literacy Study

Educational phenomena are seldom measured without error. Errors are introduced because the sampling and estimation procedures used are imperfect. Appropriate standard errors must therefore be calculated and reported, so that readers can take the extent of measurement error in the data into consideration when interpreting the results of the indicator calculations. The following Tables 1 and 5 show the jackknifed standard errors of sampling for the estimates reported in indicators R04 and R05. Tables 2, 3 and 4 offer additional important information about the mean scores, the standard errors, and the number of cases involved in the calculations.

Table 1. Standard errors for Population A, Population B, and the difference between Population A and Population B reading scores [a]

	Population A	Population B	SE difference reading
Belgium (French community)	5.9	4.3	7.27 (0.06)
Canada (British Columbia)	4.5	3.1	5.50 (0.02)
Denmark	5.1	2.5	5.70 (0.01)
Finland	4.3	2.3	4.88 (0.01)
France	5.8	4.4	7.29 (0.05)
Germany (TFGDR)	6.1	3.5	7.00 (0.01)
Germany (FTFR)	6.4	2.5	6.83 (0.02)
Greece	5.6	2.2	6.02 (0.02)
Iceland	0.0	0.1	0.00 (0.00)
Ireland	6.2	5.1	8.01 (0.03)
Italy	6.1	3.3	6.96 (0.02)
Netherlands	6.1	4.6	7.67 (0.03)
New Zealand	5.8	6.0	8.34 (0.01)
Norway	3.3	2.6	4.23 (0.01)
Spain	3.6	3.0	4.66 (0.02)
Sweden	4.5	2.4	5.06 (0.01)
Switzerland	4.3	3.3	5.39 (0.03)
United States	4.9	5.1	7.10 (0.03)

a) The standard errors for Population A were computed from the following formula: $(SE_A^2 - SE_B^2)^{1/2}$; the standard errors for Population B and for the difference were based on jackknife estimates. SE difference reading is the five-year difference in reading and was computed as (Population B – Population A).

Table 2. Means and standard deviations for all three scores

Five-year difference in reading						
Between country results							
Between country mean Pop A	Between country mean Pop B	Between country mean Difference	Between country STD Pop A	Between country STD Pop B	Between country STD Difference
342.68	500.78	159.53	31.018	23.90	24.09

Annex 3 – Technical notes

Table 3. Number of cases employed in the calculations (unweighted)

	Number of cases LOW amount	Number of cases MODERATE amount	Number of cases HIGH amount	Number of cases UNKNOWN amount
Belgium (French community)	520	1 714	294	205
Canada (British Columbia)	843	2 825	665	556
Denmark	654	2 455	491	313
Finland	149	720	346	164
France	232	1 693	484	219
Germany (TFGDR)	193	1 153	396	221
Germany (FTFR)	555	2 784	619	563
Greece	432	2 073	973	464
Iceland	783	2 522	426	124
Ireland	455	2 291	642	225
Italy	590	1 919	453	127
Netherlands	692	2 432	340	284
New Zealand	371	1 961	507	296
Norway	374	1 481	305	147
Spain	1 517	5 543	1 101	324
Sweden	499	2 264	577	329
Switzerland	789	4 286	1 104	341
United States	473	1 980	603	420

Table 4. Weighted number of cases used in the calculations

	\multicolumn{4}{c}{(Percentage estimates are based on these figures)}
	Weighted N LOW amount	Weighted N MODERATE amount	Weighted N HIGH amount	Weighted N UNKNOWN amount
Belgium (French community)	583.9	1 650.2	274.6	224.4
Canada (British Columbia)	837.5	2 832.0	662.3	535.7
Denmark	996.9	2 451.8	472.5	249.6
Finland	142.8	713.4	357.0	164.3
France	237.5	1 689.2	473.3	218.1
Germany (TFGDR)	184.6	1 145.6	401.8	119.7
Germany (FTFR)	558.0	2 762.4	620.6	269.3
Greece	440.4	2 060.8	974.4	446.1
Iceland	783.0	2 522.0	426.0	115.0
Ireland	500.2	2 267.7	608.6	262.5
Italy	612.1	1 896.0	435.4	120.8
Netherlands	713.1	2 400.6	339.0	284.5
New Zealand	395.8	1 944.2	492.2	291.3
Norway	386.0	1 476.4	300.2	129.0
Spain	1 527.7	5 510.7	1 137.1	309.6
Sweden	510.6	2 253.9	557.4	285.5
Switzerland	831.7	4 280.8	1 104.5	312.1
United States	495.8	1 944.2	587.7	388.9

Annex 3 – Technical notes

Table 5. Jackknifed standard errors for amount of reading indicator

	SE for percentage estimates			
	SE percentage LOW amount	SE percentage MODERATE amount	SE percentage HIGH amount	SE percentage UNKNOWN amount
Belgium (French community)	1.38	1.40	0.82	0.79
Canada (British Columbia)	0.67	0.91	0.62	0.62
Denmark	0.88	0.85	0.63	0.47
Finland	0.84	1.51	1.34	1.00
France	0.84	1.16	0.95	0.69
Germany (TFGDR)	0.86	1.30	1.29	0.68
Germany (FTFR)	0.85	0.93	0.64	0.47
Greece	0.62	0.95	0.87	0.72
Iceland	0.00	0.00	0.00	0.00
Ireland	0.99	1.11	0.81	0.62
Italy	1.02	1.10	0.70	0.52
Netherlands	1.11	1.31	0.57	1.19
New Zealand	0.82	1.07	0.87	0.67
Norway	0.99	1.08	0.86	0.55
Spain	0.68	0.67	0.54	0.30
Sweden	0.74	0.83	0.79	0.58
Switzerland	0.72	0.87	0.70	0.52
United States	0.95	1.13	0.74	0.90

INDICATORS R11 to R15

See the notes to P01 - P06.

Annex 4 – Glossary

Apprenticeship

In calculating the indicators, the apprenticeship programmes are classified as belonging to formal education. Such programmes typically involve an alternation between learning in an educational institution (ordinary or specialised) and learning through work experience programmes, which may include highly organised training in a firm or with a craftsman. The apprentices and the firm (or craftsman) are bound by a legal agreement. Even though only a part of the training occurs in schools, it is considered as a full-time activity, because it covers both theoretical and practical training. Apprenticeship programmes are classified as technical or vocational programmes in upper secondary education (ISCED 3).

Bonferoni

The Bonferoni adjustment is used in international comparisons of the mean achievement scores of students. The procedure involves an adjustment to the test of statistical significance, by dividing the *alpha* level of the significance test into $n(n-1)/2$ categories, where n represents the number of countries being compared.

Continuing education and training

Continuing education and training for adults refer to all kinds of general and job-related education and training organised, financed or sponsored by authorities, provided by employers or self-financed.

Curriculum

Intended curriculum

The intended curriculum is the subject matter content to be taught as defined at the national level or within the education system level. It is embodied in textbooks, curriculum guides, the content of examinations, and in policies, regulations, and other official statements produced by the education system.

Implemented curriculum

The implemented curriculum is the intended curriculum as interpreted by teachers and made available to students. It is set in a pedagogical context that includes teaching practices, aspects of classroom management, use of resources, teacher attitudes, and teacher background.

Early childhood education

Education preceding the first level (pre-primary). All types of establishments or group settings aimed at supporting and stimulating the child's social and intellectual development are included in pre-primary education. The pre-primary starting age is put at the typical starting age in countries where that age is clear and unambiguous. In countries where no exact starting age can be given – due, for example, to an integration of education and pre-primary childminding, with a gradual augmentation of the educational side of things – the starting age is put at three years.

Earnings

Earnings refer to annual money earnings, i.e. direct pay for work before taxes. Income from other sources, such as government aid programmes, interest on capital, etc., is not taken into account. Mean earnings are calculated on the basis of data only for all people with income from work.

Educational attainment

Educational attainment is expressed as a certain highest level of education, defined according to the ISCED system, completed by a percentage of the adult population (25 to 64 years-old).

Educational Research and Development (R&D)

Educational R&D is systematic, original investigation or inquiry and associated developmental activities concerning: the social, cultural, economic and political context within which education systems operate; the purposes of education; the processes of teaching, learning and personal development; the work of educators; the resources and organisational arrangements to support educational work; the policies and strategies to achieve educational objectives; and the social, cultural, political and economic outcomes of education.

Educational R&D personnel

The major categories of R&D personnel are researchers, technicians and equivalent staff, and other supporting staff. Post-graduate students are counted as researchers, but reported separately within that category. The categories are defined as follows.

Researchers

Professional researchers engage in the conception or creation of new knowledge, products, processes, methods and systems, and in managing the projects concerned. This category includes managers and administrators engaged in the planning and management of the scientific and technical aspects of researchers' work. The supervision of post-graduate study by academic staff is included as part of R&D activities. Post-graduate students engaged in independent research for a higher degree are counted as R&D personnel, although they may not be receiving income or other employee benefits towards their study.

Technicians and equivalent staff

Persons whose main tasks require technical knowledge and experience in relevant fields. They participate in R&D performing scientific and technical tasks involving the application of concepts and operational methods, normally under the supervision of researchers.

Other support staff

Skilled and unskilled persons, and secretarial and clerical staff participating in R&D projects or directly associated with such projects.

Annex 4 – Glossary

Full-time equivalent personnel in educational R&D

The number of full-time equivalent personnel involved in educational R&D is the number of person-years contributed to educational R&D by all persons employed directly on R&D projects as well as by those providing direct services, such as R&D managers, administrators and clerical staff. The calculation of full-time equivalence is based on total working time, i.e. more than "normal" working time if activities involving R&D occur outside normal hours. By this definition, no person can be working more than one person-year on R&D activities in any year. For example, an academic who spends 30 per cent of his/her time over a year on R&D (and the rest on teaching and administration) would be counted as contributing 0.3 person-years to R&D. A research assistant who worked full-time on an R&D project for six months would be contributing 0.5 person-years.

Employed population

Employed population refers to all persons above a specific age who during a specified brief period, either one week or one day, were in paid employment or self-employment. It includes both those in civilian employment and in the armed forces.

Enrolment: Full-time and part-time

Students are enrolled full-time if they attend a programme that is classified as such by the institution or the authorities. Otherwise they are enrolled as part-time students. In some countries no distinction between full-time and part-time students is made at certain levels.

Expenditure: Capital and current

Capital expenditure refers to expenditure for assets that will be used for many consecutive years (e.g., buildings, major repairs, major items of equipment, vehicles, etc.), even if the financing of these assets is reported in a single financial year. For example, if a school is built in 1993, and if the construction costs are entirely accounted for in the 1993 budget, then the asset will be included as capital expenditure for that budget year.

Current expenditure refers to educational goods and services whose lifespan should not in theory exceed the current year (e.g., salaries of staff, educational supplies, scholarships, minor repairs and maintenance, administration, etc.). Conventionally, minor items of equipment are treated as current expenditure even if the corresponding physical asset lasts longer than one year.

Expenditure: Public and private

Public expenditure refers to the spending of public authorities at all levels. Expenditure by the Ministry of Education or an equivalent public authority that is not directly related to education (e.g., culture, sports, youth activities, etc.) is, in principle, not included. Expenditure on education by other ministries or equivalent institutions, for example Health and Agriculture, is included.

Private expenditure refers to expenditure funded by private sources – mainly households, private non-profit institutions, and firms and businesses. It includes: school fees; materials such as textbooks and teaching equipment; transport to school (if organised by the school); meals (if provided by the school); boarding fees; and expenditure by employers for initial vocational training.

Gross domestic product

The gross domestic product (GDP) is equal to the total of the gross expenditure on the final uses of the domestic supply of goods and services valued at price to the purchaser minus the imports of goods and services.

Gross salary

The sum of wages (total sum of money that is payed by the employer for the labour supplied) minus the employers' premium for social security and pension (according to existing salary scales). Bonuses that constitute a regular part of the wages – such as a thirteenth month or a holiday or regional bonus – are included in the gross salary.

Index of years in education completed

This index is calculated by summing across ISCED levels the product of the fraction of workers in the occupational group who have completed education at a particular level and the typical number of years required to complete that level.

ISCED

ISCED refers to the *International Standard Classification for Education*. This classification, developed by UNESCO, is used by countries and international agencies as a means of compiling internationally comparable statistics on education. According to ISCED, educational programmes may be classified as follows:

- Education preceding the first level (pre-primary)   ISCED 0
- Education at the first level (primary)   ISCED 1
- Education at the lower secondary level   ISCED 2
- Education at the upper secondary level   ISCED 3
- Education at the tertiary level, first stage, of the type that leads to an award not equivalent to a first university degree   ISCED 5
- Education at the tertiary level, first stage, of the type that leads to a first university degree or equivalent   ISCED 6
- Education at the tertiary level, second stage, of the type that leads to a post-graduate university degree or equivalent   ISCED 7
- Education not definable by level   ISCED 9

Annex 4 – Glossary

Labour force participation rate

The labour force participation rate is calculated as the percentage of the population in different age groups who are members of the labour force. The labour force is defined in accordance with the definitions used in the *OECD Labour Force Statistics*.

Leavers from education

Leavers from education are defined as students who have successfully completed a programme at one level of education, have not completed a higher level, and are not (at the beginning of the reference year) enrolled in full-time education or training.

Non-university tertiary education

Non-university tertiary education is used for tertiary education programmes at ISCED level 5. In some systems, the programmes at this level (i.e. those not leading to a university degree or equivalent) do not lead on to other programmes in higher education; in other systems such programmes allow students who successfully complete their studies at ISCED level 5 to proceed to university degree programmes in the same field. The term "articulation" is used to distinguish the latter type of ISCED 5 programme from the former, "terminal" one. For example, the "Associate Degree", awarded after two years of study in the United States, is not regarded as a university degree for international purposes; it is coded as an ISCED level 5 qualification. This also applies to the *diplôme d'études universitaires générales* (*DEUG*) in France.

Public and private schools

Public schools are organised by public authorities. They normally provide open access without any distinction of race, sex, or religion.

Private schools are normally organised independently of the public authorities, even though they may receive a small public funding.

Private schools predominantly publicly funded are schools that obtain most of their funding from public authorities, even though these schools are not formally part of the public school sector.

Government dependent private institutions are organised independently of public authorities, but receive more than 50 per cent of their funds from the public sector.

Independent private institutions are organised, financed and controlled by private individuals or bodies; they receive less than 50 per cent of their basic funds from the public sector.

Purchasing power parities

Purchasing power parities (PPPs) are the rates of currency conversion that equalize the purchasing power of different currencies. This means that a given sum of money, when converted into different currencies at the PPP rates, will buy the same basket of goods and services in all countries. Thus PPPs are the rates of currency conversion which eliminate differences in price levels between countries. The purchasing power indices used in this publication are given in *OECD Education Statistics, 1985-1992*.

Relative earnings from work

Relative earnings from work are defined as the mean annual earnings from work of individuals with a certain level of educational attainment divided by the mean annual earnings from work of individuals whose highest level of education is the upper secondary level.

Teachers

A teacher is defined as a person whose professional activity involves the transmitting of knowledge, attitudes and skills that are stipulated in a formal curriculum programme to students enrolled in a formal educational institution.

This definition does not depend on the qualifications held by the teacher. It is based on three concepts: activity, thus excluding former teachers who no longer have active teaching duties; profession, thus excluding people who work occasionally or in a voluntary capacity in schools; and formal programme (curriculum), thus excluding people who provide services other than formal instruction (e.g., supervisors, activity organisers, etc.), whether the programme is established at the country, district or school level. Schools principals without teaching responsibilities are not counted as teachers.

In vocational education, teachers of the "school-part" of apprenticeships in a dual system are included in the definition, and trainers of the "in-company-part" of a dual system are excluded.

Head teachers without teaching responsibilities are not defined as teachers, but classified separately. Head teachers who do have teaching responsibilities are defined as (part-time) teachers, even if they only teach 10 per cent of their time.

Former teachers, people who work occasionally or in a voluntary capacity in schools, people who provide services other than formal instruction e.g., supervisors or activity organisers, are also excluded.

Annex 4 – Glossary

Full-time equivalent teacher

A teacher who has a full-time appointment teaches 100 per cent of the normal teaching hours for a teacher in a specific country. Since the normal teaching hours may differ from country to country, it is impossible to express FTE in person-hours. Thus, a full-time teacher may teach more hours per week/year in one country than in another. The teaching hours of part-timers (also principals who are teachers for a part of the week), can be expressed in FTE by calculating the ratio of the teaching hours of the person under concern and the normal teaching hours for a full-timer.

Teaching hours

Teaching hours (expressed in units of 60 minutes) per week refer to the number of hours per week a full-time appointed teacher is teaching a group of students in a specific country.

Usually, the units of time in which teaching takes place (periods) are less than 60 minutes, which will make a conversion into hours necessary.

Tertiary education

Tertiary education refers to any programme classified as either ISCED level 5, 6 or 7. Entry to a programme at tertiary level requires as a minimum condition of admission the successful completion of a programme of education at the second level. In some countries evidence of the attainment of an equivalent level of knowledge, or the fulfilment of specific conditions such as a combination of age and/or work experience, is accepted as conferring eligibility for enrolment in tertiary education programmes. Tertiary education is divided into university and non-university sectors.

Theoretical age group

In classifying education by level, there is an assumption that, at least for the regular school (and in most cases university) system, a student can proceed through the system in a standard number of years. If it is assumed that the student starts school at the modal age and does not repeat any year, then the ages at which a student begins and completes each cycle or level can be calculated. These are the theoretical age ranges that correspond to each level in the school system. Using a transformation key that relates the levels of a school system to ISCED, the theoretical age range for each ISCED level can be derived.

Total labour force

The total labour force or currently active population comprises all persons who fulfil the requirements for inclusion among the employed or the unemployed as defined in *OECD Labour Force Statistics*.

Total population

All nationals present in or temporarily absent from the country and aliens permanently settled in the country. For further details, see *OECD Labour Force Statistics*.

Unemployed

The unemployed are defined as persons who are without work, seeking work and currently available for work. The standardized unemployment rate is the proportion of the unemployed as a percentage of the labour force.

University education

University education refers to any programme classified as either ISCED level 6 or 7 that leads to a university degree or equivalent. ISCED level 6 covers programmes leading to the award of a first university degree or a recognised equivalent qualification. If appropriate conditions are satisfied, this qualification allows a student to go on to a programme at ISCED level 7. These programmes lead to a university degree at post-graduate level. Some countries do not distinguish, for purposes of international data reporting, between ISCED level 6 and level 7.

Upper secondary education

Upper secondary education (ISCED level 3) is also described as second level, second stage education. It includes general, technical or vocational education for students who have completed the first cycle of secondary education (i.e. second level, first stage education: ISCED level 2). Apprenticeship programmes are included as are teacher training programmes offered at this level. Upper secondary education (ISCED 3) may either be "terminal" (i.e. preparing students for entry directly into working life) and/or "preparatory" (i.e. preparing students for tertiary education).

Second programme

If a student has completed a normal or regular sequence of upper secondary education (ISCED 3) and has graduated from that sequence (i.e. obtained the certificate or diploma) and then enrols in upper secondary education again in order to pursue another programme, he or she is said to be in a second upper secondary educational programme. If the student then completes that programme (i.e. obtains an additional certificate or diploma), he or she is a graduate of a second (or subsequent) upper secondary educational programme.

Annex 5 – Participants in the INES Project

As mentioned in the Foreword, many people have contributed to the CERI project on the development of international **IN**dicators of **E**ducation **S**ystems (INES). This annex lists the names of the country representatives, policy-makers, researchers and experts on educational measurement and statistics who have actively taken part in the preparatory work leading to the publication of this edition of *Education at a Glance*. The OECD wishes to thank them all for their valuable efforts.

I. Policy Review and Advisory Group

Mr. Tom ALEXANDER (OECD)
Ms. Jeannine FENEUILLE (France)
Mr. Alan GIBSON (United Kingdom)
Ms. Jeanne GRIFFITH (United States)
Mr. Walo HUTMACHER (Switzerland)
Mr. Ulf LUNDGREN (Sweden)
Mr. Marino OSTINI (Switzerland)
Mr. Claude THÉLOT (France)

II. National Co-ordinators

Mr. Antonio AUGENTI (Italy)
Ms. Monique BÉLANGER (Canada)
Ms. Virginia BERKELEY (United Kingdom)
Ms. Birgitte BOVIN (Denmark)
Mr. Bertil BUCHT (Sweden)
Mr. Nicolaas DERSJANT (Netherlands)
Mr. Heinz GILOMEN (Switzerland)
Mr. Sean GLENNANE (Ireland)
Mr. Jan de GROOF (Belgium)
Mr. Georges HENRY (Belgium)
Mr. James IRVING (New Zealand)
Mr. Toshikazu ISHINO (Japan)
Mr. Gregory KAFETZOPOULOS (Greece)
Mr. Reijo LAUKKANEN (Finland)
Ms. Mafalda LEONIDAS (Portugal)
Ms. Dawn NELSON (United States)
Mr. Friedrich PLANK (Austria)
Mr. Johan RAAUM (Norway)
Mr. Aristotelis RAPTIS (Greece)
Mr. Ingo RUSS (Germany)
Mr. Claude SAUVAGEOT (France)
Mr. Paul Inge SEVEREIDE (Norway)
Mr. Thorolfur THORLINDSSON (Iceland)
Mr. Alejandro TIANA (Spain)
Mr. Paul VOLKER (Australia)
Mr. Ziya YEDIYILDIZ (Turkey)

Annex 5 – Participants in the INES Project

III. Technical Group on Education Statistics and Indicators

Mr. Ruud ABELN (Netherlands)
Mr. Paul AMACHER (Switzerland)
Ms. Birgitta ANDRÉN (Sweden)
Mr. Fred BANGERIER (Switzerland)
Mr. Michele BARBATO (Italy)
Ms. Birgitte BOVIN (Denmark)
Mr. Jan van DAMME (Belgium)
Ms. Gemma DE SANCTIS (Italy)
Mr. Paul ESQUIEU (France)
Mr. Sully FAIK (Belgium)
Mr. Pierre FALLOURD (France)
Ms. Patricia FOURMY (Belgium)
Mr. Leonid GOKHBERG (Russia)
Mr. Siegfried HANHART (Switzerland)
Mr. Heikki HAVEN (Finland)
Mr. Tom HEALY (Ireland)
Mr. Max van HERPEN (Netherlands)
Ms. Carmen HIGUERA TORRON (Spain)
Mr. Ulrich HOFFMANN (Germany)
Mr. Walter HORNER (Germany)
Ms. Vladimira JELINKOVA (Czech Republic)
Mr. Gregory KAFETZOPOULOS (Greece)
Ms. Alison KENNEDY (United Kingdom)
Mr. Felix KOSCHIN (Czech Republic)
Mr. Norihiro KURODA (Japan)
Mr. Johan LASUY (Belgium)
Ms. Emel LATIFAOGLU (Turkey)
Mr. Joseph LAUTER (Luxembourg)
Mr. Andrzej OCHOCKI (Poland)
Mr. Laszlo LIMBACHER (Hungary)
Mr. Douglas LYND (Canada)
Mr. Robert MAHEU (Canada)
Ms. Aurea MICALI (Italy)
Ms. Inger MUNKHAMMAR (Sweden)
Ms. Isabel MUÑOZ JIMENEZ (Spain)
Mr. Wolfgang PAULI (Austria)
Mr. Nicholas POLE (New Zealand)
Mr. Johan RAAUM (Norway)
Mr. Aristotelis RAPTIS (Greece)
Mr. Jean-Claude ROUCLOUX (Belgium)
Mr. Ingo RUSS (Germany)
Mr. Horacio SANTOS (Portugal)
Mr. Paul Inge SEVEREIDE (Norway)
Mr. Joel SHERMAN (United States)
Mr. Thomas SNYDER (United States)
Mr. Walter STUBLER (Austria)
Mr. Matti VAISANEN (Finland)
Ms. Annik VANBEVEREN (Belgium)
Mr. Paul VOLKER (Australia)
Mr. Hiroshi YAMAMOTO (Japan)

IV. Network A on Educational Outcomes

Lead country: United States

Network leader: Mr. Eugene OWEN

Ms. Gertrudes AMARO (Portugal)
Mr. Henrik BÜLOW-HANSON (Eurostat)
Ms. Rubi CARDEL-GERTSEN (Denmark)
Ms. Chiara CROCE (Italy)
Mr. Bernard ERNST (France)
Mr. Guillermo GIL (Spain)
Ms. Marit GRANHEIM (Norway)
Ms. Aletta GRISAY (Belgium)
Mr. Douglas HODGKINSON (Canada)
Mr. Thomas KELLAGHAN (Ireland)
Mr. Gerbo KOREVAAR (Netherlands)
Mr. Kimmo LEIMU (Finland)
Mr. Mark NEALE (United Kingdom)
Mr. Lusio PUSCI (Italy)
Mr. Jules PESCHAR (Netherlands)
Mr. Sten PETTERSSON (Sweden)
Mr. Friedrich PLANK (Austria)
Mr. Dominique PORTANTE (Luxembourg)
Ms. Rosemary RENWICK (New Zealand)
Mr. Dieter SCHWEDT (Germany)
Mr. Erich SVECNIK (Austria)
Mr. Uri Peter TRIER (Switzerland)
Mr. Luc Van de POELE (Belgium)
Mr. Robert WOOD (United Kingdom)

Annex 5 – Participants in the INES Project

V. Network B on Student Destinations

Lead country: Sweden

Network leader: Mr. Bertil BUCHT

Mr. Nabeel ALSALAM (United States)
Ms. Regina BARTH (Austria)
Mr. Kenneth BENNETT (Canada)
Ms. Anna BORKOWSKY (Switzerland)
Ms. Birgitte BOVIN (Denmark)
Mr. Vassilios CHARISMIADIS (Greece)
Mr. Fayik DEMIRTAS (Turkey)
Mr. Sverre FRIIS-PETERSEN (Norway)
Mr. Michel-Henri GENSBITTEL (France)
Ms. Kjersti GRINDAL (Norway)
Mr. Tom HEALY (Ireland)
Mr. Maurice van der HEIDEN (Netherlands)
Ms. Dagmar HEIER-HILLENKAMP (Germany)
Mr. Max van HERPEN (Netherlands)
Ms. Carmen HIGUERA TORRON (Spain)
Mr. Graham JONES (United Kingdom)
Mr. Joseph LAUTER (Luxembourg)
Ms. Christine MAINGUET (Belgium)
Ms. Aurea MICALI (Italy)
Mr. Nicholas POLE (New Zealand)
Ms. Aila REPO (Finland)
Ms. Emilia SAO PEDRO (Portugal)
Mr. Klaus SCHEDLER (Austria)
Mr. Michail SKALIOTIS (Eurostat)
Mr. Luc Van de POELE (Belgium)
Mr. Paul VOLKER (Australia)

VI. Network C on School Features and Processes

Lead country: Netherlands

Network leader: Mr. Jaap SCHEERENS

Mr. Dante ANSALONI (Italy)
Ms. Bodhild BAASLAND (Norway)
Ms. Giovanna BARZANO (Italy)
Ms. Maria do CARMO CLIMACO (Portugal)
Mr. Alan CLARKE (United Kingdom)
Mr. Philippe DELOOZ (Belgium)
Mr. Pol DUPONT (Belgium)
Mr. Jean-Claude EMIN (France)
Mr. Rainer FANKHAUSER (Austria)
Mr. Steen HARBILD (Denmark)
Mr. Sean HUNT (Ireland)
Mr. Arno LIBOTTON (Belgium)
Mr. Heikki LYYTINEN (Finland)
Ms. Marilyn McMILLEN (United States)
Mr. Ramon PAJARES BOX (Spain)
Mr. Jacques PROD'HOM (Switzerland)
Mr. Ferry de RIJCKE (Netherlands)
Ms. Laura SALGANIK (United States)
Mr. Reinhard SCHANZ (Germany)
Mr. Walter SCHWAB (Eurostat)
Mr. Eugen STOCKER (Switzerland)
Mr. Erik WALLIN (Sweden)
Mr. Ziya YEDIYILDIZ (Turkey)

Annex 5 – Participants in the INES Project

VII. Network D on Expectations and Attitudes to Education

Lead country: United Kingdom

Network leader: Mr. Archie McGLYNN

Mr. Gustave BERNARD (Belgium)
Mr. Roel BOSKER (Netherlands)
Ms. Birgitte BOVIN (Denmark)
Ms. Carol CALVERT (United Kingdom)
Ms. Carmen CASTANHEIRA (Portugal)
Mr. Maija-Leena CLARKSON (Finland)
Mr. Frans DAEMS (Belgium)
Mr. Ronald DELEMONT (Switzerland)
Mr. Jan van DOMMELEN (Netherlands)
Ms. Leyla KUCUKAHMET (Turkey)

Ms. Agnès LEYSEN (Belgium)
Mr. John MacBEATH (United Kingdom)
Ms. Marcella MAZZOCCHI (Italy)
Mr. Alain MICHEL (France)
Mr. Mats MYRBERG (Sweden)
Mr. Paul PLANCHON (United States)
Ms. Laura SALGANIK (United States)
Mr. Erich SVECNIK (Austria)
Ms. Consuelo VELAZ DE MEDRANO (Spain)
Mr. Peter WHITTEN (Eurostat)

VIII. Other Experts and Consultants to INES

Mr. Stephen BARRO (United States)
Mr. Alfons Ten BRUMMELHUIS (Netherlands)
Mr. Jon COHEN (United States)
Mr. Kjell HARNQVIST (Sweden)
Mr. Olof JOS (Sweden)
Ms. Anja KNUVER (Netherlands)
Mr. Phillip McKENZIE (Australia)
Ms. Isobel McGREGOR (United Kingdom)
Mr. Jay MOSKOVITZ (United States)

Ms. Lana MURASKIN (United States)
Mr. Allan NORDIN (Sweden)
Mr. Kenny PETERSSON (Sweden)
Mr. Rien STEEN (Netherlands)
Mr. Jason TARSH (United Kingdom)
Mr. Roger THOMAS (United Kingdom)
Ms. Gonnie VAN AMELSVOORT (Netherlands)
Ms. Nadine de WACHTER (Belgium)

IX. OECD Unit for Education Statistics and Indicators

Ms. Véronique BIRR, Statistical Assistant
Mr. Norberto BOTTANI, Head of Unit
Ms. Jocelyne CARVALLO, Secretary
Ms. Anne-Marie CROSS, Secretary

Ms. Catherine DUCHÊNE, Statistical Assistant
Ms. Wendy SIMPSON, Administrator
Mr. Andreas SCHLEICHER, Administrator
Mr. Albert TUIJNMAN, Administrator

OECD PUBLICATIONS, 2 rue André-Pascal, 75775 PARIS CEDEX 16
PRINTED IN FRANCE
(96 95 02 1) ISBN 92-64-14405-6 - No. 47831 1995